To Joshua, who asks me every few weeks, "Mommy, did you finish the robot yet?"
To Orly, who I hope will have a super-housewife robot of her own someday.
To Mike, who could use one now.

Case-Based Reasoning

Janet Kolodner
Georgia Institute of Technology

Morgan Kaufmann Publishers, Inc.
2929 Campus Drive, Suite 260
San Mateo CA 94403

Publisher and Editor   *Michael B. Morgan*
Assitant Editor and Permissions   *Douglas Sery*
Project Management   *Professional Book Center*
Design, Composition, Figure Rendering   *Professional Book Center*
Copyediting   *Virginia Rich*
Cover Design   *Terry Earlywine*

Library of Congress **Cataloging-in-Publication Data**
Kolodner, Janet L.
     Case-based reasoning / Janet Kolodner.
       p. cm.
     Includes bibliographical references and index.
     ISBN 1-55860-237-2
     1. Expert systems (Computer science)   I. Title.
  QA76.76.E95K64   1993
   006.3'3--dc20   93-35703
                                                      CIP

Printed in the United States of America
97 96 95 94 93 5 4 3 2 1

Morgan Kaufmann Publishers, Inc.
Editorial Offices
2929 Campus Drive, Suite 260
San Mateo, CA 94403

Contents

PART II The Case Library: Representing and Indexing Cases

16   Conclusions, Opportunities, Challenges   563

Preface

Every working professional I know wants a wife, the old-fashioned kind—one who will wait on him or her, do the household tasks, and in general, make life easier. I want one of these too. I call it the super-housewife robot.

There are lots of things I want my robot to do: plan and make meals; do the housecleaning, laundry, dishwashing, and chauffering; keep me informed of things on my schedule that are easily forgotten; pay the bills; warn me of problems that might arise or anything abnormal it discovers while performing its duties. I want it to learn from its mistakes; I won't like it if mistakes are repeated. I'd like it to be able to manage its time well. It ought to get better at scheduling activities over time, finding out about pitfalls and time sinks and not falling into them. In general, I want it to do the things that will allow me to have more leisure time, and I want it to do those things well enough so that I won't be tempted to do them myself.

My robot is going to have to do many of the same things I do from day to day. It will have to be a good planner and problem solver, it will have to both reason and act, and it will have to learn from its experiences how to do things in the way I want them done. And it will have to work in real time—no time to figure everything out from scratch all the time.

Over the past several years, several projects in my lab have been aimed at creating this super-housewife robot. JULIA is a meal planner. EXPEDITOR schedules household tasks. MEDIC worries about combining planning and execution. MEDIATOR mediates children's disputes. The projects, of course, have much broader applicability than my robot. JULIA is the prototype for a design problem solver, and its heuristics could just as well be used for architectural or mechanical design as for meal planning. EXPEDITOR could be used to schedule army maneuvers just as well as it could be used to schedule household tasks. MEDIC was designed to be a doctor and is now being tested in an underwater robotics domain. And MEDIATOR can reason about world crises as well as about children's disputes.

The super-housewife robot, then, is a combination of all the reasoners we hope to build someday. How can we build these reasoners that can design, plan, schedule, negotiate, integrate planning with activity, and learn and do it all in real time? We might be tempted to look at all these tasks separately and solve each of them alone, but that would probably be a mistake. I keep the super-housewife robot in mind because I want to solve these problems in a parsimonious way. I want the solutions to all these problems to be sufficiently similar that we can put them into one cognitive architecture and make them run in conjunction with one another. And I want learning to be integrated with reasoning, not to be built on top.

I'm not the first to dream the dream of the ultimate intelligent machine, nor am I the first to propose a way to build it. I am proposing *case-based reasoning* as a means of getting there. In case-based reasoning, new problems are approached by remembering old similar ones and moving forward from there. Situations are interpreted by comparing and contrasting them with previous similar situations. Stories are understood and inferences are made by finding the closest cases in memory, comparing and contrasting with those, making inferences based on those comparisons, and asking questions when inferences can't be made. And learning happens as part of the process of integrating a new case into memory.

This approach is appealing for a variety of reasons. First, the process is relatively simple. It allows a reasoner to copy what has been done before even if the reasoner doesn't understand what is going on. We all perform mindlessly from time to time. With all the demands on our time and thoughts, we need to. And so might the super-housewife robot or the Mars rover or any other intelligent machine. Case-based reasoning allows a reasoner to solve problems with a minimum of effort. Second, case-based reasoning provides a way of dealing with an uncertain world. If we can't predict what might happen with certainty, or if we are missing knowledge we would like to have, we depend on the world's being continuous. What was true yesterday is likely to be true today. Cases record the past, giving us and our computers a way to make assumptions about the present. Third, the process seems intuitively plausible. It seems like what we, as people, do quite often. This plausibility has several implications. It might be easier to capture an expert's knowledge in the form of cases than in the form of rules, so building expert systems might be easier in a case-based paradigm. And, if we understand human reasoning well enough to mimic it in a computer, then we might use the results not only to build automated systems but also to build interactive systems that interact with people in a natural way.

Though we are still far from building the super-housewife robot, I believe case-based reasoning provides the basis for a cognitive model that will allow us to build it someday and, in the meantime, will allow us to build a variety of automated and interactive systems that can help us with our tasks in the workplace, in the home, and even (dare I say it?) on the battlefield (though I would prefer that we solve our problems by more peaceful means—perhaps case-based negotiators can help with that). This book presents the state of the art in case-based reasoning. It provides our current answers to many questions: how to represent knowledge in cases, how to index cases for accessibility, how to implement retrieval processes for efficiency, how to adapt old solutions to fit new situations, and so on. It is also honest about the open problems.

In writing this book, I've tried to address two audiences: the cognitive science and artificial intelligence research communities, who want to find out more about the ins and outs of case-based reasoning as it relates to research they are doing, and members of the expert-systems building world, who want guidelines for building working systems. Sometimes it was easy to address both; other times hard. A section at the end of chapter 1 gives some guidelines for reading the book, different ones for each of the two communities. In trying to address both, I found that the book grew and grew, and that in the end, I hadn't addressed some issues as thoroughly as I had wanted to. The cognitive model behind case-based reasoning is discussed at length, for example, but recent experimentation testing the psychological implications of work done in the case-based reasoning community is missing. Methodologies for addressing system-building issues are covered, but code and pseudocode for implementing these approaches is missing. The components of a case-based system are covered in detail, but the learning that emerges from the system as a whole is only covered briefly.

In the end, I was afraid that maybe I had not tied the pieces together well enough. But the book was long, and I didn't think readers would want to read another chapter (I certainly didn't want to write one). The solution is the case library of case-based reasoning systems in the Appendix. I sent e-mail to people I knew who had written case-based systems, and they passed my message on to others. I asked for descriptions of their systems and the lessons they had learned. The result is quite exciting—I didn't know there were so many case-based systems out there, and I didn't know there were so many fielded ones. And many of the lessons learned are informative not only for those just getting started but also for those of us who are experts.

I learned a variety of lessons myself from the replies. For example, shallow indexing of a flat memory, similar to an inverted index, is by far the most common means of indexing case-based systems—I wouldn't have guessed that. I added more text to the book about the ins and outs of such a scheme after I learned that. I also wouldn't have guessed that the nearest-neighbor approach to matching and ranking cases was so extensively used or that there were so many variations on choosing a best case. Nor did I know how large some case libraries are—one is over twenty thousand cases, and many others have thousands of cases. Surprisingly, those systems do retrieval efficiently using the simplest retrieval methods. I was also surprised, though I shouldn't have been, by the huge variations in sizes of cases. Some cases are only a few attributes big, others are several hundred kilobytes large. I suspect that the largest case libraries that use simple methods for retrieval work well on small cases but would be hard to scale up to large cases, but I don't know. There are also several lessons about the representational form of cases. One lesson is that though case representations should be fully expressive, they (or their indexes) need to be structured in flat rather than structured form for easy matching. And many people reported on their use of *snippets*, parts of cases of varying sizes, in solving problems. In addition, I learned some lessons about some things that perhaps should have been covered in the book—things that were so obvious to me that they didn't make it into the book but obviously not so obvious to system builders. That's not to belittle system builders; rather, it is a statement about how little teachers often know about what their students need to learn. In any case, the Appendix does tie the pieces of a case-based system together, and I highly recommend reading it. My thanks to all of you who replied to my request for information.

For those who want more information than is in this book, let me recommend some additional reading. First, Schank and Abelson's (1977) *Scripts, Plans, Goals, and Understanding* and Schank's (1982) *Dynamic Memory* provide the history behind the creation of case-based reasoning. Case-based reasoning was conceived in the late 1970s while I was a graduate student at Yale (Roger Schank was my advisor), and the first systems began to be built in the early 1980s, by my students and Roger's. At the same time, members of the AI legal reasoning community, most notably Edwina Rissland, were looking at the role of cases in argumentation. As the world began to be populated with people working on case-based reasoning, several books were published that capture snapshots of the case-based reasoning world. *Experience, Memory, and Reasoning*, by me and Chris Riesbeck (1986), holds a snapshot of 1984 case-based reasoning capabilities. The 1988, 1989, and 1991 Defense Advanced Research Projects Agency (DARPA) Case-Based Reasoning Workshop proceedings (Kolodner 1988b; Hammond 1989c; Bareiss 1991) hold snapshots of case-based reasoning research and development in those years. Riesbeck and Schank's (1989) *Inside Case-Based Reasoning* provides a snapshot of work in case-based reasoning at Yale. More recently, the most influential of the Ph.D. theses on case-based reasoning have been published as books (Hammond 1989a; Bareiss 1989a; Ashley 1990; Hinrichs 1992; Leake 1992b). I recommend all of them—they are the cream of the crop.

There are several people who deserve my thanks, whose input or support was critical in making this book a reality. I began collecting and collating much of the material in this book back in 1989 when Chris Riesbeck and I put together the first CBR Tutorial at National Conference on Artificial intelligence (AAAI). I thought it would be easy to compile a book from that; the material was essentially in place, and I had presented it many times. I was wrong. In any case, I thank Chris for all the material in here that came from our long discussions and from the transparencies we prepared. Several people have reviewed the manuscript and pieces of it along the way. Ray Bareiss and Eric Domeshek deserve the greatest thanks. Both were always available to read chapters fast and gave wonderful advice. Many other people read and commented on individual chapters: Bob Simpson, Tom Hinrichs, Mike Cox, Anthony Francis, Anna Zacherl, Ashok Goel, Ashwin Ram, Kris Hammond, Bill Mark, and Kevin Ashley come to mind right now. There were others. Nick Duncan and Joshua Bleier helped put the references together. There were also several anonymous reviewers along the way. Thanks to everyone. The deficiencies, of course, are all mine.

Much of the work reported in this book has been funded by individual National Science Foundation (NSF), Office of Naval Research (ONR), and DARPA contracts to the individuals working on the research. These agencies took the lead in making CBR a reality. The funding that paid for my projects and partially funded my time as I wrote the book has come from NSF (under grants IST-8608362 and IRI-8921256), ONR (under contract N00014-92-J-1234), Army Research Institute for the Behavioral Sciences (ARI) (under contract MDA903-90-K-0112), DARPA (under contracts F49620-88-C-0058, monitored by Air Force Office of Scientific Research (AFOSR), and N00014-91-J-4092, monitored by ONR), and IBM.

Now for thanking the most important people, my support network. First is the set of people who have helped me juggle all the things that I almost let fall while I was writing the book, especially in the past six months—my research scientists, Terry Chandler, Eric Domeshek, Mimi Recker, and Linda Wills, who took care of my technical life, and my assistants, first Jeannie Terrell and then Cindi Anderson, who kept everything else at work in order. Second, I want to thank Mike Morgan, who has been patient through all of the delays. He acted as if he was sure I could do it when I wasn't so sure—I don't know if he meant it or not, but it helped. Unfortunately, it was only a few weeks ago, rather than a year ago, that I finally understood his best advice—"Make it perfect in the second edition." Third, I want to thank the members of the computing and cognitive science communities at Georgia Tech for not dumping more responsibilities on me in the past year than I could handle. Thanks to all of you.

Finally, I thank my husband, Mike, who has made things run around the house, and my kids, Joshua and Orly, who have tried their hardest to understand why I've had to be at work late, why they can't use the computer, and why I didn't make it to any soccer games. All have given their love and support throughout, especially at times when I needed it most. Thanks, guys—I love you and couldn't have done it without you.

Janet Kolodner
Atlanta, GA

FIGURE CREDITS

The publisher gratefully acknowledges permission to reproduce the following material:

Figure 2.1–2.4 From Hammond, K.J. (1989). *Case Based Planning: Viewing Planning as a Memory Task*, Academic Press, Boston, MA.

Figure 2.7 From Barletta, R. and Hennessy, D. (1989). "Case Adaptation in Autoclave Layout Design," in *Proceedings of the Case-based Reasoning Workshop*, DARPA, Hammond, K. (ed.).

Figure 2.9 From Dupuy, T.N. (1987). *Understanding War: History and Theory of Combat*, New York: Paragaon House.

Figure 2.10 From Ferguson, W. et al. (1992). "ASK Systems: An Approach to the Realization of Story-Based Teachers," *The Journal of the Learning Sciences*, Vol. 2, Lawrence Erlbaum Associates, Hillsdale, NJ, pp. 95–134.

Figures 2.11 From Domeshek, E. and Kolodner, J. (1992). "A Case-based Design Aid for Architecture," in *Artificial Intelligence in Design '92*, Gero, J. (ed.), Kluwer Academic Publishers, Boston, pp. 497–516.

Figures 4.5, 4.6 From Kolodner, J.L. (1984). *Retrieval and Organization Strategies in Conceptual Memory: A Computer Model*, Lawrence Erlbaum Associates, Hillsdale, NJ.

Figure 5.9 From Goel, A.K. et al. (1991). "Towards a Case-Based Tool for Aiding Conceptual Design Problem Solving," in *Proceedings of the Case-Based Reasoning Workshop*, DARPA, Bareiss, R. (ed.).

Figure 5.10 From Ferguson. W. et al. (1992). "ASK Systems: An Approach to the Realization of Story-Based Teachers," *The Journal of the Learning Sciences*, Vol. 2, Lawrence Erlbaum Associates, Hillsdale, NJ, pp. 95–134.

Figure 5.11 From Domeshek, E. and Kolodner, J. (1992). "A Case-based Design Aid for Architecture," in *Artificial Intelligence in Design '92*, Gero, J. (ed.), Kluwer Academic Publishers, Boston, pp. 497–516.

Figures 5.12–5.15 From Simpson, R.C. (1985). *A Computer Model of Case-based Reasoning in Problem Solving: An Investigation in the Domain of Dispute Mediation*, Ph.D. Thesis, Technical Report No. GIT-ICS-85/18, School of Information and Computer Science, Georgia Institute of Technology.

Figure 5.16–5.18 From Koton, P. (1989). *Using Experience in Learning and Problem Solving*, Ph.D. Thesis, CS Department, Massachusetts Insitute of Technology.

Figures 5.21–5.24 From Goel, A. (1989). "Integration of Case-Based Reasoning and Model-Based Reasoning for Adaptive Design Problem Solving." Ph.D. Thesis, Department of Computer and Information Science, The Ohio State University.

Figure 5.25 From Dupuy, T.N. (1987). *Understanding War: History and Theory of Combat*, New York: Paragaon House.

Figure 5.26, 5.27 From Redmond, M.A. (1992). *Learning by Observing and Understanding Expert Problem Sovling*, Ph.D. Thesis, Technical Report No. GIT-CC-92/43, College of Computing, Georgia Institute of Technology.

Figures 6.2, 6.3, 6.4, 6.14 From Schank, R. and Osgood, R. (1990). *A Content Theory of Memory Indexing*, Technical Report No. 2, Institute for Learning Sciences, Northwestern University.

Figure 8.10 From Kolodner, J.L. (1984). *Retrieval and Organization Strategies in Conceptual Memory: A Computer Model*, Lawrence Erlbaum Associates, Hillsdale, NJ.

Figures 9.8, 9.9 From Gentner, D. (1988). "Analogical Inference and Analogical Access." In *Analogica*, A. Prieditis (ed.). Los Altos, California: Morgan Kaufmann.

Figure 10.3 From Simoudis, E. (1991). *Retrieving Justifiably Relevant Cases from a Case Base Using Validation Models*, Ph.D. Thesis, CS Department, Brandeis University, Waltham, MA.

Figures 11.4–11.7 Adapted from Simpson, R.L. (1985). *A Computer Model of Case-based Reasoning in Problem Solving: An Investigation in the Domains of Disparate Mediation*, Ph.D. Thesis, Technical Report No. GIT-ICS-85/18, School of Information and Computer Science, Georgia Institute of Technology.

Figures 11.21, 11.22 From Koton, P. (1989). *Using Experience in Learning and Problem Solving*. PhD. Thesis, CS Department, Massachusetts Institute of Technology..

Figures 11.31–11.34 From Goel, A. (1989). "Integration of Case-Based Reasoning and Model-Based Reasoning for Adaptive Design Problem Solving." Ph.D. Thesis, Department of Computer and Information Science, The Ohio State University.

Figure 13.2 From Bareiss, E.R. (1989). *Exemplar-Based Knowledge Acquisition: A Unified Approach to Concept Representation, Classification and Learning*, Academic Press, Boston, MA.

Figures 13.3, 13.4 From Bareiss, E.R., Porter, B.W., and Weir, C.C. (1989). "Protos: An Exemplar-Based Learning Apprentice." *International Journal of Man-Machine Studies*, 29:549–561.

Figures 13.10–13.13 Courtesy of Cognitive Systems, Inc.

PART I

Background

1

What Is Case-Based Reasoning?

1.1 INTRODUCTION

A host is planning a meal for a set of people who include, among others, several people who eat no meat or poultry, one of whom is also allergic to milk products; several meat-and-potatoes men; and her friend Anne. Because it is tomato season, she wants to use tomatoes as a major ingredient in the meal. As she is planning the meal, she remembers the following:

> I once served tomato tart (made from mozzarella cheese, tomatoes, dijon mustard, basil, and pepper, all in a piecrust) as the main dish during the summer when I had vegetarians come for dinner. It was delicious and easy to make. But I can't serve that to Elana (the one allergic to milk).

> I have adapted recipes for Elana before by substituting tofu products for cheese. I could do that, but I don't know how good the tomato tart will taste that way.

She decides not to serve tomato tart and continues planning. Because it is summer, she decides that grilled fish would be a good main course. But now she remembers something else:

> Last time I tried to serve Anne grilled fish, she wouldn't eat it. I had to put hot dogs on the grill at the last minute.

This suggests to her that she shouldn't serve fish, but she wants to anyway. She considers whether there is a way to serve fish that Anne will eat.

> I remember seeing Anne eat mahimahi in a restaurant. I wonder what kind of fish she will eat? The fish I served her was whole fish with the head on. The fish in the restaurant was a fillet and more like steak than fish. I guess I need to serve a fish that is more like meat than fish. Perhaps swordfish will work. I wonder if Anne will eat swordfish? Swordfish is like chicken, and I know she eats chicken.

Here she is using examples and counterexamples of a premise (Anne doesn't eat fish) to try to derive an interpretation of the premise that stands up to scrutiny.

The hypothetical host is employing *case-based reasoning* (CBR) to plan a meal. In case-based reasoning, a reasoner remembers previous situations similar to the current one and uses them to help solve the new problem. In the example, remembered cases are used to suggest a means of solving the new problem (e.g., to suggest a main dish), to suggest a means of adapting a solution that doesn't quite fit (e.g., substitute a tofu product for cheese), to warn of possible failures (e.g., Anne won't eat fish), and to interpret a situation (e.g., Why didn't Anne eat the fish? Will she eat swordfish?).

Case-based reasoning can mean adapting old solutions to meet new demands, using old cases to explain new situations, using old cases to critique new solutions, or reasoning from precedents to interpret a new situation (much as lawyers do) or create an equitable solution to a new problem (much as labor mediators do).

If we watch the way people solve problems, we are likely to observe case-based reasoning in use all around us. Attorneys are taught to use cases as precedents for constructing and justifying arguments in new cases. Mediators and arbitrators are taught to do the same. Other professionals are not taught to use case-based reasoning but often find that it provides a way to solve problems efficiently. Consider, for example, a doctor faced with a patient who has an unusual combination of symptoms. If the doctor has seen a patient with similar symptoms previously, he or she is likely to remember the old case and propose the old diagnosis as a solution to this new problem. If coming to that diagnosis was time-consuming in the earlier case, this method is a big savings of time. Of course, the doctor can't assume the old answer is correct. He or she must still validate it for the new case in a way that doesn't prohibit considering other likely diagnoses. Nevertheless, remembering the old case allows the doctor to generate a plausible answer easily.

Similarly, an auto mechanic faced with an unusual mechanical problem is likely to remember other similar problems and to consider whether their solutions explain the new one. Click and Clack, the mechanics on National Public Radio's "Car Talk," talk about their past experiences all the time. Doctors evaluating the appropriateness of a therapeutic procedure, or judging which of several are appropriate, are also likely to remember instances using each procedure and to make their judgments based on previous experiences. Problem instances of using a procedure are particularly helpful here; they tell the doctor what could go wrong, and when an explanation is available explaining why the old problem occurred, they focus the doctor on finding the information he or she needs to make sure the problem won't show up again. We hear cases being cited time and again by our political leaders in explaining why some action was taken or should be taken. Many management decisions are made based on previous experience. In addition, the "case method" of teaching is used extensively in law and business.

Cases provide context for discussing more abstract issues, and they provide illustrations of those abstract guidelines that students remember and apply in later reasoning.

Case-based reasoning is also used extensively in day-to-day commonsense reasoning. The meal planning example is typical of the reasoning we all do from day to day. When we order a meal in a restaurant, we often base decisions about what might be good on our other experiences in that restaurant and those like it. As we plan our household activities, we remember what worked and didn't work previously and use that to create our new plans. A child care provider mediating an argument between two children remembers what worked and didn't work previously in such situations and bases his or her suggestion on that.

In general, the second time we solve some problem or do some task is easier than the first because we remember and repeat the previous solution. We are more competent the second time because we remember our mistakes and go out of our way to avoid them.

Case-based reasoning suggests a model of reasoning that incorporates problem solving, understanding, and learning and integrates all with memory processes. Briefly, the following premises underlie the model, which will be presented in greater detail in later chapters:

- Reference to old cases is *advantageous* in dealing with situations that recur. Reference to previous similar situations is often *necessary* to deal with the complexities of novel situations. Thus, remembering a case to use in later problem solving (and integrating that case with what is already known) is a necessary learning process.

- Because descriptions of problems are often incomplete, the further step of understanding or interpretation of the problem is a necessary prerequisite to reasoning. A case-based reasoner cannot recall a relevant case unless it understands the new situation it is in. On the other hand, as problem solving progresses, a reasoner may gain a better understanding of a situation, allowing more relevant cases to be recalled than could have been done earlier. This suggests that understanding or interpreting a situation is a necessary part of the reasoning cycle and both a prerequisite to problem solving and a corequisite during problem solving. But the need for problem understanding is not specific to case-based reasoning. Any form of reasoning requires that a situation be elaborated in enough detail and represented in enough clarity and with appropriate vocabulary to allow the reasoner to recognize the knowledge it needs (whether general knowledge or cases) to reason about it.

- Because no old case is ever exactly the same as a new one, it is usually necessary to *adapt* an old solution to fit a new situation. Adaptation compensates for the differences between an old situation and a new one.

- Learning occurs as a natural consequence of reasoning. If a novel procedure is derived in the course of solving a complex problem and all goes well in its execution, then, in effect, a new procedure is learned for dealing with this new class of situations. The procedure is embodied in the experienced case, and the case is indexed in memory such that it is retrievable when its procedure can be used advantageously. If instead problems are encountered in using this new case in a new situation, the reasoner is warned that the procedure in the case is faulty or that its indexes (representing its range of applicability) are inaccurate. An attempt is made to analyze the results of the new situation and to fix its problems. The new situation, stored in the case library, embodies a refinement or modification of the reasoning knowledge found in the original case. Its indexes designate when it is useful, and indexes associated with the old case are refined, based on this analysis, so that it is retrieved only when its procedure is known to be appropriate. This incremental learning process results in the learning of new procedures, their refinement, and the learning of when each is appropriately used.

■ Feedback and analysis of feedback through follow-up procedures and explanatory reasoning are necessary parts of the complete reasoning/learning cycle. Without evaluation processes based on feedback, learning could not happen, and references to previous experiences during reasoning would be unreliable. Follow-up procedures include explaining failures and attempting to repair them.

These premises suggest that the quality of a case-based reasoner's reasoning depends on five things:

1. The experiences it has had
2. Its ability to understand new situations in terms of those old experiences
3. Its adeptness at adaptation
4. Its adeptness at evaluation and repair
5. Its ability to integrate new experiences into its memory appropriately

The less experienced reasoner will always have fewer experiences to work with than the more experienced one. But, as we shall see, the answers given by a less experienced reasoner won't necessarily be worse than those given by the experienced one if the reasoner is creative in its understanding and adaptation and if it has had at least some relevant experience.[1] It is important, then, that a case-based reasoner start with a representative set of cases. A representative set covers the goals and subgoals that arise in reasoning and both successful and failed attempts at achieving those goals. Successful attempts are used to propose solutions to new problems. Failed attempts are used to warn of the potential for failure.

The ability to understand a new problem in terms of old experiences has two parts: *recalling* old experiences and *interpreting* the new situation in terms of the recalled experiences. The first we call the **indexing problem**. In broad terms, it means finding in memory the experience closest to a new situation. In narrower terms, we often think of it as the problem of assigning indexes to experiences stored in memory so that they can be recalled under appropriate circumstances. Recalling cases appropriately is at the core of case-based reasoning.

Interpretation is the process of comparing the new situation to recalled experiences. When problem situations are interpreted, they are compared and contrasted to old problem situations. The result is an interpretation of the new situation, the addition of inferred knowledge about the new situation, or a classification of the situation. When the solutions to problems are compared to old solutions, the reasoner gains an understanding of the pros and cons of doing

---

1. In fact, if the novice reasoner has, by chance, had an experience particularly relevant to a new novel situation, its answers can be equal to those of an expert.

something a particular way. We generally see interpretation processes used when problems are not well understood and when there is a need to criticize a solution. When a problem is well understood, there is little need for interpretive processes.

Adaptation is the process of fixing up an old solution to meet the demands of the new situation. We shall see that nine methods for adaptation have been identified. They can be used to insert something new into an old solution, to delete something, or to make a substitution. Applying adaptation strategies straightforwardly results in competent but often unexciting answers. Creative answers result from applying adaptation strategies in novel ways.

One of the hallmarks of a case-based reasoner is its ability to learn from its experiences, as doctors might do when they commit to memory a hard-to-solve problem so that they can solve it easily another time. In order to learn from experience, a reasoner requires feedback so that it can interpret what was right and what was wrong with its solutions. Without feedback, the reasoner might get faster at solving problems but would repeat its mistakes and never increase its capabilities. Thus, **evaluation** and consequent **repair** are important contributors to the expertise of a case-based reasoner. Evaluation can be done in the context of the outcomes of other similar cases, can be based on feedback, or can be based on simulation.

A case-based reasoner's performance improves in two ways. It becomes *more efficient* by remembering old solutions and adapting them rather than having to derive answers from scratch each time. If a case was adapted in a novel way, if it was solved using some novel method, or if it was solved by combining the solutions to several cases, then when it is recalled during later reasoning, the steps required to solve it won't need to be repeated for the new problem.

Case-based reasoners also become *more competent* over time, deriving better answers than they could with less experience. One of case-based reasoning's forte's is helping a reasoner to anticipate and thus avoid mistakes it has made in the past. This is possible because the reasoner caches problem situations, indexing them by features that predict its old mistakes. Remembering such cases during later reasoning provides a warning to the reasoner of problems that might come up, and the reasoner can work to avoid them.

Within artificial intelligence (AI), when one talks of learning, it usually means the learning of generalizations, either through inductive or through explanation-based means. Though the memory of a case-based reasoner notices similarities between cases and can therefore notice when generalizations should be formed, inductive formation of generalizations is responsible for only some of the learning in a case-based reasoner. Case-based reasoning achieves most of its learning in two other ways:

- Through the accumulation of new cases
- Through the assignment of indexes

New cases give the reasoner additional familiar contexts for solving problems or evaluating situations. A reasoner whose cases cover more of the domain will be a better reasoner than one whose cases cover less of the domain. One whose cases cover instances of failure as well as success will be better than one whose cases cover only success. New indexes allow a reasoner to fine-tune its recall apparatus so that it remembers cases at more appropriate times.

That is not to say that generalization is not important. Indeed, the cases a case-based reasoner encounters give it direction in the creation of appropriate generalizations, that is, those that can be useful to its task. How can that work? When several cases are indexed the same way and all predict the same solution or all can be classified the same way, the reasoner knows that a useful generalization can be formed. In addition, the combination of indexes and predicted solution or classification also give the reasoner guidance in choosing the level of abstraction of its generalizations. Some case-based reasoners use only cases; others use a combination of cases and generalized cases. Even when a case-based reasoner does not use generalizations to reason, they are useful in helping the reasoner organize its cases.

Case-based reasoning is not the first method that combines reasoning and learning, but it is unique in making learning little more than a byproduct of reasoning. A case-based reasoner that remembers its experiences learns as it reasons; feedback from early experiences gives it insight for solving later problems. Reports of fielded case-based reasoners bear this out. CLAVIER (Hennessy and Hinkle 1992; Barletta and Hennessy 1989; Mark 1989), for example, configures composite parts for loading in an autoclave. In over a year of use at Lockheed, its case library grew from 20 to over 150 cases, it became a more efficient problem solver, and its solutions became more accurate. At the same time, it served as a corporate memory for those who work on the shop floor. It accumulated the experiences of all those workers in its memory, learning not just what one of them had been able to learn but the things all of them had learned.

Such projects also show that learning does not have to be a major piece of the computer program. Though learning procedures can be quite complex, even in a case-based system, a large proportion of what a system needs to learn to improve its performance requires little additional mechanism beyond the case-based reasoning the system does.

1.2 WHAT IS A CASE?

The intuition of case-based reasoning is that situations recur with regularity. What was done in one situation is likely to be applicable in a similar situation. If we know what worked in a previous situation similar to the new one, we start with that in reasoning about the new situation.

This is quite different from the way AI practitioners and psychologists have been taught to think about knowledge. When we discuss knowledge representation in AI, we usually think about making the knowledge as general as possible so that it is widely applicable. Models tell us how devices work, and we might try to apply the model of a heart, for example, across many different patients. The goal in formulating models is to capture what is common across a variety of similar objects. Though some rules are very specific, the goal is to formulate rules that are generally applicable. Why, then, should we want to emphasize specific knowledge tied to specific situations?

General knowledge certainly has advantages. Of particular import is the economy of storage it allows. If we can represent all hearts using one model, there is less to store. Similarly, our general knowledge allows us to deal with uncertainty. We may not know exactly what the flow of blood is into a particular heart, but the model gives us a way of approximating it closely enough so that we can reason about that heart without knowing all the details.

But general knowledge also has its disadvantages. One big one is the issue of operationalization (Mostow 1981). General knowledge may provide a framework for reasoning, but applying some general piece of knowledge to a particular situation can be arbitrarily difficult. Mostow (1983) gives the example of playing the card game hearts. A general rule in hearts that guides play is "Avoid taking points." The problem with this rule is that it is expressed too abstractly—the terms it uses are unintelligible to the novice player and mean a variety of specific things to the expert. Using the rule requires that players be able to recognize situations when points are likely to be taken, that they be able to predict when they will be in such a situation, and that they be able to plan so that they won't be in such a situation.

Three tactics, for example, that operationalize "Avoid taking points" are "Play a lower card than has already been played," "If you are the first player or don't have a low card, play the lowest one you have," and "If you don't have a card in the suit that was played, use the opportunity to throw a high card from another suit." It is these tactics and others like them that the expert hearts player uses in order to avoid taking points, and it is these tactics that the novice player needs to learn. We can imagine that this learning is accomplished by keeping track of the ways the general rule has been operationalized over time and reusing strategies and tactics, gradually learning under what circumstances each applies. These are the cases.

Another disadvantage of general knowledge is that although it covers the normal, it doesn't tell us much about how to reason about situations that are different from the norm. A model of the human heart, for example, tells us how to reason about a normal working heart or one that is misbehaving in the usual ways. But it may not be good for reasoning about a heart that is functioning in some way different than expected, for example, a heart with a structural defect.

The problem gets worse as available knowledge is less and less complete. Lighting designers, for example, have models suggesting how much lighting is needed given the size of the room; the color of the walls, carpets, and furniture; and the task to be done. The models work very well when walls and furniture are medium- to light-colored (what we usually see) but don't work at all if walls, carpets, and furniture are all very dark or very light. A different model might be constructed for those situations, but the knowledge needed to form those models is not available. Cases can be used to cover those situations and, in fact, are used when lighting designers reason about these types of situations. In short, models make a closed-world assumption that is difficult to transcend—impossible, in fact, when the necessary general knowledge is not available. A case-based reasoner, by contrast, deals with the incompleteness of the knowledge it has by adding cases that describe the situations its other cases don't account for.

Cases, which represent specific knowledge tied to specific situations, represent knowledge at an *operational* level; that is, they make explicit how a task was carried out or how a piece of knowledge was applied or what particular strategies for accomplishing a goal were used. In addition, they capture knowledge that might be too hard to capture in a general model, allowing reasoning from specifics when general knowledge is not available. Another advantage of cases is that they chunk together knowledge that belongs together. A reasoner that uses cases is saved from having to compose a lot of decontextualized pieces of knowledge with each other to solve a problem. The case caches compositions of knowledge that have been made already.

Cases come in many shapes and sizes. They may cover a situation that evolves over time (as in designing a building or following a patient through several illnesses), they may represent a snapshot (as in choosing a particular type of window for a building or recording a judge's ruling), or they may cover any size time slice in between those extremes. They may represent a problem-solving episode (as do medical and architectural cases), associate a situation description with an outcome (as in legal cases), or do some combination.

What is common to all cases is that they represent an experienced situation. That situation, when remembered later, forms a context in which the knowledge embedded in the case is presumed applicable. What the doctor did in some situation for some patient was applicable to that situation. What the architect did in one situation is tied to that situation. What the judge ruled based on some particular set of circumstances was right for that situation. When a similar situation arises, those decisions and the knowledge that went into making them provide a starting point for interpreting the new situation or solving the problem it poses.

Several questions arise from this discussion. First, we might consider the relationship between cases and general knowledge. Then, we might wonder whether all experiences are worth storing as cases, and if not, which ones are? We'll consider the second question first, as its answer gives insight into the answer to the first.

Consider the following: You brush your teeth every morning. The toothpaste is in a particular place. The toothbrush is in a particular place. You pick up the toothbrush, put toothpaste on it, maybe run it under the water, put the toothbrush in your mouth, and so on, each day. What are the cases? We could think of each individual toothbrushing experience as being a separate case. Certainly each is a separate experience. There is something unsatisfying, however, about thinking about storing each in memory as a separate case, perhaps because we find it very hard to distinguish these individual experiences one from another. On the other hand, we can imagine remembering the time you put hair conditioner on the toothbrush instead of toothpaste or the time you were at a friend's house and had to search for the toothpaste or the time you finished up the toothpaste and had to go downstairs to get another tube and sprained your ankle on the way down. Each of those seems like a case worth remembering. Why do these seem like memorable cases, but the normal, everyday toothbrushing experience doesn't?

Memorable cases seem to be experiences that are different from the norm or different from what was expected. But what about the "normal" experiences, the ones in which everything went as expected? These seem to be merged together in our memories into generalizations or composite cases. The minor differences are blended to define these generalizations or composite cases, and the ones we seem to remember distinctly are those that are different. Traditionally, those generalizations have been called *schemata* (Bartlett 1932; Rumelhart and Ortony 1977; Brewer and Nakamura 1984) by the psychology community. Schank and Abelson (1977) defined particular kinds of schemata, called *scripts,* that capture generalizations about common, day-to-day recurrent activities, and several psychologists (Reder and Anderson 1980; Smith, Adams, and Schorr 1978) have proposed ways in which blending might happen.

What about the relationship between generalized schemas and cases? Schank's (1982) *Dynamic Memory* proposes structures called MOPs (memory organization packets) that serve as both repositories of generalized knowledge and organizers of cases. MOPs hold general knowledge describing types of experiences in their *content frames,* and they index cases according to the ways they differ from those norms. Lebowitz's IPP (1983a, 1983b) and my own CYRUS (Kolodner, 1983a, 1983b, 1984) were the first implementations of MOPs and the forerunners of case-based reasoning programs. Organizational structures and methods will be discussed in detail in chapter 8; for now, MOPs can be thought of as repositories for general knowledge and cases as specializations of those general models. The two are connected through a complex indexing web.

Cases worth remembering, then, are experiences that are different in some way from what was expected. They record major variations from the norm. Indeed, what makes a good case evolves over time as normative expectations change. If I have a new bathroom installed, for example, and my toothbrush and toothpaste are in different places relative to the sink than they were previously, I will have to learn a new routine for toothbrushing—my hand will have to learn to go to a different place to pick up the props. The first time I use this new sink, I must behave differently than I did when I brushed my teeth at the old sink. This is different from the old norm, and this new experience represents a case. As I gain experience using this sink, however, all my experiences become merged together into a new set of norms, a new script, or the content frame for a new MOP. My individual experiences are no longer different from the norm and no longer represent distinguishable cases.

There are several points this discussion makes. First, it implies that cases are not the only type of knowledge our intelligent systems need in order to function. If we were building a full cognitive model, we would want to include in it both cases and abstractions of those cases. Second, it implies that the organization of abstractions and cases in a memory changes dynamically over time and with experience. What might start as a new experience, different from the norm, may eventually become the norm. In a full cognitive model, memory's organizational and representational structures need to change to reflect these changes.

Given this cognitive stance, I must now admit, however, that most of our current implemented case-based reasoners make little use of general or abstract descriptions of situations, relying almost completely on cases for these descriptions. The major reason for this is that researchers have been trying to see how far cases could carry a reasoner. The answer, as we shall see, is that they can carry a reasoner pretty far. But we have also found places where general knowledge is helpful. When general knowledge is available, it can guide the choice of indexes (as in KRITIK [Goel 1989]), the means of determining how well a new situation matches a stored case (as in CASEY [Koton 1988a, 1989]), and the choice of adaptation strategies (as in KRITIK and CASEY). In our running systems, general knowledge tends to be recorded in adaptation strategies and in the *models* (Hayes 1985; Forbus 1988; De Kleer and Brown 1984) that some adaptation and matching procedures use.

If our reasoners use only cases to describe situations, then how do they deal with the general situation, the one that is the norm? In order to keep knowledge uniform, systems tend to represent both normative experiences and distinguished ones as cases. Normative experiences are only represented in systems once, however, so that case libraries are not overwhelmed with redundant knowledge. PROTOS (Porter, Bareiss, and Holte 1990; Bareiss 1989a), for example, calls these *prototypical cases,* and it begins its reasoning by attempting to use one of these.

This brings us to another complication. Our case-based systems are having new experiences each time they are used. We want to record those experiences in their case libraries so that they can evolve into better reasoners over time. But if we put every experience in that is different in any small way from those that are already in the library, it could easily become overwhelmed with all the cases.

Thus, we must consider whether every experience in which a difference is encountered is worthy of recording in a case library. Our intuitions tell us probably not. If the toothpaste happens to be a few inches to the left of where I expected and I am able to easily compensate for the difference with no ill effects, then the experience is probably not worthy of being recorded. Recording it will not add enough efficiency or capability to the reasoning system to make it worth using the extra memory. But if that few inches requires me to reach farther than normal, causing me to pull a muscle, we would probably all agree that this experience would be recorded as a distinguishable case by a person and should be recorded in a system.

So, how can we distinguish which experiences with differences are worthy of being remembered as separate cases? The answer to this question is difficult to formulate. One way we might distinguish is by *whether their difference makes a difference*. That is, did it have any effects that could not have been predicted based on the norms? Did I have to do any extra reasoning to compensate for the difference? Or did it cause something to happen that could not have been predicted from the norms that made a difference to future activity or reasoning? Did it cause me to wonder about something that I would not have noticed otherwise? Or did it allow me to learn something I need to know to do an important task (as in IVY [Hunter 1989a; Ram and Hunter 1992])? If I merely move my hand differently to pick up the toothpaste and I do it pretty automatically with no ill effects, then there is no extra reasoning I do, nor is there any effect that could not be predicted. Thus, there is no need to record the experience as a separate case. But if the toothpaste is on a high shelf and I have to figure out how to get it down, or if I pull a muscle as a result of reaching too far, something different from the norm is happening, and a case should be recorded.

The bottom line here is this: *If the difference is instructive such that it teaches a lesson for the future that could not have been inferred easily from the cases already recorded, then record it as a case.*[2] Otherwise, the experience can be seen as a minor variation of the norm. When I figure out how to get the toothpaste down from a high shelf, I am doing reasoning that can be saved and reused later—a lesson about how to get something from a particular high shelf. When I pull a muscle, I am learning about the possible ill effects of a particular action. The lesson here is a warning against putting myself in that kind of situation again.

Just as what constitutes a difference changes over time, so does what constitutes a lesson. The normal way of doing something is a lesson if it is not already known. As it is repeated over and over, however, with no new information, there will be no lesson in the experience and therefore no new case recorded. Cases, then, don't represent only differences. They may also represent norms that were different from prior knowledge at the time they were experienced. Recording cases when their differences are instructive but not when they could have been easily inferred is a way of using one representation for both normative and unique knowledge.

We must also consider what kinds of lessons cases should teach. Perhaps the best guideline we can give is that cases recorded in a case library should contribute to achieving the goals of the reasoner. As people, we have a wide variety of goals. Any small difference from a norm might teach a lesson relevant to one of our goals. Thus, from the point of view of the cognitive model, it is difficult to predict exactly which cases should be recorded, when, and for

---

2. Of course, now we must consider what *easily inferred* means. I will punt here, saying that this is something a system builder must determine for his or her domain and task.

what intentions. For a machine, however, it is somewhat easier. Our automated systems normally have a limited number of goals. Some are goals for action (move the block), others are goals for reasoning (identify the patient's disorder; evaluate the design of the building; design a heat pump; compare two instances and show the differences).

Among other lessons a case can teach are how to achieve a goal, how to achieve several goals in conjunction, or the kinds of problems that might arise in achieving a goal (what might go wrong). A case has an important lesson to teach if the reasoner has derived a new way of achieving the goal, if it has put considerable effort into adapting an old way of achieving a goal, if a failure to achieve a goal is noticed, if the effect of some situation causes a new goal to arise, or if it is unable to achieve one of its goals.

The discussion has seemed to digress somewhat from what a case is. But, in fact, several principles of cases have been uncovered here:

- A case represents specific knowledge tied to a context. It records knowledge at an operational level.
- Cases can come in many different shapes and sizes, covering large or small time slices, associating solutions with problems, outcomes with situations, or both.
- A case records experiences that are different from what is expected. Not all differences are important to record, however. Cases worthy of recording as cases teach a useful lesson.
- Useful lessons are those that have the potential to help a reasoner achieve a goal or set of goals more easily in the future or that warn about the possibility of a failure or point out an unforeseen problem.

The definition of a case that we can cull from this discussion is this:

A case is a contextualized piece of knowledge representing an experience that teaches a lesson fundamental to achieving the goals of the reasoner.

The discussion also provides guidelines for high-level answers to some questions that system designers ask. Which cases should I put into the system? Those that teach something fundamental to the goals of the reasoner. How do I recognize the boundaries of cases in an ongoing situation? Any parts of a situation that contribute to the lesson it teaches belong in the representation of the case. How should I break my huge case into pieces? According to the lessons it teaches. More detailed answers to these questions can be found in chapter 5.

Finally, the discussion teaches us about the content of cases. We can see that there are two parts to a case:

1. The lesson(s) it teaches
2. The context in which it can teach its lesson(s)

The second of these we call the case's *indexes*. They tell us under what circumstances it is appropriate to retrieve the case. Chapters 6 and 7 discuss choice of indexes. The case's lessons are its content. The bulk of chapter 5 addresses representation of this content. Its emphasis is on the content of cases, that is, the knowledge that must be included in them in order to make their lessons usable.

This emphasis is somewhat different from the usual one on form seen in discussions of knowledge representation. Our experience has shown that the particular representational format used is less important than getting the content of the representations right. Of course, there are some general lessons of knowledge representation that should not be ignored in representing cases (e.g., the form and content of generalization hierarchies). System implementors must understand formal options, but we will not emphasize them here.

1.3 MAJOR CBR ISSUES: COMPOSITION AND SPECIFICITY

Reasoning, under the traditional view of reasoning in both artificial intelligence and cognitive psychology, is largely a process of remembering abstract operators and composing them with each other. Case-based reasoning takes an alternative view. Rather than viewing reasoning as primarily a composition process, case-based reasoning views reasoning as a process of remembering one or a small set of concrete instances or cases and basing decisions on comparisons between the new situation and the old instance. There are several important implications of this view that provide insight about the set of issues case-based reasoning researchers choose to concentrate on in research and system building:

■ Case-based reasoning emphasizes the use of concrete instances over abstract operators. It regards large chunks of composed knowledge as the starting point for reasoning. Though there may be smaller and more abstract chunks of knowledge in memory, they derive from cases and are thus secondary to them.[3]

■ Case-based reasoning emphasizes manipulation of cases over composition, decomposition, and recomposition processes. Though we do not claim that composition processes are never used in reasoning, we do claim that reasoning using cases comes first and that composition of operators is more or less a last resort.

Emphasis, in case-based reasoning, is on the use of concrete instances, because they can provide more guidance in solving a new problem than can abstract operators. The major reason for this is that concrete instances provide operational knowledge. They show application and use of knowledge that abstract operators do not supply. The hearts example from the previous section points this out. An abstract strategy that says, "Don't take points," is far less useful than concrete rules that specify how to behave in particular point-taking situations. There is agreement within AI circles that it is more efficient to use *strong knowledge* (knowledge specific to a problem) than *weak knowledge* (domain-independent generally applicable knowledge) in solving problems. In fact, the bias is so strong that almost all intelligent computer programs are built such that they use the most specific knowledge they have available to solve a

---

3. Of course, we must consider where generalizations come from and which are the kinds most likely to exist.

problem before resorting to more generally-applicable knowledge. Operationalization is the major reason why—when knowledge being used is more specific, less inference has to be done to figure out how to apply it. SOAR (Laird, Newell, and Rosenbloom 1987; Newell 1992) and ACT* (Anderson 1983), two computational models of human cognition, also use this heuristic. SOAR's chunking procedures save compositions of operators that have worked in the past, and preference functions in both models prefer more specifically applicable knowledge chunks over more generally applicable ones when several could apply to a new situation.

It is a common assumption, then, in both AI and psychology, that the use of more specific knowledge is *more efficient* than the use of less specific knowledge. Case-based reasoning takes this assumption seriously, concentrating on the use of highly specific knowledge in reasoning. Rather than looking at how specific knowledge can arise from the use of abstract operators, case-based reasoning concentrates on specific knowledge and asks (secondarily) what kinds of general knowledge are useful and how useful general knowledge can be built up from concrete instances. Rather than concentrating on decomposition and recomposition processes, case-based reasoning concentrates on manipulating large chunks.

Using specific knowledge to reason can also be *more accurate* than using generalizations. PROTOS (Bareiss 1989b; Porter, Bareiss, and Holte 1990) provides empirical evidence of this. PROTOS diagnoses hearing disorders using a case-based classification algorithm. In one experiment, its performance is 50 percent more accurate than performance of generalization-based classification programs. CHEF (Hammond 1986a, 1986b, 1989a), a case-based planning program, and JULIA (Hinrichs 1992; Hinrichs and Kolodner 1991), a case-based design program, also suggest that concrete instances can provide more accuracy. Both programs use their cases to point out potential pitfalls in problem solving, allowing previously made mistakes to be avoided.

Interestingly, model-based reasoning (Hayes 1985; de Kleer and Brown 1984; Forbus 1988) takes a similar approach, emphasizing the use of large chunks of general knowledge over composition of smaller rules. But case-based reasoning goes one step further. Models cover the normative situation; cases cover more novel situations. Models are static knowledge structures; they don't change. Collecting cases allows a reasoner to change its behavior over time, covering more of what is novel as it gains experience. The premise in case-based reasoning is that once a problem has been solved, it is often more efficient to solve the next similar problem by starting from the old solution rather than by rerunning all the reasoning that was necessary the first time. CASEY (Koton 1988a, 1989) gives us empirical evidence of this claim. CASEY, which diagnoses heart failures and is built on top of a model-based diagnosis program, uses the same knowledge to solve problems that the model-based program uses. When it has a case available, its reasoning is two to three orders of magnitude faster than the model-based reasoning program, and it is equally accurate.

There is one other major difference between the approach of case-based and model-based reasoning. Model-based reasoning is designed for domains in which a phenomenon is well enough understood that its causality can be represented accurately in a formal language. Case-based reasoning, by contrast, excels in covering "weak-theory domains," domains whose phenomena we don't yet understand well enough to record causality unambiguously. This feature allows case-based reasoning to be used in domains where model-based reasoning cannot be applied.

The case-based reasoning paradigm has a bias against the problem decomposition and recomposition implied by composition of operators, because composition is a highly complex process. When problems are entirely decomposable into noninteracting parts, decomposition and recomposition are easy. As problems become less and less decomposable into non-interacting parts, however, recomposition becomes harder and harder. Traditional methods must be stretched beyond their original intent to deal with these problems. Such problems, which I like to call *barely decomposable*, can be more efficiently solved by methods that don't have to break them into pieces.

This is especially true when the model of the domain is largely unknown, as is the case with CLAVIER (Barletta and Hennessy 1989; Hennessy and Hinkle 1992; Mark 1989), a system that produces parts layouts for curing in an autoclave. CLAVIER works in a very poorly understood domain. About all that is known is what has worked well and not worked well in the past. Not only are interactions between the component parts of the problem still unknown, but little is known about what the component parts of the problem are. Those who have studied the domain agree that traditional composition-based (rule-based) methods for solving its problems would not have worked. Case-based reasoning, however, works quite well. Though old cases don't solve problems completely, they provide almost-correct solutions that enable CLA-VIER to avoid decomposition completely. Instead, it solves problems by remembering an old successful case and adapting it to fit the new situation.

Case-based reasoning allows a problem to be solved as a complete unit. If a similar problem has been solved previously, it can provide the glue that holds barely decomposable problems together. Rather than dealing with hard recomposition problems, the reasoner has only to fix up those parts of the old solution that don't fit the new situation. Though some decomposition is necessary to solve some large problems, case-based reasoning provides a way to minimize it. Several of our case-based design programs provide illustrations of cases providing this glue. CLAVIER's cases minimize decomposition in a domain where it would be nearly impossible to solve the problem by decomposing it because the interactions between the parts are unknown. JULIA (Hinrichs 1992; Hinrichs and Kolodner 1991), by contrast, works in a relatively well-understood but not codified commonsense design domain, meal planning. The component parts of its problems are well known, as are many but not all of the interactions between those parts. But the interactions between the parts are complex and dynamic. As component parts of a solution are solved, they add to the interactions. Using an old case as a general framework for solving a problem makes the majority of the interactions explicit from the start, making solution of the components less complex. The reasoner still has to use subgoals to focus on component parts of the problem, but they are solved in the context of a framework that connects them to each other. Though we are not claiming that a more traditional problem solver could not plan meals, we are claiming that the process is more efficiently and naturally done using a case-based approach. CYCLOPS (Navinchandra 1988, 1991), which designs landscapes, uses cases similarly.

1.4 PROCESSES AND ISSUES

Whenever an approach relegates the traditionally conceived processes to a secondary position, it must propose alternative primary processes. We continue in this section by discussing case-based reasoning's primary processes and presenting the issues that must be encountered in designing solutions. To inform that discussion, we first review the purposes cases serve and then present the primary processes those purposes imply.

Cases serve two sorts of purposes when they are recalled:

- Cases provide suggestions of solutions to problems.
- Cases provide context for understanding or assessing a situation.

As suggestion providers, cases provide ballpark solutions that are adapted to fit a new situation. The reasoner in the initial example used cases in this way to suggest several main dishes and to suggest means of adapting one of them for someone allergic to milk. As context providers, cases provide concrete evidence for or against some solution or interpretation that can drive interpretation or evaluation procedures. In the initial example, the case of Anne eating mahimahi in a restaurant provides concrete evidence that Anne does indeed eat some fish, helping the reasoner to figure out why Anne didn't eat the trout she was served and whether she might eat some other fish. Case-based reasoning is thus a process of "remember and adapt" or "remember and compare." Though some composition is necessary to solve large problems, composition of rules, knowledge, or cases is not the primary process. And, rather than remembering abstract operators, case-based reasoning recalls concrete instances.

People use cases for both these purposes: to help us understand and assess situations and to help us solve problems. As our examples show, in the general course of reasoning, we tend to interleave these processes according to what is needed at the time. We can't solve a problem when we don't understand the situation it is embedded in; we often need to solve problems in order to understand the implications of a situation well. We evaluate our solutions by projecting their results using assessment methods, and we may need to solve new problems in the course of evaluation. For simplicity, however, it makes some sense to refer to two different styles of case-based reasoning. In problem-solving situations, we tend to emphasize the use of cases to propose solutions; in interpretive situations, we tend to emphasize using cases for criticism and justification.

This discussion suggests the primary processes required for case-based reasoning. First and foremost, partially matching cases must be retrieved to facilitate reasoning. Thus, **case retrieval** is a primary process, as is its component process, **partial pattern matching** and its adjunct process, **case storage** (also called **memory update**). In order to make sure that poor solutions are not repeated along with the good ones, both styles of case-based reasoning **evaluate** their solutions.

The two styles of case-based reasoning, however, each require that different reasoning be done once cases are retrieved. In problem-solving CBR, a ballpark solution to the new problem is **proposed** by extracting the solution from some retrieved case. This is followed by **adaptation**, the process of fixing an old solution to fit a new situation, and **criticism**, the process of critiquing the new solution before trying it out. In interpretive CBR, a ballpark interpretation or desired result is **proposed**, sometimes based on retrieved cases, sometimes imposed from the outside (as when a lawyer's client requires a certain result). This is followed by **justification**, the process of creating an argument for the proposed solution, done by a pro-

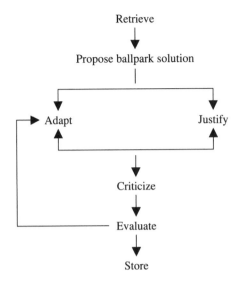

FIGURE 1.1 The Case-Based Reasoning Cycle

cess of comparing and contrasting the new situation with prior cases, looking for similarities between the new situation and others that justify the desired result and differences that imply that other factors must be taken into account. Sometimes justification is followed by a **criticism** step in which hypothetical situations are generated and the proposed solution applied to them in order to test the solution.

These steps and styles are in some sense recursive. The criticize and adapt steps, for example, often require new cases to be retrieved. There are also several loops in the process. Criticism may lead to additional adaptation; so might evaluation. And when reasoning is not progressing well using one case, the whole process may need to be restarted from the top with a new case chosen. Figure 1.1 summarizes their relationship.

In the following sections, we give a short overview of each step and discuss some of the issues that must be addressed to explain it and make it work well on the computer.

1.4.1 Case Retrieval

Remembering is the process of retrieving a case or set of cases from memory. In general, it consists of two substeps:

Recall previous cases. The goal of this step is to retrieve "good" cases that can support reasoning that comes in the next steps. Good cases are those that have the potential to make relevant predictions about the new case. Retrieval is done by using features of the new case as indexes into the case library. Cases labeled by subsets of those features or by features that can be derived from those features are recalled.

> **Select the best subset.** This step selects the most promising case or cases to reason with from those generated in step 1. The purpose of this step is to winnow down the set of relevant cases to a few most-on-point candidates worthy of intensive consideration. Sometimes it is appropriate to choose one best case; sometimes a small set is needed.

There are several big problems that must be addressed to make retrieval happen. First, we must give the computer a means of recognizing that a case is applicable to a new situation. This is the **matching**, or **similarity-assessment**, problem. When two cases obviously look alike, that isn't too hard. It is fairly easy, for example, to see how a program could recognize that one summer meal served to vegetarians is similar to another one with the same description. But sometimes cases that are most applicable don't look very similar to the new situation on the surface, and it is necessary to dig deeper to realize that they are similar.

Football and chess strategies, for example, have much in common, though the concrete features of the games are dissimilar. One is played on a board, the other on a field; one has pieces, the other people; one has teams competing with each other, the other individuals. What they have in common are more abstract features shared by competitive games. There are two sides in opposition; each wants to win; each wants the other side to lose; both games involve planning and counterplanning; both involve positions on a playing field, though it is an actual field with people for football and a board with pieces for chess. Nevertheless, we might expect a chess expert who knows how to plan a fork in chess to notice the potential in a football game for setting up a fork.[4]

One way to deal with this problem is to use more than just the surface representation of a case for comparison. Cases are also compared at more abstract levels of representation. To make this happen we must discover which of the abstract ways of representing a case are the right ones to use for comparisons. We call this the **indexing-vocabulary** problem.

We must also give the computer elaboration capabilities. Sometimes so little is known about a new situation that there is little basis for comparing it with other situations. Sometimes what is known is in too raw a form for comparison, and additional features of the situation need to be derived from it. We call this the **situation-assessment** problem. In predicting who will win a battle, for example, the ratio of defender strength to attacker strength is predictive, but neither defender strength nor attacker strength by itself is. Cases need to be judged similar based on the ratio (a derived feature) rather than the individual values (surface features). Similarly, judges make their decisions based on evaluative assessments of a situation such as the degree of violence exhibited and the extent to which the defendant was provoked. Such information is not available in raw cases but must be derived from the facts of the situation. When a judge uses cases to evaluate a new situation, the most useful ones will be those that are similar on these elaborated or derived descriptors. The issue here is to come up with a way of elaborating situation descriptions and generating derived features for cases in an efficient way. We

---

4. A fork is a situation in a competitive game where two or more possibilities for a good move are possible for one side. Blocking either move results in the opponent doing the other one and gaining advantage. In football, one can set up a fork, for example, by sending two receivers into the zone covered by one defensive back. The ball is passed to whichever receiver the defensive back chooses not to cover.

need guidance in generating derived features because some are expensive to derive, and even if all were cheap, it would be expensive to generate all possible derived features of a case.

A third issue is **retrieval algorithms**. How can we search a massive case library in an efficient way to find appropriate cases? We shall see that initial approaches to this problem attempted to find organizational strategies for cases so that search of the case library would be limited to potentially relevant cases only. More recently, the approach has been to find representational forms for a case's indexes that can be matched efficiently by a parallel machine. The assumption here is that with parallel machines, the bottleneck is in the matching algorithms rather than in the search algorithms.

Together, these problems comprise **the indexing problem**. Broadly, the indexing problem is the problem of retrieving applicable cases at appropriate times (despite all the problems cited above). In general, it has been addressed as a problem of assigning labels, called **indexes**, to cases that designate under what conditions each case can be used to make useful inferences. These labels have been treated much like indexes in a book. Old cases are indexed by those labels. Programs use a new situation as a key into that index and find appropriate cases by finding the case with the best-matching index. Researchers are working on specifying what kinds of indexes are most useful, designating vocabularies for indexes, creating algorithms and heuristics for automating index choice, organizing cases based on those indexes, searching memory using those indexes, and choosing the best of the retrieved cases. There is a tension between using indexes to designate usefulness and direct a search while at the same time not allowing them to overly restrict what can be recalled. This is one of the most important issues in case-based reasoning.

1.4.2 Proposing a Ballpark Solution

In the next step, relevant portions of the cases selected during retrieval are extracted to form a ballpark solution to the new case. In problem solving, this step normally involves selecting the solution to the old problem, or some piece of it, as a ballpark solution to the new one. In interpretation, this step involves partitioning the retrieved cases according to the interpretations or solutions they predict and, based on that, assigning an initial interpretation to the new problem.

For example, a problem solver attempting to plan a meal focuses on the meal plan of a recalled case and uses it as its ballpark solution. Or, if it is attempting to derive some piece of a meal plan, it focuses on the analogous piece in the old case. Thus, when JULIA is trying to design an easy-to-prepare and cheap meal for twenty people, if it remembers a meal in which antipasto salad, lasagne, broccoli, and spumoni were served, that solution will be the ballpark solution after this step. When it is trying to choose a main dish, if it is reminded of the same case, lasagne (its main dish) will be its ballpark solution to that goal.

An interpretive program, in this step, decides which of the possible interpretations to begin reasoning with. PROTOS (Bareiss 1989a), a program that diagnoses hearing disorders, uses a coarse evaluation function to distinguish which of the many possible diagnoses proposed by the recalled cases is most appropriate to its new case. Though the ballpark solution is correct only about half the time, it provides classification procedures with a place to start in interpreting the other half of its problems.

There are several issues that arise in constructing a ballpark solution. First is the question of how appropriate portions of an old case can be selected for focus. An old case could be quite large, and it is important that the parts of it with no relevance to the new situation not get in the way. It is possible, however, that seemingly unrelated parts of an old case can provide guidelines. The best answer we have to this problem so far is twofold: First, the goals of the reasoner determine where to focus in the old case. The reasoner focuses attention on that part of the old case that was relevant to achieving the reasoner's current goal in the past. Thus, if the reasoner is trying to derive a solution, focus is on the previous solution. If the reasoner is trying to derive a particular part of a solution, focus is on that part of the solution in the previous case. If the reasoner is trying to interpret a situation, its classification in the old case is the focus. Second, the internal structure of the old case, especially the dependencies between different parts of the case, tell the reasoner how to expand focus in relevant ways. Thus, when the reasoner focuses on the solution or classification in an old case, those features of the case that led to selection of that solution or classification are also in focus.

Another issue has to do with how much work to do in this step before passing control to adaptation or justification processes. Often there are relatively easy and automatic, some would say *commonsense*, adaptations that can be made in an old solution before it undergoes the scrutiny of harder adaptation processes. For example, in labor mediation, adjustment of salary and other benefits based on cost of living is an expected adjustment. Such adjustments might also be made to old interpretations before creating arguments for them. Especially in interpretive reasoning, making easy adjustments in this step before harder reasoning kicks in may be more advantageous than making adjustments after arguments have been mounted. This way, argumentation is based on a more realistic solution.

A third issue has to do with choice of an interpretation in interpretive reasoning. If one can get to the "right" answer no matter where one starts, then choice of a first alternative is merely an efficiency issue. However, if all alternatives are not connected in some way, initial choice of a first alternative might affect accuracy. Thus, where to begin in doing interpretation is a real issue.

1.4.3 Adaptation

In case-based problem solving, old solutions are used as inspiration for solving new problems. Because new situations rarely match old ones exactly, however, old solutions must be fixed to fit new situations. In this step, called **adaptation**, the ballpark solution is adapted to fit the new situation. There are two major steps involved in adaptation: figuring out what needs to be adapted and doing the adaptation.

Issues in adaptation arise from both steps. We start by considering adaptation itself. For any particular domain or task, we can come up with a set of adaptation strategies or heuristics. We can implement those and create a working system. This approach is rather *ad hoc,* however. One big question we must address is whether there is a general set of adaptation strategies that we can start with for any domain and that provide guidelines for defining specialized adaptation strategies. Taking the meat out of a recipe to make it vegetarian is a strategy specific to recipe adaptation, for example, but it is a specialization of a more general strategy that we call *delete secondary component*. This strategy states that a secondary component of an item can be deleted if it performs no necessary function. For each type of adaptation strategy, we must also designate the knowledge necessary for its application.

Also important in adaptation are methodologies for evaluating which parts of an old solution need adaptation to fit the new one. One way to identify what needs adapting is to notice inconsistencies between old solutions and new needs and, based on that, choosing what should be adapted. Some of the bookkeeping methods developed elsewhere in AI (e.g., reason-maintenance, constraint propagation) are useful here but are used in different ways than in their original formulations.

1.4.4 Evaluative Reasoning: Justification and Criticism

In these steps, a solution or interpretation is justified, often before being tried out in the world. When all knowledge necessary for evaluation is known, one can think of this step as a validation step. However, in many situations, there are too many unknowns to be able to validate a solution. We can criticize solutions using all the techniques of interpretive case-based reasoning, determining, in effect, whether the derived solution is the best alternative. We do this by *comparing and contrasting* the proposed solution with other similar solutions. This step requires a recursive call to memory processes to retrieve cases with similar solutions. For example, if there is an already known instance of a similar situation's failing, the reasoner must consider whether or not the new situation is subject to the same problems.

We might also propose hypothetical situations to test the robustness of a solution. Yet another way to criticize a solution is to run a simulation (coarse or high-fidelity) and check the results.

Criticism may require retrieval of additional cases and may result in the need for additional adaptation, this time called *repair*.

Major issues here include strategies for evaluation using cases; strategies for retrieving cases to use in interpretation, evaluation, and justification; the generation of appropriate hypotheticals and strategies for using them; and the assignment of blame or credit to old cases.

1.4.5 Evaluative Testing

In the next step, the results of reasoning are tried out in the real world. Feedback about the real things that happened during or as a result of executing the solution are obtained and analyzed. If results were as expected, further analysis is not necessary in this step, but if they were different than expected, explanation of the anomalous results is necessary. This explanation requires figuring out what caused the anomaly and what could have been done to prevent it. It can sometimes be done by case-based reasoning, that is, by reapplying a previous explanation.

This step is one of the most important for a case-based reasoner. It gives the reasoner a way to evaluate its decisions in the real world, allowing it to collect feedback that enables it to learn. Feedback allows it to notice the consequences of its reasoning; this in turn facilitates analysis of its reasoning and explanation of things that didn't go exactly as planned. This analysis, in turn, allows a reasoner to anticipate and avoid mistakes it has been able to explain sufficiently and to notice previously unforeseen opportunities that it might have a chance to use later.

Evaluation is the process of judging the goodness of a proposed solution. Sometimes evaluation is done in the context of previous cases; sometimes it is based on feedback from the world; sometimes it is based on simulation. Evaluation includes explaining differences (e.g., between what is expected and what actually happens), justifying differences (e.g., between a proposed solution and one used in the past), projecting outcomes, and comparing and ranking alternative possibilities. Evaluation can point out the need for additional adaptation, or repair, of the proposed solution.

1.4.6 Memory Update

The new case is then stored appropriately in the case memory for future use. A case comprises the problem, its solution, plus any underlying facts and supporting reasoning that the system knows how to make use of. The most important process at this time of memory update is choosing the ways to "index" the new case in memory. Indexes must be chosen such that the new case can be recalled during later reasoning at times when it can be most helpful. It should not be overindexed, however, because we would not want it recalled indiscriminately. This means that the reasoner must be able to anticipate the importance of the case to later reasoning. Memory's indexing structure and organization are also adjusted in this step. This problem shares all of its issues with the first: We must choose appropriate indexes for the new case using the right vocabulary, and we must at the same time make sure that all other items remain accessible as we add to the case library's store.

1.5 APPLICABILITY OF CASE-BASED REASONING

In the remainder of this book, we will be discussing the technical details of case-based reasoning, but before moving to that we spend just a little more time on the advantages and usefulness of the method.

1.5.1 Range of Applicability and Real-World Usefulness

We start by considering why doctors, or anybody else trained in the practice of making logical decisions, would make case-based inferences. After all, doctors are trained to use facts and knowledge, and case-based reasoning looks like something based on hearsay. The answer is simple. Doctors are trained to recognize disorders in isolation and to recognize common combinations of disorders. They also know the etiology of disorders, that is, how they progress. But they cannot be trained to recognize every combination of disorders, and the knowledge they have of disease processes is time-consuming to use for generation of plausible diagnoses. If they have used their knowledge of disease process to solve a hard problem once, it makes sense to cache the solution in such a way that it can be reused. That is, once they have learned to recognize a novel combination of disorders, if they remember that experience, they will be able to recognize it again, just as they recognize more common combinations, without the difficult reasoning necessary the first time. Logical medical judgment comes in later in deciding whether or not the patient does indeed have the proposed set of diseases.

Similarly, we can't expect a computer program to be seeded with all the possible combinations of problems it might encounter. Nor can we expect it to have efficient algorithms for generating plausible solutions from scratch all the time. A model-based troubleshooting system, for example, might know very well how something functions. That doesn't necessarily mean that it can generate solutions to problems easily, especially when more than one fault could be present at any time. Similarly, though a causal model may be helpful in verifying a design, it may not provide enough information to be able to generate designs in underconstrained or overconstrained situations. Just as case-based reasoning provides a way for people to generate solutions easily, it also provides a way for a computer program to propose solutions efficiently when previous similar situations have been encountered. This doesn't mean that causal reasoning is without merit. On the contrary, it must play the role that the medical doctor's logic plays after a solution is proposed. The causal model–based system needs to work along with the case-based system to identify changes that must be made in an old solution, to ensure valid adaptations, and to verify proposed solutions. Indeed, CASEY (Koton 1988a, 1989) and KRITIK (Goel 1989; Goel and Chandrasekaran 1989) do just that, CASEY for the task of heart failure diagnosis and KRITIK for design of simple mechanical objects.

Case-based reasoning is useful to people and machines that know a lot about a task and domain because it gives them a way of reusing hard reasoning they have done in the past. It is equally useful, however, to those who know little about a task or domain. Consider, for example, a man who has never done any entertaining yet has to plan the meal specified in the Introduction. His own entertaining experience won't help him. But if he has been to dinner parties, he has a place to start. If he remembered meals he'd been served under circumstances similar to those he has to deal with, he could use one of those to get started. For example, if he could generate a list of large dinner parties he has attended, he could, for each one, figure out whether the dishes were easy to make and inexpensive, and when he remembered one, adapt it to fit. Alternatively, if he has had to make food decisions before and his sister has always helped him do that, his interpretation of this situation as a kind of food problem would tell him to call his sister for advice. Or, if he remembers parties but doesn't know how to determine how easy items are to make, he could interpret that as a food decision, remember that his sister gives good advice on that, and call his sister for that advice.

Case-based reasoning is also useful when knowledge is incomplete and/or evidence is sparse. Logical systems have trouble dealing with either of these situations because they want to base their answers on what is well known and sound. More traditional AI systems use certainty factors and other methods of inexact reasoning to counter these problems, all of which require considerable effort on the part of the computer and none of which seem intuitively very plausible. Case-based reasoning provides another method for dealing with incomplete knowledge. A case-based reasoner makes assumptions to fill in incomplete or missing knowledge based on what its experience tells it, and goes on from there. Solutions generated this way won't always be optimal, or even right, but if the reasoner is careful about evaluating proposed answers, the case-based methodology gives it a way to generate answers easily.

Though the advantages of case-based reasoning are easily evident when an old solution is fairly close to that needed in the new case, case-based reasoning also can provide advantage even if the old solution is far from what is needed. There are two possibilities. Those features of the remembered case that must be ruled out in the new situation can be added to its description and a new case recalled, or the recalled case can be used as a starting point for coming up with a new solution. When there is considerable interaction between the parts of a solution, then even if large amounts of adaptation are required to derive an acceptable solution, that may still be easier than generating a solution from scratch. And the case provides something concrete to base reasoning on.

In short, case-based reasoning reduces the cognitive load involved in interacting with a complex real-world environment.

1.5.2 Advantages and Disadvantages of CBR

Case-based reasoning provides many advantages for a reasoner.

- Case-based reasoning allows the reasoner to propose solutions to problems quickly, avoiding the time necessary to derive those answers from scratch.

The doctor remembering an old diagnosis or treatment experiences this benefit. Although the case-based reasoner has to evaluate proposed solutions, as any reasoner does, it gets a head start on solving problems because it can generate proposals easily. There is considerable advantage in not having to redo time-consuming computations and inferences. This advantage is helpful for almost all reasoning tasks, including problem solving, planning, explanation, and diagnosis. Indeed, evaluation of CASEY (Koton 1988a) shows a speedup of two orders of magnitude when a problem has been seen in the past.

- Case-based reasoning allows a reasoner to propose solutions in domains that are not completely understood by the reasoner.

Many domains are impossible to understand completely, often because much depends on unpredictable human behavior—the economy, for example. Others nobody understands yet—for example, how some medications and diseases operate. Other times, we simply find ourselves in situations that we don't understand well, but in which we must act anyway, for example, choosing which graduate students to accept into a program. Case-based reasoning allows us to make assumptions and predictions based on what worked in the past without having a complete understanding.

- Case-based reasoning gives a reasoner a means of evaluating solutions when no algorithmic method is available for evaluation.

Using cases to aid in evaluation is particularly helpful when there are many unknowns, making any other kind of evaluation impossible or hard. Solutions are evaluated in the context of previous similar situations. Again, the reasoner does its evaluation based on what worked in the past.

■ Cases are useful in interpreting open-ended and ill-defined concepts.

This is one use attorneys put cases to extensively, but it is also important in everyday situations. In the example above, cases were used to determine what was included in the concept "fish Anne won't eat." The performance of PROTOS (Bariess 1989a; Porter, Bareiss, and Holte 1990) in classifying hearing disorders when little information is known shows that a case-based methodology for interpretation can be more accurate than traditional methods based on necessary and sufficient conditions when classifications are ill defined.

■ Remembering previous experiences is particularly useful in warning of the potential for problems that have occurred in the past, alerting a reasoner to take actions to avoid repeating past mistakes.

How can this work? Remembered experiences can be successful or failed episodes, that is, situations in which things did not turn out exactly as planned. Consider again the reasoner trying to plan a meal. He or she can be helped considerably, for example, by remembering a meal that was supposed to be easy to prepare and inexpensive and instead was hard to make because some of the ingredients were hard to obtain in manufactured form and had to be made from scratch. The reasoner is warned, by this case, to avoid those ingredients or to make sure they are available before committing to a menu.

■ Cases help a reasoner to focus its reasoning on important parts of a problem by pointing out what features of a problem are the important ones.

What was important in previous situations will tend to be important in new ones. Thus, if in a previous case, some set of features was implicated in a failure, the reasoner focuses on those features to ensure that the failure will not be repeated. Similarly, if some features are implicated in a success, the reasoner knows to focus on those features. Such focus plays a role in both problem-solving and interpretive case-based reasoning. In interpretive case-based reasoning, justifications and critiques are built based on those features that have proven responsible for failures and successes in the past. An attorney, for example, focuses on those aspects of a new situation that mattered in previous cases. In problem solving, a reasoner might attempt to adapt a solution so that it includes more of what was responsible for previous successes and less of what was responsible for failures.

Of course, there are also disadvantages in using cases to reason:

■ A case-based reasoner might be tempted to use old cases blindly, relying on previous experience without validating it in the new situation.
■ A case-based reasoner might allow cases to bias him or her or it too much in solving a new problem.

- Often people, especially novices, are not reminded of the most appropriate sets of cases when they are reasoning (Gick and Holyoak 1980; Gentner 1989).

Relying on previous experience without doing validation can result in inefficient or incorrect solutions and evaluations. Retrieval of inappropriate cases can cost precious problem-solving time or lead to costly errors that can be avoided by more incremental methods.

People do find case-based reasoning a natural way to reason, however, and the endeavor of explaining the processes involved in case-based reasoning might help us to learn how to teach people to reason better using cases. In addition, the case memory technology we develop is beginning to allow us to build decision aiding systems that augment human memory by providing the appropriate cases while still allowing the human user to reason in a natural and familiar way. And we can make sure our programs avoid negative types of behavior.

1.6 COGNITIVE MODEL, OR METHODOLOGY FOR BUILDING EXPERT SYSTEMS?

Is case-based reasoning a model of people, or is it a methodology for building intelligent systems? I've been somewhat schizophrenic about this issue up to now, sometimes referring to people doing case-based reasoning, sometimes referring to machines that use the method to reason. Case-based reasoning is both, and explorations in case-based reasoning have been of both the ways people use cases to solve problems and the ways we can make machines use them.

1.6.1 Case-Based Reasoning and People

There is much evidence that people do, in fact, use case-based reasoning in their daily reasoning. Some of that evidence is hearsay—we have observed it. Other evidence is experimental. Ross (1986, 1989), for example, has shown that people learning a new skill often refer back to previous problems to refresh their memories on how to do the task. Research conducted in our lab shows that both novice and experienced car mechanics use their own experiences and those of others to help them generate hypotheses about what is wrong with a car, recognize problems (e.g., a testing instrument not working), and remember how to test for different diagnoses (Lancaster and Kolodner 1987, 1988). Other research in our lab shows that physicians use previous cases extensively to generate hypotheses about what is wrong with a patient, to help them interpret test results, and to select therapies when several are available and none are understood very well (Kolodner, unpublished). We have also observed architects and caterers as they recall, merge, and adapt old design plans to create new ones. Researchers at GTE found that engineers' reasoning about what could go wrong with phone switching networks used cases extensively (Kopeikina, Bandau, and Lemmon 1988). Others have observed strategic planners, economists, and stock-market analysts using case-based reasoning.

The programs we build are an attempt to understand the processes involved in reasoning in a case-based way. There are several important potential applications of an understanding of the way people solve problems in a natural way. First, we might build decision-aiding systems for people that can help them retrieve cases better. Psychologists have found that people are comfortable using cases to make decisions (Ross 1986, 1989; Klein and Calderwood 1988; Read and Cesa 1990) but don't always remember the right ones (Holyoak 1985; Gentner 1989). To alleviate this problem, the computer can be used as a retrieval tool to augment people's memories. Second, we might create teaching strategies and build teaching tools that teach based on good examples. If people are comfortable using examples to solve problems and know how to do it well, then one of our responsibilities as teachers might be to teach them the right examples and effective ways to index them. Third, if we understand which parts of this natural process are difficult to do well, we can teach people better how to do case-based reasoning. One criticism of using cases to make decisions, for example, is that it puts unsound bias into the reasoning system, because people tend to assume an answer from a previous case is right without justifying it in the new case. This tells us that we should be teaching people how to justify case-based suggestions and that justification or evaluation is crucial to good decision making. If we can isolate other problems people have in solving problems in a case-based way, then we can similarly teach people to do those things better.

1.6.2 Building a Case-Based Reasoner

As a method for building intelligent reasoning systems, case-based reasoning has appeal because it seems relatively simple and natural. Though it is hard to get experts to tell you all the knowledge they use to solve problems, it is easy to get them to recount their war stories. In fact, several people building expert systems that know how to reason using cases have found it easier to build case-based expert systems than traditional ones (Barletta and Hennessy 1989; Goodman 1989; Simoudis 1992). A big problem in reasoning in expert domains is the high degree of uncertainty and incompleteness of the knowledge involved. Case-based reasoning addresses those problems by having the reasoner rely on what has worked in the past. Case-based systems also provide efficiency. While we find first-principles problem-solving systems spending large amounts of time solving their problems from scratch, case-based systems have been found to be several orders of magnitude faster (Koton 1988a, 1989).

There are several different kinds of case-based reasoning systems one might build. At the two extremes are fully automated systems and retrieval-only systems. Fully automated systems are those that solve problems completely by themselves and have some means of interacting with the world to receive feedback on their decisions. Retrieval-only systems work interactively with a person to solve a problem. They act to augment a person's memory, providing cases for the person to consider that he or she might not be aware of, but the person will be responsible for hard decisions. There is a whole range of systems in between, some requiring more on the part of the person using the system, some requiring less.

There are also several purposes one might create a case-based reasoning system to serve. We might want it to solve problems, to suggest concrete answers to problems, to suggest without providing answers (i.e., to give abstract advice), or to just act as a database that can retrieve partially-matching cases. Much as has been the case with database systems, we can foresee case-based systems interacting with a person or another program. Interacting with a person, we can see an executive who is doing strategic planning asking for cases to help in deriving or evaluating a solution. The CSI Battle Planner (Goodman 1989) provides this type of capability now for battle planning. CLAVIER (Barletta and Hennessy 1989; Hennessy and Hinkle 1992), in its current version, provides this for engineers who configure layouts of parts for an auto-clave. Several experimental systems (e.g., ARCHIE [Goel, Kolodner et al. 1991; Pearce et al. 1992; Domeshek and Kolodner 1991, 1992], the ASK systems [Ferguson et al. 1992], and ORCA [Bareiss and Slator, 1991, 1992]) are investigating what is necessary to provide this kind of aid for complex problems. Or, we can imagine a tutoring system that accesses a library of examples to use in teaching.

What is required for the simplest of systems is a library of cases that coarsely cover the set of problems that come up in a domain. Both success stories and failures must be included. And, the cases must be appropriately indexed. This library, along with a friendly and useful interface, provides augmentation for human memory. And automated processes can be built on top of it incrementally.

1.7 A NOTE TO READERS

This book was written with two audiences in mind, each with different interests. Cognitive sci-entists and artificial intelligence researchers reading the book will be interested, I expect, in the conceptual and cognitive models behind case-based reasoning, wanting to hear the how-tos of building systems only after motivation and justifications for methods are presented. I expect that builders of systems are more interested in the how-tos of system building, often losing patience with long preliminary conceptual discussions.

This book addresses case-based reasoning as both a cognitive process and a methodol-ogy for building intelligent systems. In most chapters, discussion is of models of case-based reasoning that have been developed up to now, first discussing the reasoning methods them-selves, then discussing methods for implementing methods. The book both provides guidance for systems builders and spells out the psychological significance of the work, but it may not be organized optimally for either cognitive scientists or system builders.

Thus, I provide this guide to reading the book for those who want to know where they can find the things they are interested in. The introductory section to the book continues with three more chapters, presenting several case-based reasoners that have been developed and introducing the reasoning tasks case-based reasoning supports and the cognitive model it im-plies. I assume that all readers will want to read chapters 2 and 3, the presentation of systems and the discussion of tasks case-based reasoning can support. Some readers, however, will not be interested in chapter 4, which presents the cognitive model. Those readers can easily skip that chapter; its content will not be necessary for understanding the methods presented in other chapters.

The book continues with four parts. Part II (chapters 5, 6, and 7) discusses the case library, exploring case representation and selection of indexes for cases. Part III (chapters 8, 9, and 10) discusses algorithms for update and retrieval of the case library. Discussion includes pattern matching, retrieval and update algorithms, situation assessment, and choice of most useful cases. Part IV discusses processes for case manipulation. Adaptation and the control of adaptation are presented in chapters 11 and 12; chapter 13 presents interpretive compare-and-contrast processes. Chapter 14 addresses control issues inherent in systems that use multiple cases. In Part V (chapter 15), issues in building case-based systems are discussed. Included in that chapter is discussion of how one might decide whether a system should be autonomous or interactive and how to use the case-based reasoning model as a starting point for developing interactive case-based and story-based systems for decision support, advisement, aiding, and training.

For the most part, chapters and sections are organized so that conceptual issues are addressed first, with methods presented later. Though I believe that an understanding of conceptual issues will allow system builders to make the best use of the presented methods, some readers may want to focus on methods first, referring only to those conceptual issues they feel they need to understand to make the methods work. These readers will want to read chapters 5 and 7 of Part II in their entirety but may want to skip large parts of chapter 6 on first reading. They will want to read Part III sequentially, skipping those sections that are too conceptual. In Part IV, those readers who are building problem-solving systems will want to read chapters 11 and 12, reading 14 only if their reasoners will use multiple cases to solve a single problem and 13 only if their systems will be responsible for evaluating derived solutions. Those building interactive systems to assess situations or evaluate and repair solutions derived by a human user will want to concentrate on chapter 13 first, moving on to the other chapters in that section only as needed for their task.

Readers interested mostly in the cognitive model and in conceptual issues will find the book more straightforward to read. Such readers should read chapters until they find them more technical or methods-based than they are looking for and then skip to the next chapter.

All readers will benefit by returning to chapters 2 and 3, and perhaps even chapter 1, after reading the remainder of the book. These chapters will serve to pull together the disparate issues addressed in the separate chapters. The appendix of systems at the end of the book is also meant to serve that purpose.

1.8 SUMMARY

Case-based reasoning can mean adapting old solutions to meet new demands, using old cases to explain new situations, using old cases to critique new solutions, or reasoning from precedents to interpret a new situation or create an equitable solution to a new problem. A case-based reasoner learns as a byproduct of its reasoning activity. It becomes more efficient and more competent as a result of storing its experiences and referring to them in later reasoning.

In a departure from traditional methods of reasoning investigated by AI researchers and psychologists, case-based reasoning views reasoning as a process of remembering one or a small set of concrete instances or cases and basing decisions on comparisons between the new situation and the old one. Decomposition and recomposition are, as a result, deemphasized, as is the use of general knowledge. Instead, emphasis is on the manipulation of knowledge in the form of concrete specific instances. Large chunks of composed knowledge are seen as the starting point for reasoning.

A case, however, is more than a large chunk of composed knowledge. It is a *contextualized* piece of knowledge representing an experience, and any case worth recording in a case library (whether human or machine) teaches a lesson fundamental to achieving the goals of the reasoner who will use it. Cases are *indexed* by combinations of their descriptors that predict the situations in which they will be useful. Cases represent knowledge at an operational level.

They come in many different shapes and sizes, covering large or small time slices, associating solutions with problems, outcomes with situations, or both.

Because case-based reasoning integrates reasoning and learning, it is not enough for a case-based reasoner to stop reasoning after it derives a solution. Rather, it must continue by collecting feedback about its solution and evaluating that feedback. Without evaluation processes based on feedback, learning could not take place reliably, and case-based reasoning itself would be too unreliable to depend on.

The quality of a case-based reasoner's reasoning depends on the experiences it has had, its ability to understand new situations in terms of those old experiences, its adeptness at adaptation, and its adeptness at evaluation and repair. The major processes employed by a case-based reasoner are case storage and retrieval, adaptation, and criticism.

Case-based reasoning is applicable to a wide range of real-world situations, ranging from knowledge-rich situations in which construction of solutions is complex to knowledge-poor situations in which cases provide the only available knowledge. It has many advantages, allowing a reasoner to propose solutions to problems quickly, to reason in domains that are not well understood, to evaluate solutions when algorithmic methods are not available, to avoid previous problems, and to focus on important parts of a situation. Its major disadvantages are all linked to using cases poorly to reason, for example, relying too heavily on their proposals without evaluating them. Yet case-based reasoning is a natural way of reasoning for people and one showing considerable promise for machines.

There are several kinds of case-based systems that might be built. Automated systems solve problems from start to finish. If we take case-based reasoning seriously as a cognitive model, however, we can think about building systems that can interact with people in a natural way to solve problems. The simplest of these uses the machine's case library to augment the memory of a person, leaving the human user to reason based on retrieved cases.

2

Case Studies of Several Case-Based Reasoners

In this chapter, we present case studies of several case-based reasoners. Through this presentation, readers should begin to understand better the types of tasks case-based reasoning can be used for and the types of input, knowledge, and reasoning architectures that go into making a case-based reasoner run. We present six automated reasoners:

1. CHEF as a case-based planner
2. JULIA as a case-based designer
3. CASEY as a case-based diagnosis program
4. HYPO as a case-based interpretive program
5. PROTOS as a case-based classification program
6. CLAVIER as a case-based program that is in use and saving its company money

We then discuss several hypothetical and real "retrieval-only" case-based systems. These are interactive systems that help a person perform a reasoning task or that provide advice.

For each system, we discuss its domain and task, the knowledge it uses, its input, its architecture, and the reasoning it does. The representations, knowledge, and reasoning used in these programs will be discussed in far more detail in later chapters of this book as we discuss the ways in which each of the components of a case-based reasoner can be implemented. Note that each system presented was chosen because it is representative of a class of case-based systems. Thus, some systems whose pieces are discussed extensively later in the book (e.g., MEDIATOR) are not presented in detail in this chapter. Readers can find out more about those systems by consulting the Appendix.

2.1 CHEF

CHEF is a case-based planner (Hammond 1986a, 1986b, 1989a). It takes as input a conjunction of subgoals that it needs to plan to achieve, and its output is a plan. Its domain is recipe creation. Recipes are viewed, in CHEF, as plans. They provide the sequence of steps that must be carried out to achieve the creation of some dish. Thus, CHEF's input is goals that recipes can achieve (e.g., include fish, use stir-frying method, achieve savory taste); its output is a recipe (plan) that can achieve those goals.

As a case-based planner, CHEF creates its plans by recalling old plans that worked under similar circumstances and modifying them to fit its new situation. Thus, its first step in creating a plan is to retrieve an old recipe that fulfills as many of its new goals as possible. To enable reminding of this sort, CHEF indexes its plans by the goals they achieve. Beef and broccoli, for example, is indexed by several goals, among them `include beef`, `include a crisp vegetable`, `use method stir-fry`, and `achieve taste savory`.

Next, CHEF adapts the old plan to fit the new situation. It does this in two steps. First, it reinstantiates the old plan. That is, it creates an instance of it that substitutes new objects for the ones used previously. If it is creating a chicken and snow peas recipe, for example, from its beef and broccoli recipe, it substitutes chicken for beef and snow peas for broccoli in the old recipe. To do this, CHEF needs to know something about the roles its objects play in the old plans. CHEF has fairly limited knowledge of this, and the particular method it uses to know what should be substituted for what is to look at the similarities between the objects in the old and new situations and substitute those items in the new situation that are most similar to objects in the old one. Because chicken and beef are both defined as meat, for example, it decides that they correspond; similarly for broccoli and snow peas—both are vegetables.

In its second adaptation step, CHEF applies special-purpose *object critics* to modify the old plan for the new situation. A typical one says that duck must be defatted before stir-frying. It looks something like this:

```
After doing step: bone the duck
             do: clean the fat from the duck
        because: the duck is now fatty
```

This critic is associated with the object *duck*, and each time it is used in a recipe, the critic is fired off. If there is a step of boning the duck in the recipe being created, a step is added after that one specifying that the duck should be defatted.

Object critics most often add special-purpose preparation steps to a plan (e.g., deveining shrimp, chopping items into pieces of the right size, deboning, defatting). They are CHEF's way of encoding knowledge about special procedures associated with the use of objects within its domain. Their use during adaptation shows the interplay between the use of experience and general knowledge in a case-based reasoning system.

After reinstantiation and application of critics, CHEF has a complete plan. Many planners would stop there and be finished. Remember, though, that a hallmark of case-based reasoning is that a reasoner learns from its experiences. If the planner stopped with creation of its plan, it would have no feedback to tell it whether its plan worked or didn't work. Without that feedback, there is little basis for learning. The reasoner could store the new plans it created, but it would have no way of knowing later on whether it was repeating a plan that worked or one that didn't. In addition, in complex situations, it often isn't possible to predict what will and will not work with certainty. Only trying plans out in the complexity of the real world can provide that insight.

CHEF therefore goes on to use its plan and collect feedback about how it worked. When a plan works well, it is finished. It stores the plan in memory and goes on to its next task. When a plan doesn't work as expected, however, CHEF attempts to learn from the situation. It creates a causal explanation of why the plan didn't work and uses that to index into its general planning knowledge, which it uses to *repair* the faulty plan.

CHEF tries its plans by running them in a simulator that provides feedback much like that the world would supply (to the extent that the world is captured in the simulator). When it runs its original recipe for beef and broccoli through the simulator, for example, it finds that the broccoli turns soggy. It recognizes this as a failure of the plan and attempts to explain why it happened. In this case, it finds that extra liquid in the pan caused the broccoli to cook too much and that the extra liquid is a side effect of a previous step and does not directly achieve any goal. CHEF thus classifies this failure as a `side-effect:disabled-condition:concurrent`. That is, a side effect of one step disabled a condition of another step, and the side effect and disabled condition happen concurrently with each other. Associated with this sort of failure, CHEF has three repair strategies: splitting and re-forming steps in the plan, altering the plan to get rid of the side effect, and finding an alternative plan. It chooses to split and re-form.

We need to consider now how CHEF can recognize the failures of its plans. The answer is that after CHEF creates a plan, it does the equivalent of trying it out in the world (by running it in its simulator). This feedback enables it to notice whether its plans were successful or not by comparing real results (from the simulator) to expected results. A program might also recognize failures by projecting the results of its plans as well as it can, predicting their results, and then comparing those projections to its expectations.

Another thing we should consider is the classifications CHEF uses to categorize its failures. As can be seen from the one used in this case, CHEF's explanations are in terms of causal relationships between goals, plans, and steps of plans that provide a general vocabulary for describing general planning situations. These situation descriptions function similarly to the critics in HACKER (Sussman 1975) and NOAH (Sacerdoti 1977), though they are more flexible than those critics. Each describes a general plan failure situation and points to a variety of strategies for repairing that sort of failure. The major difference between these structures, called TOP (Schank 1982; Hammond 1984), and the critics in NOAH and HACKER is that TOP organize information about these sorts of situations, whereas critics are rules that associate one repair with each failure type.

CHEF chooses a repair strategy by first looking to see if there are any similar cases stored in the TOP that suggest a repair and then checking the suitability conditions for each repair plan to see which is most appropriate. It applies an appropriate repair plan and fixes its faulty plan.

CHEF continues with one more step before it is finished. It updates its understanding of the world so that it will be able to anticipate and not repeat the mistake it has just made. To do that, it figures out what the predictors of this type of failure are and uses those as indexes to a warning that a failure might happen. It chooses its indexes by examining the previously

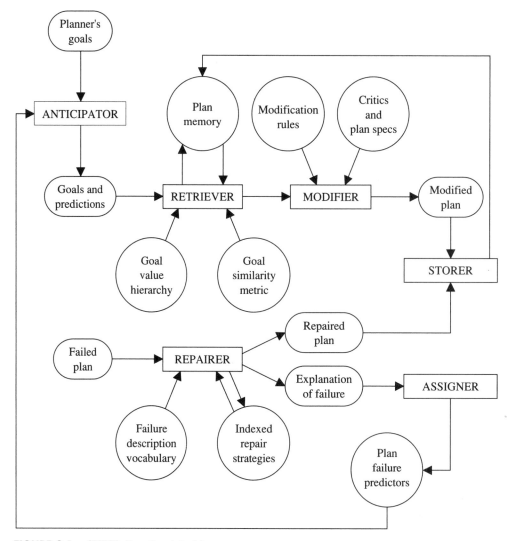

FIGURE 2.1   CHEF's Functional Architecture

derived explanation of this failure, extracting from it those parts that describe environmental features responsible for the failure. It uses this index to index both the case with the failed plan, which acts as a warning case, and the case with the repaired plan, which provides it a way to plan around that particular problem. For the beef and broccoli recipe, the best predictor is that the vegetable being stir-fried needs to remain crisp. This becomes an index to the faulty beef and broccoli recipe, which warns of the potential for sogginess and for the repaired beef and broccoli recipe, which provides a way to keep the vegetable crisp.

   After indexing the new plan by the effects it avoids, CHEF is able to anticipate, and thereby avoid, making the same mistake in the future. It does this by inserting one additional step in its planning process before plan creation: anticipation of failures. In this step, which is its first, it looks specifically for plans with goals similar to its current ones that failed, and it adds to the description of its current situation that it should avoid such failures.

Figure 2.1 shows the pieces of CHEF's architecture. Rectangles represent its functional units, circles represent its knowledge sources, and ovals represent the input and output of each functional process. A portion of CHEF's output, shown in Figures 2.2 and 2.3, traces the steps CHEF uses in creating and correcting the beef and broccoli recipe. Figure 2.4 shows how CHEF uses what it has learned from that experience to anticipate and avoid the same failure in making chicken and snow peas at a later date.

```
RETRIEVER:
Searching for plan that satisfies--
    Include beef in the dish.
    Include broccoli in the dish.
    Make a stir-fry dish.

Found recipe -> REC2 BEEF-WITH-GREEN-BEANS

Recipe exactly satisfies goals ->
    Make a stir-fry dish.
    Include beef in the dish.

Recipe partially matches ->
    Include broccoli in the dish.
        in that the recipe satisfies:
            Include vegetables in the dish.

MODIFIER:
Building new name for copy of BEEF-WITH-GREEN-BEANS
Calling recipe BEEF-AND-BROCCOLI

Modifying recipe: BEEF-AND-BROCCOLI
to satisfy: Include broccoli in the dish.

Placing some broccoli in recipe BEEF-AND-BROCCOLI

--Considering ingredient-critic:
    Before doing step: Stir-fry the -Variable-
        do: Chop the broccoli into pieces the size of chunks.
--ingredient-critic applied.

Projected results:
    The beef is now tender.     The dish now tastes salty.
    The dish now tastes savory. The dish now tastes sweet.
    The broccoli is now crisp.  The dish now tastes like garlic.

SIMULATOR:
Executing recipe.
```

FIGURE 2.2   CHEF's Steps in Creating Beef and Broccoli

REPAIRER:
Checking results.

Checking goals of recipe -> BEEF-AND-BROCCOLI ...

The goal: The broccoli is now crisp is not satisfied.
   It is instead the case that: The broccoli is now soggy.

Changing name of recipe BEEF-AND-BROCCOLI
to BAD-BEEF-AND-BROCCOLI

Explaining the failures ...

ANSWER: The step: Stir-fry the sugar, soy sauce, rice wine, garlic,
                cornstarch, broccoli, and beef for three minutes enables the
                satisfaction of the following goals:
                     The dish now tastes savory.
                     The beef is now tender.
                But the same step results in thin liquid in the pan from the
                beef, resulting in the failure

Found TOP TOP1 -> SIDE-EFFECT:DISABLED-CONDITION:CONCURRENT
   It has 3 repair strategies associated with it:
        SPLIT-AND-REFORM
        ALTER-PLAN:SIDE-EFFECT
        ADJUNCT-PLAN

Applying TOP to failure in recipe BAD-BEEF-AND-BROCCOLI
Asking questions needed for evaluating strategy:
        SPLIT-AND-REFORM ...

Implementing plan -> Instead of doing step: Stir-fry the sugar, soy sauce,
   rice wine, garlic, corn starch, broccoli, and beef for 3 minutes
Do: S1 = Stir-fry the broccoli for 3 minutes.
    S2 = Remove the broccoli from the result of action S1.
    S3 = Stir-fry the sugar, soy sauce, rice wine, garlic, cornstarch, and
            beef for 3 minutes.
    S4 = Add the result of action S2 to the result of action S3.
    S5 = Stir-fry the result of action S4 for a half minute.
Suggested by strategy SPLIT-AND-REFORM.

ASSIGNER:
Building demons to anticipate failure.

Building demon: DEMON0 to anticipate interaction between rules:
"Meat sweats when it is stir-fried."
"Stir-frying in too much liquid makes vegetables soggy."

```
Indexing demon: DEMON0 under item: MEAT
by test: Is the item a MEAT?
Indexing demon: DEMON0 under item: VEGETABLE
by test: Is the item a VEGETABLE and Is the TEXTURE of item CRISP?

Goal to be activated: Avoid failure of type SIDE-EFFECT:DISABLED-CONDI-
TION:CONCURRENT exemplified by the failure "The broccoli is now soggy" in
recipe BEEF-AND-BROCCOLI.
```

FIGURE 2.3   Repairing Beef and Broccoli

```
ANTICIPATOR:
Searching for a plan that satisfies--
    Include chicken in the dish.
    Include show peas in the dish.
    Make a stir-fry dish.

    Collecting and activating tests.
Fired: Is the dish STYLE-STIR-FRY?
Fired: Is the item a MEAT?
Fired: Is the item a VEGETABLE and Is the TEXTURE of item CRISP?

Chicken + Snow Pea + Stir-frying = Failure
    "Meat sweats when it is stir-fried."
    "Stir-frying in too much liquid makes vegetables soggy."
    Reminded of BEEF-AND-BROCCOLI
    Fired demon: DEMON0

Based on features found in items: snow peas, chicken, and stir-fry adding
goal: Avoid failure of type SIDE-EFFECT:DISABLED-CONDITION:CONCURRENT exempli-
fied by the failure "The broccoli is now soggy" in recipe BEEF-AND-BROCCOLI.

RETRIEVER:
Searching for plan that satisfies--
    Include chicken in dish.
    Include snow pea in dish.
    Make a stir-fry dish.
    Avoid failure of type
        SIDE-EFFECT:DISABLED-CONDITION:CONCURRENT

Found recipe -> REC9 BEEF-AND-BROCCOLI
...
```

FIGURE 2.4   Anticipating and Avoiding a Previous Failure

In a final note about CHEF, we consider for a moment some of the knowledge CHEF needs to do its job. CHEF's most powerful knowledge source is its case library, which indexes its plans such that they are accessible to guide later planning. Another powerful knowledge source are its TOPs and the strategies they hold that help CHEF repair its failed plans. Another knowledge source is its object critics, which help it to adapt old plans to fit new circumstances. Another powerful but largely hidden knowledge source is its semantic memory, which holds the definitions of the terms it uses. CHEF uses its definitions of terms for a variety of purposes, including partial matching and finding the correspondences between cases. Finding a case that matches best requires both direct matching of symbols and partial matching based on the meaning of symbols. For example, if beef and broccoli is indexed by the goal "include a crisp vegetable," and CHEF is trying to create a recipe for chicken and snow peas, it will know that the beef and broccoli is a good match only if it has defined snow peas as a crisp vegetable. Instantiating an old plan with new objects also requires that CHEF know the definitions of its terms—it needs to know that broccoli and snow peas are both vegetables, for example, to know that one should be substituted for the other. CHEF represents its terms as frames and organizes them with respect to each other in a semantic network.

CHEF proposes a new approach to planning that allows it to avoid many of the problems of more traditional planning systems. Some of its advances are based on the fact that it reuses plans and therefore can be more efficient than other planners. Some are the result of the fact that it incrementally repairs its plans and learns from the experience. As a result of this learning and the anticipation step performed before attempting to derive a solution, CHEF can predict problems before they happen, allowing it to compose plans that avoid previous mistakes. The combination of these benefits is attained because CHEF views planning as a memory task rather than as a construction task, closing the loop between reasoning, execution, and learning.

2.2 CASEY

CASEY (Koton 1988a, 1988b, 1989) is a case-based diagnostician. As input it takes a description of its new patient, including normal signs and presenting signs and symptoms. Its output is a causal explanation of the disorders the patient has. The causal explanation connects together symptoms and internal states. Figures 21 and 22 in chapter 11 show several of the explanations CASEY has constructed.

CASEY diagnoses patients by applying model-based matching and adaptation heuristics to the cases it has available. It has a case library of approximately twenty-five cases, all of which were diagnosed by the Heart Failure Program (Long et al. 1987). CASEY is built on top of the Heart Failure Program, a model-based diagnostic program that diagnoses heart failures with unprecedented accuracy. CASEY's model-based matching and adaptation heuristics are domain-independent and are as accurate as the domain model they are applied to.

When presented with a new patient, CASEY searches its case library to see if it knows of a similar case and, if so, uses that to diagnose the new patient. If it has no similar case, it passes the case on to the Heart Failure Program, which diagnoses it and returns its results to CASEY to use another time. CASEY uses a two-step process to do case-based diagnosis. First it searches memory for similar cases and uses model-based *evidence rules* to determine which of the partially matching cases that are retrieved are sufficiently similar to suggest an accurate

No.	Feature Name	Value for Old Case (David)	Value in New Case (Newman)
1.	Age	72	65
2.	Pulse rate	96	90
3.	Temperature	98.7	98.4
4.	Orthostatic change	absent	unknown
5.	Angina	unstable	within-hours & unstable
6.	Mean arterial pressure	107	99.3
7.	Syncope	none	on exertion
8.	Auscultation	murmur of AS	unknown
9.	Pulse	normal	slow-rise
10.	EKG	normal sinus & LV strain	normal sinus & LVH
11.	Calcification	none	mitral & aortic

FIGURE 2.5 Differences CASEY Must Reconcile

diagnosis. Then, it applies model-based *repair rules* (adaptation strategies) to adapt the old diagnosis to fit the new situation.

An example will illustrate. CASEY must diagnose a new patient, Newman. Among other things, Newman is 65 years old, has a pulse rate of 90, a temperature of 98.4, within-hours and unstable angina, mean arterial pressure of 99.3, syncope on exertion, slow-rise pulse, EKG normal sinus and LVH, and mitral and aortic calcification. CASEY's retrieval functions return to it an old patient, David. David was 72, with pulse rate of 96, temperature of 98.7, and so on. Figure 2.5 shows the differences between Newman and David. While there are many similarities between the two cases, there are also many differences, and in order to validate that David provides a good context for diagnosing Newman, those differences must be reconciled.

This is where CASEY's evidence rules come in. These rules specify under what circumstances differences can be reconciled. In general, whenever matching is being done, there will be some features of the old case that match nothing in the new case (e.g., orthostatic change in Figure 2.5) and some in the new case that match nothing in the old case (e.g., syncope and calcification in Figure 2.5). In addition, there will be some dimensions on which some of the values are different in the old and new cases (e.g., age, pulse rate, and temperature in Figure 2.5). CASEY's evidence heuristics examine the role each descriptor plays in the previous diagnosis and the role all the new descriptors could play in the same diagnosis, and it attempts to match these outlying features to each other. If it is successful, the match is validated. If not, the old case is discarded and another is tried.

For example, one of CASEY's evidence rules says that if two symptoms are both manifestations of the same internal state, then they can be considered to match each other. CASEY's causal model of the heart states that LV hypertrophy can manifest itself as "ekg: lvh" or "ekg: lv strain." Applying that rule and using that part of the model, the EKG values in the two cases can be reconciled with each other. Both play the same role, although their values are different. Another evidence rule says that an extra symptom in the new case that is not present in the old could be a manifestation of some internal state known to exist in the old case. If it is, then the difference is reconciled—the role it plays is as manifestation of a known internal state. This is what allows the aortic valve calcification in the new case to be reconciled with the old diagnosis.

Using its evidence rules, CASEY does, in fact, reconcile all the differences between Newman and David. It goes on to create an explanation of Newman's disorders by adapting David's diagnosis. CASEY uses a set of domain-independent model-based repair rules to do its adaptation. Each of its repair rules is associated with one or more of the evidence rules. CASEY keeps track of which evidence rules apply, and it applies the corresponding repair rules at adaptation time. For example, when two values, one of which is present in the new case and one in the old, both play the same role in the diagnosis, a repair rule adapts the old diagnosis to fit the new situation by substituting one value for the other one. When a feature of the new case has been identified as a manifestation of a known internal state, the old diagnosis is adapted by inserting in it an evidence link that connects the internal state to the new symptom. Figures 11.21 and 11.22 in chapter 11 show how CASEY adapted David's diagnosis to fit Newman. Notice in particular the connections to LV hypertrophy in the lower right corner and the insertion of aortic valve calcification in the upper right corner of Figure 11.22.

Chapter 9 gives the details of CASEY's evidence rules, and chapter 11 gives the details of its repair strategies. I won't attempt to describe all of them here. The important thing to remember is that a combination of four knowledge sources work together in CASEY to validate potential matches and to adapt old diagnoses to fit new situations:

1. General-purpose evidence and repair rules predicated on general causal knowledge
2. A causal model of the device being reasoned about (the heart, in this case)
3. The old case, including its problem description and its solution (in the form of a causal explanation)
4. The problem description in the new case

Though the causal model and cases change from domain to domain, the evidence and repair rules are domain-independent and can be used over the wide range of domains for which causal models are available.

One of the major problems that arises in CASEY is that retrieving cases based only on similarity of surface features would result in poor retrieval. In CASEY's domain, and indeed in many medical domains, the same disorder can manifest itself in many different ways, and different disorders can look very similar to each other at the symptom level. Retrieval based only on available signs and symptoms, then, would cause CASEY to retrieve many inappropriate cases and, even worse, to miss some applicable ones. CASEY compensates for this by indexing cases by both their surface features and the internal states that are part of their diagnoses. Upon retrieval, it infers plausible diagnostic states for its new case before doing retrieval and retrieves based on a combination of plausible diagnostic states and signs and symptoms. A case is considered a good match and a candidate for validation to the extent that its internal states match the plausible internal states of the new case and, secondary to that, the correspondence between the surface features of the two cases.

Another major concern with respect to CASEY and its domain is accuracy. Can we rely on a case-based program to create solutions to problems requiring accuracy? As stated previously, the Heart Failure Program, which CASEY is built on top of, is an unusually accurate heuristic program with a well-defined causal model guiding its reasoning. Evaluation of CASEY showed that it was equally accurate (Koton 1988a, 1989). If we look at what CASEY added to the Heart Failure Program, we see that it added a set of heuristic rules that are guided by the same model that the Heart Failure Program uses. Our conclusion, then, is that CASEY gets its accuracy from the Heart Failure Program's model, and that its heuristics do not detract from its accuracy.

At the same time, CASEY performs far better than the Heart Failure Program when we measure its efficiency, showing a speedup of two to three orders of magnitude when it holds a relevant case in its case library. Cases provide a starting point for constructing a causal explanation, and the time put into searching the space to construct one from scratch is avoided. Our conclusion, based on these studies, is that case-based reasoning has the potential to speed up our model-based programs considerably without loss of accuracy.

2.3 JULIA

JULIA (Hinrichs 1988, 1989, 1992; Hinrichs and Kolodner 1991) is a case-based designer that works in the domain of meal planning. As in other design domains, problems are described in terms of constraints that must be achieved, and solutions describe the structure of an artifact that fulfills as many of those constraints as possible. As in other design domains, problems are large. In general, they cannot be solved by finding one old case that mostly covers the solution and adapting from there. Rather, problems usually must be decomposed into component parts to be solved separately. Yet, component parts interact strongly with each other, requiring some mechanism for keeping track of their relationships.

JULIA solves this problem by combining case-based reasoning with constraint posting and propagation. Its case-based reasoner proposes solutions to problems and warns of the potential for failures. Its constraint mechanisms keep track of the relationships between the component parts of the item being designed. The interaction between the two comes in the indexing vocabulary JULIA uses for its cases. Because constraints describing the relationships between parts of an artifact are so important in synthesizing design components, JULIA uses these constraints to index its designs.

Constraints in design can come from several different places, though all must be treated similarly during reasoning. Some constraints come from our general knowledge of the artifact being designed. For example, in a meal, the major ingredients of dishes should not be repeated across dishes or courses of the meal. Another general rule is that the tastes of dishes in a meal should be compatible. Another is that the meal should be nutritionally balanced. Others are imposed by the new problem. In a particular meal, for example, a client might specify that dishes be easy to make or that some particular ingredients be used or that some dietary constraints be imposed.

In order to create meals that fulfill both general requirements and the requirements of a particular situation, JULIA must use both general knowledge (about meals) and specific requirements imposed by the client as it is reasoning. This means that in addition to using cases as a knowledge source, and in addition to the particular specifications of a new design case, JULIA must have general knowledge about the kinds of artifacts it is designing. JULIA stores this sort of knowledge in its *object prototypes*. JULIA's object prototypes correspond to different kinds of meals it knows about, for example, normal American dinners, European dinners, buffet-served meals, and one-course meals. Each prototype specifies its structure and the relationships between its parts. A normal American dinner, for example, includes an appetizer course; a salad course; a main course with a main dish and two side dishes, one of which is a vegetable side dish and the other a starch; and a dessert course. They are sequenced in a certain way, and we know, for each, what the approximate size of the dishes are. We also know the relationships between the dishes in the courses. For example, their caloric content, when taken as a whole, should not be excessive, and they should be nutritionally balanced. Their tastes should be compatible, especially the dishes served in the same course. We also know that the more informal the dinner, the more likely that one or more of the courses will be dropped, and several other prototypes (including one-course meals) describe such meals.

JULIA uses both cases and object prototypes as it is doing design. Though it prefers to use cases to suggest its solutions (because they are more detailed), it uses meal prototypes to suggest frameworks for solutions when cases are not available to do that. Though object prototypes are not exactly cases, they play a similar role to that played by cases—they provide large chunks of normative information to the reasoner without the reasoner's having to derive it from scratch.

In a typical problem-solving session, JULIA is told about the new problem. It first attempts to fill in missing information that it knows to be important to meal planning. Some information it is able to fill in by inference; other things it must ask the client. It begins constructing a solution by attempting to find a case that closely matches the specifications of its new problem. If it finds one, it establishes that as its solution framework. If not, it chooses an appropriate prototype and establishes that as its framework. In its next step, it reconciles the requirements of the new situation with the framework it has established. This is where its constraint methods begin their work. The requirements of the new problem are imposed on top of the framework that has been established, and their implications are propagated throughout the framework. In some places there are conflicts. JULIA adapts the framework to fit the new situation in those places. In other places, nothing specific is filled in, but the combination of constraints imposed by the prototype and constraints imposed by the new situation provide guidelines for filling it in. JULIA uses case-based reasoning to fill those in.

JULIA continues by focusing on some aspect of the solution and using case-based reasoning to construct its solution. Each case-based reasoning step involves recalling appropriate pieces of cases that fulfill, as well as possible, the designated constraints for that piece of the solution and then adapting what is retrieved appropriately. Each time JULIA fills in some value in its ongoing solution specification, that value's effects are propagated throughout the rest of the design. When conflicts are encountered, JULIA attempts to adapt the solution to reconcile the conflicts. Failing that, it attempts to adapt the problem specification by minimally relaxing some constraints. It resorts to backtracking only if it cannot resolve conflicts by one of these methods.

Meanwhile, there are two interruptions to the process that might happen as JULIA is constructing its solutions. The client might interrupt with a new demand, or the retriever might find a case that warns of the potential for failure. New demands from a client are particularly interesting, as they have the potential to violently disrupt the ongoing design. In one of JULIA's cases, for example, the client announces late in the design process that there will be vegetarians coming. JULIA must repair its design to accommodate the vegetarians. It treats such interrupts the same way it treats conflicts that arise in the normal course of design. It first attempts to adapt what it has done so far and then attempts to relax constraints, and only after those two methods fail does it resort to backtracking.

This sort of interrupt is common in design, by the way. An architect was recently recounting to me an experience he had designing a major university building. Initially, the clients had made no specifications about the facade of the building. The architects had decided to make it poured concrete. When the design was almost finished, the clients decided they wanted a brick facade. The basic shape of the building was kept, but the structural work, which had been aimed toward the concrete facade, had to be completely redone. Attempting adaptation first and constraint relaxation second before backtracking serves to limit the change needed to accommodate a new specification.

The second type of interrupt JULIA deals with comes from its own retriever, which might recall a case that warns of the potential for failure. When this happens, JULIA stops what it is doing and considers whether the failure might happen. If, indeed, there is the potential for failure in this situation, it updates its specifications accordingly and continues. A case might warn, for example, that there might be vegetarians coming to dinner who need to be accommodated. JULIA asks the client if indeed this is so and, if so, treats it as a new demand, exactly as described above.

JULIA's adaptation strategies are quite simple and explained in some detail in chapter 11, so I won't go into detail here. In short, JULIA does two kinds of adaptation. It can make substitutions in its ongoing solution, or it can change the structure of its ongoing solution.

The following sequence shows JULIA's reasoning as it designs an inexpensive and easy-to-prepare meal for the AI research group at Georgia Tech. It is told that it should use tomatoes and cheese as major ingredients.

```
How can I help you?
    (host tom)
    (guests jlks-research-group)
    (cost cheap-meal)
    (ease-of-prep easy)
    (ingredients (tomato cheese))
```

JULIA chooses its most general meal prototype to start, and propagates the constraints of this problem specification into that framework. For example, it knows that one of the members of jlks-research-group does not eat veal and adds that as a constraint. It continues by trying to elaborate the problem specification through inference and questioning. One inference it tries to make is the choice of a cuisine. Tomatoes and cheese suggest two cuisines to it, Mexican and Italian, and JULIA asks the client which he prefers, to which he replies, "Italian." Had JULIA been able to decide by itself, it would have.

The decision to serve Italian cuisine requires JULIA to alter the meal framework it has developed so far. In Italian cuisine, there is an extra course, the pasta course, and the appetizer course is specialized to antipasto. It uses its Italian-meal prototype to do this.

JULIA continues by trying to fill in more details about the meal before it actually starts suggesting dishes. It uses recalled cases to do this. Here, it recalls a previous case that was cheap, easy to prepare, and Italian that was informal and served buffet style. It suggests this combination to the client:

```
What do you think about informal and buffet?
    ok
```

JULIA goes on to fill in details of the meal itself. JULIA concentrates on filling in details course by course (component by component). However, if it finds a single case that can suggest many of the components, it tries to use that case. Here, the same case that suggested an informal meal served buffet style also suggests a main course: lasagne as the main dish with garlic bread on the side and red wine to drink. JULIA queries the client about those choices.

```
Would you like lasagne, garlic bread, and red wine?
    yes
```

This initiates another change to the solution structure, however. Recall that an Italian meal has a standard structure that includes a pasta course. Recall also that meals have general constraints on them that suggest that main ingredients not be duplicated across dishes. The lasagne in the main course violates that constraint. JULIA uses an adaptation critic called "two birds with one stone" to decide that with lasagne in the main course, no pasta course is necessary, and it removes the pasta course from the solution framework. Lasagne in the main dish also conflicts with starch in a side dish, and using the same adaptation critic, it removes the starch side dish from the main course.

JULIA sees that designation of the main course remains incomplete and continues working on it. It focuses now on coming up with a vegetable side dish. It retrieves an Italian dinner with a pasta main dish that had a vegetable side dish and suggests its side dish to the client.

```
What do you think about brussels sprouts with garlic and parmesan for a
vegetable side dish?
    sure, and vegetarian constraint
```

The client agrees but throws in a new constraint. There will be vegetarians coming to dinner. JULIA propagates this constraint throughout the solution in progress. It further specifies the antipasto in the appetizer course—it must be a vegetarian one. But it conflicts with the lasagne that has already been chosen as the main dish. JULIA attempts to adapt the lasagne to make it suitable. It does this by substituting a known variant that is vegetarian. In doing this, it avoids the need to retract everything that depends on the lasagne (here, the garlic bread and the wine).

```
There's a contradiction, but we can salvage the plan by substituting
vegetarian-lasagne for lasagne.
```

JULIA is finished with the main course and moves on to the appetizer, which is already constrained to be vegetarian and an antipasto. The only antipasto it knows about has meat, but it uses its adaptation rules to delete some ingredients and substitute others to synthesize a vegetarian alternative.

```
How about vegetarian-antipasto for an appetizer?
   good
```

The problem solver now focuses on dessert. The case retrieved previously that suggested lasagne also suggests coffee and spumoni messina for dessert. The client agrees, and JULIA is finished.

JULIA's case representations are shown in chapter 5. Its problem specifications look the same but are filled in more sparsely. In addition to the processes described in this short description, JULIA uses reason maintenance procedures that work along with its constraint propagation procedures to notice conflicts in its designs in progress. It also has procedures for maintaining the integrity of its designs as it modifies their structures and accepts constraints late in the process. JULIA's basic structure has six components:

1. The *goal scheduler* maintains an agenda of design goals. This is the part of the program that provides focus on various parts of the design (e.g., the main dish, a side dish, the appetizer). It also associates plans with its goals that guide the order in which it decomposes and achieves them. JULIA always prefers to achieve a goal without decomposing it, but if no case is available to allow it to do that, the goal scheduler decomposes the goals.

2. The *case retriever* searches memory for similar cases. Problem descriptors and constraints are used for indexing and ranking cases.

3. The *adaptation engine* transforms cases and design components based on constraint violations. It uses a small set of primitive transformation rules.

4. The *constraint poster* (Stefik 1981) propagates values and constraints.

5. The *reason maintenance system* (Doyle 1979) maintains justifications for and against candidate decisions and records the consequences of decisions and sources of values. It also notices conflicts that are propagated by the constraint poster.

6. The *structure maintenance system* ensures that the representation of the solution is internally consistent and consistent with the goals of the problem solver.

These modules are coordinated by a control strategy composed of two nested cycles of control. The *problem reduction cycle* reduces goals to subgoals, schedules them, and evaluates whether they are achieved. The *constraint satisfaction cycle* calls upon the constraint poster, case retriever, and adaptation engine to formulate constraints, propose plausible values from cases, evaluate and adapt those values as necessary, choose among alternatives, and propagate constraints.

Helping these processes are some large stores of knowledge. JULIA has several hundred cases. In addition, it knows several hundred dishes and their recipes and knows about the ingredients of each. Its semantic memory holds a taxonomy of concepts such as types of food, dishes, social events, meals, and courses. It also contains problem-independent domain knowledge in the form of plans, constraints, and cases.

Designers talk about three levels of design tasks: routine, innovative, and creative design. Where does JULIA stand with respect to these? When JULIA takes an old design and reuses it, it is doing rather routine, mundane design. Sometimes, however, old designs provide a starting point, but considerable adaptation is needed to merge the suggestions of several old cases or even to make the suggestions made by one case fit the new situation. It is in these circumstances that JULIA moves into innovative and even creative design. I don't know how we could test where JULIA ranks on the scale of creativity, but discussions with human designers who are considered quite innovative tell us that JULIA is performing many of the same mental acts they perform, using the same sorts of knowledge, and dealing with the same sorts of contingencies and assumptions. Alas, this does not mean that we can seed JULIA with knowledge about buildings and ask it to design one. That would be a knowledge engineering feat beyond most of us. But it does suggest that we've captured much of what designers do, and that perhaps the model of design that JULIA represents could be the starting point both for creating autonomous design programs and for creating computer programs that can help people do design.

2.4 HYPO

HYPO (Ashley 1990; Ashley and Rissland 1988a) is an interpretive reasoner that works in the domain of law. It was the earliest of the interpretive case-based reasoners, and over its lifetime, it has become one of the most sophisticated. HYPO takes as input a legal situation, and as output it creates an argument for its legal client. It can take the defendant's or the plaintiff's side in a dispute and is equally good at creating arguments for either. It's particular domain of expertise is nondisclosure cases. Typically, in these cases, a secret of some company has been disclosed to a competitor who is then able to take advantage of it, for example, by coming out with a competing product quickly. But not all cases of disclosing trade secrets are illegal, and the task of the program is to decide, for any case, whether or not the disclosure was legal and to create an argument supporting its decision.

HYPO's reasoning process has several steps in it:

1. Analyze the case for relevant factors. That is, figure out which of its many descriptors are the relevant ones to pay attention to.
2. Retrieve cases that share those factors.

3. Position the retrieved cases with respect to the new one. That is, separate the cases into those that support the point the arguer wants to make and those that support an opposing point.

4. Select the most on-point cases from each set. These are the cases that share the most relevant factors with the new situation.

5. Argue the issue. This is where the arguments get created. In general, HYPO's arguments are what are called three-ply arguments. The most on-point case that can support its point is chosen to make the point. Then the strongest case that makes the opposing point is chosen to counter it. Differences between the two cases are examined, and cases that can address those differences and that support the arguer's point are chosen to rebut the counterargument. Several arguments are made, each based on different initial cases, different counterarguments, and different rebuttals.

6. The analysis done while arguing the issue is used to explain and justify the arguer's point.

7. Hypothetical cases are created and used to test the analysis that has been created. Hypotheticals have never happened, but they test the limits of the analysis in ways that real cases might not be able to.

The argument step is the major one in this process. In that step, similarities and differences between old and new cases, and between several old cases, are identified and reasoned about. Chapter 13 holds a concrete example of HYPO's performing each of these steps within the disclosure domain. It is easier, however, to illustrate the process using a simpler, more commonsensical domain.

Here, we imagine George, who is about to turn thirteen, arguing with his overprotective parents about going to the movies to see *Little Shop of Horrors*.[1] They don't want him to go. He wants to go. The first thing George has to do in arguing his case is to analyze the relevant factors. *Little Shop of Horrors* is rated PG-13, and he is not yet thirteen, so age is a factor. Related to age as a factor is maturity. Rating of the movie is also a relevant factor here. Other factors that George knows are important in determining whether one can go to the movies are how far away it is from home, what night of the week it is, and whether one has finished one's homework or not. He determines, however, that none of these is important here.

George recalls cases in which age, maturity, and movie rating were factors. In one, his sister, who is older, was allowed to see the same movie. In another, his friend Noah, who is his best friend (hence of approximately equal age and maturity) was allowed to see it. In another, he was not allowed to see another PG-13 movie a year before. The first two cases support his point; the last doesn't. Of those that support his point, both share the same factors with this one—age, maturity, and rating. Both seem to be equally on point. Thus, George could appropriately create an argument based on either. He decides that the better argument will be based on what his parents have allowed his sister to see; the case of Noah will be used as backup.

He creates a three-ply argument based on these cases. First, he argues that he should be able to see the movie because his sister was allowed. He anticipates that his parents will focus

---

1. From (Ashley 1990).

on the differences between the new situation and that of his sister, pointing out that she is older and therefore more mature. He will then use the Noah case to show that neither age nor maturity are necessarily appropriate here, because there is an example of someone of the same age and maturity being allowed to go. The argument itself goes something like this.[2]

> **George**: That's not fair. You let Sarah see that movie. (Sarah is his older sister.)
> **Parents**: Sarah is three years older than you.
> **George**: Why does that make a difference?
> **Parents**: You're not mature enough for that movie.
> **George**: Noah's parents let *him* go see it. (Noah is George's best friend.)

Of course, George's parents, at this point, might point out that there are factors beyond age and maturity that are crucial. They might point out that the movie is too far away or that George hasn't finished his homework yet. Using these new factors, George might recall other cases and use them to fashion a new argument. Having fashioned that argument, he might test it by creating hypothetical situations. For example, if his parents tell him the movie is too far away, he might recall a case in which a movie was farther away and he was allowed to go. Looking at the differences between those cases, however, he might find that he was allowed to go because another movie his parents wanted to see was playing in the same theater. He might fashion a hypothetical based on that, asking his parents whether, if this movie was playing somewhere where they wanted to go, they would take him there. When a hypothetical case gives positive feedback, it is sometimes possible to shape reality to match the hypothetical. George may be able to show his parents that, indeed, the movie is playing somewhere that is also playing a movie they want to see.

HYPO shows us several important things about case-based argumentation. First, it shows us the importance of compare-and-contrast procedures for understanding situations and makes clear some of the steps involved in that processing and what cognitive processes and knowledge are necessary to engage in such reasoning. Its other contributions are in the specifics it tells us about those steps. For example, it proposes strategies for argumentation. How do we choose the case to use for rebuttal? How will the other side choose a case to use for counterargument? Rebuttal can be simple, but when several cases are available, it is good to use the one that can make the strongest argument. It might make the strongest argument because it covers more points or because it comes from a higher authority (as in the George example). And HYPO proposes strategies for creating hypothetical situations that can help in testing an argument. In addition, HYPO tells us what we, as knowledge engineers, must do to make our programs perform argumentation. In particular, we must seed them with the factors that are the important ones in a domain or give them the capability of computing those factors. The strategies HYPO uses to create arguments, those it uses to create hypothetical cases, and what goes into choosing factors are all presented in more detail in chapter 13.

Though law is HYPO's domain, its areas of expertise are open-ended or open-textured concepts and argumentation, and these are also areas in which it has contributions to make. Chapter 13 has a long explanation of what open-textured means, and I won't repeat that here.

---

2. Adapted from (Ashley 1990).

Suffice it to say that many of the concepts that we think we understand well are very poorly defined. For example, a sign on a store might say, "No pets allowed." Does this mean our blind friend with a seeing-eye dog can't take her dog in? A recipe you are following says, "Salt abundantly." How much salt are you supposed to put in? We encounter open-textured concepts on a daily basis, and we must interpret them. We do much of that interpretation based on our experiences. We know how much salt we've used in the past to make pasta, for example, and if the new recipe is one for pasta, we use what we've used in the past—that tells us what "abundantly" means. If we haven't had experience cooking, we are less likely to be able to understand what these ambiguous concepts mean.

Similarly, we all engage in argumentation on a regular basis. Often, we must decide between several alternatives. How do we decide? We weigh the benefits of each. We consider the possible effects. We try to anticipate or project what might happen in each circumstance. We often think about other situations as we are doing this. This process is very similar to the argumentation that HYPO does, and its analysis can give us guidance on building programs that can do commonsense reasoning, on building programs that can help people make decisions, and on the things we need to teach people to make them capable arguers.

2.5 PROTOS

PROTOS (Bareiss 1989a; Porter, Bareiss, and Holte 1990; Bareiss, Porter, and Weir 1988) implements both case-based classification and case-based knowledge acquisition. Given a description of a situation or object, it classifies the situation or object by type. When it misclassifies an item, its expert consultant steps in and informs PROTOS of its mistake and what knowledge it needed to classify the item correctly. PROTOS's domain of expertise is audiological (hearing) disorders. Given a description of the symptoms and test results of some patient, PROTOS determines which hearing disorder that patient has. Its expert consultant is an expert audiologist. It has also been applied to other tasks, for example, recognizing an agent's emotional state.

Case-based classification, as PROTOS implements it, is quite simple. The classification of a situation or object is determined by finding the object or situation it already knows about that is the closest match to the new object. PROTOS assigns to the new item the same classification assigned to its closest match.

PROTOS's searches for a closely matching case using two major steps. First, it narrows its search to a most likely candidate. Then, based on qualities of the match between its most likely candidate and the new item, it follows pointers around the case library in search of better matches. It repeats this second step until it either finds an acceptable match or fails.

This process is a simple implementation of generate-test-debug (Simmons and Davis 1987; Simmons 1988). PROTOS first guesses what category its new problem fits into by looking at how the important features of the new case overlap with important features of categories of hearing disorders it knows about. It verifies that hypothesis by attempting to match its new case to exemplars in the hypothesized category to see if it can find a good match. If it finds a match, it is finished. If it doesn't find a match, it uses the results of its matching process to select a better hypothesis. This process is guided by its knowledge of the kinds of classification mistakes that are common in its domain. In response to misclassifying a case due to strong resemblance to cases in the wrong category, PROTOS adds links from the wrong to the right category that allow it to avoid making the same mistake in the future.

A simple example will illustrate. PROTOS must diagnose a hearing ailment described by the following properties:

> s-neural(milk,gt2k), ac-relex-u(normal), ac-reflex-c(normal), o-ac-reflex-u(elevated), o-ac-reflex-c(normal), tymp(a), speech(normal), air(normal), history(noise), notch-at-4k, static(normal), age (greater-than-65)

It first attempts to narrow its choices. It does this by identifying the categories these symptoms are associated with and choosing the one that is associated with the largest number of important given symptoms.

> Reminded of: cochlear-noise, cochlear-age-and-noise, cochlear-noise-hered, mixed-poss-noise-om, otitis-media,...
> The strongest reminding is: cochlear-noise

It then attempts to match its new case to the most prototypical of the cases of cochlear noise.

> Choosing case p8594R as the most prototypical exemplar of cochlear-noise.
> This match is deficient.

PROTOS's strongest reminding is correct about 50 percent of the time. Because PROTOS uses only surface features of its new cases to choose a candidate item for matching, it is not surprising that its first candidate often is not a good match to its new item. PROTOS's next step is to use the results of its match combined with associations built into the case memory to find a better candidate. There are several differences between the prototypical exemplar of cochlear noise and its new case, one of which is that the new case has the property age(greater-than-65) and the old one does not. This particular difference is associated with a link in memory that associates the first case PROTOS considered to another that differs from it by this feature. PROTOS follows that link to the new case and chooses that case as its new candidate case. It considers whether this new candidate case is a good match for its new case.

> Traversing difference link labeled age(greater-than-65). Found p827R, a case of cochlear-age-and-noise.
> This match is very close.
> Patient has cochlear-age-and-noise.

Indeed, the match is a good one, so PROTOS assigns to the new case the classification assigned to the case it matched well: cochlear age and noise.

Two capabilities make PROTOS's case-based classification process work.

1. Its case library records a rich set of semantic connections between its categories and cases that allow it to identify likely matches in its case library.

2. Its match process can identify correspondences between components of candidate cases and new items even when those components look quite different from each other.

PROTOS has four kinds of connections between its cases and categories. *Reminding links* associate features with categories, allowing a best guess at a category to be chosen initially. *Prototype links* connect categories to items that most typify the category. *Difference links*, or indexes, record important differences between items. They connect items to each other according to their differentiating features. These two kinds of links allow a first best candidate to be chosen from a category, and they also allow movement from candidate item to candidate item, according to the differences between the candidate item and the new item identified by the match procedure. *Censor links* are also labeled by descriptors and are used to rule out connections that might otherwise be made.

PROTOS's match process uses a combination of two kinds of knowledge.

1. A (often incomplete) model of the item it is attempting to identify that includes functional, causal, correlational, and taxonomic relations
2. Associations between functional components and their implementations in real artifacts or situations

It matches by finding functional correspondences between the components of two items. If it is asked to match a normal four-legged chair to a chair with a pedestal, for example, it uses its model of a chair to recognize that the pedestal on the second chair is playing the same role as the legs on the normal chair, and it allows the match. One match is better than another to the extent that corresponding components are more like each other.

PROTOS's knowledge acquisition process is driven by failures in its classification process. When it is unable to correctly identify the category of an input, it engages in a conversation with an expert that results in the addition of new knowledge and revision of its memory connections. The expert provides PROTOS with appropriate explanatory knowledge that allows PROTOS to associate the specifics of a new case with its functional knowledge. Communication between the expert and PROTOS is through a fixed vocabulary of causal, functional, correlational, and taxonomic relationships. If PROTOS had initially misclassified its case, it also adds *difference links* to its memory that will keep it from making the same misclassification in the future.

An example will illustrate. PROTOS has just been asked to classify the following disorder:

```
air(moderate), bone(normal), speech-intell(normal), tymp-pr(negative),
tymp-peak(flat), ipsi-AR(absent), contra-AR(absent), other-i-AR(normal),
other-c-AR(absent)
```

PROTOS chooses `otitis media` as its most likely candidate classification and attempts to match this new case to its most prototypical case of `otitis media`. All the matches between features of the new case and the prototypical one are direct except for a match between air(moderate) in the new case and air(abnormal) in the prototypical case. PROTOS matches these two features to each other, however, because its generalization hierarchy tells it that air(abnormal) is a generalization of air(moderate). The expert rejects the match, telling PROTOS that its generalization is okay but that the match, nevertheless, is a poor one. The expert is telling PROTOS, in essence, that the knowledge it used to make the match between the new case and the prototypical one is okay, but it should have explored more alternatives. PROTOS therefore seeks to identify the failure in its search process that led it to stop once it identified this possible match.

PROTOS does this by redoing its reasoning in search of some other route that would have arrived at the correct solution. If it finds one, it updates its pointers appropriately. Here, PROTOS regresses to the step that caused it to identify otitis media as a possible classification. It attempts to redo this step by considering whether any of the other classifications it was considering at that point were appropriate ones. It finds that malleus fixation was also a possibility, and it attempts to match its new case to an exemplar of that category. It succeeds at that match and asks the teacher whether it is a good one. The teacher agrees that it is the appropriate answer. PROTOS now considers what knowledge it would have needed to allow it to choose this category originally by examining and asking questions about weaknesses in the new match. It notices that the exemplar it matched its new case to has a feature air(severe) that has no match in the new case and asks the expert to explain that. The expert explains:

air(moderate) has generalization air(abnormal) which has specialization air(severe)

PROTOS goes on to ask about several correspondences it made to enable the match that were weak, and the teacher replies with similar explanations for those, which PROTOS installs in its model. PROTOS then installs the new case as an exemplar of malleus fixation.

PROTOS has now refined its knowledge about audiology so that it can do a better job of matching. And it has installed its new exemplar so that it can use it in the future to recognize similar cases of malleus fixation. But it must still make sure that it does not get confused between otitis media and malleus fixation in the future. To ensure that, PROTOS installs a difference link labeled air(moderate) between the exemplar it originally used and the new case.

In the future, this difference link will be used to alert PROTOS that a new case it thinks is otitis media might be a case of malleus fixation if the property air(moderate) is present. The process will be like that shown in the first example. There, a difference link labeled age(greater-than-65) and connecting cochlear noise to cochlear age and noise allowed PROTOS to correctly identify its new case as cochlear age and noise even though it originally looked more like cochlear age.

PROTOS is interesting in being one of the few case-based reasoning programs that has been evaluated extensively (Porter, Bareiss, and Holte 1990). Evaluations of PROTOS were of the effort it expended to do its task, its overall accuracy, and its accuracy relative to both other classification programs and human novices and experts. Evaluations of PROTOS's effort during classification show that it attempts between four and eight matches each time it does classification, and that 85 to 90 percent of its correct matches are arrived at through traversal of prototypicality links, while the remaining 10 to 15 percent are through traversal of difference links. PROTOS was 90 percent accurate over its entire 200-case corpus, but after running its entire corpus and engaging in knowledge acquisition discussions with the expert for each case it misclassified, PROTOS was 100 percent accurate in classifying its 24 test cases. After moderate knowledge acquisition, then, PROTOS performs quite accurately, accessing most of its correct matches through prototypicality links but in 15 percent of the cases relying on difference links to do classification correctly.

When we compare PROTOS to other classification programs, the significance of the case-based method of classification becomes more apparent. The most powerful classification program at the time PROTOS was developed was ID3 (Quinlan 1986). When ID3 was seeded with PROTOS's 200 training cases and then tested on its 24 test cases, ID3 was able to correctly classify only 38 percent of the test cases, while PROTOS could correctly classify all of them.[3] In particular, PROTOS excelled on cases with many missing features. In PROTOS's domain, cases are usually described by only about eleven features, while the domain itself is defined in terms of fifty-eight features. Methods like ID3, which define their categories in terms of necessary and sufficient conditions, work best when all examples are described by the presence or absence of all the domain's features. PROTOS's case-based method, by contrast, can work with whatever features are available.

Since then, ID3 has been extended and is a more powerful classifier than it was, able to work with examples with new feature values (Duran 1988). Evidence from PROTOS continues to point to the case-based method's being superior for "outlyer" cases, however. Several variants of ID3 that were augmented to deal with missing features and seeded with PROTOS's 200 training cases were still able to correctly classify only 77 percent of the 24 test cases (Porter, Bareiss, and Holte 1990). This percentage is roughly equivalent to the 81 percent of the test cases that PROTOS classified correctly through accessing prototypical cases in categories. PROTOS seems to excel at classifying the "outlyer" cases, that is, those that are only weakly prototypical whose descriptions share little with the general description of the category itself. Classifying such cases can be confusing, as these cases tend not to fit well into any category—they may have salient features of several different categories (consider *whales*, for example, or *penguins*). If PROTOS has seen such outlyers in the past and been confused about what category they belong to, it will have installed difference links allowing it to classify such outlyers correctly in the future.

2.6 CLAVIER

CLAVIER (Mark 1989; Hennessy and Hinkle 1992; Barletta and Hennessy 1989) is a system for configuring the layout of composite airplane parts for curing in an autoclave. It is up and running at Lockheed in California. Given a set of parts that need curing as input, it designs the

---

3. This number has been disputed by some who claim that the version of ID3 that was used was missing a trivial extension and, as a result, was unable to classify any cases with feature values not present in the training set. For example, if it had never seen a green apple before, this version of ID3 could not have classified a Granny Smith apple correctly. Extending ID3 as it should have been extended would have resulted in some of the misclassified cases' being classified correctly. Thus, we probably should not take the specifics of this number seriously. When we discount those cases that ID3 should have been able to classify, however, we still find that PROTOS is more powerful.

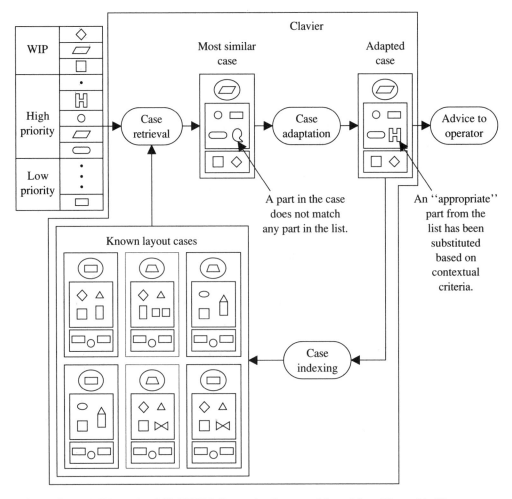

FIGURE 2.6 A Schematic of CLAVIER's Reasoning Process. Adapted from Figure 3 in Hennessy, D.H. and Hinckle, D. (1992). "Applying Case-Based Reasoning to Autoclave Loading," *IEEE Expert*, 7(5), pp. 21–26.

layouts for several loads of the autoclave that will cure all the parts, getting as many of them cured on time as possible. As stated earlier, the task of autoclave loading is a black art. A causal model of what kinds of layouts work simply doesn't exist. In fact, the air currents in different autoclaves create different conditions across autoclaves. Thus, experience curing particular kinds of parts in a particular autoclave is necessary before loading can be done efficiently. Fortunately, the expert at Lockheed kept a file of the loads he had done in this autoclave, and Barletta and Hennessy, who built the original system, were able to translate that file into cases. Figure 2.6 shows a schematic of CLAVIER's process.

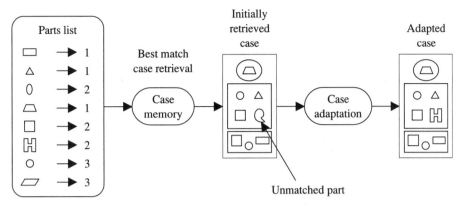

FIGURE 2.7   Input and Output in CLAVIER.

CLAVIER was seeded with approximately twenty cases and has collected over a hundred more as it has been used. The first version of CLAVIER was fully automated, and that is the one we discuss here, though the later version interacts with workers to do its job. CLAVIER takes as input a list of composite parts needing curing and has a time priority associated with each part. Parts with earlier due dates have priorities higher than those with later due dates. Its case library is made up of layouts of parts in the autoclave, both those that worked well and those that didn't. Cases are indexed by the parts they included. In its first step, CLAVIER uses the input to retrieve cases, choosing as the best case the one that includes the most parts of highest priority.

Figure 2.7 shows sample input and a case from CLAVIER's case library. The leftmost column holds the set of parts that need curing. The middle column shows a case from the case library. The rightmost column shows the solution CLAVIER produces after adaptation. Each case in the case library shows its configuration of parts. Each configuration is composed of several tables, each of which has several parts on it. The long column in Figure 2.8 shows more of CLAVIER's cases.

CLAVIER's most interesting component is its adaptation mechanism. In general, the cases CLAVIER retrieves do not fulfill its needs exactly. Usually, the difference is in one or two parts. That is, in the case that is retrieved, every part in its configuration, except for one or two, is in the list that represents the current situation. CLAVIER's adaptation task, then, is to substitute some part that needs curing for one that is not in its input. One might think that this could be done simply by considering the size or shape of the part that needs to be substituted and choosing one of equivalent size or shape. But for some technical reasons, that doesn't work.

What CLAVIER does instead is to use its experience to guide adaptation. For each piece that it needs to substitute, it looks for a table from a previous load that had the pieces on the current table plus some piece from the input set that still needs curing. It then chooses the part that table suggests. Figure 2.8 shows this adaptation process.

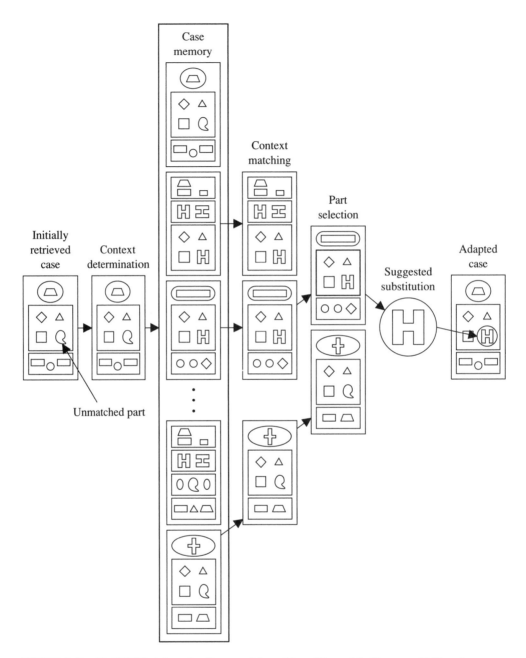

FIGURE 2.8 CLAVIER's Adaptation Process. Adapted from Figure 4 in Hennessy, D.H. and Hinckle, D. (1992). "Applying Case-Based Reasoning to Autoclave Loading," *IEEE Expert*, 7(5), pp. 21–26.

The important parts of the process, as one can guess from the illustration, are the context-determination and context-matching steps. Two kinds of knowledge are used for context determination and context matching: global knowledge providing the context in which the table is located and local knowledge describing the table itself. Global context includes such factors as the type of material used by parts in the load, the type of mold being used, and general groupings of parts types (e.g., beams, ribs, stiffeners). It allows the system to find loads with similar heat-up characteristics, thereby allowing the system to find its substitutions among cases with globally similar characteristics. Local context includes mostly spatial knowledge—where in the oven the table is and the sizes of the parts it holds. CLAVIER searches for tables that meet both the global and the local characteristics of the table that needs a part substituted.

On all counts, CLAVIER can be considered a success for case-based reasoning. As an application, it has provided Lockheed with a corporate memory of autoclave configuration knowledge and has been able to apply that knowledge on the fly. As new knowledge is acquired, it is used immediately. The daily experiences of each worker are stored in the system and available to every other worker on the shop floor. This system has already allowed less experienced autoclave operators to load the autoclave like professionals (Hennessy and Hinkle 1992).

CLAVIER was relatively easy to build, partly because the expert on the floor was keeping the right kinds of information in his files. Although loading an autoclave is a black art, the expert who gathered the information understood what it was important to keep track of. The workers on the floor were already using a case-based approach before CLAVIER was built. They kept their records in such a form that they could use them to reconfigure the autoclave later.

As a research vehicle, CLAVIER developed the idea of case-based adaptation and the use of pieces of cases in reasoning, showing the importance of both local and global knowledge in choosing the right pieces of cases. Other systems, too (e.g., CELIA [Redmond 1990a, 1992]), are showing this as a need, and we will discuss it in the chapter on case representation.

The most important advantage reported for CLAVIER has been its ability to learn. It began with about 20 cases, has over 150 at this writing, and continues to grow. As its experience has grown, it has become more accurate in its retrievals, requiring considerably less adaptation now than originally. Its knowledge has grown along with that of the human experts, adapting as they have to changes in the problem space of the domain.

In addition to its successes, CLAVIER demonstrates several difficulties related to fielding case-based applications, particularly in the areas of validating new cases and maintaining the case library. Because no theory of the domain exists, validation of the system requires validation of every individual case. The fact that it learns compounds that problem. CLAVIER is a constantly evolving system. As its case library grows, its behavior changes, making validation even more difficult. Validating individual cases does not ensure that particular cases will be retrieved. Each new case changes the functionality of the system. CLAVIER currently batches its updates to get around this problem, and its creators are working on the problem of continuous validation.

2.7 RETRIEVAL-ONLY AIDING AND ADVISORY SYSTEMS

All the systems mentioned and illustrated so far in this chapter were automated case-based reasoners. That is, given a problem to solve, they did what was necessary to solve it and produced a solution. The only role of a person in those systems was to produce feedback to let the system know how its solution had performed.

But creation of autonomous systems is only one way case-based reasoning can be used for system building. The most powerful thing about case-based reasoning, perhaps, is its fit with what people do. As we stated in chapter 1, people use case-based reasoning naturally in much of their everyday reasoning. In complex domains or those where a person is a novice, however, people do not always remember the most appropriate cases, sometimes because of bias, sometimes because they haven't yet encountered the appropriate experiences. Many people in the case-based reasoning community believe that case-based reasoning's biggest potential is in building interactive systems that can help people solve problems or teach them new domains.

The emphasis, as of this writing, in building interactive case-based systems has been on developing interactive aiding and advisory systems. Just as there are several possible roles a human advisor can play in helping us solve problems, so too are there several possible roles a case-based advisory system can potentially play. It can act merely as a browsing facility, it can provide information in response to queries, it can act as a coach, looking over the shoulders of the human and providing guidance and suggestions, or it can act as a colleague, playing a role equal but complementary to that of the human user. Those systems that have been built to date have been browsing facilities and information providers. I begin the discussion, however, with presentation of two hypothetical systems, one a coaching system, the other a query system, to give readers an idea of the range of roles a case-based advisory system can take on.

2.7.1 A Hypothetical Architect's Assistant

In this hypothetical aiding system, we see the computer acting as a design coach, helping a novice architect with design of a geriatric hospital. There are a number of issues an architect has to deal with: functionality must be appropriate, the design must fit the site, costs must be within limits, and so on. Let us assume that the computer screen is configured with a space for notes, a space for graphical manipulations, a space for the problem specification, and a space where cases are presented. Let us further assume that each case has both a picture part and a textual part. Though the presentation will show all interactions in English, let us also assume an interface in which most of the interaction is through graphics, menus, and pointing, with canned English explanations and descriptions produced by the system.

On the screen we see the new problem in the problem specification space and a representation of the site, showing its contour, size, and shape, in the graphical space.[4]

> **Problem:** Design a geriatric hospital; the site is a four-acre, wooded, sloping square;
> the hospital will serve 150 inpatients and 50 outpatients daily; offices for 40 doc-

---

4. I thank Craig Zimring for this example.

tors are needed. Both long-term and short-term facilities are needed. It should be more like a home than an institution, and it should allow easy visitation by family members.

Screen: Shows the site, its contour and shape.

The person now uses the mouse to highlight those parts of the problem specification that he or she feels need to be addressed at this point, early in the design.

Person: Highlights hospital, homeyness, provision of visitation, long-term and short-term care, and geriatric.

The computer uses those highlighted parts of the problem as preferences in finding useful cases in memory. The most useful cases will match all those features; less useful ones (that perhaps can address only some part of the problem) will match some subset of those features. The computer finds many cases and partitions them according to how well they match the highlighted criteria. It presents its ordered partitions and asks the person which he or she would like to see more detail on. At the same time, the computer does some bookkeeping (invisible right now). It keeps track of which cases in its lists achieve which of the requested features.

Computer: I know of many long-term facilities for the elderly, many acute-care hospitals, and one geriatric hospital: Wesley Woods in Atlanta. Of the acute-care hospitals, Piedmont Hospital in Atlanta is the most homey. Of the long-term facilities, the Jewish Home in Fairfield County, Conn., is closest in the type of care it provides and the ability to provide opportunities for family visitation. What would you like to see?

The person chooses to see Wesley Woods, the only geriatric hospital with both long-term and short-term facilities. The computer shows a picture of the layout of Wesley Woods and provides a commentary.

Person: Wesley Woods.

Screen: Shows picture and layout of Wesley Woods along with a description window.

Computer: The goal in designing Wesley Woods was to create a homey atmosphere. To do that, they used residential rather than institutional furnishings, forms, and materials and made sure it was cheery and colorful. They made all the corridors short so people would feel as though they were in a home-size place. The functional units of the hospital were hidden from normal sight so the patients didn't feel they were in a hospital. The design did a very good job of providing homeyness. However, there was one big problem. It was hard for patients and staff to find their way around because the views give no distinguishing landmarks or orienting features and it is not possible to see one's destination until nearly there. It looked so much like a home that patients and visitors were not sure what to do once they arrived there.

The person makes some notes based on Wesley Woods' successes and failures (make sure corridors have views, make sure corridors have distinguishing features), decides that there are large portions of that design it can borrow, and begins to manipulate that design (using icons) to make it fit the new site. It won't fit on the site because of the slope. The person adapts its design by adding a lower floor, subtracting out part of lower floor of Wesley Woods, putting the two main entries on two different levels.

The computer, which is responsible for bookkeeping, now notices that the building has entries on two levels. It knows this to be a difficult design problem and therefore attempts to retrieve cases that can help the designer. It retrieves several cases that show how to use two entrances. It interrupts the designer and makes a suggestion. The architect makes use of this information.

> **Computer:** I have several examples of hospital buildings with entrances on two levels. Georgia Baptist Hospital has lobbies on two levels, one for inpatients, one for outpatients. Brigham and Women's in Boston has entries on two levels with a two-floor lobby that combines inpatient and outpatient functions. The lobbies are connected by a ceremonial escalator.
>
> **Person**: I'll put the outpatient lobby on the bottom level and the in-patient lobby on the second level.

The computer has kept track of the goals of the designer and how they were achieved in other cases it retrieved that the designer might not have seen yet. It has a mechanism for noticing when design goals are violated by design decisions. In this case, because the inpatient entrance is above usable ground and the Jewish Home in Fairfield had provided for easy visitation by providing easy access to the usable outdoors, the program notices a violation of design goals. It also is able to retrieve another case in which, even though the ground sloped, access to the outside was easily provided. It interrupts the architect to warn of the potential problem and to suggest a solution.

> **Computer**: One of the nice features of the Jewish Home in Fairfield was the access to the outside that patients had. That's a potential problem if the inpatient lobby is on the upper floor.
>
> I know of another institution where access was important and was provided by putting patient rooms and gathering places against the same slope so people could walk right outside. In another, the two functions were divided between two different buildings, each on a different part of the slope, so everyone had access to the outside.

We do not continue with the example here, but stop to point out the responsibilities of the machine and the person. The computer has two responsibilities: bookkeeping and retrieval. The bookkeeping it does is of two varieties. First, it keeps track of the good points of designs it remembers. The Jewish Home, for example, had the advantage of providing easy access by patients to the outside. This made visitation by family members pleasant. In addition, it makes

easy inferences to make sure, to the best of its knowledge, that good points of designs it knows of are not violated and that bad points are not repeated.

The case retrieval done by the system has three purposes:

1. Cases provide suggestions.
2. Cases provide warnings of potential problems.
3. Cases help in critiquing.

The computer acts as a combination of coach and slave, providing relevant suggestions to the user while acting to serve the needs of the human reasoner. Everything the computer does is in service to the responsibilities of the person using the system. That person is responsible for the decision making itself, doing a variety of reasoning tasks:

- Adaptation
- Choice of features to consider
- Choice of cases to consider
- Evaluation of suggestions
- Evaluation of warnings
- All decision making

2.7.2 A Hypothetical Mediator's Assistant

In the architect's assistant, the hypothetical system looked over the person's shoulder and provided warnings and suggestions as necessary. In this next example, also hypothetical, we see the user requesting cases from the system to help her in answering several questions that need answering to assess the situation and to come up with a solution. This example is based on the reasoning done by PERSUADER (E.P. Sycara 1987a; K. Sycara 1988a, 1988b), a system that acted in the role of mediator in union-management disputes.

In this example, we see the mediator presented with a problem. The union wants a large salary increase, but the company cannot afford it. In order to figure out what to do, the mediator must collect some information. She wants to know why the company is losing money. The system helps her by providing several cases of companies losing money, each of which suggests a different explanation. Note again that we show English interaction because it is easy to show. The person might actually interact with the system in some other way.

Problem: Southern Airlines presents its employees with the ultimatum that if they don't take wage cuts of 8 percent, the company, which has become noncompetitive, will have to go bankrupt.

Mediator: Get me cases to suggest why the company is losing money although the industry is prosperous.

Computer:

Great Railroad Company: When they were losing money in prosperous times, it was because the union was insisting on featherbedding, an expensive and unnecessary practice.

Northern Airlines Shuttle: When they were losing money in prosperous times, it was because the management was not treating the employees well. The employees, in turn, were not as productive as they should have been.

Western Trucking: When they were losing money in prosperous times, it was because of mismanagement among the executive board. They were using the resources of Western Trucking for purposes unrelated to the company.

The mediator considers each alternative, collecting information she needs, and decides that this is a case of mismanagement. She now needs to find a solution. She adds to the representation of the problem that there is mismanagement in the company, and asks the computer to suggest solutions. The computer responds with several cases.

Computer:

Western Trucking: Management was forced to resign, and employees took a pay cut until things were back to normal. It took time to get back on the road, but consensus is that the new management did better than the old management could have.

Foobaz Airlines: Employees took a pay cut to avoid bankruptcy but management was forced to put employees on the board and give employees a share in the company. The president took things under control, firing those managers who had been involved in mismanagement. He made it clear that employees on the board were to be taken seriously. Because employees felt both responsible for their share of the company and that they were listened to, productivity went up immediately, and the company began making more money. Two years later the employees not only regained their old salaries but began making more than their counterparts at other airlines. This could not have been done without the willingness of both parties to cooperate in the agreement.

In this hypothetical example, the aiding system is taking a much more passive role than in the previous example. Even so, cases recalled by the system provide the user with much important data. We can think of this system as a smart interface for a database system. It is able to recall partially-matching cases that a decision maker can base analysis and decisions on. It is more than a database in that it does its retrieval based on the specifics of a situation and finds partially-matching cases that can be used to answer the specific questions of the user. It does not require full matching of features, nor does it require a database administrator to formulate queries. Rather, it allows the decision maker to ask the questions himself or herself and to be close to the data decisions are based on.

2.7.3 Some Real Aiding Systems

In the past two years, several real case-based aiding systems have been built and are being developed. The first was the Battle Planner (Goodman 1989). It plays a coaching role for a novice battle planner. The user describes a battle situation to the system and tells the system his or her best guess at a solution. The system then retrieves cases that can be used to critique the solution. The Battle Planner also extracts useful summary information from the collection of cases it retrieves. The user uses the cases and summary information to, first, critique his or her solution and, then, if the solution was inadequate, propose a better one. The user again asks the system to retrieve cases and continues in this way until the cases that are retrieved give no more clues about generating a better solution.

A short example will illustrate. Figure 2.9 shows the system's I/O behavior. At the top, we see that the person entered the description of the battle situation and his or her solution. Here, the mission and method fields describe the solution; the other fields describe the battle situation. The user is planning for the American (defender) side. The Battle Planner retrieves nine World War II cases, all in which the attacker wins. It provides commentary about what options and variations were tried in prior cases (and their outcomes) and then supplies a comparative analysis. Armed with that and the cases themselves if the user wants to look at them, the user reformulates his or her solution. This time, the cases retrieved tell the user that the solution is satisfactory.

The Battle Planner is not quite a query system, nor is it quite a coach, but it does perform those pieces of answering queries and coaching that are needed for aiding people doing the particular tasks of projecting the effects of a solution, analyzing those effects, and using those results to reformulate a plan. The Battle Planner has been fielded at West Point with mixed review. Many found it useful; others complained about its idiosyncratic interpretations of battles. It was developed using one of the commercially available shells. The shell it used, REMIND (Cognitive Systems 1992), provides case organization and retrieval capabilities and, based on an influence model given by the system developer, derives summary information useful for critiquing.

Several other simple retrieval-only systems have also been built. CLAVIER, presented earlier, was originally created as an automated system but has been put into production as an aiding system. Users describe a configuration problem, and the system retrieves cases that suggest a solution. The person analyzes whether a case is appropriate, adapts cases as needed, and records any adaptations and how well they worked for future use.

Several help-desk types of systems have been developed or are under development. A help-desk is an information facility set up by an organization to deal with problems users of its systems are having. It is manned by support engineers who provide "over the telephone" service assistance, generally on two kinds of problems: those due to the customer's not knowing how to perform a task and those due to system failures of various kinds. Support engineers are trained to recognize and fix certain kinds of common problems, but they don't generally engage in finding a failure's cause. Thus, a help-desk itself can only deal immediately with the simplest of problems. Harder problems are sent to somebody more expert.

Help-desk implementations, in general, look like smart database systems. The help-desk technician describes a problem to the system, and the system retrieves the closest matching similar cases, which suggest solutions. CASCADE (Simoudis 1991a, b, c; 1992) was created to aid engineers at Digital Equipment Corporation in recovering from VMS device driver failures. The help-desk technician fills in a form describing the current problem, and the system retrieves cases that suggest solutions. Suggestions made by the system allow help-desk personnel to recognize and deal with more of the problems that come their way without passing

Scenario Situation: Soviet invasion of Europe, a U.S. Division at Fulda Gap, facing a salient (bulge) in the Soviet line, with a hill behind U.S. troops.

	Attacker	*Defender*
Nationality	Soviets	U.S.
Troop Strength	3700	1100
Heavy Tanks	54	34
Light Tanks	30	30
Morale	tired	fresh
Initiative	–	+
Terrain	Rugged, mixed	
Mission	Seize hill	Hold territory
Method	Frontal assault	Static defensive line

Retrieved Cases: 9 cases from WWII, all attacker wins.

- In one battle, rapid assault → major victory
- In two other battles, delaying actions → successful second defense

Comparative Analysis: Significant factors generated by retriever from its clustering:

```
These factors favor Attacker win:
    Defender lacks reserves
    Defender lacks depth
```

		Attacker	*Defender*
	Nationality	Soviets	U.S.
New Mission and Method:		. . .	
	Mission	Seize hill	Delay
	Method	Frontal assault	Defend in depth

Retrieved Cases: 18 cases, all defender wins.

FIGURE 2.9   An Example from the Battle Planner

them on to other personnel than they could without the aid. NCR is developing a similar program to aid help-desk personnel to debug disk driver complaints.

Researchers at Apple have taken this concept one step further. NNAble (Laffey, Machiraju and Chandhok 1991a) is designed to be an integrated support and learning system that both supports help-desk personnel on the job and contributes to in-service training. To do that, they built an organizational memory into their system and integrated the case-based support system with other help facilities that enable users to get short descriptions of tasks they need to do and identify others in the organization with whom they might collaborate in solving problems.

More recently, developers have become more ambitious, attempting to build systems that aid more complex problem solving. SCI-ED (Kolodner 1991b), for example, will help elementary school teachers plan science lessons. ARCHIE-2 (Domeshek and Kolodner 1991, 1992, 1993) is designed to help architects with conceptual design of buildings. AskJef (Barber et al. 1992) is being developed to help computer interface designers make appropriate choices in laying out interface screens. The ASK systems (Ferguson et al. 1992) are browsing tools that have education as their goal. ASK-Tom teaches novice bank consultants their job. Advise-the-President teaches high-school students about contemporary American history. Common to all the systems just mentioned is the use of a kind of case called a *story*. A story is a way of presenting a case so that the lesson it teaches is clear. The same case might be presented through several different stories, each of which provides a different point of view or focuses on different aspects of the case.

In story-based systems, the premise is that the user will browse through a series of stories in each sitting, stories that are related to each other through some natural progression of goals the user has. An architect, for example, may start with the goal of investigating acoustics issues, concentrating first, say, on a particular type of room (e.g., a courtroom), moving on to another type of room, moving from there to heating and air conditioning in the same room, and so on. A novice learning about bank consulting may start by focusing on the job itself, move on to finding out more about a particular aspect of the job, look at alternatives for doing some particular task, and so on. The important thing in these systems is to make sure the system allows these natural progressions. Thus, a big issue in creating these systems is to discover a presentation scheme that clusters related stories together.

The ASK systems address this issue by using the metaphor of a novice having an advisory conversation with an expert and basing interactions with the system on conversational moves that make sense in context (Schank 1977). Given some item the novice has just asked about, the screen makes available follow-up questions the novice would be likely to ask next. An illustration from ASK-Tom (Schank et al. 1991; Ferguson et al. 1992), shown in Figure 2.10, will make this more concrete. In the middle of the screen, we see the issue the user is currently interested in—first things to find out about customers and their assets. The user, we assume, has just heard a story giving advice about that issue. Related issues the system knows about are organized around the circumference of the screen. Related stories might provide context for the advice just given, give additional detail, and so on. ASK-Tom groups these stories along several dimensions natural to a continuing conversation with the expert. Thus, the user can continue by asking for *alternatives* to doing what was proposed in the focal story, *examples* that show more specific issues that arise, expected *results* of following the advice of the story, *warnings* about what to watch out for in carrying out the advice, *opportunities* that might be taken to better carry out the advice, and *context* that might be important to the advice. Pointing and clicking on one of those boxes enables the user both to hear the story that goes with the box and to consider other relevant issues related to the new focus.

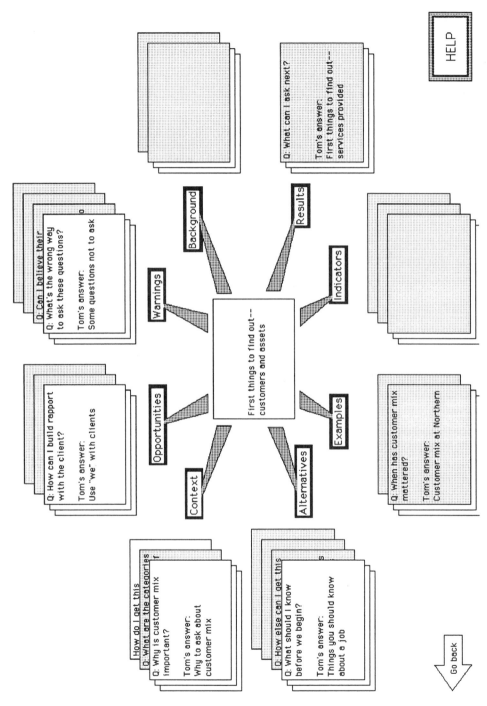

FIGURE 2.10 A Screen from ASK-Tom

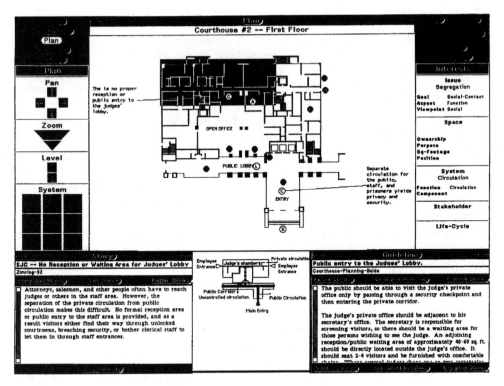

FIGURE 2.11 A Screen from ARCHIE-2

Other systems organize their stories in a graphical presentation scheme. ARCHIE-2, which gives advice about architecture, clusters its stories using a floor plan, a representational form architects are used to reading. The floor plan is annotated with stories when there is something significant to get across to the designer. Some stories in ARCHIE-2 tell about design features that didn't work and what could be done to fix them; others report on features of the design that were particularly, and perhaps unexpectedly, good. Users first describe to the system the problem they are working on, and the system retrieves buildings that are similar to the new one. The user then asks to see some aspect of the design of a building that is retrieved, and is shown a floor plan surrounded by annotations. Figure 2.11 shows an example. At the top of the figure is a floor plan with annotations around it, each giving a short description of some design feature. Beside the floor plan are controls and forms that allow users to specify design issues and floor plan pages they are interested in. At the bottom of the figure, we see what results when the user clicks on one of those annotations: additional detail about the designated story is provided, along with buttons that allow access to guidelines and other examples of similar phenomenon. AskJef, which gives advice about layout of computer interfaces, uses the layout of a computer screen similarly to organize its stories. This means of clustering seems to make sense when the advice being given is about an artifact and how it works or is designed.

The most ambitious of these story-based browsing systems is the Story Archive (Bareiss, Ferguson, and Fano 1991). It holds a wide range of stories, in the form of video clips, covering historical events, entertainment, famous people, and so on. They are indexed and cross-indexed according to issues and topics each addresses. Using an interface like the one from ASK-Tom, a user can ask for a video clip about some topic or issue and from there explore video clips about related topics. The system allows users to explore issues from several different points of view to find out how different political groups, religious groups, or *ad hoc* groups have analyzed different issues. The idea is to create an environment in which a person can learn both facts and analytical thinking skills in an enjoyable way.

Indeed, it is not a far leap from browsing systems that advise to those that teach, though some creative thinking and interface design is needed to make that leap. Advise-the-President, for example, began as a browsing system in which a student could find out about decisions presidents have made (e.g., about the Iran hostage crisis). Its most recent incarnation sets the student up as an advisor to the president, asking the student to find out as much as he or she can about an issue and the way it has been approached in the past in order to give the president advice. The indexing, presentation of stories, and connections between stories remained the same when the system moved from being a browsing system to an instructional system anchored by a task the student had to do. Changes were in the interface only.

The creation of case-based aiding systems has begun in earnest only recently, and it is too early to say exactly what their contribution will be. The potential benefits of such systems are quite exciting to think about, however (Kolodner 1991a). For novice problem solvers, such systems can provide the range of experiences they haven't had, allowing them to solve problems based on the wisdom of experts. There are several reasons novices should be able to perform better using such aiding systems than without them. First, with more cases available, they will be able to recognize more situations and the solutions or evaluations that go with those. Second, if cases that are available include failed cases, novices will be able to benefit from the failures of others. Third, novices will have available to them the unanticipated successes, and therefore the tricks, of experts that they wouldn't have otherwise. Fourth, retrieved cases will allow novices to better recognize what is important in a new situation. Cases indexed by experts and retrieved on the basis of a description of a new situation will be those that experts would recall and will show the novice ways of looking at a problem that he or she might not have the expertise for without the system. Fifth, the ability to recognize what is important will allow for better critiquing of solutions and situations. Additionally, novices will have access to obscure cases that they otherwise would not be able to make use of. These obscure cases can help with any of the tasks listed above.

Using these systems during a training period additionally provides students with a model of the way decision making ought to be done, for example, what things ought to be taken into account, and provides them with concrete examples on which to hang their more abstract knowledge. Much of the expert decision-making skill people have comes from observing experts and discussing with experts why they solved problems in certain ways. A case-based aiding system can provide at least some of that experience.

Benefits of these systems are not just for novice problem solvers, however. In some domains, there is much to remember. For tasks where there is much to remember, case-based aiding systems can augment the memories of even expert decision makers. In addition, as discussed previously, both experts and novices tend to focus on too few possibilities when reasoning analogically or to focus on the wrong cases. Case-based aiding systems can help alleviate these problems.

Nor are the benefits for problem solvers only. As development on ASK systems is showing, such systems may prove quite useful in education, serving as a means of teaching facts and thinking skills simultaneously in an environment that engages students and makes them want to learn.

2.8 SUMMARY

Six automated case-based reasoners were presented in this chapter. CHEF is a case-based planner. JULIA is a case-based designer. CASEY is a case-based diagnostic program that creates causal explanations using a combination of case-based reasoning and model-based knowledge. HYPO does interpretive reasoning in the legal domain. PROTOS does case-based classification and its case-based procedure is far more accurate than inductive approaches. CLAVIER is used at Lockheed to lay out composite parts of airplanes in an autoclave, and has been a major success as an application. It also implements a novel case-based adaptation strategy.

While this chapter has concentrated on automated case-based systems, the next chapter concentrates on the cognitive model implied by case-based reasoning. It first presents the model and then continues by discussing the implications of the cognitive model. One implication, if we consider case-based reasoning to be a good model of people, is that it can serve as the basis for guiding the creation of interactive systems that can advise and aid people doing complex cognitive tasks. Several such systems that have already been built will be discussed in that chapter.

3

Reasoning Using Cases

In chapter 1, I stated that cases were useful as a ubiquitous source of inference. As an encapsulation of experience, they provide expectations that serve as inference sources for a wide variety of inference types. In this chapter, we provide more detail about the inferences cases can support. There are two dimensions on which we will explore case-based inferences:

1. The range of *inference tasks* case-based inference supports
2. The effects of those inferences across a variety of *reasoning tasks*

Our computer programs have shown us that cases provide sources of knowledge that can be used to support almost every type of inference. MEDIATOR (Kolodner and Simpson 1988, 1989), the earliest case-based program, for example, used case-based inference to support a variety of different inference tasks, ranging from problem elaboration to solution framing to blame assignment to repair.

Our programs have also illustrated the usefulness of case-based reasoning over a variety of reasoning tasks. CHEF (Hammond 1986a, 1986b, 1989a), for example, illustrates the many roles cases can play in planning. They can help with anticipating problems that might arise, constructing solutions, and repairing solutions. The result is that a case-based planner spends less time planning, leaving more time for execution or action. JULIA (Hinrichs 1992; Hinrichs and Kolodner 1991) illustrates the roles cases can play in design. They suggest solutions and warn of potential failures, but most importantly, they allow problems that must be solved in pieces to be solved efficiently, in effect providing the "glue" that holds together different pieces of the solution. When a case suggests the framework for a design solution, the remainder of the solution can be formed by adapting pieces of the old solution in place rather than generating numerous alternative solutions that must then be fit together properly.

The range of reasoning tasks cases support can be broken roughly into two categories: problem-solving tasks, including design, planning, and diagnosis, and interpretive tasks, including understanding, justification, and projection. As the discussion in chapter 1 points out, this is somewhat of an artificial distinction, since all tasks require some degree of each. Nevertheless, it is a useful distinction for discussing the various reasoning tasks cases help with. Reasoning using cases tends to look different for problem-solving and interpretive tasks. In problem solving, cases suggest ballpark solutions that are then modified to get to a suitable solution. In interpretive tasks, several cases are compared and contrasted with each other to achieve an understanding of the new situation with respect to other things that are already known.

Cases support a wide variety of inference tasks and reasoning tasks. But though cases are a powerful source of inferences, case-based inference is not appropriate for every task and domain. Cases hold large amounts of raw knowledge in them that can serve as a source for many different kinds of inference in a whole variety of circumstances. But a major issue related to inference is "which type when?" There are some domains and tasks that are so well understood and well defined that a small number of rules suffice to reason about them. Other domains and tasks are highly technical and require the kinds of causal reasoning that models support well. Others are highly detailed and require exacting computations that no heuristic program can support. Case-based inference is probably not appropriate under such circumstances. On the other hand, some tasks and domains are so poorly understood or defined that cases provide the only reliable source of inferences. And even well-understood and well-defined tasks, domains, and models have their limitations. Their general knowledge tends to become unreliable around the edges, that is, when situations are sufficiently different from what the general knowledge covers. If cases are available that illustrate behavior at the edges of that general knowledge, they can act to augment the well-understood general knowledge found in the rules or model. Some sources of knowledge are good for evaluation but don't provide guidance about construction of solutions. Cases help with that. Even exacting computations might be helped by guidelines on how to get started or how to narrow the task.

In this chapter, the many roles of cases are discussed. We begin by discussing the many different kinds of inference tasks cases can support. We continue by exploring the different reasoning tasks case-based reasoning can contribute to. We end with a discussion of the relative merits of case-based and other reasoning methods, comparing them on efficiency, capability, and ease of system building.

3.1 CASE-BASED INFERENCE

Perhaps the greatest contribution of MEDIATOR (Kolodner and Simpson 1989) was its illustration of the variety of inference tasks case-based inference supports. MEDIATOR's task was to resolve disputes over resources, ranging, for example, from two children wanting the same candy bar to two students wanting the same book from the library at the same time to Israel and Egypt both wanting the Sinai. To solve its problems, it first had to understand the problem well. What are the real goals of the disputants? Do they want possession of the whole object, or some part of it? Do they want to own it, or just to use it for a while? Will they be happy with compromise decisions, or must it be an all-or-nothing solution? MEDIATOR's first

Understand the problem:

- Classify the problem
- Elaborate the problem specification

Generate a plan:

- Choose planning policies
- Select abstract plan
- Refine abstract plan
- Choose plan actions
- Bind plan variables

Evaluate results
Recover from failure:

- Understand the failure
- Remedy reasoning error
- Solve new problem

FIGURE 3.1   MEDIATOR's Case-Based Inference Tasks

step, then, was *problem understanding*. To do that, MEDIATOR classified disputes as physical (involving ownership of a physical object), economic, or political; inferred the goals of the disputants; and, from those results, inferred the type of solution that would be appropriate. Its next step was to *propose a solution*. Without case-based reasoning, it did that using plan instantiation methods. It chose a relevant solution plan from its hierarchy, refined it to its most specific relevant form, instantiated its variables, specified its steps, and predicted its results. Its next step was to collect feedback and to compare the real results with the predicted ones. From there, if real results were different than predicted, MEDIATOR analyzed the differences to assign blame for the failure and then remedied it.

MEDIATOR, like more traditional problem solvers, was always aware of the reasoning subgoal it was working on and had available to it "from scratch" inference rules or methods that it could use to achieve each one. Given a subgoal to achieve, MEDIATOR first attempted to find a relevant case and use case-based inference to achieve it. Only if no cases were available did it use its "from scratch" knowledge. MEDIATOR thus used case-based inference for a wide variety of inference tasks, including problem classification and elaboration tasks, planning tasks, and blame assignment tasks. Figure 3.1 lists the full set of inference tasks MEDIATOR used case-based inference for.

MEDIATOR's means of doing these tasks was to use the problem specification to find cases similar to the new situation and then to focus its attention on the part of the old case in which its current reasoning subgoal was achieved. Thus, when trying to choose an abstract plan, it would focus on the plan used to solve the previous problem. To understand a failure, it would focus on the failure classification from the recalled case. It extracted the appropriate piece of the previous case and, after checking its appropriateness, installed it in the new case. Thus, when MEDIATOR was attempting to choose a plan to resolve the Sinai dispute (Israel and Egypt both want possession of the Sinai) and recalled the Korean conflict, it focused on the plan used to solve that problem (`divide-equally`), checked the applicability of that plan for the new situation by examining its preconditions (e.g., item can be divided without losing value, a compromise solution is allowable), and because those preconditions were fulfilled, installed that plan in the solution to the Sinai dispute.

In general, each of MEDIATOR's inferences resulted in one of three things:

1. Choosing a framework for a solution, usually a frame whose slots were filled in during subsequent reasoning (e.g., during problem classification, abstract plan selection, choice of plan actions, failure explanation, and failure remedy)
2. Choosing one or several values to fill frame slots (e.g., when choosing planning policies)
3. Choosing the values of (instantiating) frame variables (e.g., when binding plan variables)

In using essentially the same case-based inference processes for tasks involved in understanding, planning, and recovery from failure, MEDIATOR demonstrates the broad applicability of case-based inference.

MEDIATOR shows that case-based inference processes have their greatest advantage in situations where a long chain of reasoning is necessary to reach a conclusion. When achieving a goal normally required many inference steps, case-based reasoning helped by suggesting a solution without the need for interim reasoning steps. In these instances, the reasoner has only to check a proposed solution for consistency, rather than generating it from scratch. In MEDIATOR, this happens during plan selection and remedy selection (done by successive refinement when no cases are available) and during recovery from reasoning failures when MEDIATOR is trying to identify the source of its error (blame assignment, done by following dependencies when no cases are available).

On one-step inference, MEDIATOR also showed the advantages of case-based reasoning. "One-step inferences" are the inferences that can normally be made with the application of one inference rule. Sometimes cases make the same suggestion an inference rule would make, showing that at least case-based reasoning is no worse than using inference rules. Other times, however, cases allowed *more appropriate* decisions to be made than could be done using general-purpose inference rules. There are two reasons for this. First, novel cases can suggest novel inferences that general-purpose inference rules might not cover. Second, cases provide control in choosing which one-step inference to make. It is not hard to imagine a domain in which many possible "easy" inferences could be made at any time. The advantage of case-based reasoning in such domains is that it suggests use of those inferences that have worked well in the past, allowing the problem solver to bypass the process of deciding among all the possible inferences it could possibly make.

3.2 CBR AND PROBLEM SOLVING

Solving problems, understanding situations, assigning blame, and each of the other tasks we want our reasoners to do require a series of inference steps. As discussed above, case-based inference can shortcut the inference process by proposing solutions, alleviating the need for the long inference chains required to construct those solutions.

In constructing solutions to problems, cases perform two major functions. They suggest almost-right solutions to problems that are then modified to fit the new situation, and they warn of the potential for failure. The host in the example in chapter 1, for example, used case-based reasoning for two solution-creation purposes: to propose tomato tart as the main dish and to suggest a means of adapting it to suit the guest allergic to milk products. She used another case to anticipate that one of the guests would not eat fish, allowing her to anticipate, and therefore plan around, that problem.

Case-based reasoning is useful for a wide variety of problem-solving tasks, including planning, diagnosis, and design. In each of these, the caching of experience in cases allows the reasoner to become more efficient, becoming more capable over time of solving problems that require the achievement of several conjunctive goals or consideration of multiple interacting constraints. Earlier we discussed the ways cases can help in making individual inferences. In this section, the global effects of those inferences during problem solving are discussed and illustrated.

3.2.1 CBR for Planning

Planning is the process of coming up with a sequence of steps or a schedule for achieving some state of the world. The state that must be achieved may be designated in concrete terms, as in, for example, designating the end state for the Tower of Hanoi problem (configure the game board such that disk 1 is on top of disk 2 is on top of disk 3, and all are on peg 3) or describing the end result of making a delivery (the box labeled "Klein" should be on the Klein driveway). Or a desired state can be designated in terms of constraints that must be satisfied, as in, for example, scheduling the gates at an airport (each flight should be assigned a gate, no two flights should be at a gate at once, no on-time flight should have to wait for a gate, and so on). The end product of the planning process is a set of steps that, when executed, are intended to produce the desired state of the world.

The earliest case-based planner was CHEF (Hammond 1989a). CHEF, as you recall, creates new recipes based on those it already knows about. Its first step is to find a single plan (old recipe) that satisfies as many of its active goals as possible. It continues by altering or adapting the old plan to satisfy the new goals that it doesn't cover, doing its adaptation by reinstantiating the old plan and applying a set of special-purpose modification rules. After trying its plans out, it repairs them appropriately using general planning knowledge.

For example, in creating a recipe that combined beef and broccoli, it remembered its recipe for *beef with green beans* and adapted that recipe appropriately. First, broccoli was substituted for green beans. Then, the set of steps used to create beef with green beans was fixed. Because broccoli is in large pieces that need to be made considerably smaller for stir-frying, the "slice the green beans into pieces of size chunk" step in the beef with green beans recipe was modified and changed to "chop the broccoli into pieces of size chunk." Next, CHEF predicted the results of its plan. If all went well, it expected, among other things, the beef to be tender and the broccoli to be crisp. It found, after it prepared the recipe (in its simulator), however, that the broccoli was soggy. Using this feedback, it explained the failure and repaired it, creating a better plan than it could have initially. Finally, it indexed the repaired plan to make it available during subsequent reasoning. By indexing it according to the kinds of problematic situations it solved (e.g., the need for a crisp vegetable), CHEF is able to recall the plan in the future to help it anticipate and avoid the mistake it made originally.

There are many problems that must be dealt with while planning. First is the problem of protections. Good plans are sequenced, whenever possible, such that late steps in the plan don't undo the results of earlier steps and so that preconditions of late steps in the plan are not violated by the results of earlier steps.[1] This requires that the effects of plan steps be projected into the future (the rest of the plan). Second is the problem of preconditions. A planner must make sure that preconditions of any plan step are fulfilled before scheduling that plan step. Thus, planning involves scheduling steps that achieve preconditions in addition to scheduling major steps themselves. These two problems together, when solved by traditional nonlinear planning methods, require considerable computational effort. As the number of plan steps increases, the computational complexity of projecting effects and comparing preconditions increases exponentially (Chapman 1987).

Case-based reasoning deals with these problems by providing plans that have already been used and in which these problems have already been worked out. The planner is required only to make relatively minor fixes in those plans rather than having to plan from scratch. A recipe, for example, is an already-worked-out plan that provides an ordering of steps that plans for and protects preconditions of each of its steps.

Case-based reasoning also suggests solutions to more complex planning problems.[2] For example, in complex real-world problems, the number of goals competing for achievement at any time can be quite high, and new ones are formed in the normal course of activity. If we try to achieve each one independently of the others, then total planning and execution time are at least the sum of the time needed to achieve each one, and probably more because of interactions. If a planner can notice the possibility of achieving several goals simultaneously or in conjunction with each other, this complexity can be cut significantly. Case-based reasoning provides a method for doing this. Previously used plans are saved and indexed by the conjunction of goals they achieve. If the conjunction of goals is repeated, the old plan that achieved them together can be recalled and repeated. The beef and broccoli recipe created in the example above, for instance, achieves several goals in conjunction: inclusion of beef in a recipe, inclusion of a crisp vegetable in a recipe, and preparation by stir-frying. If this recipe is recalled the next time these three goals must be achieved conjunctively, it will provide a framework for a solution without the need to consider each goal separately.

Another set of complexities that crop up in planning come from dealing with the relationship between planning and execution in a realistic way. Though the traditional view of

---

1. See Charniak and McDermott (1985) for an excellent explanation of these problems.

2. See Marks, Hammond, and Converse (1988, 1989) for an excellent explanation of these problems.

planning, as suggested above, was that a planner would create a plan (sequence of steps) to be executed later, the newer view of planning says that planning and execution must be combined. That is, we cannot expect a well-thought-out sequence of steps to work when executed in the real world. There are several reasons for this. First, it is unrealistic to think that all knowledge needed to plan well is known at the start of planning—we often find things out as we go along, and some things we never know for sure. Second, the world is unpredictable. Unexpected interruptions crop up (e.g., a fire alarm rings in the middle of doing some task). Agents who were unknown at the time of planning change things in an unexpected way (e.g., someone buys all the nails of a particular kind that you needed for your plan, and they are unavailable). And we can't even predict the actions of known agents all the time (e.g., someone else in the family got hungry for chocolate and ate the chocolate chips you were planning to use in your baking). In general, conditions in the world can change between coming up with a plan and carrying it out.

All this requires that our planners be able to put off at least some planning until execution time when more is known and that they be able to do execution-time repairs on already-derived plans that cannot be carried out. In addition, if the planner can anticipate execution-time problems, fewer repairs will have to be done at execution time.

Case-based reasoners are addressing many of these issues. PLEXUS (Alterman 1986, 1988), a program that knows how to ride a subway, is able to do execution-time repairs by adapting and substituting semantically similar steps for those that have failed. For example, when riding the New York subway, having ridden BART in the past, PLEXUS expects to find a machine to buy a ticket from. When it doesn't see one, it finds another plan that would achieve the same purpose as buying a ticket from a machine. It does this by finding an appropriate sibling or close cousin of the violated plan step in its semantic network. It attempts to substitute another ticket-buying plan it knows about, buying tickets from a cashier (as is done to get into the movies). It adapts that plan by substituting token for ticket, because it is a token that is necessary in the New York subway. SCAVENGER (Alterman, Zito-Wolf, and Carpenter 1991), a successor to PLEXUS, uses a similar adaptation process to learn how to operate simple devices.

CHEF (Hammond 1989a) anticipates problems before execution time by learning from its problematic experiences. When problems happen at execution time, CHEF attempts to explain them and then to figure out how they could be repaired. It stores its repaired plan in memory and indexes it by features that describe situations in which the problem is likely to recur. During plan derivation, it looks for situations similar to its current one in which plans failed and uses any it finds to anticipate the problems they point out. Later, it uses the repaired failure situations to suggest a plan that will avoid the problem it has anticipated. For example, CHEF uses its repaired beef-and-broccoli this way. It indexes it as a stir-fry with a crisp vegetable, and anytime it is creating another stir-fry recipe with crisp vegetables, it remembers this recipe, which warns it that the vegetable might get soggy and provides it with a plan for keeping the vegetables crisp during stir-frying (by separating the cooking of the vegetable from the cooking of the remainder of the ingredients and only mixing the ingredients together in the last step).

Other case-based planners address other of these problems. TRUCKER (Hammond 1989b) is an errand-running program that keeps track of its pending goals and is able to take advantage of opportunities that arise that allow it to achieve goals earlier than expected. If it needs orange juice, for example, and it sees a convenience store on its way home from work, it grabs the opportunity to buy the orange juice, even though it had not created a particular plan to do so. MEDIC (Turner 1989a, 1989b, 1989c) plans the steps in diagnosing pulmonary (lung) diseases. It is able to reuse previous plans for diagnosis but is flexible enough in its reuse to be able to follow up on unexpected turns of events. Thus, if it is tracking down a pulmonary complaint and the patient offers information about a heart condition that it had not known about previously, MEDIC analyzes which is more important to follow up. If it turns out the heart problem is more important, MEDIC interrupts its current diagnosis plan and moves to the more urgent one and will return to the original one when appropriate later. EXPEDITOR (Robinson and Kolodner 1991) plans the events in the life of a single parent who must both get the kids to school and get to work on time. It begins knowing how to achieve its goals singly and learns new procedures for achieving goals in conjunction by interleaving their steps. It also learns about common interruptions to its well-known plans (e.g., there is no cereal in the cupboard) and how to deal with those situations (feed the kids peanut butter and jelly for breakfast). Finally, it learns new plans for anticipating and avoiding failures in its plans. Though EXPEDITOR is slow in its initial planning, it gains competence over time as it is able to reuse the plans it creates. Finally, the CSI Battle Planner (Goodman 1989) shows how cases can be used to criticize and repair plans before they are executed.

A major requirement for efficient situated planning is an expressive, but efficiently accessible, representation for procedures. Each of the programs just mentioned has its own representation. SCAVENGER uses a representation called a multiplan; TRUCKER uses opportunistic memory; MEDIC uses hierarchies of several types of schemas; and EXPEDI-TOR uses MOP/scene structures. There are three things common to all these representations. First, they attempt to represent what is common to several similar plans once, and they index anomalous situations from that common core according to the recognizable characterizations of situations that call for using the specialized plan. Second, each breaks its plans into parts according to the subgoals that are pursued and makes the component parts of each of its plans individually accessible. Third, though component parts of plans are individually accessible, they are linked sequentially and/or causally to other component parts so that the full plan can be easily reconstructed if necessary. CELIA, a cognitive model of diagnostic planning, which will be discussed in chapter 4, also makes these commitments in its representations, as does PRODIGY/ANALOGY, an implementation of derivational analogy that combines heuristic search with case-based reasoning.

3.2.2 CBR for Design

In design, problems are defined as a set of constraints, and the problem solver is required to provide a concrete artifact that solves the constraint problem. Usually the given constraints underspecify the problem; that is, there are many possible solutions. Sometimes, however, the constraints overconstrain the problem; that is, there is no solution if all constraints must be fulfilled. When this happens, solving the problem requires respecifying the problem so that the most important constraints are fulfilled and others are compromised.

We can view the meal planning example in chapter 1 as a kind of design problem. As a designer, that meal planner must satisfy the likes and dislikes of her guests, keep the meal inexpensive, make the meal hearty, and use tomatoes. In addition, she must make the main and side dishes compatible with one another, must not repeat major ingredients across dishes, must make the appetizer complement the rest of the meal, and so on. Many different meals would satisfy these constraints: vegetarian lasagne would work as a main dish if one tray were made with tofu instead of cheese, and any number of side dishes and appetizers would complement it. Several other pasta dishes would also suffice as main dishes, each with any number of side dishes and appetizers to complement it. A combination of main dishes, one of which would satisfy the meat-and-potatoes people, another the vegetarians, and so on, and complementary side dishes and appetizers would also work.

Though it is convenient that there are so many possible solutions, the big problem is constructing any satisfactory solution at all. Given the many constraints, which are the important ones to focus on, and how can a solution be formed? This is the major problem facing a designer, whether a designer of meals, houses, bridges, engines, or airplanes. Constraints, which are commonly used to specify design problems, provide a means of evaluating whether a sufficient solution has been reached, but they are not, by themselves, constructive. That is, they don't point the way, by themselves, to solution alternatives.

Design cases provide illustrations of the way multiple constraints have been handled in solutions in the past. Remembering an old design case that was created with constraints similar to the new set in mind can help a reasoner construct a solution. The old case suggests a design, or at least a partial design or design framework, to the designer. In fact, designers report that their major initial design activity involves going through file cabinets and design books to see how different constraint combinations have been handled in the past. Only after this exploration do the designers of large artifacts (e.g., houses, engines, airplanes) begin to frame their solutions.

To see how this works, let's go back to the meal planner. Suppose that she remembers a meal she served to a large group of people. As required in this situation, it was easy to make in large quantities, inexpensive, hearty, and used tomatoes. In that meal, she served antipasto, lasagne, a large green salad, and garlic bread. This time, she has vegetarians coming for dinner, and one guest is allergic to milk products. The old solution doesn't quite fit—several guests who are vegetarian and one guest who is allergic to milk products won't be able to eat the lasagne. Nor will the vegetarians be able to eat the antipasto. The job now is to adapt the old solution to fit the new situation. The lasagne can be adapted to better fit the new situation by taking out the meat. The antipasto can be adapted by substituting additional cheeses and marinated vegetables for the meat. This will satisfy all constraints except the one specifying that one guest doesn't eat dairy products. The meal can be further adapted such that in one tray of lasagne, tofu cheese substitute is used instead of cheese. This adaptation of the old menu is now suitable for the new situation.

This is an example of an underconstrained problem. The constraints provide guidelines but don't point the reasoner toward a particular answer. In addition, the search space is huge, and though there are many answers that would suffice, they are sparse enough within the search space that standard search methods might spend a long time finding one. Furthermore, the problem is too big to solve in one chunk, but the pieces of the problem interact with each other in strong ways. Solving each of the smaller pieces of the problem in isolation and putting it all back together again would almost always violate some of the interactions between the parts.

Solving a problem by adapting an old solution allows the problem solver to avoid dealing with many constraints, and keeps it from having to break the problem into pieces needing recomposition. For example, the compatibility of the main and side dishes is never considered while solving the new problem because the old case provides that. Nor are ease of preparation, expense, or heartiness considered in generating a solution. The old case provides solutions to those constraints also. The problem is never broken into parts that need to be recomposed. Rather, faulty components (e.g., the lasagne) are corrected in place.

For these kinds of problems, which I like to call *barely-decomposable*, cases can provide the glue that holds a solution together. Rather than solving the problems by decomposing them into parts, solving for each, and recomposing the parts, as can be done with nearly-decomposable problems, a case suggests an entire solution, and the pieces that don't fit the new situation are adapted. Though considerable adaptation might be necessary to make an old solution fit a new situation, this methodology is almost always preferable to generating a solution from scratch when there are many constraints and when solutions to parts of problems cannot be easily recomposed. In fact, engineering and architectural design is almost entirely a process of adapting an old solution to fit a new situation or merging several old solutions to do the same.

The other major role of cases in design, as for all problem-solving tasks, is to point out problems with proposed solutions. When the meal planner in chapter 1 remembers the meal where Anne didn't eat fish, it is warned of the potential that its proposed solution will fail.

Several problem solvers have been built to do case-based design. JULIA (Hinrichs 1992; Hinrichs and Kolodner 1991) plans meals. The examples shown above are all among those JULIA has solved. CYCLOPS (Navinchandra 1988, 1991) uses case-based reasoning for landscape design. KRITIK and KRITIK-2 (Goel 1989; Goel and Chandrasekaran 1989; Goel 1991a, 1991b; Stroulia et al. 1992) combine case-based with model-based reasoning for design of small mechanical and electrical devices. They use case-based reasoning to propose solutions and use model-based causal knowledge to verify their proposed solutions, to point out where adaptation is needed, and to suggest adaptations. CADET (Sycara and Navinchandra 1989a, 1989b) also uses a combination of case-based and causal knowledge to do design.

More recently, the results of these investigations into case-based design processes have led to the creation of several case-based tools to aid human designers. ARCHIE (Goel, Kolodner et al. 1991; Pearce et al. 1992) and its successor ARCHIE-2 (Domeshek and Kolodner 1991, 1992, 1993) are being built to help architects do conceptual design, while AskJef (Barber et al. 1992) is aimed toward aiding human-computer interface designers with their task. These efforts were discussed in more detail in chapter 2.

At least one design problem solver is being used regularly in the industrial world. CLAVIER (Barletta and Hennessy 1989; Hennessy and Hinkle 1992), presented in chapter 2, is being used at Lockheed to lay out airplane components made of composite materials in an autoclave (oven). Though there is no causal model of what works and why, CLAVIER has been quite successful using cases. Based on the experiences of the human expert in charge of layout, CLAVIER can place pieces in appropriate parts of the oven and avoid putting pieces in the wrong places. It works as well as the expert whose experiences it uses, and is thus useful to

Lockheed when the expert is unavailable. CLAVIER almost always uses several cases to do its design. One provides an overall layout, which is adapted appropriately; the others are used to fill in holes in the layout that adaptation rules by themselves cannot cover.

One can also look at mediation as a kind of design in which the problem specification is overconstrained rather than underconstrained. In mediation, two adversaries have conflicting goals. It is impossible to fulfill the entire set of goals of either side. The role of the mediator is to derive a compromise solution that partially achieves the goals of both adversaries as well as possible.

In solving overconstrained problems, design specifications must be respecified while solving the problem. When overconstrained problems are solved by constraint methods, many different ways of relaxing constraints must usually be attempted before settling on a set that work. When case-based reasoning is used, a close solution to the constraint relaxation problem is provided by the remembered case, and it is adapted. MEDIATOR (Kolodner and Simpson 1989), discussed earlier, solved simple resource disputes, for example, two children wanting the same candy bar or two faculty members wanting to use the copy machine at the same time. PERSUADER (E.P. Sycara 1987a, 1987b; K. Sycara 1988a, 1988b) solved labor-management disputes. Its process was one of remembering an old precedent-setting case and then applying a series of adaptation strategies to it to create a solution for the new situation. It first applied *parameter adjustment* strategies to make relatively easy changes in an old contract, the kind that must be made all the time, for example, cost of living adjustments. This resulted in a ball-park solution. It then applied special-purpose critics to *evaluate* the ballpark solution in order to identify more specialized problems with an old contract, for example, to recognize whether or not the company could afford the contract. It then adapted the ballpark solution to repair these problems either by using an adaptation strategy suggested by another case or by applying another specialized set of critics. Finally, it used another special-purpose set of critics to adapt the solution in order to compensate for any changes that upset the equity of the old solution.

In almost all design problems, more than one case is necessary to solve the problem. Design problems tend to be large, and though one case can be used to solve some of it, it is usually not sufficient for solving the whole thing. When some case can provide a framework for a solution, other cases can be used to fill in missing details. In this way, decomposition and recomposition are avoided, as are large constraint satisfaction and relaxation problems.

MEDIATOR, PERSUADER, and CLAVIER all work this way. Some case is used to provide a framework for the solution, and other cases are used to fill in details or guide adaptation. When PERSUADER solves its problems, for example, it usually finds one old solution that covers the major points and then deals with issues that solution doesn't address by recalling other cases and using their suggestions as the basis for adding additional detail to the solution.

Other times, new problems are too big for one old case to provide a framework, and some degree of decomposition must be done before a framework can be found. JULIA deals with problems like this by using composite cases to provide a framework. For example, because it knows that dinners normally have an appetizer course, a salad course, a main course, and a dessert course, it can provide itself with a framework for solving the remainder of its problem even if it does not have a single case that covers its needs. Designers tell me that the ability to "frame" a problem is what differentiates great from ordinary designers. None of our case-based reasoners to date have focused on addressing this problem in all of its complexity. Designers, however, seem to frame problems by choosing the major points they want to address, using one or several cases to suggest a framework, and continuing from there. This suggests that case-based reasoning has much to offer the solution to this problem but that decisions about priorities are also important.

3.2.3 CBR for Explanation and Diagnosis

Explaining anamolies is prevalent in all of our problem-solving and understanding activities as people. If we read in the paper about a plane crash, we wonder why it happened. If we fail at something we are doing, we try to explain what went wrong so we won't repeat it. It we hear of someone doing something unexpected, we try to explain it. Explanation has been called the credit assignment problem and the blame assignment problem, depending on whether one is explaining a success or a failure. In general, it is the problem of zeroing in on or identifying what was responsible for something that happened. It is a problem that the AI world has been grappling with for some time.

A case-based approach to explanation (Schank 1986) says that one can explain a phenomenon by remembering a similar phenomenon, borrowing its explanation, and adapting it to fit. SWALE (Kass and Leake 1988; Leake 1992b; Schank and Leake 1989) does just that. When it hears that Swale, a racehorse in the prime of its life, died in its stall, it remembers several similar situations, each of which allows it to derive an explanation for the Swale case. When it remembers Jim Fixx dying of a heart attack after a run, it considers whether Swale had just been out for a run and if he had a heart condition that his owners had been unaware of. When it remembers Janis Joplin, it considers whether Swale was taking illicit drugs. Some explanations it can derive in this way are more plausible than others, and some require more adaptation than others. For example, in considering the Janis Joplin explanation, it must also come up with someone who wanted Swale to have the drugs (Joplin wanted them herself, but a horse can't) and a reason why that person would want Swale to have the drugs. This requires quite a bit more inference than an explanation based on the Jim Fixx experience.

As in planning and design, case-based explanation requires a retrieval mechanism that can retrieve similar cases, an adaptation mechanism to creatively modify old explanations, and a validation mechanism that can decide if a proposed explanation has any merit.

Diagnosis is a particular kind of explanation problem. In diagnosis, a problem solver is given a set of symptoms (things that are not as they should be) and asked to explain them. When there are a small number of possible explanations, one can view diagnosis as a classification problem. However, when the set of explanations cannot be enumerated easily, we can view diagnosis as explanation. A case-based diagnostician can use cases to suggest explanations for symptoms and to warn of explanations that have been found to be inappropriate in the past. The following example is from an early case-based reasoning project called SHRINK (Kolodner 1982, 1983c; Kolodner and Kolodner 1987), designed to be a psychiatric diagnostician.

A psychiatrist sees a patient who exhibits clear signs of Major Depression. The patient also reports, among other things, that she recently had a stomach problem that doctors could find no organic cause for. Though random complaints are not usually given a great deal of attention in psychiatry, this time the doctor is reminded of a previous case in which he diagnosed a patient for Major Depression who also complained of a set of physical problems that could not be explained organically. Only later did he realize that he should also have taken those complaints into account; he then made the diagnosis of Somatization Disorder with Secondary Major Depression. Because he is reminded of the previous case, the psychiatrist hypothesizes that this patient too might have Somatization Disorder with Depression secondary to that, and he follows up that hypothesis with the appropriate diagnostic investigation.

Here the doctor uses the diagnosis from the previous case to generate a hypothesis about the diagnosis in the new case. This hypothesis provides the doctor with a reasoning shortcut and also allows him to avoid the mistake made previously. In addition, the hypothesis from the previous case causes him to focus his attention on aspects of the case that he would not have considered otherwise: the unexplainable physical symptoms associated with Somatization Disorder.

Of course, one cannot expect a previous diagnosis to apply intact to the new case. Just as in planning and design, it is often necessary to adapt an old diagnosis to fit a new situation. CASEY (Koton 1988a, 1988b, 1989) diagnoses heart problems by adapting the diagnoses of previous heart patients to new patients.

For example, when CASEY was trying to diagnose the patient Newman (in chapter 2), it was reminded of another patient, David. Though they shared many symptoms, there were also differences between them. Newman, for example, had calcified heart valves and syncope on exertion, while David did not. CASEY adapted the diagnosis for David to account for these differences. Newman's aortic valve calcification was inserted as additional evidence for aortic valve disease, his syncope was inserted as additional evidence for limited cardiac output, and mitral valve disease was added to the diagnosis.

CASEY is a relatively simple program built on top of an existing model-based diagnostic program. When a new case is similar to one it has seen previously, it is several orders of magnitude more efficient at generating a diagnosis than is the model-based program (Koton 1988a, 1989). And, because its adaptations are based on a valid causal model, its diagnoses are as accurate as those made from scratch based on the same causal model.

Cases are also useful in diagnosis in pointing the way out of previously experienced reasoning quagmires. Though this normally happens as a side effect of SHRINK's and CASEY's reasoning, PROTOS (Bareiss 1989a) is designed to ensure that it happens in an efficient way. Recall (from chapter 2) that PROTOS diagnoses hearing disorders. In this domain, many of the diagnoses manifest themselves in similar ways, and only subtle differences differentiate them. A novice is not aware of the subtle differences; experts are. PROTOS begins as a novice, and when it makes mistakes, a "teacher" explains its mistakes to it. As a result, PROTOS learns these subtle differences. As it does, it leaves *difference* pointers in its memory that allow it to move easily from the obvious diagnosis to the correct one. In one instance, for example, it misdiagnosed a case as cochlear-age. When the teacher saw that, it told the program that in fact the case was one of cochlear-age-and-noise and that what differentiated the two was the age(greater-than-65) that was present in the new case but not present in other cases of cochlear-age. PROTOS rediagnosed the case correctly and inserted a *difference link* between the case of cochlear noise that had helped it make the original diagnosis and the new case, now classified as cochlear-age-and-noise. Later, when PROTOS thought a new case with age(greater-than-65) was an instance of cochlear-age, it was able to follow the difference link with that label, finding the case classified as cochlear-age-and-noise, and making a valid diagnosis first time around.

Generating a diagnosis from scratch is a time-consuming task. In almost all diagnostic domains, however, there is sufficient regularity for a case-based approach to diagnosis generation to provide efficiency. Of course, the diagnostician cannot assume that a case-based suggestion is the answer. The case-based suggestion must be validated. Often, however, validation of a suggested diagnosis is much easier than generation of a plausible diagnosis. In those kinds of domains, case-based reasoning can provide big wins.

3.3 INTERPRETIVE CBR

Interpretive case-based reasoning is a process of evaluating situations or solutions in the context of previous experience. Evaluation in context is something we do every day: My son says he has a sore throat. Do I assume it is a normal early-in-the-morning sore throat, or do I think it might be strep? It is important to evaluate and come to a conclusion because my next actions will be different depending on my interpretation of the sore throat. If I think it is nothing, I will send him to school. If I think he might really be sick, I need to make plans to take him to the doctor. Or, I am on the admissions committee at the university. I have to evaluate whether a particular applicant has what it takes to make it at my school. His test scores look good, and so do his grades, but one of his references says that he is particularly immature. Does this make a difference? Do I pay attention to that letter or not?

A common way to evaluate such situations is to remember old situations that are like the new one and to compare and contrast them. Is this new situation enough like an old one that it can be interpreted the same way the old one was? Is my son's sick complaint like other ones he's made when he's just tired, or is it more like those he makes when he is really sick? In what ways is this new applicant similar to those who have done well at my school? In what ways is he similar to those who have done less well?

We also ask what differentiates the new situation from old similar ones so that we can ascertain whether or not the old interpretation is likely to hold. Perhaps an applicant is like some who have not done well (e.g., he is, after all, immature). On the other hand, his grades and test scores are far higher than those of other immature students, and students with grades like his normally do quite well. Perhaps I know of one case of a very intelligent applicant who was also very immature but who grew and matured during his tenure at school and went on to win awards that the school was quite proud of. That tells us that it may not be so important to pay attention to the immaturity. But perhaps this student, though he has good grades and scores, doesn't have exceptional scores like the person who did so well. And so on. The cases help us "place" this applicant relative to others we have seen and whose histories we know. This placement helps us to project the future of this applicant, thereby helping us make a decision.

Supreme Court justices use interpretive case-based reasoning when they make their decisions. They interpret a new case in light of previous cases. Is this case like the old one? How is it the same? How is it different? Suppose we interpret it in some way, what are its implications? Lawyers use interpretive case-based reasoning when they use cases to justify arguments.

People on the street use interpretive case-based reasoning every day. The child who says, "But you let my sister do it," is using a case to justify his or her argument. Managers making strategic decisions base their reasoning on what's been true in the past. And we often use interpretive case-based reasoning to evaluate the pros and cons of a problem solution. An arbitrator, for example, who has just come up with a salary for a football player, might look at other players with similar salaries to judge if this new salary is consistent with other salary decisions. A battle planner might look at battles in which strategies similar to the one just chosen were used in order to project the effects of this chosen strategy.

Cases are used for interpretation and evaluation by professionals and laypeople, by children and grownups, by experts and novices, for commonsense reasoning and for reasoning in expert domains, for interpreting situations and while solving problems. Cases provide a useful basis for interpreting new situations because there are often so many unknowns that no straightforward means of evaluation is available. What kind of grade-point average is necessary to make it in the university? How mature do students have to be? It depends on the circumstances.

Interpretive case-based reasoning is most useful for evaluation when there are no computational methods available to evaluate a solution or position. Often, in these situations, there are so many unknowns that even if computational methods were available, the knowledge necessary to run them would usually be absent. A reasoner who uses cases to help evaluate and justify decisions or interpretations is making up for his or her lack of knowledge by assuming that the world is consistent. Two students with the same background and the same grade-point average are likely to perform similarly in college. At the same time, interpreting new situations based on old ones provides a way of maintaining consistency and equity over time. The legal system is based on that premise. If the law treats similar cases alike, it is equitable.

We briefly discuss three tasks in which interpretive case-based reasoning is useful: justification, interpretation, and projection. In justification, one shows cause or proof of the rightness of an argument, position, or solution. In interpretation, one tries to place a new situation in context. Projection means predicting the effects of a solution and is a process necessary in the course of complex problem solving. These tasks share the common thread of *argumentation*. Some cases will support one interpretation or effect. Others will support a different one. The reasoner must compare and contrast the cases with each other to finally come up with an interpretation of a situation.

Interpretive tasks, in turn, support a variety of reasoning goals. Classification, situation assessment, troubleshooting, and solution evaluation and repair are the most pervasive.

Interpretive processes take as input a situation or solution, and their output is a classification of the situation, an argument supporting the classification or solution, and/or justifications supporting the argument or solution.

3.3.1 **Justification and Adversarial Reasoning**

Adversarial reasoning means making persuasive arguments to convince others that we or our positions are right. Lawyers argue adversarially on a day-to-day basis. So do the rest of us as we try to convince others of our position on some issue. We also argue adversarily with ourselves when trying to convince ourselves of the quality or utility of some solution we have just derived. In making a persuasive argument, we must state a position and support it, sometimes with hard facts and sometimes with valid inferences. But often the only way to justify a position is by citing relevant previous experiences or cases.

The American legal system, like other common-law systems, is case-based. There are many rules, but each has terms that are underspecified, or *open-textured*, and many contradict each other. The definitive way of interpreting laws is to argue based on cases. Cases are used to show the meanings of underspecified terms. For example, *business-related travel* is not a well-specified term. It can be defined and its applicability to a new situation can be shown by comparing a new case that seems like business-related travel to other instances that are known to be or not to be in that category. Law thus provides a good domain for the study of adversarial reasoning and case-based justification. Much of the work in this area is in the legal domain (Rissland 1983; Bain 1984, 1986; Ashley 1990; Branting 1988, 1989).

HYPO (Ashley 1990; Ashley and Rissland 1988a), presented in chapter 2, provides a good example of case-based argumentation in the legal domain. HYPO's method for creating an argument and justifying a solution or position has several steps. First, the new situation is analyzed for relevant factors. Based on these factors, similar cases are retrieved. They are positioned with respect to the new situation; some support it, and some are against it. The most on-point cases of both sets are selected. The most on-point case supporting the new situation is used to create an argument for the proposed solution. Those in the nonsupport set are used to pose counterarguments. Cases in the support set are then used to counter the counterarguments. The result is a set of three-ply arguments in support of the solution, each of which is justified with cases. An important side effect of creating such arguments is that potential problem areas get highlighted.

Consider, for example, a nondisclosure case that HYPO argued.[3] John Smith had developed a structural analysis program called NIESA while an employee of SDRC. He had generated the idea for the program and had been competely responsible for its development. When joining SDRC, he had signed an Employee Confidential Information Agreement in which he agreed not to divulge or use any confidential information. Upon leaving SDRC, he went to work for EMRC as vice president for engineering. Eleven months later, EMRC began marketing a structural analysis program called NISA. Smith had used his development notes from SDRC's NIESA program in developing the new program. SDRC had disclosed parts of the NIESA code to some fifty customers. Now, SDRC is suing John Smith for violations of the nondisclosure agreement.

HYPO is arguing for the defendant (Smith). It uses the factors present in this case to pose a set of questions that must be answered: Did disclosure of NIESA code to fifty custom-

---

3. Thanks to Kevin Ashley for the example. Adapted from examples in Ashley (1990).

ers annul John Smith's nondisclosure agreement? Did the fact that Smith was the sole developer annul the nondisclosure agreement? Several cases are recalled, and an argument is made based on *Midland-Ross* v. *Sunbeam* that because the plaintiff (SDRC) disclosed its product information to outsiders, the defendant should win a claim for trade secrets misappropriation. However, a counterargument can be created based on differences between the two cases. In the *Midland-Ross* case, there was disclosure to many more outsiders, and the defendant received something of value for entering into the agreement. This point can be supported by *Data General* v. *Digital Computer,* where the plaintiff won even though it had disclosed to more outsiders than in the *Midland-Ross* case. However, a rebuttal is made based on that case. In *Midland-Ross*, the defendant won because the disclosures were restricted. In the *Data General* case, disclosure was by the sole developer of the new product. Using these cases, then, HYPO structures an argument that the defendant should win in a way that counters the arguments the other side is expected to make.

We see similar argumentation and justification in day-to-day argumentation. In chapter 2, for example, HYPO's method was illustrated using the arguments of an almost-thirteen-year-old who is told by his parents that he cannot go see *Little Shop of Horrors*. He uses all the cases at his disposal to plead his case. He says he should be able to see it because his sister was allowed to and because his friend, who is the same age he is, was allowed to. As his parents give their arguments (also using cases to make and justify points), we expect him to use other cases to counter those points.

In general, cases are useful in constructing arguments and justifying positions when there are no concrete principles or only a few of them, if principles are inconsistent, or if their meanings are not well specified.

3.3.2 Classification and Interpretation

Is swordfish a fish Anne will eat, or isn't it? This is the interpretive question faced by the reasoner in the beginning of chapter 1. In general, interpretation in the context of case-based reasoning means deciding whether a concept fits some open-ended or fuzzy-bordered classification. The classification might be derived on the fly (e.g., types of fish Anne will eat), or it might be well known but not well defined in terms of necessary and sufficient conditions. Many of the classifications we assume are well defined are categories of the open-ended variety. For example, we assume that a vehicle means a thing with wheels used for transportation, but when a sign says, "No vehicles in the park," it is probably not referring to a wheelchair or a baby stroller, both of which fit our simple definition. Making such distinctions is much of what lawyers are asked to do every day. Similarly, when a physician must determine if someone is schizophrenic or an audiologist must determine if someone has a particular hearing disorder, the recognition process is fraught with ambiguity. There are many ways schizophrenia can show itself, and necessary and sufficient conditions don't say how to deal with the borderline cases. And, as we see in the swordfish example, we are called on to do interpretive reasoning quite often as we do our everyday, commonsense tasks.

A case-based classifier asks whether the new instance is enough like another one to be assigned the same classification. Recall that PROTOS (Bareiss 1989a), which diagnoses hearing disorders, works like this.[4] Rather than classifying new cases using necessary and sufficient conditions, PROTOS does classification by trying to find the closest matching case in its case base to the new situation. It classifies the new situation by that case's classification. To do this, PROTOS keeps track of how prototypical each of its cases is and what differentiates cases within one classification from each other. It first chooses a most likely classification, then chooses a most likely matching case in that class. Based on differences between the case it is attempting to match and the new situation, it eventually zeros in on a case that matches its new one well and assigns the new case to the same category.

When no case matches well enough, it is sometimes necessary to consider hypothetical situations. Much of the work on this type of interpretation comes from the study of legal reasoning (see, e.g., Rissland 1986). Suppose, for example, that a lawyer must argue that his client was not guilty of violating a nondisclosure agreement because the only one he disclosed to was not technically competent to copy it. There may be several cases that justify this argument. To test it, one might create hypothetical cases that go beyond the real cases in testing boundaries. One might propose a situation in which the person disclosed to was not technical but was president of a company with technical personnel. Another might be one in which the person disclosed to was not technical, but his wife, whom he disclosed to, was. Interpretation based on hypothetical cases helps in fine-tuning an argument for or against a particular interpretation.

HYPO uses hypotheticals for a variety of tasks necessary for good interpretation: to redefine old situations in terms of new dimensions, to create new standard cases when a necessary one doesn't exist, to explore and test the limits of reasonableness of a concept, to refocus a case by excluding some issues, to tease out hidden assumptions, and to organize or cluster cases. HYPO creates hypotheticals by making "copies" of a current situation that are stronger or weaker than the real situation for one side or the other. This work is guided by a set of modification heuristics that propose useful directions for creation of hypothetical cases based on current reasoning needs. HYPO's strategies for argumentation guide selection of modification heuristics. For example, to counter a counterexample, one might propose variations on a new situation that make it more like the counterexample. Additional detail about HYPO in chapter 13 will make this clearer.

When a concept is being created on the fly, interpretation requires an additional step: derivation of a set of defining features for a category. For example, to decide if Anne will eat swordfish, one must first attempt to characterize what makes a fish Anne will eat acceptable. Otherwise, the basis for comparing swordfish with other fish she will eat cannot be known. Mahimahi, a fish she has eaten, is meatlike. Trout, which she won't eat, looks like fish. Salmon, which she has eaten, looks like a flat slab of food. The trout she wouldn't eat had its head on—it looks like a fish. The mahimahi and salmon she's eaten were made in the oven. The trout was made on the grill. These are some of the dimensions we need to use in determin-

---

4. In a previous section, we presented PROTOS as a problem solving system. Here we present it as an interpretive system. PROTOS' task, diagnosis, includes aspects of both uses of cases. It interprets open-ended concepts (classifications) using a case-based classification algorithm, and it uses an indexing scheme based on differences to avoid previously-made diagnostic mistakes. PROTOS shows us that problem solving and interpretation are not as separate as our simplified approach makes them out to be.

ing if swordfish is in the category of fish she will eat. We need to determine both the set of dimensions that it is plausible to compare things on and also the set that are relevant to the situation. This seems easy for us in the case of Anne and the fish—we probably assume that having the head on a fish is unappetizing for her, and we probably assume that the more meatlike the fish is, the better. But how do we decide that?

We currently have no explanations for this process and no computer programs that do a good job of it. HYPO is seeded with the set of dimensions that is relevant to focus on for a particular legal domain, and then each of its cases knows in particular what was focused on in it. PROTOS begins with a set of dimensions it knows to focus on, and then, as it makes mistakes, it is taught (by a person) what to focus on instead. But considerably more work is needed on this problem. It seems relatively easy to us to figure out what is important in a situation, but getting a computer to do it automatically is a challenge.

3.3.3 Interpretive CBR and Problem Solving: Projection

Much work on interpretation has centered on the legal domain and has looked at justifying an argument for or against some interpretation of the law. One should not walk away from this discussion with the impression that case-based interpretation is merely for interpretive problems, however. On the contrary, it has much usefulness as part of the evaluative or critical component of problem solving and decision making whenever strong causal models are missing. Though there has been little work in the area, the processes involved in interpretative case-based reasoning have the potential to play several important roles for a problem solver. First, if the framework for a solution is known, or if constraints governing it are known, these methods could be used to choose cases that would provide such a solution. Second, argument creation and justification result in knowledge of what features are the important ones to focus on. Knowing where to focus is important in problem solving also. Third, a side effect of compare-and-contrast methods is that the process can point out which features, if they were present, would yield a better solution. It does this by keeping track of near-miss dimensions and creation of hypothetical cases. A problem solver could use such information to inform its adaptation processes. Finally, interpretive methods can be used to predict the usefulness, quality, or results of a solution.

The clearest example of the usefulness of interpretive methods in problem solving is in projection of the effects or results of a proposed solution. Projection, the process of predicting the effects of a decision or plan, is an important part of the evaluative component of any planning or decision-making scheme. When everything about a situation is known, projection is merely a process of running known inferences forward from a solution to see where it leads. More often, however, in real-world problems, not everything is known, and effects cannot be predicted with accuracy based on any simple set of inference rules.

Consider, for example, a battlefield commander who must derive a strategy for an upcoming battle. Doctrine provides a set of rules for doing battle, and they can be used to create a first approximation of a battle plan. But doctrine gives rules for situations in general, not for particular situations in which the troops are tired, the strategies of the enemy commander are well known, it has been raining for a week, or the mountains are shaped in a way that allows a trap to be laid. In battlefield planning, as in many other situations, the little details of a situation are important to the worthiness of a plan. There are many details that could be attended to, and only some are important. And as in other adversarial situations, it is impossible to know everything about the other side, predict all of their strategies, or predict all of their reactions or counterplans. Yet a good plan must be created, and it must be evaluated based on projected results.

Cases provide a way to projecting results based on what has been true in the past. Cases with similar plans that were failures can point to potential plan problems. If a previous plan similar to the currently proposed one failed because the troops were too tired, for example, the commander is warned to evaluate whether his troops are too tired, and if so, knows to fix his strategy to take that into account. He might change the plan so that tiredness will not be a factor, give his troops a rest, or get fresh troops in for the battle. Cases with similar plans that were successes give credence to the current plan. In addition, when parts of a plan are targeted for evaluation, cases can help with that. The effects of using a particular kind of trap, for example, can be evaluated by recalling another case where a similar trap was used.

Projection is one of the most important bottlenecks facing the planning community today. A real-world planner must be able to project effects of plan steps to interleave tasks with each other, to plan late steps in a plan before earlier ones are executed, and to set up contingencies. Case-based reasoning has much to contribute to solving this problem. Though little effort has gone into automating the projection process to date, there have been attempts to build systems that can help people project the effects of a complex plan.

CSI's Battle Planner (Goodman 1989), discussed in the previous chapter, is an interactive case-based aiding system that helps a person to use cases to project effects. A student commander can propose a solution plan to the system. The Battle Planner retrieves the best-matching cases that use a similar plan and divides them into successful and failed situations. The user can examine the cases, use them to fix his or her plan, and then attempt a similar evaluation of the repaired plan. Or, the person can use the system to do a sensitivity analysis. By manipulating the details of the situation and looking at the changes in numbers of wins and losses (in effect, asking a series of "what-if" questions), the user can determine which factors of the current situation are the crucial ones to repair.

3.4 CASE-BASED AND OTHER REASONING METHODS

Case-based reasoning has a number of important contributions to make to building automated reasoning systems. Because it caches old solutions, it can shortcut from-scratch processes, warn of potential problems, and point the way out of previously experienced reasoning quagmires. An important by-product is that less time is needed for reasoning, leaving more time for action. Case-based reasoning also allows a reasoner to notice opportunities based on what has worked in the past. It provides constructive methods for creating solutions, while many other reasoning methods and knowledge sources provide primarily validation information. In addition, the fact that something worked in an old situation often provides sufficient justification for repeating it in a new situation. In this way, cases might provide a built-in way for a system to explain and justify its decisions.

A piece of good news is that some of our case-based systems have outperformed traditional expert systems. CASEY, for example, is equally accurate and two to three orders of magnitude faster than the Heart Failure Program, a model-based program that uses the same knowledge to reason. PROTOS, which diagnoses hearing disorders, was 50 percent more accurate than other classifiers in an evaluation study (Porter, Bareiss, and Holte 1990). The moral of those stories seems to be that if a causal model is well known, a case-based system can perform better than the traditional model-based one, and if problem situations are incompletely described (as PROTOS's are), then case-based methods work better than other classification methods.

People who have built case-based systems have found that they could build them easily (Goodman 1989; Simoudis 1992; Hennessey and Hinkle 1992). Communication between system experts and domain experts is relatively straightforward. Communication is through concrete examples (sometimes war stories), which experts are usually more than willing to contribute.

The major disadvantage of case-based reasoning is that it does not fully explore its solution space, meaning that some optimal solutions might not be found. But this is true of every heuristic method, and some fine-tuning can be done to make sure a system gets to answers that are good enough. Domains that require optimal answers are probably not appropriate for heuristic methods at all—case-based or other. Another disadvantage is that a case-based reasoner requires a large memory to hold its cases, which could be a problem for an owner of a small system.

How does case-based reasoning compare with other heuristic methods? In this section, we compare case-based to rule-based and model-based methods, pointing out the differences and the pros and cons of each.

3.4.1 **Case-Based and Rule-Based Reasoning**

At some level, we can think of case-based reasoning as a type of rule-based reasoning in which the rules are very large, the antecedents need to be only partially matched, and the consequents need to be adapted before they are applied. A case's problem description might correspond to a rule's antecedent, and its solution to the consequent. Rather than requiring a perfect match, we can apply the case when the match to the antecedent is good enough. And rather than applying the consequent directly, it needs to be adapted to make up for the differences between the problem statements.

Though thinking of case-based reasoning this way might provide intuitions for some people about case-based reasoning, it also obscures some of the differences between the two approaches. Some differences are what we might term surface issues; others are deeper. Perhaps the deepest issue has to do with where the research emphasis lies. In both rule-based and case-based reasoning, there are several issues of import, including the mechanisms or architecture for making the method work and the content of the knowledge that is used. Though neither can be ignored, the rule-based and case-based reasoning research communities have traditionally put different emphasis on these two things. In rule-based reasoning, the emphasis has been on the mechanism of reasoning and the form of the knowledge, with less emphasis on the content of the knowledge.[5] All knowledge (or most knowledge) is encoded in rules, but little

---

5. Clancey's (1988) work on the epistemology of rule-based systems is an important exception.

guidance is given about what the content of those rules should be. Of course, anyone building a system has had to emphasize the content of the rules and what they need to cover, but this has not been a major intellectual issue. It is left as an applications issue. In case-based reasoning research, on the other hand, the majority of intellectual emphasis has been on content issues: What kinds of content should cases have? What should the content of indexes be? What kinds of adaptation strategies do we need? What knowledge do they need to work? The majority of this book answers those questions at a conceptual level. There is little emphasis on exactly what form cases should take (e.g., frames or propositions) or exactly how adaptation strategies ought to be implemented, with the assumption that those versed in expert systems implementation will know the methodologies for carrying out the methods.

The surface differences between the two methodologies stem from that outlook plus one other deep difference—a conviction about the size knowledge chunks should be to enable reasoning. The rule-based community says they should be small chunks requiring composition. The case-based community says they should be larger, already composed, and rather than composing chunks with each other, the major activities should be comparing chunks and adapting chunks (either of which might require rules, by the way). These differences in outlook lead to the following apparent differences between the two methods:

- Rule-based reasoning: Rules in rule base are *patterns*.
  Case-based reasoning: Cases in case library are *constants*.
- Rule-based reasoning: Rules are retrieved that match the input *exactly*.
  Case-based reasoning: Cases are retrieved that match the input *partially*.
- Rule-based reasoning: Rules are applied in an iterative cycle of microevents.
  Case-based reasoning: Cases are retrieved first, approximating the entire solution at once, then adapted and refined to a final answer.
- Rule-based reasoning: Rules are small, ideally independent but consistent pieces of domain knowledge.
  Case-based reasoning: Cases are large chunks of domain knowledge, quite likely redundant, in part, with other cases.

These differences also lead to differences in knowledge acquisition. In rule-based reasoning, knowledge is extracted from experts and encoded in rules. This is often difficult to do. In case-based reasoning, most (but not all) knowledge is in the form of cases. Case-based reasoners also need the same semantic knowledge that rule-based reasoners need. In addition, case-based reasoners need adaptation rules and similarity metrics—more types of knowledge, but perhaps knowledge that is easier to acquire. Several recent studies point to the relative ease with which case-based reasoners can be built as compared to building the same rule-based systems. The first such study, done by Cognitive Systems, showed that it took two weeks to build the case-based version of the system that had taken four months to build in its rule-based form (Goodman 1989). More recently, developers at Digital Equipment Corporation found the same to hold true (Simoudis 1991b, 1992). Developers of a rule-based system for diagnosis called CANASTA spent 960 person days to complete their system, while developers of CASCADE, a case-based system with the same functionality, spent a total of 105 person days on development. If we factor in the relative worth of different types of people involved in the development (e.g., knowledge engineers, experts), then development of CANASTA, the rule-based system, comes to 1600 normalized person days, while that required to build CASCADE, the case-based system, was 193. CASCADE performs as well as CANASTA on both accuracy and efficiency.

Other claims have been made recently about the maintainability of case-based systems. Continuing with his comparison of CANASTA and CASCADE, Simoudis (Simoudis 1991b, 1992) claims that much of the time that has gone into CANASTA has been maintenance time, and that maintenance continues to be needed throughout the life of the system. On the other hand, CASCADE, the case-based system, needs almost no maintenance. This is because in a rule-based system, the addition of one rule often requires modification of several other rules. Addition of cases to a case library requires little or no modification beyond the addition of the case.

The builders of CLAVIER (Hennessy and Hinkle 1992) make a related claim. They were able to build a useful system with only about twenty cases in it to begin with and to add to its cases over time. The system was easy to build and useful from the beginning, becoming more useful over time.

There are also differences in the explanations that rule-based and case-based systems can give. A rule-based system gives rule chains as explanations. A case-based system shows cases its solutions were derived from. Is one more understandable than the other? The jury is still out. Not very much work on explaining solutions has been done in the case-based community. As more systems are built and placed in industry, we will find out how hard or easy it is for a case-based system to justify itself to a user.

3.4.2 Case-Based and Model-Based Reasoning

The intellectual commitments made by model-based and case-based reasoning are far closer to each other than are the commitments made by case-based and rule-based reasoning. Both model-based and case-based reasoning were developed as methods for bypassing reasoning from scratch. Both compose knowledge into large chunks and reason using large chunks. The differences have mostly to do with the content of the knowledge each uses and the conditions of applicability for each:

Knowledge content: Model-based reasoners store causal models of devices or domains; case-based reasoners store cases describing the way things work.

Domain applicability: Model-based reasoning is applicable when a causal model exists, that is, when a domain is well enough understood to enumerate a causal model; case-based reasoning is applicable under those conditions, but also when domains are not understood well. The set of cases plays the role of the generalized model when a domain is not well understood.

Task applicability: Model-based reasoning provides means of verifying solutions, but solution generation is unguided; case-based reasoning provides for efficient solution generation, and evaluation is based on the best cases available.

Having now gotten the differences between the two methods out of the way, it seems to me that the similarities between the two methodologies are more interesting than their differences. As stated above, both methods were developed with the goal of bypassing reasoning from scratch. Both reason using large chunks of knowledge. True, there is a commitment in model-based reasoning to emphasizing general knowledge that covers a domain, while the emphasis in case-based reasoning is on idiosyncratic knowledge, specific to particular episodes but not necessarily normative. It seems to me that all this points to the complementary nature of the two methodologies, rather than to discussions of which is better. From my point of view, neither methodology can cover the territory sufficiently by itself, and there is much in each methodology that complements the other. Models tend to hold knowledge needed for validation or evaluation of solutions but do not provide methods for constructing solutions. Case-based reasoning provides that. Case-based reasoning needs means of evaluating its solutions, guiding its adaptation, and knowing when two cases are similar, and the general knowledge in models can often provide that. There is, in fact, a tradition of integrating case-based and model-based methods within the case-based reasoning community. CASEY (Koton 1988a, 1989) integrates the two methods for diagnosis; KRITIK (Goel 1989; Goel and Chandrasekaran 1989) integrates them for design. Both of those programs reason about devices of different sorts. But even some case-based programs and approaches that deal with commonsense domains and use commonsense knowledge use a lot of model-type knowledge to reason. JULIA's object prototypes, for example, are general models of what meals are like. PROTOS's matching knowledge is in the form of commonsense models.[6] And even Schank's MOPs (Schank 1982) can be thought of as models of the commonsense world that organize cases.

Of particular import in discussing models and model-based reasoning is that as robust as a model might be for what it covers, there is no general model that can both be an efficient representation and provide wide coverage. Generalizations cover general cases, and at their edges they become less than reliable. If we try to make a model cover special cases, it begins being cumbersome and loses its efficiency. We can think about sets of models, where together a set of models can cover a domain. But even a set of models has to have edges, and it will be unreliable at those edges. Here is where the real complementariness of the two types of knowledge becomes evident. Models cover general situations but are not good at covering idiosyncracies of a domain. Cases are good at covering idiosyncracies, and though we can make them cover general types of situations, more general structures that can carry strategic and other kinds of information in them are more efficient at doing that. If we put the two together, letting each provide what it specializes in, we will be able to build robust reasoning systems that can both reason efficiently about generalized situations and cover the idiosyncracies of atypical ones. If we integrate the two with each other and index them similarly, then case-based reasoning's retrieval techniques can be used to retrieve both models and cases. In chapter 4, which is about the cognitive model case-based reasoning implies, a section will discuss this proposal in more detail using MOPs as the illustration of what the combination of models and cases can provide.

---

6. In the form of incomplete fragments.

3.5 SUMMARY

Cases are good for a variety of different inference tasks required for understanding, proposing solutions to problems, assigning blame, and other reasoning processes. In general, when cases are available, they allow a reasoner to avoid long chains of inferences, allow a reasoner to avoid assessing which of several available inference rules ought to be applied, and allow the reasoner to avoid mistakes made in the past.

Case-based reasoning has contributions to make to nearly all the different problem-solving and interpretive tasks that the artificial intelligence world has taken on. Its major contribution to problem solving is that cases suggest efficient ways of constructing solutions and warn of the potential for failure, allowing reasoners to anticipate and/or avoid problems that have arisen in the past. In addition, the efficiency gained by using case-based reasoning in planning can leave a reasoner more time to apply to action. In design, the use of cases allows a designer to concentrate on merging and adapting old solutions rather than having to worry about how to define the relationships between parts of a design, to decompose it, and to compose the pieces of the solution back together with each other. Though it seems that case-based reasoning could lead to uninteresting repetitive solutions to problems, there is no reason why it has to lead to such solutions. Even the most creative of human planners and designers use old cases to guide the creation of solutions.

In understanding and assessing situations, cases allow a reasoner to interpret or understand a situation in the context of other similar situations. Other situations can point out what to focus on and what outcomes might arise. Comparisons between old and new situations allow a reasoner to argue and justify the pros and cons of interpreting a situation or solving a problem in a certain way.

The major difference between case-based and rule-based reasoning is in the size of the chunks used for reasoning. This leads to a number of other differences, most important of which is that rule-based reasoning is a process of composing large numbers of small chunks to get to a solution, while case-based reasoning is a process of adapting small numbers of large chunks. Case-based reasoning has been shown to be more efficient in several situations.

The relationship between case-based and model-based reasoning is more complementary. Both were created to avoid reasoning from scratch, and both are committed to reasoning with large chunks of knowledge. The knowledge they use, however, is quite different, with models representing general knowledge and cases representing specific knowledge. The conclusion is that both are needed for reasoning about complex, real-world situations, especially commonsense situations in which much is unknown.

4

The Cognitive Model

4.1 A SHORT INTELLECTUAL HISTORY

Case-based reasoning derives from a view of understanding as an explanation process (Schank 1982). As we read a text or listen to a discussion, we use our knowledge about what is being written or talked about to help us tie together the pieces of what we hear. Our knowledge helps us predict what we will hear next, disambiguate words, resolve pronouns, and make connections between the disparate things being talked about. Of particular import in comprehension is making connections, or explaining the interactions of the individual things we hear. Consider, for example, the following story:

> John went to a restaurant. He ordered lobster. It was good.

Our knowledge about restaurants allows us, first, to predict that John will do what is normally done in restaurants and that he will play the role of customer. That allows us to realize, on hearing the second sentence, that "he" refers to John (because we know it is the customer who normally orders in a restaurant). We also infer that John probably sat down at a table and that he had a menu to look at. Our inferences might be wrong, but without them it would be impossible to piece together the disparate pieces of the story. When we hear that that "it was good," we assume the "it" refers to the lobster, that the lobster was cooked and brought to the table, that John ate at least some of it, and that he found it tasty. Again, our knowledge of what happens in restaurants allows us to infer all that. We also assume that John will pay the bill and eventually leave, that he was hungry when he entered the restaurant and probably no longer is, that he will leave a tip for the waiter, and so on. Our knowledge about what generally happens in restaurants allows us to explain the connections between the different pieces of the story. In the process, we hypothesize pieces of the situation that were not explicitly mentioned.

Schank and Abelson (Schank and Abelson 1977) proposed that our general knowledge about situations is recorded in *scripts* and that scripts allow us to set up expectations about what we will hear about, which, in turn, allow us to infer the relationships between the things we hear. But scripts provide only one kind of knowledge to us as we understand, and we also use knowledge about goals, plans, interpersonal relationships, the roles people play, character traits, and so on in our understanding. Representations for all these types of knowledge have been proposed (Dyer 1983; Schank and Abelson 1977; Cullingford 1978; Wilensky 1978, 1983), and computer programs that use all these types of knowledge to understand have been written. Understanding is seen as a *knowledge application* process in which explanations that tie together the individual things we encounter are formed.

This view of understanding asserts that when the appropriate knowledge structures are available, understanding is a *relatively simple* top-down process. Available knowledge structures allow the reasoner to *generate expectations*, in turn allowing the reasoner to *recognize* how something new that it encounters fits into the rest of the story. Without expectations, understanding must be more bottom-up; that is, explanations tying the pieces of the story together must be generated each time.

This is a specialized version of the standard "schema" view of reasoning that says that general knowledge is resident in memory in chunks and that reasoning is a process of applying those chunks to new situations. What was new and different about Schank and Abelson's approach was that it specified several particular types of chunks as being useful ones and proposed reasoning engines that knew how to use each type of chunk. Scripts, being sequences, are reasoned about using a script applier that knows how to fill in missing events in a sequence. Goals and plans are handled by an engine that predicts the plans someone will use, given a goal that person wants to achieve.

Schema theories are an old tradition in modern psychology (e.g., Bartlett 1932; Rumelhart and Ortony 1977; Brewer and Nakamura 1984; Thorndyke and Hayes-Roth 1979; Alba and Hasher 1983) and have been proposed as models of human memory. But, when we push schema theories to account for the full range of understanding and reasoning behaviors, do they hold up? Does Schank and Abelson's specialized schema theory hold up? Reading a story about an unusual kind of restaurant, for example, requires a fair amount of inference the first time to tie the pieces together, but understanding another story about the same type of situation is easier. The second time around, a person will generally be *reminded* of the first instance, which then performs the same function scripts and other schemas do: It provides the reasoner with expectations that allow the reasoner to interpret the story in a top-down way—by recognizing something that happens as something it is expecting rather than by having to tie the pieces together from scratch.

What do schema theories say of this kind of behavior? If pushed, researchers might say that instances themselves can be schemata too, and that it is an instance schema that is created in the first instance and used to understand the second instance above. Or, they might talk about creating general schemata from instances and say that a schema (more general than the instance itself) was created from the first instance and used in the second one. These are answers, but weak ones. The theory of scripts didn't do much better. Like schema theory, script theory was incomplete. Scripts, like schemata, hold normative knowledge, but not instance knowledge.

If remembering and using both general knowledge structures and specific instances is crucial to understanding, then our schema theories need to account for retrieval and use of both. It is this notion that guided research in Schank's research lab beginning in the late 1970s. In the same spirit in which Schank and Abelson addressed specifics about types of schemata and how to process them, research in Schank's lab continued by addressing specific questions about organizational structures and retrieval algorithms that had not been addressed previously by schema theorists. An assumption was made that the top-down understanding process itself remains the same whether it is using general knowledge structures or instances. Effort was therefore directed at defining retrieval algorithms and organizational structures that make the right knowledge, whether general knowledge or a particular instance, accessible.

The basic question asked was the following:

We have so much knowledge and so many cases available to us, how do we find the right ones?

A big piece of the answer to this question is *indexing*. Our hypothesis is that people *label* memory structures (both those holding general knowledge and those holding instances) in ways that make them accessible when needed. Memory structures are labeled according to their *type* and *the ways they differ* from other similar structures. Thus, one way we might label a visit to the original Legal Seafoods Restaurant[1] is as a *restaurant episode where we paid before we ate*. The label specifies a general context (restaurant visit), designating the general memory structure it is an instance of, along with a set of descriptors that distinguish this instance from others like it (we paid at a funny time). Labeled that way, the next time we are asked to pay before we eat in a restaurant, we can be reminded of this first case. We might also label this instance as *a restaurant visit to Legal Seafoods*. This will allow us to remember it next time we are there, allowing us to remember, perhaps, that the fish chowder or the smoked bluefish pâté is excellent, or that we waited for several hours before being seated. It is these labels, or indexes, that allow us to differentiate cases from each other. If both general knowledge and cases are labeled or indexed according to what differentiates them from other similar memory structures, then both are equally accessible by the same retrieval mechanisms.

The theory of *Dynamic Memory* (Schank 1982), proposed by Schank and his students in the late 1970s (Kolodner 1983a, 1983b, 1984; Lebowitz 1983a) and mentioned in chapter 1, presented indexing as the key to using experience in understanding. The premise was that remembering, understanding, experiencing, and learning cannot be separated from each other. Our memories, which are dynamic, change as a result of our experiences due to the new things we encounter, the questions that arise in our minds as a result of these experiences, and the way we answer these questions. We understand by trying to integrate new things we encounter with what we already know. Thus, understanding causes us to encounter old experiences as we process new ones. Those experiences provide expectations that allow the understanding process to be mostly simple and top-down. Individual experiences and general descriptions of normative experiences are both encountered as we understand; both provide the same sorts of information to understanding processes. The side effect of this process, of course, is that a

---

1. In Inman Square, Cambridge, Mass.

dynamic memory never behaves exactly the same way twice, because it changes as a result of every one of its experiences. Reasoning processes thus never encounter exactly the same knowledge on two traversals through memory.

Of primary import in this theory are means of selecting indexes and integrating general knowledge with experiences themselves. The theory of dynamic memory proposed that memory is organized by *memory organization packets* (MOPs), which have two functions: They hold general knowledge, and they organize, in a complex hierarchy, specific experiences (cases) of that general knowledge. Thus, a *restaurant visit* MOP holds general knowledge about restaurant visits (e.g., their sequence of events, the characters) and also organizes instances of going to restaurants. As suggested in earlier discussion, however, every instance of going to a restaurant may not be worth storing. MOPs store those instances in which *expectations were violated* or *anomalies were encountered,* that is, those instances in which extant expectations were inadequate for understanding the situation. Cases are indexed primarily by those anomalies, so that if a similar anomaly is encountered, the case in which it was previously encountered can be recalled and provide its expectations. Reminding, learning, and understanding thus go hand in hand.

The leap from memory structures and retrieval algorithms that allow understanding to happen to the use of cases in other sorts of reasoning is a short one. Once reminding was made central to understanding, as dynamic memory did, researchers began to ask how remindings might be useful for other cognitive tasks. Even casual observations of people suggested that remembering old situations was central to problem solving. Further observation showed that, indeed, cases were useful in problem solving: in suggesting solutions to be adapted to fit the new situation and in warning of potential pitfalls.

This caused researchers to ask another question: Could the same retrieval processes and memory structures designed to support remindings in understanding also support problem-solving? It seemed plausible that they could, and the first case-based problem-solving programs appeared soon after this question was posed. MEDIATOR (Kolodner and Simpson 1984, 1989), which solved everyday resource disputes (such as two kids wanting the same candy bar), showed the breadth of inferences cases could support and showed that case-based inference could indeed shortcut reasoning processes. JUDGE (Bain 1984, 1986), which acted like a judge sentencing juvenile offenders, showed the relationship between understanding and problem-solving processes. Problem solving in JUDGE was primarily a process of elaborating a problem description in enough detail to recall a similar case and then adapting the solution from that case to create a good solution to the new problem. CHEF (Hammond 1986a, 1986b, 1989a), a case-based planning program that created new recipes from old ones, showed how cases can be used to help a reasoner anticipate and avoid old failures.

But a major question remains. Understanding, we said, is a process that combines the use of cases with the use of general knowledge, preferring whichever can provide the most specific expectations. MOPs are memory structures that organize general knowledge and cases together in memory, making both equally accessible. Case-based reasoning, however, seems to favor cases to the neglect of general knowledge. Why? The reason is a pragmatic one rather than a theoretical one. In problem solving, as in understanding, the most specific predictions are generally the most useful ones. We want our problem solvers to make use of the most specific knowledge available. Often, this is provided by cases.

Given that there has been much research on the role of general knowledge in reasoning but little on the role of specific instances (cases), it made sense to concentrate on the role of cases. Case-based reasoning researchers have thus emphasized the role of cases and for many years deemphasized the role of general knowledge. Our case-based reasoners do make extensive use of general knowledge, but in a very different way than do traditional problem solvers. Though cases provide a starting point for solving a problem, general knowledge in case-based systems provides guidance in adapting old solutions to fit new situations, choosing indexes, matching cases to each other, and evaluating the goodness of derived solutions.

More recently, researchers are beginning to give the role of general knowledge more thought, looking at the role of *generalized episodes* (Kolodner and Simpson 1989) in reasoning. A generalized episode is more or less the equivalent of a MOP. It has the same structure as an episode, but describes a general type, not a specific episode. It is almost as specific as an episode, lacking only the details. In JULIA (Hinrichs 1992), for example, composite cases (e.g., Italian meals, buffet meals) provide the program with a framework for its solutions, and it fills detail into the framework based on specific cases. CELIA (Redmond 1990b, 1992), to be described later in this chapter, integrates the use of general knowledge (in the form of models) with case knowledge to both do diagnosis and learn how to do it better. It may be important to point out here that in moving from the use of cases to the integration of general knowledge and cases, there are assumptions and claims being made about the form and content of useful general knowledge. One claim is that big chunks representing descriptions of types of episodes are useful. More on this later.

Psychological theories and experimentation have also played a role in the intellectual history of case-based reasoning. Schank (1982) cites Gordon Bower's experiments on scripts (Bower, Black, and Turner 1979) as influential in showing that scripts were not a complete enough theory of memory representation. A less acknowledged but equally important source of inspiration for the theory of dynamic memory can be traced to Don Norman, Danny Bobrow, and members of the LNR research group at the University of California at San Diego. The LNR group had a long history of doing research that paralleled that going on in Schank's lab. Early in the 1970s, that group and Schank's group at Stanford investigated conceptual representations of knowledge (Schank 1975; Norman, Rumelhart, and LNR Research Group 1975). In the middle and late 1970s, the LNR group began developing a theory of memory and reasoning called "descriptions" (Bobrow and Norman 1975; Norman and Bobrow 1979).

The theory went something like this: Knowledge is encoded in schemata, some of which are general descriptions of things, some of which describe specific things. The process of retrieval from memory is an incremental process of describing and redescribing what needs to be retrieved. The process might retrieve something specific from the memory, it might reconstruct something that lives in the memory in several parts, or it might construct something new by combining and recombining the small schemata that are retrieved. The retrieval process itself is an incremental process with a parallel search at its core: given a description of what one is looking for (in the shape of a schema), it searches the memory in parallel and returns the best partial matches. Surrounding the parallel search are evaluation and elaboration processes. Evaluative processes evaluate what the search process returns, looking at how close the matches are and where they aren't quite right. That process sends its results to the elaboration process, which updates appropriately the description of what is being sought in the memory.

THREE ASPECTS OF MEMORY RETRIEVAL

Aspect	*Uses as input*	*Provides as output*	*Comment*
Retrieval specification:	Purposes, needs, despcriptions.	Target description, verification criteria.	May require memory retrieval.
Match:	Target description.	Memory records.	
Evaluation:	Memory records, verification criteria.	If success, terminate. If failure, revise the retrieval specification	May require memory retrieval.

FIGURE 4.1   Norman's Elaboration Process

There was more to the process the LNR group described: it took priorities and time constraints into account in its search. But that is not important to what we discuss here. Figure 4.1 shows the basic process.

This model was not the first to propose that people compose their knowledge into schemas and reason with large composed chunks, but it was one of the first to acknowledge that specific instances of schemas play the same role as schemas holding more general knowledge. And its incremental elaboration process for searching memory was novel. Looking at the theory of descriptions from the point of view of dynamic memory, it suggested many interesting questions. What kinds of schemata are there in memory? Which are the most useful ones for supporting inference and reasoning? What role do schemata holding general information play? What role do those holding specific information play? How do the two interact? How, exactly, does the elaboration process work? How, exactly, does the evaluation process work? What about the partial matching process—how is it defined? Does parallel search really look at every schema in the memory? Is there really enough parallelism for that?

Work on dynamic memory and case-based reasoning is, in many ways, complementary to Norman and Bobrow's theory of descriptions. Though the theory of descriptions proposed general mechanisms for retrieval without worrying about underlying memory organization, dynamic memory and MOPs propose a memory organization that supports reconstructive processes along with well-specified processes for retrieval that depend on that underlying organization of information and knowledge in memory. For example, Mike Williams (Williams and Hollan 1981), one of Norman's students, elaborated on the memory search process Norman and Bobrow proposed.[2] Based on a series of protocol studies, he identified several types of strategies for searching memory—strategies that specified what memory should be looking for. His research was the counterpart on the psychology side to work on CYRUS (Kolodner 1983a, 1983b, 1984) on the AI side. All that work taken together begins both to answer the

---

2. This work ultimately led to the development of RABBIT (Williams et al. 1982), an interface for a database that allowed users to refine their specifications of what they were looking for based on examination of one or several items that were returned. RABBIT can be thought of as the first interactive program based on the case-based reasoning approach, though it has never been presented that way by its authors.

questions posed by the theory of "descriptions" and to explain the intimate connections between understanding, reasoning, memory, and learning.[3]

4.2 DYNAMIC MEMORY

The premise in Schank's *Dynamic Memory* (Schank 1982) is that remembering, understanding, experiencing, and learning cannot be separated from each other. A dynamic memory changes as a result of its experiences. It understands by attempting to find the closest thing in memory to what it is trying to understand and then adapting its understanding of the old item to fit the new one. In the course of understanding, then, old experiences are remembered, providing expectations that further drive the understanding process.

Understanding, in turn, allows memory to reorganize and refine itself, in short, to be dynamic. As cases and memory structures are recalled and used, the memory gets a chance to try out the knowledge associated with its cases and categories. It may find that some expectations never hold up. This discovery may cause it to get rid of some category or case altogether or to wonder how it should be re-indexed so that it is recalled only when its expectations will hold. It may find that the expectations from some category or case are too vague. This may cause it to set a knowledge acquisition goal for itself or to examine the cases that are in that category and find new generalizations across them. It may find that the expectations from some case or category are too specific, always needing to be adapted in similar ways. This may cause it to break a category into several pieces or to decide that additional cases must be remembered and stored.

This understanding and learning cycle is not merely a process for language understanding. It is the process that drives our reasoning. Knowing where something fits in with what we already know is a prerequisite to reasoning about it. We find it hard to suggest a solution to a problem until we understand the problem. At the same time, further reasoning about the problem (based on our earlier imperfect understanding of it) may allow us to understand it better. We use what we know about a situation to find the closest match in memory, and we use that as the basis for deriving expectations and inferences. As we test those expectations and inferences, and as we gather additional information about a situation, we may find closer matches in memory, allowing us to derive better expectations and inferences. The remembering, predicting, and testing of predictions that we do as we understand and solve problems is very much the same as the remembering, predicting, and recognizing that we do as we understand stories that are told to us.

---

3. A final piece of the intellectual history of dynamic memory belongs to the Sloan Foundation and the visitor series it supported. During the 1978–79 academic year, Yale's AI lab hosted a different cognitive scientist each week for an entire year. Each visitor stayed a whole week, giving three lectures in that week and making himself or herself available to the Yale cognitive science community for in-depth discussions. During that year, Schank's MOPs and theory of dynamic memory (Schank 1982) were developed, and development of CYRUS (Kolodner 1983a, 1983b, 1984) and IPP (Lebowitz 1983a, 1983b)—two programs that modeled dynamic memory and made the processes of choosing indexes and searching memory explicit—were in full swing. Many of the visitors influenced work on dynamic memory.

4.2.1 **Reminding**

Finding the right old thing in memory is, under this view, *the key* to successful reasoning. The right thing might be a general knowledge structure (schema) representing a normative description of something, or it may be an instance of that general knowledge structure (a case). The right one is the one that can provide the best inferences.

Identifying the right thing in memory is the process we call *reminding*. Reminding, in everyday parlance, is the phenomenon of remembering an old event in the process of thinking about or talking about another one. We notice our own remindings when they are surprising. The thing we remember may be so obscure or so old that we are surprised we still remember it. Often, however, when we are reminded, we find that whatever it is we are reminded of is useful. It may provide an answer to a dilemma, it may suggest a new way of looking at something, it may suggest a pit we are about to fall into, and so on. One premise of dynamic memory is that our conscious remindings and the remembering that happens unconsciously during understanding are products of the same retrieval process.

I said earlier that indexing or labeling allows such retrieval to happen. Both memory categories (schemas) and individual instances (cases) are labeled according to the category they are in and the way they differ from the category. Our discussion would not be complete without consideration of the kinds of categories (schemas) there might be in a dynamic memory. Where do we begin in defining those?

We begin with another premise (Schank 1982):

> The structures in memory that are used for processing (i.e., the ones that provide expectations and suggest inferences) are the same ones that are used for storage.

This premise comes from our discussion of understanding. I gave an example earlier of a person reading a story about a new kind of restaurant and having to make a lot of explanatory inferences to understand the situation. That same person reading a second story about the same restaurant or the same kind of restaurant, I claimed, would have a much easier time. The expectations derived from the first episode would guide understanding of the second instance. The record of the first episode serves two purposes: It records the episode, and it provides expectations for understanding the second one. That is, it is used for both storage and processing.

The premise tells us to begin with the types of schemas that we already know are used for processing. For example, we know that situation descriptions, in the form of scripts, play a large role in understanding. We can therefore assume that situation descriptions are a useful kind of memory category. We know that knowledge structures representing goals and plans and their relationships play a large role in understanding. We thus assume, too, that the relationships between goals and plans form useful memory categories.

The premise also suggests a tool to use in figuring out more about memory categories. If storage structures and processing structures are the same, then *noticing and analyzing remindings* can be a powerful tool in uncovering the types of memory categories people use. When we are reminded in the course of understanding something, we may have been using the event we are reminded of to process the new one. Analyzing the similarities between the new item and the reminding might point us toward a taxonomy of memory categories.

We examine several remindings both to show the utility of analyzing remindings as a tool and to begin to explore the kinds of processing structures that we use in understanding and reasoning. We begin with Legal Seafoods. At the original Legal Seafoods Restaurant in Inman Square, waiters presented the bill after taking the order (before the food came). The first time I went there, I found this anomalous, as most people did. I had never been in a restaurant before where one both sat down at a table to order and paid before getting the food. The second time I went there, I was reminded of the first and was therefore able to expect that I would have to pay before eating. Many years later, when I went to the newer Legal Seafoods, I was reminded again of the original visit, and I again expected to pay after I ordered. I was surprised that they had changed their method of billing and now asked for payment at the end of the meal, just as in other restaurants. I continue to be surprised to this day each time I go into Legal Seafoods. The original index is still there, I suppose, and provides me with the expectation that I will pay before eating.

This is a kind of activity-based reminding. When engaging in or reading about an activity similar to one we've encountered before, we tend to be reminded of the earlier similar one. The purpose of such remindings seems clear. They provide expectations for understanding the new situation or guidelines for participating in it. Our compilations of the variations in recurrent stereotypical sorts of events come from first storing and then recalling the variations in these activities that we have seen. Activity-based categories (similar to scripts) seem to be useful ones for processing.

Schank tells several reminding stories in *Dynamic Memory* that show off other aspects of memory processing. One story he tells is of going to the post office and standing in line for a long time and then overhearing the person in front of him ask for one stamp. He is reminded of people who go to a service station and buy only a few gallons of gas. Both are situations in which the goal being achieved in the situation is a recurring one. Not only that, but in each situation, we know of a plan that allows us to minimize the time spent fulfilling this recurring goal. Buying a whole roll of stamps at one time allows us to avoid going to the post office again for a long while. We can subsume the goals involved in needing stamps to send an individual letter by acquiring stamps that allow us to send a bunch of letters before we need to acquire stamps again. Filling the tank of the car with gas allows us to go many miles before needing gas again. We subsume the goals of needing gas to go to individual places by achieving the goal of filling the tank.

This reminding shows us the role of goals in understanding. In understanding the post office situation, Schank was reminded of the gas station situation. But what is it about goals that was of import in this reminding? It wasn't the goals themselves. In one instance, the goal was to acquire a stamp to mail a letter; in the other, the goal was to acquire gas to be able to use the car to get somewhere. Rather, something about the nature of the goals and their relationships to other goals was important. In both, the goal was an acquisition goal. In both, the goal was one that recurs with regularity. In both, there is a well-known goal that subsumes the recurring one. Schank expected the person to pursue the subsuming goal; instead the person was pursuing the recurring one. Goals, their types, their relationships, and their statuses are all sources of predictions in understanding and grist for the construction of memory categories.

Another story Schank tells is of his daughter searching for sand dollars in the ocean. Sand dollars are a small ocean animal that can be found in knee-deep or higher water in some places. He finds her diving for the sand dollars in shallow water and asks her if she's finding any. She says no. He asks her why she's searching in the shallow water. She says it is because it is easier. Schank is reminded of the story of the drunk and the lamppost.

A drunk is looking for his keys under a lamppost. A man comes and asks if he can help him look. After looking for some time and not finding the keys, the man asks the drunk if he's sure he lost them there. The drunk says that he actually lost the keys up the street, but he's looking here because the light is better.

Why this reminding? In both of these cases, the main character has the goal of finding something. In both, there is a well-known plan for finding that thing. In both, the main character is using a more convenient plan but one that is unlikely to yield results. The similarities in these stories are about goals and plans. Plans, too, help us understand. The interesting thing about this reminding, however, is that it is not the particular plan that is similar across these stories, but rather the abstract characterization of the plan (look where convenient) in the context of similar goals (acquisition of something whose location we know) with well-known plans (look in the place where the thing is known to be). This reminding tells us that though plans are important for reminding, they are subservient to goals. From this and other examples, the inference was made that plans do not form processing categories themselves but rather inform the creation of specialized goal-based categories.

Each of these last two remindings is what we call "cross-contextual." That is, the similarities between the situations are across something other than the type of situation itself. Buying fuel and buying stamps cuts across two different scripts (post office and service station). And the stories aren't really about either script anyway. They are about the goals and plans of people doing those scripts; the scripts are incidental. Searching for sand dollars and searching for keys have in common searching, but the similarities at the raw situation level end there. Those stories, too, are about goals and plans and their interactions. Remindings, in both these instances, seem to depend on keeping track of the whole sequence of goals and plans in the situation.

Analysis of remindings suggests two very different kinds of memory structures, one kind organizing situations with similar activities, the other kind organizing situations that are similar in the interactions between goals and plans of people interacting in the situation. In Schank's *Dynamic Memory*, the first are called MOPs (memory organization packets); the second, TOPs (thematic organization packets). Both kinds play two roles: they are repositories for similar events, and they are processing structures. The major implication of using memory structures for both these roles is that they must hold the kinds of information that allows them to perform both roles. That is, they must hold expectations and other descriptive information that reasoning processes need, and they must organize their instances in a way that allows them to be extracted easily.

4.2.2 MOPs

MOPs, or memory organization packets, organize situations whose activities are similar. The general knowledge in a MOP is much like the knowledge held in the original formulation of scripts. It includes information about normative sequence of events, setting, cast of characters, props one can expect to see in the situation, standard goals of someone entering the situation, and so on. The major difference between the general knowledge in a script and that in a MOP is in the level of detail of that knowledge. When scripts were originally developed, they were defined as holding the complete sequence of events for a type of situation. Thus, the `visiting the doctor` script, for example, was defined as holding all the details of the sequence of events of going to a doctor, including the details of each of the scenes, and a separate `going to the dentist` script was defined as holding all the details of the sequence of events of going to a dentist.

The implication of this representation was that details of script scenes were repeated across all the scripts that shared each scene. The waiting room scene, for example, was stored in its entirety in both `visiting the doctor` and `visiting the dentist`. Defining scripts as big monolithic structures implied that dentist stories and doctor stories would be processed by completely different knowledge structures and would be stored in completely different places in memory, and the two would never come in contact with each other. This method turned out to be problematic for several reasons. First, it is uneconomical. Second, it prohibits making generalizations across similar scenes of disparate types of events (e.g., it would have been impossible to notice similarities between a waiting room in a doctor's office and one in a dentist's office according to the old script theory). Third, it is not consistent with people's memories. Gordon Bower and his students found this out in experiments testing the validity of scripts (Bower, Black, and Turner 1979). In particular, they found that subjects told a story about a visit to the doctor and another about a visit to a dentist confused things that happened in shared scenes of the two events. For example, they would retell the story about the visit to the doctor and insert something that happened in the waiting room of the dentist's office, and *vice versa*. Bower's results showed scripts in their original form to be a poor model of memory organization.

Describing situations in terms of MOPs attempts to correct this problem. Rather than including all the details of all the scenes in a single representation, MOPs describe situations in a more distributed way. Each situation is described by the sequence of *scenes* it is composed of, and each scene is described in a memory structure of its own, one that both holds normative descriptive information and organizes its own instances. This allows similar activities that would have been represented by several different scripts to be represented by the same MOP. Both doctor's visits and dentist's visits, for example, can be described by the `professional office visit` MOP, whose sequence of scenes includes `make appointment`, `go`, `enter office`, `waiting room`, `see professional`, and `pay`, and `leave`. Making the appointment, going, entering the office (and signing in), waiting, paying, and leaving are essentially the same, no matter what professional is being seen. The major difference is in the `see professional` scene, which is further divided into (new-style) *scripts* representing the detailed sequences of events that happen in a particular professional's examining room. These new-style scripts, like the original ones, are stereotyped sequences of events, but they cover only a single scene. Figure 4.2 shows the general knowledge associated with the `professional office visit` MOP. Note the `see professional` scene, which indexes several scripts associated with that scene.

A scene describes a setting and a set of activities that are pursued in order to achieve the goal(s) associated with the scene. The `see professional` scene is a good example. The setting is the professional's examining room. The major goal is the examination. The major activity is

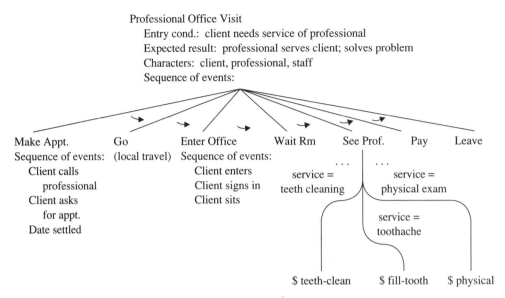

FIGURE 4.2   A MOP and Its Scenes—Professional Office Visit

the examination, whose detailed sequence happens differently depending on which professional is being seen and what the client's complaint is. Another example is ordering, as is done, for example, in a restaurant. In ordering, a client makes clear to a representative of a business establishment the service or item the client wants. The major activity is the communication needed to make that happen. Ordering can happen in a variety of different settings, and the particular accoutrements of the communication event are different depending on the setting. In a restaurant, the client looks at a menu to see what is available and then tells a waiter the things on the menu that he or she wants. In ordering from a catalogue, the client either makes a phone call to the appropriate office and tells the person who answers the code numbers of what he or she wants, where to mail it, how to pay for it, and so on, or the client writes that information on an order form. In a fast-food restaurant, one looks at the menu on the wall above and tells somebody at the counter what one wants. And so on. Though the details of the sequence of events in the scene are different, the goal and major action are the same. Figure 4.3 shows the ordering scene. Note that it has its own general knowledge describing ordering, that it indexes several scripts describing particular ways of doing ordering, and that it is pointed to by the sequence of events of several different MOPs.

Where do scripts fit in? Two paragraphs ago, I referred to old-style and new-style scripts. In both of the previous figures, several scripts were referred to. In its new style, a script is a stereotypic sequence of events, as in its original definition, but rather than describing sequences of events that cover several scenes, a script represents a stereotyped sequence of events the happens in one setting or scene. Thus, we no longer talk about the restaurant script—it is too encompassing. We can, however, refer to the restaurant-ordering script, where a menu is used to see what is available, one waits for the waiter to ask what one wants, and

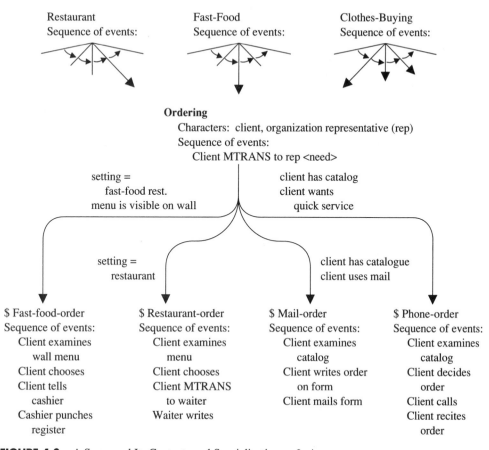

FIGURE 4.3 A Scene and Its Contexts and Specializations—Order

then one tells the waiter, who writes it down. We can also refer to the restaurant-paying script, in which the check comes, and we put down a credit card or money, and the waiter sees it and takes it and brings back a signature page or change. Restaurant-ordering is a particular way of achieving the goal of the ordering scene; restaurant-paying is a particular way of achieving the goal of the paying scene.

How do MOPs, scenes, and scripts organize events so that those that can provide the best expectations can easily be made available to reasoning processes? This is where *indexing* comes in. General knowledge associated with MOPs, scenes, and scripts provides expectations for normative situations; cases provide expectations for anomalous situations, those in which normative expectations don't hold. MOPs, scenes, and scripts thus need to index instances such that they are available to provide expectations for dealing with anomalous situations. *Cases are indexed by combinations of features that predict their applicability in an anomalous situation.* At the old Legal Seafoods Restaurant, for example, the paying scene came after the ordering scene. In other ways it was like other restaurants. Indexing the Legal Seafoods case by the feature "restaurant is Legal Seafoods" allows a previous Legal Seafoods instance to be recalled, providing the expectation that paying will come after ordering rather than at the normal time.

Scenes also index instances, but rather than indexing whole episodes, they index the pieces of episodes that pertain to them, that is, those that provide expectations that allow a reasoner to deal with the scene's anomalies. Consider, for example, the paying scene in Legal Seafoods. Because one paid before getting served, it was inappropriate to leave the tip at that time. The tip, normally part of the paying scene, needed to be done at the end of the meal, as is usually done. The restaurant MOP holds sequence of events information and therefore needs to index the Legal Seafoods event in such a way that the paying is expected *and* the tip is remembered. The paying scene, however, is the structure that needs to hold the expectations about paying itself. To store all the expectations needed to pay correctly in Legal Seafoods the second time, the paying scene stores both the initial paying component of the first meal and the tipping component at the end of that meal, indexing the paying component by "in Legal Seafoods, just ordered" and the tipping component by "in Legal Seafoods, about to leave." Expectations deriving from anomalies at the MOP level and at the scene level are combined to provide the whole set of expectations needed to process the second episode. Figure 4.4 shows the ways these structures are related and the indexing and expectations that derive from the first Legal Seafoods experience.

It is perhaps time to summarize the way all these pieces fit together. MOPs *package* scenes, by referring to their sequence as part of the MOP's descriptive information. They *index* instances that provide expectations about setting, characters, and sequence of scenes—the kinds of general information MOPs hold. Scenes *index* scripts and instances that provide expectations about how the scene will unravel in different circumstances. Scripts are *specializations* of scenes, and scenes are *components* of MOPs. Scripts index cases that specialize them, that is, that provide expectations about variations in the script. Figure 4.4 shows how some of the scenes, scripts, and instances related to going to a restaurant are connected to each other. Cases can be specializations of MOPs or scenes—they are the instances that show the specifics of situations that vary from what is expected in a significant way.

4.2.3 TOPs

The second kind of memory structure is called a TOP, or thematic organization packet. Like MOPs, they both store general knowledge describing the kinds of situations they organize, and they organize those episodes. The situations TOPs describe and organize are similar thematically. They provide a means of categorizing situations by the intentions of participants rather than by the details of the activities of situations. They capture the similarities between situations occuring across different domains.

According to Schank, TOPs are responsible for several different understanding behaviors (Schank 1982, 111):

■ Getting reminded of a story that illustrates a point

■ Coming up with adages, such as "a stitch in time saves nine," at appropriate times

- Recognizing an old story in new trappings
- Noticing co-occurrences of seemingly disparate events and drawing conclusions from their co-occurrence
- Knowing how something will turn out because the steps leading to it have been seen before
- Learning information from one situation that will apply in another
- Predicting an outcome for a newly encountered situation

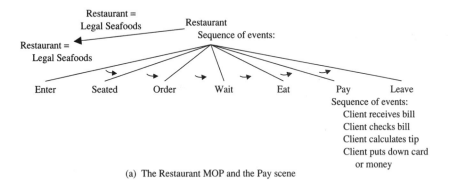

(a) The Restaurant MOP and the Pay scene

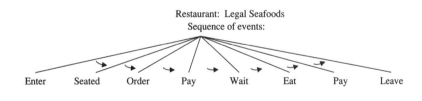

(b) The Legal Seafoods MOP

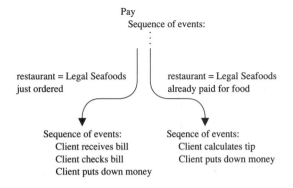

(c) The Pay scene after experencing Legal Seafoods

FIGURE 4.4   An Event Indexed in a MOP and Its Scenes

What's necessary for all these behaviors is cross-contextual reminding, that is, reminding across domains. By keeping track of relationships and conditions on goals and plans in situations, TOPs provide an organization and categorization of events that allows such reminding. We can think of *Romeo and Juliet* and *West Side Story*, for example, as both being instances of `Mutual Goal Pursuit; Outside Opposition`. Cross-contextual reminding also requires keeping track of the sequence and relationships of goals and plans in a situation while understanding or doing other kinds of reasoning.

If we look at what defines relationships between goals and plans, we can begin to appreciate the vocabulary necessary to describe and categorize events thematically. First, of course, we have the goals and plans themselves. Next, we know that goals have certain relationships to each other: they can be in competition or can complement each other, one can subsume another, one can be a subgoal of another, one can replace another, and so on. We also know that goals have a status: they can be active, be blocked, succeed, or fail. In addition, actions are carried out as parts of plans to achieve goals. Each action in a situation creates an outcome, which, in turn, provides conditions under which goals are achieved and plans are carried out. The relationships between people involved in a situation also affects the ways plans are carried out and the kinds of plans and goals someone might have. The understanding process presented in SPGU (Schank and Abelson 1977), along with analysis of remindings, suggests that keeping track of this full complement of goals, plans, conditions, interpersonal relationships, and outcomes is a natural part of the understanding process. Thus, the full set of these and their relationships make up the vocabulary set for the representational and processing categories we call TOPs.

TOPs are formed by combining goal descriptions with conditions, often about planning, specific to those goal types. Cases they organize are indexed by features that predict anomalous situations the cases provide expectations for. `Mutual Goal Pursuit; Outside Opposition`, for example, is a *goal description, condition* pair defining a TOP. *Romeo and Juliet* and *West Side Story* are both indexed in that TOP by features such as "young lovers" and "false report of death." The drunk and the lamppost story is an example of `acquisition goal, easy, but inappropriate search plan`. The two stories about buying only a gallon of fuel and buying only one stamp are examples of `recurring acquisition goal, nonsubsuming solution`.

Goal descriptions are descriptions of goals themselves (e.g., acquire money), relationships between goals (e.g., mutual goal pursuit), or types of goals (e.g., recurring acquisition goal). Conditions describe the plan or type of plan being used to achieve the goal (e.g., search plan), characterize the plan (e.g., easy, but inappropriate; nonsubsuming; strange strategy; dirty tactics), describe unusual conditions (e.g., outside opposition; difficulties along the way; outside help; normal solution won't work), describe solutions (e.g., compromise solution), describe outcomes (e.g., opponent quits; opponent gets stronger; apparent success; apparent failure; crisis abates mysteriously), or describe intents (e.g., evil intent). We shall see that this analysis has been used more recently to suggest a representational vocabulary for describing intention (social) situations, regardless of domain (Schank and Osgood 1990; Domeshek 1991a, 1991b).

4.2.4 Indexing

We now know what the categories are that allow episodes to be organized appropriately. We also know that each category indexes its members such that they are available to provide expectations in anomalous situations. To better understand what indexing entails, then, we need to better understand what constitutes an anomalous situation.

Consider again the Legal Seafoods example. Knowing that we are in Legal Seafoods allows us to expect that we will pay before eating. It also gives us expectations about what tastes good (fish chowder and bluefish pâté). The index "restaurant is Legal Seafoods" allows memory to access this case when Legal Seafoods is encountered again, allowing expectations about this situation to be accessed and used. What do we learn from this example? Two things. First, that indexes that *anticipate the special usefulness of a case* are good ones to use. Those that anticipate usefulness of a case are the ones that tell us that its specialized set of expectations are the ones that are most relevant. Here, the descriptors of the situation that anticipate the usefulness of the Legal Seafoods episode are those that *specialize the norms* of restaurant-visits, namely, that the particular restaurant is Legal Seafoods. Second, that one type of anomaly, like paying before eating, is a *violation* of predicted norms. Another type of anomaly, not shown here, is a *true surprise,* a situation in which something happens that could not have been predicted.

What other indexes allow anticipation of usefulness of this case? We can answer that by thinking about what this case is useful for. In addition to telling us what will happen or what we should order in Legal Seafoods, it tells us how to manage paying before eating (i.e., when to leave the tip). Thus, another good index for this case is the anomaly itself—the fact that we paid before eating. If we happen to be particularly fond of bluefish pâté, we may also use this case to help us derive expectations of when we will be able to order it—perhaps in seafood restaurants in Boston. Indexing the case as one that happened in a seafood restaurant in Boston will allow us to anticipate ordering bluefish pâté upon thinking about going to another seafood restaurant in Boston.

In general, there are two kinds of indexes that are useful:

1. *Differences* allow us to retrieve cases that specialize the norms.
2. *Anomalies* provide expectations for understanding or acting in similar anomalous situations.

In general, these indexes form the situation descriptors that anticipate the usefulness of a case, allowing cases to provide advice, allowing a reasoner to anticipate problems that might arise, to know how to act in a situation, and so on.

4.2.5 Reminding Revisited

The text so far has discussed reminding as a natural implication of the process of understanding. As we understand, we come across memory structures, both general and specific, that provide expectations. This natural process of traversing memory's indexing structure to find the best expectations provides remindings. Such remindings are unintentional or accidental—they happen as a natural consequence of understanding.

Other reminding is *intentional*. When we try to figure out who is the most famous person we've ever met, we might attempt to recall going backstage at the theater. In order to answer questions, whether posed by an outside person or posed by ourselves, we try to intentionally remind ourselves of things we know. We do that by hypothesizing the framework for this thing we are looking for, and we look for something like it.

The process of traversing memory structures is the same for both sorts of reminding. It is the source of the descriptions that differentiates the two processes rather than the search process itself. This is an important point because, though our discussion has been of unintentional reminding, case-based reasoning derives more from the intentional form of reminding. When we want to solve a problem, we might unintentionally think of an old situation that provides part of our solution. But more often, we must intentionally *try* to think of a situation that is similar. We might think, "If only I could remember something relevant . . . ," and then we try to be reminded.

The implication is that the remembering process that drives case-based reasoning is a two-part process. It often requires *situation assessment*, which is the process of elaborating the problem specification in such a way that something appropriate can be remembered. Though the original theory of *Dynamic Memory* does not address this process, it was addressed early on in fleshing out the theory. The process of elaborating a specification in order to be reminded was a major focus in CYRUS (Kolodner 1983a, 1983b, 1984), one of the first implementations of dynamic memory. CYRUS uses elaboration strategies to create hypothetical descriptions of events it wants to retrieve. It may not know exactly where in memory to find something it is looking for or even exactly what it is looking for, but its elaboration strategies guide its process of hypothesis. This process is similar to what we must often do to solve problems. We pose questions to ourselves and incrementally construct answers that eventually lead us toward the solutions we are looking for.

4.3 BEYOND INTENTIONAL SITUATIONS: DYNAMIC MEMORY AND MODEL-BASED REASONING

Though case-based reasoning's premises are general, the theory that underlies it concentrates on reasoning about, understanding, and remembering *intentional situations*, the kinds of situations in which agents with goals interact with the world around them. MOPs, TOPs, scenes, and scripts hold the kinds of general knowledge structures needed to hold knowledge about these kinds of situations and needed to represent these sorts of episodes, and *Dynamic Memory* concentrates on how these kinds of episodes and knowledge structures are connected to each other through their indexes.

But the cognitive model implied by *Dynamic Memory* goes beyond intentional situations. In specifying that these several kinds of generalizations are the important kinds, and in specifying that general knowledge and specific episodes are represented and indexed similarly, the cognitive model gives guidance for figuring out the types of generalizations that might be expected in other kinds of domains and how to represent their episodes.

Consider, for example, reasoning about physical devices. How can we represent these kinds of experiences? The cognitive model tells us that it is important to represent knowledge about specific types of situations and the interactions between their functional and intentional pieces. Specific types of situations here might refer to specific types of devices being reasoned about: lighting systems, hearts, automobile engines. We can think of each as combinations of subsystems that are shared across devices: for example, electrical subsystems, pumping subsystems. And each of these has components that are shared across subsystems: pumps, pulleys, conduits, for example. So we might consider representing specific situations as device models composed of device model components. These are equivalent to the MOPs and scenes.

In addition, these subsystems are related to each other. In intentional situations, people have several goals. Each goal is being carried out by some plan. These goals and plans interact with each other. There are also interactions between the goals and plans of several people. TOPs capture these kinds of relationships. In physical devices, we can find the same kinds of interactions. The electrical subsystem of the car interacts with the water circulation system in several ways, some expected, some not. The circulation system has a pump that uses electricity from the electrical system to operate. If a water hose has a leak and leaks water onto connections in the electrical system, the electrical system will fail to work. We can think about subsystems in the human body interacting with each other in similar ways.

We can also think about the reasoning of someone engaged in diagnosing or designing a device as being akin to the reasoning of someone engaged in an intentional situation. The reasoner has goals, derives plans to carry out those goals, sets expectations based on those plans, and notices anomalies when the expectations don't pan out. As in intentional situations, we can think about the goals and plans of an agent involved in reasoning about a device interacting with each other in interesting ways.

An example I like to give to my classes is this: A doctor's car has just broken down. He takes it to the mechanic, who tells him the battery is bad and replaces the battery. It breaks down again. He takes it back to the mechanic, who finds a short in a wire, replaces the wire, and tells him the car is fixed. It breaks down again. At this point, the doctor is reminded of a patient. The patient, he thought, had an easy-to-fix problem. But after he treated the problem and it seemed cured, it came back again. This happened several times. Eventually, he figured out that, in fact, he had been treating a symptom that was occuring as a by-product of another, more major problem, one whose other symptoms seemed hidden. He takes the car back to the mechanic, telling him the story and suggesting that there may be something going on in the car outside the electrical system. The mechanic finds a short in the same wire, and this time the wire is wet. Sure enough, the problem came from another subsystem. A broken hose just above the wire was leaking.

How can we explain a reminding such as this one? We can explain it only by coming up with a way of describing the car problem and the patient problem in the same terms. Both are about two subsystems interacting in unforeseen ways. Both involve attempting to solve a (seemingly) obvious problem several times with poor results. The abstract relationships between system components and their relationship to the process of carrying out a diagnosis are the vocabulary items that describe these two cases. These may be the dimensions that define the analog to TOPs for representing experiences with devices.

The discussion above tries to explain the interactions between general causal knowledge and specific case knowledge by making an analogy to the relationship between general and case knowledge defined in the theory of dynamic memory. Is this stretching the point of dynamic memory beyond what it was intended for, or is it showing its more general applicability? I'd like to think it is the latter, that dynamic memory is more than a way of organizing intentional episodes in memory. In particular, my own view of dynamic memory views MOPs, scenes, and TOPs as components of *models* of the everyday world.

Within artificial intelligence, *model-based reasoning* (Forbus 1988 gives an overview) refers to the structuring and use of general causal knowledge, usually to describe well-understood causal devices such as circuits, electrical generators, and pumps. In psychology, people talk about reasoning using *mental models* (Gentner and Stevens 1983 gives an overview), special kinds of schemas that hold functional and causal knowledge. A basic assumption of model-based reasoning is that a single general model of a class of objects or devices is sufficient for representation. Even when this is not the belief, this is the way model-based programs are generally implemented. A single model is represented that includes in it every contingency for every exceptional situation that the model builder can think of. [4]

Thinking about models in a more MOP-like way allows us to think about model knowledge as residing in a set of related memory structures. No one structure needs to hold more than its limited normative view of the world. Some other related structure will hold its exceptions. Consider, for example, our understanding of an automobile's fuel system. Some cars have carburetors, others have fuel injectors, and these make up the two major models of fuel systems. But there are differences between carburetor models and fuel injection systems—though they work more or less the same, differences in construction lead to differences in performance and differences in breakdown. We can think of a hierarchical organization of fuel systems as organizing these different models. Figure 4.5 shows what these hierarchies might look like.

So far, it looks like a traditional semantic network sort of structure. But let's add to the picture a means of acquiring new causal knowledge. Suppose a new car comes on the market. It has a carburetor that is a lot like the one on a Chevy Nova, one that a particular mechanic knows well. When the mechanic sees the new carburetor, he assumes it will perform like the one on the Nova, and treats it that way. It performs a little differently. This new case is indexed off the Nova carburetor node and is available the next time a new carburetor like this one is encountered. Rather than adding a new contingency to a monolithic model, a new node is added to the network of models that specializes a model that is already there in an appropriate way.

---

4. Two notable exceptions are the work of T. Govindaraj, an industrial engineer trying to use AI notions of model-based reasoning to implement a system to train engineers in the monitoring of steam plants on ships, and Ashok Goel's recent work integrating model-based and case-based reasoning. Govindaraj (Govindaraj 1987; Vasandani and Govindaraj 1990) found that large monolithic models of devices were too cumbersome to manage when large-scale devices were being modeled but that he could make them work by dividing models into component parts (a MOP-like approach). Goel's work, in KRITIK-2 (Bhatta and Goel 1992; Stroulia and Goel 1992), takes the next step in applying a *Dynamic Memory*–based view to the representation of models. His system uses both MOP-type and TOP-type models that are similar in spirit to what is suggested here.

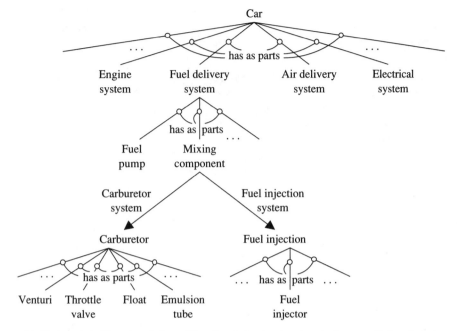

(a) Each node holds a description of function, behavior, input, output, connectivity, etc that one needs in a description of a device and its parts. The structure, so far, is MOP-like.

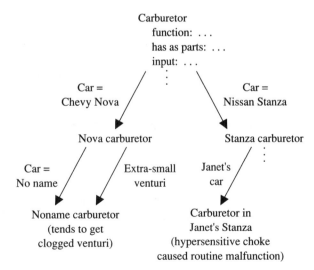

(b) Here we see particular carburetors indexed under the carburetor node. That node holds normative information about carburetors. Nodes indexed below it are exceptional or specialized cases.

FIGURE 4.5   A Distributed Mop-like Model of the Fuel System of a Car

In addition, dynamic memory adds to the conception of models a view that models of different things can share parts, and that in order to make predictions across models that configure their parts in different ways, it makes sense to represent models as packages of component parts. Just as the restaurant MOP packages together in a well-known sequential order a set of specialized scenes that in their more general forms are shared by other situations, so too does the model of the fuel system of a car package together in well-known causal orders a set of specialized functional components that, in their more general forms, are shared by other artifacts.

The theory of dynamic memory thus adds several things to the conception of models:

■ It describes the kinds of components a representation of models should have to be generally applicable.

■ It provides a way of relating models to each other.

■ It provides a way of integrating models and instances.

■ It provides a framework for thinking about the way models are acquired.

Dynamic Memory also provides guidance for representing, segmenting, accessing, and reasoning about cases involving complex devices. One segments cases according to component parts and subsystems that are shared across devices (a MOP-like representation). One integrates specific knowledge (cases) with general knowledge (models) by using packaging and specialization hierarchies of the sort proposed by MOPs. One permits access to pieces of cases and to specializations of device parts and subsystems by indexing each by combinations of features that describe the ways they violate or specialize norms and by combinations of features that describe situations in which the knowledge they hold is likely to be useful. One explains remindings across domains by positing an understanding system that tracks the interactions between parts and by proposing memory structures similar to TOPs that organize cases that share model-independent relationships with one another (e.g., a problem in one subsystem manifests as a problem in another subsystem).[5]

4.4 SOME RUNNING COGNITIVE MODELS

Several computer programs have been written with the intent of exploring and elaborating the cognitive model implied by dynamic memory and case-based reasoning. We discuss two here:

■ CYRUS (Kolodner 1983a, 1983b, 1984, 1985), the earliest implementation of dynamic memory, implemented a simplified version of MOPs and included processes for choosing indexes, reorganizing memory, making generalizations, and searching memory.

■ CELIA (Redmond 1989a, 1989b, 1989c, 1990a, 1990b, 1991, 1992), a more recent project, is a learning program that begins as a novice and learns from its own and its teachers' experiences. It integrates the use of cases and models in doing and learning to do the task of troubleshooting a car. It uses a combination of case-based, explanation-

---

5. CELIA (Redmond 1962), to be presented later, provides a model of one way of doing this.

based, and empirical learning methods, using knowledge encoded in cases and in two types of models (the model of the device being reasoned about and the model of the reasoning process), showing how the combination of experience and incomplete general knowledge in the form of models combine to allow a reasoner to become more proficient. CELIA uses its experiences both to add to its models and to augment its case memory.

4.4.1 CYRUS: A Model of Reconstructive Memory

Remembering comes naturally to people, yet psychologists do not fully understand it. Numerous psychologists have proposed that memory is a reconstructive process (e.g., Bartlett 1932; Norman and Bobrow 1979; Spiro 1979; Williams and Hollan 1981), but the specifics of the reconstructive process have been mostly neglected. CYRUS (Computerized Yale Retrieval and Update System) was conceived as a model of reconstructive dynamic memory. It focuses on the processes involved in remembering, looking both at how items are put into memory and at how they are recalled. CYRUS stored and then retrieved events in the life of Cyrus Vance when he was secretary of state of the United States (under President Jimmy Carter). Beginning with a few well-chosen MOPs, it understood and integrated new episodes from Vance's life into its memory, indexing them appropriately and creating new MOPs along the way. In response to questions, it searched its memory reconstructively to retrieve the requested facts. Using the computer as a tool allowed us to define and implement plausible processes for reconstructive retrieval.

The investigation that led to CYRUS was inspired by several observations about human memory. First, we had already noticed that people are reminded of old situations in the course of understanding, and we wanted to explain the processes that would allow that to happen. Because we already believed that general knowledge (in the forms of scripts, plans, goals, etc.) was important in understanding, doing this required an explanation of how general knowledge that we knew was important to understanding and knowledge about specific cases were integrated with each other. Second, we knew that recognition was easier than recall, and an informal investigation of our own showed us that the more detail presented in a query, the easier it was to recall whatever was needed to answer it. For example, if we asked people if they had ever met a famous person, much search was required, while if we asked them if they had ever met a famous person in a museum, they were able to answer immediately. Third, we observed that recall of lists of things is hard unless some order is imposed on the list. So, for example, people named all the people in their research group by visually walking around the space that houses the research group and naming the person who occupies each desk or office. People tended to name all the players on a sports team by enumerating the positions (a shorter list) and then naming the players in each position. Fourth, we noticed a particular organization people like to put on recall when asked to do a rather poorly defined search. When we asked people questions requiring a lot of memory search, they tended to search memory by proposing hypothetical situations in which what we were asking for might have happened and then searching for instances of those hypothetical situations. For example, when we asked people to name the most famous person they had ever met, several of our subjects reported thinking about the kinds of situations in which they might have met famous people and then recalling situations of those sorts and checking to see if any famous person was present in one (e.g., political rallies, backstage at the theater). Fifth, we noticed that people often searched for concepts different from what was requested in a question. Someone asked about museum visits, for example, might search memory for trips. The set of observations make it clear that remembering is often a process of *reconstructing what probably happened* in order to allow retrieval of the details of what did happen.

The first of these observations led us to wonder about how reminding could happen. The others began to give us clues as to the nature of memory search. The last told us that there was no need for the processes we came up with to be exact—in fact, we had an idea that if we could come up with a set of processes that searched memory in a reconstructive way, then we might be able to explain some aspects of forgetting as well as remembering. Our goal was to explain these phenomena concretely in terms of memory structures and cognitive processes, and in a way that would also allow us to make predictions about other aspects of memory. The exploration that culminated in CYRUS thus had several goals:

■ To make specific the processes and principles for organizing cases and generalized episodes (MOPs) with respect to each other

■ To make specific the processes and principles for traversing those organizational structures for retrieval and insertion

■ To make specific the processes and principles for intelligently searching a conceptual dynamic memory

CYRUS's retrieval process had several qualities to it:

■ It was reconstructive.

■ Rather than directly enumerating items from memory, it constructed descriptions of what it was looking for and then confirmed them by looking them up.

■ It worked by progressively narrowing in on a description of the item to be remembered.

■ It had strategies for deriving new target items from old ones when search for the old one was not giving results.

Retrieval worked in a two-step cycle. In the first step, a description of an item targeted for retrieval was constructed. In the second step, memory was traversed to find the targeted event. Failure to find what was targeted resulted in returning to the first step and constructing a new target, sometimes by incrementally elaborating the previous target, sometimes by applying strategies to transform it into something completely different. Two things are of interest in this process: the strategies that are available for construction and elaboration of a target item and the memory traversal process.

Suggesting Contexts for Search in CYRUS

CYRUS had three types of heuristics to effect construction and elaboration of contexts for search and a set of executive search strategies to guide their application. Constructive heuristics could suggest a type of event (context) based on known component parts and instantiate it (*component-to-context instantiation* heuristics), could elaborate or flesh out components of suggested events (*component instantiation* heuristics), and could suggest and instantiate an alternative type of event to search for (*context-to-context instantiation* heuristics). For example, when asked if Vance had talked to Brezhnev (who was then prime minister of the USSR) recently, CYRUS used a component-to-context instantiation heuristic to suggest that their discussion might have been in the context of a `diplomatic-meeting`. A component instantiation might then be used to suggest that the meeting happened in the USSR. If a meeting with that description could not be found, a search strategy would suggest searching for larger events it could have been part of and would call a context-to-context instantiation heuristic to instantiate a `diplomatic-trip` that this meeting might have been part of.

Use of all these together can be seen when we ask CYRUS if Vance's wife has ever met Mrs. Begin. To answer this question, CYRUS must first figure out what kind of event to look for, then fill in enough detail about it to differentiate the one it is looking for from other similar ones. It begins by asking itself what kinds of events it should be looking for in memory. The heuristics it uses for this are *component-to-context instantiation* ones. However, it does not have enough information in the query to choose a context for search (because it keeps track of events in the life of Cyrus Vance, and Vance is not mentioned in the question). Its strategies use information about who the participants are, however, so it uses a *component-instantiation* heuristic to infer that if Mrs. Vance were at the event, then Cyrus Vance must have been there also. That allows it to use a *component-to-context instantiation* heuristic to suggest that it should be looking for a `social-occasion`. This memory structure uses an associated *component instantiation* heuristic to infer that Menachem Begin must have been at the event also. Because `social-occasion` is quite abstract, CYRUS attempts to find additional *component-to-context instantiation* heuristics to help it make what it is looking for more concrete. One suggests that the event is also a `political-event`. Another suggests that if the episode it is trying to establish should be both a political event and a social occasion, then it might be a `state-dinner`. CYRUS now has a type of event to look for. It uses *component instantiation* heuristics associated with `state-dinner` to fill in as much as it can about the state dinner it is looking for. It looks first for a state dinner in Israel that included all four parties; if it doesn't find one of those, it will look for one in the United States. CYRUS finds a state dinner in Israel with the appropriate participants and answers the questions. If, however, it had not found a state dinner, a search strategy would have been employed to direct the search to some other type of event associated with a state dinner (e.g., a diplomatic trip) during which the discussion between Mrs. Begin and Mrs. Vance might have taken place. A *context-to-context instantiation* heuristic would have been used to construct that alternate context.

Searching CYRUS's Memory

Memory traversal was the second important piece of CYRUS's retrieval capability, but traversal cannot be discussed without discussing CYRUS's memory organization. CYRUS's memory structures are a variety of MOPs (Schank 1982) called E-MOPs. Like MOPs, E-MOPs have two functions: they store general knowledge about a type of event, and they organize individual episodes using a web of indexes. CYRUS further developed the theory of MOPs by proposing that E-MOPs and cases are arranged together in specialization/generalization hierarchies. Thus, traversal of an index in an E-MOP can lead to encountering an event or a specialized E-MOP. Figure 4.6 shows a schematic of one of CYRUS's E-MOPs.

Like MOPs, specialized E-MOPs in CYRUS hold generalized knowledge that describes the events they organize, and they, too, organize events and specialized E-MOPs through a web of indexes. In Figure 4.6, the content frame (norms, generalized knowledge) of the E-MOP called diplomatic-meeting is seen. The structure below that is its indexing structure. Triangles represent types of indexes (e.g., topic, participants' nationality), while the labels on the arcs below them represent the value of the index (e.g., Arab-Israeli peace, SALT, Israel, Egypt, USSR). Below those arcs are pointers either to specialized E-MOPs (e.g., MOP1, MOP2) or events (e.g., EV2, EV3).

Indexes in an E-MOP act as gates. They can be traversed if their values are specified. For example, if a query specifies that it is looking for an event that included persons of Israeli nationality, then the arc representing Israel under participants'-nationality can be traversed, encountering EV1, an event in which some of the participants were Israelis.

CYRUS's memory structures participate in the retrieval process in two ways. First, the structure of memory provides guidelines for retrieval processes, telling them which elaborations would be most productive. Each MOP knows what types of indexes it has (though it can't enumerate the specific ones). When traversal is stuck at an E-MOP (i.e., there is no additional specification in a query that allows further traversal), the E-MOP reports back the types of indexes it has, and elaboration processes attempt to flesh out the query along those dimensions. Second, generalizations in the content frame of E-MOPs help elaboration processes do their jobs. Diplomatic-meeting, for example, knows that its topics are usually international contracts. An elaboration heuristic attempting to hypothesize the topic of a meeting uses that specification as a framework and elaborates around it, trying to figure out what particular international contract the participants in a meeting might have been discussing.

CYRUS's memory organization, its way of choosing indexes, its methods for adding new cases to its memory and creating new MOPs, and its means of retrieval will be discussed in more detail in chapters 6, 7, 8, and 10.

CYRUS as a Cognitive Model

CYRUS's approach to long-term memory was novel for its time. Rather than looking at encoding, storage, and retrieval as separate entities, it examined them in relation to each other. Integration of new items into memory (encoding) both reflects retrieval capabilities observed in people and takes the underlying memory organization into account. Similarly, in considering memory organization (storage), we examined the constraints implied by human retrieval—its

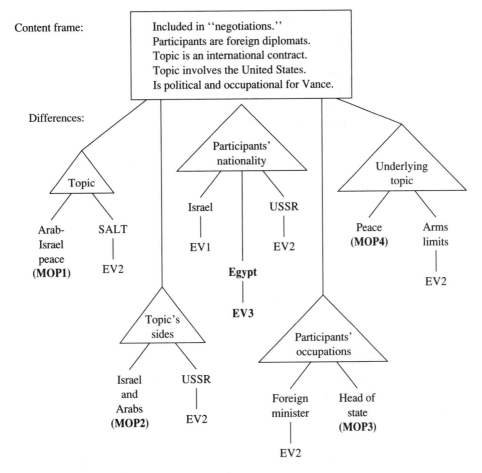

FIGURE 4.6   A Piece of One of CYRUS's E-MOPs: M-Diplomatic Meeting

successes, its failures, and the strategies it used. CYRUS looked at memory as both a process and a store, defining specific algorithms and memory structures that together define a *process model*. In addition, it emphasized *memory organization* in a very concrete way, providing a way of organizing schemata with respect to each other, defining the kinds of schemata that are useful for storing episodes, examining change in schemata over time, and studying the use of schemata in organizing individual items represented by a particular schema.

It was also novel in its view of what reconstruction is. CYRUS views reconstruction as a process of constructing a description of a target item to be found in memory, adding features to progressively differentiate it from its nearest neighbors and finally finding its hiding place in a well-organized memory. The process is a two-step cycle: coming up with a description comes first, discovering if it is in memory second. Memory's organization drives the process.

A cognitive model is as good as the processes it explains and the predictions it makes. CYRUS set out to explain reconstructive retrieval processes, but in the end explained more than that. In particular, its explanations of forgetting are interesting. According to CYRUS's model, forgetting happens for several reasons. Something might not be retrieved because a description that differentiated the targeted event from other similar ones cannot be constructed. Sometimes this is because search heuristics are not complete in their enumeration of plausible contexts for search. Sometimes it is because available general knowledge does not allow elaboration of a relevant novel descriptor. Forgetting can also happen because a question (retrieval probe) incorrectly specifies the details of an item to be retrieved. Or, a question (retrieval probe) might specify an event in a way that is different from the way it was specified at encoding. When that happens, retrieval can happen only if elaboration strategies can transform given descriptors into those that might have been recorded at the time the item was inserted and indexed in memory.

CYRUS's explanation of reconstructive retrieval can be described in a nutshell (Kolodner 1984):

> A few powerful strategies for search, combined with rich conceptual indexing, allow retrieval without category enumeration.

4.4.2   CELIA: A Case-Based Approach to the Passage from Novice to Expert

CYRUS explored the evolution of a memory as additional experiences were added to it, but it did little with those experiences once it retrieved them. CYRUS built models of the everyday world as it augmented its memory with experiences, but because its only goal was retrieval, it could not be used as a vehicle for exploring the implications of memory change for skilled performance.

CELIA (Redmond 1989a, 1989b, 1989c, 1990a, 1990b, 1991, 1992), a more recent project, explores the ways problem-solving performance changes as experiences are acquired. CELIA models the memory and reasoning capabilities of a novice troubleshooter. In trying to be as realistic as possible, some of CELIA's knowledge is encoded in cases, while other knowledge is encoded in two types of models: a model of the device being reasoned about (here, a car's fuel system) and a model of the reasoning process being carried out (here, troubleshooting). Novices, we assume, begin with incomplete, and perhaps buggy, models of both the devices they are reasoning about and the ways they need to reason to solve problems, but with experience, they both acquire new cases and update those models. CELIA thus begins with incomplete models of both device and process, and through experience, both acquires cases and adds to its models. What is particularly interesting about CELIA is that it inserts case-based reasoning and the use of cases in reasoning into a broader model of memory that reasons using several different methods and several different kinds of knowledge.

CELIA acts as an apprentice mechanic. It solves problems by itself, and in addition, it learns by watching and listening to a teacher explain his reasoning about particular cases. As it listens to and understands the teacher, it integrates those experiences and what is learned from them with what it already knows. CELIA uses case-based reasoning, but it is not a case-based reasoner per se. That is, it uses several different kinds of knowledge to reason, among them cases. While it learns new cases and new indexes, it also learns several other things and uses a variety of different learning methods.

CELIA takes as input several sequences of teacher actions and explanations collected while observing teachers in an area vocational technical school. CELIA's memory, which is meant to hold the same sorts of knowledge a student might have, holds several different kinds of knowledge: an (impoverished and possibly incorrect) causal model of how an automobile engine and all its parts work, a model (also impoverished and incorrect) of the reasoning process employed in troubleshooting, and a set of troubleshooting experiences (both those of the student and those of the student watching the expert).

As a result of its learning experiences, CELIA's knowledge improves in several ways, allowing it to perform better: it refines and elaborates its models of the device and of the diagnosis process, it collects new troubleshooting experiences, and it learns the applicability of its troubleshooting experiences.

CELIA is an *active intentional learner*. As it watches and listens to a teacher performing some troubleshooting task, it *predicts* what the teacher will do or say next. It then *observes* or listens to the teacher. When predictions don't match what the teacher says or does, it attempts to *explain the discrepancy* and learn from it. If it can't explain a discrepancy, CELIA sets itself up with the goal of acquiring whatever knowledge it thinks is necessary to explain it, watching during later experiences for the opportunity to acquire that knowledge. CELIA makes sense of what the teacher is doing and sets itself up for active learning at the same time.

Case-based reasoning's major roles are in aiding the prediction and explanation processes. Predictions that the student makes often come from previous troubleshooting cases remembered in the course of reasoning. Explanations of how it could have avoided a mistake are often in the form of cases it should have recalled that would have allowed it to make the correct prediction. In addition, CELIA internalizes its experience observing the teacher into troubleshooting cases and uses those in later problem solving.

Prediction in CELIA

CELIA's prediction process makes use of all the different kinds of knowledge it has available. It predicts what a teacher might do next by retrieving cases that can make a prediction and by using its models, preferring the predictions made by cases over other predictions. This is because its models are known to be incomplete and buggy, while its cases are known to be instances of troubleshooting sequences that have been carried out. In essense, it predicts the thing that it would be most likely to do next were it doing the problem solving itself.

After discovering descrepancies between what it was expecting and what happened, CELIA uses cases again to help it explain its mistake and repair its knowledge. Of particular importance in this step is its process of figuring out how it could have avoided its mistake. In this step, it asks itself whether it already knew what it needed to know to make the correct prediction, and if so, why it didn't make the prediction. Often, making the right prediction depends on recalling a different case than the one it recalled. When that happens, CELIA considers why it did not recall that case. In general, it is because it had it indexed poorly. CELIA refines the indexes on that case so that it would have been recalled in the current instance. It also refines the indexes of the case that made the poor prediction so that it will not be recalled under similar circumstances in the future. In this way, CELIA learns the applicability of its cases.

Making the Teacher's Cases Its Own

One other piece of CELIA related to cases is its process of making its experience watching the teacher into a troubleshooting case. Though on the surface this may seem like a trivial process, it is, in fact, quite complex. The reason is this. CELIA is trying to learn how to do a task. Every cognitive task is composed of several steps, each of which has a cognitive subgoal attached to it (e.g., I need to make a hypothesis; I need to explain something). The better the student can do at explaining why the teacher did what he did and recording that, the more useful will be the cases the student remembers. But explaining someone else's motivations is difficult. We know our own reasoning subgoals, but we have to guess at someone else's. Making the teacher's experience troubleshooting a car into a useful case for the student requires the student to analyze the things the teacher does, explain why the teacher did what he did, and connect together the different things the teacher said and did in a coherent way.[6]

CELIA's prediction process, briefly described above, is key to doing this. Its model of troubleshooting allows it to predict the kinds of reasoning subgoals the teacher might have. For example, after coming up with a hypothesis during diagnosis (one type of subgoal), one tries to verify it (another type of subgoal); hypotheses about subsystems of a device might be refined into hypotheses directed at particular components of those subsystems (another type of subgoal). CELIA's model of the device allows it to refine its predictions. For example, if the current hypothesis was that the fuel system was faulty, CELIA can use its model of the fuel system to predict that the next hypothesis will be that the carburetor or the fuel pump is not working. CELIA's cases allow it to make predictions about things that are not yet in its models. For example, if its model of troubleshooting is missing the knowledge that one must verify hypotheses after deriving them, CELIA might still be able to predict that the teacher will verify some hypothesis because it has seen that happen before in a particular case. Similarly, if its model of the fuel system is missing some major component, CELIA might still be able to predict that the teacher will make a hypothesis about that component if it has a case in which such a prediction was made.

Representation of Cases in CELIA

An issue that had to be addressed in CELIA to allow cases to provide such power was the representation of cases. The reasoner needed to be able to recall not only full cases but also the pieces of cases in which individual decisions were made. For example, CELIA might have several cases in which there is a hypothesis that the carburetor is not working. Each might show different test results when the carburetor was tested. CELIA needed to be able to skip

---

6. This was an original goal of the EBL community in trying to build learning apprentices, but EBL emphasis has shifted in recent years from attempting to understand the apprentice to generalizing explanations that are already formed.

from, say, the prototypical case in which the carburetor is discovered to be faulty to one in which an obscure problem with the carburetor is discovered. To allow such access, cases are represented as linked pieces of cases, called *snippets* (Redmond 1990a). Each snippet corresponds to a problem-solving subgoal the reasoner encountered in solving its problem. The problem solver (apprentice) has available both large cases and their pieces as it solves problems, and once a piece of a case is available, any other pieces of the case that it is connected to are also available. Thus, cases can provide a single step for the reasoner or an extended sequence of actions.

But each snippet is also indexed individually. Thus, CELIA is not confined to recalling whole cases. It can recall pieces of cases that are relevant to its new situation. It can do this because each case snippet stores the context in which it took place and records that context as an index. The next time the reasoner is in a similar situation, it can recall a piece of an old case. For example, if CELIA is in the situation described above, it may begin by using its description of the current problem to recall a case in which the carburetor is faulty. Using the same case, it may predict that a certain test should be carried out to verify the problem. After that test is carried out, however, it may see that the test result is different from the test result in the case. This tells it that the case it is currently using to make predictions is no longer applicable. It finds a snippet of a different case by asking for a snippet in which the carburetor was faulty, this particular test was carried out, and the result was similar to the one obtained. Finding such a snippet from another case, it can now predict what should be done next.

In storing its cases as snippets and indexing them individually, CELIA, in effect, implements the MOP/scene structure originally suggested in *Dynamic Memory* (Schank 1982) but not actually implemented in any of our case-based reasoning programs up to now. CELIA also makes clear how to define scenes for this class of problems: cases are broken into scenes according to the reasoning subgoals of the task being carried out. The major MOP CELIA's cases fall into is `diagnosing and repairing a car`. Its scenes include `verify complaint`, `generate a hypothesis`, `refine the hypothesis`, `verify hypothesis`, `perform test`, `evaluate test outcome`, and so on. Such scenes are shared by other troubleshooting domains and tasks, contributing to the capability of cross-contextual reminding in the troubleshooting domain.[7]

Indexing in CELIA

Indexing is another issue CELIA had to deal with. In our discussions of indexing, we shall make it clear that the more knowledge one can use in choosing indexes, the better the accessibility to cases will be. CELIA, however, begins as a novice and has no way of knowing which

---

7. This is somewhat different from the conception of scenes presented in section 3 of this chapter. There, scenes were defined according to the components and subsystems of devices. That view of scenes concentrates on organizing according to the model of the device. The view of scenes here is in the same spirit. It is a view that derives from the model of the process of troubleshooting. This breakdown facilitated learning the process. The other breakdown would facilitate learning the model. In fact, *Dynamic Memory* advocates multiple breakdowns and multiple indexing of cases and pieces of cases according to the several points of view from which the case can be interpreted. A more complete memory model would thus include MOPs and scenes of both sorts; CELIA's cases are represented and indexed only from this one point of view right now.

pieces of the context in which a decision was made are the ones that should be used as indexes. Thus, it begins with an indexing scheme that discriminates poorly but ensures that cases and snippets will be recalled whenever any piece of the context in which they took place is repeated. Indexes, then, begin as necessarily huge combinations of features early in problem solving because the novice doesn't know which pieces of what is going on are relevant to a decision that was made. Later, after using a case or a case snippet, however, CELIA discovers its usefulness. If a retrieved case or snippet proves inapplicable when recalled during later problem solving, CELIA refines that snippet's indexes so that it will no longer be recalled in such situations. If a case that should have been retrieved is not retrieved, CELIA refines its indexes so that it will be retrieved later in similar situations.

Integrating Case and Model Knowledge

CELIA also makes a contribution to our understanding of the interaction of case knowledge and model knowledge in reasoning. The goal was to integrate the use of these two kinds of knowledge in a way that is both flexible (i.e., either can be used at any time, and the one giving the better predictions is used) and consistent (i.e., the reasoner shouldn't make wildly different predictions in similar circumstances). CELIA's prediction process balances the conflicting demands of consistency and flexibility. The reasoner makes it predictions after it knows the results of previous actions. Thus, its predictions are always made on the basis of real-world occurences rather than hypothetical possibilities. In addition, the prediction process favors cohesiveness, specificity, and what has been seen to work previously over predictions made on the basis of abstract general knowledge. It would rather predict the next thing that happens in one case than predict something that happened in another case. It would rather make a prediction based on what it experienced in an earlier case than one made based on its general knowledge of how one does diagnosis. Its prediction process is in keeping with the basic premise of case-based reasoning—that concrete, specific, operational knowledge in the form of cases is easier and more beneficial to reason with than abstract general knowledge. Its prediction process illustrates a way to integrate the use of both sorts of knowledge under that assumption.

CELIA as a Cognitive Model

In addition to making some of the premises and hypotheses of dynamic memory and learning more concrete, CELIA adds to our understanding of early learning of a task and makes predictions about successful instruction.

Most interesting, perhaps, is that CELIA provides a model of learning that happens without strong knowledge of a domain or task. CELIA's learning processes allow it to bootstrap domain and task knowledge from its experiences of watching and listening to an expert problem solver. Through remembering those experiences, the student gets a good start toward being able to function in the domain. At the same time, the student identifies places where he or she is lacking knowledge. The student interacts with the expert instructor to acquire some of that missing knowledge. Learning helps both future problem solving and future learning.

Of course, it is important for the student to take an active role in learning for this to happen, and CELIA shows what such an active role means. The student should predict what the instructor will do next, observe the instructor's actions, and try to explain descrepancies. Sometimes the student will be able to explain descrepancies. Other times, the student will need to find out more in order to explain. If explanation is done well, it will at least cause the student to acquire knowledge that will allow him or her to finally derive an explanation, sometimes by asking the instructor, sometimes by looking in a book, sometimes by waiting for another experience that will provide it.

The instructor plays a crucial role in apprenticeship learning, but using the instructor to directly implant knowledge in the novice is unreasonable. CELIA shows that demands on an instructor don't have to be excessive if the student takes responsibility for actively following the instructor's example. The instructor's job is to solve problems in front of students, to provide explanations at times when he or she thinks students may not have all the knowledge they need to follow the solution, to answer questions, and to give hints when students are having trouble. Effective apprenticeship requires the student to ask questions and requires the instructor to provide the right level of hints and explanations. Of course, additional effort must be put into giving more concrete guidelines about what those hints and explanations need to look like.

CELIA also shows some of the reasoning processes that it might be important to teach to students. Students should perhaps be taught what being an active intentional learner means: being coached at making predictions, noticing descrepancies, and explaining them. Questions that allow explanations to be formed should be encouraged. It might also be important to impart to students a means of maintaining flexibility in their reasoning—the kind of flexibility that CELIA maintains in making its predictions.

When experiments were run on CELIA (Redmond 1992), one of the interesting things they showed was that the acquisition of cases was more useful in ensuring successful problem solving during early learning than augmentation or refinement of domain or task knowledge. Cases provide the specifics used in prediction and explanation, and, if acquired, they can guide problem solving and prediction well. Experimentation with CELIA shows that early in learning, remembering cases is the most powerful form of learning and other forms do not provide as much of an advantage. This is due partly to the limited domain knowledge a novice has. With little domain knowledge, a novice can't form explanations easily about what is going on. Acquisition of cases, however, allows the novice to store new domain knowledge associated with the kinds of situations it is useful in. Later in the learning process, when many cases have been acquired, that domain knowledge can be migrated out of the cases to form a general model of the domain. Early on, however, the student does not know enough about applicability of the new pieces of knowledge he or she is acquiring to build a coherent model. Much experience is required for the applicability of knowledge to be learned.

CELIA shows that an important kind of experience comes from watching and listening to an instructor solve problems. Many of the skilled professions employ this kind of instruction already; for example, the trades employ apprenticeships, and medicine requires doctors to serve internships and residencies. CELIA suggests that such experiential situations be integrated early into the curriculum. CELIA shows that even when the student knows little, such experiences can be enlightening, more so, perhaps, than the mere accumulation of facts.

CELIA also suggests some minimal amount of knowledge that the student should have in order to make the most of such experiences. The student should have at least some idea of the set of steps involved in the reasoning process and the reasons the steps are done (e.g., diagnosis means coming up with a hypothesis and checking it out) and should have some basic knowledge about the subsystems and component parts of the device being reasoned about (e.g., the car has a fuel system and an electrical system; the fuel system is made up of a fuel pump, a carburetor, and so on, connected to each other in certain ways with certain kinds of conduits). It is less important for the beginner to have a strong knowledge of the domain and task, however, than to have had commonsense experiences with the reasoning process and with devices. For example, students who don't know the steps of car diagnosis but who have had the experience of having a problem with some device explained to them and finding it was an inaccurate description will be able to understand the importance of verifying a client's complaint when they see the teacher doing it and will be able to add that subtask to their model of car diagnosis. Students who don't know exactly how the fuel pump is connected to the carburetor will be able to make inferences about what might be going wrong if they understand the general concept of conduits, perhaps through experience with common household plumbing.

CELIA's Testable Predictions

CELIA models the ideal apprentice. It doesn't model the student who is having trouble, nor does it model the one who doesn't follow what the teacher is doing. As a model of the ideal, however, it can tell us much about the kinds of situations that enable successful learning. In particular, it makes the following testable cognitive predictions:

> Learning by observing and listening to an expert leads to significant increases in performance after only limited exposure to examples if the student plays an active role in understanding what the expert is doing.

CELIA's performance increased considerably as a result of its experiences observing the teacher solve problems. We cannot claim, however, that merely collecting sequences of actions is what made CELIA's performance improve. Key to its improvement was that it analyzed those cases, explaining to itself (as best it could) the teacher's actions and making those experiences its own. That is, it always explained to itself *why* each step of the process was being carried out. This is consistent with research on self-explanation (Chi and Van Lehn 1991; Chi et al. 1989).

> During early learning of a task and domain, a collection of cases is the single most useful type of knowledge acquired. Refining and adding to models of the domain and task result in far less improvement in capabilities.

CELIA adds to its models and refines its indexes in addition to adding cases to its case library, and it has access to all that knowledge when it reasons. Cases provide only one of its knowledge sources. But when ablation studies were run to see where CELIA's increase in performance was coming from, the most significant increases were coming from having more cases available. When its ability to use its cases during problem solving was removed, so was much of its capability. Note that CELIA is not biased toward use of cases or collection of case knowledge such that this result is built in. It learns as much as it can from each of its experiences, collecting cases and adding to its models each time. Though it prefers to make predictions based on cases, it is able to use its other knowledge fully. Early in learning, that knowledge is buggy and incomplete. It grows much slower than the case library does.

> It is difficult to improve the accuracy of case retrieval early on. Attempts to make students aware of when their knowledge is applicable may not succeed, because they are missing crucial domain knowledge. As domain knowledge acrues, this problem abates.

This result says that early in learning students will put poor indexes on cases because they do not have enough knowledge to be able to determine the applicability of their knowledge. One could point it out, but they may not have enough knowledge to understand the explanation. As they make mistakes and are forced to analyze the indexes on their cases, indexing becomes better. And as students learn more, they are better able to index cases appropriately the first time. Thus, experience, especially experience that induces failure, is a key to improving accuracy.

- It is better to present a variety of types of problems early on rather than concentrating on several very similar ones.
- Repeated presentation of the same problem will not lead to long-term improved performance. Variations on a problem work better.

These two results come simply from the statistics of experiments that were run, but they make a lot of sense. Experience with a wide variety of problems seeds the space of experiences broadly, implying that cases will be used often to make predictions. The use of cases to make predictions, even if the wrong predictions are made, is important, because it gives the reasoner an opportunity to refine its indexing and learn when its experiences and the things it knows are applicable. Seeding the case library with many similar cases means that later in problem solving, cases will be recalled to make predictions less often. At the same time, experience with variations of a problem allows a particular piece of the space to be examined from many different perspectives, allowing the applicability of the knowledge acquired to be learned. Are these two results contradictory? No. The first says that broad exposure should be given early on. The second says that if a student is having trouble with some concept, then give variations of the problem to the student to work on as drills, not the same one over and over.

Of course, also at issue is the sequencing of problems. CELIA has little to say about that, but other work (e.g., PROTOS) suggests that sequencing from more to less prototypical problems would result in the most effective learning.

4.5 SUMMARY OF CLAIMS

The cognitive model behind case-based reasoning, inspired by Schank and Abelson's *Scripts, Plans, Goals, and Understanding* and by Schank's *Dynamic Memory* and its descendants, make claims in several areas:

- It proposes a means of organizing and retrieving episodic knowledge, both general and concrete, in a memory.
- It proposes a set of primary processes required for reasoning using cases.
- It proposes a natural way of integrating learning with other reasoning processes.
- It proposes a set of principles for determining the kinds of generalizations that are useful when learned.

Case-based reasoning takes the next step, looking at the ways in which retrieved events are used for reasoning.

4.5.1 The Structure and Organization of Knowledge

- Knowledge is in the form of specific events and generalizations of specific events. Both are organized in the same memory structures, both are indexed in the same ways, and both are accessed by the same retrieval processes. We refer to specific events as *cases*.

Dyamic Memory tells us that both general knowledge and case knowledge are important in understanding and reasoning. Thus, while case-based reasoning concentrates on the role individual episodes play in reasoning, there is no commitment to cases being the only form of knowledge in memory. Rather, the commitment is to cases being the primary generators of inferences and to considering only those kinds of generalizations that can directly derive from cases, that is, those that can be noticed in the normal course of understanding and solving problems. We shall return to that claim later.

The other major commitment is to the means of accessing knowledge in memory. This is a commitment to *indexing*. The claim is that each knowledge structure in memory, whether it holds general knowledge or case knowledge, is labeled by important combinations of its descriptors. This claim further states that experiences recorded in memory include descriptors that were obvious and evident when the event was perceived and also inferred descriptors derived in the process of reasoning about the experience and creating the knowledge structures it resides in. Any of that knowledge is available to use in an index.

Furthermore, the claim implies that given a specification of something to be retrieved from memory, either a general knowledge structure or a case might be retrieved. As in other AI programs and cognitive models, whatever matches the memory probe most specifically is returned.

4.5.2 Primary Processes

- Understanding and assessment underlie all reasoning. Items in memory are remembered because they are encountered as part of the process of understanding. The basic reasoning process, then, is *remember and manipulate*.

Knowledge access, or remembering, is a key part of reasoning. And because specifically-applicable items are preferred by retrieval processes over less specific ones during retrieval, primary reasoning processes must include those that know how to manipulate cases, that is, those that can reason based on the specifics of cases that are retrieved.

Cases we are reminded of are encountered by our memories as they are trying to understand a new situation. Understanding is a process of integrating a new experience with what is already known, finding the place in memory where it would reside if we already knew it. Figuring out where a new item fits into the general scheme of things we already know allows appropriate inferences and predictions to be made.

When memory is given a partial description of a new situation, it uses that description to guide memory search, looking for the most specific place in memory to place the new experience. But often, a partial description is not sufficient for useful search, and elaboration is required to allow the most usefully similar extant knowledge to be found. Elaboration is a process of fleshing out a description of a situation, often making it more specific. It is guided by general strategies of the sort CYRUS implements, and it is highly dependent on what is already in memory. Elaboration, also called *situation assessment*, is an important part of remembering.

Search processes that are key to understanding allow a reasoner to determine where a new item fits into the general scheme of things that are already known. These processes stop their search at particular places in memory, and knowledge that resides in those memory locations is available for reasoning. We refer to this knowledge as being *retrieved*. Reasoning processes use knowledge that is retrieved to make inferences and predictions. If search processes make available the most specific similar items in memory (e.g., cases), then reasoning processes must be able to manipulate those specific items.

The case-based reasoning community has spent considerable time studying the ins and outs of two kinds of manipulation processes: *adaptation* processes and *interpretation* processes. Adaptation processes modify an old solution to fit a new situation, facilitating case-based problem solving. Evaluation processes compare and contrast a new situation to old ones that are retrieved, facilitating the anticipation and avoidance of old problems and the evaluation of the goodness of proposed decisions and solutions. Chapters 11 through 14 provide in-depth descriptions of these processes. Another type of case-manipulation process that still needs attention is *merging*, the process of taking suggestions from several different cases and merging them into a solution.

4.5.3 Dynamic Memory and Learning

A major claim of the cognitive model is this:

■ Memory is dynamically changing with each new experience.

As a result of this dynamic change, we can't expect our memories to act exactly the same way any two times, even given the same problem to work on. Though a reasoner might understand

and solve the same problem the same way a second time, the experiences it has had in between might change it such that it will act differently the second time than the first.

Dynamic change is learning, and the cognitive model makes claims about particular kinds of learning that are useful. One can think of this claim as a specific claim about the ways memory dynamically changes over time.

- ■ A dynamic memory with indexed general and specific knowledge learns in several different ways:
  - □ It acquires new cases.
  - □ It re-indexes cases it already has.
  - □ It creates new generalizations.
  - □ It learns what to pay attention to.
  - □ It learns new ways to index cases.

New cases are acquired with each new experience. New experiences are understood by accessing memory structures (both general and specific) that provide expectations. Those cases are indexed into memory according to the ways they violate expectations that previous experience has compiled.

Sometimes, an old case is recalled in understanding or solving a new one, and it is found not to be appropriate to the new situation. As a result, the relevance of that case is reanalyzed and it is re-indexed based on our new understanding of it.

As several similar experiences are encountered, their similarities are extracted to create new general memory structures (MOPs). As described above, these general structures hold normative knowledge that can be used to direct search of memory, to help with reconstruction, to answer questions, to provide expectations, and so on.

As we begin learning a new domain, we pay attention to the things our previous experience tells us are important. We don't understand new domains well, however, and our old experience may not be able to predict everything well. As we make mistakes and encounter failures, however, we take the opportunity to explain to ourselves what went wrong, in the process uncovering misconceptions in our thinking and deriving new expectations. These expectations move us toward paying attention to the right details. They also point to new ways of indexing cases.

Finally, we use our old experiences to solve new problems by merging and adapting old solutions with each other. We begin with a set of simple adaptation methods, and as we use them and debug them, we index them better and refine them, as a result getting better at adaptation. Some adaptation guidance comes from modifying or refining old adaptation heuristics; other guidance comes through the chance adaptation of a case that works—that case provides guidance for adaptation under similar circumstances.

4.5.4 The Structure and Role of General Knowledge

Another claim concerns the kinds of representational structures we can expect to find in a dynamic memory and the kinds of generalizations that play a first-class role.

- The kinds of generalized knowledge structures we can expect to find in memory are of two sorts:
  - ☐ General descriptions of particular kinds of situations
  - ☐ Generalizations of the ways intentional and functional components of situations interact with each other
- They can be found in two sizes:
  - ☐ Individual units
  - ☐ Composed units

Within the framework set up in *Dynamic Memory*, the two kinds of generalized knowledge correspond to MOPs and TOPs. MOPs are general descriptions of specific types of situations, for example, going to restaurants, going on trips, visiting a museum. TOPs describe the way intentional components of situations interact with each other, that is, the relationships between goals and plans that are active in a situation.

Dynamic memory also tells us about breaking up larger episodes into smaller parts. Composed units (MOPs) describe particular kinds of episodes. Individual units (scenes) describe the component parts of these episodes that are shared across composed units. Ordering, for example, is something we do in restaurants, at several different kinds of stores, through catalogs, and through decorators. The particular setting of the situation is different for each, but the basic intent and major action is the same. The intent is to let someone who can fulfill our desire for something we want to buy know what it is we want to acquire; the major action is to communicate what we want to that person. Whether we write it on an order form, or tell someone over the phone, whether we do it in the context of ordering in a restaurant or ordering from a catalog, the intent and basic action are the same.

One additional type of general knowledge predicted by case-based reasoning's cognitive model is adaptation methods, our knowledge about how to modify an old solution to fit a new situation. Though we predict such knowledge exists in the memory, we have fewer specific claims to make about the structures it lives in. We assume such knowledge is indexed according to the situations in which it can be appropriately used, and we assume that indexes are modified as adaptation methods are used and fail. We also know something about the way some adaptation methods are created. For example, CHEF creates adaptation rules as a result of analyzing failed situations and noticing that had a single small modification been made in the failed solution, it would have worked. We know much about specific kinds of adaptation methods that work (they are detailed in chapter 11). More work is needed, however, before we can make claims about exactly where they fit in memory's networks.

4.6 EVIDENCE OF CASE-BASED REASONING IN PEOPLE AND ITS IMPLICATIONS

The cognitive model presented in this chapter is what some psychologists call an *invented model;* that is, inspired by observations of human behavior, a plausible model was created to explain that behavior. Computer programs built to mimic observed behavior contributed to fleshing out of the model. Model creators always kept their eyes on what was known about people to make sure the invented model was consistent with what is known (Bower, Black, and Turner 1979; Graesser and Nakamura 1982; Lichtenstein and Brewer 1980), and particular parts of the model have been tested experimentally on people (Barsalou 1988; Barsalou and Bower 1984; Reiser 1986a, 1986b, 1988; Reiser, Black, and Abelson 1985; Reiser, Black, and Kalamarides 1986; Seifert and Gray 1990). But the model as a whole has not been tested. Do people have MOPs in their heads? Do we have TOPs? We don't know.

We do know, however, that people find case-based reasoning a natural way to reason. Psychologists observing the problem-solving and decision-making procedures of people see them using case-based reasoning under a variety of circumstances. Ross (1986, 1989), for example, has shown that people learning a new skill often refer back to previous problems to refresh their memories on how to do the task. Research conducted in my lab shows that both novice and experienced car mechanics use their own experiences and those of others to help them generate hypotheses about what is wrong with a car, recognize problems (e.g., a testing instrument is not working), and remember how to test for different diagnoses (Lancaster and Kolodner 1987, 1988). Other research in our lab shows that physicians use previous cases extensively to generate hypotheses about what is wrong with a patient, to help them interpret test results, and to select therapies when several are available and none are understood very well (Kolodner, unpublished). We have also observed architects and caterers recalling, merging, and adapting old design plans to create new ones.

Klein and Calderwood (1988) observed expert decision makers in complex, dynamically changing situations. These experts use analogs to understand situational dynamics, generate options, and predict the effects of implementing an option in several different naturalistic decision-making situations. They observed experts using cases both to suggest solutions that were then adapted and to evaluate solutions and situations. In the naturalistic situations they observed, use of analogs was far more important than application of abstract principles or rules or conscious deliberation about alternatives. Analogs, or cases, provided concrete manifestations of the rules or principles that allow them to be applied easily. Cases also alerted decision makers to causal factors operating during the incident and helped them to anticipate what might happen if a course of action was implemented, to suggest options, and to reassure themselves that an option has worked and can be relied upon. The primary power of cases, claims Klein (Klein et al. 1988), is that they allow the decision maker to deal with unknown and uncertain information. An analog reflects the ways variables affected solutions in the past. In the same study, Klein and Whitaker found that case-based method is much more reliable than unstructured prediction when there are many unknowns.

Read (Read and Cesa 1990) observed people using old cases for explanation of anomalous occurrences, and found them particularly adept at doing that when the anomalous event reminded them of a personal experience.

The conclusion we draw from these studies is that reasoning using analogs is a natural process for people, especially when there is much uncertainty or many unknowns and during early learning. People know well how to use analogs to reason, and use of analogs in reasoning (at least for experts) results in reliable solutions.

Evidence also points out, however, a number of difficulties people have in using cases to reason. Some people use case-based reasoning blindly, relying on previous experience without validating it in the new situation. A case-based reasoner might allow cases to bias him or her or it too much in solving a new problem (Gilovich 1981). Moreover, often people are not reminded of the most appropriate sets of cases when they are reasoning (Brooks, Allen, and Norman 1989; Holyoak 1985; Gentner 1989).[8] In addition, when there is much to remember, people cannot always access the right cases when they need them.

Novices have a variety of other problems. They cannot do case-based reasoning well for two other reasons. First, they are missing the experiences they need to make good case-based decisions. Second, they are missing the experiences that tell them which parts of a situation are the important ones to focus on; that is, their criteria for judging similarity of cases is deficient.

This set of observations has led some members of the case-based reasoning community to look at the ways we might use case-based reasoning to help people reason better. The fact that people use cases easily but don't always know or remember the right ones coupled with the fact that we know how to build case libraries that do remember cases at the right times has led the case-based reasoning community to concentrate a great deal of effort recently on the design and creation of interactive case-based aiding and decision support systems, some of which were described in chapter 2 (e.g., Kolodner 1991a, 1991b; Domeshek and Kolodner 1991, 1992; Ferguson et al. 1992). In such systems, the computer holds a store of cases and makes them available to people at appropriate times, leaving it up to the human user to make

---

8. Much of the experimental work among the analogy community shows that it is far easier to get people to be reminded of an appropriate event when surface features match (e.g., Ross 1986; Holyoak 1985; Gentner 1989), that when situations are similar along only more abstract features, reminding its inhibited. One way to interpret these results is to claim that people are reminded only on the basis of surface features, that thematic features and structural features play no role in human reminding. There are some who make this claim.

Interpretation of these results based on *Dynamic Memory* is different. *Dynamic Memory* claims that the features people have available to them to enable reminding are those that are derived in the normal course of reasoning. Looking back at the early reminding experiments, we see that most ask subjects to be reminded of situations or stories without asking them to become involved in reasoning about those situations. Without reasoning about the situations, subjects have nothing but surface features describing a new situation available to them. No wonder that is all they can use for reminding!

Those experiments that do ask subjects to reason about a situation use only novice subjects and therefore really test only novice reminding. Never in any of those experiments do subjects have considerable knowledge and deep understanding of the kinds of situations they are reasoning about. Thus, they are unable to derive relevant thematic or structural descriptors. Viewed this way, the experiments show that *novices* tend to use surface features for reminding and therefore tend to be inappropriately reminded or unable to be reminded. But there are no claims that those experiments make about reminding and indexing in general.

Recent experimentation on reminding inspired by the theory of *Dynamic Memory* has put people in situations where they must reason deeply about a problem they are working on (e.g., Seifert and Gray 1990; Faries and Reiser, 1988, 1990). Their remindings are then collected. These experiments show evidence that structural and thematic descriptors of a situation indeed play an important role in human reminding when such descriptors are derived in the normal course of reasoning. Most recently, experiments and modeling done by Lange and Wharton (1993) show quite robustly that when put in a situation in which derivation of deep features is required for understanding or reasoning, those features play a primary role in reminding.

There have also been claims made that indexing is a poor way to think about retrieval and that it doesn't match what people do (e.g., Thagard and Holyoak 1989; Waltz 1989). This claim, I think, misunderstands what indexing is. The implementation of indexes as pointers may very well be a poor match to people. But the broader view of indexes as identifiers (discussed further in chapter 10) does not require a particular implementation and hasn't been shown to conflict with the human model.

decisions based on the cases that have been provided. Such a system can augment the memory of its human user by providing, at appropriate times, the relevant experiences of others. But because people are better at dealing with aesthetics, ethics, creative adaptation, and judgment, the real decision making is left to the human user. The computer provides cases to human problem solvers at appropriate times to help them with such tasks as coming up with solutions, adapting old solutions, critiquing and evaluation solutions, and warning of potential problems.

Another challenge is following up on the model's implications for education and training. Case-based education is based on the notion that stories tend to make the facts we hear more compelling, and we therefore remember them better. A system that can teach facts in an interesting way will make learning more exciting. Several systems are being developed with this in mind. Advise-the-President and ASK-Tom (Fergusen et al. 1992), both mentioned in chapter 2, are *story-based* systems that index interesting stories in a case library. They then allow students to browse the library, controlling their own learning experience.

Case-based training, on the other hand, has as its goal implanting appropriate cases in the head of a student, cases representing the kinds of situations the student will encounter on the job. Training of this type is by no means new. What case-based reasoning adds, however, is the notion that giving students representative experiences alone is not enough. Each experience must be presented such that it will be indexed appropriately by the student. The big research issue, of course, is figuring out strategies for doing that. CELIA provides a first attempt at doing this, showing us how crucial knowing the need to learn something is to learning it and indexing it. CELIA thus suggests that we put students in situations where they have the goal to learn whatever is being taught before we try to teach it. Still, there is more research to do in dealing with this issue.

The challenge in building such systems is to be able to represent, segment, and index cases appropriately so that they can be retrieved at appropriate times and presented to users in accessible ways.

PART II

The Case Library: Representing and Indexing Cases

A case-based reasoning system can only be as good as its memory of cases. The case memory has two parts: a *case library,* which serves as a repository for cases, and a set of *access procedures.* Together, the library and its access procedures make cases accessible when retrieval cues are provided to it and incorporate new cases into its structures as they are experienced, in the process maintaining accessibility of the items already in the library. This section discusses the case library. Part II of the book discusses access procedures.

There are several questions we must address in building a case library. Some have to do with case representation.

- What is a case?
- What component parts does a case have?
- What kinds of knowledge does a case need to encode?
- What representational formalisms and methodologies are most useful in representing case?

Other issues pertain to choosing a case's indexes. The *indexes* of a case act like indexes to books in a library. A case's indexes are combinations of its important descriptors, the ones that distinguish it from other cases. Just as we use the card catalog in a library to direct us toward books that are likely to fulfill our reading needs, retrieval algorithms use a case's indexes to select cases likely to fulfill the needs of the reasoner.

The *indexing problem* is the problem of making sure that a case is accessed whenever appropriate. This means the case should be indexed so as to be accessible whenever appropriate, and also that retrieval algorithms be able to use those indexes to get the right cases out at the right times. The loaded word here is *appropriate*. When are the appropriate times for a case to be accessed? Our answer, which will be discussed in considerable detail, is that a case is appropriately retrieved if it has the potential to help the reasoner fulfill his or her or its goals. Indexes, then, should be those features of a case that predict its usefulness.

There are thus a wide range of issues associated with choosing indexes:

■ What kinds of goals do reasoners have that a case might contribute to fulfilling?
■ How should we label or index cases so that we can recognize their applicability in the future?
■ What guidelines are available for this process?
■ How can the computer automate the process?

The other major issue associated with choosing indexes is the indexing and representational vocabulary to be used. Some vocabulary is specific to domains. For example, every medical domain has its own set of symptoms that it pays attention to and that must be represented. But there are also some vocabulary items that cross domains. And if we expect our case-based reasoners to be able to have the same sorts of cross-domain remindings that people exhibit and to make the same kinds of analogies, then we must address the content of the indexes that allow those kinds of remindings to happen—the vocabulary items that describe abstract relationships that hold across domains. The third set of issues we address in this section, then, are those associated with indexing vocabulary:

■ What vocabulary should we use to describe and index cases?
■ How do we choose domain-related vocabulary items?
■ What abstract descriptors hold across domains?

In this section of the book, we address this whole range of issues. Chapter 5 begins by discussing what a case is and continues by discussing case content. Guidelines for choosing the content of cases are presented. However, implementation of the guidelines in a system is largely a pragmatic concern. Because the particular components needed in a case depend a lot on what cases will be used for in a system, chapter 5 continues by giving examples of case representations from several systems and explaining why those representations were appropriate for those systems. These examples also serve to show the many different representational formalisms that can usefully be employed to encode cases in the computer.

Chapters 6 and 7 discuss indexing. Chapter 6 begins with a discussion of what makes a good index. It continues by discussing means of choosing vocabulary for describing cases. Indexes are chosen from that vocabulary. It goes on to present a generally applicable cross-domain vocabulary and its implications. Chapter 7 presents methodologies for choosing a case's indexes, both by hand and by computer. It beings with guidelines people can use to examine a case and determine its appropriate indexes. The second part of the chapter presents methods for choosing indexes automatically by computer.

Overall, our conceptions of the problems that must be addressed are somewhat ahead of our implementational know-how. For example, we can look at a case and recognize how to index it, but it is harder for a computer to do that evaluation. Thus, the pros and cons of different implementation choices are presented, at least to the extent that we are aware of them.

A final issue in building a case library is choosing the right cases to insert into it. That issue is addressed in chapter 15, which discusses the details of building case-based reasoning systems.

5

Representing Cases

In chapter 1, we discussed what a case is. Our discussion uncovered several principles about cases:

- A case represents specific knowledge tied to a context. It records knowledge at an operational level.
- Cases can come in many different shapes and sizes, covering large or small time slices, associating solutions with problems, outcomes with situations, or both.
- A case records experiences that are different from what is expected. Not all differences are important to record, however. Cases worthy of recording as cases teach a useful lesson.
- Useful lessons are those that have the potential to help a reasoner achieve a goal or set of goals easier in the future or that warn about the possibility of a failure or point out an unforeseen problem.

We concluded that a case is a contextualized piece of knowledge representing an experience that teaches a lesson fundamental to achieving the goals of the reasoner. We also concluded that a case has two major parts: *the lesson(s) it teaches* and *the context in which it can teach its lesson(s)*. The lessons it teaches comprise the case's content; the context in which it can teach those lessons are its indexes. Indexes record under what circumstances it is appropriate to retrieve the case. Chapters 6 and 7 discuss choice of indexes.

In this chapter, we address pragmatic issues related to representing a case's content. In particular, we focus on four issues:

1. What component parts does a case have?
2. What kinds of knowledge does a case need to encode?
3. What formalisms and methodologies are appropriate for representing cases?
4. How can we recognize the boundaries of cases, and how can they be devided into chunks of the right size?

Our emphasis will be on the content of cases, that is, the knowledge that must be included in them in order to make their lessons usable. As we discuss content, however, we will illustrate many of the forms cases can take. Means of choosing a vocabulary for describing cases will be discussed in chapter 6, in the discussion of vocabularies for indexing.

5.1 COMPONENT PARTS OF CASES

What component parts does a case need to be useful? There are two answers that people usually recognize as important immediately: the *description of the problem* that was being solved or the situation being understood and the *description of its solution*. With these two case components, new problems can be solved in a case-based way by first finding a relevant case (by selecting the case whose problem descriptions match the new situation best) and then adapting the solution to that problem to the new situation.

This is the way CASEY (Koton 1988a, 1989) works. Its cases have problems and solutions. In diagnosing cardiac problems, it takes as input a description of the new problem, finds the closest matching case in memory by comparing the new problem to descriptions of old ones, and then adapts the solution to the case it chooses to fit the new situation. CASEY shortcuts reasoning needed to get to a solution by using a case-based approach, and its answers are as accurate as those computed by the Heart Failure Program (Long et al. 1987), its model-based companion program.

Any reasoner whose cases have just these two components can be used to shortcut reasoning. In situations with many unknowns, however, using reasoning based on cases that record only problems and solutions can lead to severe inaccuracies. In particular, if one takes into account only the unevaluated solutions to old cases in proposing new solutions, it is just as easy to suggest poor solutions as good ones. CASEY is so accurate because the only solutions it stores are good ones and because its domain model is fairly accurate.

What if CASEY's model were not so accurate, however? Suppose CASEY started as a novice and didn't know so much about the causal connections between symptoms and disease states. It would make mistakes. If it mindlessly used the knowledge it had to solve problems and stored every problem and solution, it would get to its answers more efficiently over time, but it would repeat its mistakes as often as its good solutions. If, in addition, however, it received feedback about its solutions, it could reason about whether it should repeat an old solution or not. Mistakes shouldn't be repeated; successes should. If, in addition, it stored interpretations of its feedback, it could use cases to augment its sketchy model of how the heart works, becoming more accurate over time as a result.

There are certainly some domains that are well understood and where we can be sure that correctly solved cases will guide a reasoner to good solutions. In complex and commonsense domains, in domains where much is unknown, and in domains where much is unpredictable, however, the situation is more like that of the novice CASEY, the one with an incomplete model that makes mistakes because it is missing vital knowledge. A reasoner in these situations needs to be able to analyze whether a suggested solution is likely to work or not. A reasoner in these situations would be helped by cases recalled during problem solving that warn of the potential for failure. When much is unknown or unpredictable, previous cases provide some clues about the problem situation and can be used to predict the effects of a proposed solution.

In order to support these tasks, *outcome* must be represented in cases along with problems and solutions. What happened as a result of applying the solution? Was it successful? Did it fail? With outcome included in cases, a reasoner can suggest solutions that worked and use cases with failed solutions to warn of potential failures. It can also evaluate whether repeating an old solution will result in the outcome it wants in the new situation.

To summarize, there are three major parts to any case, though for any particular case they may not all be filled in:

1. **Problem/situation description**: the state of the world at the time the case was happening and, if appropriate, what problem needed solving at that time.
2. **Solution**: the stated or derived solution to the problem specified in the problem description, or the reaction to its situation.
3. **Outcome**: the resulting state of the world when the solution was carried out.

Thinking about case representation from the point of view of these three kinds of case components provides a useful framework for representing cases. It also begins to give us a way of specifying what kinds of knowledge needs to be in cases in order for different tasks to be carried out. Cases that include a problem and solution, for example, can be used in deriving solutions to new problems. Those with a situation description and outcome can be used in evaluating new situations. If, in addition, the case has a solution specified, it can be used in evaluating proposed solutions and in anticipating potential problems before they occur.

The information encoded in each of these categories also has a bearing on how useful a case can be during reasoning. A case is as useful in later reasoning as the information it holds. There are several items that might be represented in an outcome, for example. The base-line is execution feedback, that is, what the state of the world was after (and while) the solution was carried out. With this information, a case-based reasoner can anticipate potential problems and project the outcome of new solutions to aid in evaluation. If, in addition, the case includes an *explanation* of why an outcome came about (i.e., the causal connections between the initial situation, the solution, and the outcome) and the way in which it was repaired, the case can also be used for guidance in repairing a similar failure in the future.

Similarly, if the solution part of a case designates only a solution, it can be used to help in proposing a solution to a new case. If the solution includes in addition a record of its derivation, then the old *solution method* can be attempted in cases where the old solution is inapplicable. If the derivation includes connections between the problem description, the situation, and the solution, they can be used to help in guiding adaptation.

In the next subsections, the content of each of these pieces of a case representation will be discussed. In the following section, several case studies will show how the needs of a particular reasoner have been taken care of in its case representations. The form of each of those representations will also be discussed.

5.1.1 The Content of Problem Representations

The problem or situation description part of a case encodes the state of the world as reasoning begins. It might represent a problem that needs to be solved or a situation that needs to be interpreted, classified, or understood. In general, a case-based reasoner determines whether an old case is applicable to a new situation by examining the similarities between descriptions of the problem in the old situation and the new one.[1] If a new situation is sufficiently similar to an old problem description, that case is selected. Thus, a problem representation must have sufficient detail to be able to judge the applicability of the case in the new situation.

There are three major components of a problem representation:

1. Goals to be achieved in solving the problem
2. Constraints on those goals
3. Features of the problem situation and relationships between its parts

The **goals** in a problem description describe the aims of the actor in the situation. In general, the reasoner is striving to achieve its goals or fulfill its aims successfully. Goals can be abstract or concrete, overarching or narrow. The overarching goal of a diagnostician, for example, is to derive a diagnosis for a situation. As part of that process, the diagnostician may have the subgoal of deriving a logical competitor set or interpreting a test result. Which goal belongs in a problem situation depends on what lesson the case is aiming to teach. If a case is teaching about what diagnosis is appropriate given a set of symptoms, then the "diagnose" goal belongs as the goal of the case. If, on the other hand, it is an example of interpreting a particular test, then the "interpret test result" goal is recorded as the goal.

In problem-solving situations overarching goals include "diagnose," "create," and "plan," and often they further specify what should be diagnosed, created, or planned. JULIA, for example, has the overarching goal in its cases of creating a meal, while CHEF has the overarching goal of creating a recipe. In interpretive situations overarching goals include "understand," "explain," and "evaluate," and these too might specify what in the situation is to be understood or explained or evaluated. JULIA, for example, may sometimes want to evaluate the goodness of some piece of its solution and other times want to evaluate the solution as a whole.

Subgoals come from a variety of sources. Some are subgoals of a reasoning process (e.g., "remember," "adapt," "decompose"). Others are subgoals specific to a reasoning task (e.g., hypothetico-deductive reasoning used in diagnosis is a process of forming a partial hypothesis, collecting data to support it, fitting the new hypothesis into the larger hypothesis,

---

1. It's actually somewhat more complicated than this, but for now, this is an appropriate intuition.

etc.). Many times these subgoals are specialized for particular domains (e.g., the doctor may have a subgoal of collecting particular data). Other subgoals describe reasoning quandaries (e.g., "resolve inconsistency"). The particular goals and subgoals that are recorded in a case depend on the task and domain the reasoner is working in.[2]

Constraints are the conditions put on goals. CHEF's goal, for example, is generally to create a recipe. Each time it has different constraints—it must use some set of ingredients or create a certain taste or use some particular method or keep within some caloric or cost boundary. MEDIATOR's overarching goal is to resolve disputes, but each time it has different constraints—it can resolve disputes in a way that involves compromise, or it can create all-or-nothing solutions. JULIA creates meals and must keep in mind the likes and dislikes of people who will eat the meal, caloric content, cost, and so on. All these are constraints.

Features of the problem situation is the catchall that holds any other descriptive information about the situation relevant to achieving the situation's goals. In a medical diagnosis program, for example, a patient's symptoms and test results are necessary descriptors of the situation that the reasoner needs to do diagnosis. Though constraints are the conditions that *must* be attended to in constructing a solution; other features of the situation include anything else that *might* be taken into account in achieving the situation's goals. A meal planner, for example, may not be constrained by what's in the refrigerator, but what the refrigerator holds may influence the type of meal that is planned. What is in the refrigerator is included in the problem description if it affected the solution to the problem. A labor mediator might not be constrained by the company's financial status, but he or she will tend to come up with different kinds of solutions depending on what that financial status is. Financial status of the company is included in the features part of the problem description if it distinguishes the usefulness of several different solutions.

Some examples will illustrate the contents of several different kinds of problem descriptions. We begin with a typical case from the MEDIATOR. Two sisters want the same orange, presumably to eat it. The goal of the reasoner is to resolve the dispute. There are no constraints on that goal initially (though later it might be constrained to be either a compromise or all-or-none type of solution). Features of the situation include the fact that there are two disputants, sister1 and sister2; that they both want the same orange, orange1; that they both want to eat the fruit of orange1; and that this is a dispute situation. Figure 5.1 shows how these descriptors divide into goal, constraint, and situation descriptions.[3]

We continue with an example from CHEF's domain: recipe creation. Let's say our reasoner wants to create a recipe that includes beef and broccoli, that tastes spicy, and that is made by stir-frying. The goal of the reasoner is to create a recipe. Constraints on the recipe are that it include beef as an ingredient, include broccoli as an ingredient, have spicy taste, and be prepared by stir-frying. There might be certain ingredients and spices available in the refrigerator and pantry, the cost of the new ingredients that must be bought might need to be below a

---

2. Chapter 14 discusses the types and sources of reasoning goals in more detail.

3. Figure 5.12 shows an actual representation from MEDIATOR of this case. In fact, MEDIATOR records only the situation descriptions and constraints (if they exist) of its cases. MEDIATOR does not record goals because it really has only one goal—to resolve disputes.

```
Goal: resolve dispute
Constraints:
Situation description:
    isa: dispute-situation
    disputants: sister1, sister2 (sisters sister1 sister2)
    disputed object: orange1
    dispute:
      stated goals:
         (goal sister1 (possess sister1 orange1))
         (goal sister2 (possess sister2 orange1))
      inferred goals:
         (goal sister1 (ingest sister1 (fruit orange1)))
         (goal sister2 (ingest sister2 (fruit orange1)))
```

FIGURE 5.1   The Contents of One of MEDIATOR's Problem Descriptions

certain amount, there might be several things already cooking on the stove and not much burner space available, and so on. A full problem representation for a super-housewife robot that needs to make a stir-fry meal with broccoli and beef might look like the problem description in Figure 5.2. [4]

Situations that require explicit problem solving (e.g., design and planning tasks) emphasize goals and/or constraints in their problem representations. But situations requiring understanding or interpretation tend to have a fairly simple goal (e.g., diagnose, understand) and emphasize descriptors of the problem situation. The example from MEDIATOR illustrated that, so will an example from PROTOS. Here the program, acting as an audiologist, must diagnose a hearing problem. It is given the results of a set of audiological tests. Its goal is to diagnose by classifying this case into one of its known categories of hearing disorders. The results of the audiological tests describe the problem situation and comprise the bulk of the problem description. Figure 5.3[5] shows one of PROTOS's cases.[6] CASEY's problem descriptions,

---

4. CHEF's representations are different from what's shown here in two ways. First, CHEF's cases themselves don't record their goal (create a recipe) or take features of the problem situation into account, the former because its goal is always the same, the latter because it does not use situation information in creating its plans. It is, however, easy to extrapolate from CHEF a bit and imagine the kinds of situation features that might describe a recipe-creation case in the real world. That's what we've done here. Second, Hammond (1989a) refers to CHEF's constraints as its goals. I prefer to refer to recipe creation as CHEF's major goal and to its other descriptors as constraints. What I call its constraints describe the conditions on the recipe-creation goal—it can't just be any recipe; it has to be one that includes certain ingredients, has a certain taste, and so on.

5. Based on a figure in Bareiss (1989a), page 59. Note that the attribute-value representation of the items in the situation description are abbreviations of standard tests and their results. "S-neural (mild, gt4k)," for example, means that there is evidence of mild hearing loss above 4KHz, while "ac-reflex-u(normal)" means that the uncrossed acoustic reflex is normal.

6. In actuality, PROTOS does not record its goals and constraints: PROTOS has only one goal, to diagnose, and there are no constraints put on it. Only the details of the situation it needs to diagnose are important to its reasoning.

```
Problem:
   Goal: (create dish)
   Constraints:
      (include broccoli)
      (include beef)
      (taste spicy)
      (preparation stir-fry)
   Situation:
      (available broccoli)
      (unavailable red-peppers)
      (available beef)
      (frozen beef)
      (broken front-right-burner)
      (available ginger)
      (available scallions)
      (available-money $5.00)
      (available-time 2 hours)
      ...
```

FIGURE 5.2   A Hypothetical Recipe Creation Case Including Goal, Constraints, and Situation Description

```
Problem Description:
   Goal: diagnose
   Constraints:
   Situation Description:
      s-neural(mild, gt4k)        tymp(a)
      s_neural(mild, lt1k)        speech(normal)
      ac_reflex_u(normal)         air(mild)
      ac_reflex_c(normal)         history(vomiting)
      o_ac_reflex_u(normal)       history(dizziness)
      o_ac_reflex_c(normal)       history(fluctuating)
```

FIGURE 5.3   A Problem Description from PROTOS's Domain. (Adapted from Bareiss, 1989.)

though they describe heart problems rather than audiological problems, are very similar. Its goal is always to diagnose, there are no constraints on that goal that it deals with, and the bulk of its problem descriptions are in its situation description, which holds descriptions of patient signs and symptoms.

HYPO is also an interpretive program. It generally has the goal of creating an argument for one side or the other in a legal situation. The bulk of its problem descriptions are situation descriptions and include two kinds of information relevant to describing legal cases:

1. What claims were involved in the case
2. What factual features the court considered important in connection

Figure 5.4 shows the situation description part of one of its problem descriptions.[7] In this case, a company called USM has taken a company named Marson to court for trade secrets misappropriations. USM alleged that Marson had used its trade secrets to create a new product and gain a competitive edge. The problem description describes the two companies, the products they make, and the knowledge necessary for making those products (only part of which is in the figure).

As can be seen from these examples, some problem situations emphasize all three—goals, constraints, and situation description—others emphasize only one or two of those. In general, reasoners that have only one overarching goal they know how to achieve and that store their cases in one big chunk (more on this later) tend to deemphasize their goals. Goals of a case don't distinguish one case from another, so recording the goal doesn't add information to the problem description. Other reasoners deemphasize one or more components of the problem situation because they don't use that information. CHEF, for example, creates recipes but doesn't worry about whether the ingredients to make the recipe are there or whether the burners are available. Thus, it doesn't need a description of the world—it doesn't use that information to create its recipes.

In general, problem solvers are concrete about goals and constraints, while interpretive programs tend to concentrate on situation descriptions. These are only tendencies, however, and what needs to be included in a problem description depends on how a case will be used in the future and what information will be needed later to determine whether a new situation matches it well. The more involved in real-world action a problem solver is, for example, the more it needs situation descriptive information. It is that information that distinguishes the utility of one case from that of a similar one. In contrast to CHEF, EXPEDITOR (Robinson and Kolodner 1991) and RUNNER (Hammond 1989b), for example, both execute their plans. Thus, plans are created taking into account many concrete details of the situation in which the plan is carried out. Solving problems such as these requires access to situation descriptions.

When systems are implemented, deemphasized pieces of problem descriptions are often not even recorded in the problem representation. CHEF records neither its goal nor its situation descriptions, recording only relevant constraints. PROTOS, CASEY, and HYPO record only situation descriptions; none records goals or constraints. Pieces of the problem description that are recorded in representations are the pieces that get used in reasoning. Extraneous information is usually left out.

There are two general guidelines that should be followed in deciding which descriptive information belongs in a problem description:

1. Include in the problem description all descriptive information that was explicitly taken into account in achieving the case's goals.
2. Include in the problem description the kinds of descriptive information that are normally used to describe cases of this sort.

---

7. Taken (very freely) from Ashley (1990).

```
Situation description:
   date: Aug 29, 1979
   parties:
     USM
         isa: corporation
         competitors: Marson
         product-list:
            USM-machine
               a kind of: blind-rivet-machine
               used for: rivet-manufacture
               market: rivet-buyers
               technology used: rivet-design, rivet-manufacture
               competitors-products: marson-machine
               developer: USM
               project-start: 1954
               project-end: 1959
               knowledge-used: about-USM-machine
               security-measures: minimal-measures, access-to-premises-
                   controlled, restrictions-on-entry-by-visitors, employee-
                   nondisclosure-agreements
               security-breach-list: nil
              similarities-with-competitive product: nil
      Marson
         isa: corporation
         competitors: USM
         product-list:
            Marson-machine
               a-kind-of: blind-rivet-machine
               used-for: rivet-manufacture
               market: rivet-buyers
               technology used: rivet-design, rivet manufacture
               competitors-products: USM-machine
               developer: Marson
               project-start: 1961
               project-end: 1964
   roles of the parties: (plaintiff USM) (defendant Marson)
   claims: (claim USM (trade-secrets-misappropriation Marson))
   results: (competitive-advantage-gained Marson)
            (security-measures-adopted USM)
```

FIGURE 5.4   A Situation Description from a Legal Case

The first guideline says that whatever was explicitly relevant should be recorded. It allows the system to ignore features that are relevant but left implicit because they never vary. The second guideline is necessary for accessibility. At least some portions of the case description are used for indexing and judging the degree of similarity between a new situation and an old case.

The best cases to retrieve, of course, are those that are similar along dimensions known to be relevant to solving a problem. But because those things may not all be known when a new case is described, there needs to be an alternate way of determining best matches.

This guideline is particularly important for weak-theory domains. We often know there is a connection between certain problem descriptions and solutions without being able to characterize it well. Including the descriptive information in a case description that we *think* provides those connections allows the reasoner to function as if the causal connections were well understood.

In general, the closer old case descriptions are to descriptions of new situations, the easier retrieval and matching will be. Thus, case descriptions should include the kind of information that naturally describes the situation: what would normally be included in descriptions of new problems to be solved or new situations to be interpreted. If new scenerios are described in terms of goals and constraints, then cases should include that information in their problem descriptions. If new scenerios are described richly in terms of descriptive features, then old cases should be described in that way.

This designation is not without complications. Sometimes a problem is naturally described not just by the problem description but also by features of its solution-in-progress. How does this affect what belongs in a problem description? Sometimes a problem is described in one way to begin with but, after some reasoning, gets redescribed in a more correct or more sophisticated way. Which should be used as the problem description? We will return to these issues after completing the discussion of case representation.

5.1.2 The Content of Solutions

There are many different types of solutions. The solution to a design problem is the artifact that was designed. The solution to a planning problem is the derived plan. The solution to an interpretive problem is the interpretation or classification finally assigned to the case. The solution to an explanation problem is the explanation. The solution is, in short, the concepts or objects that achieve the goals set forth in the problem description, taking into account the specified constraints and other specified contextual features.

With a solution in place, a reasoner that retrieves a case can use its solution to derive a new solution. But solutions also have other components that aid adaptation and critiquing. Listed below are the ones the research community has identified as useful:

- The solution itself
- The set of reasoning steps used to solve the problem
- The set of justifications for decisions that were made in solving the problem
- Acceptable solutions that were not chosen (and reasoning and justifications that go with them)
- Unacceptable solutions that were ruled out (and reasoning and justification that go with them)
- Expectations of what will result upon deployment of the solution

We've already described what a solution is. Here, we will briefly discuss each of the other parts to a solution specification and what each is useful for. As adaptation and evaluation are presented in more detail in later chapters, the rationale for including each of these in the solution to a case will become clearer.

Reasoning steps. Several case-based reasoners (e.g., ARIES [Carbonell 1986], JULI-ANA [Shinn 1988a, 1988b], JULIA [Hinrichs 1992; Hinrichs and Kolodner 1991]) record the set of reasoning steps used to derive a solution in their case representations. This allows those reasoning steps to be repeated in later problem solving. The easiest way to illustrate the usefulness of such information is to take readers back to college calculus and probability courses. In those courses, the teacher generally works out problems on the board, specifying the set of steps used to solve the problem. In addition, the book walks students through the steps needed to solve a problem. When students are presented with a new problem, they leaf through the book and their notes to find the problem closest to the one they now have to solve and repeat the solution steps used in the old problem. Because of all the intermediate calculations that have to be done and the fact that the relationship between problem features and solutions is very complex, adapting an old solution to solve the new problem is out of the question. On the other hand, the old solution gives guidelines for solving the new problem by providing a set of steps that, if carried out, will result in a solution. JULIA uses such guidelines to figure out how to divide its design problems into manageable chunks. JULIANA uses old solution steps both for that and to guide adaptation of an old solution. ARIES uses old solution steps to guide the entire solution procedure for new problems, exactly as described above.

This part of the solution specification looks like a list of the inferences that were made on the way to the solution. First I did *x,* then *y,* and so on. Each also has associated with it the sources of knowledge used to make the inferences. For example, if a reasoner derived a piece of a solution by remembering a case and adapting it a certain way, the means of derivation is recorded as a case-based inference, the case inferred from is specified, and the adaptation heuristics applied are recorded. One inference JULIA makes, for example, is to serve a version of tomato-bake without any milk products in it. The knowledge it represents about how it derived the solution is shown in Figure 5.5. This representation states that the reasoning done was to make a case-based inference, that the case it is based on is Late Summer Tomatoes, and that the way it was adapted was to apply a transformation rule called delete-secondary-ingredient specifically applied to the ingredient cheese from the main-dish of that meal.

What a recording of reasoning steps used looks like depends at least in part on the kinds of reasoning a system has available. ARIES, for example, can follow old reasoning chains or can apply operators as it is solving problems. The steps in its cases look like lists of operators that were applied and the bindings of their variables. JULIA makes case-based inferences, as

```
Reasoning:
   Step1:
      a-kind-of: case-based inference
      source-case: Late Summer Tomatoes
      adaptation: delete-secondary-ingredient (cheese, main-dish)
```

FIGURE 5.5   A Reasoning Step

shown, and its recordings of the steps used to solve a problem show the individual case-based inferences it makes—for each, its source case and adaptation heuristics applied to modify the old solution to fit the new situation. Systems that solve problems by constructing rule chains might record the rules used.

Justifications.   Justifications also provide a way of guiding adaptation of an old solution. In one of JULIANA's cases, for example, it was adapting a meal served in summer to the winter. In the summer meal, melon had been served, but it is unavailable now. Justifications associated with that part of the solution stated that melon was chosen because it is a summer fruit, the season was summer, and it was inexpensive. Substituting the current season (winter) in that justification, JULIANA is provided with guidance in choosing a fruit for the new meal: it should be a winter fruit because the season is winter, and it should be inexpensive. Based on that justification, JULIANA considers apples, pears, and oranges but does not consider grapes or blueberries or raspberries as substitutes for melon.

Justifications serve two additional purposes. First, they provide guidance during evaluation of a solution. If parts of a previous solution are justified, one way to evaluate whether the results of an old solution will hold in the new situation is to examine whether the properties that justified parts of the old solution are present in the new case. In one of its cases, for example, JULIA decides to serve two main dishes because constraints on ingredients of the main dish overconstrain it. The two dishes it served were grilled salmon and nondairy garden tomato bake. In a later situation, JULIA is reminded of this case when it is trying to come up with a tomato dish. In addition to finding a suggestion for a tomato dish, it sees that there were two main dishes served. It wonders whether it should serve two main dishes at the meal it is planning now. Consulting the justifications for serving two main dishes at that meal, it finds that the reason was that ingredients were overconstrained. That not being the case in the new situation, it decides that one main dish is enough. Figure 5.6 shows JULIA's justification for serving several dishes (rather than one), the reasoning it did to make that happen, and the two main dishes it decided upon.

Second, justifications guide index selection. The justifications for some choice or solution say what it was about the world that was important in coming to that conclusion. The purpose of indexes is to specify what is important about a case, and what was important about the world in solving a problem gives strong clues for indexing. The case in Figure 5.6, for example, would appropriately be indexed as a case where the ingredients slot of a main dish was overconstrained. The solution it proposes, and the lesson it teaches for such situations, is to increase the choice and serve two main dishes. In the next chapter, this will become clearer.

```
main-dishes
   Reasoning:
     Step1: Increase choice (main-dish)
   Justification: Overconstrained ingredients slot
   Value:
      main-dishes 2: grilled salmon
      main-dishes 1: good-garden-tomato-bake
```

FIGURE 5.6   Justification for Serving Two Main Dishes

```
main-dishes1: good-garden-tomato-bake
   Ingredients:
      rule-out: dairy-products
   Justifications: Contains tomatoes
                   Cost = inexpensive
                   Host = *JLK*
   Reasoning:
      Step1:
        a-kind-of: case-based inference
        source: Late Summer Tomatoes
        justification: Contains tomatoes
                       Cost = inexpensive
                       Host = *JLK*
        adaptation: delete-secondary-ingredient (cheese, main-dish)
           justification: violates (ingredient (cheese),
                                     constraint (rule-out (dairy-products)))
```

FIGURE 5.7 Reasoning Steps and Justification for Nondairy Garden Tomato Bake

Note that justifications and reasoning steps are related to each other quite closely. Justifications can provide the rationale both for solutions themselves and for the means of deriving solutions. In general, whenever an inference is applied to compute some value, the justifications for the inference or the value are also recorded. Figure 5.6 shows one instance of a justification-reasoning pair. There, the justification justifies the use of the reasoning step (i.e., choice was increased because of an overconstrained ingredients slot). Figure 5.7 shows another illustration, this time of the justification for serving nondairy garden tomato bake (reasoning for that is shown in Figure 5.5). When JULIA chooses to serve nondairy garden tomato bake, it does so because it contains tomatoes and is inexpensive and because the recipe it is derived from has been served before by this host. The use of the particular case-based inference it makes is also justified, by the fact that the dish it recalls almost fits the bill but its cheese ingredient violates the constraint not to use dairy products.

In the illustrations above, justifications are shown as annotations on a framelike structure, and their actual form has been fairly ambiguous. Programs that have recorded justifications generally use one of the common notations used in reason maintenance (e.g., Doyle 1979).

Alternative solutions. Another useful piece of information about a solution is what alternatives were available but not chosen. When a case is recalled, unused acceptable alternative solutions can also be used in deriving new solutions. Though their outcomes cannot be evaluated, they provide an alternative means of solving a problem if other means are ruled out. Alternative solutions that were ruled out also provide guidance in evaluating proposed solutions. A solution that was ruled out previously might appropriately be ruled out again.

Expectations about outcome. Another useful piece of knowledge that can be included in a solution representation is expectations about what the outcome will be. When a

```
Expectations:
   if-ok: (ingest sister1 (fruit (piece1 (orange1))))
          (ingest sister2 (fruit (piece2 (orange1))))
```

FIGURE 5.8   One of MEDIATOR's Expectations About Outcome

solution is created, the reasoner usually has expectations about what will result when it is carried out. The reasoner may also have expectations about particular problems that might arise and might know what will result in those cases. If these expectations are associated with cases, the reasoner can determine if a solution is as expected by matching what has actually happened with what was predicted. MEDIATOR, for example, knows that there is something wrong with its solution to the Orange Dispute when one sister bakes with her orange peel and throws away the fruit, because it expects that each sister will eat her half of the fruit. Expectations can be of what will happen if all goes right or of particular outcomes that signal failure. Figure 5.8 shows MEDIATOR's expectations upon proposing that the orange be divided in half.

5.1.3 The Content of Case Outcomes

The outcome of a case specifies what happened as a result of carrying out the solution or how the solution performed. Outcome includes both feedback from the world and interpretations of that feedback.

Baseline outcome information includes feedback from the world detailing what happened as a result of (or while) carrying out or deploying a solution, along with a determination of its success and/or whether expectations were met. With such information, a reasoner can anticipate potential problems and predict the outcome of a proposed solution. Outcome can include more, however. In particular, if expectations are violated or if the solution failed, outcome might also include the explanation for the problem and what was done to repair it. There are thus several parts to outcome:

- The outcome itself
- Whether or not the outcome fulfilled or violated expectations
- Whether the outcome was a success or a failure
- Explanation of the expectation violation and/or failure
- Repair strategy
- What could have been done to avoid the problem
- Pointer to next attempt at solution (result of applying repair)

The most obvious component part of outcome is the feedback itself, that is, the things that actually happened in the world as a result of carrying out or deploying the solution. The outcome of a design case tells us how the design performed in the world and how it lived up to the goals specified for it, for example: Was it easy to build? Could it be used effectively? Did users like it? Did managers like it? Was it aesthetically pleasing? The outcome of a planning problem tells us what happened as a result of (or during) plan execution. And so on. After an orange is divided between two children, for example, the outcome might be that both eat it, or it could be that the first child eats it and the second makes juice with her piece.

In addition to the outcome itself, some interpretive information is useful to record and save in a case. One important piece of interpretive information is whether or not a solution succeeded in achieving the case's goals. An annotation about success or failure attached to a case allows a case-based reasoner to begin to predict whether an old solution should be attempted or not. For example, a reasoner should repeat solutions that worked but not those that failed.

Another interpretation of outcome is the degree to which expectations were met or violated. When a solution is created, a reasoner has expectations about what its results will be. A solution might succeed at achieving stated goals but violate expectations. Similarly, a solution might fail to achieve goals, but the failure might be expected. Annotations about whether expectations are met and under what circumstances they are met or not met gives a reasoner a way of predicting results in an uncontrollable world. In addition, expectation violations show a reasoner that it is missing information. Interpretations of expectation violations give the reasoner guidance about what it should learn.

A record of success or failure allows a reasoner to decide if it wants to repeat an old solution or not. A record of real outcome allows more sophisticated reasoning. It allows a reasoner to recognize the potential for unexpected side effects, thus allowing it to anticipate potential problems. It also allows a reasoner to make predictions about what success will look like and to evaluate whether a suggested solution is an appropriate one.

At the same time, while success or failure can be derived from outcome as needed, once a derivation of success or failure or of meeting expectations is done, it makes sense to record it rather than having to repeat the computation another time. This recording and computation are not without their complexities, however. There may be several ways to judge the success of a solution, and if there are several, then a single recording of success won't be sufficient. The layout of offices in a building, for example, may be good with respect to wayfinding but poor when judged on the amount of group interaction it allows. The outcome of a case may need to record outcomes from several different points of view. If there are several ways to measure outcome, each might need to be part of the case representation.

When an outcome is as expected, there isn't much more to record. However, when an outcome violates expectations or when a solution fails, human reasoners usually wonder why. They often try to explain the violation, that is, to find out what was wrong with the solution that caused the expectation to be violated. They attempt to derive a repair if the outcome was poor. And if the outcome was bad, they consider how it could have been avoided, if unexpectedly good, how it can be repeated.

When an outcome is different than expected, recording such information can help the reasoner perform better in the future. If case representations include explanations of failures in them, they can be helpful in explaining later failures. If they are indexed by features of the world that were responsible for the failure, they can be used to anticipate and avoid potential failures in the future. If, in addition, they include the way the problem was repaired, the case can be used later to help repair similar problems, and sometimes it can be used to suggest alternative solutions. A recording of how the outcome could have been avoided or can be repeated can also help in anticipating problems, and this information is quite useful in choosing indexes for the case.

Finally, it is often useful to record a pointer to follow-up attempts to solve the same problem. Recording follow-up attempts allows a reasoner on the verge of failure to be led to an alternative solution that might be better. A special case of this happens when a problem solver in a confused state recalls an old case based on its incorrect interpretation. If the outcome of that case is recorded along with a pointer to the attempt to resolve it when interpreted correctly, the confused problem solver can be led out of its confusion. This happens in both MEDIATOR (Kolodner and Simpson 1989) and PROTOS (Bareiss 1989a). If MEDIATOR were told that two kids wanted the same avocado, it would assume they both wanted to eat it and be reminded of the failed Orange Dispute episode. That reminding would warn it to be careful that it got the goals of the disputants interpreted correctly and would point it to the successful Orange Dispute episode, in which the orange was divided according to the part of the orange each disputant wanted. If, in fact, one disputant in the avocado dispute wanted the seed to plant, the pointer to the follow-up Orange Dispute suggests a solution immediately. The outcome from one of MEDIATOR's cases is shown in Figure 5.14.

PROTOS also stores pointers to follow-up attempts, but as *difference links*. When a diagnosis attempt fails, PROTOS gets feedback about what it should have noticed to get to the correct diagnosis and installs a difference link between the case it was reminded of that led it to failure and the diagnostic category or case that provides the right answer. It labels the difference link with the features of the new situation that it should have paid attention to. In this way, if the reasoner is again led to the erroneous case, if the new case shares features with the difference link, it finds a pointer to a better solution.

5.2 THE ISSUE OF CASE PRESENTATION

Now that we know what is helpful in a case representation, the next question becomes how we represent all that knowledge. Artificial intelligence provides us with a wide range of representational formalisms (e.g., frames, semantic networks, predicate notation, rules) that can be used to represent the contents of a case in a form the computer can read. As the examples in the next section will show, case-based reasoners have been built using the whole variety of these formalisms. The important thing has been to get the knowledge into some format in a way that works rather than designating one or another format as the appropriate one for representing cases.

But there is another issue related to representation that must be addressed when systems need to interact with people. Representations that are easy for a computer to read are not necessarily easy for a person to read. And much of what it would be useful to represent in a case is, for all intents and purposes, beyond what we know how to represent using these formalisms. ARCHIE (Pearce et al. 1992; Goel, Kolodner et al. 1991) provides a case in point (Figure 5.9). ARCHIE was designed to be an aid to an architect. The idea was that the architect would specify his or her problem to ARCHIE and ARCHIE would recall cases and present them to

Goal

O-GOAL: Organization Type	Academic Officer
O-GOAL: Group Interaction	Semi-Important
O-GOAL: Face to Face Contact	Semi-Important
O-GOAL: Frequency of Visitors	Frequently
O-GOAL: Time at Office	Frequently
O-GOAL: Time in Meetings	Infrequently
O-GOAL: Image Importance	Trivial
O-GOAL: Information Sources	Computer / Face to Face / File
O-GOAL: Outside Communication	Frequently
O-GOAL: Computer Use	Important
O-GOAL: Lab Space	Important
O-GOAL: Security Requirements	Highly Secure
O-GOAL: Growth Need	Semi-Important
O-GOAL: Budget	N/A
C-GOAL: Floor Layout	Closed
C-GOAL: Gross Area	N/A
C-GOAL: Total Area	N/A
F-GOAL: Adjustability	Trivial
F-GOAL: Aesthetics	Semi-Important
F-GOAL: Furniture Budget	N/A
F-GOAL: Modularity	Not a Factor
F-GOAL: Storage Needs	Important
F-GOAL: Storage Needs-Books	Semi-Important
F-GOAL: Storage Needs-Files	Not a Factor
F-GOAL: Worksurface Area (sq ft)	15

Picture

Plan

Case Name	CIRCA
C-PLAN: Ambient Lighting Type	Flourescent
C-PLAN: Natural Lighting Amount	Majority Natural Light
C-PLAN: Natural/Artificial Lighting Ratio	0.50
C-PLAN: Number of Floors	5
C-PLAN: Space Shape	Angular
C-PLAN: Total Area	5500
P-PLAN: Group Layout	One Group
P-PLAN: Workgroup Division	Core Border
P-PLAN: Workgroup Shape	Angular
P-PLAN: Common Spaces	Copier Room / Corridor / Lab Area / Meeting Room / Waiting Room
P-PLAN: Number of Conference Rooms-Shared	0
P-PLAN: Number of Conference Rooms-Unshared	1
P-PLAN: Partition for Manager	Permanent Wall
P-PLAN: Partition for Support Staff	Furniture
P-PLAN: Partition for Worker	Permanent Wall
P-PLAN: Partition Height for Manager	To the Ceiling
P-PLAN: Partition Height for Support Staff	Desk Level
P-PLAN: Partition Height for Worker	To the Ceiling
P-PLAN: Area of Manager Office	250
P-PLAN: Area of Support Staff Office	200
P-PLAN: Area of Worker Office	150
F-PLAN: Furniture for Manager	Traditional
F-PLAN: Furniture for Support Staff	Traditional
F-PLAN: Furniture for Worker	Traditional
F-PLAN: Has Task Lighting?	False
F-PLAN: Adjustable?	False
F-PLAN: Modular?	False
F-PLAN: Shared Workspace	No Space
F-PLAN: Storage Types	File Drawers / Floor Shelves / Pedestals

Result

O-OUTCOME: Individual Satisfaction	Highly Satisfied
O-OUTCOME: Group Interaction	Unplanned Interaction
O-OUTCOME: Distraction Control	Highly Controllable
O-OUTCOME: Distraction Frequency	Infrequently
O-OUTCOME: Accessibility	Difficult to Access
O-OUTCOME: Noise Level	Background Noise
O-OUTCOME: Privacy-Auditory	High Privacy
O-OUTCOME: Privacy-Visual	High Privacy
O-OUTCOME: Security	Highly Secure
C-OUTCOME: Lighting Quality	Good Lighting
C-OUTCOME: Lighting Quality-Artifical	Good Lighting
C-OUTCOME: Lighting Quality-Natural	Satisfactory Lighting
C-OUTCOME: Lighting Problem Comments*Glare is a	
C-OUTCOME: Air Problem Commens*Individual	Moist
C-OUTCOME: Air Quality	1
C-OUTCOME: Air Temperature	Good Temperature
C-OUTCOME: Color Scheme Aesthetics	Agreeable
P-OUTCOME: Partition Cost for Manager	0
P-OUTCOME: Partition Cost for Support Staff	0
P-OUTCOME: Partition Cost for Worker	0
P-OUTCOME: Partition Design Aesthetics	Agreeable
P-OUTCOME: Partition Finish Aesthetics	Bland
F-OUTCOME: Furniture Cost for Manager	8000
F-OUTCOME: Furniture Cost for Support Staff	4000
F-OUTCOME: Furniture Cost for Worker	4000
F-OUTCOME: Total Cost	80000
F-OUTCOME: Within Budget?	N/A
F-OUTCOME: Adequate Space?	Agree
F-OUTCOME: Adequate Storage?	Strongly Agree
F-OUTCOME: Ease of Adaptability	Agree
F-OUTCOME: Furniture Color Aesthetics	Bland
F-OUTCOME: Furniture Design Aesthetics	Agreeable
F-OUTCOME: Furniture Finish Aesthetics	Agreeable

FIGURE 5.9 A Case from ARCHIE

161

the architect, who would then solve the problem using the cases as guides. Figure 5.9 shows a picture of a typical case from ARCHIE.[8]

ARCHIE's cases represent knowledge about the design of buildings. The first column in Figure 5.9 holds the problem specification of one of ARCHIE's cases. The middle column holds the solution. The last column holds outcome information. All the guidelines for what to include in a problem specification, solution, and outcome are followed in this representation. But there's clearly something wrong. Although ARCHIE's frame representations provide a nice synopsis of the case for a computer, people looking at representations like this can't take anything away with them. It's too much information, and it isn't in an easily comprehensible form.

Though we need to represent solutions in symbolic notations in order for the computer to reason about them, it is sometimes useful to explain at least some parts of a case in text or pictures to make its contents more accessible to a person who might be using it to reason. The pointers discussed earlier tell us what needs to be included in a case for it to be useful, but they don't imply that all the content has to be in machine-usable form. The parts of a case that a human needs to access for reasoning need to be in human-comprehensible form. Sometimes this means pictures, sometimes text, sometimes charts, CAD output, videos, sound. The list could go on and on.

Going back to ARCHIE, we can imagine what an architect might need to look at to understand a case, and indeed ARCHIE provides some of that. An architectural aiding system, and any system dealing with objects that must be visualized, should store a picture of its solution in addition to a description of it. The picture allows the user to visualize the solution and might also be the means of integrating the case-based system with a CAD or other type of drawing system that the designer normally uses. The layout in the lower left-hand corner of Figure 5.9 was ARCHIE's concession to visualization.

Other information that could be useful to the architect is lessons that the case has to offer. Indeed, this is what case-based reasoning is good at—using cases to make lessons accessible and concrete. And indeed, ARCHIE attempts to do this by integrating *annotation boxes* into the framelike representation. One of these boxes can be seen in the top right corner of the figure. Others are buried among the fields in the rightmost column and can be expanded by the user to get the full English-language story. In ARCHIE, then, some of the information is formated in a human-digestible way. So why am I complaining about ARCHIE?[9] ARCHIE makes concessions to people but doesn't go far enough. ARCHIE's cases each have a variety of lessons to teach, and it does record those lessons and make them accessible, but they are buried in the presentation in such a way that they are hard to see.

Several other systems do a better job than ARCHIE of presenting cases well. The Battle Planner (Goodman 1989) was the first serious attempt to build a usable, interactive case-based

---

8. ARCHIE was built using the Cognitive Systems' CBR Shell, now called REMIND.

9. Since ARCHIE is my program, I feel I can be hard on it, though perhaps I am being too hard on it because it is my program. While I consider ARCHIE a failure as a case-based aiding system, it has a lot of instructive lessons to teach.

system. Its cases are small, and their important parts can be represented completely in a single screen or less. Figure 5.25 shows one of its cases.

More recent interactive case-based systems use video, graphics, sound, and other media to present cases in an understandable and compelling way. The ASK systems (Ferguson et al. 1992) use video clips and text to present their cases. ASK systems are built around a system architecture meant to support the construction of advice-giving systems. Figure 5.10 shows a screen from one of those systems, ASK-Tom (Schank et al. 1991; Ferguson et al. 1992). To make the user aware of what cases are available and what they are about, ASK systems help the user select a theme (e.g., when to say no at a high-spot review). They then organize one-line descriptions of cases in stacks around that central theme according to the way they address it. One stack, called *alternatives*, for example, holds cases that show alternatives to the central theme. Another stack, called *warnings*, holds cases that instruct on what to watch out for. The stack called *examples* holds examples of carrying out the theme. And so on. Users click on the case they want to see and are shown a video clip that tells the story. ASK systems represent only their indexes in machine-usable form. The full content of the cases is in the videos.

Another example of a system that does better than ARCHIE is ARCHIE-2 (Domeshek and Kolodner 1991, 1992, 1993), ARCHIE's successor. While ARCHIE made concessions to people's needs, ARCHIE-2 is built around the needs of its users. Figure 5.11 shows a picture of its presentation style. In ARCHIE-2, graphical representations and lessons learned are the central pieces of the presentation of a case on the screen. As shown in the figure, the central and largest part of ARCHIE's screen shows the graphical presentation of the building being presented. Here, it is shown as a floor plan, but elevations and photographs can serve the same purpose. The graphic is marked according to the lessons it has to teach, and those lessons are shown as short annotations around the sides. The user chooses which of the lessons he or she wants to see, and a longer, more descriptive English-language description of the lesson is made available (at the bottom). Icon buttons representing building functions allow the user to specify which kinds of lessons he or she wants to see. Zooming and page-turning buttons allow the user to navigate the set of graphics available. The three boxes along the left side allow the user to specify the kinds of design issues he or she is interested in. While the themes in ASK systems tie together a series of related cases, the graphics in ARCHIE tie together lessons that comprise a larger case.

This book is not about software engineering or human-computer interaction, so I won't spend more time on presentation issues. Systems builders should be aware, however, that such issues are of paramount importance in building interactive systems, case-based or otherwise, and need to be taken seriously as a system is being designed.

5.3 CASE STUDIES

A question to consider at this point is which parts of the representation need to be in machine-usable form and which need to be human-usable. Obviously, anything a person has to interact with should be presented in a way that the person can digest. But what does the computer need? It depends upon the computer's responsibilities. A computer program that needs only to retrieve cases needs to represent only those portions of the case needed for retrieval in

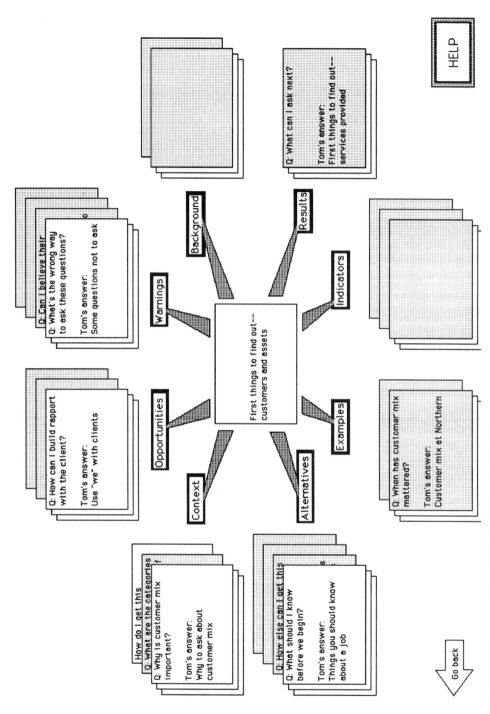

FIGURE 5.10 Presentation of Available Cases in ASK-Tom

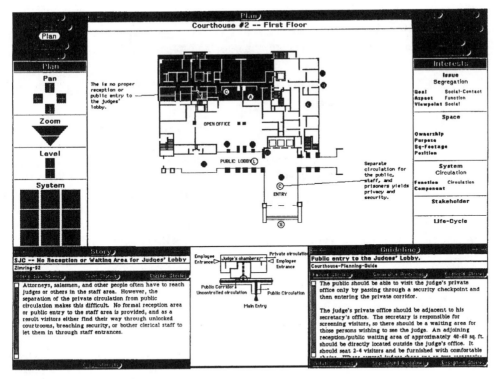

FIGURE 5.11 A Screen from ARCHIE-2

machine-usable form. One that will help with or do adaptation needs to have what it needs for that task in a format it can use.

We don't answer the question explicitly right now because there hasn't been enough presented yet about how cases are used to make the answer comprehensible. Given, however, that there are usually at least some pieces of a case that need to be represented in machine-usable form, it makes sense to explore how that can be done.

Cases have been represented using a variety of notations. CASEY and PROTOS both use attribute-value representations. MEDIATOR's representations are structured as frames. CHEF's are a hybrid: a frame representation organizes case information, but slot fillers in the frame representation are formatted using first-order predicate calculus. Representations in the Battle Planner use a flat slot-filler format reminiscent of database records. As long as they include the appropriate descriptors, problem descriptions can be represented in almost any format.

In this section, representations from several systems are presented to illustrate what the contents of some real cases look like and to show how different representational formats have been used for case representation. Though there are many types of information that are useful in a case, for any particular application, there may be no need to record all of them. It is difficult to give guidelines about what to record other than to analyze your task and record what's needed. Hopefully, these examples will serve to make this guideline more concrete. Except for the Battle Planner, all the systems presented in this section are automated case-based reasoners and thus represent all their knowledge in machine-usable form.

5.3.1 MEDIATOR: Highly Structured Representations, Broad But Not Deep

MEDIATOR (Kolodner and Simpson 1989), recall, solved everyday resource disputes in a commonsense way. It could figure out how to split a candy bar between two kids and what to do if two students wanted the same library book at the same time, and it could even suggest a solution to the dispute between Israel and Egypt over the Sinai. It used case-based reasoning for a variety of reasoning tasks: to help it elaborate problem descriptions, to help it solve problems, to help it explain failures, and to help it propose repairs. Because MEDIATOR used cases to carry out all these tasks, its case representations are broad, including representations of the problem, its solution, and its outcome. Because MEDIATOR does no adaptation to speak of, its representations of solutions are quite sparse (they don't need to include much more than the solution itself), but because it focuses on explaining and repairing its failures, its representations of outcomes are relatively complete.

MEDIATOR's case representations are very highly structured and are implemented in a frame system. Figures 5.12 through 5.15 show MEDIATOR's representation of the Orange Dispute. As mentioned previously, in the Orange Dispute, two sisters want the same orange. MEDIATOR assumes they both want to eat it and solves the problem by having one sister cut the orange in two and the second choose her half. When the second sister uses her peel for baking and throws away the pulp, MEDIATOR realizes it made a mistake. It explains its error, placing the blame on its inference that both sisters wanted to eat the orange. It then solves the problem again, this time suggesting that the first sister get the fruit and the second the peel.

Figure 5.12 shows the way MEDIATOR represents the problem description (the slot filler for the slot problem. It is a physical dispute (a kind of problem) between sister1 and sister2, both people and both with the goal of ingesting orange1, the disputed object.[10] Most of MEDIATOR's representation is a description of the situation, or problem features. MEDIATOR does not represent its goals explicitly. When it sees a problem of type M-Physical-Dispute, it knows that its goal is to resolve the dispute. When it sees a problem of type M-Failure-Recovery, it knows that its goal is to explain and repair the failure. Nor are constraints on its goal obvious in the representation. MEDIATOR does not have constraints on its goals.

Figure 5.13 shows the solution to the Orange Dispute. MEDIATOR's solutions have two parts: a plan with bound variables and a set of predictions about the expected state of the world after the plan is carried out. We can see that its solution plan for this case is "One cuts, the other chooses," and that if everything goes as planned (if-results-ok), then each sister will ingest her piece of the orange.

The outcome portion of the Orange Dispute, shown in Figure 5.14, has several parts. MEDIATOR records feedback from the world (feedback), its evaluation of the feedback with respect to its success or failure (evaluation), its interpretation of its mistake and how it

---

10. Indentations in the representation show successive levels of frames and their slots.

```
Mediation-1:
(M-MEDIATION isa M-PROBLEM
   problem: orange-dispute-0
           (M-PHYSICAL-DISPUTE
             characters:
                 party1: sister1 isa person
                         goal: (*INGEST* (actor sister1) (object orange1))
                 party2: sister2 isa person
                         goal: (*INGEST* (actor sister2) (object orange1))
             disputed-object: orange1
             arguments:
                 arga: arguer: sister1
                       support: (*phys-control* (actor sister1)
                                                (object orange1))
                 argb: arguer: sister2
                       support: (*phys-control* (actor sister2)
                                                (object orange1))
             goal-relationship: competition )
```

FIGURE 5.12   Orange Dispute, Problem Specification

repaired the problem (both in remediation), and a pointer to the next attempt at solving the problem (next).

The feedback here states that sister1 ingested her piece of the orange (piece1) and that sister2 baked a cake, in the process doing some preparation with the peel of the orange (peel1). The solution is marked as a failure. The remediation slot records both MEDIATOR's explanation of its reasoning error and its means of resolving the error. Here it inferred the goals of the disputants poorly (a M-WRONG-GOAL-INFERENCE), a kind of poor problem elaboration (M-POOR-ELAB), which is in turn a kind of misunderstanding, which is a kind of reasoning failure. MEDIATOR was the actor who made the mistake (recorded in the actor slot of M-WRONG-GOAL-INFERENCE). Its means of repairing its reasoning error was to make a new inference based on the feedback it received. This is shown as the plan of the filler of the remediation slot. After carrying out this repair, it reinterprets the original problem as one in which sister2 had the goal of wanting the peel of the orange (rather than the orange as a whole). Its next attempt at solving the problem (mediation-2) works off of that interpretation. Mediation-2 in Figure 5.15 shows MEDIATOR's representation of the reinterpreted problem.

```
plan: M-ONE-CUTS-OTHER-CHOOSES
   with cutter = sister1; chooser = sister2
predictions:
     if-results-ok:
         ((*INGEST* (actor sister1) (object piece1))
          (*INGEST* (actor sister2) (object piece2)))
```

FIGURE 5.13   Orange Dispute, Solution Specification

```
feedback: ((*INGEST* (actor sister1) (object piece1))
           ($BAKE (actor sister2) (object cake1)
                  (instr ($PREPARE (actor sister2) (object peel1)))))
evaluation: failure
remediation: remediation-1
  (M-FAILURE-RECOVERY isa M-PROBLEM
     problem: (M-WRONG-GOAL-INFERENCE isa M-POOR-ELAB isa
                M-MISUNDERSTANDING isa M-REASONING-FAILURE
                    actor: MEDIATOR
                    reasoning problem: MEDIATION-1)
     plan: M-USE-ACTUAL-EVENTS
     predictions: goal (sister2) = (*phys-cont* (actor sister2)
                                                (object peel2))
     feedback: nil
     evaluation: success )
next: mediation-2 )
```

FIGURE 5.14   Orange Dispute, Outcome Specification

5.3.2 CASEY: Concentrating on Situation Description and Solution, Proposition-Based Representations

CASEY (Koton 1988a, 1989) diagnoses heart problems. As input, it receives extensive information about the signs and symptoms, history, and results of lab tests performed on its patient. CASEY solves each problem and goes on to the next one, without ever receiving feedback on whether it performed well or badly.[11] It therefore did no follow-up reasoning. It concentrated on doing an exacting job of creating a solution (i.e., a diagnosis) but did not try to anticipate problems or evaluate its solutions. Its problem specifications are lists of data; its solutions are in the form of causal networks.

CASEY's representations are almost the opposite of MEDIATOR's in several dimensions. Whereas MEDIATOR's representations are very structured, CASEY's are almost free-form and use a proposition-based representation. MEDIATOR's record almost all parts of the problem; CASEY's record only the problem specification and the solution. MEDIATOR's solutions are sparse; CASEY's are quite detailed, including both the solution itself and the means by which it was computed.

A case in CASEY is a frame with three major slots in it: the problem, the solution, and a justification for the solution. The problem slot is filled with a list of propositions describing the symptoms of the patient. The solution slot is filled with a list of propositions describing the patient's diagnostic state. In general, these propositions form a causal network. Some state of the patient causes some other state, which in turn causes some symptom to appear. Or, alterna-

---

11. In fact, CASEY performed quite accurately. CASEY is one of CBR's success stories. Readers should recall that CASEY was built on top of a model-based program called the Heart Failure Program (Long et al. 1987) and performed as accurately, but several orders of magnitude faster, than its model-based colleague.

```
Mediation-2:
(M-MEDIATION isa M-PROBLEM
   problem: orange-dispute-1
          (M-PHYSICAL-DISPUTE
             characters:
                party1: sister1 isa person
                       goal: (*INGEST* (actor sister1)
                                        (object orange1))
                party2: sister2 isa person
                       goal: ($BAKE (actor sister2) (object cake1)
                                    (instr ($PREPARE
                                               (actor sister2)
                                               (object peel1))))
             arguments:
                arga: arguer: sister1
                     support: (*phys-control* (actor sister1)
                                               (object fruit1))
                argb: arguer: sister2
                     support: (*phys-control* (actor sister2)
                                               (object peel1))
             disputed-object: orange1
             goal-relationship: concord )
   plan: M-DIVIDE-AGREEABLY
        with party1 = sister1; party2 = sister2
             part1 = fruit1 ;(= fruit (orange1))
             part2 = peel1 ;(= peel (orange1))
   predictions:
      if-results-ok:
        ((*INGEST* (actor sister1) (object (fruit (orange1))))
         ($PREPARE (actor sister2) (object peel1)))
   feedback: none
   evaluation: success )
```

FIGURE 5.15 Corrected Orange Dispute

tively, some symptom provides evidence for some internal state of the patient. The justification slot shows the case the solution was derived from and the basis on which that case was retained as a good match.

Figures 5.16, 5.17, and 5.18 show parts of several of CASEY's cases. Figure 5.16 shows one of CASEY's problem descriptions: a list of patient descriptors. Figure 5.17 shows a solution to a case. It is shown in graphical form for readability. Internally it is represented using a set of propositions. Figure 5.18 shows CASEY's record of how it derived the solution shown in Figure 5.17. It records that it derived the solution from another case called Margaret and shows on what basis it justifies the match between the new case and the old one.

```
((patient-name "natalie") (age 62) (sex female)
 (dyspnea on-exertion) (orthopnea absent) (chest-pain anginal)
 (angina unstable) (syncope/near-syncope none) (palpitations none)
 (nausea/vomiting absent) (cough absent) (diaphoresis absent)
 (hemoptysis absent) (fatigue absent) (therapies none)
 (blood-pressure 146 81) (heart-rate 86) (arrhythmia-monitoring normal)
 (resp 14) (temp 98.3) (appearance anxious) (mental-status conscious)
 (jugular-pulse normal) (pulse slow-rise) (auscultation s2 murmur)
 (s2 soft-a2) (murmur systoic-ejection-murmur)
 (apex-impulse laterally-displaced) (parasternal-impulse normal)
 (chest clear-to-auscultation-and-percussion) (abdomen normal-exam)
 (extremities normal-exam) (ekg lv-strain normal-sinus)
 (cxr calcification cardiomegaly) (calcification mitral aortic-valve)
 (cardiomegaly lv))
```

FIGURE 5.16   A Problem Description in CASEY

5.3.3   CHEF: Representing a Solution Plan

CHEF's (Hammond 1989a) representations take the middle road in terms of structure: less structured than MEDIATOR but more structured than CASEY, less inclusive than MEDIATOR but more inclusive than CASEY.

CHEF's task was recipe creation, a planning task. Given the goal of creating a recipe and a set of constraints on its solution, CHEF derived a step-by-step plan (recipe) for some new dish. After creating a recipe, CHEF "tried it out in the world." That is, its simulator ran the recipe. When something didn't work (e.g., the broccoli was soggy, or the soufflé fell), CHEF attempted to explain the failure and repair the failed plan.

The description of CHEF's cycle of reasoning sounds very similar to MEDIATOR's: create a plan, try it out, receive feedback, explain any failures, and repair. Its representations, however, are quite different. MEDIATOR used its explanations to do case-based explanation. Thus, it needed to record explanations of its failures. CHEF, however, does not use its explanations to reason about later cases. Thus, it does not record them in its cases. Instead, it uses its explanations to determine how its cases should be indexed. It puts any explanatory information necessary for retrieval into the indexes but not into the cases.

Thus, the primary pieces of CHEF's case representations are their problem descriptions and their solutions. Solutions, being plans, are represented as plans. The particular plan representation CHEF uses is taken from Charniak and McDermott (1985). Objects used in the plan are separated out from the steps themselves. Plan steps refer to the objects as variables. Any particular plan shows the way the variables are bound.

Figure 5.19 shows one of CHEF's cases. The problem representation shows the constraints CHEF started with in creating this plan. The solution shows the recipe it created. The `ingredients` portion shows the objects used in the plan. They are each named and assigned a value. Although CHEF does not do this, one could also think about describing each object by function. The `actions` in the plan are also each named so that they can be referred to, and each

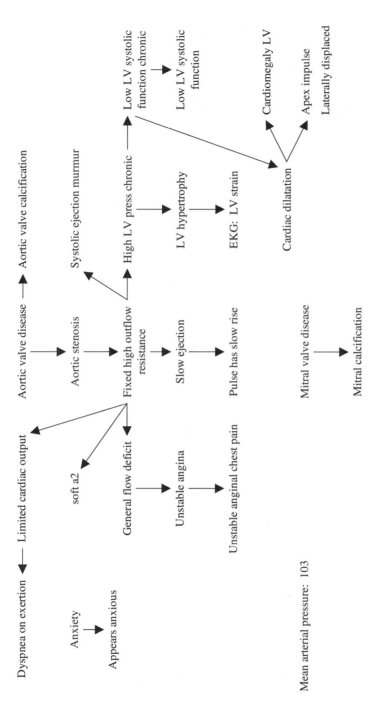

FIGURE 5.17 One of CASEY's Solutions

```
((transferred-from "margaret" node-64)
 (same-qualitative-region
   (mean-arterial-pressure:103 mean-arterial-pressure:104)
   rule: (high blood-pressure))
 (definite-cause (calcification mitral) mitral-valve-disease)
 (new-state aortic-valve-disease)
 (causes aortic-valve-disease aortic-stenosis)
 (other-evidence (pulse slow-rise) slow-ejection)
 (other-evidence (s2 soft-a2) fixed-high-outflow-resistance)
 (other-evidence (apex-impulse laterally-displaced) cardiac-dilatation)
 (other-evidence (cardiomegaly lv) cardiac-dilatation)
 (supports-existing-state (cardiomegaly lv) lv-hypertrophy)
 (no-evidence high-sympathetic-stimulation))
```

FIGURE 5.18   Justification of One of CASEY's Solutions

```
Problem:
   (include tofu)
   (taste hot)
   (style stir-fry)

Solution:
   (ingredients
      ingr1 (tofu lb .5)
      ingr2 (soy-sauce tablespoon 2)
      ingr3 (rice-wine spoon 1)
      ingr4 (cornstarch tablespoon .5)
      ingr5 (sugar spoon 1)
      ingr6 (broccoli lb 1)
      ingr7 (r-pepper piece 6))
   (actions
      act1 (chop object (ingr1) size (chunk))
      act2 (marinate object (result act1)
                    in (& (ingr2) (ingr3) (ingr4) (ingr5))
                    time (20))
      act3 (chop object (ingr6) size (chunk))
      act4 (stir-fry object (& (result act2) (ingr7))
                    time (1))
      act5 (add object (result act3) to (result act4))
      act6 (stir-fry object (result act5) time (2)))
   (style stir-fry)
```

FIGURE 5.19   One of CHEF's Cases: Broccoli with Tofu. (Hammond, 1989.)

action refers to ingredients it needs by variable name and to other actions by their names. Actions are represented in a predicate notation, but a framelike notation holds the many predicate clauses together as a unit. As we will see later, a representation that separates objects used in the solution from the solution itself allows easy reinstantiation at adaptation time.

5.3.4 JULIA and KRITIK: Representing Design Cases, Concentrating on the Solution

Like CASEY, JULIA (Hinrichs 1992; Hinrichs and Kolodner 1991) puts most of its effort into creating solutions. JULIA's domain, however, is not as well specified as CASEY's, and much of JULIA's job involves anticipating potential problems, creating on-the-fly solutions, and evaluating the solutions it creates. JULIA's task is design, and JULIA designs meals. Most of JULIA's problems are too large to be solved as a whole. Thus, JULIA solves problems by breaking them into parts. One of its tasks is to maintain the constraints that hold parts of a problem together. JULIA sometimes reasons from whole cases, but more often it makes inferences based on pieces of old cases.

Because JULIA does extensive adaptations that require knowing the basis on which old decisions were made, JULIA keeps track of why it made the decisions it made. Thus, its representations of solutions include justifications for decisions made in the course of problem solving and a recording of the inference rules and heuristics used to solve the problem. Solutions also include the constraints that tie pieces of the solution together. JULIA keeps track of justifications, inference rules, and constraints by attaching annotations to slots in its representation.

In Figure 5.20 we see a partial representation of a case from JULIA.[12] JULIA uses frames to structure its cases and divides the slots in frames into units (Hinrichs 1992) according to their functional roles. For example, it has a set of character slots, which includes the roles `eaters` and `preparers` and `servers`. `Eaters` organizes a set of slots including `host` and `guests`. Both play the `eater` role, and both have other roles associated with them as well.

Another set of slots associated with a meal is its `descriptors`, divided into `primary-descriptors` (including `cost`, `cuisine`, and `ingredients`) and `secondary-descriptors` (including `eating-config` and `ease-of-prep`). A third set is its sequence of events, designated as `events`. This set groups the parts of the meal, divided into `appetizer` course, `salad` course, `main-course`, and so on. Parts of the meal can be thought of as the component parts of the artifact being designed. They are tied together by a set of constraints that specify their relationships.

Design is an iterative process, and design of large artifacts needs to take into account decisions made about some piece of the design as formulations of other pieces are being constructed. Thus, what is a solution at one time during design becomes a part of the problem description later on. As a result, JULIA does not differentiate between problem specification slots and solution description slots. Instead it records the sources of its slot fillers. The `cuisine`

---

12. The indentation in the figure represents the assignment of slots and embedding of frames in the computer. JULIA's actual representations have a fair amount of indirection in them (e.g., justifications are themselves complex frames whose names are inserted in slots of the real representations.) The figure is meant to give the flavor of what knowledge is associated with what other knowledge in JULIA's representations. For more detail, see Hinrichs 1992.

slot, for example, is filled with AMERICAN-CUISINE. It was filled via an inference and is part of the solution. This is designated by showing its source (a memory lookup based on the constraint coming from guest GUEST2 that the food be plain [GUEST2 is a meat-and-potatoes man]). The designation of host as *JLK*, on the other hand, is part of the problem specification. Its source is the *CLIENT*. For compactness, we leave out the source in the figure when it is the CLIENT.

Special constraints on a problem derive from initial specifications, and JULIA also keeps track of where those constraints derive from. *JLKS-SISTER-IN-LAW, for example (a filler of the guests slot), is a vegetarian who is allergic to milk products, while GUEST2 is a meat-and-potatoes man. JULIA's constraint propagator gathers these initial constraints and propagates them to the remainder of the problem. Thus, we see that the dishes slot of the main-course has milk and meat and fish ruled out as ingredients, based on the fact that *JLKS-SISTER-IN-LAW designates them as constraints on her eating. The same slot has normal-tasting-foods and substantial-foods ruled in based on GUEST2's presence as a guest. Later the problem solver finds that this set of constraints overconstrain it, and it solves the problem by deciding to serve two main dishes. It partitions the constraints among its two choices, leading to the main-dishes-1 slot of the main-course designating that milk, meat, and fish are ruled out and the main-dishes-2 slot of the main-course designating that the food must be normal tasting and substantial. Similarly, the fact that we want to use tomatoes is initially recorded in the ingredients slot and propagated to the main-dishes slot of the main-course. And so on.

In addition to keeping track of the sources of its constraints, JULIA keeps track of why it made the decisions it made. We see this most clearly on several of the dish slots of the main course. GOOD-GARDEN-TOMATO-BAKE is justified by the fact that it includes tomatoes and that it is inexpensive (two of the designated constraints). It was derived by recalling the main dish of the Late-Summer-Tomatoes case and transforming it by deleting the milk products. Similarly, the decision to include two main dishes is justified by the fact that the slot was overconstrained, and the procedure for dealing with the overconstraint was increase-choice, resulting in two main dishes.

As we shall see, JULIA's careful bookkeeping helps it to determine where adaptation is needed, constrains its adaptations, and allows it to solve problems that must be solved in parts in a case-based way.

KRITIK (Goel 1989, 1991b; Goel and Chandrasekaran 1989), which is also a design problem solver, uses a different method for justifying its solutions. KRITIK designs mechanical devices and electrical circuits. Figures 5.21 and 5.22 show one of KRITIK's solutions, a a simple electronic circuit. We see the schematic of the design in the first figure and its functional description in the second.

KRITIK creates new designs by adapting old designs, making extensive reference to a causal model describing how the old design works. Thus, every design also holds a causal explanation of how its components work together to produce the indicated effect. This causal model acts as a justification for the design as a whole. While the functional representation shows how the pieces are connected to each other and shows the general effects of those con-

```
name PROBLEM-2
isa (M-MEAL)
reasoning: REFINE-MEAL-1
characters:
  eaters:
    host *JLK*
      source: *CLIENT*
    guests *JLKS-SISTER-IN-LAW* *GUEST2* *GUEST3*
setting:
  time: APRIL-11
  locale: *JLKS-HOUSE*
descriptors:
  primary-descriptors:
    cost: INEXPENSIVE-MEAL
    cuisine: AMERICAN-CUISINE
      source: memory-lookup
        justification: (prefer taste *normal-tasting*)
          source: *GUEST2*
    ingredients: TOMATO
  secondary-descriptors:
    eating-config: SITTING
    ease-of-prep: EASY
events:
      appetizer: appetizer-course
      salad: salad-course
      main: main-course
      dessert: dessert-course
main-course:
  dishes:
    constraints: (rule-out ingredients (*milk* *meat* *fish*))
                  source: *JLKS-SISTER-IN-LAW*
              (prefer taste *normal-tasting*)
                  source: *GUEST2*
              (prefer heavy-light *substantial*)
                  source: *GUEST2*
              (prefer ingredients (*fish*))
                  source: *CLIENT*
  main-dishes:
        Reasoning: Increase Choice
        Justifications: Overconstrained Ingredients Slot
    main-dishes-2: GRILLED-SALMON
      Constraints: (prefer taste *normal-tasting*)
                   (prefer ingredients (*fish*))
```

FIGURE 5.20 A Case from JULIA (continued next page)

```
  main-dishes-1: GOOD-GARDEN-TOMATO-BAKE
     Constraint : (rule-out ingredients (*milk* *meat* *fish*))
     Source: case - Late Summer Tomatoes
     Justifications: - Contains tomatoes
                     - Cost = inexpensive
                     - Host = *JLK*
     Reasoning: Transform by deleting dairy products
  side-dishes:
    veg-dish: STUFFED-GREEN-PEPPERS
    starch-dish: WILD-RICE
  beverage: WHITE-WINE
dessert-course:
  dishes: BROWNIES
  drink: MINT-TEA
 ...
```

FIGURE 5.20   (continued). (Adapted from Hinrichs, 1992.)

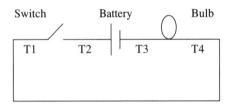

FIGURE 5.21   A Design from KRITIK

nections, the causal model shows how the underlying physics allows those effects to happen. The causal model associated with this design can be found in Figures 5.23 and 5.24. [13]

Rather than justifying each of its design decisions individually as JULIA does, KRITIK justifies its solutions as a whole by constructing a causal model that explains how the solution works. Why can KRITIK justify its solutions, while JULIA needs to justify its decisions? The answer, I believe, has three parts. First, KRITIK's problems are smaller than JULIA's. KRITIK never has reason to access or consider some piece of a solution independent of the whole. A monolithic justification supports its processing very well. JULIA would have trouble with such a justification structure unless it could easily access pieces of the justification. Second, KRITIK's solutions are entirely tied together by a well-known causal model. Any model of meal planning is necessarily incomplete, and any explanation of the decision making done to plan a meal will necessarily have holes in it. Third, KRITIK can derive a new causal model for any new design quite easily, by adapting the model from the one case it used to derive its answer. JULIA uses many cases to derive an answer; creating a one-piece causal model would

---

13. KRITIK computes causal explanations for its new designs by adapting the causal explanation of the old design. The whole process includes choosing an old case, adapting its solution to fit the new situation, verifying that solution, and then adapting the old causal explanation to create one for the newly designed object.

BEGIN FUNCTION ProduceLight RedBulbCircuit

GIVEN:

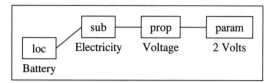

MAKES:

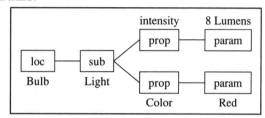

STIMULUS: Force on Switch

BY: BehaviorProduceLightRedBulbCircuit
END FUNCTION ProduceLight RedBulbCircuit

FIGURE 5.22   Representing a Design's Function in KRITIK

BEGIN BehaviorChangeModeSwitch

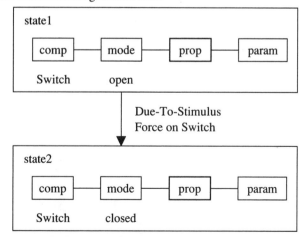

END BehaviorChangeModeSwitch

FIGURE 5.23   A Simple Causal Justification from KRITIK

BEGIN BehaviorProduceLightRedBulbCircuit

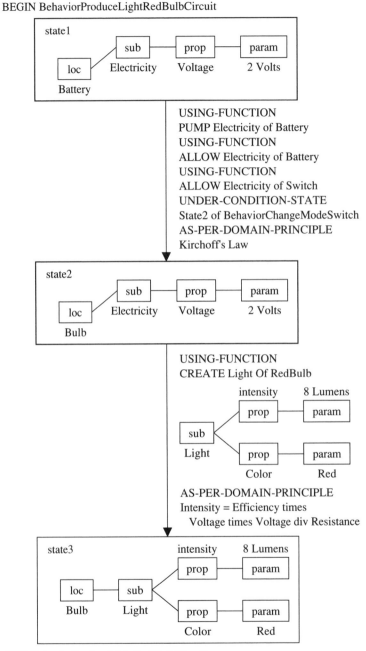

END BehaviorProduceLightRedBulbCircuit

FIGURE 5.24   A Complex Causal Justification from KRITIK

be quite hard. It is easier for JULIA to maintain its justifications on a decision-by-decision basis than to attempt to construct a unifying explanation for its solution.

Design programs are not the only ones to use causal models to justify solutions. PROTOS (Bareiss 1989a), a diagnostic program, also uses a causal model for that purpose.[14] PROTOS diagnoses hearing disorders. Like CASEY, PROTOS's specifies problems in terms of a list of descriptors of its patients. Its solutions are quite different, however. While CASEY's solutions are in terms of internal states of the patient contributing to the symptoms, PROTOS's solutions merely name the disorder the patient has. Its process of diagnosis, however, requires a knowledge-based matching procedure that determines how the symptoms of the new patient justify the diagnosis. PROTOS justifies its solutions using the results of this match.

5.3.5 HYPO's Representations: Concentrating on Situation Description

Except for MEDIATOR, most of the systems illustrated above concentrate their efforts on problem solving. The resulting representations therefore have sophisticated problem specifications and solutions but don't specify outcomes with much sophistication. HYPO (Ashley 1990), by contrast, concentrates its efforts on justifying an outcome. Its case representations are rich in the kinds of descriptors necessary for that task.

HYPO's representations concentrate on situation descriptors, never considering goals and constraints. Figure 5.4 shows one of HYPO's problem descriptions. As can be seen in that figure, the description of the situation is quite complex, including both descriptions of the agents (companies) involved in the dispute and descriptions of the general market situation, the relative advantages of each, what each did in the situation in question, what was achieved by this action, and what the claimant is requesting in its lawsuit. Outcomes in HYPO are merely the judge's ruling in a case and the basis for the opinion, but problem descriptions capture sufficient information to justify and understand the outcome so that it can be used intelligently in later reasoning.

5.3.6 Formlike Representations

The moral of the illustrations just considered is that the particular representational format used is less important than getting the content of the representations right. Experimental systems are generally written in LISP and use whatever kind of representational structure the researcher is comfortable with that also supports the processing that needs to be done. The result of implementing those experimental systems is that we can now specify what needs to go into the content of a representation.

An easier representational structure than any shown so far, and a structure that will work if one knows the content one wants to put into the cases, is a formlike representation. Such representations are reminiscent of database entries. Each case is represented by a set of fields and their values. Representations are flat, that is, there are no embedded structures.

---

14. PROTOS's models are partial models acquired from its teacher in response to problem solving failures. No attempt is made to insure the consistency of a model. Models are stored in a semantic network form.

Cognitive System's CBR Shell, now called REMIND (Cognitive Systems 1992), facilitates using formlike representations in building case-based decision aiding systems. The philosophy behind REMIND is that it acts as a memory augmenter for a human user. The human describes a problem to REMIND, and it recalls similar cases and presents them to the human user. The user reads those cases and uses them to create or criticize his or her solution.

REMIND allows three kinds of slots:

1. Input fields hold information known at the beginning of problem solving.
2. Calculated fields are derived from the input fields.
3. Output fields hold outcome information and are blank in a new case.

An example from the Battle Planner (Goodman 1989), the first substantial program written using REMIND, will illustrate. The Battle Planner takes as input a description of a battlefield situation and a description of a first-cut solution derived by the user from standard military doctrine. It derives several fields, including `strength ratio`, from its inputs. Derived or calculated fields provide additional information that unanalyzed fields cannot provide. For example, the strength ratio of an attacker and defender is more useful in predicting outcome than is the absolute number of forces each side has. Cases that are retrieved provide feedback about what has happened in situations matching that of the current battle when the proposed solution was attempted. Based on retrieved cases, the user criticizes his or her initial solution, repairs it, and repeats the process until satisfied with the solution. Figure 5.25 shows one of the Battle Planner's battles.

In addition to illustrating a form-filling representation, this case also illustrates the use of unstructured commentaries and other annotations on cases. As stated earlier, when a person is going to interact with a system, it is useful to present the output in a notation that a person can use. This case shows one way of doing that. The information shown in the text is not needed for retrieval or inference in this system. Rather, it is information that a person seeing this case could make use of. Accordingly, it is represented in a way that a person can easily use. When graphical notations are needed, they can be added to cases in a similar way. The important guideline when representing cases is that everything that the computer program must use to do its job must be in a format it can use; anything not needed by the program that will be used only by a human can be put into a representation the person can use easily.

Of course, formlike representations and textual annotations are not the only ways to make cases people-readable, and indeed, for some applications, they do not work well at all. As shown in several examples in section 5.2, some applications require more graphical presentations and others require a means of letting the user know what information or cases are available. For many simple applications, however, formlike representations have been shown to be quite useful.

5.4 ADVANCED ISSUES

In addition to the content of cases, there are a number of other issues that must be addressed with respect to case representation. When cases are very large, for example, it sometimes makes sense to subdivide them into smaller parts. In addition, problem specifications change

INPUT:

Feature	Attacker	Defender
Op. Unit	Jap 24th Div (−)	US 7th Inf Div (+)
Commander	Lt Gen Amamiya	MG Arnold
Troops	6850	15350
MBT	0	67
Lt-Tank	0	73
Artillery	60	198
Tac Air	0	175
Reserves	not a factor	
Depth	not a factor	
Force Superiority	Disadvantage	Advantage
Terrain	Rugged Mixed	
Weather	Dry Sunny temperate	

DERIVED FIELDS:

Feature	Attacker	Defender
Strength Ratio	0.45	2.24

OUTCOME:

Feature	Attacker	Defender
Victor	Win	Loss
Mission Accomplishment	7	3
Resolution	Breakthrough	Withdraw/Delay
Attrition (%/day)	0.70	18.30
Casualties	60	550
Armor Losses	10	30

Unstructured Graphics and Text Commentary (*Note: this is not the same battle as above*):

(Okinawa, World War II)
   In an attempt to strike at what the Japanese believed were seriously weakened US forces, the Japanese Okinawa defenders launched a counterattack against the US 7th Infantry Division. The Japanese attack failed largely due to massive defense artillery fire and the initiative of individual US soldiers. Japanese Banzai charges were repulsed by artillery and heavy weapons fire.

FIGURE 5.25   A Case from the Battle Planner

over time as reasoning progresses. We need to consider how to represent those changes. Finally, cases often need to be extracted from continuous environments. How do we do that extraction? We address these three representational issues in the remainder of this chapter. Overall, the answer to each question derives from the guideline given in chapter 1: If it teaches a lesson for the future, call it a case.

5.4.1 Grain Size of Cases: Monolithic Cases or Distributed Cases?

Cases come in many shapes and sizes. A case describing the design of a house, for example, may include a case of designing the outside of a house, a case of kitchen design, several cases of bathroom design, and so on. A case of curriculum planning might include several cases of lesson planning and several cases of experiment planning. A case of medical diagnosis might include a case of interpreting a particular diagnostic test and another case of planning further testing.

Our discussions so far have centered on representing individual cases. In general, cases are related to other cases along the same dimensions that relate events to each other. An event can be part of another larger event; a case can be part of another larger case. An event can be causally connected to another event; a case can be causally connected to another case. An event can be sequentially related to another event; a case can be sequentially related to another case. An event can contain smaller episodes; a case can contain other cases. It follows that large cases might *package* other cases that are related causally, sequentially, or partonomically.

In talking to people about how they use cases to solve problems and in analyzing protocols of people using cases to solve problems, it is clear that people access pieces of cases to solve problems even when a case as a whole seems far from the new case. For example, one physician I interviewed in a protocol study remembered six different case pieces in the course of solving one complex problem: one helped him evaluate the ambiguous results of a stress test, another helped him evaluate the potential for growth of the aneurism that needed treatment, another warned of the potential for problems in using a particular medical procedure he was considering, and three helped him determine if a set of symptoms that were present were important to take into account in solving the major problem. Each of these was only part of a larger case, and none of the larger cases were very good matches themselves to the new situation when taken as a whole. Mark's (1991, 1992; Mark and Schlossberg 1990) study of design and designers shows that they too use small pieces of design cases to solve new problems. As they break large design cases into smaller parts to solve them, they recall similar smaller parts of old cases that help them with design. A simple example will illustrate more concretely.

> You are planning a vegetarian Thanksgiving dinner. You can't use a traditional Thanksgiving dinner case to help you plan the main course, but you do find a festive vegetarian autumn meal with a main course menu that is almost appropriate. You are now planning the dessert course. The most useful reminding here is probably the dessert course of a traditional Thanksgiving meal. Remembering it, however, requires that access be to the dessert course itself independent of the rest of the meal. Otherwise, the "vegetarian" part

of the probe, which is inconsistent with a traditional Thanksgiving meal, might preclude reminding of a meal with a Thanksgiving dessert.

There are two requirements for enabling recall of case parts.

1. The representational scheme must make parts of cases easily accessible.
2. The indexing scheme must index case parts as if they are independent units.

If we think of pieces of cases as cases themselves, then the representational problem boils down to a means of organizing related cases in such a way that they can be accessed in clusters as needed. That is, a whole case (consisting of smaller pieces) must be as accessible as any of the parts of the case. There are two ways to do this:

1. Represent cases monolithically with large cases containing their pieces as parts. This will require, in addition, a scheme for locating appropriate case pieces within the larger case. Index the case by both its own indexes and those of its pieces.
2. Represent the pieces of large cases as cases and provide links allowing full cases to be reconstructed. Index cases and their pieces individually.

MEDIATOR represents cases using the first method. Explaining the Orange Dispute, for example, is embedded in the case of solving it (see Figures 5.12, 5.13, and 5.15). MEDIATOR locates pieces of cases within the whole case by associating access guidelines with each of its problem-solving subgoals. Its explanation subgoal, for example, knows to look in the `explanation` slot to find the case part it must use to reason.

JULIANA and CELIA use the second method. Reports about CELIA describe the representation scheme well (Redmond 1990a, 1992).

- Cases are divided into subparts, called *snippets* (Kolodner 1988).
- Each snippet represents pursual of some reasoning goal (or set of goals pursued in conjunction).
- Each snippet contains information pertaining to pursuit of its goal(s). This includes the snippet's problem description, actions taken in pursuit of its goal(s) (real actions or mental actions), and pointers to related snippets.
- Links between snippets preserve the structure of the reasoning. Each snippet is linked to the snippet for the goal that suggested it and to the snippets for the goals it suggests.
- A full case is represented by a header that holds global information about the case and a set of causally connected case snippets.
- Each snippet is independently indexed, as is the full case.

A snippet's problem description includes a pointer to the case header, the goal being pursued, and the problem-solving context surrounding pursual of the goal. The problem-solving context describes the problem solving that has gone on previous to pursuing the snippet's subgoal, including relevant subgoals that have been pursued and the results of actions taken so far. Figure 5.26 shows the contents of one snippet, and Figure 5.27 shows the snippet structure of a full case.

```
CASE-TEST-HYPOTHESIS-130

CONTEXT
Internal
  Ruled-In     (Lean (Position (Idle-Mixture-Screw)))
  Ruled-Out    (Low (Position (Idle-Speed-Screw)))
               (Lean (Position (Idle-Mixture-Screw)))
               (Incorrect (Position (Throttle-Dashpot)))
  Tests-Done-N-Results
        (Temperature Engine-System (When (Stalls Engine-System)) Cold)
           (Hot (Temperature Engine-System))
        (Stalls Engine-System)
           (Stalls Engine-System)
        (Small (Distance Throttle-Dashpot-Stem Throttle-Lever))
           (Not (Small (Distance Throttle-Dashpot-Stem Throttle- Lever)))
  Fixes-Done    (Increase (Position (Idle-Mixture-Screw)))
  Solution: NIL
  Current-Hypoth     (High (Contains Carburetor-Float-Bowl Fuel))

Global
  Complaint          (Stalls Engine-System)
  Other-Sympt        (Rough (Run Engine-System))
  Frequency          Weekly
  How-Long           2months
  Amb-Temp-@-Fail    Any
  Weath-@-Fail       Rainy
  Car-Type           (1981 Ford Granada)
  Car-Owner          Davis Cable
  Participants       Mark Graves, David Wood
  Location           Mikes-Repair-Shop
  When               2843569149

PURSUIT OF GOAL
Goal    G-TEST-HYPOTHESIS
Test    (High (Contains Carburetor-Float-Bowl Fuel))
Test-Method
        (Turn-Off Engine-System)
        (Remove Carburetor-Air-Horn-Screw)
        (Remove Carburetor-Air-Horn)
        (Ask (Level Fuel Carburetor-Float-Bowl) Scale-On-Carburetor-Float- Bowl)
Test-Tools      Screw-Driver
Test-Result     (High (Level Fuel Carburetor-Float-Bowl))

LINKAGE
Link-Down       CASE-INTERPRET-TEST-140
Link-Up         CASE-GENERATE-HYPOTHESIS-125
Prev-Hypothesis (High (Contains Carburetor-Float-Bowl Fuel))
```

FIGURE 5.26   Example Snippet from CELIA

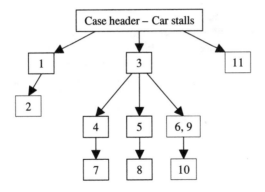

Diagnosis Actions (in order presented)

1. Hyp – Loose connected spark plug
2. Test – Loose connected spark plug (neg.)
3. Hyp – Malfunction carburetor
4. Hyp – Lean idle mixture
5. Hyp – Low idle speed
6. Hyp – High float level
7. Test – Lean idle mixture (neg.)
8. Test – Low idle speed (neg.)
9. Hyp – High float level (restate)
10. Test – High float level (neg.)
11. Hyp – Malfunction control system

FIGURE 5.27 Case Snippet Structure for a Case from CELIA

There are two major differences between the two representational schemes presented. One has to do with the process of accessing parts of cases independently of the whole. The other has to do with support of generalization. When representing cases using large cases with embedded parts, access is first to a case, then to its relevant part. To make this easy, each index to a case needs to specify which part of the case it is indexing. When representing cases as pieces, access to case pieces is more direct, but access to the case as a whole requires extra work. In choosing one scheme over the other, consideration should be given to predominant access needs: Will access usually be to whole cases or to case pieces?

While the first difference between the schemes is an efficiency issue, the second is a qualitative difference. When cases are represented in individual parts, the memory can notice similarities between parts of cases and has the potential to create generalizations about case parts. For example, a system that represents meals in pieces has the potential to make generalizations about autumn desserts, vegetarian main courses, or appetizers with cheese. It is much harder to make generalizations about similar parts of dissimilar cases in a system that represents cases as monolithic wholes.

Indeed, this is the rationale behind MOPs (Schank 1982), a predecessor of case-based reasoning. Representations using scripts (monolithic) didn't allow the reasoner to notice similarities between, for example, doctor's visits and dentist's visits. When episodes were broken down into component parts, however, it was possible to notice similarities across divergent kinds of episodes, to make generalizations about those component parts, and to use those generalizations to make predictions in new unknown situations sharing those parts. Initial approaches to case-based reasoning ignored MOPs and represented cases as monolithic wholes. As case-based reasoning is getting more sophisticated and being applied to more complex problems, however, representations implied by MOPs become more and more necessary.

We might think of snippets, then, as corresponding to scenes of MOPs. An issue that came up in representing MOPs and one that comes up in representing cases is the grain size of component parts. How do we divide a case into its snippets? CELIA divides its cases according to reasoning goals because it is a reasoner whose purpose is to learn the reasoning goals associated with diagnosis. Using reasoning subgoals as determiners of snippet grain size has advantages. Cases will be of varying sizes, and the reasoner will have cases available to help in reasoning whatever the size of the problem he or she is solving. This should not be interpreted to mean, however, that a system should represent its cases using low-level subgoals to determine the grain size of snippets. Indeed, Schank never discusses subgoals at all in proposing scenes as the components of MOPs.

More recently, as builders of case-based reasoning systems have begun to attempt to represent cases of considerable size and complexity, a consensus has been developing that cases should be divided according to the lessons they teach. This answer is, of course, related to the definition of a case given in chapter 1. If a case is a contextualized lesson, then it makes sense to divide a case into pieces that teach lessons—each of those, in fact, fits the definition of a case. As the necessity of dividing cases into component parts has been discovered, a new vocabulary for referring to cases and the lessons they teach has been derived. The word *case* is generally reserved for talking about an experience; it contains many *stories*, each of which is a retelling of the case or some piece of it that teaches a lesson or makes a point.

In general, then, what constitutes a coherent piece of a case is a pragmatic issue and depends on the reasoning the system does or supports. A system builder will have to determine the kinds of subgoals the system will have (for an automated system) or the kinds of subgoals someone using the system will have and will need help with (for an aiding system). It is these subgoals that determine what a relevant lesson is and therefore what comprises a case snippet.

We can illustrate using ARCHIE-2. As described previously, ARCHIE-2 is a case-based aiding system for an architect. In determining what was the right grain size for case pieces (called *stories* in ARCHIE-2), we looked at two different things: the kinds of subgoals architects have and the kinds of stories architects tell each other. We found that their subgoals as they did design were rather *ad hoc* and unpredictable, but that they had common topics. In particular, they center around several different things: a structural piece of a building, a functional subsystem of a building, and *design issues* (Domeshek and Kolodner 1991, 1992). We also found that the stories architects tell center on these same sorts of topics. In our current analysis, the pieces of cases that ARCHIE-2 records and presents to architects are those that tell a story about the interaction between two or more of those dimensions, for example, lighting (a functional subsystem) in the classrooms (a structural piece), security (a design issue) at the entrances (a structural piece of the building), how the accoustical system (a functional subsystem) kept noise (a design issue) to a minimum in courtrooms (a structural piece).

5.4.2 Evolving Problem Descriptions

Often the description of a problem evolves over time. JULIA, for example, may start knowing that it has to create a meal that vegetarians can eat, but it may find out only later that because someone is allergic to milk products, it cannot use milk in any of its dishes. MEDIATOR starts out assuming that the two sisters in the Orange Dispute want the orange to eat it. It later finds out one wants to bake with the peel. Problem descriptions evolve because new specifications are added late (e.g., the reasoner didn't think of them at the time the problem was originally specified), because new specifications are discovered during problem solving, because over-constraint or inability to solve the problem as described causes new specifications to be added, or because feedback during problem solving or after a solution is initially derived points out wrong assumptions that were made in initial specification.

In addition, one can think of a problem description changing naturally over time as a problem is incrementally solved. Problems that are solved in several steps inherit their partial solutions as part of the problem description. In one of JULIA's scenerios, for example, it starts by knowing that it needs to plan a meal for twenty people that should be easy to make and cheap. It decides that Italian cuisine with some sort of pasta dish would solve the problem. This partial specification of the solution now becomes part of the problem description as it attempts to refine its plan. After it decides to serve lasagne as the main dish, that too becomes part of the problem description as it searches for cases to help it solve the remainder of the problem. Knowing it is going to serve lasagne as the main dish keeps it from suggesting an additional starch dish elsewhere in the meal.

When a problem description evolves over time, which of the several descriptions should be used to describe the case? The initial description? The first embellishment? The final embellishment? All or some of the descriptions in between?

In general, implementors record new case descriptions only when there is a discrete change in the problem definition. Otherwise, problem specifications are as described in the end. In solving the Orange Dispute, for example, the problem description evolved many times.

In the beginning, all that was known was that two sisters wanted the same orange. After inference, MEDIATOR added to that description that they both wanted to eat it. After additional inference, MEDIATOR added that the two sisters' goals were in conflict. Later it added that a plan called "One cuts, the other chooses" should be used to solve the problem, and so on. Later it found that it had made a poor inference along the way and that its initial interpretation and therefore its initial solution were wrong. It reinterpreted the problem as one in which one sister wanted to bake with the peel of the orange and continued solving the problem from there.

One could think of a dozen or so different problem descriptions for this problem. MEDIATOR recorded two different problem descriptions, and each had a different solution along with it (as shown earlier). MEDIATOR's heuristic was that as long as reasoning could continue incrementally with no backup, the same problem was being solved. The problem representation it saved was the final one it had at the time it either finished or had to back up. After backup, one could consider the situation a new case requiring a different problem representation.

MEDIATOR could have decided to save just the final problem description along with its solution. But there is an advantage to saving mistaken problem descriptions: a new problem might be mistakenly described in the same way in the future. If a case with a similar problem description is found, it can point the way to a correct problem interpretation.

JULIA uses a different method. As a problem description and solution are filled in, JULIA updates it, constantly refining the problem description as it is solving the problem. JULIA saves only one problem description, but keeps track of its old decisions in the ruled-out facet of each slot. It indexes the case in multiple ways. Some indexes are derived from previous descriptions of the problem.

The advantage of saving the fully embellished problem description as the description of the case is that it is more generally applicable than any partial description could be. The key to case retrieval, after all, is partial matching. A fully embellished problem description can be partially matched in a variety of ways, making the case description applicable in a wide variety of future situations. By creating a new case with a new problem description when the problem description is qualitatively changed, MEDIATOR's method keeps solutions to different problems separate from each other. In keeping all incremental descriptions and all partial solutions as annotations on cases, no matter whether the problem is qualitatively changed or not, JULIA keeps all the same information but in a way that makes it harder to access poor solutions directly. In making a decision about which way to record cases, one must ask whether it would be helpful to access previous poor solutions individually or not.

5.4.3 Boundaries of Cases: Representing Cases in Continuous Environments

A case is a snapshot of a situation. It's easy to imagine when to take the picture when a situation has clear boundaries. In a one-shot diagnostic situation, the case is defined by the patient's symptoms (and history), the diagnostic decision, and the feedback designating success or failure. In a design situation, the case is defined by the specifications, the designed artifact, and the feedback designating how it functions in the world.

In continuous environments, however, it isn't so obvious where the cases start or end. Consider, for example, a flexible manufacturing environment. An operator sits in front of a terminal managing the process for hours at a time. Is the entire session a case, or some part of it? Which parts? How can we identify them? Battlefield planning situations are similar. A general collects information continually, refining decisions continually. What are the cases? The harried housewife's situation is the same. She may be working continuously for hours interleaving different tasks she has to do. Is the whole several-hour session the case? Is each particular thing she does a case? Which combinations of things she does are cases? The issue of case boundaries comes up even within seemingly discrete design and diagnostic situations; feedback can happen over long periods of time and continuously.

Situations in which case boundaries are not obvious are often situations in which planning and execution are interleaved. Many real-world scheduling problems, like operation of a flexible manufacturing system and housework, are like this. Many monitoring and control problems are like this too, especially the ones in which monitoring and action are interleaved. Monitoring a battlefield is an example of this, as is monitoring a nuclear power plant or a satellite, or controlling a processing plant. A processing plant controller, for example, watches to make sure that the machines are behaving as they should. When behavior begins to deviate from what's expected, the controller adjusts controls to repair the deviation. An example will make the problem concrete:

> I am operating a flexible manufacturing system over a period of three hours. During that time, I do a lot of standard scheduling things: I move items from one queue to another, from a queue to a machine, and so on. Also during that time, I run into several problems:
>
> ■ I notice that I need to gather a set of items of type X to run them through a batch process. Several of these X parts are needed right now in order that a job not be late. I solve this problem by finding all items of type X (in the queue and not yet in the queue) and sending them all through the procedures needed to get them ready for the batch process. This works, except that now another job that I thought would be on time is held up a little.
>
> ■ I notice that an important part is in the overflow buffer. I take it out and put it where it belongs, in the queue for one of the machines. I wonder how it got into the overflow buffer, and I realize that the "work in progress" queue must have overflowed. I wonder how I could have avoided that. I realize that I need to check the contents of that queue before putting items into it and to be selective in putting things into it when it is close to full.

The session is made up of many actions, miniplans, and decisions, some related and some not. Out of these, two stand out. In the first, I grab an unforeseen opportunity and learn a pitfall of the procedure I employ. In the second, I notice a problem, fix it, and figure out how to avoid it in the future. Where is the case(s)? Is the big situation a case? What about each of the two marked ones? What about any of the rest of the episode?

Treating the three-hour session as one big case seems infeasible for several reasons. First, as explained above, the chunks are too big to allow the reasoner to extract interesting generalizations or trends. Second, what kind of useful problem description could we create for the entire three-hour episode? The situation changes over time, and no one description is useful for predicting access to the many smaller episodes lurking inside. The problem discussed above comes up here: which problem descriptions are the ones to use in describing the episode. The problem is different here, however, because the big episode cannot be specified very well independently of its parts—many of its parts relate to each other only on the basis of happening at the same time. There is no big problem to be solved subsuming the entire episode. Third, the entire episode holds a lot of unorganized information in it. Even if we were able to index it well enough so that the episode could be accessed appropriately, it might be hard to find any of the smaller episodes buried in it in any organized way.

One way to represent situations like this is to identify a set of discrete cases within the larger episode and to record each of those. There are two reasons one might want to create a case: when there is some lesson that can be learned from the situation and when it confirms, lends credence to, or denies some hypothesis made previously (also teaching a lesson). This happens under the following circumstances:

- An expectation fails, and the unexpected consequences are meaningful to the situation.
- An expectation fails, is fixed, and then is explained.
- Serendipity is noticed.
- A situation matches the predictive part of a hypothesis.
- Old solutions are combined in ways that haven't been done before.

Going back to the example, this definition yields an answer to the question, Where are the cases? Both marked pieces of the episode should be recorded as cases. In both, an expectation fails, is fixed, and is then explained. In both, something is learned. In the first, a pitfall of a procedure is learned. In the second, a method of avoiding a problem is learned. What about the whole episode? Is it a case? Only if the situation as a whole has a lesson to teach or affects some hypothesis. Are there any other pieces of the episode that should be recorded as cases? Any pieces that fit the definition should be recorded. For example, if during the episode, the operator discovers a new way of moving something from a queue to a machine, a case should be recorded.

Another way of summarizing what the cases are is to say that cases are states of the world that give guidance in doing the tasks that the reasoning system has to do. That is, a case exists when there is something important to record. Recognizing the beginning of a case is an opportunistic process guided by failed expectations.

Once a case is recognized, of course, all the necessary case components must be pulled out of the whole big situation. Whether done automatically or by hand, a record of the entire continuous process needs to be kept to allow this to happen.

Although many continuous situations seem appropriate for case-based reasoning, there has been little work done in this area. The major work is an experimental system called NETRAC being built by GTE (Kopeikina et al. 1988; Brandau, Lemmon, and LaFond 1991) to control telephone switching. So that the computer doesn't have to automatically determine where the boundaries of cases are, they keep the entire record of an episode but index its parts. Case representations are quite complex. In general, the problem of automatically determining case boundaries is hard and has not been addressed. However, in many situations, a person can easily identify case boundaries and the parts of the continuing situation that belong in the case record.

5.5 SUMMARY

Cases have three component parts: a situation or problem description, a solution, and an outcome. The situation description records the state of the world at the time the case was taking place, and if appropriate, what problem needed solving at that time. The solution records the solution to the problem specified in the problem description. The outcome records the resulting state of the world after the solution was carried out.

Cases do not always record all these things. Cases that include a problem and solution can be used in deriving solutions to new problems. Those with situation description and outcome can be used in evaluating new situations. A case with all three components can be used, in addition, for evaluating proposed solutions and anticipating potential problems before they occur.

Cases might record more or less detail in each of these components. In general, a case is as useful in later reasoning as the information it holds. The more *relevant* types of information it holds in it, the more different kinds of inference a case will support. For example, there are several represented in an outcome. With execution feedback only, a case-based reasoner can anticipate potential problems and project the outcome of new solutions. If, in addition, the case includes an explanation of why its outcome came about and the way in which it was repaired, the case can also provide guidance in repairing a similar failure in the future.

Cases can be represented in a variety of different forms on the computer. Programs have been built using propositional representations, frame representations, formlike representations, and combinations of the three. What is important is that the form of the representation be appropriate for the reasoning that needs to be done. Portions of cases that the machine will use to reason need to be represented in a way that enables that reasoning. Portions of cases that people will use to reason with should be presented in a form that a person can easily interact with.

A number of advanced issues come up in building case-based systems with complex cases. Some cases are very large (e.g., the case of designing a building) and need to be broken into smaller pieces. Our guideline for doing this is to consider for each case what lessons it teaches and to consider the large case a collection of these lessons (variously called snippets and stories by different implementors). One can find all the lessons a case has to teach by considering the subgoals the reasoner had to consider in solving the problem and looking for the advice the case has to give for each of those subgoals. In continuous situations, it is difficult to recognize the boundaries of cases. For those situations, individual cases are recognized for each lesson the situation has to teach, and whichever parts of a situation contribute to the lesson it teaches belong in the representation of the case. Problem representations change over time, and we must know when to treat the case as several cases. The suggestion made is that cases be broken into several cases when the reasoning to solve the problem becomes discontinuous, that is, when an expectation failure changes the course of reasoning and the reasoner must, in essence, back up to some previous understanding of the situation and continue from there.

The discussion of advanced issues was somewhat abstract and perhaps hard to follow by those who have not yet built a case-based system. Parts of that section will become more clear in later chapters of this book and as one gets experience building case-based systems. This is a section to return to when problems of using complex cases arise.

A major issue with respect to representing cases has not been addressed in this chapter: the choice of vocabulary items for describing situations, their solutions, and their outcomes. This issue is addressed in the next chapter, in the context of choosing a vocabulary for indexing.

6

Indexing Vocabulary

The biggest issue in case-based reasoning is retrieval of appropriate cases. How do people remember the right ones at the right times? How can we make the computer do the same (or better)? As we stated earlier, we call this problem the **indexing problem**. The indexing problem has several parts. First is the problem of assigning labels to cases at the time that they are entered into the case library to ensure that they can be retrieved at appropriate times. In general, these labels designate under what circumstances the case might have a lesson to teach, and therefore when it is likely to be useful. They are used at retrieval time to judge the appropriateness of an old case to a new situation. Second is the problem of organizing cases so that search through the case library can be done efficiently and accurately. Related, of course, is the problem of retrieval algorithms themselves. In this chapter and the next, we concentrate on the first problem, that of assigning labels to cases to designate the situations in which they are likely to be useful.

On first thought, the indexing problem seems fairly easy. After all, indexers have been writing indexes for books and indexing books in card catalogs for many years. They seem to have a standard method—so what makes the problem hard?

There are several answers. First, many indexers don't do a very good job. There don't seem to be very good guidelines for choosing indexes that universally give good results. The goodness of indexes in books seems to depend on the good sense and expertise of the person doing the indexing. The better the indexer understands the domain, the better the index tends to be. If, in addition, the indexer understands the tasks the user will be engaged in when using the index, the index will tend to be even better. Second, we want to be able to automate the index-selection process. To do that, we need to be very specific about what makes a good index and how to choose them.

One of my recent experiences can be used to illustrate the complexities of choosing good indexes. I returned from Spain, where I had tasted a Spanish version of hot chocolate that I wanted to make for my kids. Soon after my return, I had found a recipe in one of my cookbooks, but I had never made it. Now I was looking for the recipe again. I knew which cookbook it was in, but I had a lot of trouble locating it in there. I looked in the index under "Spanish cuisine." It wasn't listed there. I looked under "chocolate." It wasn't listed there either. I looked in the chapter called "Spanish Specialties." It wasn't there either. I looked for a chapter called "Drinks" or "Beverages" and couldn't find one. I finally looked in the index under "hot chocolate" and found it. I turned to the page, found that it was called "Castillian hot chocolate," and found that it was in the desserts chapter. Being interested in indexing, I wondered whether I could have found it had I remembered its name. So I looked in the index; that wouldn't have helped—it wasn't listed that way either. It was, however, listed as a chocolate dessert (dessert, chocolate).

What was wrong with the index to this book is that it didn't anticipate the circumstances under which someone might be searching for this recipe. It was listed as "hot chocolate" and as a dessert, but it was not listed as a beverage or as a Spanish dish. The indexers did not anticipate that someone might have wanted to find a Spanish way of making a hot chocolate drink, one that is quite different from the common American hot chocolate, and that therefore might not be thought of as hot chocolate. Nor did they anticipate that someone might want to look it up under its Spanish name—chocolaté. In Spain, it is a beverage, drunk for breakfast, not a dessert, yet the indexers listed it only as a dessert and neglected to anticipate that someone might want to look it up based on the function it serves in its native Spain. They didn't anticipate that someone might have some chocolate around and want to find recipes that used chocolate. The indexers of the book were depending on the person who wanted to find the recipe to generate the American name for it (hot chocolate) or to think of it as a dessert rather than as a beverage.

There are several indexing issues being illustrated here:

■ Indexing has to anticipate the vocabulary a retriever might use.

In indexing the Castillian hot chocolate as "hot chocolate," the indexers began to do this, but in the end they didn't follow through. They didn't think that a retriever might want to access it based on its foreign name—chocolaté.

■ Indexing has to be by concepts that are normally used to describe the items being indexed, whether they are surface features or something more abstract.

Hot chocolate is a beverage, and this particular version of it is specific to Spanish or Castillian cuisine. Both of these are normal descriptors of the dish and should have been used for indexing. It is anticipated that Americans, the readers of the book, will use it as a dessert, and indexing it by this concept (as the indexer did) makes sense but is not enough.

- Indexing has to anticipate the circumstances in which a retriever is likely to want to retrieve something (i.e., the task context in which it will be retrieved) and the descriptors the retriever is likely to have available to describe the item he or she or it wants to retrieve.

There are several tasks the retriever might be engaged in in looking up this recipe. The retriever might be looking for a way to use chocolate, might be looking for a chocolate beverage, might be looking for a chocolate dessert, might be looking for a Spanish beverage, and so on. In indexing this dish only by its American counterpart (hot chocolate) and the fact that it is a chocolate dessert, the indexers severely restrict the circumstances in which it is easy to access this recipe.

The point here is that indexes represent an *interpretation* of a situation, one that takes into account the way someone might think about that situation and the circumstances in which he or she might want to remember it. Indexing items this way allows a retriever to retrieve the most useful cases even though they may not be described by the same surface descriptors. In the cookbook example, this meant retrieving something described as a dessert when the retriever had a beverage in mind.

In chapter 1, I gave another example of retrieval based on features other than surface ones. I said that even though football and chess are quite different, we might expect someone who knows chess well to notice a fork opportunity in a football game. Given that chess and football share few surface descriptors, how could this happen? Both football and chess are competitive games. As competitive games, they share many abstract features. Each side is attempting to beat the other by setting up situations in which the other team is at a disadvantage. It is these abstract features that might be similar across such different activities. If all the chess expert noticed about the football game were its surface features (two teams, a funny-shaped ball, a field of a certain size and shape, and so on), we would never expect him or her to notice similarity to a game of chess. It is because the expert is able to describe football along more abstract dimensions that the similarity can be noticed. In this case, the similarities are that both are competitive games and in both cases, one team is positioned such that the other team can respond in either of two ways; whichever way is chosen leaves an opening for the first team. Sometimes cases need to be judged similar even though they share few surface features, so retrieval and matching procedures must do their work based on more than just surface features.

In fact, sometimes similarity of surface features should be ignored in favor of similarity across more useful descriptors. Owens (Owens 1989b) gives an example of that. A shop scheduler is trying to expedite the production of a particular part by having two machines work on it at the same time. He has many cases available to provide guidance:

- Some in which he had successfully or unsuccessfully tried to speed up production
- Some in which he had tried to use those two machines together
- Some involving the manufacture of exactly that type of part on the same day of the week while it was the same temperature outside

Let us assume that outside temperature and day of the week have little to do with this particular production procedure. Given this assumption, even though the cases in the third set have many facts in common with the current situation, they are not as likely to provide good advice in the new situation as those from the first two sets. The difference is that those in the first two sets share a common purpose with the new situation.

There are several points to be made by these examples. The first is that *features to be used as indexes must be chosen carefully if the most useful cases are to be recalled from the case library.* Choosing indexes according to surface features that are easy to extract from a case may be less useful than indexing by complex combinations and compositions of features that distinguish cases from each other by the lessons they can teach or by the purposes they fulfill. Though such features require computational effort to derive, indexing by these features makes cases appropriately accessible and allows the retriever to retrieve useful cases. Indexing by such "deep" features is particularly important when a case can be used across domains, allowing it to be recalled under quite diverse circumstances. To allow this to happen, domains, tasks, and cases must be analyzed to determine which concepts should most appropriately be used for description. These concepts make up the indexing and representational vocabulary.

Second and related to my first point, *the features of a case that are useful as indexes often go beyond the surface features of the case*. The fact that a speedup of production is being attempted or that two machines are being used at the same time are not surface features of a description of a shop. Yet they are more useful in retrieving cases than are the surface features (part x is on machine y, the temperature in the shop is z, the day is Tuesday, and so on) under at least some circumstances. Similarly, the plans, goals, and tactics of a chess player or a football coach may not be part of the surface representation of the situation, but they are important descriptors of the situation that allow cross-contextual or out-of-context remindings. The implication here is that *choice of good indexes may require an interpretation or elaboration process during which the interesting functional features of a situation are derived.* Indexes are chosen from that set.

Our examples thus show that there are two parts to the problem of choosing indexes. First, we need to find out which ways of describing or representing a case are the right ones to use so that cases can be compared with each other along appropriate dimensions. That is, tasks and domains must be analyzed to find the functionally relevant descriptors that should be used to describe and index cases. We call these descriptors the **indexing vocabulary**.

Interesting to consider here is where the indexing vocabulary comes from. To the extent that cases are represented symbolically, a case's indexes are a subset of the case's description or representation. Thus, *index vocabulary is a subset of the vocabulary used for full symbolic representations of cases.*[1]

---

1. This being claimed, however, it is important to keep in mind that symbolic representations of the full contents of cases are necessary only to the extent that the reasoner needs to reason about the cases. Fully automated case-based reasoners, of course, need full representations of their cases so that they can adapt them and/or use them for evaluation. Retrieval-only case-based systems, such as those embedded in aiding systems, browsing systems, and tutoring systems, however, often do not need to represent the contents of their cases symbolically, but only need to represent each case's indexes, the part of the case description needed for retrieval.

Thus, in specifying guidelines for choosing a vocabulary for indexes, we are also providing guidelines for choosing a vocabulary for describing or representing cases. The previous chapter described the types of information that must be represented in cases. The discussion of vocabulary in this chapter gives guidelines for choosing the dimensions and symbols (slots and fillers) for symbolically representing those aspects of a case.

Second, for any particular case, we need to be able to designate which parts of its description, or which of its features, should act as its indexes. For any particular case, we need to be able to assign labels that designate the situations in which that case could appropriately teach a lesson. This process is called **index assignment** or index selection. Indexing vocabulary tells us what sorts of descriptors should be used for some class of cases. Index assignment is the process of choosing identifying descriptors for a particular case.

Research on indexing over the past decade has led us to conclude that good indexes are features and combinations of features that distinguish a case from other cases because they are predictive of something important in that case. Put another way, indexes are those combinations of features of a case that describe the circumstances in which a reasoner might find the case useful during reasoning. Indexes might be those combinations of features of the case that were responsible for failure or the features that were responsible for success. Cases recalled because the features responsible for failure are matched in the new situation can be used to help a reasoner anticipate and avoid problems that happened in the past or help the reasoner to critique a solution. Cases recalled because features responsible for its good solution are matched in the new situation are helpful in suggesting solutions to new cases.

Notice that this is a functional and pragmatic approach to the issue of indexing. We look at the tasks a case might be used for (e.g., suggesting a solution, anticipating a failure) and choose as indexes those of its features that describe when it can be useful for each task. This is a fundamentally different approach to indexing than has been taken traditionally in information retrieval and database work. In those conceptions of indexing, features chosen as indexes, that is, those that produce the branches in the organizational structure, have been the ones that divide the set into partitions of approximately equal size. The ideal is to keep the organizational structures balanced. A feature is a good discriminator if it helps balance the organizational structure. In our conception of the problem, by contrast, we require distinguishing features to distinguish cases from each other for some purpose. We are not concerned with balancing the organizational structure. Rather, we are concerned with cutting it up into conceptually useful pieces.

Analysis of remindings coupled with experience in building case-based reasoning systems has led the CBR community to propose several guidelines for choosing indexes for particular cases:

- Indexes should be predictive.
- Predictions that can be made should be useful ones, that is, they should address the purposes the case will be used for.
- Indexes should be abstract enough to make a case useful in a variety of future situations.
- Indexes should be concrete enough to be easily recognizable in future situations.

Application of these guidelines results in indexes being selected that differentiate cases from each other in useful ways, making it possible for a retriever to retrieve cases appropriate to a new situation.

In this chapter, we begin by discussing the qualities of good indexes, then use the rest of the chapter to discuss indexing vocabulary. We begin that discussion by looking at breadth and specificity issues related to indexing vocabulary, then present a cross-domain indexing vocabulary that has been used extensively in experimental systems, and then consider the broader vocabulary lessons it teaches. In the next chapter, we cover index assignment, presenting computational methods for selecting those aspects of a case's description that belong in its indexes. In chapters 8, 9, and 10, we continue the discussion of indexing by exploring the relationship between indexes and retrieval algorithms. In those chapters, the roles indexes play in the retrieval process and the ways they can be implemented are made more concrete.

6.1 QUALITIES OF GOOD INDEXES

Good indexes are predictive, and the predictions they make should be useful ones. Good indexes are abstract enough to provide coverage but concrete enough to be recognizable. The vocabulary used for indexes must allow those descriptors that make good indexes to be represented. In this section, we discuss in more detail what each of these qualities means.

6.1.1 Predictive Features

We begin by explaining what *predictive* means. As explained in chapter 5, at the most basic level, a case is a description of a problem, an attempted solution, and the outcome of carrying out the solution. Some aspects of the case were taken into account in coming up with the solution and were responsible for choices made about the solution. Other aspects were responsible for parts of the outcome. Aspects of the case that were taken into account in coming up with a solution are predictive of the part of the solution they suggested. Aspects of the case that were responsible for its outcome are predictive of its outcome. Because aspects of a case are represented as descriptors of the case, we can define predictive features as *those combinations of descriptors of a case that were responsible for solving it the way it was solved and those combinations that influenced its outcome.*

Some examples will illustrate. First we consider a meal that was a failure because some guest, a vegetarian, could not eat the main dish, which was meat. The combination of descriptors, *guest was a vegetarian* and *meat was an ingredient in the main dish*, were responsible for the failure. If we see that combination of descriptors again in a meal we are planning, we can predict the same failure (the vegetarian won't be able to eat the main dish). They are predictive of a particular outcome.

Predictive descriptors can also predict better-than-expected outcomes. Consider a cook who decided to try a new recipe that included a combination of novel ingredients, for example, peanut butter, ginger, and eggplant. She might have been leery of the result but willing to take a chance. The dish turned out to be quite good; eggplant, peanut butter, and ginger complemented one another well. This combination of descriptors, *peanut butter is an ingredient, gin-*

ger is an ingredient and *eggplant is an ingredient*, were responsible for a successful outcome, the tasty dish. If a dish with this combination of descriptors is being considered again, this case can be used to predict that it will be tasty. Alternatively, if these ingredients are available again, this case can be used to suggest a dish that combines them.

Two more examples will complete the illustration. Consider now a patient who had a novel set of symptoms. The doctor considered many different diagnoses and tried many different treatments before finally figuring out what the combination of disorders was and what treatment was effective. The combination of symptoms, which are both responsible for the difficulty in reasoning and predict a diagnosis and treatment, are a good index. Finally, consider a legal decision that was determined by a loophole. Those features of the case that enabled the loophole are the predictive ones. They allowed the loophole to be used in this case and, if seen again, predict that the loophole can again be used.

Predictive features are found by a *post hoc* analysis that takes into account the best available theory of causality. Before a case is experienced, one cannot know which of its features are predictive ones. It is only after it has been experienced that one can analyze what went into understanding the experience or solving the problem and determine which of its features and feature combinations were the predictive ones. Chapter 7 presents two approaches to choosing indexes by *post hoc* analysis—one requires analysis of each individual case; another depends on an analysis of the domain.

6.1.2 Abstractness of Indexes

Although cases are specific, indexes to cases need to be chosen so that the case can be used in as broad a collection of situations as appropriate. As stated earlier, that often means that indexes should be more abstract than the details of a particular case. Consider, for example, a case from CHEF. CHEF has just created a recipe for beef and broccoli, a stir-fried dish. When it first created the recipe and tried it out, it found that the broccoli got soggy. It fixed the order of the steps in the recipe so that the broccoli remained crisp. There are several ways this case could be indexed, among them the following:

- *Dish is prepared by stir-frying*, *dish includes beef*, and *dish includes broccoli*
- *Dish is prepared by stir-frying*, *dish includes meat*, and *dish includes a crisp vegetable*

The first set will allow this case to be recalled whenever beef and broccoli are to be stir-fried together. This index, however, would not be able to distinguish whether this case or some other involving another protein and vegetable is a better partial match when attempting to stir-fry chicken and snow peas. A reasoner that recalled both this recipe and one for tofu with spinach based on indexes specifying ingredients only would have a difficult time determining that the beef and broccoli recipe is more applicable—because its vegetable, like the snow peas, is crisp. Indexing the case according to an abstract description that captures what is important about the case (the second set of descriptions) allows a retriever to focus immediately on the features of a case that point out its applicability. These descriptors point out the **range of applicability** of the case and make the case **generally applicable**.

6.1.3 Concreteness of Indexes

The danger of abstract indexes is that they can be so abstract that only through extensive inference would the reasoner ever realize that a new situation had those descriptors. Thus, *while indexes need to be generally applicable, they need to be concrete enough so that they can be recognized with little inference.* Consider another example from CHEF to illustrate this. CHEF has just created a new recipe for a strawberry soufflé. It created this dish by adapting a recipe for vanilla soufflé. When it first made the soufflé, it fell. CHEF figured out the problem—that the liquids and leavening were not balanced; there was too much liquid for the amount of leavening in the recipe. It also figured out that the extra liquid was due to the juice in the strawberries. It solved the problem by increasing the leavening to counter the effect of the liquid in the strawberries. There are many ways this case could be indexed, among them the following:

- *Dish is of type soufflé* and *liquids and leavening are not balanced*
- *Dish is of type soufflé* and *dish includes strawberries*
- *Dish is of type soufflé* and *dish includes fruit*
- *Dish is of type soufflé* and *dish has a lot of liquid*

The last three are clearly better indexes than the first because their features are recognizable directly without inference. The last is okay but probably not quite as good as the middle two because it is hard to tell the difference between too much liquid and the right amount. The middle two are most concrete and recognizable, and of them, the third, which mentions fruit rather than strawberries, is more generally applicable.

6.1.4 Usefulness of Indexes

A final consideration in choosing indexes is the criterion of **usefulness**. *Indexes should be chosen to make the kinds of predictions that will be useful in later reasoning.* In general, any issue that came up in solving one problem could come up again in another one. A case can be useful in giving guidance about any reasoning issues that came up in solving it. And it can be useful in predicting outcome along any dimensions of its outcome that are unusual. Thus, each of the combinations of its descriptors that describe the circumstances in which it can give useful guidance are useful as indexes.

In practice, however, a particular case-based reasoner or decision aider will make or guide only some subset of decisions that must be made. Thus, *useful indexes are those that label a case as being able to give guidance about the decisions that reasoner deals with.*

We have distinguished five kinds of reasoning decisions that case-based reasoners are often called on to make: solution generation, anticipation of potential problems, explanation of reasoning errors and failures, recovery from reasoning errors and failures, and evaluation of proposed solutions. Analysis of the kinds of indexes that are useful in retrieving cases to support making these kinds of decisions leads to the following three guidelines for choosing indexes useful for the different reasoning goals the reasoner is called on to do or support (Kolodner 1989).

■ To use cases to help generate solutions to problems, index on combinations of descriptors responsible for choice of a particular solution, solution component, or solution method.

■ Index on descriptors responsible for failures in order to make the case useful for

☐ Anticipating potential problems

☐ Explaining reasoning errors and failures

☐ Recovering from reasoning errors and failures

■ To use cases for evaluating proposed solutions, index on combinations of case descriptors that were responsible for each case's outcome *and* on combinations of descriptors that describe outcomes.

We illustrate each in turn.

Consider first a reasoner that must choose a means of achieving its goals, a type of solution generation problem. Indexing cases by goal-constraint-feature combinations that were responsible for selecting a particular means of achieving its goal will allow the reasoner to use cases to suggest means of achieving its goals. Recall the tomato tart meal presented in chapter 1. Several goals were achieved in its solution: the reasoner chose a main dish that fit its constraints, and it figured out how to adapt a dish with milk products for a guest allergic to milk. It should thus be indexed two ways using the first guideline:

> Goal: choose a main dish
> > Constrained by: dish should not include meat or poultry or fish; dish should be easy to make
> > Other features: tomatoes are available
> Goal: adapt a dish
> > Constrained by: dish should not include milk products
> > Other features: dish has cheese as an ingredient

The first will help the reasoner generate a solution when it needs to choose a main dish that is vegetarian and easy to make. The second will help the reasoner adapt a dish with cheese when milk products are ruled out.

An example from CHEF illustrates the second guideline. Recall that the first time CHEF makes beef and broccoli, the broccoli gets soggy because it is cooked along with a meat that requires a relatively long cooking time. CHEF analyzes what went wrong and repairs this recipe. The descriptors responsible for the failure are that meat and a crisp vegetable were being stir-fried together. Indexing by the combination of these features (cooking method is stir-fry; meat is an ingredient; a crisp vegetable is an ingredient) allows CHEF to recall this case whenever it is stir-frying a crisp vegetable and a meat, letting it anticipate that the vegetables might get soggy and suggesting the repaired plan that cooks them separately as a solution. CHEF can also recall this case when it is trying to explain why some vegetable stir-fried with meat got soggy. This case allows it to explain that the vegetable got soggy because it was cooked along with the longer-cooking meat. It also provides a means of fixing the new recipe—by separating the cooking of the two ingredients and merging them together only at the end, as was done in repairing the beef and broccoli recipe.

An illustration of the third guideline comes again from the opening example in chapter 1. Recall that that reasoner remembered a case where Anne came to dinner and grilled fish was served. Anne didn't eat the fish, and hotdogs were put on the grill at the last minute. What was responsible for the failure in this case was that Anne was a guest and fish was served. Indexing on this combination of features allowed the reasoner to use this case in its evaluation of its new solution. Because in the new case, too, Anne is a guest and fish is being served, this case is recalled, suggesting that the same outcome will recur.

Because a single case might be useful for a variety of purposes, it makes sense here to mention a natural implication of these guidelines: *A case may have several indexes associated with it, each representing a description of a different type of situation in which it might be useful.* Consider again the strawberry soufflé example. Analyzing it again based on the criteria of usefulness, the first descriptor feature set (including *liquids and leavening are not balanced*) would be a good index in a system that helps a person to determine how to recover from its failures and knows how to assign blame for failures when they occur. If the same system helps with the creation of solutions, the third descriptor set (including *dish includes fruit*) is also a good index.

6.2 CHOOSING VOCABULARY

We know that indexes should be predictive, useful, generally applicable, and recognizable. We know that each case should have an index describing each type of situation in which it has the potential to be applicable. The discussion of index qualities provides a first cut at helping us understand what a vocabulary for representing indexes has to cover. Its most important lesson is that we need our vocabulary to cover relevant similarities rather than just surface features. We ensure that by focusing indexing on the relevant features of a case, that is, those features and sets of features that, if encountered again, can predict something useful about some new situation. Sometimes such features are the surface features of the cases, but other times they correspond to more abstract, deeper descriptors. Missing, however, are concrete guidelines for the content of indexes.

Any vocabulary for representation has two parts to it: a set of dimensions that the vocabulary covers and a set of symbols representing the values that comprise the description of that dimension. One can think of these as the slots and fillers of a frame representation or the predicates and arguments in a first-order predicate calculus representation. Thinking simply about the problem, then, we can think of choosing vocabulary as choosing slots for a frame representation and symbols and symbol structures to use as fillers for those slots.

The discussion in chapter 5 already gives us some guidelines for doing this. We know that a case is represented by its situation description, its solution, and its outcome. Because indexes are chosen from a case's description, we know the kinds of things that must be represented by an indexing vocabulary.

But that discussion doesn't tell us anything specific about which dimensions to use for representation, which symbols to use, or what level of detail the representation should be at.

Of all the possible ways of describing a case's situation, solution, and outcome, which are the ones that ought to be used?

There are two sets of materials that can be examined to determine this.

1. **The functional approach:** We examine a corpus of available cases and the tasks that must be supported, looking at what each case can be used for and the ways it needs to be described to make it available.

2. **The reminding approach:** We examine the kinds of remindings that are natural among human experts who do the designated task, looking for relevant similarities between new situations the experts are put in and the cases they are reminded of, to find out which kinds of descriptors are the important ones for judging similarity and in what circumstances.

The results of either of these analyses will tell us what dimensions are the important ones to focus on, the range of values each can take on, and the level of detail that is advantageous in a representation.

This analysis is done keeping three things in mind:

1. The range of tasks the case-based reasoner is responsible for
2. The range of cases available to support those tasks
3. The degree and directions in which the system will be expanded in the future

The first allows us to constrain the vocabulary to only what is needed for the designated tasks. The second acts to both constrain and broaden. If only cases from a particular domain are available, it tells us to constrain the vocabulary to cover only the domain. If cases that are available span domains, it tells us that dimensions and vocabulary must be chosen to be more generally applicable. The third warns us that if we make the choice of index vocabulary too narrow to begin with, then we may not be able to easily expand a system later.

The bottom line in choosing indexing vocabulary is this: *Indexing vocabulary must capture those dimensions of the domain that need to be captured for reminding that is useful.* The level of detail required in symbols used for representation is determined by how specifically similar cases must be to provide credible advice.

This is pragmatic advice that follows from the qualities of indexes presented earlier: Indexes should allow useful remindings. If we can determine, for any domain and task, the dimensions that are useful for judging similarity, then we know what dimensions the vocabulary must cover. When we determine how detailed and how specifically applicable advice from cases needs to be to adequately cover the assigned tasks, we can determine the level of detail that must be captured in the symbols representing values for each dimension. How to do this will be the task in the rest of this section. Discussion begins by looking at the coverage a vocabulary has to provide and continues with presentation of the functional methodology for determining the dimensions that an indexing vocabulary for a particular task and domain needs to capture.

It would be worthwhile, before launching into discussions of vocabulary, however, to give a warning. Coming up with a complete and correct set of dimensions and vocabulary terms that is efficient in terms of matching, covers everything, and is adequately expressive is a monstrous, if not impossible, task. Just when a domain has been analyzed almost in its entirety, a counter example might be discovered that shows a fault in the vocabulary. There is no way to ensure against that and no way to prove that the vocabulary is right. Nevertheless, there is a need in any system for a vocabulary that works. The spirit of vocabulary-definition endeavors needs to be to propose a vocabulary that *works most of the time*. It should make intuitive sense, provide reasonable coverage, be reasonably expressive, and support a large number of remindings. The more the vocabulary can cover, the better it is, but there is no way to show that it is correct other than to use it in large working programs.

The methods and vocabularies presented throughout the rest of this chapter should be interpreted and evaluated keeping this warning in mind. There may be ways to make methods and vocabularies better, and every implementor who has a better way should use it. The name of the game, however, is to analyze available cases to come up with a manageable set of symbols, each of which carries discernible and differentiable meaning with it, and to use it across large numbers of cases.

6.2.1 Determining Coverage

Figuring out which dimensions of a domain should be covered in a vocabulary and which symbols should be used to represent values in those dimensions requires examining two things:

- A representative corpus of available cases
- The range of tasks that those cases are being asked to perform

Given a range of cases that a case-based reasoner has available and a description of the situations in which the case-based reasoner will be expected to perform, the vocabulary used for indexing should allow the reasoner to recall useful cases.

Without going into the specifics of vocabulary, an example will illustrate how the task of the reasoner and the available cases determine the needs of a vocabulary. Let us assume that we are creating a system to play chess. The tasks it is responsible for are determining strategy and, based on that strategy, choosing moves. Only chess games are available as cases. We might examine a set of chess games to determine how to index. Upon examination, we find that determining strategy or moves requires indexing board positions according to positions of several of the important pieces, positions of one side's important pieces with respect to the other side's pieces, positions of pieces that can counter the other side's important pieces, and relative positions of pieces that work together. In addition, we find that determining strategy requires indexing sequences of boards according to the strategic plans they carry out, the conditions for carrying out those plans (in terms of both strategic advantage and board position), and so on. If the only cases that are available are chess cases and the only two tasks the system will ever be asked to carry out are strategic planning and move selection in a chess game, then one would use this analysis to choose dimensions for representation. One might have a dimension representing the position of each piece, a dimension representing strategic position, a dimension representing groupings of pieces, and so on. In other words, the dimensions and symbols used for representation are those used to describe chess games in chess terms.

Now, let us assume that we want to create a system with the task of planning strategy for two-sided competitive games. A wide range of cases are available, covering several games. Moreover, each case must be indexed so that it can give advice for a wide variety of games. Even though football and chess are quite different, for example, a chess case might point out a fork opportunity in a football game. The indexing vocabulary here must provide a representational formalism that allows a chess game to be recognized as similar to a football game. Given that chess and football share few surface descriptors, this can only happen if the vocabulary allows both to be described according to more abstract features. A chess game indexed in this system is thus described in more domain-independent terms than were used to describe the chess game above. Instead of describing the chess game using a chess vocabulary, it must be described using the vocabulary of competitive games, a more abstract vocabulary that talks about opposing sides, competitive advantage, strategic plans, counterplans, and their interactions.

This vocabulary needs to cover similarities between cases from a wide variety of related domains. We might begin by examining the similarities between games played on fields, for example, soccer and football, which are relatively similar, and then branch out to board games, for example, chess, refining the vocabulary to cover the broader range of competitive games. A combination of generally applicable and game-specific dimensions and symbols will be used. The set of dimensions, perhaps, might be applicable across the whole set of competitive games, with the specifics of any game captured by using symbols specific to the game it represents to fill the values for those dimensions.

Let us now consider the goal of creating a more general-purpose advice-giving program to give advice about a wide range of issues encountered when people interact with people. Its cases describe the relationships between people, organizations, and countries, including instances of conflict and cooperation. This system might still include a chess game or two (perhaps one illustrates the pitfalls in counting on victory; perhaps another illustrates how perseverance pays off), but now the vocabulary needs to be even more different. One might describe these situations in terms of goals and subgoals, the plans used to carry out those goals, the interactions between the goals of several individuals, the interactions of plans and goals, thematic descriptions of people that lead one to make predictions about the plans they will carry out, and so on. To derive the vocabulary here, we might begin with competitive games, if we have already analyzed those, and discover more general ways to express the interactions between people and interactions between teams, perhaps according to the relationships of their goals to one another. We would examine a wide range of interaction situations: for example, management situations, negotiations situations, common everyday resource disputes, the planning and counterplanning of siblings against each other.

The specificity of index vocabulary depends on the tasks that must be supported. In the general-purpose advice-giving system, for example, the specifics of a chess game may not need to be represented in an index. In the chess advisor, they do. If cases are to be used for both tasks, the indexing vocabulary needs to cover the specifics of chess games and also describe each in terms of interactions between opponents.

We can sum up as follows: Given a task and a range of cases, indexing vocabulary should provide sufficient coverage to enable a task to be accomplished, without being over specific or over abstract. On the other hand, vocabulary should be chosen taking into account future directions a system might be expanded for—other tasks its cases might be asked to accomplish and other corpora of cases that might become available.

In the next section, we introduce two methods for examining cases and tasks to determine the needed vocabulary. There are three things to keep in mind as dimensions and symbols are chosen.

■ The indexing vocabulary should be general enough to cover the range of tasks the case-based reasoner is responsible for and specific enough to make the differentiations that are needed for that task. However, there is no need to make the vocabulary more general or more specific than what is required for the designated task.

This rule allows us to constrain the vocabulary to what is needed for the designated tasks. If a system is tasked to do lesson planning for elementary school, for example, then we confine our indexing to the construction and evaluation of lesson plans being put together for elementary school children. Though some cases make points applicable to adult education and others make points applicable to parenting, we don't need to make the indexing vocabulary cover those. At the same time, we make sure we include domain-specific dimensions that are relevant to teaching elementary students. For example, level of maturity is important in describing the readiness of children, allowing differentiation between lessons appropriate for less mature and more mature children. If we were indexing cases for adult education, level of maturity might not be necessary.

■ The indexing vocabulary should cover the range of cases that the case-based reasoner will use.

Some systems will have domain-related cases only. Others will have cases that span domains. While some descriptors are domain-specific (e.g., the maturity of children), the vocabulary that describes features that span domains should be consistent across cases, allowing cases from the several available domains to be indexed similarly with respect to shared features. This allows cross-domain retrieval to be done. If we had both teaching and counseling cases in a system that was giving advice about interacting with children, for example, we would want to index both by the important descriptors they share, that is, intellectual maturity of the child, degree of understanding of the concepts in the case. This guideline acts to both constrain and broaden. If only cases from a particular domain are used, it tells us to constrain the vocabulary to cover only the domain. If cases that are available span domains, it tells us that dimensions and vocabulary must be chosen to be more generally applicable.

■ The indexing vocabulary should anticipate the degree and directions in which the system will be expanded in the future.

narrow to begin with, then we may not be able ... ows that a system will be greatly enhanced in ... enhancements and make sure the vocabulary either allows those enhancements or can be easily upgraded.

The important point is that the vocabulary has to match the needs of the reasoner—the ... that it ... out and the range of cases that it has to reason with.

...g Index Vocabulary

Choosing an indexing vocabulary for a domain and task requires examining a corpus of cases in the context of a set of tasks they provide guidance for. Earlier, we noted two methods for ...ing this, the functional approach and the reminding approach.

Using the functional methodology, we collect cases from the domain that are representative of both problems that arise and are solved in the domain and solutions to those problems. We then examine that corpus, keeping in mind the tasks it must support. We identify, for each case, the points it can make, the situations in which each point is applicable, and the ways the case needs to be described to make it available to make each of its points.

Using the reminding methodology, we collect and examine the kinds of remindings that ... natural among human experts who do the designated task. We first attempt to explain how each reminding could have happened by designating what makes the two cases similar. We then consider what changes or descriptions that would allow such remindings and, from there, propose dimensions of ... situation and specific vocabulary items that can describe those dimensions and that would have allowed the remindings. Using this method, our conjectures about what makes two situations similar give us our clues as to what the vocabulary needs to include. After examining a variety of remindings, a vocabulary that covers the whole set is derived.

Either way, the goal is to discover dimensions that are important ones to focus on in judging similarity, the range of values each can take on, and the level of detail that is advantageous in a representation. The reminding methodology is illustrated in chapter 4 and also in section 4 of this chapter. Thus, we focus our attention in this section of the chapter on the functional approach.

...for Choosing ... Indexing Vocabulary

The functional methodology focuses on the purposes of indexes: to designate the situations in which some lesson a case can teach might be relevant. There may be many lessons any case can teach and many packages of expectations it can provide. Depending on the circumstances in which the case is remembered, a different one of its lessons needs to be extracted and used. The approach here to identifying indexing vocabulary for a task and domain is to derive indexes for a corpus of cases and then to derive a vocabulary that can cover the set. The idea is as follows:

1. Collect a representative set of cases. Overall, cases should be representative of the problems that arise in the domain, the contexts in which problems arise, solutions, and solution outcomes.

2. Identify the points each case can make, or the lessons it can teach.

3. Characterize the situations in which each case can appropriately make each of its points, making sure to include in the characterizations the task the reasoner is engaged in and the reasoning goals in those circumstances.

4. For each, describe indexes that would allow the case to be recalled in each designated situation, making sure that descriptions of indexes are both abstract enough to be generally applicable and concrete enough to be recognizable.

5. Choose a set of dimensions and symbols that allow the content of those indexes to be represented.

To be more concrete about this process, we must identify the kinds of points cases can make, specify how to characterize situations profitably, and provide guidelines that allow indexes to be chosen based on the qualities of indexes presented in the previous section. But first we present an example that will be used for illustration throughout:

> A teacher is teaching about discovery and design in the context of building wind machines. The students, who are in the fifth and sixth grades, have to design and build vehicles that will be propelled by the wind. Fans are available for testing the built vehicles. Students are encouraged to use incremental means of designing—they should test their vehicles, explain their failures, modify them based on the explanations, and so on. Aides are available to help with construction. Some students are working in small groups; others are working alone. The students have chosen their own groups to work in. Some students are very successful at using the incremental design method, are designing and building novel vehicles, are having a great time, and seem to be discovering a lot about wind propulsion. Others, however, are having trouble evaluating what is wrong with their designs and repairing them. When their designs don't work, they are simply throwing them away and starting again from scratch. Other students are having trouble putting together the things they have designed; their manual dexterity is not up to the level of their creativity. The teacher is glad that she thought to have aides available to help the students with their building. They provide construction help to those who need it, relieving her of that duty and giving her the opportunity to make herself available to the students who are having trouble with the evaluation step. Except for the best students in the class, those students who are working in groups are having an easier time than those working alone.

There are a number of circumstances in which this case could be useful.

■ A teacher is putting together a design course and wants to teach learning from failure. She wonders what kinds of experiences to give the students to go along with that lesson. This case proposes a student exercise: building wind machines. It also shows what kinds of materials are needed for that (both the building materials and the evaluation materials [the fan]) and the importance of allowing the evaluation to happen in the classroom.

■ A teacher is at the beginning of a design session and sees the kids throwing away their designs and starting over from scratch. If he is reminded of this case, he learns that this is a common problem for fifth and sixth graders and younger children. He might choose to gather them together in a group and talk about issues in evaluation and incremental design before they continue with the exercise, or he may try to find additional adults to help in the classroom so that he can give those who need additional help the attention they need.

■ A teacher is planning a design project for her fourth graders. This case suggests something they can build. It also suggests that extra teaching aid is needed in the classroom both to help with construction and to help students evaluate and incrementally repair their designs.

■ A teacher is planning a building project for his fifth graders and trying to determine how much extra help he needs in the classroom. This case suggests the tasks they are needed for (construction and help with evaluation) and gives some idea about how much help each child might need. It shows how much help was used for construction. The teacher might have to compute how much more is needed to help with evaluation too.

■ A teacher is trying to justify the need for aid in the classroom. This case shows the need in two ways.

■ A teacher is trying to identify what concepts kids need to learn before beginning a design project. In this case, they were short on evaluation skills. The teacher may decide that that is a topic to discuss before they begin their projects, or she may decide to structure the set of classes so that they begin discussing evaluation at the time when they start having to evaluate their designs.

The goal is to describe a set of indexes that will make it retrievable in each of these situations, and then, after examining other cases, to design a vocabulary that can be used to designate its indexes.

The Kinds of Lessons Cases Can Teach: Points

The first step in analyzing an individual case is to identify the points it can make or the lessons it can teach. We use a method here of listing the kinds of points cases tend to make and then analyzing each case to discover the lessons of each kind that it teaches. The rationale is this: If we can list the kinds of points cases tend to make, then we have a chance to systematically analyze each case, extracting from it the points it makes of each type.

A simple analysis of cases suggests four broad classes of points cases can make.

Conditions for success: They can make points about how to achieve some goal. If a goal was accomplished successfully in one situation by some method, the method is likely to work in another similar situation.

Conditions for failure: They can point out when failures are likely. If some failure happened in one situation, it is likely to happen in a similar situation.

Predictions of outcome: They can report outcomes.

Explanations of outcome: They can provide explanations of outcomes, or why things turned out the way they did.

Any case might make several points, each of which is appropriate in different situations or contexts.

The case in the example makes several points:

Point 1: Many fifth- and sixth-grade students are missing the skills that allow them to analyze their work by themselves and discover what the problems are. If you put them in such a situation, they will fail (a condition for failure, a prediction of outcome, and an explanation of outcome).

Point 2: To successfully complete projects involving complex analysis, provide individual attention to those students who need it (a condition for success and a prediction of outcome).

Point 3: To successfully complete building projects with fifth and sixth graders, provide extra construction aid (a condition for success and a prediction of outcome).

Point 4: To successfully complete complex projects, have kids work in groups (a condition for success and a prediction of outcome).

Characterizing Situations in Which Points Are Appropriately Made

The next step is to attempt to characterize the kinds of situations in which points can profitably be made. There are several components to such a characterization:

- The reasoning goal the point supports (e.g., constructing a solution).
- The task the reasoner is engaged in (e.g., putting a lesson plan together).
- Situation descriptors that, in conjunction with the goal and task, specify the circumstances in which a case can appropriately make a point (e.g., students are in fifth grade, the concept being taught is evolution, discussion is about dinosaurs).

The previous section listed the types of reasoning decisions case-based reasoners are often responsible for: constructing solutions; predicting failures; explaining reasoning errors, failures, and anomalies; recovering from reasoning errors and failures; and evaluating proposed solutions. Recall that each of these has associated with it guidelines for index selection. For example, to anticipate failures, one indexes a case by those of its features that were responsible for its failure.

Specifying circumstances in which a case can be useful in terms of reasoning goals makes it easy to select the index assignment guidelines that ought to be applied. But how can an indexer know which reasoning goals a case's point can support? This task is made simple by the fact that points that cases can make are aligned with reasoning goals. Cases that make points about conditions for failure, for example, can help a reasoner predict failures, explain

Points a Case Makes	*Corresponding Reasoning Task*
Conditions for success: tells how to do something (e.g., achieve some goal, perform some task, recover from a failure, adapt some solution)	achieve a constructive task, (generating a solution or piece of one or recovering from a failure)
Conditions for failure: predicts problems that might arise	anticipate potential problems explain failures recover from failures evaluate proposed solutions
Predictions of outcome: reports outcome	project outcome (in order to evaluate proposed solutions)
Explanations of outcome: tells why something happened the way it did	explain failure or other anomoly

FIGURE 6.1   Points and Reasoning Tasks

failures, recover from failures, and evaluate proposed solutions. Those that make points about conditions for success can help a reasoner to construct and evaluate solutions. And so on. Figure 6.1 associates the points cases can make with the reasoning goals they support.

We continue with the example to illustrate. The sample case makes four points and needs to be indexed individually for each. We have already identified the points it makes; the next step is to describe the situations in which each has the potential to be relevant.

- The first point presents a condition for failure: If you put fifth and sixth graders in a situation in which they need to analyze their work, they will fail. This point allows a reasoner to anticipate a potential problem and to evaluate outcome (two goals) whenever a teacher is putting a plan together or evaluating a plan (two tasks), when the plan involves having fifth or sixth graders analyzing their work individually (situation descriptors).

- The first point presents an explanation of an anomaly: The reason fifth and sixth graders cannot easily complete projects requiring them to incrementally analyze and refine their work is because they do not yet have the skills to analyze complex failures. This point allows a reasoner to explain a failure (goal) in situations in which fifth or sixth graders were unable to complete a project of this kind (situation descriptors).

- The second point provides conditions for success and prediction of outcome: Even if difficult analysis is necessary, when help is available, students can often complete the analysis successfully. This point allows a reasoner to recover from a real or potential plan failure (goal) when complex analysis is necessary in a lesson (situation descriptor). It allows a reasoner to generate a successful solution (goal) under the same circumstances. And it allows evaluating outcome (goal) when a plan involves complex analysis and when individual help is available (situation descriptors).

■ The third point also provides conditions for success: To successfully do building projects with fifth and sixth graders, make extra help available to aid with construction. This point allows a reasoner to generate a solution (goal) when putting a lesson plan together (task) and considering doing a building project with fifth or sixth graders (situation descriptors).

■ The third point also predicts outcome: When you put extra helpers in a classroom to help with a construction project, construction will be successful. This point allows a reasoner to evaluate a solution (goal) in which extra helpers are added to a classroom during a building project (situation descriptors).

■ The fourth point predicts outcome and provides conditions for success: To successfully complete complex projects, have kids work in groups. This point allows a reasoner to generate a solution (goal) when students will be working on complex projects (situation descriptors). It also allows evaluation of a derived solution (goal) when complex projects will be worked on and kids are working in groups (situation descriptors).

Describing the Indexes That Are Needed, Describing the Vocabulary That Is Needed

The previous step identified the many situations in which a case is expected to be profitably recalled. In this step, those situation descriptions are turned into indexes. There are two parts to this step:

■ Use guidelines associated with reasoning goals to identify the content of each index.
■ Specify the content at the correct level of detail.

When this step is complete, it is fairly simple to designate what needs to be covered in the indexing vocabulary. The dimensions and symbols in the indexing vocabulary must provide a way of representing symbolically the content of cases' indexes. In this subsection, we look at how each of the types of reasoning goals provides guidelines for index selection, and we show how each works in choosing indexes for this case. We also point out the contributions of each analysis to choosing vocabulary. We analyze each type of reasoning goal in turn.

Achieving constructive goals.   A constructive goal is a goal to construct or choose a solution. In case-based reasoning, these goals mostly look like choice goals—the reasoner finds a case that provides an almost-right solution that is chosen to solve the problem. Constructive goals include such things as choosing solutions to fulfill constraints, choosing strategies to use in solving a problem or reasoning through a situation, choosing an adaptation strategy, and choosing a means of repairing a solution.

What do situations in which constructive subgoals are being achieved have in common? In all, there is a goal to construct some piece of a solution, there is a partial solution, there are a set of constraints on the solution being constructed, and there is a state of the world to contend with. The partial solution, constraints, and state of the world affect the way the goal can be achieved. When a reasoner is trying to achieve a constructive goal, old situations in which a similar constructive goal was achieved under the same sorts of conditions can provide useful information.

> *A useful index for retrieving cases that can help a reasoner achieve a constructive sub-goal combines the goal that was being achieved with the conditions of the world that led to the goal's being achieved in that particular way.*

When those conditions are met in the context of that same goal in the future, this case will appropriately make its point or tell its story.

Three examples from the teaching case above illustrate this guideline. That case made two points with respect to achieving constructive subgoals:[2]

Point 3: To successfully do building projects with fifth and sixth graders, make extra help available to aid with construction.

Point 4: To successfully complete complex projects, have kids work in groups.

In point 3, the teacher's goal was to have the class complete a project requiring building and design. Success was due largely to providing extra help in the classroom for the children. Conditions of the world that led to choosing to achieve the goal that way were that the students were of a certain age (fifth and sixth graders) at which their manual skills, required for building, are behind their design capabilities. In the future, when a teacher wants to do a project requiring building with fifth and sixth graders, this case can provide guidelines. These features together form one useful index for this case.

In point 4, the teacher's goal was to have the group complete a relatively complex project. Here the goal is to work on a project. The major condition of the world that led to choosing to have the class work in groups was that the project was of high complexity. These features together form another useful index for this case. If recalled when another teacher is trying to get a class to successfully complete a project that is seen as relatively complex for the group, it suggests that the teacher have the class work together in groups on the project.

From this analysis, we now know that an index vocabulary needs to be able to specify goals of teachers in terms of activities the students are engaged in (e.g., building) and that two dimensions constrain that goal: the age or maturity or knowledge-state of the students (fifth and sixth grade) and the level of complexity of a project. We still are not sure exactly how to represent each of these or the level of detail each requires. That will be ascertained after looking at many more cases. Other cases, for example, tell us that completion of activities such as building is usually a secondary goal, the primary goals of teachers being that students learn certain facts or skills.

We also analyze the descriptors we've derived to see if they are generally applicable and recognizable. Here, we have probably made our situation descriptors generally applicable enough, but we must ask if they are sufficiently recognizable. Can a teacher, for example, easily recognize when a task is of high complexity, or does the indexing need to be more specific

---

2. Point 2 is also a point about a constructive subgoal but of a particular kind—recovery from a plan failure. It will be covered later.

than that? I tend to err on the side of making indexes specific—in this case, designating for point 4 *design* (the specific complex activity these students were engaged in) and *analysis* (the particular difficult step) in the index. I also like to err on the side of redundancy, indexing the case to make this point by all the designations `activity is design, complexity of activity is high,` and `activity step includes analysis` when describing the teacher's teaching goal. Under any of these circumstances, a teacher should consider having students work in groups. The next example discusses how to add these designations to the indexing vocabulary.

Anticipating potential problems.   Anticipation of potential problems requires a different kind of indexing. Here, the goals of the reasoner are not as important to retrieval. Rather, the reasoner needs to retrieve any similar case where a failure was encountered. Any one of those can warn the reasoner about a potential pitfall.

> To enable retrieval of cases that can be used to anticipate potential problems, failure cases are indexed by the combinations of their descriptors that were responsible for their failure.

The lessons any case can teach about failure are useful whenever the combination of descriptors that describe the circumstances for failure is encountered in the future.

Recall what happened in the presented case and the point about failure that the case teaches. Fifth and sixth graders were to incrementally develop wind vehicles, building a vehicle, trying it out, analyzing its failures, and repairing the design accordingly. Instead, they threw away designs that didn't work and started over from scratch. That case made an important anticipatory point:

Point 1: If you put fifth and sixth graders in a situation in which they need to analyze their work, at least some will be unable to complete the task.

We need to index the case by the combination of its descriptors responsible for the failure. The teacher has already determined that it was the analysis step that was difficult for the kids. Thus, "activities requiring analysis" is a good candidate for part of the index. The rest of the index needs to designate in what circumstances such tasks will lead to failure. The case tells us that fifth and sixth graders are unable to do analysis. Thus, we might index by the set of features "student activity requires analysis" and "students are in fifth and sixth grades."

From this, we know that another dimension of the indexing vocabulary is reasoning skills required in order for students to complete an activity. This tells us that activities should be described not just by name (e.g., building) but also by component skills that they require (e.g., analysis). The contribution here a dimensional analysis of "activity."

The level of abstraction or detail required in an index comes up here also. When we look at the index that has just been derived, we see that it is easy to recognize what grade students are in, and that that designation seems generally applicable. But is "activity requiring analysis" sufficiently recognizable? We may all have our own opinions of that, some of us believing that we would be able to recognize that easily, others thinking that it would be hard to recognize. Let us, for a moment, take the side of those who think it is hard to recognize. The guideline tells us that we must substitute something more concrete for this descriptive piece of the index. The case gives us a clue as to what we might substitute: incremental debugging of a design requiring the steps of build, evaluate, and repair. This is the task the students were actually involved in that required analysis, and it was the evaluate step that was failing.

From this, we discover that it is advantageous to describe activities in terms of the specific component mental skills required, that a broad-brush description of mental skills may not be sufficient.

Explaining and recovering from reasoning errors. Cases that point out the potential for failure can often be used to help explain a failure or to point to a means of recovering from one—two other common reasoning goals (Kolodner 1987).

> *Indexing by features that predict failure also supports the retrieval of cases that can help with explaining and recovering from reasoning errors.*

If our teaching case is recalled while trying to derive a lesson plan in which students are required to do an analysis step, it will point to the potential for failure (point 1) and suggest a solution (point 2). But if it is not recalled while deriving a lesson plan (perhaps the teacher did not realize the extent of analysis that was required), the plan might fail. The teacher then will attempt to figure out why it failed and what he or she might do to make the lesson work better. At this point, the teacher has available the description of the situation he or she started with plus a description of what happened in class. Cases with combinations of those features can be recalled. In particular, what happened here was that students began building their projects, tested them, and then when they didn't work, threw them away and started over. Indexing by this set of descriptors allows the case to be recalled when a teacher is trying to explain a particular failed outcome (point 1).

Suppose that in the new case children in fifth grade were designing electrical circuits. The teacher followed the lesson plan suggested by the science manual. The students began building their circuits. They would put a circuit together and test it, and when it didn't work, they would take it all apart and start over. The teacher notices this, realizes that this is not what the children should be doing, and wonders why they are failing and what he or she can do to compensate so that they can perform better. The teacher notices that they should be doing incremental building, evaluation, and repair. This allows the teacher to remember the wind vehicle case.[3] That case provides an explanation for the students' failure: fifth graders are unable to do the evaluation step that this task requires. It also suggests one solution: Give extra help to those who need it. If most students in the class need help, the teacher may translate that into preparing a class session in which incremental evaluation is discussed as a problem-solving technique.

Alternatively, the teacher may have already explained the failure and simply be in need of a suggestion about how to recover from it. This requires indexing the case so that point 2 can be made:

---

3. Or, it allows the teacher's computer assistant to recall it and present it.

Point 2: To successfully complete projects requiring complex analysis in a fifth- or sixth-grade class, provide individual help to those students who need it.

The goal the teacher was trying to achieve here was to have the class successfully complete a project requiring analysis even though some kids were not yet able to do that task. Success was achieved through noticing who needed help with analysis and providing individual help to those students. Conditions of the world that led to choosing to achieve the goal that way were that there was someone available with the time to provide that aid to students. An appropriate index for the case based on this point designates that the teacher's goal is recovering from a plan failure when some kids are incapable of analysis required in the plan. One also might also consider adding to the index that help was available in the classroom. To decide if that condition belongs in the index or not, one considers what is necessary in the index to make the case generally applicable. Here, adding that condition makes the case less applicable than leaving it out. We want the case to be available whenever a teacher is trying to recover from a failure such as this—the suggestion from this case may cause the teacher to find extra help on the spot, even if it is not available at the time of the failure.

What does all this tell us about indexing? An indexing vocabulary that can represent student behavior while engaged in an activity will allow this case to be recalled when this sequence of behaviors repeats itself. Thus, we need to be able to represent student behaviors. Some of the symbols for representing student behavior will coincide with symbols used to represent component skills that make up activities (e.g., building, evaluating, repairing). But that symbol set covers only *expected* student behavior. A dimension must be added to log missing and/or faulty behaviors (e.g., here, the evaluating/analysis step was either skipped or not done well enough), and the set of behaviors already identified needs to be incremented to include common faulty behaviors (e.g., throwing things away).

Projecting outcome and evaluating solutions. Projecting outcome and evaluating solutions requires another type of index.

> *To retrieve cases appropriate to projecting outcome, index cases by sets of features that were responsible for its outcome.* When the outcome is failure, these are the same features that make the case available to help with anticipation of failure. Cases can also help predict successful outcomes, however, and to do that, they must be indexed by the combination of their features that predict success.

There was much that did not work well in our teaching example, and we have discussed those things, but there was one thing that worked well:

Point 4: Students working in groups were able to tackle the complexities of the assigned problem better than those working alone.

The positive outcome here is that students in groups worked well. The situation here is that the problem was relatively complex given the background of the students. The two fea-

tures that belong in an index that will help in projecting outcome are that the assigned problem
was relatively complex and that students worked in groups. Given these two features in
another situation, this case can be recalled. Recalling it will allow the reasoner to see that, at
least in this situation, those working in groups were able to complete the work more successfully. The reasoner will also see that the particular problem being worked on was a design
problem and will compare and contrast the two situations with each other to determine if the
outcome in the old situation is likely to repeat in the new one.

We learn here that the indexing vocabulary for these cases should include a dimension
for the types of groupings of students as they engage in activities. They might work as individuals or in several kinds of groups.

Explaining anomalies:

*For cases to help with explanation, index by the combinations of their features that pre-
dict that the explanation is an appropriate one.*

One lesson the teaching case teaches is why fifth and sixth graders cannot easily complete projects requiring incremental analysis and refinement:

Point 1: The reason fifth and sixth graders cannot easily complete projects requiring
them to incrementally analyze and refine their work is that they do not yet have
the skills to be able to analyze complex failures.

When is this explanation appropriate? A reasoner will normally try to explain an anomaly after
it has occurred. Thus, this explanation should be retrieved after a similar anomaly has occurred.

This discussion suggests that in order to support explanatory capabilities, cases should
be indexed by the sets of features that describe an anomalous situation requiring explanation.
In this case, the anomalous situation is that the fifth and sixth graders, who were working on a
project requiring incremental analysis and refinement of their work, were unable to complete
their projects successfully. Indexing this case by this description will ensure that the next time
fifth or sixth graders are unable to complete an assignment of the same sort, this case will be
retrieved. The case will suggest that the students are missing analysis skills.

This is an outcome description, and there are two components of outcome that are
important in describing this case: the expected outcome (successful completion of the activity
by everybody) and the actual outcome (failure of most to complete the activity successfully).
Representing both is important to distinguish between this case, in which successful completion was expected, and another, in which the teacher knew that the activity was difficult and
didn't expect everybody to complete it. Dimensions of this outcome designation, whether
expected or actual, seem to include the expected or actual outcome itself (success or failure),
who that outcome is applied to (the whole class versus some part of it), and the part of the case
to which it is applied (the student activity).

Do the Indexes Cover All Circumstances?

A final step in analyzing individual cases might be to see if the chosen indexes do their job. This might be done by designating several concrete circumstances in which the case should be useful and asking whether the chosen indexes allow retrieval in these circumstances. Several concrete circumstances in which this case is applicable were presented along with the case. It is left to the reader to discover how each of these circumstances is covered by the chosen indexing scheme.

Choosing Representational Dimensions and Symbols

The discussion above showed the contributions this case makes to choosing a vocabulary to support lesson planning. Many dimensions and symbols for representing indexes for this task and domain fell out of the analysis of the usefulness of this case. One determines the full set of dimensions and symbols needed to index cases by doing a similar analysis of usefulness over a representative set of cases. A representative set covers the set of issues that arise in doing the designated task or tasks in the designated domains and the set of situations in which the tasks are carried out. Chapter 15 discusses how to choose a representative set of cases to seed a case library.

There are two guidelines to remember as indexing vocabulary is being derived—one technical, the other commonsense.

■ The symbols and dimensions used should provide coverage, be adequately expressive, and should each carry discernible and differentiable meaning.

The goal in choosing representational conventions is to allow matching functions to be both efficient and accurate. I will leave it to the AI and expert systems textbooks to make clearer what this means technically. Cullingford (1986) has a particularly good set of chapters about choosing representational vocabulary.

Pragmatically, one comes to understand this guideline as the indexing vocabulary is developed and as the case library is initially used. If cases that should have been retrieved are not recalled because retrieval and matching functions cannot identify the cases as appropriate, inadequacies of the indexing vocabulary are uncovered. This brings us to the second guideline, the commonsense one.

■ Developing an indexing vocabulary is an incremental, pragmatic process.

The indexing vocabulary developed using a representative set of cases. It is tested and then incrementally refined by specifying representative situations and seeing whether the vocabulary makes appropriate cases available. The set of dimensions and symbols is refined based on inabilities of the vocabulary to represent indexes such that appropriate cases can be retrieved. A representational scheme that accepts barely matching cases as good matches needs to be made more discriminating. One that fails to show the similarities between similar cases needs to be made more expressive.

6.3 TOWARD A GENERALLY APPLICABLE INDEXING VOCABULARY

The discussions so far provide guidance on how to choose vocabulary for any single case-based reasoner being built. One can examine remindings and/or examine the potential utility of individual cases and derive a vocabulary that covers the sets of descriptors these analyses show to be important in reminding. But, alas, with guidelines like these, system developers are left to derive a new indexing vocabulary for each new domain they encounter. Individual developers will certainly get better over time, recognizing the similarities between domains they have addressed and new ones, borrowing the dimensions and vocabulary from those domains.[4]

On the other hand, if we could characterize domains and specify the dimensions, and perhaps some of the vocabulary, for each type of domain, then system developers would have an easier job. Indeed, a major goal of the CBR research community is to find a **generally applicable indexing vocabulary**, a theory of the representational content of indexes that crosses domains.

With generally applicable indexing vocabularies available, the job of the knowledge engineer would surely be far easier. A new domain would not have to be analyzed anew to figure out which are its important dimensions. Though there is much in any domain that is specific to the domain, we could at least give knowledge engineers or system builders a place to start in defining representations and indexing content when building a case-based reasoner for a new domain. If we can provide a set of dimensions for indexing that are commonly important ones, the knowledge engineer's job would be to *identify* the domain-specific symbols consistent with dimensions known to be important rather than also having to *discover* the important dimensions.

There are other benefits, too, to discovering generally applicable vocabularies. If developers working in the same domain shared vocabulary, then they could also share case libraries. In addition, using shared vocabularies would allow case-based reasoners to use cases from a variety of domains as they reason, much as people are able to do. Within-domain cases are certainly useful in suggesting specific solutions, but often the cases that can shed the most light on a situation come from quite different domains.

Consider, for example, a case from JULIA's domain. JULIA is attempting to plan a meal and has been concentrating on choosing a main dish. Its main dish, however, seems to be overconstrained, resulting from needing to fulfill the dietary requirements of a large group of picky eaters, each of whom has different requirements. JULIA can find no one main dish that satisfies everyone. Its dilemma, at this point, is to figure out how to deal with its overconstrained slot. It has no meal-planning case in which it had to deal with this particular kind of overconstraint. If JULIA could remember an experience designing a text editor for two different bosses, each of whom insisted on a different means of interacting with the system, however, its solution might be obvious. The solution in that case was to deal with the overconstraint by providing two different solutions in the overconstrained part of the design (i.e., two different

---

4. Case-based vocabulary construction!

interfaces) and making the rest of the design work well with both. Using this case, JULIA would recognize the need to provide several different main dishes.[5]

Coming up with generally applicable vocabularies also has implications for cognition. Many in the case-based reasoning community would like to explain the cross-domain remindings we see in people. Why should the chess expert recognize the football fork? How can we explain a doctor's reminding of a difficult-to-diagnose patient when the car mechanic is having trouble figuring out what is wrong with a car? How can we explain the many out-of-domain remindings we all have in the course of a normal day? We know there is similarity involved in these remindings, but what are the dimensions of that similarity? Furthermore, looking at case-based reasoning as a cognitive model, we must believe that people somehow make use of what they know about an old domain (e.g., diagnosing people) to figure out what is important to pay attention to in a new one (e.g., diagnosing cars).

Discovering generally applicable vocabularies will allow us to make our case-based reasoners more powerful, to make the job of the knowledge engineer easier, and to discover the deep basis for similarity that allows cross-domain remindings to happen in people.

The Universal Index Frame (UIF, Schank and Osgood 1990) represents the first attempt that has been made within the CBR community to create a generally applicable descriptive vocabulary. The UIF covers the broad range of *intentional domains*, that is, domains that are about interactions between agents with goals. Competitive games (e.g., chess, football, soccer) are intentional domains, as are any other domains in which interpersonal interactions and the goals of several parties are important (e.g., management, negotiations, sibling relationships). Thus, with this vocabulary, we can explain how a football expert could be reminded of a football experience while playing soccer or chess or while managing employees in a new business. And we can give knowledge engineers working on one of these domains guidelines about what sorts of situation descriptors are the right ones to use for indexing if they are working in one of the domains the UIF covers.

Unfortunately, we will also see that although its name implies universality, the Universal Index Frame is not entirely universal. It does cover a broad range of domains, but it leaves out much. For example, there is no effort to define dimensions that allow visual kinds of remindings or those that allow remindings in the context of reasoning about devices. Nor does the UIF give explicit guidelines for choosing domain-specific dimensions and vocabulary items.

The UIF's name is misleading for another reason also. It was derived as a means of representing indexes, and its creators had in mind that one would index cases by filling in a complete UIF structure to represent them. Hence, it was called an *index frame*. In fact, it has turned out to be something quite different: a set of dimensions and symbols that *describe* cases across the intentional domains. Filling in the frame it provides results in a symbolic description of a situation. The indexes for a case can then be chosen from that set of descriptors.

The UIF does, however, provide a way of looking at the choice of indexing vocabulary that has much applicability as new kinds of domains and indexes are approached. In the next section, the UIF is presented in considerable detail, and in the following section, its broader implications and the lessons it teaches are explored. Some readers will not want to know the details of the Universal Index Frame; others will begin to wonder why so much detail is being

---

5. JULIA actually solves this problem with an adaptation heuristic. It does not do cross-contextual reminding.

provided. Such readers should at least read the first portion of the next section, up to the beginning of section 6.4.1, but can safely skip the details, skipping to section 6.5 and coming back to the details later if portions of following sections are not clear.

6.4 THE UNIVERSAL INDEX FRAME: A VOCABULARY FOR INTENTIONAL SITUATIONS

Before the days of case-based reasoning, there was much focus in Schank's group at Yale and in his students' AI groups on understanding stories about people interacting with each other. An important process in understanding those stories, and in understanding those kinds of situations, is tracking the goals of the agents (Schank and Abelson 1977). If we know what goal an agent has, we can predict the plans he or she will use to achieve the goal. If we know about several goals an agent has, or if we know about several agents, each of whom has goals, we make predictions about the actions of the agents based on our understanding of the way goals tend to interact. Similarly, we know a great deal about the way plans and the steps of plans interact, and we make predictions about what will happen in different situations based on that knowledge. The point here is that knowledge about plans and goals and the interactions of agents with plans and goals helps us make sense of many of the stories we read and, indeed, large pieces of our lives. Tracking those goals seems to be a natural and automatic cognitive activity in people.

The vocabulary of goals, plans, and their interactions provides a representational formalism for describing situations in which agents interact with each other, whether it is in a competitive game situation or a common day-to-day encounter. We call these *intentional situations* (Schank and Abelson 1977). This representational vocabulary also provides the basis for describing the similarities between events that are very different from each other on the surface. Schank's (1982) *Dynamic Memory* gives many examples of people's being reminded of old situations based on new ones because the goal/plan structure of the two situations was similar.

In one example, he is telling a story about how he likes his steak really rare and his wife won't prepare it that rare for him. The person he is talking to remembers a time when he wanted his hair cut really short. The barber did not believe he wanted it that short and refused to cut it as short as he wanted it. In both cases, one agent needs another to do something for him. In both, the thing that he wants the agent to do is an extreme version of what the agent normally does. In both, the agent ignores the extreme thing the person wants and instead carries out the normal plan. Goals and plans and their interactions in the two cases are very similar.

In another example, Schank's daughter was searching for sand dollars in shallow water in the ocean, when sand dollars can be found more plentifully in deeper water. When asked why she was looking for them in shallow water, she said that it was easier. When they hear this story, many people are reminded of the drunk and the lamppost story. In both situations, a person has a goal of finding something, usually carried out by looking in the place where it is most likely to be found. Instead, in both cases, the person substitutes a plan that is easier to carry out but cannot yield results.

Another example Schank cites is being reminded of *Romeo and Juliet* upon seeing *West Side Story*. Many people are reminded of one when they encounter the other. Why? There are several reasons. At the level of surface similarities, both are about young lovers, clan rivalries, and tragic death. At the level of goals and plans, in both, the young lovers make plans to spend the rest of their lives together despite the objections of their parents, and in both, the lovers don't coordinate their plans for reaching their mutual goal well enough, resulting in tragedy.

In each of these instances, major similarities between the cases are at the levels of the goals and plans of the agents and their interactions. Let's examine these similarities in more detail to see what dimensions and descriptors are required to describe these sorts of similarities. We begin with the steak and haircut stories. They are similar in a variety of ways:

- Goal type: satisfaction goal
- Goal characterization: extreme version of normal goal
- Plan: use agent to provide service
- Expectation failure: normal goal fulfilled by agent rather than expected one
- Explanation of failure: alternative belief by agent

We see that the type of goal, some sort of characterization, an abstract characterization of the chosen plan, a description of the expectation failure, and the explanation of the failure are all involved in explaining the similarities between these two stories. Let us assume for now that we have discovered the first set of dimensions for describing similarities between intentional situations. But let us not be so quick to assume that we have discovered the descriptors of all intentional situations. We'll examine the other two examples to discover some of the other kinds of similarities such situations can have.

We move on to the sand dollars and the drunk under the lamppost situations. They have an overlapping but different set of dimensions in common:

- Goal: possess object
- Plan: search for object
- Plan characterization: easy method
- Expectation failure: object not found
- Explanation of failure: lack of common sense (or lack of ability)

While in the first example, it was the goal type that the two situations had in common, here it is the goal itself. The first example had a special characterization of the goal. This one does not—it is a normal possession goal. This situation, by contrast, characterizes the plan. In both, it was the easy search that was pursued as opposed to the smart search.

Romeo and Juliet and *West Side Story* have a different set of descriptors. Here, it is not only the goal itself that is important but also that there is a goal held mutually by two parties, and that it is a high-priority goal. Also important here are the conditions under which the goal is being pursued (outside opposition), a characterization of the plan being used (each plans separately), the outcome of the plan (death), and the explanation of the failure to achieve the goal (lack of coordination).

- Goal relationship: mutual goal pursuit
- Goal conditions: outside opposition
- Plan characterization: each plans separately
- Outcome: death
- Explanation of failure: lack of coordination

As we examine the similarities between the different events in these examples, we can begin to see the dimensions on which intentional situations need to be described and the sorts of abstract descriptors that need to be used to promote remindings across domains. Such dimensions as the goals of agents, types of goals, some characterizations of goals, plans that were carried out, some characterizations of those, failures that arose, and their explanations are each important aspects of an index that captures what is relevant in intentional situations. In addition, the difference between what was expected and what happened or the difference between one person's point of view and another's with respect to these descriptors often needs to be described in an index (e.g., one person expected the other to fulfill his or her wishes, the other did something else; the young lovers expected to be able to spend the rest of their lives together, but instead one or both died).

In *Dynamic Memory* (Schank 1982), Schank proposed organizing structures called thematic organizational units, or TOPs, as organizers of cases that are thematically similar to each other, that is, those that share common goals and plans and goal/plan interactions. In his conception, TOPs are defined by common combinations of goal-goal, goal-plan, and plan-plan interactions, each serving as a category for cases. A TOP classifies cases that have more or less the same goal/plan structure. The one that describes *Romeo and Juliet* and *West Side Story*, for example, is `Mutual Goal Pursuit against Outside Opposition`.

In this conception, goals, plans, and their interactions provide a vocabulary for defining abstract categories of events or cases. Each category carries with it both general knowledge about what to do and not to do in those situations and specific instances illustrating what happens in these kinds of situations. `Mutual Goal Pursuit against Outside Opposition`, for example, holds general information saying that secrecy is needed in attaining goals and that the path to achieving the goal will be difficult. *Romeo and Juliet* is one of the cases it knows about, and, in particular, it knows that this story is a case of planning individually without coordination. If another instance of mutual goal pursuit with outside opposition is encountered by a memory of this sort, its general information will tell the reasoner that secret planning is in order. If it knows that the planning of the agents with mutual goals is not being coordinated, it recalls *Romeo and Juliet* to show what the consequences of such planning in these kinds of situations could be.

If a case can be recognized as falling into one of these abstract categories, knowledge organized around the category (both general knowledge and specific cases) provides guidelines for acting. Hammond implemented this view of memory and planning in CHEF (Hammond 1989a), which used knowledge associated with its TOPs to repair failed plans.

It makes sense, then, to describe cases by their goals, plans, and goal/plan interactions, the case's thematic structure. That is, these same goals, plans, and goal/plan interactions that provide a vocabulary for defining thematic categories can also provide a vocabulary for indexing. If the same thematic structure is used both to define categories that hold planning information and to index, then the categories a case falls into can be recognized, as can similarities between cases. If two cases have the same thematic structure, they fall into the same thematic category, and it is likely that one can contribute suggestions for thinking about the other. The thematic structure of a case serves as an index linking the case to its thematic classification. It also serves as an index to other cases with the same thematic structure.

The Universal Index Frame (UIF, Schank and Osgood 1990) builds on this conception, using the dimensions and vocabulary of goal/plan interactions to structure the descriptions of intentional situations. Thus, it emphasizes the recording of goal- and plan-related information in indexes and uses the typology of goals and plans presented in *Scripts, Plans, Goals, and Understanding* (Schank and Abelson 1977) and *Dynamic Memory* (Schank 1982) as the vocabulary for its dimensions. In particular, it specifies a set of dimensions for indexing based on goal/plan interactions, and it suggests that the interactions between the goals and plans of several characters or those of a single character are a crucial part of the index. The Universal Index Frame commits to the following claims about the content of indexes. Some are claims about indexes for intentional situations; others are claims about indexes in general.

1. Indexes can record both **content** and **contextual** specifications. Context sets the stage, describing the state of the world when the episode took place; content specifies salient pieces of what happened in the episode. In an intentional situation, the contextual part holds setting information and tells us the relationships between the characters.

2. A case is worth remembering (storing away in the memory) when it is different from what is expected in some noteworthy way. It violates our expectations either because *some expectation failed* or because *something truly surprising happened*. Indexes specify whether the situation was an expectation failure or a surprise and along what dimension that expectation violation occurred. Indexing is **anomaly-based**, and the major anomaly an index is centered around is designated as a piece of the case's context. Anamolies represent differences between several views of a situation, sometimes the expected view and what really happened, other times the views of several agents. In describing a case, one describes several views and the differences between them. Indexes, too, capture the relationships between several views of a situation.

3. A case can have many indexes associated with it. Each index corresponds to a single interpretation of the case, concentrating on one lesson the case teaches, and records a set of criteria for retrieving the case from that point of view.

4. There are certain aspects of intentional situations that seem to take part in reminding. These make up the component parts of the index and are the *dimensions* of the representation. Values along a relevant subset of these dimensions are designated to create an index. These aspects include

   ■ Thematic relationships between the characters
   ■ The goals, beliefs, emotions, tasks, and plans of the characters and the results of carrying out the plan

- The relationships between the goals, beliefs, emotions, tasks, and plans of the different characters
- The way in which the episode differed from what was expected along these dimensions

5. For each dimension important to indexing intentional situations, a first pass has been made at deriving the vocabulary for filling the slots.

Figure 6.2 shows the structure for a full description of a case using the Universal Index Frame. Words in small letters in the second column indicate the type of concept that is allowed to fill each slot. The frame has three parts: the context grid, the content grid, and the global slots. The content grid represents the content of the story. The global slots (anomaly and setting) and the context grid set up the case's context.

The **content grid** is the representational mechanism that captures the content of the situation from several different relevant points of view. Content is presented as a grid with rows representing the goals and plans of the characters and columns designated for each point of view. The column at the far left of Figure 6.2 shows the full set of descriptors that are captured in the UIF. The top three slots (viewer, view, and agent) designate whose point of view is being captured in the column. The *viewer* is the one looking at the situation, the *agent* is the central character, and the *view* tells us what sort of description it is (of the ideal situation, the expected one, the perceived one, what the viewer wants, and so on). The other slots describe the situation from that point of view.

To represent relationships between multiple points of view, one view is recorded in one column and another in another column, and the relevant differences between them are recorded in the "anomalies" column at the far right. To represent the difference between what was expected and what happened, for example, expectations are recorded in one column, what really happened in another, and the difference on the far right, as in Figure 6.3, which shows the content grid for the sand dollars situation. Here, view 1 shows the ideal view of the situation, view 2 shows what the viewer perceived, and the anomaly column shows that this is a plan expectation failure. That is, a different plan than was expected was carried out.

The **context grid** keeps track of the relationships between the characters if there are several characters. In *Romeo and Juliet*, for example, there are four main characters: Romeo, Juliet, Romeo's family (the Montagues), and Juliet's family (the Capulets). Romeo has the relationship *lover-of* with Juliet, and he is a *member-of* the Montague family. The Capulets and Montagues are *enemies-of* each other. And so on. Figure 6.4 shows the full context grid for this case.

The **global slots** capture contextually relevant information that doesn't fit in either of the other two parts of the index. In implementations to date, it has held the setting, a description of the physical location of the situation, and the anomaly in the situation, the thing that makes this case different from the norm and therefore worth recording. As discussed earlier, there may actually be several anomalies in a case, each represented in the "anomalies" column of the content grid, but the one in the global slots portion of the case is the most important one. This portion of the index could be extended to include other information as necessary.

```
ANOMALY: anomaly
SETTING: setting
CONTEXT GRID:

                Thematic
                roles
                _____

                _____

                _____

CONTENT GRID:
    Slot-names              View 1          View 2    ......    Anomalies
    _____

    Viewer                  agent
    View                    view
    Agent                   agent
    _____

    Anticipatory-affect     affect
    Pre-task-belief         belief
    Task                    task
    Theme                   theme
    Goal                    goal
    Plan                    plan
    Result                  impact
    Side+                   impact
    Side-                   impact
    Resultant-affect        affect
    Post-task-belief        belief
    _____

    Delta-affect
    Delta-belief
    Trade-off
```

FIGURE 6.2   The Universal Index Frame (UIF)

```
    Slot-names          View 1              View 2              Anomalies
    _____

    Viewer              R                   R
    View                ideal               perceived
    Agent               daughter            daughter
    _____

    Task                search              search
    Goal                possess obj         possess obj
                        (sand $)            (sand $)
    Plan                use-approp-         adapt-inapprop-     plan exp-
                        mechanism           mechanism           failure
```

FIGURE 6.3   A Sample Content Grid Showing Two Views of the Sand Dollars Episode

Thematic Roles	Romeo	Juliet	Montagues	Capulets
Romeo	- - - - -	lover-of	family-of	
Juliet	lover-of	- - - - - -		family-of
Montagues	member-of		- - - - - - -	enemy-of
Capulets		member-of	enemy-of	- - - - - - - -

FIGURE 6.4 A Sample Context Grid

We continue in this section by examining the dimensions for representation specified in the UIF and the vocabulary it provides for each dimension. The goal here is not to make readers fluent at using the Universal Index Frame, but rather to give readers an idea of what a generally applicable vocabulary might look like, where it might derive from, and the considerations that must be taken into account in creating one. Those who want to use the Universal Index Frame are urged to read the reports describing it in detail (Schank and Osgood 1990). Those who are not interested in the specifics of the UIF can safely skip to section 6.5.

6.4.1 Specifying Content

We will begin by looking at the **content** part of the index, the part that specifies what happened in an episode. One of the hallmarks of the content of intentional stories is that there is always more than one view in any situation. This may be because there are multiple people, each approaching the situation with his or her own set of goals, beliefs, and expectations; because one person brings multiple interacting goals or beliefs to a situation; or because what happened in a situation was different from what was wanted, feared, or expected. Examples of the first include the steak and haircut stories. An example of the second happens when someone has goals in conflict (e.g., a liquor store owner being robbed at gunpoint has the conflicting goals of saving his money and preserving his life) or when the goals of a person interact in an unexpected or opportune way (e.g., John wants to go to the movies and he needs to make some money; the mother next door calls and asks him to babysit for her kids, telling him that it would be nice if he would take them to the movie he wants to see). The third is exemplified by the drunk and the lamppost story and the sand dollar story. The person viewing the situation has two views: the ideal view (what should have happened) and the perceived view (what happened instead).

The index, then, needs to be able to describe each episode from multiple points of view. It is not just the multiple points of view, however, that make an intentional situation noteworthy. Rather, an episode is noteworthy when multiple points of view interact with each other in unusual ways. Suppose John wants to go the movies and wants to make money, and he solves the problem by first going to the movies and then mowing the lawn. The episode is not all that interesting, because there is no unusual interaction between the goals; they were easily achieved sequentially, the usual way. It is only when he is able to achieve the usually conflicting goals at the same time that the episode becomes memorable. Thus, another piece of the index's content is the relationship between the views.

Each point of view in an intentional situation brings with it goals, beliefs, plans, and emotions, some of which are present at the beginning of the episode, others of which are the result of what happens in the episode. The UIF thus suggests the following descriptors (dimensions) for each point of view:

- *Anticipatory affect*: the emotions of the character going into the situation
- *Pretask belief:* relevant beliefs of the character going into the situation
- *Task*: the task the actor is actively engaged in as the episode plays itself out
- *Theme*: relevant thematic relationships, roles played by the character, character traits, and lifelong ambitions that the character brings to the situation
- *Goal*: the character's relevant goal
- *Plan*: the plan the character uses or intends to use in the situation
- *Result*: the major impact of what happened in the situation
- *Positive side effects*
- *Negative side effects*
- *Resultant affect*: the emotions of the character leaving the situation
- *Posttask belief*: relevant beliefs of the character leaving the situation (i.e., what he or she learned from the situation)
- *Change in affect*: a characterization of the degree of change in the character's feelings as a result of the episode

We now know the dimensions that should be used to represent indexes for intentional situation. What about the vocabulary for each piece of it? What kinds of views are there? What relationships are there between views? What is the vocabulary for affects? beliefs? tasks? themes? goals? plans? impacts? These vocabularies come partly from previous research about plans, goals, themes, and so on and partly from analysis of a variety of different remindings. We start with the dimensions of a single view and then present the different kinds of views and their relationships.

The complexity of the task of defining vocabulary for these dimensions varies widely with dimensions. Values for some dimensions are relatively easy to define and are short, concise lists (e.g., affect, task). For others, it is impossible to enumerate the range of values that can fill the slot, but a typology of values is fairly straightforward (e.g., goal). Others require a multidimensional typology (e.g., themes, plans). That is, we can't enumerate the list of values, nor can we find a single way of dividing it by types. Rather, we can find a set of dimensions on which to characterize the values. For others, we can't come up with a standard vocabulary at all (e.g., beliefs). In fact, beliefs are about many of the other categories plus more. There is also wide variation in the expressiveness of the vocabulary chosen for different dimensions, sometimes due to the complexity of representing the concepts, sometimes because there is a need to be more or less expressive. Goals, for example, are expressed fairly succinctly. Results, on the other hand, are in a highly simplified form. Rather than representing real results, the UIF has in it a qualitative characterization of the impact of the result. This is partly because of the complexity of representing results in a detailed way and partly because analysis of remindings shows that there are certain characterizations of results that seem to guide reminding; the details of results aren't all that important in judging similarity across domains.

I thus repeat the warning given at the beginning of this chapter. Coming up with a complete and correct set of dimensions and vocabulary terms is a daunting, perhaps impossible task. The vocabulary to be presented here is an attempt to cover as much as possible, be intuitively reasonable, be reasonably expressive, support a large number of remindings, and work most of the time. The UIF is a vocabulary in progress, incomplete in places and probably incorrect in places, needing to be used extensively so that it can be fleshed out, made more comprehensible, and made more consistent. It has been used to represent the indexes of a thousand or so cases so far. It may need to be used on ten thousand or more before it is complete.

Affect.   The vocabulary of affects and emotions is used to specify both anticipatory and resultant affects (Ortony, Glore and Collins 1988). What is needed here is a vocabulary that captures our commonsense view of our own feelings and emotions. What are the ways we feel that cause us to act or react in certain ways? The UIF proposes four types of emotions. *Cognitive* emotions get at the degree to which a character is attracted to or repulsed by some aspect of a situation, the degree to which the character can focus mental effort, and the degree to which the character is alert to external events. *Plan/goal* emotions are those that express the protagonist's expectations about a situation. *Sensation* emotions are the "raw" affect felt by the individual. *Self-image* emotions are those that are related to self-confidence and that predict how conservative or radical an agent's goals might be. These emotions are related to confidence, initiative, and security. Also represented in the UIF is a characterization of the change in affect from beginning to end of an episode. A change is always related to some particular emotion. Figure 6.5 lists the affect vocabulary.

VOCABULARY OF EMOTIONS:

Cognitive emotions: disgusted, disinterested, distracted, bored, neutral, curious, attracted, fascinated, alert, confused.

Plan/goal emotions: desperate, fearful, nervous, resigned, hopeful, neutral, excited, surprised, reassured, relieved, satisfied, disappointed.

Sensation emotions: anguished, despondent, sad, distressed, neutral, content, pleased, happy, joyful, hateful, furious, angry, pained, uncomfortable, comfortable, pleasured, irritated, grateful, sympathetic, loving.

Self-image emotions: self-pity, neutral, gloating, shamed, embarrassed, guilty, vindicated, proud, shy, bold, insecure, secure.

VOCABULARY OF EMOTIONAL CHANGES:

Changes of affect: intensification, attenuation, extinguishing, positive, inversion, negative inversion, same, neutral.

FIGURE 6.5   Representing Affect: Used for `anticipatory affect` and `resultant affect` Slots, It Captures Our Commonsense View of Our Own Feelings and Emotions

---

Generating alternatives: `search`
Predicting outcomes: `project`
Making decisions: `choose`
Beginning an action: `initiate`
Monitoring an action: `execution`
Ending an action: `terminate`
Explaining a failure: `explain`
Fixing something that went wrong: `repair`

FIGURE 6.6   Task Vocabulary: Used to Represent the Cognitive Activity an Agent Is Engaged in

Task.   A character's task is the cognitive activity he or she is actively engaged in when the episode occurs. This aspect of the representation is motivated by psychological results (Seifert 1988) showing that putting people in a task situation similar to that in a previous episode facilitates reminding. A person is likely to remember episodes of *explaining* while doing explanation, *preparation* while doing preparation, and so on. The task vocabulary proposed by the UIF is listed in Figure 6.6.[6]

Themes.   The next category of terms, themes, is quite a bit more complicated than either emotion or task. Themes (Schank and Abelson 1977) organize and predict plans and goals and tend to persist over long periods of time. They tend to reflect who a person is. Themes are associated with a person's interpersonal relationships (e.g., parent, husband), roles he or she plays (e.g., chairperson, teacher, advisor), character traits (e.g., honesty, trustworthiness), and long-term ambitions (e.g., to become president). A list of themes could be very long and very *ad hoc*. But themes are similar to each other in several ways. We all recognize, for example, that parent-child and advisor-advisee relationships are similar to each other, and we recognize that sometimes the parent role is similar to the boss role. What is needed is a set of dimensions on which to characterize themes that allows those similarities to be recognized. Given such a set of dimensions, individual themes can each be defined according to where they fall on each dimension.

Concentration in the UIF has been on interpersonal themes, which come up more extensively than the others in intentional situations. Interpersonal themes are described along four dimensions: thread membership, initiation control, termination control, and performance control. Figure 6.7 lists the full vocabulary. Thread membership gets at the aspect of the person's life that the theme is active over: for example, social life, education, and home life. The interpersonal theme *father,* for example, is a `family life` theme, while *committee member* might be a `community life` or `career` theme, and *lover* is a `romantic life` and perhaps `home life`

---

6. Notice that the tasks listed here are similar to the tasks listed previously in this chapter in the discussion about points, but not exactly the same. The set listed here represents the tasks agents in a case are engaged in and provides a vocabulary for representing the indexes of cases, allowing cases to be differentiated from each other based on tasks a character in the case is engaged in. The other set was created for the purpose of guiding selection of indexes and represents the reasoning of someone using a case. The different roles that cognitive task is playing result in two different breakdowns.

Thread membership: social life, community life, state, economic life, career, formal education, religion, home life, family life, romantic life

Initiation control: mutual consent, provider/dependent, master/slave, independent control, external control, circumstantial control

Termination control: same vocabulary as initiation control

Performance control: inducements, enforcements, third-party control

FIGURE 6.7   The Vocabulary for Representing the Four Dimensions of Interpersonal Themes

and/or `family life` theme. Themes that share a common thread tend to share goals, values, plans, control, and so on.

The other three aspects of interpersonal themes, as defined by the UIF, have to do with control—the kind and extent of control each agent can exercise over the other in a relationship. Initiation control characterizes how the relationship can be initiated. Termination control characterizes how it can be ended. Performance control characterizes how one can get the other to do something.

An interpersonal theme is defined by describing where it fits in each of these four dimensions. The *parent* theme, for example, fits the `family life` and `home life` threads, is initiated by `provider/dependent` control with the parent as provider, can be terminated only by `external control` or `circumstantial control`, and includes both `inducement` and `enforcement` controls on performance. The *child* theme is described by essentially the same dimensions, but puts the child in the opposite role in several of the control relationships. Though interpersonal themes themselves need to be defined as the situation warrants, defining where each theme fits on this set of dimensions will allow a matcher to determine the similarity of two themes with different names. *Parent* and *thesis advisor,* for example, are similar in that both have `provider/dependent` initiations and have similar performance control definitions.

Goals.   With goals, we move back to more familiar ground. The AI and psychology literatures both claim that goals play a large role in guiding behavior. A person follows a particular plan because it is one that can help him or her to achieve some current goal. One shows emotion as a result of achieving or not achieving goals. One problem in indexing a case by the goal of a character is to decide which of the many goals the person has at any time is the one to record. For example, a person who takes a book out of the library to read it might want to read it to learn about some subject, and might want to do that to be knowledgeable in a disciplinary field, and might want to do that to become a professor or an inventor or an entrepreneur. Which is the right goal to record in an index?

The solution proposed in the UIF is to record the highest-level goal that has a direct effect on the events in the case. The convention is that the recorded goal should be general enough to subsume more specific goals in the hierarchy during matching without being so abstract that it is useless. For example, if in some case a book was not available and the person therefore took out another book on the same subject, the goal of learning about that subject would be applicable. If the person instead took out a book on a different subject, but in the

PERFORMANCE GOALS:

execute-action *(action)*

ACHIEVEMENT GOALS:

achieve *(state, value)*
maintain *(state, value)*
possess *(object)*
achieve-victory *(opponent, action, victory criterion)*

KNOWLEDGE ACQUISITION GOALS:

gain-knowledge *(fact description)*
learn-explanation *(causal description)*
assess goal achievement *(goal, time, agent)*
predict result of action *(action, time, agent)*
decide on something *(set criterion)*

GOALS PERTAINING TO GOALS:

avoid goal achievement *(goal)*
achieve goal for another *(goal, agent)*
agent achieves goal *(goal, agent)*

FIGURE 6.8   Vocabulary of Goals Represented in the UIF

same disciplinary area, we would assume that the goal of learning the discipline was the active one.

There are four general classifications of goals that have proven useful for indexing intentional situations: performance goals, achievement goals, knowledge acquisition goals, and goals pertaining to goals. A performance goal is a goal to do something, and is represented simply as execute-action *(action)*. An achievement goal is a goal to be in some state. A knowledge acquisition goal is a goal to know something. One might want to know a fact or an explanation, or want to form an opinion about goal satisfaction, action results, or what meets a criterion. Goals pertaining to goals include wanting to avoid achieving a goal, wanting to achieve a goal for sombody else, or wanting someone else to achieve a goal. Figure 6.8 lists the goals that the UIF uses.

Goals are specified in the UIF by their type, as shown in Figure 6.8. In addition, each has other specifications associated with it, also shown in that figure, such as the objects or actions the goals apply to. Though goal types are well defined in the UIF, their specifications are not as well specified. Why? For two reasons. First, though goal types are domain-independent, many of the specifications that go with them are associated with the domain the goal is applied to. Second, many goal specifications are composed of other pieces of an index.

Note also that goals play a central role in the UIF. Other portions of the UIF are often filled in based on some relationship to the specified goal. For example, plans are usually chosen to achieve goals, results are the results of a plan with respect to a goal, and a task is usually done in service to a goal. If there is a choice of several goals that might be specified in a description of a case, the one chosen should be the one that has a relationship to one or more of these other specifications.

Plans.   What would it mean to have a vocabulary for plans? Similarly to themes, there are so many different plans one could use; their enumeration is probably intractable. Indexing by plans, then, means *coming up with some means of characterizing plans that allows them to be compared with each other in a meaningful way.* That is, plans should be described according to the planning issues that arise in them that are common across other plans. This includes issues of dealing with other agents (including fellow planners, counterplanners, authority, peers, employees), dealing with resources (e.g., acquiring them, using them, keeping the supply steady, sharing them, policies for acquiring and using them), getting and providing information (e.g., finding it, gaining access to it, giving access to it), access to tools, dealing with time (e.g., interleaving tasks, sequencing them according to some policy, combining tasks in the same time slot, delaying tasks), and so on. Plans, in the UIF, are specified along these dimensions as shown in Figure 6.9. Note that the representation of plans is the least specified and most *ad hoc* of the vocabulary categories. Though we know some of the common dimensions of plans, the list is by no means complete. This is an area in which additional work is needed in coming up with both dimensions and vocabulary for representation.

Results and impacts.   The final category we must specify is results. Results of an event can be almost anything: another causally related event, a change of state, a change of emotional state, a change of belief, and so on. In trying to define what needs to be specified in a result, the definers of the UIF had to analyze what it was about results that was taken into account in reminding. Their claim is that there are four important pieces of results that should be recorded: emotions or affects resulting from an episode, new beliefs believed as a result of the event, direct impacts resulting from the event, and side effects resulting from the event.

- Characterizations of other agents who are involved: partners, counterplanners, authority, peers, employees
- Necessary aspects of dealing with resources: acquiring them, using them, keeping the supply steady, sharing them, policies for acquiring and using them
- Means of getting and providing information: finding it, gaining access to it, giving access to it
- Needed tools
- The way time is dealt with: interleaving tasks, sequencing tasks according to some policy, combining tasks in the same time slot, delaying tasks

FIGURE 6.9   Sample Dimensions of a Representation for Plans and Some Sample Values They Can Take

`Resultant affects`: emotions resulting from an episode
`Change in affect`: changes in degree of an emotion resulting from an episode
`Posttask belief`: new beliefs of the case's agents derived as a result of the event
`Results`: direct impacts resulting from the event
`Positive side effects`: positive side effects resulting from the event
`Negative side effects`: negative side effects resulting from the event

FIGURE 6.10   Six Dimensions for Representing Results; Each is a Slot of the UIF

These are represented in six results slots of the UIF, as summarized in Figure 6.10. Note that this set of descriptors of results characterizes the episode's result in an abstract way but does not describe the concrete result (i.e., what happened) itself.

The attempt to characterize results in a domain-independent way led to a shorthand for representing results, called **impacts**. *Results* and *side effects* slots are filled with impacts, and there are three kinds: impacts on goals, emotional impacts, and cognitive impacts. Emotional impacts are new emotions that arise and changes in extant emotions. Because they have already been discussed, we discuss only goal impacts and cognitive impacts here. Goal impacts refer to effects on some character's goal (e.g., it was achieved, it was blocked). Representing a goal impact requires designating the goal that is impacted, who has the goal, and the impact on the goal. Cognitive impacts are changes of belief or knowledge state resulting from an event, including such things as expectation failure, expectation generation, and belief generation. The full set is listed in Figure 6.11. Representing a cognitive impact requires designating whose cognition and which expectation, explanation, or belief were impacted.

Though results are represented quite simply, they can be quite complex. The complexity is seen in the many different kinds of results that are represented in the UIF. Together, some quite complicated results can be represented. A failure despite extreme effort, for example, is represented as a combination of (1) a pretask belief that significant resource expenditure is necessary to achieve a goal, (2) the result that the goal is blocked, (3) the negative side effect that large amounts of efforts were expended, and (4) the posttask belief that resource expenditure will not achieve this goal. Representing triumph depite overwhelming odds is simple. There are two parts to the representation: (1) a pretask belief that the difficulty of achieving the goal will cause it to be blocked and (2) the result that the goal is achieved. Representing ironic success is also possible, though it has more parts: (1) pretask belief that a goal is threatened by its own preconditions, (2) the result that the goal is achieved, (3) resultant affect of surprise, and (4) a posttask belief that the preconditions indeed serve the goal.

Representing multiple views.   A single view of an episode is recorded by filling in values for each of the dimensions listed above. More interesting than representing a single view, however, and more vital for indexing in intentional situations, is the recording of the relationships among multiple views. This is perhaps the greatest contribution of the UIF, specifically designating that the relationships among views of a situation are important to capture in an index.

The first task in allowing the relationships among views to be captured is to define the different kinds of views of a situation that there might be. The UIF defines six views.

GOAL IMPACTS:

Goal is achieved: `achieved`
Goal is partially achieved: `served`
Goal is blocked (permanently or temporarily): `blocked`
It is anticipated that the goal will be blocked: `threatened`
The goal might be blocked: `inhibited`
Another mutually exclusive goal was achieved: `clobbered`
No more attempts to achieve the goal will be made: `aborted`
A new goal is added: `created`
The goal no longer serves its supergoal: `disconnected`
The goal's importance has increased: `promoted`
Importance has decreased: `demoted`

COGNITIVE IMPACTS:

An expectation failed: `expectation failure`
A new expectation was generated: `expectation generation`
An expectation was fulfilled: `expectation fulfillment`
An explanation was generated: `explanation generation`
An explanation was found to be faulty: `explanation failure`
An explanation was fulfilled: `explanation fulfillment`
A new belief was generated: `belief generation`
An extant belief was modified: `belief modification`
An extant belief was reinforced: `belief reinforcement`
A shift of attention resulted: `attention shift`

FIGURE 6.11   A Vocabulary for Goal Impacts and Cognitive Impacts

---

`Expected` is what the viewer expected to see, `perceived` is what the viewer observed (directly or indirectly), and `actual` is what actually happened. This view is used only when what was perceived and what actually happened are different. Otherwise, `perceived` is used. `Ideal` is what should have happened, from the point of view of the viewer, if everything had happened optimally. `Wanted` is what the viewer wants to happen, and `feared` is a scenerio the viewer feels would be negative if it happens. Figure 6.12 summarizes.

`Expected`: what the viewer expect to see
`Perceived`: what the viewer saw
`Actual`: what actually happened
`Ideal`: what should have happened, from the point of view of the viewer
`Wanted`: what the viewer wanted to happen
`Feared`: a negative scenerio the viewer did not want

FIGURE 6.12   Representing *Views* of a Situation

Representing a single view requires designating a viewer, that viewer's point of view, and the character being viewed, along with all relevant dimensions that describe a situation from that point of view. Representing multiple views is done by placing several views side by side. Figure 6.3 shows what this looks like for the sand dollar story. The viewer in both cases is "R," but one view shows what R thinks is the ideal view of the situation, the other shows what R saw. In both cases, his daughter was the main character being viewed. In the ideal view, her task was to search with the goal of possessing sand dollars and to use the appropriate plan. In the perceived view, she searched with the goal of possessing sand dollars but used an inappropriate plan.

The same representational vehicle can be used to show two different people looking at the same situation but with different interpretations of it, a person viewing a situation with two major goals in mind (a goal conflict), the failure of a plan to behave as expected, and so on. What is needed now to complete the picture is a way of designating which differences between the views are the ones to focus on and a way of designating the reason for the difference. For that, we look to a representation of anomalies.

Representing anomalies. We record cases when they are different from what is expected in some useful or interesting way. A case that is different from what is expected is different by virtue of some anomaly. That is, there is some discrepancy between values in different views of a situation. In the UIF, representations of anomalies are defined on two dimensions: whether the anomaly is a `surprise` or an `expectation failure`, and the anomalous dimension of the content: `goal`, `plan`, `task`, and so on. When a person uses an inappropriate plan to achieve a goal (as in the sand dollars story), the anomaly is an `expectation failure` associated with the `plan`. If a novel set of ingredients is being combined to make some dish and it turns out delicious (a pleasant surprise), the anomaly is a `surprise` associated with an actor's `belief`. As we saw in Figure 6.3 earlier, the plans in the ideal view and the perceived one disagree with each other. The plan was different than expected; thus it is an expectation failure. Figure 6.13 summarizes the two kinds of anomalies.

There may be several anomalies in a situation. Any combination of content descriptors could be anomalous across views. The goal could be anomalous, as well as the plan, as well as the task, and so on. Anomalies can be associated with each of the content dimensions of an index, and a case might have several anomalies recorded in it. Consider, for example, the following story (Schank and Osgood 1990):

> Bill has just moved in with a new office mate, who has an undergraduate degree in paleontology. Bill is trying to get acquainted and begins to talk to him a bit about dinosaurs to be polite. As he gets into the discussion, however, he finds that he is quite interested in the topic and asks more and more questions. Eventually, the new office mate is turned off and decides he doesn't like Bill. Bill is taken by surprise.

One way to represent this situation is as an anomaly between Bill's expectations about what would happen in meeting a new office mate and his perception of what did happen. Looking at the situation this way, there are four anomalies present. First, the expected goal was to get acquainted, while the actual goal pursued was to find out more about dinosaurs. Second,

Expectation failure: something expected did not materialize, or something else was done instead

Surprise: something that could not have been predicted happened

FIGURE 6.13 Two Kinds of Anomalies

the expected plan was to promote goodwill, while the plan that was actually used was to request information. Third, it was expected that the goal of getting acquainted would be achieved, while what actually happened was that it got more or less ignored and therefore disconnected in the course of the dialogue. Fourth, there was no side effect expected, but instead there was a negative side effect of clobbering the get-acquainted goal. Figure 6.14 gives a graphical view of these differences. Notice that four different anomalies are recorded.

6.4.2 Specifying Context

The picture of the content part of an index is now complete. What is left is to discuss the context-setting part of the index. What needs to be in there? For intentional situations, three components have been designated as context-setting: the major anomaly the situation addresses, the setting of the situation, and the interpersonal relationships among the characters.

Though there may be many anomalies in a situation, the major anomaly in the context specification of a case records the one anomaly that supersedes all the others. Because it needs to supersede the others, what is needed is a more abstract recording than in the content part of the case. There are three types of anomalies represented in the context part of a case: anomalous behavior, anomalous phenomena, and anomalous belief. Anomalous behavior is someone

Slot-names	View 1	View 2	Anomalies
Viewer	Bill	Bill	
View	expected	perceived	
Agent	Bill	Bill	
Task	explain	explain	
Goal	do-goal: get- acquainted	know-goal: dinosaurs	surprise
Plan	promote goodwill	request - information	surprise
Result	achieve	disconnect	result exp-failure
Side-neg		clobber (achieve do-goal)	side-effect exp-failure

FIGURE 6.14 A Sample Content Grid Showing Two Views of the Office Mate Episode

doing something unexpected. Anomalous phenomena is something unexpected happening. An anomalous belief is one that is surprising or turns out to be incorrect. Any can be expectation failures or surprises. Thus, the two dimensions anomalies are recorded on at this level are `sur-prise` versus `expectation failure`, and `behavior`, `phenomena`, and `belief`. The sand dollars case and the office mate case are both examples of `behavior expectation failure`. All the anomalies were behavior anomalies, and though some were surprising and others were expectation failures, the expectation failures seem to be more vital to the description of the story.

The setting of a situation is where it physically takes place. There is not much to say about that. The representation of interpersonal relationships has already been discussed above, and those that actually take part in the construal of the situation represented by the index are recorded in the content of the case. The contextual part of the case represents the full range of interpersonal relationships among the characters in the story. These relationships set the stage for the story itself.

6.5 GENERALLY APPLICABLE INDEXING SCHEMES: LESSONS ILLUSTRATED BY THE UIF

The UIF addresses indexing of cases so that they can be recalled across contexts. It concentrates on representing thematically similar components of cases, but does not deal much with representing the details of situations. When a case-based reasoner is confined to solving problems in some particular domain, however, emphasis on thematic information becomes less important than emphasis on the details of situations. A civil engineer building a bridge, for example, wants to see the way other bridges with similar spans and similar opportunities for ground support have been done. If working with a new material, he or she may want to examine the details of bridges and perhaps other artifacts that have been built with that material to see how the material behaves, how it holds up, what kinds of supports it needs, and so on. The indexes needed here are not thematic; they need to specify details of the situation.

Nevertheless, the UIF is important, both because it gives a first approach to coming up with a universal indexing scheme for a broad range of cases and because it is the first attempt to codify the types of information that might be included in an index. There are a number of lessons we can take away from the endeavor, whether or not we use this particular indexing scheme and vocabulary in our own systems, whether or not we need our indexing schemes to be universal, and whether or not we are building pragmatically oriented CBR systems or more experimental ones.

6.5.1 Indexes Correspond to Interpretations of Situations

Perhaps the most important lesson to be drawn from the UIF is that the best indexes are based on interpretations of events rather than on the raw events themselves. Indeed, the cognitive model behind case-based reasoning predicts this. It tells us that features available to use for reminding are all those that are derived in the process of reasoning about a situation—trying to understand it or trying to solve its problem. Thus, the features we use for indexing need to be drawn from that set. The UIF provides a framework for capturing interpretations of situations drawn while reasoning about them. An interpretation of a situation has the important details in it; it leaves out the descriptors that play less significant roles.

The particular types of interpretations found to be useful in describing intentional situations are *anomalies*, and it is these kinds of interpretations that the UIF captures. Once one makes a commitment to some kind of interpretation, one can choose dimensions for representation based on what's needed to describe such interpretations. That's what the UIF does. Its dimensions capture the descriptors one needs to describe anomalies in intentional situations.

Of course, the types of interpretations that we use to describe intentional situations are different from those we use for other kinds of situations. An analysis of the ways one tends to describe episodes in a domain can lead one to the kinds of interpretations needed for that domain.

The idea of capturing interpretations rather than full descriptions is important because it frees the indexer from having to create a full representation of a situation. One represents only as much of a situation as is needed to reason about it, and one indexes only to the level of detail needed for relevant reminding.

6.5.2 Capturing Relationships Among Components of an Episode

A related lesson the UIF teaches is about the kinds of descriptors one should think about capturing in indexes. Our first inclination, when we think about indexes, is to think about the indexes in books. Such indexes are created from individual features of a concept and simple combinations of features. The first inclination of most people, when they attempt to build an indexing system for cases, is to index them the way they would be indexed in a book.

The approach in the UIF is different. In particular, it stresses the importance of *capturing relationships among components of a case* in a case description, hence, in an index. It is not just enough to combine features to create an index, the combinations of features themselves might compose into something that needs to be referenced in describing a case or in indexing it. In the UIF, composition is in two ways: across several views of the same content dimension (e.g., goals, plans, themes) and down the set of content dimensions for any one view. Each view, in the UIF, is a complex descriptor of the case that has attributes associated with it (whose view it is, from what point of view the case is being looked at, and who its major character is). And the values along each dimension of the content each form complex features that have the "anomaly" attribute associated with them. For example, if the plan in two views is different, the anomaly attribute comments on the difference.

Overall, the UIF allows indexes to capture large, complex combinations of features. An arbitrarily large subset of the description of a case might act as one of its indexes—there is no attempt to make indexes compact. If a case library is large, then large complex combinations and compositions of features might be necessary to identify the best-matching case. In addition, the combinations of features that are composed in the UIF are quite a bit more complex than what we normally see in books.

The UIF provides a new way to think about indexing, and creators of indexing schemes for case libraries should put much thought into what needs to be captured before settling for simple descriptors and simple combinations of descriptors as indexes. Simple combinations are also important, but more complex compositions of features that capture the interpretations of situations and relationships among descriptors may buy precision and power that simple descriptors can't provide.

6.5.3 The Specificity of Indexes

Many of us think about indexes as needing to be highly specific and detailed. But what needs to be captured in an index depends on the task the cases will be put to and the dimensions of similarity between cases. Much of what is recorded in the UIF is abstract or is a characterization of a specific without being specific itself. This is because the UIF's goal was to come up with a scheme that would allow reminding across domains. Analysis of such remindings in people showed that the specifics of situations were not as important as the more abstract designations of goal relationships, goal-plan relationships, emotional impacts, changes of belief, and impacts on goals. As the result of that analysis, effort was put into characterizing these components of situations at an abstract level rather than looking at how to record their details. Results, for example, are never recorded specifically in an index. Rather, their impact is recorded.

That being said, it is important to recognize that some domains do require more detail in their indexes. And necessary details must, of course, be recorded. But creators of indexing vocabularies should not neglect more abstract kinds of descriptors. It is important, in creating an indexing vocabulary, to analyze what makes cases similar[7] to see which aspects of cases are the important ones to represent. Much effort can be saved if it is found that some details of situations don't need to be represented in indexes. Much power can be gained if those abstract descriptors that facilitate reminding are made part of the indexing vocabulary. Of course, one should not make indexes so abstract that they cannot be recognized.

6.5.4 Surface Features and Abstract Features in Indexing and Reminding

Often details do need to be represented in indexes. Abstract features are useful for some tasks, but for others, cases that are the same across domain-specific dimensions are most useful. A question to consider at this point is the role of surface features and surface similarity in reminding. If we consider intentional situations, our intuitions are that if we know of several cases that are thematically similar, we will tend to be reminded first of the one of those that is most similar on surface characteristics. Within a thematic category, cases that are similar on surface features might contribute more specific or refined expectations than cases that are less alike on the surface.

Suppose, for example, that a person knew about *Romeo and Juliet* and also knew about a plot among some of the workers of an organization to leave the organization and form another one. When this person heard about the plot, in fact, he was reminded of *Romeo and Juliet*, since in both there was work toward a mutual goal in the face of outside opposition. Upon

---

7. E.g., by examining the natural remindings of people doing the designated task.

remembering *Romeo and Juliet*, he gave advice to the conspirators that they should make sure they coordinated their plans with each other to avoid tragedy. Suppose, now, that this person goes to see *West Side Story*. Which situation is he more likely to remember? *Romeo and Juliet,* or the organization story? Both are in the same thematic category: mutual goal achievement in the face of outside opposition. Unless there are other thematic components in common between *West Side Story* and the organization story, I would contend that it is more likely that this person will be reminded of *Romeo and Juliet* than the organization story. Why? Because though both cases are equally similar on thematic grounds, *Romeo and Juliet* is also similar on surface characteristics.

The example shows us that indexing vocabulary, even for intentional situations, needs to include both abstract and situation-specific vocabulary. We might want retrieval algorithms to put priority on thematic or relational similarity, and then to prefer cases that are similar in other ways. Such a vocabulary will cover intentional situations, those where agents with goals attempt to achieve their goals. And it is intended to support the full range of reasoning one might do about such situations, including the tasks that come up in understanding such situations, those that come up in taking part in them, and those that come up in conversing about them.

Though the UIF was designed with the capture of thematic information in mind, it also includes places for recording at least some of the details of a situation. One represents goals, for example, by representing the type of goal and what it is applied to in the world. If someone wants to possess a book, it is represented as a `possess` goal applied to the object `book`. The possession part is thematic; the object part (book) represents specifics of the situation. Similarly for each of the other slots.

The lesson here is that a generally applicable vocabulary does not have to neglect the recording of domain-specific information about a case. Rather, *it should provide generally applicable dimensions where domain-specific descriptors can be recorded*. The more domain-independent are the dimensions used for indexing cases, the more chance there is to extend case libraries so that they can be used for several different tasks. The more domain-independent are the dimensions used for indexing cases, the more generally applicable guidelines we have available for going about the task of choosing domain-specific vocabulary: the dimensions tell us what sorts of domain-specific descriptors we should concentrate on.

6.5.5 Modularity and Redundancy in an Indexing Scheme

Another lesson to take from the UIF representation is that modularity in an indexing scheme is worthwhile. The UIF is modular in several ways. It separates out global information, contextual information, and content information. It separates out what is true before an event takes place, what happens during the event, and what is true after. It separates out different views of the same event. Such modularity is good because it provides a systematic way of viewing a case that is likely to result in coherent capture of its description. It causes the indexer to think systematically about a case's description.

But modularity also leads to redundancy. Some descriptors can be found in several places in the descriptive vocabulary. The UIF is redundant in two ways, in its recordings of anomalies and in its recordings of relationships among people. Each is recorded both as a context-setting feature and as a descriptor of the content of the situation. Each is recorded specifically in the places it belongs in the content part of the index and more abstractly in the context.

Redundancy, in turn, has its advantages and disadvantages. The major disadvantage, of course, is the extra space it requires for storage. But the major advantage outweighs this. The redundancies in the UIF stem from two goals: (1) making evident important parts of the representation by making them prominent and (2) allowing each part of the index to stand alone. The representation of anomalies in the UIF illustrates both. Anomalies are represented as part of the content representation of a case, associated there with the case component they describe. One can read across a line of the UIF that has an anomaly recorded and see the several values for that component of the case description and what type of anomaly the differences represent. A single line of the UIF can stand alone as a piece of a case's description. The major anomaly in a situation is elevated by including it in the global slots of the case. There, it is singled out by placing it in a more prominent part of the case description.

6.5.6   Describing Cases and Indexing Cases: The Differences

The frame that gets filled in by UIF vocabulary items was originally conceived as a frame for representing a case's indexes. The idea was to fill in one or several UIF frames completely for each case and to use the full combination of features represented in each frame to index the case. This worked well for some systems the UIF was created for (e.g., ABBY [Domeshek 1991a, b, c]). These systems had as their task to give abstract advice about a situation. In ABBY, for example, the user tells the system a story (by filling in a UIF form), and the system finds all the relevant stories in its memory to tell in response. The UIF was good for doing this. It allowed systems to find every case in a system that partially matched the new situation.

But the task of these systems required little discrimination between those cases that matched better and those that matched worse. When the UIF frames were used as indexes in systems that needed to choose cases that could best address the needs of a reasoner, the UIF frame, by itself, couldn't do the job (Bareiss, personal communication; Burke, personal communication). One reason was that it encompassed too large a description of each situation without designating which of its many features and combinations of features were more important than other ones. Though it provided a good abstract description of each case, because each of its features are equally important, it did not provide discriminatory power—the power to differentiate which of several partially matching cases had the potential to be more useful in reasoning.[8] In SPIEL (Kass et al. 1992, forthcoming; Burke and Kass 1992), a

---

8. We shall see this problem come up again when we discuss redundant discrimination nets in chapter 8.

system that tells stories for pedagogical reasons, this problem was solved by adding detail to UIF representations and by indexing stories, in addition, by pedagogical goals they can address.[9]

The UIF provides a set of symbols and dimensions that are applicable for describing cases across a variety of domains. It provides the vocabulary needed to index cases across those situations. But useful indexes are chosen for cases only by selecting out from a full description of a case those combinations of descriptors that can support a reasoner's purposes. Some of these descriptors are captured in the UIF; others are not. Methods presented in the next chapter tell us how to choose task-oriented indexes for cases.

6.6 BEYOND THE UNIVERSAL INDEX FRAME

How universal is the Universal Index Frame and its vocabulary? Thematic vocabulary captures interactions among people and interactions among the goals of an individual person. It captures those things at the level of goals, plans, and themes active in the situation. There are several things it leaves out. First, as discussed earlier, it is light on representing specifics of a situation. Second, there are important classes of events it does not capture. Third, it makes no claims about remindings based on visual or other sensory information. Addressing the first issue requires analysis much like that described earlier in the chapter. We must look at what tasks the system has to do and what kinds of similarities among cases, if specified in indexes, would allow useful remindings. The second and third issues, though quite interesting, require analyses that simply have not been done yet.

It is worth pointing out, however, one class of events that the UIF does not capture that has similar breadth and complexity to intentional situations and that, when solved, will provide much guidance to case-based reasoners involved in diagnosis and design. That important class of events, presented briefly in chapter 5, is experiences reasoning about objects and devices. Consider, for example, a car mechanic who is trying to diagnose and repair a particular automobile. He finds the faulty component and replaces it, but the owner comes back a week later with the same problem. The same component is broken, and he replaces it again, assuming he put in a faulty part the week before. This goes on several times, until finally, he begins to wonder whether something else is causing this component to break. He finds that the cooling system has a pinhole leak that is dropping water onto this component and making it short out. There's not enough water leaking to notice that the cooling system is faulty, but there is enough for it to affect another subsystem of the car engine.

How do we describe this case abstractly? From the intentional point of view, our car mechanic has the goal of fixing the car but is thwarted by an unknown action caused by another agent (in this case, an object, an agent without goals). This is one way to look at the story, but it is not the only way. It is also a story about seemingly separate subsystems of a mechanical device interacting with each other in unexpected ways. More specifically, a minor

---

9. Though UIF descriptions of stories are entered into SPIEL by hand, the system automatically chooses indexes for pedagogical goals based on a set of heuristics that interpret story descriptions to determine which kinds of pedagogical goals they can achieve.

problem in one subsystem caused more drastic problems in other subsystems that were related only spatially. This point is about how devices work, not about plans and goals.

Unfortunately, the work of defining a universal framework and vocabulary for describing and indexing cases involving objects and devices has not been done yet. As the example illustrates, as in intentional situations, the framework will have to emphasize interactions and types of interactions between parts. As in describing intentional situations, there might very well be a need for an equally complex indexing structure that includes both context and content and that specifies relationships and interactions. Views might represent expected behavior of the device (or one of its subsystems) and actual behavior. Though the work of defining this framework and vocabulary hasn't been done yet, the UIF suggests a direction to take in pursuing it. Further research on qualitative reasoning may also contribute to creating this vocabulary.

What can we expect of such a framework and vocabulary, when they are created? They will be able to support the recording of indexes for all the different kinds of devices that exist and the reasoning one can do about such devices, including diagnosis, repair, and design. They will allow experiences in one design or diagnosis domain to be recalled when working in another one. If, for example, the mechanic in the story went to medical school and was having trouble with a diagnosis problem, we might expect him to recall this case and wonder whether there might be interactions between the bodily subsystems going on that are not the expected ones. The framework and vocabulary will also provide guidelines to system implementors telling them the sorts of things to record and the vocabulary with which to do that recording in these domains.

Will there ever be one universal framework and vocabulary for indexing? The framework for case representation given in chapter 5 is probably as close as one can get to a universal framework for representing indexes. Indexes, like representations of cases, need to be able to record situation descriptions, solution descriptions, and result descriptions. The particular details of what needs to go into each depends largely on the task and domain. A universal framework that can cover every sort of case and every sort of reasoning goal would probably be so abstract that it would be useless. What would be useful, however, is to determine what broad classes of cases there are and to create indexing frameworks for each. Intentional cases is one broad class; reasoning about devices and artifacts is another; there are others as well.

What do we do until the universal framework and vocabulary are developed? We must continue to build systems and index cases the best we can, using functional guidelines for index selection to discover which dimensions of a domain are the important ones to record in indexes. In the process, we must learn as much as we can about the commonalities of cases across domains so that we can aim toward more universal indexing schemes for a wide variety of domains. Intentional domains were the first to be codified because there had been many years of research analyzing and understanding the ins and outs of cases and remindings over that broad class. The same sort of analysis has been being done over the past few years in reasoning about devices, and it is beginning to be time to codify the themes and framework for indexes across those device domains. Codifying other types of domains will follow.

6.7 SUMMARY

The indexes of a case designate in what circumstances the case should be retrieved. If we think about every case as teaching a set of lessons, then indexes represent the circumstances under which a lesson a case teaches should be taught. There are four properties a useful index has: It should be predictive. It should make useful predictions. It should be easy to recognize. It should be generally applicable.

Most important to a theory of indexing is a theory of the content of indexes. Approaches to discovering a content theory of indexing within the case-based reasoning community have been from two points of view. The functional, or pragmatic, point of view examines the kinds of cases that are available and the tasks they must support to identify the dimensions and symbols that, if used as indexes, will allow the available cases to cover the range of assigned tasks.

The reminding approach looks to remindings to point out the particular concepts that tie together cases from a domain or set of domains. It aims toward a set of descriptive dimensions and vocabulary items for filling those dimensions, trying to be as generally applicable as possible but also keeping in mind that each domain is likely to have its own domain-specific vocabulary. The Universal Index Frame comes from this tradition.

Because the indexes to a case are a subset of the case's description or representation, the vocabulary one has available for indexing cases can only be as good as the representational or descriptive vocabulary that is available. Theories of indexing vocabulary are really representational theories—they describe the representational dimensions that are needed to describe cases, though the cases themselves may have much more detail in them than do the indexes.

Though indexing vocabulary gives guidelines on the symbols that should be used to represent and index cases, procedures are also needed for choosing those representational dimensions that should be used to index each case, that is, to describe it uniquely and usefully. A content theory of indexing needs both components—the vocabulary and the guidelines for using it. Equally important to indexing is a set of processes for using indexes to retrieve cases from memory. The next chapter and the chapters in the section on case retrieval discuss these two issues.

7

Methods for Index Selection

If we consider again the examples and guidelines from the last chapter, we see that though the guidelines for choosing indexes are each fairly straightforward and understandable, their combination and implementation could be quite complex. Indexing by the combinations of features responsible for failure, for example, requires computation of those features. This process, commonly called *blame assignment*, is computationally complex, if not intractable. The process for figuring out why something succeeded, often called *credit assignment*, is the flip side of blame assignment and equally complex. Indexing by features that led to choosing solutions can, in principle, be done easily if the reasoner itself has solved the problem and kept track of the reasoning that led to its solution. But case libraries often need to be seeded with cases that the reasoner itself has never solved.

Two kinds of heuristic methods for automating index selection have been proposed that bypass these complexities. One kind chooses its indexes based on a checklist provided by the system builder. That is, the system builder tells the system which kinds of features (dimensions) it should use for indexing. Each case is indexed by the dimensions found on the checklist. The best checklists are lists of features known to be predictive; this kind of procedure chooses as indexes *features that tend to predict solutions and outcomes*. Another kind of index-selection procedure concentrates on extracting *differences* between the new case and other cases in the case library. In practice, these two kinds of methods usually need to be combined so that only those predictive features that are also distinguishing are chosen as indexes.

Both of these methods are computationally simple and require little knowledge on the part of a computer program. But both choose large numbers of indexes for cases, and though indexes tend to be predictive, they aren't guaranteed to be predictive in each individual case. Because indexes are not confined to usefully predictive features, case retrieval must be a two-step process when these methods are used (Kolodner 1989): In the first step, indexes are used to choose partially-matching cases. In the next step, the more useful cases are chosen from those.

A third kind of index selection method uses *explanations* of why a solution worked or didn't work as a basis for choosing indexes. These procedures choose indexes that are usefully predictive. These methods, unlike the first two, are highly knowledge-dependent and computationally complex. Using these methods, each case is indexed by the features that were important in solving it or by features that were responsible for its failure. When stored indexes are so chosen, a large percentage of the cases that are recalled are useful for further reasoning. The advantage of this method, then, is that it allows better identifiers to be associated with cases. The major disadvantage is that this method requires large amounts of computation and knowledge, so it cannot be easily used in large, broadly applicable real-world systems and it is not easily applied when domain theories are weak or nonexistent.

The division in types of methods for choosing indexes is paralleled by a set of indexing philosophies. One philosophy says that because correct indexes are hard to compute, it makes sense to analyze the domain and task and find out what kinds of features and feature combinations *tend* to be the predictive ones. Cases are then indexed by those of their features that tend to be good ones for indexing, but individual cases are never analyzed for the particular features they have that are predictive. The rationale here is that if we have been able to analyze the domain and task well enough, then we will usually be able to choose good indexes by this method. Though we will miss some unusual cases and retrieve some that should not be retrieved, overall the behavior of the retrieval processes will be just fine. Checklist-based approaches support this philosophy.

The second philosophy of indexing says that indexes should be chosen as individually as possible for each case. Choosing indexes specially for each case according to what was responsible for its failures and successes will provide very accurate retrieval later. Explanation-based approaches support this philosophy.

In fact, neither philosophy on its own seems to be able to solve the problem well enough. Indexing by features that tend to be predictive results in large numbers of cases being retrieved, making it necessary to run a separate process that chooses the most useful ones. Running a separate process, by itself, would not be bad, but because cases have not been analyzed individually to determine the relationships of their descriptors to their outcome, much of the knowledge needed to determine usefulness of cases is missing. On the other hand, if cases are indexed accurately, then a system can retrieve cases based only on predictions about its usefulness that were made at the time the case was put into the case library. It will miss cases that were not marked appropriately at the time they were added to the case library, and it may fail to find some interesting and useful partially-matching cases.

In other words, by the explanation method, it can only remember cases in situations it had anticipated their being useful for. There's something counterintuitive about this—people tend to feel that they get reminded of cases they were not expecting to remember, and that those cases can turn out to be very useful in guiding their reasoning. So though the first method is perhaps too broad, the second method by itself is too restrictive. Some principles for combining the two are needed. Several recent investigations (Kolodner 1989; Simoudis 1991b, 1992) propose using a coarse indexing scheme based on tendencies to drive initial retrieval and a more fine-grained indexing scheme for selecting the best cases from those retrieved in the first pass.

We shall see that though automated procedures exist for choosing indexes, they are deficient. Checklist-based approaches are sometimes too inaccurate and hard to control, while explanation-based approaches require huge amounts of knowledge, making their automation prohibitive for large domains. Though both methods are useful in narrow domains, neither method provides enough computational power to build systems that can automatically make decisions about indexing for all cases when domains are broad. Guidelines for index selection provided in the previous chapter, by contrast, are more generally applicable but are quite abstract. Our research goal is to create automated index-selection methods that implement those abstract guidelines and make them concrete. Until automated procedures catch up to guidelines for index selection, however, another way to index cases is to have a knowledge engineer use those guidelines to choose indexes for cases by hand.

In this chapter, the full range of procedures for choosing indexes is presented. We begin by presenting a method people can use to choose a case's indexes. This will give readers a feel for what indexes need to cover. After that, automated procedures for index selection are presented, along with the pros and cons of each.

7.1 CHOOSING INDEXES BY HAND

Methodology for choosing indexes of cases parallels the methodology presented in the previous chapter for determining the indexing vocabulary needed in a domain. One first determines what a case can be useful for and then designates the circumstances under which it could be useful. Using index selection guidelines associated with the different kinds of reasoning decisions the case can support, a first set of descriptors is chosen from that set of features. Those descriptors are massaged to make sure the index is generally applicable, and each component is described in a way that is recognizable. In an additional step, the description is translated into the symbolic vocabulary of the reasoning system. Figure 7.1 sums up the steps.

The first two steps designate the lessons the case teaches, or the points it makes, and for each, the circumstances in which those lessons can usefully be taught. As stated in the previous chapter, lessons can be about what is likely to happen or what should be done in some situation. Either way, it is important to be able to designate the circumstances the point is relevant to. It is these circumstances that become the case's indexes. Steps 1 and 2 help the indexer to identify the lessons and the circumstances in which they could appropriately be taught. In step

1. Determine what the case could be useful for by designating its points with respect to the set of tasks the reasoner is being asked to carry out.
2. Determine under what circumstances its points would be useful for each of these tasks.
3. Translate the circumstances into the vocabulary of the reasoner.
4. Massage the circumstances to make them as recognizable and generally applicable as possible.

FIGURE 7.1 Steps in Assigning Indexes to Cases

3, they get put into the right form and get represented appropriately. In step 4, they get generalized appropriately.

We will look at two cases to illustrate and motivate explanation of each step in this process. First, consider the following case that indexes must be chosen for.

> **Problem:** Twenty people were coming to dinner, it was summer and tomatoes were in
> season, we wanted a vegetarian meal, and one person was allergic to milk prod-
> ucts.
>
> **Solution:** We served tomato tart (a cheese and tomato pie). To accommodate the per-
> son allergic to milk, we used tofu cheese substitute instead of cheese in one of
> the tarts.

The first step in choosing indexes is to determine what the case could be useful for.
There are two possible uses for this case:

1. It provides conditions for success when choosing a vegetarian main dish with tomatoes:
   Choose tomato tart to feed vegetarians in the summer.
2. It provides conditions for success when trying to accommodate a person allergic to milk
   when a main dish with cheese is being served: *When trying to adapt a dish with cheese
   in it for someone who eats no milk products, use tofu cheese substitute.*

Determining what a case could be useful for is an introspective process on the part of the
indexer. A case is useful to the extent that it has lessons to teach. The first step gets at the lessons the case teaches. A case's lessons are guidelines that it provides for dealing with similar
situations; the case itself illustrates those guidelines. People generally find it easy to look at a
case and recognize some of the lessons it teaches, but the goal is to determine the full range of
lessons a case teaches and to index it for all of those. How can that be done?

One way to get at the lessons a case can teach is to consider the kinds of uses cases are
put to in the system. Do they suggest solutions? Do they point out the potential for failure? Do
they help in projecting results? For any particular system, the useful lessons a case can teach
are those that are of a type the system knows how to use. The indexer thus asks of each case,
Which of the tasks that case-based reasoning supports in this system can this case provide
guidelines for? When we look at this case, we see that it provides guidelines for construction
of a solution and for choice of an adaptation method, two kinds of solution creation decisions.

Another way to determine a case's usefulness is to consider the kinds of points cases can
make (as described in chapter 6), to designate which points of each type the case makes, and to
select from the set those points that can promote the case-based reasoner's goals.

In the second step, we ask the indexer to get a bit more specific. The indexer needs to
look at each general task the case provides guidelines for and to consider whether there is a
specific part of that task the case supports or whether the task can be further specified. Looking at this case, we see that it supports choice of a main dish, a particular part of solution creation, and that it supports adaptation when a dish has cheese, a more specific specification of
the task.

Note that there may be many ways of further specifying a task. At this point, the particular specification chosen is not all that important. Later steps will sort that out. The important thing in this step is to consider what the possibilities are.

Having answered these questions, the indexer now knows what lessons the cases teaches and what parts of the reasoning process it addresses. The next step in choosing indexes is to determine under what circumstances this case would be useful for each of the purposes designated in step 1. Sometimes this question will have been answered by the time step 1 is done. Sometimes, additional reasoning is needed. Going back to our example, we see that for the first use of this case, there are two circumstances when it would be useful, and for the second purpose, there is one.

1. First,

   ■ Goal is to choose a main dish, dish is to be vegetarian, dish is to include tomatoes
   ■ Goal is to chose a main dish, dish is vegetarian, time is summer

2. Main dish has cheese as an ingredient, one or a few guests are allergic to milk products, goal is to accommodate those guests

Note again that different people will have different ways of specifying these circumstances. For example, one person may see the circumstances as pertaining to a main dish with cheese, others to any dish with cheese. This step, like the first, has the purpose of getting some specification down on paper. The next two steps normalize that specification.

The goal in step 1 is to determine what a case can be useful for (the lessons it teaches). The goal in step 2 is to determine when it can usefully teach each of its lessons. We specify when a lesson can usefully be taught by providing descriptions of situations when it would be appropriate to recall it. After some massaging, this is what becomes the case's indexes.

In step 3, these situation descriptions are translated into the vocabulary of the reasoner. In this third step, the person choosing the indexes is asked to put what he or she has been thinking about into a representation the case-based reasoning system can use.

This is a step that a simple tool can help with. Every system that is written represents its cases using a vocabulary of dimensions (represented by predicates or slots) and symbols that are allowed to fill its slots or the roles in its predicate representations. This structure and vocabulary need to be made explicit to the indexer in this step. The user needs to be presented with a representational structure to be filled in along with the set of legal values that can fill each dimension. The indexer translates his or her thoughts into representational vocabulary by filling in the form provided.

How does it work here? Let's suppose that an index in this hypothetical system is provided with the following dimensions, or slots:

```
guests
host
cuisine
ingredients
```

```
preparation method
dishes
    salad
    main dish
    sides
    beverage
    dessert
    dessert-beverage
reasoning goal
constraints
season
results
```

Let us further suppose that some of these slots have further substructure. Each dish, for example, has the following possible descriptors.

```
cuisine
taste
texture
ingredients
preparation method
constraints
```

We represent an index by filling in the slots, giving us the three indexes in Figure 7.2 for this case. Each column represents a single index for the case. The first (index1) shows that the case is applicable when the reasoner is trying to choose a main dish and the main dish must use tomatoes and be vegetarian. The second (index2) says that it is applicable when the reasoner is trying to choose a main dish that needs to be vegetarian and it is summer. The third column (index3) shows that the case is applicable when the reasoner is trying to adapt a main dish that has cheese in it so that it has no milk.

In step 4, we massage the designated indexes to make them as recognizable and and generally applicable as possible. There are two ways to generalize an index. One can generalize the vocabulary item that fills the slot (e.g., "tomato" becomes "salad vegetable"), or one can generalize a slot itself (e.g., "main dish" becomes "dishes"). Generalizing a slot means moving something that is in a specific slot to a corresponding slot at a higher level in the representation. Here, the representation is of an abstract object, a meal, with parts. Generalizing a slot means moving a descriptor from a slot of a part of the item to a slot representing a bigger part of it.

What kind of generalization is appropriate here? For each filled-in piece of the index, we must ask whether the vocabulary item could be generalized in some way that continues to designate the importance of the case, and we must ask whether the description should be moved to a more prominent place in the representation. Let's look at index1 first. We might try to generalize "vegetarian" to "food restriction," but then tomato tart would not necessarily be an appropriate suggestion. So this vocabulary item seems appropriate. We might try generalizing "tomatoes" to "salad vegetables," but then tomato tart wouldn't make much sense either. So that one, too, is at the right level of generality.

	index1	index2	index3
guests			
host			
cuisine			
ingredients			
preparation method			
dishes			
salad			
main dish			
constraints	vegetarian	vegetarian	no milk
ingredients	tomatoes		cheese
sides			
beverage			
dessert			
dessert-beverage			
reasoning goal	choose main	choose main	adapt dish
constraints			
season		summer	
results			

FIGURE 7.2   Three Indexes for the Tomato-Tart Meal

We then consider whether we ought to generalize "choose main dish." One can generalize the conditions specified by a goal by considering whether the lesson is also appropriate to the goal it is subservient to. "Choose main dish" is subservient to "design meal." We must therefore ask whether this case provides any guidance when a reasoner must design a meal with a vegetarian main dish with tomatoes. In fact, it does provide that guidance; it suggests a whole meal that fits those constraints. Tomato tart is the main dish; other dishes served with it are also suggested.

One question we must ask when we generalize is whether to index by *both* the specific and the generalized descriptor or only by the generalized one. That is, should we index using both "choose main dish" and "design meal" or only by "design meal"? The answer depends on the types of experiences the system is going to have and the things it is most likely to use its cases for. If a system uses cases to help it achieve both abstract goals (like "design meal") and more specific ones (like "choose a main dish"), and if a case can address both, then it makes sense to index on both. Let us make that assumption. Thus, we create a new index based on the first one that designates its goal as "design meal."

Generalizing a goal, however, brings some other complexities with it. A generalized goal might pertain to a bigger part of the problem. If it does, then it might be appropriate to move those descriptors that describe the piece of the case the more specific goal refers to to a level in the representation where they are better associated with the new goal. Here, we generalized the "choose a main dish" goal, which is associated with the main dish of the meal, to "design a meal," which is associated with the meal in general. Thus, it is worth considering whether some of the descriptors that referred to the main dish should be generalized to refer to the meal. In particular, the question is whether the vegetarian constraint and the designation of ingredients associated with the main dish would be better placed as descriptors of the meal as a whole. Associated with the main dish, the index would designate that this case is appropriate when the goal is to design a meal and the main dish should be vegetarian and have tomatoes. Moving both to be descriptors of the meal would mean that this index designates that this case is appropriate when the goal is to design a meal that is supposed to be vegetarian and have tomatoes. Or, one can be moved but not the other. The indexer must make this choice based on knowledge of the domain, aiming to index the case so that it can be easily recognized as applicable during later problem solving. We choose to move both descriptors so that they describe the meal as a whole. The representation for this index (index4) is shown in the first column of Figure 7.3.

Generalization of index2 and index3 proceeds similarly. Considering index2, we find that we don't want to generalize the vegetarian constraint, that we don't want to generalize the season, but that it makes sense to generalize the goal and create a new index based on that. We then move the vegetarian constraint that goes with the main dish so that it covers the whole meal (as we did in generalizing the first index), in essence, specifying that this case provides guidelines for a reasoner trying to design a meal that should be vegetarian when the season is summer. We see this index (index5) in the second column of Figure 7.3.

Considering the third of the original indexes (index3), we see that we cannot generalize the "no milk" constraint, because the guideline provided ("use tofu cheese substitute") is fairly specific to that. Nor can we generalize the ingredient "cheese" for the same reason. When we consider the goal ("adapt"), we find that we cannot generalize that and still have a relevant lesson to teach. On the other hand, we might notice that it is being applied to main dishes only, and we might want the adaptation suggestion to be available anytime a dish with cheese needs its milk products removed. We do that by moving the designated constraints from the main dish dimension of the meal to the more general dish dimension, as shown in the third column of Figure 7.3 (index6). Figures 7.2 and 7.3 show the whole set of indexes for this case.

We now look at all the terms we are using in our indexes to determine if they are sufficiently recognizable. Here, all are.

We look at the case in which Anne didn't eat the grilled fish as another example. Here, the circumstances are that Anne and a bunch of other people were invited to dinner. The main dish was barbecued whole trout. When it was brought to be table, Anne stated that she didn't eat fish, and hot dogs, which were available and are quick to make, were put on the grill for her as a substitute.

We start by considering what this case can be useful for. It is useful for two things:

- It predicts a condition for failure by telling us something that Anne won't eat: *Anne doesn't eat grilled trout.*
- It provides a suggestion for success in the condition of needing to recover from a plan failure; that is, when we have just barbecued and someone won't eat the food: *When finding out that someone won't eat the main dish at the last minute, and when the grill is on, use hot dogs.*

	index4	**index5**	**index6**
guests			
host			
cuisine			
ingredients	tomatoes		
preparation method			
dishes			
constraints			no-milk
ingredients			cheese
salad			
main dish			
constraints			
ingredients			
sides			
beverage			
dessert			
dessert-beverage			
reasoning goal	design meal	design meal	adapt-dish
constraints	vegetarian	vegetarian	
season		summer	
results			

FIGURE 7.3   Three More Indexes for the Tomato-Tart Meal

For each, we consider under what circumstances it would be useful for each of these.

- For the first, when Anne is a guest and grilled whole trout is to be served.
- For the second, when food has been barbecued and someone doesn't like what was made.

We then translate into representations that the system can use. We use the same structure as earlier, filling it in as in Figure 7.4. Each column designates the index associated with one of those circumstances.

We look at each index to see if it is generally applicable and recognizable. Examining index7, we ask whether "grilled whole trout" is generally applicable? Is it only when we are serving grilled whole trout that we want to remember this case, or can we describe when it can be useful more generally? If Anne doesn't eat grilled whole trout, then there are probably other fish dishes she won't eat either. But how should "grilled whole trout" be generalized? There are a number of ways to do it. The question we must ask here is what really caused Anne not to eat—is it because she doesn't like fish? because she doesn't like it barbecued? because she doesn't like trout? because she doesn't like fish with the head on? Whichever of these is the answer to why Anne didn't eat the fish determines the generality of this piece of the index. Let's assume for now that Anne just doesn't like fish. Then we include that in the index. We check to see if it is recognizable. It is. We therefore specify the main dish as "fish" in the index, substituting that for "grilled whole trout."

	index7	index8
guests	Anne	
host		
cuisine		
ingredients		
preparation method		
dishes		
salad		
main dish	grilled whole trout	fish
preparation method	barbecued	
sides		
beverage		
dessert		
dessert-beverage		
reasoning goal		
constraints		
season		
results		no eat

FIGURE 7.4 Two Indexes for the Meal Anne Didn't Eat

Obviously, a person doing indexing needs to be knowledgeable about the cases and the domain to be able to index well. Equally obvious, whatever the expertise of the indexer, there are bound to be idiosyncrasies in the indexing each individual does. The four steps of this process are designed to get as many of the idiosyncrasies of indexing out of the process as possible. There is redundancy in what is considered in each step and some overlap between the steps. The idea is to get indexers to consider everything that needs to be considered at some point in the process, realizing that everyone won't necessarily consider everything at the same time. Some people looking at the Anne case, for example, might generalize the circumstances when the case is applicable by designating that the relevant main dish is "fish," and never considering that "grilled whole trout" should be part of the index. Others will choose "grilled whole trout" early on and then need to generalize. Some will be able to designate circumstances when a case is applicable in step 1, when the goals it gives guidelines for are being considered. Others will need to consider goals by themselves first and then figure out the circumstances later.

The piece of the process that acts to decrease idiosyncratic indexing the most is putting indexes into a representation that the case-based reasoning system can use. Though steps 1 and 2 encourage the indexer to think about the indexes conceptually, steps 3 and 4 provide indexers with a way of turning their conceptual descriptions of indexes into uniform representations. Providing indexers with a form to fill out and a restricted set of symbols that are allowed to fill those slots forces them to designate their indexes in a standard way. To see how this works, consider the first example again, that of serving tomato tart. After steps 1 and 2 of choosing indexes for that case, one might designate a goal the case achieves as "accommodating a person allergic to milk products" or "adapting a dish with cheese for a person allergic to milk." In step 3, however, the indexer is forced to figure out how to represent this goal using the fixed set of available vocabulary items. Presumably, either one of these conceptual representations of the index would lead the indexer to designate "adapt" as the goal this case provides guidelines for.

7.2 CHOOSING INDEXES BY MACHINE

In some systems, it will be reasonable and advantageous to index cases by hand. When the cases are quite complex, when their indexes need to be accurate, and when the knowledge needed to understand cases well enough to choose their indexes accurately is not concretely available or is too complex to insert into the computer, hand indexing is needed.

Other times, however, it is advantageous for the computer to do the indexing job, especially if problem solving and understanding are already automated. We begin by presenting three methods for automated index selection. The checklist-based method depends on a person's producing a credible list of features that are useful for indexing. It is based on the philosophy that one can index credibly by the kinds of features that tend to be predictive ones. The explanation-based method automates the human-guided index-selection method presented in the previous section. Its philosophy is that cases should be analyzed individually to assign credit and/or blame for its successes and failures and that indexes should be assigned accurately for each case. It is highly knowledge-dependent, requiring the computer to derive explanations and reach conclusions. The difference-based method allows indexes chosen by either of these two methods to be specialized for the case library—leaving in an index only those of its features that differentiate it from other similar cases. After discussing each method in detail, means of choosing between them are discussed.

7.3 CHOOSING INDEXES BASED ON A CHECKLIST

Programs that choose indexes based on a checklist index all cases on a fixed and well-specified set of dimensions. MEDIATOR, for example, indexes on type and function of a disputed object, type of disputants, relationship between disputants, and so on. Thus, it indexes the Orange Dispute as a dispute over a piece of food, over something edible, between kids, between sisters, and so on. These are the types of features that MEDIATOR's creator (Simpson) found to be usefully predictive when he analyzed the problem domain.

CHEF indexes cases on texture and taste of food, preparation method, and ingredients. These are the types of features CHEF's creator (Hammond) found to be usefully predictive when he analyzed the recipe creation domain. Beef and broccoli is indexed as a recipe whose preparation method is stir-fry, that includes beef as an ingredient, that includes broccoli as an ingredient, that includes a crunchy vegetable, and that tastes savory.

HYPO indexes legal cases of nondisclosure along dimensions of how many people were disclosed to, whether a nondisclosure contract had been signed, and so on. It indexes tax cases in other ways. CASEY indexes cases on symptoms and disorders, because matches on those features predict that an old solution will fit a new situation.

Given a checklist, the process of index selection is easy. For each dimension on the checklist, find or compute the value along that dimension that describes the case, and choose it as an index. An example from CHEF will show this concretely.

CHEF has just created a recipe for chicken and snow peas. It was made by stir-frying, and CHEF dealt with the problem of interactions between a meat and a crisp vegetable in creating it. CHEF's checklist for indexing cases specifies indexing by major ingredients, method of preparation, taste, and interactions. Applying its checklist to this case, it chooses the following as indexes:[1]

- ingredient = chicken
- ingredient = snow peas
- preparation method = stir-fry
- taste = savory
- interactions = includes meat and a crisp vegetable

Though this method of automated index selection makes the computer's job easy, the method is only as good as the checklist created by the system builder. An incomplete checklist will result in insufficient indexing; a checklist that doesn't discriminate between important and unimportant dimensions will result in overindexing and retrieval of too many cases. There are several issues that must be considered in setting up these checklists:

- Guidelines and procedures for creating a checklist
- Making sure the checklist is contextually sensitive
- Selecting consistent indexing vocabulary

Our discussion of the universal index frame addressed this third issue. The UIF attempts to provide an indexing vocabulary for one important and ubiquitous kind of case, and it gives guidelines for choosing vocabularies for other types of domains. The first two issues are discussed in the next sections.

7.3.1 Creating a Checklist

Though the checklist method doesn't require the computer to follow guidelines for choosing good indexes, it does rely on a system builder to analyze a domain in order to create a good checklist. The system builder must be careful to make the checklist usefully predictive. The best lists are informed by the criteria listed in the previous chapter; that is, the features put on a checklist should be those that make useful predictions. They must be easily recognizable, but they should describe the case at an abstract enough level to make it generally applicable.

The system builder must analyze the problem the computer will be carrying out to determine the tasks it must do or support. For each of those tasks, he or she must determine the kinds of features, or dimensions, that tend to be important in making the inferences necessary

---

1. A note about CHEF's indexing method: CHEF, in fact, uses two indexing methods. It uses a checklist to index its cases for plan selection. To index them for anticipation of failures, it uses explanation-based explanation. A paragraph later in the chapter explains why.

to complete those tasks. Finally, for each of those dimensions, the system builder must make sure indexing vocabulary is appropriately concrete and/or abstract.

MEDIATOR, for example, did a number of tasks in case-based ways, including problem elaboration, plan selection, and failure explanation. For each of these tasks, the system builder (here, Bob Simpson), examined a selection of problems to figure out which features tend to predict solutions. MEDIATOR's problem elaboration concentrated mostly on elaborating disputant's goals, and for this, the type of object was most important. When a disputant wants possession of a physical object, for example, it is usually to use it in its functionally appropriate way. Thus, indexing by type of object, where type implies function, is appropriate (e.g., fruit, book). Choosing dispute mediation plans, by contrast, requires taking into account various properties of disputed objects (e.g., Does it have separable parts and what are they? When split, do both parts still have value?), properties of the goals (e.g., Can it be partially achieved and still be considered achieved?), and requirements of the disputants (e.g., Are they willing to compromise?); failure explanation requires knowing the plan that failed, the concrete physical result of the failure, and the disputants' goals. MEDIATOR indexed cases by all these features and by their abstractions. The Orange Dispute, for example, is indexed by the fact that its disputed object is an orange (concrete), a fruit, a food, and a physical object; that it has separable parts; and that it can be divided without losing value; that its disputants are willing to compromise; and that the goals of the disputants can be partially fulfilled.

The following steps summarize a process for setting up that checklist:

- List the tasks that case retrieval will support.
- For each task, determine the kinds of features that tend to predict solutions.
- For each task, determine the kinds of features that tend to predict outcomes.
- For each kind of feature, compute the set of useful generalizations of the feature, and make sure that features chosen are recognizable (available during reasoning).
- Create the checklist by collecting the complete set.

The following heuristics intuitively describe the kinds of features that belong on an indexing checklist.

- Choose the kinds of features that tend to predict outcomes.
- Choose the kinds of features that tend to be predictive of other features.
- Choose the kinds of features that tend to make the kinds of predictions the reasoner needs.
- Choose the kinds of features that tend to discriminate.

An example will show how the process works. Our domain is layout of composite parts in an autoclave (CLAVIER's [Barletta and Hennessy 1989; Hennessy and Hinkle 1992] domain). An autoclave is a large convection oven. Here it is being used to cure parts of airplanes created using composite materials. The important thing is for airflow in the oven to allow all parts to cure at the same rate. Some large parts require a lot of time; some small parts require less time; but if airflow can be maximized around the larger parts and decreased around the smaller parts, they can be made to require the same time to cure. As in CLAVIER, cases represent layouts of parts that have worked and have not worked. The reasoner uses cases for two tasks: (1) to suggest layouts for new assemblages of parts and (2) to suggest substitutions for parts from the old case that don't exist in the new case.[2]

We begin by describing the tasks. The reasoner starts with a list of parts that need to be cured. It must design a series of layouts of parts that will cure each part successfully. It designs one layout at a time until all parts are accounted for. Figure 7.5 shows several autoclave layouts. We see that each is composed of several tables, and each table has one or several parts on it. In designing a layout, the reasoner's first task is to choose an overall layout that has the potential to work. The reasoner does this by choosing from among the autoclave layouts it knows about. Any layout it chooses, however, will generally be only a partial match, not a complete one. Many parts in the chosen layout will correspond directly to parts that need to be cured in the new situation, but there will always be some parts from the recalled layout that are not in the list of parts to be cured. The task now is to substitute something that needs to be cured for an unmatched part of the layout. This can be done by using the individual tables in the different layouts as cases and choosing a table whose parts are composed of parts from the recalled layout that are matched in the new situation and other parts from the new situation that are not yet assigned a place in the autoclave.

We now consider the construction of an indexing checklist. Recall that to do that, we must take into account the tasks the case-based reasoner needs to use its cases for and determine what kinds of features are predictive of good solutions for that task. Let's consider suggestion of layouts first. What are the predictors of good solutions? Because cases represent layouts that have worked and have not worked, because layouts specify how to configure pieces with respect to each other, and because the same types of pieces are cured over and over again, the combinations of pieces themselves can predict good and bad solutions. Thus, the *pieces in a layout* are a major part of its index. Layout is a black art—nobody is sure of the reasons why some layouts work and some don't—so there are really no other descriptors of whole layouts that can predict when an old case will be useful and when it won't.

Next, then, we must ask about generalizations of the features we have chosen. There are four generalizable aspects of parts that come to mind as possibly appropriate for indexing: size, rough shape, mass, and composition. For each, we must consider whether it is predictive in any way of whether a layout is applicable. Of those that are potentially useful, we must ask if the descriptor is easy to recognize. To answer these questions, we must do a careful analysis of the domain.

We ask the experts to tell us what they know about which features are important to success—what do they take into account as they try to configure parts in the autoclave? They tell us that all four generalized descriptors are potentially predictive. Size predicts how much air can get around the piece, and things of about the same size allow approximately the same amount of air around them; rough shape tells in what direction the air disperses as it goes around the piece, and pieces of about the same shape seem to disperse air the same way; and

---

2. Note that this analysis is a rather simplistic one. Thus, there is no claim being made here that these indexes are correct or that they would work well if they were used. Real expertise in the domain is necessary to make the right decisions. The example, however, does provide an illustration of the considerations that must be taken into account in choosing an indexing checklist.

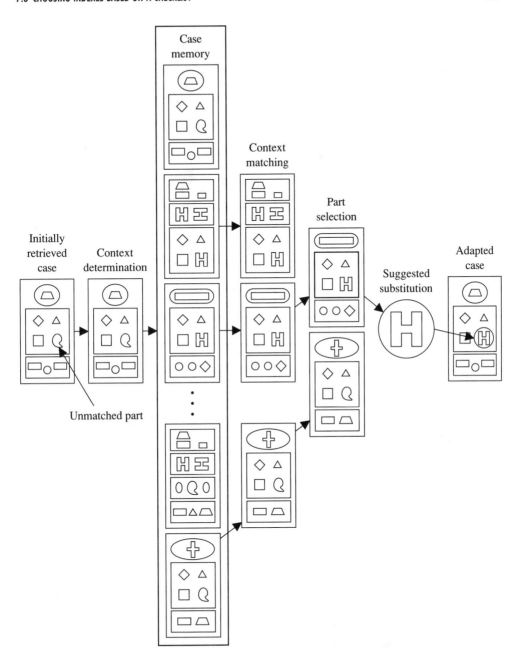

FIGURE 7.5 Autoclave Layout—CLAVIER's cases. From Figure 3 in Hennessy, D.H. and Hinckle, D. (1992), "Applying Case-Based Reasoning to Autoclave Loading," *IEEE Expert*, 7(5), pp. 21–26.

mass and composition predict how much time a part needs to cure. We are also told, however, that this is too much information to take into account right away, and that because of the interactions between the sizes, shapes, and masses of all the parts, they don't actually take that information into account at this point, except for the exceptionally large pieces and the exceptionally small ones and a few with special shapes that seem to have to be put in particular places in the oven. They do take composition into account, however.

What does this tell us about building our indexing checklist? There are several choices here. One is to follow the instructions of the experts and index only by composition. The other is to index by the other potentially predictive features also even though the experts don't find them useful. The intuition here is that the computer can deal with complexities of interactions easier than a person can. If we decide to do the indexing, then for each of the four ways of generalizing, we must choose descriptive vocabulary (e.g., for size, large, small, medium-sized), and we must consider which are easy to recognize. Another way of saying this is that we must consider which are available or easy to compute. Let us suppose that size and mass are easy to compute but that rough shape is difficult. We therefore index by the composition, size, and mass of each piece.

Let us return to the second task we want case-based reasoning to support: substitution of one part for another. We ask the expert how he decides which parts from the new list of parts to be cured can be substituted for parts from an old layout. He explains that he chooses a table from some old layout that is positioned in the autoclave similarly to the way the new table is positioned, that has parts of the same composition, and that shares relevant parts with the new table. He tells us that he prefers a table where every part is matched exactly in the new situation, but that if he can't find that, he chooses a table where most parts match. When some parts don't match exactly to something in the new situation, they need to match something closely in size and mass. This tells us that tables should be indexed by what their parts are made of (composition), their position in the autoclave, the parts they hold, and the sizes and masses of each of those parts.[3]

Can we generalize these? Here, we can think about dealing with the generalization process by choosing a descriptive vocabulary for size and mass that captures similarities along those dimensions. Using centimeters to describe size and grams to describe mass, we have absolute measures of size and mass, but it might be more useful to match by some qualitative value—Is it relatively small? relatively large? huge? Is it featherweight? lightweight? superheavy? Such qualitative descriptors of these features will allow two items of unequal but functionally similar size to be easily recognized as such.

This analysis has allowed us to determine that both complete layouts and tables must be indexed, and it has allowed us to derive two checklists, one a list of indexes for complete layouts, the other a set of indexes for tables. Are we finished? Will it work? As with any knowledge engineering endeavor, there is much fine-tuning that must be done after initial construction of the list. Use and evaluation of the scheme will be necessary before it is as good as it can be. There are several places in this scheme that we can anticipate as problematic based on the

---

3. CLAVIER, in fact, chooses a table based on a combination of *global* information about the layout (e.g., what its parts are made of) and *local* information about the table itself (e.g., its relative location, its parts). Hennessy and Hinkle (1992) give a good description of CLAVIER's indexes and its means of doing substitution.

analysis already done. At one point in the analysis, for example, we decided to index layouts by size and mass even though the experts told us that was too much to consider. When we try to use the indexing scheme, we may find it is too unwieldy and that indexing on those features causes a lot of computation to be done. We may then get rid of those indexes and see if retrieval is accurate enough without them.[4] If so, we leave them out. If not, we consider how they can be modified in some way so as to allow accuracy in a manageable way. Another thing we did was to choose vocabulary for each dimension. When we put the scheme into action, we may find that though the dimensions on our checklist make sense, the particular vocabulary we have chosen for each dimension is not good enough. When we try out the system, we may find that substituting something that is featherweight for another thing that is featherweight does not work. We must then analyze why. We may find that such substitutions don't work, meaning we must upgrade the substitution process. Or we may find that the grain size of the symbols used in the representation is poor; perhaps featherweight needs to be further divided into two categories. Alternatively, it may need to be combined with a size descriptor so that relatively small featherweight items can be recognized as curing differently than relative large or huge featherweight items.

7.3.2 Maintaining Context Sensitivity

One particular problem in creating good lists of indexing dimensions is that indexing requirements change with context, even within the same or very similar domains. A job recruiter, for example, might consider eye color to be important in recruiting models but not in recruiting computer programmers. Who a host is for a dinner is important in indexing typical social dinners, but for a state dinner, the nationality of the host is also important. In nondisclosure cases, the number of people disclosed to is important, but in tax cases, it isn't.

There are two techniques for maintaining context sensitivity of indexing checklists:

- Use several checklists, each organized around a different well-known context.
- Keep track of how useful individual indexes are, and modify lists as some are found not to be useful.

Both methods allow indexing checklists to be specialized for different contexts. The first provides a way of initially specifying indexes for different contexts. The second provides a way of specializing those lists to remove some indexing terms from consideration.

The most extensive use of context sensitive index checklists can be found in CYRUS (Kolodner 1983a, 1983b, 1984), discussed in chapter 4. CYRUS, recall, was an event memory that stored events from the life of Cyrus Vance when he was secretary of state of the United States. CYRUS was a fact-retrieval system and model of human long-term memory, and its task was retrieval. When asked a question, CYRUS recalled events that could answer the question. CYRUS predates case-based reasoning itself, but its memory forms the model for the case libraries of many case-based systems that came after it.

---

4. In CLAVIER, indexing by individual pieces for this task seems to be sufficient.

CYRUS knew about several different kinds of events, and had indexing checklists (called *predictive feature lists*) associated with each. It first determined what type of event it was dealing with (e.g., diplomatic meeting, state dinner, VIP trip) and then chose indexes for the event based on the lists associated with that type. Diplomatic meetings, for example, are indexed by political roles of the participants, classes those roles fit into, nationalities of the participants, occupations of the participants, political leanings of the participants, topic, place, participants, and issues underlying the topic. VIP trips, on the other hand, are indexed by destination, mode of travel, types of events included in them, and so on.

Because several of the types of events CYRUS knew about had similar predictive feature lists associated with them, and because one of the goals in building CYRUS was to make the memory as generally applicable as possible, CYRUS grouped events into abstract categories and associated predictive feature lists with each of those. Thus, the diplomatic meeting category didn't have all the feature types listed above associated with it. Rather, some of those features were associated with international political activities and some were associated with occupational activities, two abstract event categories diplomatic meetings belongs to. Only those specific to diplomatic meetings were actually associated with that event category. Figures 7.6, 7.7, and 7.8 show some of the information associated with each of those event categories.

Checklists associated with abstract event types allow easy computation of the types of indexes that might prove useful. But they don't specify which values along those indexing dimensions are predictive ones, and in some subcontexts, a dimension may not be predictive. CYRUS, for example, indexed international political events by, among other things, the political positions of the participants. In general, knowing the political position of a participant might predict a variety of other attributes of the event. For diplomatic meetings, this attribute is generally predictive of whether the conclusion arrived at will be approved by the government, the tone of the meeting, and the content of the meeting. Some particular political positions, however, seem to have no predictive value in some contexts. CYRUS found, for example, that it could make no predictions about diplomatic meetings from the fact that a participant was a foreign minister. Though, in general, it continued to index events by the

```
norms:
  participants' occupation type = political
  participants' occupation class = diplomat
  topic type = international contract
  included in other international political activities
  includes other international political activities
  initiated by international conflict

predictive features:
  political roles of participants (e.g., negotiator)
  classes those roles fit into (e.g., diplomat)
  nationalities of the participants
  polities on the sides of any dispute or contract being discussed
  political leanings of participants
```

FIGURE 7.6   International Political Activities. (Kolodner, 1984.)

```
norms:
    participants are in occupational roles
    included in other occupational activities
    includes other occupational activities

predictive features:
    occupations of the participants
    roles of the participants in the event
    classes those roles fit into
```

FIGURE 7.7 Occupational Activities. (Kolodner, 1984.)

political positions of their participants, it discontinued indexing diplomatic meetings along that dimension when the participant was a foreign minister. Later, it found that when a diplomatic meeting was with a Soviet diplomat, there was no position in government that it encountered that made useful predictions. It thus discontinued indexing by position in government when participants were Soviets and the event type was diplomatic meeting.

Note that if checklists are to be associated with different contexts, then the reasoner must have a way of associating context with a case. CYRUS knew of approximately twelve different categories of events and classified events using a set of simple discriminations. The classification task can be hard, however. There is a trade-off between the benefits of using contextually sensitive checklists to guide indexing and the costs associated with classifying cases and identifying them with available contexts. The more sensitive the checklists, the harder it tends to be to distinguish contexts from one another, making context identification an expensive operation.

```
norms:
    isa: international political activity, occupational activity
    participants: diplomats of countries involved in contract being discussed,
                  acting in the role of negotiator.
    location: conference room in capital city of country of an important
              participant
    topic: international contract
    duration: one to two hours

predictive features:
    topic, place, participants
    sides of the topic
    issue underlying the topic (e.g., peace)

nonpredictive features:
    participant's occupation = foreign minister
    participant's occuation = head of state
```

FIGURE 7.8 Diplomatic Meetings

7.4 DIFFERENCE-BASED INDEXING

How can a memory know that some indexed feature is not predictive? How can it know that an indexed feature *is* predictive? Both require keeping track of what is the same across cases indexed in similar ways. CYRUS knew that it could make no predictions about meetings in which the main participant was a foreign minister because it kept track of similarities between the first several meetings with foreign ministers and found that they had nothing in common except the things common to all meetings.

The purpose of indexing is to differentiate cases from one another so that at retrieval time, retrieval algorithms can choose best-matching cases from the case library. The guidelines presented at the beginning of the chapter represent our theory of what kinds of features best differentiate cases from each other. But, as we discussed previously, the computations that must be done to calculate these combinations of features can be intractable.

When a memory keeps track of what is common across similar cases, it has a means of discovering which features of a case differentiate it from other similar cases, and it can choose as indexes those features that differentiate cases. If almost all `diplomatic meetings` are in Washington, D.C., for example, then indexing by the place when a meeting is in Washington is pretty senseless. It won't help differentiate one event from another. Indexing on `place is Washington` would mean that almost all diplomatic meetings would be indexed the same way. On the other hand, place is a good index for a meeting in Geneva. If most meetings are in Washington, the index `place is Geneva` differentiates this meeting from others.

Of course, not all features that are different across similar cases make useful indexes. The size of the meeting room, for example, might differentiate two meetings from each other but might not be predictive of anything important in either case. There is no point in indexing by size of room if it doesn't enable any inferences. To ensure that a difference-based index selector selects only predictive features, difference-based indexing must be combined with some method of choosing predictive features. We shall see in the next section how it has been combined with checklist-based index selection. In such a scheme, memory restricts its indexing to the subset of predictive features that also discriminate, that is, those that make predictions that are different from the normal ones or allow inferences different from the normal ones to be made.

In chapter 8, we discuss several means of organizing cases in a case library. Some of those methods provide ways of keeping track of similarities across similar cases. Shared-feature networks, as well as several variations of discrimination networks and redundant discrimination networks, support this capability. We will hold off the discussion of keeping track of similarities between cases until that time.

7.5 COMBINING DIFFERENCE-BASED AND CHECKLIST-BASED METHODS

Checklist-based indexing methods designate which dimensions to focus on in indexing. Difference-based methods designate which values along any dimension are useful for indexing. A combination of these two approaches allows indexing on only those values along a predictive dimension that differentiate a case from other similar ones. CYRUS's algorithm for index selection shows how this combination works.

1. Select a classification for the case.
2. Select types of features (using contextually sensitive checklists) that are known to be predictive. These dimensions have indexing potential.
3. For each, compute its value for this case (resulting in dimension-value pairs).
4. From these, get rid of
   ■ Dimension-value pairs known to be nonpredictive in this context
   ■ Normative dimension-value pairs

This algorithm allows CYRUS to index only on the subset of indexable features that are not similar across cases. In the first step, the case is classified to determine which contextual information should be brought in in choosing indexes. In the next step, dimensions for indexing are chosen. This is done using contextually sensitive lists of predictive features. In the third step, CYRUS finds the value for each dimension on its list. At the end of this step it has created a set of *dimension-value* pairs (e.g., place = Geneva). It then deletes from its list all pairs that it knows to be similar across cases of the type it is trying to index (normative pairs) and all pairs it has found not to be predictive.

A complete example from CYRUS will make the process more concrete. Figures 7.6, 7.7, and 7.8 show the information CYRUS has about `international political activities`, `occupational activities` and `diplomatic meetings`. In addition, CYRUS knows and uses the norms of activities involving Cyrus Vance.

CYRUS wants to index the following diplomatic meeting:

Cyrus Vance has a meeting with Andrey Gromyko in Belgium about SALT.

CYRUS firsts decides that this is a `diplomatic meeting`. It then collects the set of dimensions that are appropriate for indexing a diplomatic meeting. Because a `diplomatic meeting` is an `international political activity` and an `occupational activity`, the list of dimensions for indexing includes everything in the `predictive features` lists of each of those event types.

In the third step, CYRUS uses that list of dimensions to create dimension-value pairs that can serve as the indexes for the case. It creates the following list:

1. participant1's occupation = foreign minister
2. participant2's occupation = secretary of state
3. class of participant1's occupation = diplomat
4. class of participant2's occupation = diplomat
5. participant1's political role = negotiator
6. participant2's political role = negotiator
7. participant1's nationality = Russian
8. participant2's nationality = US

9. participant1's political leaning = Communist
10. participant2's political leaning = Capitalist
11. topic = SALT
12. topic type = international contract
13. topic participants = United States and Russia
14. topic's underlying issue = arms control
15. participant1 = Gromyko
16. participant2 = Vance
17. place = Belgium

In the next step, CYRUS deletes from the list of potential indexes all the pairs that are either normative or known not to be predictive. Pair 1 is deleted because the occupation of foreign minister is known not to be predictive in `diplomatic meeting` contexts. Pairs 2, 4, 6, 8, 10, and 16 are deleted because they are the norms for activities involving Vance. Pairs 3, 5, and 12 are deleted because they are the norms for `international political activities` and `diplomatic meetings`. The set of pairs that are left correspond to features of the case that are known to be predictive and that differentiate this meeting from others:

- participant1's nationality = Russian
- participant1's political leaning = Communist
- topic = SALT
- topic participants = United States and Russia
- topic's underlying issue = arms control
- participant1 = Gromyko
- place = Belgium

Note that the norms associated with CYRUS's categories are not necessary conditions for membership in the category but rather note the common attributes of items in the category. A diplomatic meeting, for example, could be for the purpose of planning a trip or later set of meetings. Though it would still be a diplomatic meeting, its topic type (planning) is different from the normative topic type (international contract). That meeting would be indexed by this difference from the norm (topic type = planning). The scheme keeps track of the ways in which similar cases tend to be similar and indexes cases that differ from those norms according to their differences (i.e., by the features that discriminate them from other similar cases). This issue will come up again as we discuss organizations for case libraries in chapter 8.

7.6 EXPLANATION-BASED INDEXING

Difference-based and checklist-based indexing methods provide a simple means of computing potentially predictive features to use as indexes. But they have a major flaw. They choose indexes based on a model of the kinds of features that are *usually* predictive but don't analyze cases *individually* for their predictive features.

This causes two problems: extra features are often chosen for indexing that are not predictive in a particular case, and some features that are predictive in that case, but not in general, are not indexed. Because these methods don't always discriminate cases well enough from each other, retrieval based on indexes chosen by these methods results in many superfluous cases being retrieved. A separate ranking process must sort the cases that are recalled to determine which are the most appropriate.

Explanation-based indexing methods are aimed at choosing indexes appropriately for individual cases. The reasoner attempts to explain why the solution worked or didn't work, and then uses explanation-based generalization methods to generalize the explanation (Hammond 1987, 1989a; Barletta and Mark 1988). Indexes are then chosen from the content of the generalized explanation. In explanation-based indexing, domain knowledge is used to determine which facts of a case are the most relevant and which can be safely ignored. Some examples will illustrate.

In the first example, we see explanation-based choice of indexes that will help the reasoner to avoid a mistake it has just made. CHEF has just derived a recipe for strawberry soufflé. It made the recipe and the soufflé did not rise. CHEF asked itself why the soufflé didn't rise. Using its domain knowledge, CHEF came up with the following explanation tying the solution and state of the world to the plan's outcome: a side effect of using the strawberries was that the extra liquid they had in them disabled the necessary condition of balance between liquids and leavenings required for rising. The concrete feature of the situation that was responsible for the side effect was that the strawberries produced more liquid than the available leavening could handle. An explanation-based index for this case would include in it that the recipe is of type soufflé and it includes strawberries. This index isn't quite good enough: it doesn't serve the criteria of being generally applicable. A more generally applicable index can be found by generalizing the features of the situation that are responsible for the failure to the most abstract point where the explanation can still hold. In this situation, any fruit will cause the same problem, and the index "recipe is type soufflé and dish includes fruit" is chosen.

How does this method work? After the reasoner discovers it has made a mistake, it attempts to explain it or to assign blame. After explaining the mistake, it extracts from the explanation the concrete recognizable features of the situation that were responsible for the problem. It then generalizes those features to the point where they are still concrete but where the explanation that was derived can still be applied. Suppose "strawberries" are defined as a "fruit," and that in turn is defined as a "food." The explanation for the failed soufflé continues to hold if we substitute "fruit" for "strawberries." It fails to hold, however, when we try to substitute "food" for "fruit"—not all foods generate liquids. We discuss this process in more detail below.

Note the difference between the results of this method of selecting indexes and checklist-based methods. This method chooses as indexes only those features that are responsible for the failure, that is, those features that, if seen again in a later case, will predict the failure seen in this case. Checklist- and difference-based methods have no means of distinguishing which of many potentially predictive and differentiating features are responsible for the failure and will index by many more features. The facts that the dish includes strawberries and that it includes fruit will be chosen as indexes because those features differentiate this case from other soufflé cases and because ingredients are potentially predictive dimensions of recipes.

But so might the fact that an ingredient has seeds be chosen as an index, because that is a potentially predictive dimension when a dish includes fruit.

A second example will illustrate explanation-based choice of indexes that can help a reasoner derive a solution. To support this task, the reasoner indexes on features found to be useful in achieving a goal: those that were responsible for solving the problem the particular way it was solved. JULIA has just planned a meal and chosen to make tomato tart as the main dish. It chose tomato tart because it is summer and tomatoes are in season and because Jeanette, a vegetarian friend, is coming for dinner. These are the features responsible for JULIA's achieving the goal `choose main dish` in this particular way. This explanation of why this solution was chosen ties a piece of the problem to its solution. Generalizing this explanation (of why the goal was achieved by choosing tomato tart), JULIA indexes the case the following two ways:[5]

1. The goal is to choose a main dish, it is summer, a vegetarian guest is coming, and tomatoes should be included.
2. The goal is to design a meal, it is summer, a vegetarian guest is coming, and tomatoes should be included.

The first allows tomato tart to be suggested when a reasoner is attempting to choose a main dish. The second allows the entire tomato tart meal to be recalled when the goal is to design a meal, making its entire menu available early on in the reasoning.

This choice of indexes is accomplished by having the reasoner keep track of what went into making each of its decisions and how those decisions affect other decisions. Here, JULIA knows its concrete justifications for choosing tomato tart. Some derive from the problem statement (a vegetarian is coming), some from the state of the world (it is summer). Each of these considerations is then generalized. Resulting indexes describe situations in which a goal might be achieved in a similar way in the future. JULIA also knows that choosing a main dish is subservient to designing a meal and is the most important subgoal of that goal. Thus, once it has indexed this case as one that can achieve the subgoal of choosing a main dish, it also indexes it as one that can achieve the more major goal of designing a meal.

The explanation-based index selection process has the following steps:

1. Create an explanation.
2. Select relevant observable features from the explanation.
3. Generalize those observable features as far as possible, making sure the resulting generalizations are also observable. The original explanation must still apply, given this general description.
4. If the index supports a solution-creation goal, then
   - Append additional information specifying the goal the case achieves.
   - Generalize the goal appropriately and repeat the process.

We explain each in turn and end with an illustration of the complete process.

---

5. Using reasoning similar to what was described in the previous discussion of this case.

7.6.1 **Creating an Explanation**

An explanation is a chain of inferences that ties together several parts of a case. Sometimes, as in the JULIA example above, an explanation ties together input and solution. Other times, as in the CHEF example, an explanation ties together input, solution, and outcome. Explanations are generally done for a reason, and there are two major reasons explanations are needed:

1. To explain how a goal was achieved or how a solution was created
2. To explain why a failure happened

Explanations, then, tend to answer one of two questions: What did the reasoner do to create this solution to this problem? Or, Given the input, solution, and state of the world, why did the particular outcome occur?

A case-based reasoner that chooses its indexes using knowledge-rich explanatory methods must have some means of creating explanations. Creating an explanation can be done by a variety of methods, including theorem proving, case-based explanation, and others. MEDIATOR and SWALE (Kass and Leake 1988) use case-based methods of explanation. CHEF builds full causal explanations by forward and backward chaining of rules describing causality. What all these systems have in common is that they build explanations of anamalous outcomes after the fact. That is, they wait until a plan has been carried out and try to explain the poor results based on the state of the world, input, the plan being carried out, and available causal information. The explanations that are built tie together input information, a solution, and an outcome. Indexes chosen based on these kinds of explanations provide access to cases that can help a reasoner to anticipate previously encountered failures and to explain similar failures if they come up again.

Another means of creating explanations takes advantage of the fact that a reasoner can keep track of and know why it made its decisions. When a reasoning trace is recorded, it can be used as an explanation connecting input considerations and state of the world to some part of the solution. JULIA, in the example above, kept track of the reasoning it did in choosing tomato tart as a main dish. This reasoning serves as an explanation of the decision. Explanations of this sort are helpful in choosing the kinds of indexes that will make a case available in similar solution-creation situations that come up in the future. Cases retrieved on the basis of these explanations will help the reasoner propose solutions to similar problems as they arise.

We will not explain in detail how explanations can be built. The problem is beyond the scope of this book and is, in fact, one of those truly complex AI-complete problems that will continue to be studied for years to come. It is a problem that is getting quite a bit of attention recently in the machine learning community, where the major issue under scrutiny is how to create explanations when knowledge is incomplete or inaccurate (DeJong and Mooney 1986; Mitchell, Kellar and Kedar-Cabelli 1986; Schank 1986). Though the problem of building explanations has not been solved in general, there are methodologies that can be made to work in constrained situations, as evidenced by the complex explanations created by CHEF.

Case-based explanation may turn out to be the most practical way of creating explanations. In case-based explanation, explanations are created on the basis of old explanations of similar kinds of situations (Schank 1986). SWALE (Leake 1992b; Schank and Leake 1989; Kass and Leake 1988), for example, is able to explain the sudden death of Len Bias, a all-star basketball player, by recalling the case of Jim Fixx. Jim Fixx, who was a seemingly healthy jogger, died of a heart attack soon after jogging. The heart attack was caused by undue stress on the heart, which had a defect that had been previously undiagnosed. Using that case as the basis for its explanation, SWALE hypothesizes that Len Bias must have had an undiagnosed heart defect and that he must have been jogging, which put so much stress on his heart that he had a heart attack. SWALE eventually adapts this explanation to make it fit Len Bias better, ultimately concluding that the stress on the heart must have been caused by wind sprints, a kind of running basketball players do. Though this was not the true explanation of Len Bias's death (he overdosed on cocaine), it is a plausible explanation that many people came up with before learning the truth.

SWALE creates explanations by keeping a library of **explanation patterns** (Schank 1986) indexed by the situations in which they have the potential to be appropriate. Explanation patterns are closely tied to real cases. Though explanation patterns are more general than cases, they are indexed and used in similar ways. They are accessed through partial matching of salient features, and they require adaptation to be used. Several examples throughout the book illustrate SWALE's means of explanation. KRITIK (Goel 1989, 1991b) also creates explanations in a case-based way. Its task is design of small devices, and the explanations it creates are causal explanations of how the device works. It uses case-based reasoning to create new devices, then creates explanations of how the new device works by adapting the explanation of the device it derived the new design from. CASEY's diagnosis task can also be thought of as a case-based explanation task.

7.6.2 Selecting Observable Features

Explanations can be quite abstract, and it is important that indexes be concrete enough to be recognizable. CHEF, for example, explains that the strawberry soufflé didn't rise because there was an imbalance of liquids and leavening. This is clearly too abstract to index on. It is not easily recognizable, even by experienced bakers.

But there is more to the explanation of the failure than this abstract description of the problem. Explanations tie together real-world observations and real-world constraints and are therefore tied to concrete real-world features that are recognizable. The imbalance of liquids and leavenings, for example, is caused by a side effect of the "pulping the strawberries" step of the recipe. The particular side effect is that liquid is created. Pulping the strawberries is a step of the recipe because strawberries are being used in the recipe.

Having strawberries in the recipe is a concrete observable feature in the explanation. If strawberries are used in a soufflé again, they will cause the same problem: the soufflé won't rise. Indexing on the concrete feature ingredient = strawberries will allow the reasoner to recognize that it is in one of these problematic situations.

In this step of the process, observable features are selected from the explanation that has been built. These are the real-world features the explanation is grounded in.

7.6.3 Generalization

In the third step, observable features are generalized as much as possible. The intuition here follows from the guideline that indexes should be as generally applicable as possible. CHEF's soufflé recipe, for example, won't rise no matter what fruit you substitute for strawberries, because any fruit will produce too much liquid. A more generally applicable index than `ingredient = strawberries` would be `ingredient type = fruit`. Indexing this way, the case can be recalled whenever a soufflé with fruit is being planned. When recalled, it warns the reasoner that the soufflé runs the risk of not rising, and if the reasoner had found a solution that worked for this recipe, the recalled case would also provide a revised solution or a method of adapting the new recipe.

The question, of course, is, How much generalization is appropriate? Why not generalize "fruit" to "food" or to "liquidy food" in this example, for instance? This question has a three-pronged answer. First, observable features can be generalized as much as the explanation allows, providing that the index remains concrete and recognizable and provides discriminability. "Food," for example, is not a relevant generalization for two reasons: foods don't all cause liquids to be emitted, and "food" does not discriminate—all ingredients are foods.

The second part of the answer is that observable features can be generalized only in ways that available generalization procedures allow. If the only available generalization procedure is to walk up a generalization hierarchy, then only concepts found in the generalization hierarchy can be chosen as indexes. Using this generalization procedure, "liquidy food" can be chosen as a feature for indexing only if it is a category of food in the abstraction hierarchy and if "fruit" is one of its descendants. Other generalization procedures (e.g., one that can collect a subset of attributes from an item) might be able to form the generalization "liquidy food" more easily.

The third part of the answer is that observable features should be generalized only to the point where they remain both observable and easily interpreted. Even if a generalizer can form the concept "liquidy food," it may not be appropriate to use it as an index because it is ambiguous and therefore not easily interpreted or recognized.

7.6.4 Dealing with Solution-Creation Goals

When we initially showed a set of good indexes for the tomato tart meal at the beginning of this section, the indexes each had a goal attached to them. Why? An index needs to specify the situations in which a case should be appropriately retrieved, that is, the situations in which it will help a reasoner with its reasoning. Cases that can help with evaluating a solution are useful any time a similar situation comes up—only matching of situational features is necessary. But cases that aid with construction of solutions are really only useful in the context of constructing the pieces of the solution they apply to.

We can use the CHEF and JULIA examples to illustrate. In the CHEF example, the strawberry soufflé has just fallen. The indexes chosen predict under what circumstances this failure might happen again—when fruit is used in a soufflé. Under what circumstances might recall of this case be useful? Whenever a baker or chef is making a soufflé with fruit in it. If recalled before execution of such a recipe, it warns of what might go wrong, pointing out that additional reasoning might be necessary before carrying out the task of making the soufflé. If recalled during preparation of the soufflé, it makes the same warning, this time telling the baker to do some additional reasoning before continuing. If recalled after the soufflé is finished and has fallen, it provides an explanation of why the soufflé fell. Predicting failure, or any other outcome, is potentially useful during any reasoning or execution step of a plan or design. Cases that predict outcome are the ones that help with evaluation.

Suggesting solutions, however, really only makes sense when the reasoner is trying to construct a solution. When it is trying to evaluate a solution, remindings of alternative solutions can get in the way. There are a lot of satisfactory ways of solving most problems; once one is chosen, there is often little benefit in considering another. Thus, when cases suggest solutions, it makes sense to mark them as such by attaching to them the goal they help achieve. Because tomato tart fulfilled the goal of choosing a main dish, that goal is attached to it as part of its index.

In fact, appending a goal to an index that supports solution creation is prescribed by the functional analysis of indexes presented in the previous chapter. We said there that indexes in support of solution creation need to have the achieved subgoal included as part of the index.

But is the index we've come up with so far sufficient? Do we want to recall the tomato tart case only when we are considering what to serve as a main dish? Wouldn't it be more efficient to be able to recall that meal, in addition, when we're trying to construct a meal for the summer that uses tomatoes and is vegetarian, that is, before we break the problem into component pieces? Recalling this case early in problem solving would allow the reasoner to construct a solution framework early on, allowing it to bypass much problem decomposition. Attaching the goal of choosing a main dish is too specific to support that. What is needed in addition is an index that specifies more general goals the reasoner might be attempting to achieve that the case can help with. This tells us that generalizing goals in our indexes is as important as generalizing other descriptive features. Goal specifications, too, need to be generally applicable.

Making goal specifications generally applicable requires knowing which of the many subgoals of a goal are its primary goal achievers. Designing a meal, for example, has among its subgoals choosing an appetizer, choosing a main dish, choosing side dish 1, choosing side dish 2, choosing a beverage, and choosing dessert. Some are primary to the meal-planning task (e.g., choose the main dish); others are secondary (in this case, the rest). We generalize the goal for primary subgoals, but not for secondary ones. Because choosing a main dish is the primary subgoal of designing a meal, we specify the goal it is subgoal to in an index as well as specifying it. Thus, the goals we want this case to support are "choose a main dish" and "design a meal." This case provides guidelines for achieving both when vegetarians need to be served, tomatoes need to be used, and it is summer. The process, in general, is to examine the solution-creation subgoal that is being explained to see if it is a primary subgoal of any goal. If it is, then the index selection process is repeated for that goal.

In effect, what I'm prescribing here is a method of allowing indexes for a case to *trickle up* from the decisions that were made in creating its solution. The case is good for guiding decisions similar to those that were made in solving it. It is also good for guiding decisions that those decisions affected. And so on. The tomato tart case can help a problem solver choose tomato tart under the conditions it was chosen before; it can also help a problem solver choose a whole menu that includes tomato tart. The process of generalizing goals in an index supports identifying a wide range of lessons the case can teach and indexing over that whole set.

7.6.5 Some Examples

We illustrate the entire process using the tomato tart case. Recall that JULIA has just planned a meal and has decided to serve tomato tart as the main dish. It chose tomato tart because it is summer, a vegetarian friend is coming to dinner, and it is told to use tomatoes. Along with the tomato tart, it is serving a green salad, red wine, and bread. For dessert, it is serving gelato. There are a number of subgoals JULIA had to achieve in designing this meal—among them choosing each of the dishes. In indexing the case, we want to ensure that we make solutions to each of its subgoals available to it in the future when it tries to achieve the same subgoals. We also want the case to be recallable early in problem solving so that its entire menu can be suggested.

Creating an explanation. Before creating an explanation, the system must choose the subgoals it will explain. It is appropriate to index each of the subgoals it spent time attempting to achieve; thus, it must explain each of those. We will illustrate using only the selection of a main dish. Here, it is trying to explain how a subgoal was achieved. To do that, it retrieves its record of the justifications for achieving that subgoal. Here, the justification has the following components:

- Dish should include tomatoes.
- Jeanette, a vegetarian friend, is coming to dinner.
- If vegetarians are coming to dinner, the food should be vegetarian.
- Dish should be easy to prepare.
- Dish should be delicious.
- Dish should be appropriate for summer.

Making an explanation out of it, we add the result, that tomato tart was chosen.[6]

Selecting relevant observable or recognizable features. The next step is to select relevant observable features from the explanation. Any features that are part of the explanation are relevant. Observable features are those that we can see and those that are easy recognizable or known without inference. In this domain, that includes the guests and constraints that are given as part of a problem statement. Thus, the observable features include the following:

- Jeanette is a guest.
- Dish includes tomatoes.

---

6. This explanation is somewhat incomplete. Some systems might want to connect the pieces better than these are connected. This explanation, however, is sufficient for the job we need to do.

■ Dish is easy to prepare.

■ Dish is appropriate for summer.

Generalizing observable features.   We then need to generalize those features, making sure they remain observable or easily recognizable. We generalize the guest Jeanette by looking to see what description of her was relevant to the explanation. The fact that she is vegetarian is what was taken into account. Were we to substitute any other vegetarian in the problem statement, the result would remain just as appropriate. Thus, the fact that a guest is a vegetarian is a good generalization of "Jeanette." Is that recognizable? We often know whether our guests are vegetarians, so we will consider that a fine generalization.

Can we generalize that the dish uses tomatoes? No, because that is a specific of the problem specification that is addressed directly in the solution. There is no generalization of it that would render the solution still applicable. If I want to use red peppers in a meal, this dish will not be a good suggestion, even though both red peppers and tomatoes are salad vegetables. Nor is there any generalization of "easy to prepare" or "appropriate for summer." Thus, the descriptors we are left with include the following:

■ A guest is vegetarian.

■ Dish includes tomatoes.

■ Dish is easy to prepare.

■ Dish is appropriate for summer.

Additional steps for indexes in support of solution creation.   In the next step, we consider what kind of explanation this is. Because it is an explanation of how to achieve a goal, it is in support of solution creation. Thus, we have two more steps. We must append the subgoal it supports to the descriptor set we have derived, and we must consider whether the subgoal should be generalized and the process repeated. Appending the subgoal this descriptor set supports, we get the following explanation-based index:

■ Goal is to choose a main dish.

■ A guest is vegetarian.

■ Dish includes tomatoes.

■ Dish is easy to prepare.

■ Dish is appropriate for summer.

Considering generalization of the subgoal, we look to see what "choosing a main dish" is subservient to. We find that it is subservient to "designing a meal." We also look at the relationship between these two goals and find that choosing a main dish is a primary subgoal of designing a meal. Thus, we also choose indexes for "design a meal" using a similar process.

In choosing indexes to support this goal, we begin by seeing what decisions were made as it was achieved. This will be the basis for the explanation that is created. Thinking a bit about what went into creating the solution, we can see that the explanation is likely to be quite complex if we take everything that was considered into account in our explanation. One way of cutting that complexity is to create the explanation taking into account only major decisions that were made, that is, only the reasoning done in support of primary subgoals. Thus, we construct an explanation that includes only the things those primary subgoals took into account as they were being achieved. The process, from there, is the same.

To make sure the process is clear, let's continue with another example. JULIA once again has to plan a meal for the summer. Once again, it is told that tomatoes are in season and should be used and that the meal should be easy to make. It is also told that one of its guests is on a low-cholesterol diet. It remembers the tomato tart meal. Its problem now is that the tomato tart contains a lot of cheese and is high in cholesterol. It therefore derives for itself the subgoal of adapting tomato tart to lower the cholesterol. It does this by substituting skim-milk mozzarella cheese for the regular mozzarella the recipe calls for. How should this case be indexed?

Creating an explanation.   What has to be explained? Here, the reasoner needs to justify why it adapted the tomato tart by substituting skim-milk mozzarella. It knows that the major subgoal it addressed in solving this problem was an adaptation subgoal, adapting the main dish for a person on a low-cholesterol diet. This is the subgoal it knows it must justify. The justification for its decision to adapt the dish by substituting skim-milk for whole-milk mozzarella is that it needed to create a low-cholesterol dish, tomato tart was being considered as a dish, the cholesterol in tomato tart's cheese was too high, and skim-milk cheese is an acceptable substitute for regular cheese.

Selecting relevant observable features.   The need for the dish to be easy to make and low in cholesterol (both given as part of the problem specification), and the fact that tomato tart has already been chosen (a fact about the situation) are observable and relevant.

Generalizing observable features.   Easy to make and low in cholesterol cannot be generalized. Tomato tart can. Here we generalize it by finding a description of it that is more general and continues to justify the decision that was made. A general way of describing the tomato tart that does that is that it is a dish with cheese as a main ingredient.[7] The generalized features, then, are that the dish be easy to make, that it be low in cholesterol, and that it has cheese as a main ingredient.

Appending goal information.   Because this index is in support of a solution-creation goal, we must append that goal to the list of features to get the full index. The goal we append is "choose an adaptation method." We must also consider the goals this goal is subservient to and consider whether an index in support of those goals is appropriate also. This goal is a subgoal of choosing the main dish, and it is, in this case, an important subgoal of that goal. Thus, we might also want an index in support of that goal. To compute that, we would recover the set

---

7.   EBG methods talk about using the inference rules that were used to construct the explanation as the guidelines for generalization. One can generalize things such that the explanation still holds. For more details on this generalization process, see the EBG and EBL literature (e.g., DeJong and Mooney 1986; Mitchell, Kellar and Kedar-Cabelli 1986).

of decisions that went into constructing low-cholesterol tomato tart as a filler for the main dish and repeat the process.

7.7 COMBINING EXPLANATION-BASED, CHECKLIST-BASED, AND DIFFERENCE-BASED METHODS

Though explanation-based methods provide a method of choosing useful indexes, there is no guarantee that chosen indexes will discriminate a case from other similar cases. Explanation-based methods can be combined with difference-based methods to make this happen. Explanation-based methods can be used to generate a set of useful indexes, and difference-based methods can be used to subtract out those features that don't discriminate.

Another problem that comes up with explanation-based methods is that they are only as good as the domain model the explanations are created from. In many of the domains case-based reasoning is useful for, complete domain models don't exist. One way to deal with this lack is to combine explanation-based with checklist-based methods of choosing indexes. CABER, a troubleshooting system (Barletta and Mark 1988; Barletta and Kerber 1989), illustrates how this can be done. The system they built was aimed at recovering from faults in robotic cells. The domain model could account for some pieces of an explanation but was not complete enough to build full explanations of faults. Checklists were used to keep track of which kinds of features tend to be predictive, and explanation-based methods were used to the extent that domain knowledge was available. Those features found to be relevant to an explanation were given *priority* status as indexes, and other potentially relevant features were given *secondary* status. Barletta and Mark used this status in order to organize cases in hierarchies in the memory. Such status could also be used to determine which of two partially-matching cases is a better match.

Hammond solved the problem of incomplete domain knowledge another way in CHEF. He used checklist-based index selection for those indexes that helped with plan selection because his best model of what kinds of plans can be used with different kinds of foods were the cases themselves. However, he used explanation-based index selection to choose the kinds of indexes that predict potential failure. One might ask why, if he had a causal model that was good enough to detect failures, he didn't use it to choose indexes for correctly generated solutions. Using the causal model is quite time-consuming, and it is not always necessary to know the minute details of why things work. In addition, our models of why things fail aren't always good enough to explain why things succeed. CHEF's causal model was not complete enough to explain why every success story was a success. The fact that things work is often model enough. Failures, however, prompted CHEF to do deeper reasoning, making time-consuming causal reasoning and the indexes that can be created that way worth the time.

7.8 CHOOSING AN AUTOMATED INDEXING METHOD

One set of methods chooses as indexes features that tend to be predictive. Another set uses deep knowledge to choose the right set of indexes for each case. Either method can be combined with difference-based procedures that select from the chosen indexes only the ones that differentiate the case from other similar cases. How can an indexing method be chosen? And when is it appropriate to combine a basic index selection method with difference-based procedures?

Choosing an automated indexing method depends on two things: how hard it is to create explanations and how exact the indexing needs to be. If it is easy to create explanations, then explanation-based methods for choosing indexes are preferred, because they are more exact. Though explanation itself is difficult, when a reasoner's domain is constrained enough, its explanation process is not necessarily hard. CHEF, for example, was able to derive explanations of why its recipes failed because the set of conditions it had to consider was highly constrained by the relative simplicity of its domain.

Even when explanation is hard, it is sometimes possible for a system to interact easily with a person to create explanations. PROTOS, for example, cannot create explanations of its failures on its own, but it does provide a way for a person to explain its failures to it. Based on those explanations, it is then able to choose indexes for its cases. MEDIATOR created explanations of its reasoning failures by posing questions based on its previous reasoning to a person who provided answers. MEDIATOR's explanation method was based on TEIRESIUS (Davis 1982), a knowledge aquisition system that predates case-based reasoning by many years but remains one of the standards for knowledge-acquisition systems embedded in expert systems shells.

The second consideration in deciding if explanation-based or checklist-based methods of index selection should be used is how exact the indexing needs to be. For some problem domains, almost any case that is remembered will provide guidance in deriving solutions. In meal planning, for example, the range of potentially good solutions is huge, and adaptation is easy. Thus, any case that is somewhat similar helps in beginning to generate a solution. Indexing by what tends to be predictive would work just fine in that domain; there is no need to use explanation-based methods unless an unusual amount of precision is required.[8]

In other situations, more exact indexing works better. A system that provides cases to people to use for an exacting design task might be tedious to use if it recalled too many hard-to-adapt or inapplicable cases. For such a system, cases need to be indexed so that they are recalled only when directly applicable.

The level of detail the problem solver is working on also seems to have a bearing on whether retrieval needs to be constrained or not. At more abstract levels of problem solving, for example, when the framework for a solution is being created, there is more tolerance for consideration of barely-matching cases. In setting up a framework, the problem solver is looking for alternatives that can be incorporated to make a solution novel. At the more detailed levels, however, when much of the framework is in place, problem solving is more goal-directed and less tolerant of barely-applicable retrievals.

All that being said, there may be a need for exact indexing, and it may, at the same time, be difficult or impossible for the system to create its own explanations. How should a system builder proceed? Here, it makes sense to assign indexes by hand.

---

8. JULIA uses explanation-based methods to make some points about design. A simple meal-planning program, however, would not need to be so intricate.

A further consideration in choosing an indexing method is the organizational structures and retrieval algorithms that are available. As we shall see in chapter 8, the method of index selection interacts with organizational structures and retrieval algorithms. Some organizational structures (e.g., redundant discrimination networks) were created with indexing based on tendencies of features to be predictive in mind.

Whether or not to use a difference-based method also depends on the organizational structures and retrieval algorithms chosen for a system. When indexes are used as search restrictors (e.g., in discimination networks and redundant discrimination networks), it is useful to use difference-based methods to ensure that the redundancy of indexing is kept under control. When they are used only as identifiers (e.g., in methods based on parallel retrieval schemes), subtracting out the differences from the indexes is unnecessary.

There are trade-offs between ease of indexing and retrieval accuracy that must be considered in choosing an indexing method. Neither method is perfect in all situations. Using checklists to index by dimensions that tend to be predictive is computionally simple, but retrieval algorithms will necessarily miss some cases that should be retrieved and retrieve many items that only superficially match. On the other hand, this method makes retrieval of partial matches very easy. When such methods are used, retrievers usually retrieve many cases—some of which are relevant to the reasoning at hand and some of which are not—and a sorting algorithm must be applied to the retrieved cases to choose the more appropriate ones from the set.

Indexing by explanation-based methods, by contrast, provides more exact indexing. Cases are labeled by the features and combinations of features that are known to identify the situations in which it is useful. Retrieval algorithms, then, can retrieve fewer and more appropriate cases. The downside of this sort of indexing is that cases are indexed specifically for situations they are known to be useful for. It is possible that a case can be useful in unanticipated ways, and indexing according to explanations alone might keep it from being recalled in those situations.

7.9 SUMMARY

Automated index selection procedures are based on one of two approaches to indexing. In one approach, cases are indexed by features and dimensions that tend to be usefully predictive across the domain. The checklist-based method to indexing is used under this approach. The domain is analyzed, and the set of dimensions that tend to be important ones are computed. These are put in a checklist, and all cases are indexed by their values along these dimensions. In the other approach, cases are analyzed individually to find which of their features are predictive ones, and cases are indexed by those features. The explanation-based method implements this approach.

Neither approach is perfect. Checklist-based approaches are easy to implement and computationally simple, but they tend to overindex by unimportant features and to miss indexing on important dimensions novel to a particular case. Explanation-based methods are computationally complex and require a great deal of knowledge, but provide more accurate indexing. Accuracy, too, however, has its advantages and disadvantages. Less accurate indexing makes retrieval of partial matches easier but results in many largely inappropriate cases being retrieved; more accurate indexing results in retrieval of fewer cases and more appropriate ones but makes retrieval of unanticipated partial matches more difficult.

People tend to be better at choosing indexes than any of our computer programs to date. Thus, for practical applications, it makes sense to have people choose the indexes for cases. The process of choosing indexes begins with a set of conceptual steps in which the indexer considers what sorts of descriptions would make good indexes. These steps are followed by a set of steps that require the indexer to specify the indexes in the vocabulary of the case-based reasoner and to generalize indexes appropriately. This process can be enhanced by a simple tool that presents to an indexer the set of dimensions that make up the legal descriptors an index can have and, for each dimension, the set of legal vocabulary items that can fill it.

PART III

Retrieving Cases from the Case Library

In previous chapters, we discussed how to represent cases and how to choose appropriate indexes for them. In these next chapters, we explore how to retrieve the cases stored in the case library. The task is this:

> Given a description of a problem or situation along with some notion of the reasoning the reasoner is engaged in, retrieval algorithms must find one or a small set of useful similar cases.

Notice that we are asking the retriever to retrieve not just *similar* cases, but rather cases that are *usefully similar* to the new situation. An example will illustrate what "usefully similar" means.

> A host is planning a meal for a set of people who include several vegetarians, one of whom is also allergic to milk, several unadventurous eaters, and her friend Anne. Because it is tomato season, she wants to use tomatoes as a major ingredient in the meal.

The case library holds the following cases:

> **Meal1:** It was summer, the meal had to be easy to prepare; grilled trout was served, Anne was a guest; Anne didn't eat because she doesn't like grilled fish.
> **Meal2:** It was summer, there were vegetarian guests; we wanted to use tomatoes; the meal had to be easy to make; tomato tart was served.

Meal3: It was summer; the guests were unadventurous eaters; grilled hot dogs and hamburgers were served.

Meal4: Elana, who is allergic to milk, came to dinner. Yuppie pizza was served. To accommodate Elana, some of the pizza was made with tofu cheese substitute.

If we examine the similarities between each of these cases and the new situation, it's hard to say which case is most similar to the new one. When we begin to consider usefulness, however, choice of a best case becomes clear. If the reasoner is trying to choose a main dish, Meal2 and Meal3 are better than the others. If the reasoner is considering serving grilled fish and trying to evaluate it as a main dish, then Meal1 is best. If the reasoner is considering serving tomato tart and trying to figure out how to adapt it to get rid of the cheese, then Meal4 is best.

The example shows that retrieving cases that are similar to the new situation along just any dimensions isn't enough. Some dimensions are more important to pay attention to than others in judging similarity. And the importance of dimensions changes along with the reasoner's goals. A case that is *useful* is one that is similar to the new problem along dimensions that help the reasoner perform its given tasks or achieve its goals.

There are several processes that go into retrieving useful cases and several issues that need to be addressed. First, we must have some means of identifying which cases have the potential to be most useful. This is done by *matching and ranking* procedures. The pattern matching community and many of those in the analogical reasoning community find it natural to talk about identifying items that are most similar to a new item. They define mapping and matching algorithms that know how to compare two items to each other and score their degree of match. Indeed, degree of match is an important component of determining usefulness of a case. But determining the degree of usefulness of a case also requires consideration of what purpose the case will be put to after retrieval and what case dimensions were relevant in the past in determining outcome. These considerations allow matching procedures to determine which dimensions of a case are important to focus on in judgming similarity.

Because the *indexes* of a case mark which of its dimensions are the more important ones to focus on in judging similarity, matching algorithms can use indexes as a guide in dtermining which features to focus on for similarity judgments. But because any case might be indexed in multiple ways, matching algorithms must be able to distinguish which indexed features to focus on at any time.

For this reason, input to retrieval algorithms includes both a description of the new situation and also an indication of what the reasoner will use the case for. Usually this description is in terms of reasoning tasks to be accomplished or reasoning goals to be achieved. Matching and ranking procedures use this description to determine which features of a case are the most important to focus on in judging similarity.

Retrieval, then, is more than just setting cases up in one's favorite data structures and applying its algorithms. The reasoner must focus on appropriate dimensions of cases and might need to be guided by the reasoner's goals. Chapter 9 discusses matching and ranking procedures, focusing first on what they need to take into account, then on the building blocks of the process, and then on several algorithms and heuristics for determining the degree of match of two cases and for ranking cases for usefulness relative to some new situation.

A second important component of retrieval are *retrieval algorithms* themselves. These are the processes that know how to search the case library to find cases with the potential to match the new situation well. Matching procedures are applied to those cases identified by retrieval algorithms as potentially useful.

As we know from studies of data structures and algorithms, one cannot discuss algorithms for retrieval without also discussing the structures those algorithms must search. A list is searched differently, for example, than a complex tree structure. It is the same in discussing retrieval of cases. Different organizations of cases give rise to different algorithms for retrieving them. A list of cases, for example, requires different kinds of retrieval algorithms than a complex tree or graph structure. Each has its advantages and disadvantages. One can be sure in a flat memory (a list) that the best case will be retrieved, but if the memory is large, it may take too much time. Complex tree structures, by contrast, require less computation to get to a useful case, but they do not guarantee that the best-matching case will be retrieved.

Chapter 8 discusses several different possible organizations for cases, the algorithms required for retrieval in each, the way each uses indexes, and the advantages and disadvantages of each. It also discusses processes for building those organizational structures and for maintaining their structures over time as new cases are added to the case library. Several kinds of algorithms are discussed. Some are serial, and some are parallel. Some build complex hierarchical structures; others do not. Some use indexes to build structures that discriminate cases from each other at a very fine grain size; other structures discriminate more coarsely; others hardly discriminate at all.

Retrieval algorithms and matching functions are, indeed, the major pieces of case retrieval. There is, however, one additional piece to the process that needs discussions. That piece is called *situation assessment*. Situation assessment is the process of analyzing a raw situation and elaborating it such that its description is in the same vocabulary as cases already in the case library. To see what this means, consider the raw description of a fight:

> John punched Joe in the nose. Joe punched John back, knocking him down. John got back up again, this time with a knife in his hand. He tried to stab Joe. Joe pulled out his gun and shot John, killing him.

This description gives us the sequence of events in the fight, but there is much missing. We can see that the violence escalated, starting with punching and moving on to stabbing and finally to shooting. We can see that Joe was acting, at least partially, in self-defense, that is, that his motive was saving himself from John, who had started the fight. We can guess that Joe was scared and John was angry. We might wonder what Joe did to provoke John, if anything. Though none of these descriptors is in the sequence of events itself, they are all descriptors of the case. And some are descriptors that, if known, help a reasoner to draw conclusions about the situation.

Suppose, now, that you are a judge who must sentence Joe. In sentencing Joe, you must consider whether you think this is murder or manslaughter and whether Joe was justified in shooting or not. If Joe was acting in self-defense, then you can draw the conclusion that there was some justification for the action that led to the death and, therefore, that it was an act of manslaughter. If you can derive no justification, you will call it murder. You will sentence Joe differently depending on which it is. He may be sentenced to only five years in prison for manslaughter, but twenty or more for murder.

Noticing that the violence escalated, that it was initiated by John, that Joe had to defend himself, and perhaps even that Joe was scared are all important to determining the sentence. They are also the features that are useful in comparing this situation to others to make sure that the proposed sentence is consistent with other similar crimes. It is these descriptors, rather than those in the raw description of the case, then, that are useful as indexes to cases. It makes little sense to index by who the fighters were or what weapons they used—neither of those is predictive of how to sentence the crime, and neither is generally applicable enough to be worth indexing on. It makes more sense to index cases by whether the killer was defending himself, whether the fight was initiated by the killer or the person who was killed, and so on. If cases are indexed in the case library by those dimensions, then retrieval of useful cases can happen only after those dimensions are inferred for a new situation.

Situation assessment is tricky, however. There are always innumerable features of new situations that could be elaborated, some of which are quite expensive to infer. And often, old cases need to be retrieved to help with elaborating a new situation. Thus, though situation assessment is an important component of retrieval, it must be controlled. Chapter 10 discusses the relationship between indexing and retrieval, focusing on the situation assessment process and also discussing the several ways of implementing indexing and the effects of different indexing schemes on accuracy, efficiency, and flexibility of retrieval.

Putting it all together, the (idealized) process goes like this: The reasoner asks the retriever for cases by describing its new situation and its current reasoning goal. The new situation is analyzed. Its description is elaborated by situation assessment procedures, which determine what the indexes for the new situation would be if it were stored in the case library. Retrieval algorithms use the case and computed indexes to search the case library. As they search, they call on matching procedures, either to assess the degree of match between the new situation and cases that are encountered, or to assess the degree of match along an individual dimension. Retrieval algorithms return a list of partially-matching cases, each of which has at least some potential to be useful in case-based reasoning. Ranking procedures analyze the set of cases to determine which of them has the most potential to be useful. That set is returned to the reasoner.

An analogous process is carried out when cases are inserted in the case library. Index-selection procedures determine the way the case should be indexed. Insertion algorithms use those indexes to insert the case appropriately into the case library's organizational structures. In general, they do the same sort of search done by retrieval algorithms. They look for a place to insert the case rather than for a place to retrieve a similar case from, but the two searches are exactly the same. One expects to find a similar case in the place where the new case would be inserted. At this point, the two processes diverge. Where retrieval algorithms rank the usefulness of retrieved cases here, insertion algorithms invoke insertion algorithms to insert the case in the case library and reorganize its organizational structure as necessary. (Figure P.1 shows the steps of the two processes.)

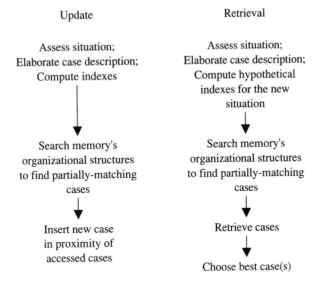

Update	Retrieval
Assess situation;	Assess situation;
Elaborate case description;	Elaborate case description;
Compute indexes	Compute hypothetical indexes for the new situation
Search memory's organizational structures to find partially-matching cases	Search memory's organizational structures to find partially-matching cases
Insert new case in proximity of accessed cases	Retrieve cases
	Choose best case(s)

FIGURE P.1   Update and Retrieval Processes

In the next chapters, these processes are presented in detail. We begin, in chapter 8, by discussing the different ways of organizing of the case library and the algorithms for searching each of the structures. Chapter 9 discusses matching and ranking procedures. Chapter 10 discusses situation assessment and provides more detail about the relationship between indexing and retrieval.

8

Organizational Structures and Retrieval Algorithms

We can think of a case library as a special kind of database. Like a database, it stores large numbers of records. Like those of a database, its retrieval algorithms must be able to find appropriate records when queried. And like a database, it must be able to do its job efficiently. Even though the library may hold thousands or tens of thousands of cases, it must find the appropriate ones in a reasonable amount of time.

In the field of databases, solving the efficiency problem has been seen as the key to success. Database researchers have put most of their efforts into designing organizational structures for records and algorithms that can traverse those structures quickly. Researchers addressing case-based reasoning have also put a lot of their efforts into making retrieval efficient. Case-based reasoning will be ready for large-scale problems only when its retrieval algorithms are sufficiently robust and efficient to handle thousands and tens of thousands of cases.

Like database search, retrieval of cases from a case library can be seen as a massive search problem—but with a twist. No case in the case library can ever be expected to match a new situation exactly, so search must result in retrieval of a *close partial match*. Partial match algorithms are quite expensive, however. Because of the expense, retrieval must be directed in some way so that matching is only attempted on those cases with some potential relevance to the new situation.

Because partial matching is so important, the algorithms used to search a database won't, in general, work for searching a case library. Database algorithms require the fields of a query to match items in the database exactly or to be instances of the types specified in the query. That is, if a query specifies that a field must be filled by a primary color, then only items with values red, blue, or yellow will be retrieved. If a field in a query specifies that it needs to be filled by the value red, then only items with value red in that field will be retrieved. Items with value `orange` or `fuchsia` in that field will not be retrieved, though both colors are close matches to red. Partial matching requires that matches such as these be allowed.

The case-based reasoning community has thus had to develop its own algorithms for search. Because partial match is expensive, the focus has been on finding efficient ways to partition the search space so that full partial matching need be done on only a small number of cases. Search algorithms thus are aimed at making a first cut at distinguishing which cases have potential relevance to a new situation.

Previous chapters have discussed indexing as a way of distinguishing what is important about a case, and indeed, indexes play a large role in many of the search algorithms and organizational structures used in case libraries. Indexes are used in many algorithms to organize cases and direct search through the organizational structures of the case library. If matching colors is important, for example, then cases will be indexed by color in some organizational structures, telling search processes that this is a feature to attend to in searching. If partial matching of colors is important, then the index might be on families of colors rather than colors themselves (e.g., the red family, the blue family), allowing retrieval algorithms to recognize two items as potential matches even though the values in their slots are not exactly the same. Alternatively, search algorithms might call matching functions to determine how closely the differing values in a new situation and old case correspond. A partial match within some range of appropriateness is acceptable.

Despite the need for new approaches to search, however, there continue to be important parallels to database algorithms. Each algorithm for searching a database corresponds to an organizational structure, a way of organizing the items in the database. In general, each search algorithm knows how to search one type of organizational structure. One set of algorithms can search B-trees; another set is designed to search heaps.

Algorithms for searching a case library, too, are each associated with a different organizational structure. The qualities of the search algorithms associated with each organizational structure parallel the qualities of the structures. Some organizational structures are bushy and meant to be searched in parallel; they are searched using breadth-first algorithms. Other organizational structures are deep; they are searched by depth-first algorithms. Some are meant for serial machines; others, for parallel machines. Algorithms reflect that distinction. Some organizational structures discriminate items from each other coarsely; others discriminate more finely. Algorithms for searching these types of structures differ in the way they interact with matching functions.

A further parallel has to do with the relationship between retrieving items from organizational structures and building those structures. As in database access, the same search strategies are used to support both tasks. During both retrieval and updating, search algorithms look for the place in the case library where an item belongs. That is the place the item will be inserted during update and also the place most likely to hold a similar item during retrieval. As in discussing the organizational structures in databases, one cannot discuss retrieval without discussing the way the structures are constructed and maintained over time as new items are inserted. Thus, as we discuss organizational structures and retrieval algorithms, we must also discuss algorithms for building and maintaining each type of structure.

In this chapter, we discuss several different organizations for cases, and along with each, the algorithms required for retrieval and update and the organization's advantages and disadvantages. The organizations and algorithms that will be presented vary in several ways. Some structures are hierarchical; others are more flat. Some structures discriminate coarsely; others discriminate more finely. Some algorithms are inherently parallel; others are serial. Depending on the discriminating power of the structures, each uses matching and ranking functions differently. Some retrieve large numbers of cases, then apply matching and ranking functions to winnow down the numbers. Others apply matching functions during the search, resulting in small numbers of cases being retrieved.

In general, the efficiency of retrieval depends on the amount and complexity of matching that must be carried out; its accuracy depends on the specificity of indexes. Each scheme attempts to partition the cases such that retrieval is both efficient and accurate. The goal is for search strategies to select out a small number of potentially relevant cases, and at the same time to make sure that at least some cases that have the potential to be most useful are in that set. The particular organizational structures and algorithms that are appropriate in any application depend largely on the number of cases in the case library, the complexity of indexes, the number of different tasks the case library must support, and the variability of indexes across those tasks.

We begin with the simplest structures and algorithms and continue with more complex ones. Several schemes will be discussed.

- Flat memory, serial search (optionally augmented by shallow indexing or partitioning)
- Shared feature networks, breadth-first graph search
- Prioritized discrimination networks, depth-first graph search
- Redundant discrimination networks, breadth-first graph search
- Flat memory, parallel search
- Hierarchical memory, parallel search

8.1 A NOTE ABOUT MATCHING

Case retrieval, no matter the method, requires a combination of search and matching. Organizational structures are searched to find potentially matching cases, and each is judged for its potential usefulness. This judgment is done by matching functions. In some schemes, search and matching are sequential; in others, they are interleaved.

The process of judging the usefulness of a case can be quite complex, and several methods for matching are discussed in chapter 9. It is necessary before discussing retrieval, however, to discuss the rudiments of matching. There are two concepts to focus on: importance of a dimension or descriptor to judging similarity or usefulness and degree of match of the values along a dimension.

In general, some dimensions or descriptors of a case are more important in judging usefulness than others. A good matching algorithm or heuristic takes into account which features of a case are more important and scores cases for usefulness according to those criteria. For example, if the reasoner is attempting to choose a plan to achieve a goal, then a match between the current goal and a goal in an old case are most important; next in importance are matches between the constraints that guide how the goal must be achieved; and next in importance are matches to the descriptive features that went into choosing the plan previously. Matches on other features are ranked considerably lower in importance. A case that matches on important features but not on less important ones needs to be judged a better match (or more useful case) than one that matches on less important features but does not match on important ones.

At the same time, some dimensions might match each other across cases only partially. One case might have the dimension color specified as red, another orange. Red and orange match better than red and blue but not as well as red matches red. A matching function or heuristic also needs to take into account the degree of match along specific dimensions.

The extent to which one case matches another depends on both these things. Cases that match well on important dimensions are better matches than those with less similarity across important dimensions. Cases that match well on important dimensions are better matches than those that match well on less important dimensions. As we discuss retrieval in the next sections, the extent to which a case matches a retrieval specification will play a large role in the discussion. It is not important now to know exactly how the extent of match is computed, but it is important to understand what goes into that computation:

- The degree of match along each dimension
- The importance of each dimension

Keeping this in mind should be sufficient to understand the advantages and disadvantages of each organizational structure and retrieval algorithm presented. Matching and ranking will be discussed in detail in chapter 9.

8.2 A SET OF CASES

The following set of cases, taken from MEDIATOR (Kolodner and Simpson 1989), will be used throughout this chapter to show the way the different organizational schemes and their retrieval algorithms work. Let us assume that the following cases are in the case library:

Candy: Two children want the same chocolate bar. Their mother has one break it in half; the other choose the half he or she wants. Each child gets half the candy bar and eats it. (a physical dispute)

Orange1: Two teen sisters want the same orange. Their mother has one cut it in half, the other choose her half. Each gets half of the orange. One sister eats her portion of the fruit; the other bakes with the peel of her half. The mother realizes her solution failed and considers what she might have done wrong. She realizes that she misunderstood the goal of the second sister and wrongly assumed that sister wanted to eat the fruit of the orange, when in fact she wanted to bake with the peel. (a physical dispute)

Orange2: Two teen sisters want the same orange. One wants to eat the fruit; the other wants to bake with the peel. Their mother has the second sister extract the peel from the orange and then give the fruit to the first sister. Both sisters are satisfied. (a physical dispute)

Korea: The leftists and the rightists both want control of Korea. After considerable fighting with no decisive victor, it is decided to divide the country between the two groups: the rightists get the south, and the leftists get the north. (a physical dispute)

Panama: Both the United States and Panama want control of the Panama Canal—the United States for security reasons, the Panamanians because the canal is on their land. After considerable negotiations, it is decided that Panama can retain land and economic rights to the canal because it is on their territory, but that the United States will retain security rights because they paid for its construction and require that it be open. (a political dispute)

The following case will be the one that must be resolved, the one that retrieval algorithms must find a useful match for.

Sinai Dispute: Egypt and Israel both want the Sinai. There has been considerable fighting prior to these negotiations.

The reasoner assumes that this is a physical dispute because it is a dispute over physical territory that both sides want. It is attempting to come up with a solution.

Let us assume the following importance rankings: Similarity of dispute type is more important than similarity of goals, which is more important than similarity of disputed object, which is more important than similarity of disputants.

8.3 FLAT MEMORY, SERIAL SEARCH

In a flat memory, cases are stored sequentially in a simple list, array, or file. Cases are retrieved by applying a matching function sequentially to each case in the file, keeping track of the degree of match of each case and returning those cases that match best. The simple algorithm is shown in Figure 8.1.

In a flat memory, this case is matched against each case in memory, and the best matches are returned. Matching the Sinai Dispute against each of the others yields the following results:

	dispute-type	goals	object	disputants
Candy:	match	match	no	no
Orange1:	match	match	no	no
Orange2:	match	no	no	no
Korea:	match	match	partial	partial
Panama:	no	no	partial	partial

The Korean conflict is the best match and is retrieved.

There is no organization put on top of the cases in this scheme, and the retrieval algorithm is very simple. The matching heuristics, in fact, do all the work here.

There are advantages and disadvantages to such a scheme. The major advantage is that the entire case library is searched. As a result, the accuracy of retrieval is a function only of how good the match functions are. If matching heuristics are good, then the best-matching case will always be retrieved. Another advantage is that adding new cases to the case library is cheap.

For every case in memory, match input to case.
Return the best match(es).

FIGURE 8.1   Flat Memory, Serial Search Algorithm

There are also major disadvantages to such a scheme, however. The biggest disadvantage, of course, is that the scheme is expensive. As the case library gets large, so does the time needed for retrieval. A scheme like this works when a library is small but quickly gets overwhelmed as the library grows.

There are several variations on the flat memory that can help alleviate the inefficiencies.

■ Shallow indexing
■ Partitioning of the case library
■ Parallel retrieval

A shallow indexing scheme is similar to the inverted indexes used in database systems.[1] Indexing is one level deep. Each descriptor chosen as an index points to those cases that include it in their representations, and before matching, one selects out only those cases that are pointed to by descriptors specified in the new situation. Rather than attempting match over the entire case library, one uses these indexes to choose out cases that are worth applying match functions to because they share at least one important feature with the new situation.

There are two considerations to deal with in using this variation. One is which dimensions to include in the set of indexes. Such an indexing scheme works only to the extent that indexing is by discriminating features, that is, those that can differentiate out the cases that are worth paying attention to. An indexing scheme that is too specific will result in omission of some potentially useful cases. One that is too encompassing won't cut down the number of retrieved cases significantly.

A second consideration is how to allow partial matching along dimensions. The best case could conceivably be one where there are no direct matches in any specified dimension, all dimensions being close partial matches. Unless a way of allowing retrieval based on partially-matching values in dimensions can be found, such a scheme will keep these kinds of cases from being retrieved. One way to achieve this is by indexing cases not only by their observable features but also by derived features that capture partial similarities. For example, one might use dimensions such as disputant-type and object-type to represent disputes, each meant to capture an important characteristic feature of a dispute. The Sinai dispute and Panama disputes have the value country for the disputant-type dimension; the Candy and Orange Disputes have value person.

It is important to choose such dimensions and designations so that they capture similarities at appropriate levels. For example, the disputant-type in the Korean Conflict is political party, not a direct match to country in the Sinai dispute, thus disallowing retrieval of that

---

1. An inverted index file associates indexing terms with each item indexed by that term. It thus adds indexing to the otherwise flat scheme.

case as a potential partial match. If the Korean Conflict is a good partial match to the Sinai Dispute, and if it ought to be retrieved based on the similarity of disputants, then another dimension might need to be used for indexing, say `disputant-type-type`, that takes as values such concepts as `political organization`, a useful generalization of `country` and `political party` for this domain and task. Features that are added to the representation may also capture important composite descriptors of events (e.g., that the disputant was a person and it was a political dispute). What is important is to index on those descriptors that allow accurate retrieval in this first step.

This scheme has been used in many running case-based reasoning systems, both in research systems with small case libraries and in fielded systems with case libraries of any size. It works best when features used as indexes are those that allow small numbers of cases to be retrieved and when indexes are sufficiently descriptive to ensure that at least some of the potentially most useful cases are retrieved. It also seems to work well when matching functions are fast, no matter what the size of the initially retrieved set (within limits, of course). It is used often with nearest-neighbor numerical matching schemes (to be described in chapter 9). It is also used with selection schemes that evaluate the applicability of cases based on objective criteria and with preference schemes.

The second variation is to partition the case library and to make available to the system a means of recognizing which partition a new situation falls into. Upon retrieval, those criteria are checked, appropriate partitions for the new situation are chosen, and matching is against only cases from selected partitions. For the dispute cases, for example, we might divide them into political disputes, economic disputes, and physical disputes, provide a means of determining which category a new situation fit into, and attempt matching only on cases within the appropriate category. When partitions get large, some secondary means of organization is often necessary to further guide the selection of potentially useful cases. For this scheme to work reliably, partitions must be chosen carefully.

The third variation is to search the library in parallel. One way to do this is to apply matching functions in parallel to the whole library. If the case library is larger than the number of processors available, another way is to use parallel machinery to select out appropriate cases using the shallow indexing scheme and then to apply matching functions to those cases in parallel, or alternatively, to select out appropriate partitions and apply matching functions in parallel to the cases in those partitions. Other parallel schemes will be discussed in a later section of this chapter.

Figure 8.2 summarizes the advantages, disadvantages, and variations in using a flat memory organization.

8.4 HIERARCHICAL ORGANIZATIONS OF CASES: SHARED FEATURE NETWORKS

When a case library is large, there is a need to organize cases hierarchically so that only some small subset needs to be considered during retrieval. This subset, however, must be likely to have the best-matching or most useful cases in it.

The machine learning community gives us several inductive clustering methods (e.g., Fisher 1987; Michalski and Stepp 1983; Cheeseman et al. 1988; Quinlan 1986) that can be

ADVANTAGES:

■ The whole case library is searched; accuracy is a function of quality of matching functions.

■ Adding new cases is cheap.

DISADVANTAGES:

■ It is expensive when the library is large.

VARIATIONS:

■ Use shallow (one-level) indexing to reduce set of candidates.

■ Partition the library.

■ Search in parallel.

FIGURE 8.2   Flat Memory, Serial Search: Advantages, Disadvantages, Variations

---

used to do this job. The intuition is this: If you can cluster together cases that are similar to one another and figure out which cluster best matches the new situation, then only items in that cluster need be considered in finding a best-matching case. Hierarchies are formed when clusters are broken down into subclusters and so on.

Inductive clustering methods generally look for similarities over a series of instances and form categories based on those similarities. The set of mediation situations listed above, for example, might be broken into "physical disputes" and "political disputes." Alternatively, it might be broken into "disputes over land masses" and "disputes over food."

One way of determining which are the right clusters is to cluster on sets of features that are shared among large numbers of items. Another way is to cluster on individual features that divide the set into clusters of equal size. Another way is to cluster in individual features that differentiate small groups of items from the others.

Each clustering method yields different clusters. Clustering the cases above the first way, we would get two clusters based on the disputed object's type and disputant type: disputes over food between kids and disputes over land between countries. Clustering the second way, we would get the same two clusters. Clustering the third way, we would get "physical disputes" and "political disputes." The political disputes are differentiated from the rest, and physical ones can be further subdivided using the same clustering heuristic.

Shared-feature networks provide a means of clustering cases so that cases that share many features are clustered together. Each internal node of a shared-feature network holds features shared by the cases below it. Items without those features live in or below that node's siblings. Leaf nodes hold cases themselves. Figure 8.3 shows one way the mediation cases can be organized in a shared-feature network.

To retrieve a case from a shared-feature network, a sort of breadth-first search is done. The input (new situation) is matched against the contents of each node at the highest level in the graph. The best-matching node is chosen. If it is a case, the case is returned. Otherwise, if it

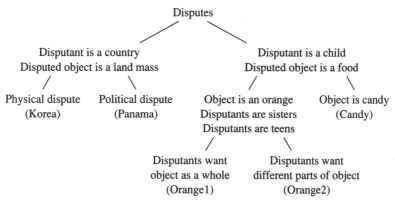

FIGURE 8.3   A Shared-Feature Network

Let N = the top node.
Repeat until N is a case:
      Find the node under N that best matches the input.
Return N.

FIGURE 8.4   Retrieving a Case from a Shared-Feature Network

---

is an internal node, the same thing is repeated among its descendants. This continues until a case is returned. Figure 8.4 shows the algorithm.

Searching for the Sinai Dispute in the network shown in Figure 8.3, we see that the top node is empty. Therefore, we match the Sinai Dispute against the contents of each node at the second level. It matches the left node better ("disputant is a country"). We repeat the procedure at the next level down, this time seeing if it matches "physical dispute" or "political dispute" better. "Physical dispute" matches better, and Korea is returned.

Building such a structure is equally simple. Figure 8.5 shows the basic algorithm. A clustering method is used to partition the cases. As just mentioned, clustering can be based on the sets of features shared by large numbers of cases, individual features that divide the set into clusters of equal size, or individual features that differentiate small groups of items from the others. The node representing each cluster is seeded with the set of features shared by all cases in the cluster. The clustering method is then applied to the cases in each partition to partition the group of cases at the next level.

After clustering the cases this way, the tree can be incrementally updated using the algorithm in Figure 8.6 as new cases are added to the case library.[2] Incremental update involves finding the place in the tree where the new case fits best and installing it appropriately.

---

2. Alternatively, the criterion in step 4 can be tightened or loosened. Rather than building a new node at the top level whenever a new case doesn't match all the features in an already existing node, the node that is already in the structure can be modified and the new case put under it. This will result in a less bushy tree.

1. Choose a clustering method.

2. Create a top node for the tree. Call it N.

3. Let C be the set of cases needing organization.

4. Put any features shared by all the cases in C into N.

5. Partition C using the clustering method. Create a node for each partition, attaching each as a successor to node N.

6. For each partition,

   (a) Create a node Ni.

   (b) If it contains more than one case, then repeat step 4, with N = Ni, C = the cases in the partition.

   (c) Else, put the features of the one case into node Ni.

FIGURE 8.5   Constructing a Shared-Feature Network

The major advantage of a shared-feature network is that it makes retrieval more efficient than when cases are organized in a list. Rather than having to attempt matches to all cases, it considers only a subset of cases. The method does have its disadvantages, however. Adding cases to the case library requires work. With a flat memory, cases just get added to a list. With a shared feature network, cases must be placed in the right place in the network as they are added. In addition, the network requires space. Thus, the total space required to store the case library is larger than the space required for the cases themselves. These added costs are outweighed by retrieval benefits, however, since space is usually not expensive, procedures for building and maintaining the network are not overcomplex, and retrieval, which is done more often than building and maintaining, is vastly more efficient.

There is, however, an additional consideration to keep in mind in assessing the advantages and disadvantages of shared-feature networks, one that has a bearing on retrieval over

---

1. Beginning at the top level, compare the new case to cases already at that level, finding the node it matches best. Call it N.

2. Does the case share all features in node N? If so, move down to the next level and go to step 1.

3. Is node N a leaf node (a case)? If so, gather all the shared features of node N and the new case, and put them in node N. Build two new nodes, N1 and N2, and make them successors to node N. In node N1, place the features from the old node N that are no longer in node N. In node N2, place the features of the new case that are not specified in the new node N.

4. Otherwise, create a new node m at the same level as node N. Put the new case into it. Make N's parent M's parent.

FIGURE 8.6   Incrementally Updating a Shared-Feature Network

time. That is the issue of keeping the network optimal. Keeping such a network optimal can be expensive. The incremental algorithm will maintain the organization set up at the time the network was created. But as new cases are collected, initial discriminations might not be the best ones, and the network might have to be rebuilt. But even more important is the question of optimality itself.

What does it mean for such a network to be optimal? The most straightforward definition would probably be that the optimal network is one in which retrieval time is kept as small as possible and the cases that are retrieved are those that are best for the job. Though I've presented clustering methods, I've given no guidelines for choosing a method that will set up a network with these two conditions satisfied.

Suppose, for example, that we needed to find the best match to a political dispute between two children over a bag of oranges. One party wants to keep the oranges until there is time to make juice from them. The other wants to eat the oranges now. Both are willing to share the oranges, and both want to do their orange activity with the other child. What case matches this one better? The Panama Dispute, or the first orange dispute? Using the network above, Orange1, the first orange dispute, would be retrieved. But perhaps it is better to retrieve another political dispute. Remembering the Panama Dispute might suggest that this one be solved by dividing rights to the oranges. Using the network above, the Panama Dispute could not be retrieved in this situation.

What is retrieved from the network depends on the organization of the network and the content of the internal nodes. If the hierarchy of nodes in the network corresponds to the importance of features, then important features will be considered first and clusters of cases that match best on those features will be extracted and considered further. If, however, unimportant features are high in the hierarchy, there is a chance that cases that share important features with the new situation will not be retrievable.

Using the relative importance of features to guide building of a network for the five mediation cases, the network in Figure 8.7 would be built. It first clusters cases according to the type of dispute, then according to the goals of the disputants, then according to several dimensions of the disputed objects. Using this network, the system would retrieve the Panama Dispute when the political dispute over the orange was described to it.

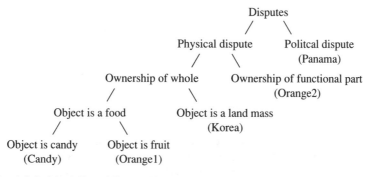

FIGURE 8.7   A Prioritized Shared-Feature Network

ADVANTAGES:

■ Partitions better than a list, making retrieval more efficient than serial search.

DISADVANTAGES:

■ Adding cases is a complex operation.
■ It is hard to keep the network optimal as cases are added.
■ Extra space is required for organization.
■ To provide accurate retrieval for several reasoning goals, several shared-feature networks, each prioritized differently, might be needed.
■ There is no guarantee that some good case won't be missed.

FIGURE 8.8   Shared-Feature Networks: Advantages and Disadvantages

There is one last consideration in discussing shared-feature networks. In discussing indexing, we said features take on different importance depending on the reasoner's reasoning goals. If one wanted to use prioritized shared-feature networks in a reasoner that had to support the solution to a variety of reasoning goals, several shared-feature networks would have to be set up, each prioritized with respect to a different reasoning goal.

Figure 8.8 summarizes the advantages and disadvantages of shared-feature networks.

8.5 DISCRIMINATION NETWORKS

Shared-feature networks cluster together similar cases. As a side effect of clustering, these networks discriminate cases. Clustering is primary; discrimination is secondary.

An alternative organizational scheme that both clusters and discriminates is a discrimination network (Feigenbaum 1963). The major difference between discrimination networks and shared-feature networks is in the priorities put on clustering and discrimination. In discrimination networks, discrimination is primary, while clustering happens as a side effect.

In a discrimination network, each internal node is a question that subdivides the set of items stored underneath it. Each child node represents a different answer to the question posed by its parent, and each child node organizes the cases that have its answer.

As in shared-feature networks, it is important to compare items along more important dimensions before less important ones to ensure that the cases that match along more important dimensions are retrieved. This is accomplished in a discrimination net by placing more important questions higher in the hierarchy than less important ones.

Figure 8.9 shows the prioritized discrimination net for the five mediation cases. The first discrimination is on dispute type, because that is designated as the most important feature. Next is discrimination on disputant goals and features of those goals. The "disputant goal" question and "ownership" question both address disputant goals. Next is discrimination on the disputed object, first by part, then by its type. In this net, questions about each dimension are

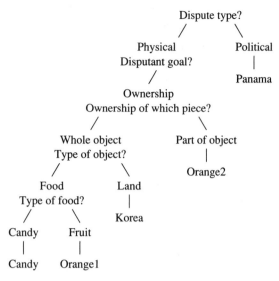

FIGURE 8.9 A Prioritized Discrimination Network

asked before going on to the next dimension. If there had been several disputes over land or food, the next discrimination would have been based on disputant attributes.

The algorithm for finding items in a discrimination network is specified in Figure 8.10. Starting at the top of the network, the first question is asked of the input (new case). The node corresponding to its answer is selected, and the question on that node is asked. This continues until a single item is found at a leaf node of the network.[3]

Searching for the closest case to the Sinai Dispute, described in section 8.2, we ask what type of dispute it is, find it is a physical dispute, and follow that branch. We then ask what the disputant goals are. Both disputants have the goal of ownership, so we follow that branch. We then ask which piece of the object the ownership goal is applied to, and find that both parties want the entire object. We follow that branch. We ask what type of object, get the answer land, and find the Korean Dispute at that leaf.

Let N = top node of tree.
Repeat until N is a case:
      Ask question at N of the input.
      Let N = subnode with the answer that best matches the input.
Return N.

FIGURE 8.10 Searching a Discrimination Network

---

3. We show a tree, but any branch on the tree could combine with another one, creating a directed acyclic graph (DAG).

1. Let N = top node of the tree. Let C = new case to be added. Let P = prioritized list of questions for nodes.

2. If N holds a case, save it as C1, and let N ask the next question in P. For each answer A to this question, add a subnode to N with A as its answer and with C or C1 as its value (unless both C and C1 give the same answer A; then let the N = new node, let N hold C1, and repeat this step).

3. Else (if N is not a case): Ask question in node N of C. Let A = its answer. If there is already a subnode with A as the answer, let that node = N, and go to step 2.

4. Else (if there is no subnode with A as the answer): add a subnode to N with A as the answer to the question in N, and put C in that node.

FIGURE 8.11   Building a Prioritized Discrimination Network

Building a prioritized discrimination net is fairly simple also. One begins with a prioritized list of features. To build the net, the first feature in the list is put in the top node. Branches are built for each value of that feature found in a case. If we begin with the Korean Dispute and the Panama Dispute, for example, and ask for the type of dispute, we get two answers: physical from the Korean Dispute and political from the Panana Dispute. Two branches are thus added to the tree, one with each answer, and each dispute is hung from its branch. If we ever add an economic dispute to the tree, another branch with value economic will be added. As cases are added to the tree with specifications the same as those already indexed in the tree, additional branches are built to discriminate the cases from one another. In a prioritized tree, the next question inserted in the tree is always the next feature from the prioritized list. If the two cases being compared along that dimension hold the same value, then a single branch is built, and another question node is built for the next feature in the list. This continues until the two items are discriminated (put in different branches of the tree).[4] Figure 8.11 shows the algorithm for building a prioritized discrimination network.[5]

Discrimination networks share most of the advantages and disadvantages of shared-feature networks. They subdivide the set of cases, making search more efficient than in an unorganized list, but the networks themselves take up space in memory. One must be careful to organize the network well to make sure that the best cases are always retrieved, and one can never guarantee that some good case won't be missed.

There are several advantages of discrimination networks over shared-feature networks, however. One is efficiency. Asking single questions of an input and traversing arcs corresponding to the answers can be implemented more efficiently than can matching subnodes, the major procedure needed to transverse shared-feature networks.

The other advantages are more conceptual. First, it is easy to understand the connection between the indexes discussed in the previous chapter and the organization of cases in discrim-

---

4. In a discrimination net or tree that is not prioritized, the next question is computed by looking at the similarities and differences between the items being discriminated and asking a question that differentiates them.

5. Charniak et al. (1987) provides considerable detail about programming discrimination networks.

ination networks. There is a direct mapping between attributes of indexes and questions on network nodes, and between values along dimensions and answers to questions. In effect, the questions at the nodes, coupled with their answers, are the indexes for the cases.

Second and related, in discrimination networks, attributes are separated from values, as in the most coherent indexing schemes. When attributes and values are separated, it is easier to track which attributes have been useful ones than when they are not. Keeping track of which indexes have been useful ones is harder in shared-feature networks, where the connection between indexes and clusters is less apparent.

On the other hand, shared-feature networks do have one advantage over discrimination nets. In a discrimination net, a wrong turn at a high node can keep the reasoner from reaching the desired leaf node. In a shared-feature network, there is less likelihood of this happening, because indexing is on several features at a time.

8.6 A MAJOR DISADVANTAGE

Both shared-feature networks and discrimination networks share one last important disadvantage. When an input is incomplete, neither kind of network gives guidance on how to continue search when a question in the discrimination network cannot be answered.

Suppose, for example, that two people are arguing about office space. Both want the same space. Is it a political dispute or a physical dispute? We might not know and might not be able to figure it out without collecting more information and doing a lot of complex inference. What is each of their goals? Do they want to own the space or control it? We may not know that either. Suppose the space is a large one, encompassing a suite of offices. Does each disputant want the whole space or just a part of it? We may not know that.

Traversing a discrimination network efficiently requires having answers or being able to compute answers to all the questions encountered on the nodes. If answers cannot be found or computed, there are three options: end the search, continue searching on all daughter paths, or choose the most plausible alternative path. All options are problematic (Porter, Bareiss, and Holte 1990). We don't want to have to end a search just because some piece of information is missing. An item can be a good partial match and still be missing some information. Continuing the search along all daughter paths is equally unsatisfying, though for a different reason. Once we allow search to continue on all descendants, we have violated the point of the discrimination network; we are no longer using it to control search. Choosing the most plausible alternative path is perhaps the most satisfying alternative, but it requires either additional computation to look ahead in the tree or the addition of knowledge that can be used to make the decision without looking ahead.

Figure 8.12 summarizes all the advantages and disadvantages of discrimination networks.

8.7 REDUNDANT DISCRIMINATION NETWORKS

Redundant discrimination networks provide an answer to the missing-information problem. A redundant discrimination network organizes items using several different discrimination networks, each with a different ordering of questions. The networks are searched in parallel. If the

ADVANTAGES:

- All those of shared-feature networks.
- Retrieval is more efficient than in shared-feature networks, because traversing arcs can be implemented more efficiently than matching subnodes.
- Understanding of connection between indexes and network organization is intuitive.
- Attributes and values are separated, making tracking of the usefulness of features easy.

DISADVANTAGES:

- All those of shared-feature networks.
- It is not clear how to deal with missing information.
- It is easier in a discrimination network than in a shared-feature network for a wrong turn at a high node to get in the way of good retrieval.

FIGURE 8.12 Prioritized Discrimination Networks: Advantages and Disadvantages

answer to a question in one network is missing, search in that network is discontinued but continues in the other networks. Because of the redundancy in the network, at least one of the networks will usually find a matching case if one exists.

Because of the significant overhead involved in redundant discrimination, these networks usually are combined with shared-feature networks to keep the redundancy under control. As in a discrimination network, each internal node of the network holds the answer to the question above. Each holds several additional questions that discriminate items below it. As in a shared-feature network, each internal node also records similarities between items indexed to that node. Redundancy of indexing is kept under control by eliminating those similarities from consideration as further discrimination is done. The network in Figure 8.13, from CYRUS (Kolodner 1984), illustrates.

CYRUS, recall, was one of the first implementations of dynamic memory (Schank 1982). As in *Dynamic Memory*, its organizational structures are called MOPs (memory organization packets). Each MOP has two functions. It holds general knowledge about the shared features of cases it organizes, and it holds an organizational structure that indexes those cases. Nodes in the tree either hold single cases (EVn in the figure) or are sub-MOPs of their parent MOPs (MOPn in the figure) and themselves redundant discrimination networks. In Figure 8.13, triangles represent questions, and labels on arcs represent answers. Boxes are MOPs and sub-MOPs. They hold the list of features shared by *most* cases under them and have an indexing structure below them. This illustration from CYRUS captures just a few of the discriminations CYRUS makes for diplomatic meetings. Chapter 7 lists the entire set of features CYRUS uses to index diplomatic meetings. CYRUS indexes redundantly on each feature whose value is not already known to be normative (i.e., in the shared features of the node).

One searches such a network using the algorithm in Figure 8.14. Following this algorithm to find a diplomatic meeting between Cyrus Vance and Menachem Begin in New York

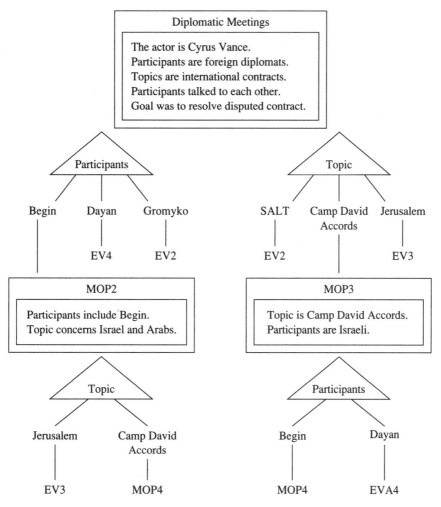

FIGURE 8.13   A Redundant Discrimination Network from CYRUS

and about Jerusalem, in the first step, the questions at level 1 of the graph are asked: Who are the participants? What was the topic? Arcs corresponding to the answers, Begin and Jerusalem, are then traversed, arriving at MOP2 and EV3. EV3 is an event and is collected. MOP2 is an internal node in the network, and the process continues from there. MOP2's questions are

Discriminate in parallel on each of the networks.
Return the entire set, that is, union, of cases found.
Match the new situation against each case in the set to find the best of those cases.

FIGURE 8.14   Searching a Redundant Discrimination Network

1. Determine which MOP the new case should be indexed in.
2. Compute the set of indexes to be used to index the case in that MOP by computing potential indexes and then deleting from the set features that are norms of the MOP and features known not to be predictive.
3. For each index, follow the procedures set out below.

FIGURE 8.15 Building a Redundant Discrimination Network: The Steps

asked: What was the topic? The arc corresponding to its answer, Jerusalem, is traversed, arriving (by another route) at EV3. That final set, EV3, is then matched against the input and found to match sufficiently.

Building redundant discrimination networks (Kolodner 1983b, 1984) is more complicated than building either discrimination networks or shared-feature networks. In short, the features to be used for indexing are first computed as described in chapter 7. Depending on whether an attribute-value pair is already in the network or not, processing continues differently. If the attribute is not yet there (the triangles), it is added, and an arc for its value is added that points to the new case. If the attribute is already there but the value from this case is not there yet, an arc for the new value is added that points to the new case. For example, to add a meeting between Vance and Moshe Arens into the structure shown in Figure 8.13, an arc labeled Arens would be added to the triangle in the top level labeled participants. If the attribute and its value are already there (e.g., another meeting with Gromyko), then a new level of discrimination is built (if one is not already there). Similarities between cases are gathered up and placed in new MOPs, and cases are discriminated in multiple ways by features that differentiate them. If the new level of discrimination is already there (e.g., if we were adding another meeting with Begin), the new case is indexed following the whole process recursively. In several additional steps, the similarities that are gathered and saved are checked and updated as additional cases are added, and indexing is adjusted based on necessary changes to those lists. These steps, in effect, compute generalizations about cases. Figures 8.15, 8.16, and 8.17 summarize the process. More detail can be found in publications about CYRUS (Kolodner 1983b, 1984).

Index creation: IF there is no prior index in the current MOP for a relevant feature of a case, THEN

■ Construct an index.
■ Index the case by that index.

Indexes are constructed in one of two ways. If the index's attribute is not yet indexed, a node corresponding to that attribute is added to the network, indexed from the current MOP. An arc labeled by the value is added to the node corresponding to the attribute. The arc points to the new case. If the index's attribute is already discriminated, but its value is not, an appropriate arc is added pointing to the new case.

FIGURE 8.16 Building a Redundant Discrimination Network: Indexing Cases

The advantages of redundant discrimination networks include all the advantages of discrimination networks, along with a few others. First, because cases are indexed in multiple ways, there are many different independent paths that can be followed to find a case. Second, as described earlier, the problem of missing features is solved. Third, the process of adding new cases to memory results in generalizations being made about groups of cases. Though CBR itself doesn't use generalizations, they can provide a useful addition to case-based reasoning. CYRUS uses generalizations created this way to help with situation assessment.

There are also disadvantages. Again, all those associated with discrimination nets apply equally here. In addition, networks require a lot of extra memory space. It is also expensive to

---

MOP creation: IF there is one case indexed at an index point for a new case, THEN

- Create a new MOP at that point (in place of the case).
- Extract the similarities between the two cases, and add those as shared features (norms) of the new MOP.
- Index the two cases in the new MOP by following the procedure in Figure 8.15.

MOP refinement: IF there is a MOP at an index point for the new case, THEN

- Index the new case in that MOP by following the procedure in Figure 8.15.
- Check the validity of the shared features (norms) of this MOP.
- Update the shared features as necessary using the heuristics below as appropriate.

Deleting sub-MOPs (discovering and recovering from undergeneralization): IF a sub-MOP indexes a large majority of the cases in its parent MOP, and if the parent MOP holds a reasonable number of cases, THEN

- Delete the index to the sub-MOP.
- Add shared features of the sub-MOP to the shared-feature set of the parent MOP.
- Delete the sub-MOP.

Recovering from false generalization: IF a shared feature has been disconfirmed, THEN

- Remove it from the MOP.
- Create an empty sub-MOP indexed by that feature.
- Gather up other features disconfirmed at the same time, and install the whole set as the shared-feature set of the new sub-MOP.
- Mark the new sub-MOP as *once-generalized*, designating that though we know there are cases that should have been indexed there, because of thinking the index was a shared feature of the parent, those cases were never indexed by this feature. This will be a sign to search-strategies that such cases do exist but will need to be found elsewhere.

FIGURE 8.17   Building a Redundant Discrimination Network: Adding and Refining Nodes in the Network

---

update the network when new items are added. Finally, the retrieval algorithm can return too many barely-matching cases in the first steps, requiring full matching procedures to be applied to large numbers of cases.

The problem here is that there is no implementation of priority in redundant discrimination networks. Indexing is done on all relevant features at all levels of the network. Without priorities in shared-feature and discrimination networks, some important cases could be missed. Without priorities in redundant discrimination networks, many cases that are similar but not potentially useful are retrieved. Though matching functions that take priorities into account can be used to select useful cases after retrieval, this can be inefficient if networks allow too many cases to be retrieved.

Another problem with the scheme presented is the limited way it can accommodate partial matching. In redundant discrimination networks, as in discrimination networks, partial matching is carried out by indexing mechanisms. The system builder anticipates the sorts of partial matches that will be needed and indexes on those derived features. Because in CYRUS, for example, the occupations of meeting participants are deemed relevant for partial matching, CYRUS indexes on the occupations of meeting participants. It can recognize that Andrey Gromyko and Moshe Dayan, who were both foreign ministers, are similar because it indexes by their occupation. But its search processes would not be able to retrieve cases in which the tempers of two diplomats were the same because it does not index on personality traits.[6] For some problems, more flexible partial matching is needed as part of the retrieval process.

Several different schemes have been developed to augment the basic principles of redundant discrimination. The goal has been to make retrieval more directed and partial matching more flexible, while keeping the advantages of redundant indexing.

We begin with CASEY (Koton 1989). As she was developing CASEY, Koton found that some case features were a lot more predictive of a common solution than others. In particular, plausible internal states seemed to be the key to finding a good match. CASEY's organizational scheme, based on this discovery, was to index cases first on internal states, discriminating on other types of features only after that baseline discrimination was done. In effect, Koton simply added priority to the redundant discrimination scheme.

The downside, of course, of adding priority to redundant discrimination networks is that the capability of finding cases when features are missing is diminished. Koton took care of that problem two ways: by making sure that those important features were known, or at least hypothesized, by the time retrieval was done, and by maintaining a separate case library indexed by surface features that the system could fall back on if there was too much missing to make good plausible hypotheses. Inference of important features is called *situation assessment* and is discussed in chapter 10.

The major result of this scheme was that only cases that could plausibly match the input were returned. Cases matching on a random set of surface features never had to be considered. Another result was that considerable ranking of cases could be done as retrieval was happening rather than having to apply the matching function to every retrieved case. The matching

---

6. If it retrieved such cases based on some other index, its matching procedures would later be able to recognize their similarity. The problem is that retrieval based on similarity of this sort is impossible if it is not anticipated in the indexing scheme.

function needed to do only a check for appropriateness of a case rather than a check through a whole set of cases to see which was the best fit.

In implementing MEDIATOR (Simpson 1985), Simpson was concerned with the abstractness of indexes and ways of being able to notice a partial match along some dimension, for example, noticing that a dispute over an avocado partially matches a dispute over an orange because the disputed object in both is a type of food. Should the Orange Dispute be indexed as a dispute over food or a dispute over an orange? Should a Lebanese meal be indexed as a meal with "cuisine = Lebanese" or "cuisine is a type of Middle Eastern cuisine"? CYRUS's answer was to index on both, allowing partial and specific matching to be done but creating significant redundancy. MEDIATOR instead indexed on the most general descriptor that could be recognized and then added a discrimination of a more specific sort when the general descriptor got overwhelmed. Thus, it indexed the Orange Dispute first as a dispute over food, but when it had seen several disputes over food, it added a new level to the discrimination network that discriminated on type of food. These new levels are generally added between two levels that already exist in the network.

JULIA's (Hinrichs 1992) answer combines CASEY's scheme with MEDIATOR's and adds additional partial matching flexibility. Like CASEY, JULIA prioritizes its indexing, indexing first on goals, then on cuisine constraints, then on cost, and so on. Like MEDIATOR, it indexes based on more abstract descriptions and adds discriminations about specifics as the need arises. In addition, JULIA integrates matching and retrieval by applying matching heuristics as it traverses the redundant discrimination network. It asks the question in the node, but rather than traversing the arc that contains the answer to the question, it traverses the one or ones with best-matching answers to the question. One question in JULIA's network, for example, asks what the ingredients of the main dish are. One arc emanating from that node is labeled chicken. As the network is traversed to find partially-matching cases, JULIA allows that arc to be traversed not only when the main dish in its problem case has chicken as an ingredient, but also when it designates poultry (subtype matching), chicken salad (subset matching), chicken wings (partonomic matching), or duck (taxonomic matching), if there is no more specific match on some other arc. Complex matching is done during retrieval, but there is little need for ranking of retrieved cases when retrieval is complete (because of the prioritization) and opportunities for finding partial matches are enabled by the complexity of the match during retrieval.

Figure 8.18 summarizes the discussion of redundant discrimination networks.

8.8 FLAT LIBRARY, PARALLEL SEARCH

Up to now, the schemes presented have been serial ones. We have looked at how best to organize a set of cases so that a single sequential processor can get the best-matching cases out. When parallel processing is added to the picture, other considerations come up.

On first glance, people often comment that with a parallel scheme, all the indexing and all the organizational schemes we have been discussing become obsolete. And, indeed, with a massively parallel machine, one can apply match functions to all cases at once to rank them. However, if we think of the indexing problem as the problem of predicting under what circum-

ADVANTAGES:

■ All those of discrimination networks.

■ Many different paths to each item in the network, allowing retrieval even when features are missing in a probe.

■ Generalizations are formed as cases are added.

DISADVANTAGES:

■ All those associated with discrimination networks except the inability to deal with missing features.

■ Much extra memory space is needed to store networks.

■ Procedures for adding new cases are expensive.

■ Indexing may not discriminate well enough, resulting in the retrieval of barely-matching cases.

■ Limited accommodation of partial matching.

VARIATIONS:

■ Add priority to the discrimination scheme: eliminates retrieval of barely-matching cases (CASEY).

■ Index on more abstract descriptions of features first, more specific ones later: accommodates partial matching (MEDIATOR).

■ Combine both variations: accommodates partial matching even better (JULIA).

FIGURE 8.18 Redundant Discrimination Networks: Advantages, Disadvantages, Variations

---

stances a particular case will be appropriately retrieved, then the indexing problem doesn't go away—it merely moves into the matching function. In a parallel scheme, indexes may not be needed to direct search; however, some designation of what to prioritize in matching and ranking cases is still needed. Matches on some features and combinations of features rank higher than matches on others, and cases that match on more important features are better matches than cases that match on less important features.

One way to use a SIMD-parallel machine[7] as a case memory is to store cases as feature vectors, putting each feature vector into a processor (Kolodner 1988a; Kolodner and Thau 1988). Retrieval is done by matching the input case to all feature vectors in parallel (Figure 8.19).

---

7. SIMD-parallel means "single instruction, multiple data." In a SIMD-parallel machine, the same instruction is applied to several pieces of data at the same time.

For all cases in memory, match case to input.
Return the best matches.

FIGURE 8.19 Parallel Retrieval on a Flat Memory

There have been several implementations of such a scheme. The first was MBR (Stanfill and Waltz 1986, 1988), implemented in the Connection Machine. Case representations in MBR (for memory-based reasoning) parallel the representations in databases. Feature vectors hold the surface features of cases; case representations have little in the way of deep or derived features. The matching function in MBR is computed by the program based on the probabilities of cases' having each feature. There is no indexing per se in MBR. Rather, it depends on the case library's holding a representative set of cases from which a match function can be computed. Retrieval is based on a weighted match that uses every feature in a case. MBR proved itself a fast algorithm, but it was never tried out on the kinds of domains in which similarity must be computed based on derived features.

A descendant of MBR, called *validated retrieval* (Simoudis 1991b, 1992), deals with that problem. Taking advantage of parallelism, in its first step, like MBR, it uses the algorithm above to retrieve all cases that match on available features of its new situation. In a second phase, it examines the cases it retrieves to see which derived features of the new situation are worth computing. Derived features are descriptors of a situation that are either hard to acquire or expensive to compute. They can be extracted from a new situation, but they require time and/or effort, sometimes considerable. In validated retrieval, only those derived features that retrieved cases identify as important are computed. Retrieval is attempted a second time, again using the parallel retrieval algorithm, using these features as part of its probe. Cases include as features both available features and deeper derived features that experts identify as important to judging similarity in a domain.

A third implementation can be found in Abby (Domeshek 1989, 1991a). Abby's procedure is different from the others in two respects. First, rather than matching on the full descriptions of cases, Abby uses the parallel matching scheme to match the potential indexes of a new situation to the indexes of cases is the case library. That is, rather than storing and searching the space of cases, Abby stores and searches the space of indexes. Abby's indexes are quite fine-grained and include all the important thematic information in each case and some of its particulars. They are similar in kind to Universal Index Frame (Schank and Osgood 1990) indexes. The second difference between Abby's scheme and the other parallel schemes is that its algorithm is not based on Connection-Machine-type SIMD parallelism, but is a parallel retrieval scheme based on *connectionist* parallelism. Explanation of the scheme is beyond the scope of this book, but more information can be found about it in "What Abby Cares About" (Domeshek 1991a).

The advantages of parallel retrieval schemes are obvious. The basic algorithm is easy. Matching and retrieval happen in one step. Adding new cases to the case library is easy because there is no organization on top of the cases that needs to be maintained.

ADVANTAGES:

- The whole library is searched; accuracy is dependent only on matching functions.
- It is fast.
- Adding new cases is easy.

DISADVANTAGES:

- Expensive hardware is needed.
- Simple match functions limit sensitivity to context in matching.

VARIATIONS:

- Allow parallel search procedures to use simple, but robust, matching functions to choose a set of potentially useful cases. In a second pass, apply more accurate matching functions to choose the best case or cases.
- Search in the space of indexes rather than the space of cases.
- Some implementations take advantage of SIMD-parallelism; others take advantage of connectionist parallelism.

FIGURE 8.20   Flat Library, Parallel Search: Advantages, Disadvantages, Variations

Expensive hardware is needed to make the scheme work, however. Furthermore, the simplest kinds of match functions that work best on SIMD machines limit sensitivity to context in matching. If contextual considerations and partial matching along the vector are taken into account in the matching, the simplicity of the match procedure can be compromised. In some cases, the needs of the matching function and those of the parallel scheme may come into conflict.

Figure 8.20 summarizes the advantages, disadvantages, and variations of parallel search on a flat memory.

8.9 HIERARCHICAL MEMORY, PARALLEL SEARCH

The advantage of a flat memory is that no maintenance is required. The disadvantage is that connections between cases in memory are not maintained. Shared-feature networks and discrimination networks of both sorts provide a way of designating the commonalities among cases. Though parallel machines may not require an organization to be imposed on items in a case library, it is often advantageous to do so. Hierarchies provide economical ways of specifying normative information and of organizing inferences. What we would really like then, is to have our cake and eat it too; that is, we want both the advantages of a hierarchical memory and the advantages of a parallel retrieval algorithm, a way of having a parallel algorithm take advantage of a hierarchy placed on top of a set of cases.

Examining redundant discrimination networks gives some clues as to how this can be done. Redundant discrimination nets, remember, are searched in a breadth-first way, the serial implementation of a parallel algorithm. Though implementations have been on serial machines, there are some obvious places where MIMD-parallelism[8] could be added to make the retrieval process more efficient. One processor might ask a question and then determine which arc is the appropriate one to follow, arrive at a new node, call in additional processors for the questions on that node, and so on. For finer-grained parallel processing, one might attach a processor to each arc in addition and, at the end of a matching cycle, rank the partial matches along each arc.

One can also think of parallel algorithms that take advantage of a hierarchical structure without depending on discriminations to guide search. Memory could be organized hierarchically (using, e.g., MOPs and sub-MOPs) in a way that makes sense but without indexes discriminating sub-MOPs and cases from each other. Each case and each node in the hierarchy is assigned a processor. In such a scheme, retrieval is achieved by broadcasting each attribute-value pair of a new situation into memory, lighting up every node in the hierarchical structure that has that pair. The most specific node in each part of the hierarchy that has any points gathers up the points in its antecedent nodes, and the ones with counts over some threshold win. A matching function is then applied to each one of those, taking the importance of features into account. This is more or less the scheme implemented in PARADYME (Kolodner 1988a; Kolodner and Thau 1988).

There are several ways the scheme could be made more sophisticated. One could give more points (importance) for some matching pairs than others, alleviating the need for a separate matching function at the end. Each node (case or generalized case) might know how many points a particular pair is worth, or the system in general might know which pairs are worth more than others.

Advantages of such a scheme parallel the advantages of other hierarchical schemes and the advantages of parallel schemes. Cases, as well as generalizations of cases, are maintained in the memory and are equally accessible. Cases that are similar to each other are stored close to each other in the case library, allowing the potential for browsing in the neighborhood of a retrieved case to see what else is there. At the same time, retrieval is efficient.

Disadvantages are somewhat more difficult to ascertain, because there have been few implementations of such a scheme. One disadvantage that is evident parallels a disadvantage of redundant discrimination networks: Retrieval is likely to turn up many barely-matching cases, requiring much work from matching functions after retrieval algorithms have done their work.

Advantages and disadvantages of this scheme are summarized in Figure 8.21.

---

8. MIMD-parallelism means "multiple instructions, multiple data." That is, the many different processors each carry out different instructions in parallel.

ADVANTAGES:

- Same as other hierarchical schemes.
- Same as other parallel schemes.
- Generalizations are accessible by the same algorithms that access cases.
- Efficient retrieval.

DISADVANTAGES:

- Difficult to ascertain, because few implementations.
- Retrieval likely to access many barely-matching cases.

FIGURE 8.21   Hierarchical Organization, Parallel Search: Advantages and Disadvantages

8.10 DISCUSSION

Now that algorithms for organizing and searching a case library have been presented, several issues related to search can be explored. The first I address is the contributions of parallelism to case retrieval. Certainly, parallel algorithms can speed up retrieval, making it more efficient. But parallelism has made a more substantial contribution to research on case retrieval: It has led researchers to look at indexes in a new light, promising more efficiency in the future, I think, than can be accomplished by merely making old algorithms parallel. Next, we look at the issue of hierarchical versus flat organizational structures. It is clear that hierarchical structures allow increased efficiency, for both serial and parallel algorithms. They also add other capabilities to a system. Next, we look at the relationship of search to matching.

8.10.1 A Note on Parallelism

It seems to be a given in computer science that hardware advances happen much more quickly than the software advances that are needed to take advantage of them. So it is also in case-based reasoning. When case-based reasoning was in its infancy (late 1970s, early 1980s), parallelism in both hardware and software was mostly a dream. Researchers were working on parallel hardware, but its implications had not yet reached the psyches of most software people. It was easy to think in terms of the kinds of parallelism embedded in breadth-first search, but other kinds of parallelism (e.g., of the sort required for connectionist networks or constraint networks) were on the minds of only a few researchers specializing in those areas. Thus, though the case-based reasoning community knew that fast retrieval algorithms were a necessity for making case-based reasoning viable, making algorithms parallel was not a high priority. Instead, priority was put on the conceptual elements of making retrieval efficient—the problem of indexing cases such that their appropriateness to a situation could be recognized, the indexing problem. The issue of how to implement an efficient system that could use indexes was a secondary problem.

Nevertheless, the first implementations of case memory (in CYRUS [Kolodner 1983a, 1983b, 1984] and IPP [Lebowitz 1983a]), though on serial machines, were implemented as breadth-first searches that could, in principle, be carried out in parallel on the right hardware. These implementations of redundant discrimination networks used indexes to guide search of memory's organizational structure. Only those pathways marked by features present in a retrieval key (the new situation) were followed in searching the case library.

For many years, the implementations that came after CYRUS tended to concentrate on indexing issues and mostly ignore the creation of new retrieval algorithms. The case libraries in MEDIATOR, PERSUADER, and JULIA, for example, all use variations of CYRUS's redundant discrimination networks. CHEF and JUDGE use (nonredundant) discrimination networks, an easy-to-implement way to organize the case library. Their domains were simple enough that a prioritized ordering of discriminations was sufficient to get the retrieval behavior from the systems that was needed to support the processes these systems concentrated on (adaptation, repair, and situation assessment).

Later, DMAP (Riesbeck 1986), though still on a serial machine, was implemented with more fine-grained parallelism in mind. CYRUS's scheme, in effect, stores cases and their generalizations (MOPs) in the processors of a parallel machine. It allows one index per case to be matched in each parallel cycle. DMAP, by contrast, distributes an individual case over several processors, allowing several indexes per case to be matched simultaneously in each parallel cycle. Indexes in DMAP, as in CYRUS, serve to direct search through organizational structures. As in CYRUS, only those parts of the structure labeled by features in the retrieval key (new situation) are accessible through DMAP's algorithms. Implementation of PARADYME on the Connection Machine (Kolodner 1988a; Kolodner and Thau 1988) took explicit advantage of the inherent parallelism in DMAP, making retrieval quite fast (complexity linear relative to the size of the probe).

These implementations all have implicit parallelism in them, and certainly their efficiency can be significantly increased by implementing them on parallel machines. Despite the fact that they were implicitly parallel, however, constraints put on organizational structures and on retrieval algorithms were those required for serial search—search is restricted as much as possible early on so that a minimum of the case library needs to be accessed. Efforts were made to minimize the number of cases examined, a serial way of achieving efficiency.

As parallel machinery became more common, however, the case-based reasoning community began looking at efficiency from a parallel point of view—minimizing the number of parallel cycles the system must carry out rather than minimizing the number of serial operations. Looking at efficiency this way led to new ways of thinking about retrieval. Rather than trying to minimize the number of cases examined, researchers began trying to minimize the number of individual matching steps (e.g., by making networks more bushy and less deep) and limit the complexity of inferences that need to be carried out (e.g., Kolodner 1989; Gentner and Forbus 1991; Gentner, Ratterman, and Forbus 1993; Simoudis 1991b, 1992). In validated retrieval (Simoudis 1991b, 1992), for example, retrieval algorithms get started by retrieving cases based only on available or easy-to-obtain information about a new situation. An inference-free search based on a coarse indexing scheme retrieves all cases that share subsets of these features with the new situation. The complex inference required to identify best-matching cases, which cannot always be done in a parallel way, is limited to those features suggested by retrieved cases. Indeed, this and other implementations show that taking advantage of parallelism can greatly increase the efficiency of retrieval processes.

The major conceptual advance that has come from taking parallelism seriously, however, has been a new way of conceptualizing indexes. Indexes were always thought of as identifiers for a case—they are the features of the case that describe its essence best. In thinking serially, however, indexes had always been given another role—they were used to restrict search through the case library. Search algorithms were only allowed to follow paths labeled by indexes. With parallel algorithms, however, indexes didn't have to play that role anymore. After all, in a scheme that matches a new situation to bunches of cases in parallel, it makes no difference whether ten cases or several hundred or even more are matched simultaneously. Indexes could now be thought about primarily as *labels* (Owens 1993) or *annotations* (Kolodner 1989) on cases, serving as their identifiers.

Thinking about indexes this way, researchers have begun to derive retrieval schemes that manipulate indexes rather than searching organizational structures. Abby (Domeshek 1991a), for example, implements a conceptually complex indexing scheme (akin to the Universal Index Frame) as simple-to-manipulate binary-feature vectors. All processing during retrieval happens on these vectors. Though it is not implemented in a parallel system, Domeshek outlines the way a fine-grained, layered connectionist network could use the representations to find the best partially-matching index to a new situation. ANON (Owens 1989a, 1989b, 1993) shows how a parallel scheme that works on a case's indexes (labels) can be used to limit inference of missing features.

The combination of addressing efficiency issues from a parallel point of view and looking at indexes as labels on cases has led to several implementations in which multiple indexing schemes are used. Validated retrieval (Simoudis 1991b, 1992) uses coarse indexes for initial retrieval of partially-matching cases, then augments the description of the case it is looking for with more fine-grained descriptive features and attempts retrieval again. PARADYME (Kolodner 1988a; Kolodner and Thau 1988) uses the equivalent of a coarse-grained indexing scheme to find partially-matching cases[9] and then uses more fine-grained indexes to find the best of several retrieved cases. Its coarse-grained indexes are the significant descriptive features of the case (computed, perhaps, using a tendency-oriented or checklist-based scheme). Its fine-grained scheme designates which combinations of features, when found together, distinguish each case from others in the case library (computed using an explanation-based scheme). One phase puts it in the right ballpark. The second chooses from among those cases.

In my opinion, the approach to retrieval that allows indexes to be used as identifiers without the baggage of also physically indexing the case library holds significant promise in making retrieval of partially-matching cases efficient. It is a relatively new approach, however, and more research and development are needed before we can say exactly what it will be able to accomplish.

---

9. PARADYME has been described as using no indexes for retrieval, and it is true that it does not use indexes to partition the case library and direct search. On the other hand, one can think of its case descriptions as providing a coarse indexing scheme for that initial retrieval.

8.10.2 Advantages of Hierarchical Organizations

When parallel algorithms were first being considered, computer scientists enthused about parallelism and not so happy about retrieval strategies that search only part of the case library told us that now we wouldn't have to build hierarchies into our case libraries—we could use flat organizations and create generalizations (that would be at the nodes of generalization hierarchies) on the fly from retrieved cases. And indeed, parallelism does have that advantage. The entire case library can be searched at once without a great deal of winnowing down of the search space as search progresses. When cases are retrieved, their similarities can be extracted, and generalizations can be formed on the fly. But these enthusiasts were overly optimistic on two counts: First, we need to remember that parallelism is always limited by the number of processors available. When a case library is very large, the use of indexing schemes to partition the search space will continue to be needed, even in highly parallel processing environments. Second, hierarchies play several important roles beyond winnowing the search space, and it would be a mistake to conclude that they are unneeded in all these roles.

When implementing serial search procedures, hierarchical organizations are required once the case library reaches an appreciable size. They partition the case library so that only a relevant portion of it is accessed. A flat organization of cases can't provide that partitioning. Hierarchical organizations allow efficient implementation of serial retrieval algorithms. Some parallel schemes use hierarchies; others don't. Whether or not there is an algorithmic advantage to hierarchies depends on the requirements of the chosen search algorithm and the size of the case library; for any particular application, this can be easily computed. But even in parallel implementations, hierarchies have several advantages over and beyond their contribution to the efficiency of retrieval.

Their first advantage is that the internal nodes in hierarchies provide a place to store generalized knowledge associated with clusters of cases. Shared-feature networks, for example, store general knowledge about different kinds of cases in the same structures that organize those cases for efficient retrieval. General knowledge might be used for a variety of reasons in a system. Keeping indexing under control and guiding clustering of cases, guiding situation assessment or elaboration of a new situation, and guiding adaptation are just three of the many roles general knowledge can play. When generalized knowledge is stored in a network close to the cases it applies to, it can be accessed by the same procedures that access cases, and knowledge applicable to a particular kind of situation can be found easily by walking around the hierarchy.

A hierarchical organization also provides a way to visualize the relationships between several similar cases. By looking at a well-constructed hierarchy, one can see which cases are more closely related to each other than others. HYPO (Ashley 1990; Ashley and Rissland 1988a), for example, organizes partially-matching cases in a hierarchy called a *claim lattice* that allows a user of the system to see what issues each case addresses and what sorts of results each implies. Figure 9 in chapter 13 shows a claim lattice. The REMIND case-based reasoning system-building tool shows paths through its hierarchies that it used for retrieval, allowing users to visualize the relevant similarities and differences between several retrieved cases.

From a cognitive point of view, hierarchical organizations also make sense. In the introductory chapters, I discussed model-based reasoning and its relationship to case-based reasoning. A mental model is a general description of a device or process. It gives the general picture of how the device or project works, but including in it all possible idiosyncrasies would make it burdensome to reason with. An alternate conjecture is that mental models and cases exemplifying the model are stored together in memory, with cases indexed from models and accessible while reasoning, using the model when a new situation differs from the model in the same way a case does (just as in MOPs). This integrated organization of cases and models allows reasoning about the general case and reasoning about novel situations to both occur naturally and stem from the same memory structures.

8.10.3 Integrating Search and Match Functions

Searching the case library's organizational structures is only one piece of a retrieval process that also includes situation assessment, index selection, matching, and ranking. Though it is useful for expository purposes to present these processes separately, in reality, they depend on one another and often are quite closely integrated. The relationship I'd like to discuss here is that between matching and search functions.

The discussion of matching at the beginning of this chapter looked at what needs to be considered in matching two cases to each other. The extent to which two cases match each other, I said, depended on a combination of the importance of each dimension of a case and the degree of match of each of the corresponding features of the two cases. Matching two cases, or a new situation and a retrieved case, to each other does indeed require these considerations. When we match two cases to each other to determine how well they match each other, we call it an *aggregate match*.

Several of the search functions we have discussed call aggregate match functions as they do their job. Algorithms for serial and parallel search of a flat case library both include a call to these functions as part of their processing. In serial search, each case in the library is matched to the new situation, a match score is computed for each, and the one with the best score is chosen. In parallel search, all the cases in the library are matched against the new situation in parallel, a match score is computed for each, and the one with the best score is chosen.

Algorithms that use a shared-feature network call aggregate match functions several times as they are searching their network, though rather than asking them to match full case descriptions to each other, they ask the match functions to match partial descriptions in the nodes of the network to the new situation. For each layer of the network that is searched, aggregate match functions are called to match the new situation to each of the nodes in that layer of the network. The node with the best match score is chosen, and its descendants are matched similarly.

Discrimination networks (both the redundant and nonredundant kinds), however, use matching functions differently. Rather than matching full or partial case descriptions to the new situation, discrimination networks target some dimension of the new situation, asking for its value and matching that value to values labeling the arcs in the network. Consider, for example, the network in Figure 8.9, and let us assume that we are looking for a match to the Sinai Dispute. The first question in that network asks what type of dispute the new one is.

Search functions ask that question of the Sinai Dispute, extracting the value `political` from it in response to that query. It is now up to match functions to decide which of the two values resident in the network for types of disputes is a better match to `political`. Those functions determine that the value `political` on the left side of the network matches exactly, and search continues from there. Matching of this sort is called *dimensional* matching.

Dimensional matching means assessing the similarity of fillers of the same functional role or dimension in two cases. Because labels on arcs of a discrimination network are the extracted values from cases organized in the network, the same dimensional matching functions used to match case dimensions to each other are used to match a dimension of a new situation to a label in a network.

Dimensional matching can be simple, as in this example, or harder if no exact match to the value from the new situation fits an arc of the network. A network might, for example, have the values `red` and `green` in it as answers to a question about color, but a case might have the value `orange` in that dimension. It is then up to dimensional match functions to assess whether `orange` matches `red` or `green` better and if it matches either of them well enough to be considered a partial match.

Match functions themselves will be described in the next chapter, so I will not attempt to explain how this can be done here. What I do want to make clear here, however, is the relationship between dimensional match functions and search functions. When attempting to discriminate which of several values is a better match to the new situation, search functions call dimensional match functions to do the job. In the algorithms above, this happens when a discrimination network is being searched and functions must decide which of several branches to traverse.

To say that discrimination schemes ask for dimensional matching while most other schemes ask for aggregate matching, however, only expresses a piece of the relationship between search and match functions. Sometimes both sorts of matching are called upon during search. Redundant discrimination networks, for example, follow several different paths in parallel during search and may retrieve many cases, some of which are better matches than others. Dimensional matching functions are called during the search, but aggregate matching functions are called after the set of candidate cases is recalled to winnow out the better cases. When search functions retrieve many candidate cases, aggregate match functions are called after the search to choose the better matches.

Both types of matches may also have to be done when retrieval is based on only a small subset of available features. The new situation might match the retrieved case on a set of indexed dimensions but may not match it well enough so that the case can is a useful one. Consider, for example, an attempt to retrieve a meeting between Andrey Gromyko and Cyrus Vance about Middle East peace from the network in Figure 8.13. After one discrimination (participant = Gromyko), we find EV3, but when we examine it, we find that it is a meeting about strategic arms limitations. After retrieving cases from a discrimination network that discriminates on only a small subset of the dimensions of situations, the goodness or usefulness of the retrieved case can be validated using aggregate match procedures.

8.11 SUMMARY

Retrieval algorithms can be described several different ways. They can be parallel or serial. They can run on hierarchical or flat organizational structures. Depending on the indexing they use, they can interact with dimensional matching functions, aggregate matching functions, or both.

Several retrieval algorithms were discussed in this chapter. Serial search on a flat memory has the advantage of being easy to implement and doing a full search of the case library, but it gets slow as the case library grows. As a library gets large, some means of partitioning it must be used to make search algorithms efficient. Shared-feature networks partition the case library according to the sizes of the sets of features shared by cases. Searching such a network is more efficient than serial search, but well-matching cases can be missed if the network isn't also prioritized. In addition, as a case library gets large, it is hard to keep a shared-feature network optimal, and the complex matching that must be done in searching such a network makes search inefficient.

More efficient are prioritized discrimination networks. In these networks, the case library is subdivided one dimension at a time, dividing first on the most important dimensions. Disadvantages of this scheme, however, are that it has trouble dealing with missing features in a probe (new situation), and if a system's cases are used for several different tasks, several different networks, all prioritized differently, might be needed.

Redundant discrimination networks deal with the missing features problem. In a redundant discrimination network, multiple discriminations are done at each level of the network. Though they allow best-matching cases to be found, they also return barely-matching cases, and a second phase of matching must be done to choose the best case or cases from those returned by search algorithms. Several variations on these networks have been developed, however, that allow more accurate retrieval.

One might think that parallel retrieval algorithms would be far more efficient than serial ones, and indeed, they can be. But the major impact of parallelism on case retrieval has not been to increase efficiency but rather to allow indexing to be thought of as a process of label assignment rather than a process of pointer assignment. Though parallelism can make algorithms faster, no matter how much parallelism is available, there will still be a need to partition the case library intelligently when case libraries are very large.

9

Matching and Ranking Cases

The ability to distinguish which of several partially-matching cases have the potential to be more useful than others is key to making case-based reasoning work. Retrieval algorithms direct search to appropriate places in memory, accessing cases with some potential to be useful, but it is up to matching and ranking heuristics to choose useful cases from that collection.

Choosing the best, or most useful, cases is primarily a partial-matching process. The process begins while searching the case library for partially-matching cases, when search processes ask matching functions to compute the degree of match along certain dimensions represented as indexes. Based on this series of dimensional matches, search functions collect a set of cases that partially match the new situation. After this set has been collected, a more comprehensive evaluation of degree of match is done, this time taking into account the importance of match along each dimension. We refer to this process as *ranking*. The importance of each dimension of a representation is a function of, among other things, the purpose for which retrieved cases will be used. Ranking procedures choose those cases that can best address the reasoner's purpose.

Several processes are necessary to compute degree of match reliably. We need a way of determining which features of two cases correspond to each other, a means of computing the degree of match between corresponding features, and a way of determining and recording the importance of features to a match. Matching and ranking procedures are designed to carry out these processes.

An example from CASEY will motivate these and other issues. CASEY is attempting to derive a diagnosis for a new patient, Newman. It remembers an old case, David. Both patients are male. Both have anginal pain. Neither has fatigue or cough. Newman is 65 years old, David is 72. Newman has a pulse rate of 90, Dave's was 96. Newman's temperature is 98.4, David's was 98.7. David had no orthostatic change. We don't know anything about orthostatic

No.	Feature Name	Value in Old Case (David)	Value in New Case (Newman)
1	Age	72	65
2	Gender	male	male
3	Pulse-rate	96	90
4	Temperature	98.7	98.4
5	Orthostatic-change	absent	
6	Chest-pain	anginal	anginal
7	Angina	unstable	within-hours & unstable
8	Mean-arterial-pressure	107	99.3
9	Palpitations	none	none
10	Syncope	none	on exertion
11	Fatigue	absent	absent
12	Cough	absent	absent
13	Auscultation	murmur of AS	
14	Pulse	normal	slow-rise
15	EKG	normal sinus & lv strain	normal sinus & lvh
16	Calcification	none	mitral & aortic

FIGURE 9.1   Comparing Two Cases from CASEY

change for Newman. Newman has syncope (shortness of breath) on exertion, while David had none. Figure 9.1 shows some of the similarities and differences between the two cases.

The task is to determine how good a match David is to Newman and whether the solution in David's case is likely to provide a good ballpark solution to Newman's situation. CASEY's first step is to compare corresponding values of each case to each other. If most corresponding features of two cases match, there's a good chance the cases are a good match. Comparing corresponding values to each other requires figuring out which features of each case correspond to which features of the other. It is easy to recognize the correspondence of some features because they have the same name.[1] Age in one corresponds to age in the other, gender to gender, temperature to temperature, and so on. Other correspondences are not as easy to make. We'll return to those later.

Next CASEY looks at how closely corresponding values match each other. Along some dimensions, it is easy to recognize how close the feature-values are to each other. Certainly, the two values filling "gender" correspond to each other, as do the values of "chest-pain." They are equal. It is harder to recognize how close values are when they don't match exactly, however. How well does "age 72" match "age 65," for example? How well does a temperature of 98.7 match a temperature of 98.4?

---

1. Though, as we shall see, similarly named features do not always correspond to each other.

We need a means of recognizing when values are qualitatively the same, or in the same ballpark, and when they are far apart. When measuring the health of a person, a temperature of 98.7 is qualitatively the same as a temperature of 98.4, age 72 is qualitatively the same as age 65, but normal and slow-rise pulse are qualitatively different from each other—one is in the normal range; the other signifies a problem. Similarly, no calcification, a normal condition, is very different from mitral and aortic calcification. A means of qualitatively comparing values is needed.[2]

In addition to knowing the degree of match of corresponding features of cases, it is also important to know how important each difference or similarity is to computing degree of overall match of the cases. If calcification is key to determining if a diagnosis holds, for example, then lack of match on that feature severely discredits the match. On the other hand, if it is irrelevant to the match, then the fact that there is a difference along this dimension should affect the degree of match very little, if at all. In general, a new situation that matches an old one well along dimensions that justify the old solution is a better match than one that matches less well on those dimensions or that matches well on less relevant features.

We can draw the conclusion, then, that in order to compute the degree of match of two cases, we need to be able to compute how close corresponding values in the two cases are to each other and how important each dimension is to justifying a solution. This was the basis for match presented in chapter 8, and indeed it is adequate in simple cases. But further analysis of the CASEY example shows that the matching process can be more complicated than that. For example, sometimes the degree of match of two corresponding values is not as important as whether the new value is consistent with the purpose the case will be put to.

Slow-rise pulse (in the new case), for example, is not a good match to normal pulse (in the old case), but it is consistent with the diagnosis from the old case. Slow-rise pulse can be a manifestation of slow ejection. Because the old case (David) suggests that Newman may have slow ejection, slow-rise pulse is consistent with the current hypothesis. Similarly, although in the old case there was no calcification, calcification of the aortic valve in the new case is consistent with the suggested diagnosis of aortic valve disease—it is a normal manifestation of that disease. Because slow-rise pulse and aortic calcification are consistent with the old diagnosis, the fact that neither manifested itself in the old case is irrelevant.

Thus, though it often makes sense to assume that matching values along a dimension correspond to each other, we can't always assume that major differences along some dimension rule out a match. The lesson to be learned from this example and, indeed, from many of CASEY's examples, is that when values along a dimension differ qualitatively from each other, it may not be appropriate to use their degree of match to determine the degree of match of the cases. Rather, another process that checks values in the new situation for consistency with the old solution may be more appropriate. This means that, in some situations, *situation descriptors with the same names may not correspond to each other*.

---

2. Such comparisons must, of course, be done in context. When evaluating the health of a person, a temperature of 98.7 is close enough to 98.4 to consider them the same. If some medication worked quite differently below 98.6 than above that temperature, however, and one needed to predict whether the medication was appropriate, then the two readings would have to be considered quite different.

The process that CASEY uses to check consistency determines which dimensions of a new case correspond *functionally* to which dimensions of the old case (or if there is any corresponding value at all). Slow-rise pulse, for example, which could be a result of "slow ejection," a portion of the diagnosis in the old case, corresponds functionally to whatever resulted from "slow ejection" in the old case. It has no correspondence to the "pulse" dimension from the old case—the dimensions, though named the same, play different roles in the two cases.

CASEY's processes for determining consistency of values in a new situation and finding appropriate correspondences between features of two cases are elegant in their simplicity. But CASEY's processes assume that the only reason one would retrieve a case is to support construction of an explanation. CASEY assumes only one purpose for its matches.

Much complexity is added to partial-matching processes when they must manage multiple *contexts* as part of the matching process. Context, here, refers to aspects of the environment that affect the match process. The purpose to which a retrieved item will be put, represented by the reasoner's goals, is the most prominent component of a match's context. The meal planning example in the introduction to Part III of this book, for example, shows that, depending on the goal of the reasoner, different features and combinations of features are more important than others in determining similarity and relevance of a case. In that situation, each of the partially-matching cases matches the new situation to about the same degree when the goal of the reasoner is not considered. When the goal of the reasoner, or the purpose to which the case will be put, is brought into the picture, however, it becomes clear which of those cases are more appropriate matches.

In the CASEY example, the retrieved case was to be used to guide diagnosis or derivation of a solution. It was appropriate to consider the consistency of given features of the new case with the diagnosis, or explanation, in the old case because the aim was to reuse that old diagnosis to explain the new patient's symptoms. Had the goal been to use the case differently, say, to determine a treatment, a means of determining consistency based on that purpose would have been more appropriate.

Computing degree of match of corresponding features, determining which features correspond to each other, and determining importance of features are all most reliably done in the context of the goals of the reasoner. The implication is that a reasoner that uses cases in support of several different reasoning goals might need several different matching and/or ranking schemes.

But the purpose a case will be put to is not the only factor that determines what to focus on during matching. The importance of a case dimension to a match also varies according to the contribution it made to solving some other similar problem or to affecting its outcome. If some feature or set of features was important in figuring out the solution to a similar problem or in predicting its results, it is likely to be equally important to take into account in solving the new problem. Thus, another way to assign importance to dimensions of a case is to give them importance equal to their relative importance in the old case. Another component of context, then, is what was relevant previously.

Under this scheme, features of the new situation have no fixed importance. Rather, importance is assigned differently to dimensions depending on which case from the case library is being matched to. In effect, a match function is computed individually for each case in the case library, depending on which of its features were the important ones. Relative similarity of the new case to each old one is judged in the context of the old case. Those features of an old case that were important previously are given high importance in judging similarity.

If a vegetarian is served meat at a meal and doesn't eat it, for example, the combination of features *some guest was vegetarian* and *meat was served* play a prominent role in that case. Because their combination had not been considered in planning the meal, the meal failed—someone did not enjoy eating. Because of the high importance of these features in predicting failure in this case, these features are given high importance when judging the degree of match between a new situation and this case. In that way, retrieval of this case can be assured, allowing the reasoner to anticipate the potential for failure and to plan around it. Similarly, if in another case, the facts that guests were vegetarians and using tomatoes was a high priority led to a decision to serve tomato tart, then the features *some guest was vegetarian* and *include tomatoes in the ingredients* are given high priority when matching to that case.

The big issue that comes up in schemes such as this is assigning importance values to dimensions of cases in the case library. Sometimes importance can be assigned using explanation-based index selection methods (the most common way). Other times, it makes more sense to compute importance on the fly, based on the relative importance of a dimension when judged over the whole set of similar cases. HYPO, for example, takes this approach (Ashley and Rissland 1988a).

All this being said, it is worthwhile to point out that, as in CASEY, in many applications, the reasoner only has one goal, so that though we need to understand the role of context in matching, implementations often do not need to explicitly consider context while computing degree of match. In other applications, partial match can be computed simply because the degree of variation in what is important is relatively small across cases and across purposes the cases will be put to. In other situations, there is simply little need to be precise during retrieval. Any case will work as a starting point, and through adaptation, a sufficient solution will be reached.

This chapter presents both partial matching and ranking procedures, the combination of which allows a reasoner to select useful or most-useful cases. The chapter begins with a set of definitions. It continues by concentrating first on the building blocks for these two processes, that is, their individual components. After they are presented, it presents several ways of putting those components together to support several different matching and ranking schemes.

9.1 SOME DEFINITIONS

At the risk of boring readers, some definitions are in order before going into the mechanics of partial pattern matching and ranking. Some procedures to be described are static (determined a priori and fixed), others are dynamic. Some are based on absolute ranking schemes (a match score is assigned); others are based on a relative ranking that weighs degree of match along different dimensions against each other. Some match whole cases to each other; others match one dimension at a time. Procedures that will be discussed combine aspects of each of these, and it will be easier to discuss the matching and ranking procedures themselves after presenting the various ways of describing matching and ranking functions.

9.1.1 Dimensions, Descriptors, and Features

The words *feature, descriptor,* and *dimension* have been used rather freely and interchange-ably up to now to mean some aspect of a case's representation. It is time to be more precise about the meanings of these terms. A **descriptor** of a case is an *attribute-value pair* used in the description of a case. Descriptors can describe aspects of the problem or situation description, the solution, or the outcome. They can refer to surface features, abstract features, structural features, or relations between features: anything that would be used to provide a description of the situation the case represents. **Dimension** refers to the attribute part of a descriptor. When we compare cases along a dimension, we are extracting corresponding descriptors from two cases and comparing their values. When we refer to the *value along some dimension* or a *feature value,* we are referring to the value of some descriptive clause given the attribute. **Feature** has been used up to now both ways. Sometimes we refer to the dimension as a feature; sometimes we have referred to the descriptor as a feature. In general, *feature* will mean descriptor from now on, that is, an attribute-value pair.

Some examples of simple descriptors are "age = 72," "pulse-rate = 96," "EKG = normal sinus & lv strain," "main dish = lasagne104." A more complex or abstract descriptor might describe the relationship between two surface descriptors, for example, "goal relationship = competitive," or some abstract description of the case, for example, "motivation = self-defense," or "abstract explanation = side effect of one subsystem caused second subsystem to fail."

A dimension of a case can be the attribute part of some descriptive clause, or it can refer to some aspect of the case derived from several of its dimensions (and eventually recorded as an attribute of the case). Some dimensions, then, are composed from other dimensions. Suppose, for example, that a car's coolant hose is slowly leaking water onto an electrical connection, causing the electrical connection to sometimes short out and in turn causing the fuel pump to periodically not pump fuel. One level of description of this situation is at the level of the components and their malfunctions: "nonworking component = fuel pump," "periodicity of malfunction = periodic." Another relates specific components to each other to form a causal explanation: "causal explanation = small leak in the coolant hose causes water to drip onto electrical connection causes electrical short causes fuel pump to stop pumping." Another level of description gives an abstract characterization of the problem: "abstract explanation = side effect of malfunction of one subsystem causes an otherwise healthy subsystem to fail." The causal explanation is composed from several other dimensions. The abstract explanation is a *derived* dimension, derived from the causal explanation, and serves as the category for the explanation.

A case can have any and all of these levels of description. We refer collectively to all descriptive attributes of a case as its *dimensions.* Depending on the purpose of a match, different dimensions and different types of dimensions are more or less important to determining degree of match. CASEY's evidence rules, for example, provide a way of matching causal explanations at the level of specific components. CHEF's TOPs and indexing structure provide a way of recognizing similarities between cases at the level of the abstract descriptions of their causal explanations.

9.1.2 **Choosing What to Match**

Matching procedures can match a dimension of one case to a dimension of another or a whole case to another case. The first is a **dimensional match**, the second an **aggregate match**. When we match age 62 to age 74, we do a dimensional match. We match features along one dimension—age. Dimensional matching is done by looking at the relationships between symbolic values in a semantic network or other hierarchical knowledge structure by comparing numeric values or by comparing values qualitatively.

During search, retrieval functions often request dimensional matches. For example, traversing a discrimination network requires extracting or computing the value of an appropriate dimension of a case. The value is then matched to appropriate labels on arcs of the network, and the branch whose label matches best is followed.

When a candidate set of partial matches has been collected and better-matching cases need to be extracted from that set, aggregate matching is required. Usually, the description of the new situation (a new case) is matched to each case selected from the case library (an old case). Cases are compared along dimensions of the problem description and whatever exists of a partial solution. Most case-based reasoners, including CHEF, JULIA, CLAVIER, and the Battle Planner, do this type of matching. It is appropriate whenever cases that look alike are solved similarly.

Under this scheme, cases are compared to each other dimension by dimension, taking into account the importance of each dimension to the match. A score representing the degree of match of one case to another is computed by combining individual dimensional match scores. Aggregate match scores are sometimes computed by a numeric evaluation function that combines the degree of match along each dimension with a value representing the importance of the dimension. Other times, they are computed by a compare-and-contrast procedure that takes into account the relative degree of match along each dimension and weighs the degree of match of several cases to see which has the potential to be most useful.

Aggregate match processes usually compute dimensional match scores for all dimensions that are part of the aggregate match or accept those match scores as input. In matching David and Newman, for example, CASEY's match functions compute dimensional matches for each of the dimensions of the David and Newman cases. In doing an aggregate match, the matcher begins by assuming that similarly named dimensions of a new situation and a case correspond to each other, and it computes dimensional matches for each. When values in corresponding dimensions do not match each other and when dimensions of a new situation or a case have no obvious dimensional correspondents, consistency-driven matching procedures (as in CASEY) are used to determine correspondences and guide dimensional match.

In other situations, matching is of the desired outcome in the new situation and the outcome of some case in the case library. For example, if a meal planner is trying to figure out what a particular picky eater will eat, it might look for cases with outcome similar to the one it is striving for: the picky eater ate and was satisfied. After finding cases like this, the reasoner can infer the kinds of foods this picky eater will eat.

Alternatively, matching can be of the desired outcome in the new situation and the outcome projected by some case in the case library. In essence, in this situation, multiple solutions for the new situation are computed and their outcomes projected. The best outcome is chosen. One might do this when it is important to come up with a good solution immediately and when computing a solution is relatively cheap. For example, a doctor might choose a treatment for a severely ill person by deriving each of the possible treatments and evaluating the patient's prognosis for each. The treatment with the best prognosis is chosen. Cases are used two times in this process: to suggest treatments and to project their effects.

9.1.3 Matching and Ranking

Matching is the process of comparing two cases to each other and determining their degree of match. **Ranking** is the process of ordering partially-matching cases according to goodness of match or usefulness. When we match cases, we can either produce a score that signifies degree of match, or we can simply determine if yes, a case matches sufficiently, or no, it doesn't. When we rank cases, we determine which of several cases, all of which match partially, is better than the others. Often, ranking procedures use the output of matching procedures to order partially-matching cases according to their usefulness.

Sometimes, however, the relationship between matching and ranking is more complicated. Some schemes, for example, use multiple matching and ranking steps. CASEY, for example, begins by using retrieval functions to choose partially-matching cases, focusing its dimensional matches on those features it knows to be most important. It then does a coarse ranking of those cases, scoring cases that match on more surface features higher than those that match on fewer. Finally, it applies its causal matching procedure to choose a case to reason with, matching cases in the order of their coarse ranking and stopping as soon as it finds a sufficiently good match. Its retrieval phase finds cases with the potential to be good matches; its coarse ranking procedure makes a first cut at ranking those. Its final matching process is both more expensive and more reliable than its first two steps, and any case that passes its tests is useful for deriving a solution.

9.1.4 Global and Local Matching Criteria: Taking Context into Account in Matching

Matching criteria designate the relative importance of different dimensions of a representation to a match. As the earlier example shows, some dimensions are more important than others in determining degree of similarity and usefulness of a retrieved case. In general, the degree to which a particular dimension is important in determining degree of similarity is dependent on the context of the match. Context of match, remember, refers to aspects of the match environment that affect the matching criteria. Two aspects of context that are important are the purpose to which a case will be put and the degree to which features have been important previously under similar conditions.

Matching criteria can be assigned **globally**, across the whole case library or large partitions of it, or **locally**, over a single case or subset of the case library. When matching criteria are assigned globally, only one or a small number of matching criteria are used, and they have little sensitivity to context. Such a scheme is appropriate when cases are used for only one purpose or when the relative importance of dimensions varies little with purpose. More context sensitivity is achieved when matching criteria are assigned more locally, that is, to a smaller set of cases, varying the criteria according to both aspects of context.

Global matching criteria result in a static matching scheme. There is little or no variation in the matching functions that are used. When more context-sensitive criteria are used and the matching criteria become more local (associated with one or a small number of cases or conditions), matching becomes more dynamic. There are two types of dynamic matching schemes. In some, matching criteria are computed on the fly by comparing and contrasting the cases that are available and weighing them against each other in a variety of ways (e.g., HYPO [Ashley and Rissland 1988a]). Most dynamic schemes, however, choose from a set of available matching criteria the one that makes the most sense given the task to be carried out. In these systems, several different matching schemes are available, each assigned a set of conditions under which it is to be used.

Matching criteria are often inserted into a function that computes degree of match. We refer to such a function as an **evaluation function**. An evaluation function uses matching criteria, or **dimensional importance values**, to compute degree of match between a new situation and a partially-matching case.

9.1.5 Absolute and Relative Matching and Ranking

Some matching schemes result in the computation of a **score** that specifies the degree of match between one case and another. Other matching schemes result in the computation of a **comparison structure** that records the degree of match of dimensions of a case to the dimensions of a second case. Ranking can result in an ordered list or a structure that shows the relative degree of match of several different cases. The schemes we will examine all compute scores.

The match score that is computed, whether for a dimensional match or an aggregate match, might be absolute or relative. An **absolute match score** is computed independent of other cases. Usually, absolute scores are numerical values and are computed by a numerical function. They could, however, be qualitative values and be computed by qualitative reasoning processes. Absolute scores can be computed by static or dynamic evaluation processes. Each of the numerical schemes we will look at computes an absolute match score.

A **relative match score** requires comparison to other cases. While an absolute scoring procedure computes a number that describes the degree of match between a new situation and a case, relative scoring builds an argument for some ranking of the cases with respect to the new situation. This argument, which states on what basis some case is better than others, provides an explanation of the ranking. HYPO does this sort of ranking through argumentation. PARADYME does it through a preference scheme. In general, relative schemes are ranking schemes rather than matching schemes, and in general, they do their work by comparing comparison structures to each other. Usually, relative ranking is done by dynamic ranking procedures. We present a preference scheme that does relative ranking at the end of this chapter. Discussion of relative ranking using argumentation is left for chapter 13.

9.1.6 Input to Matching and Ranking Functions

There are up to five inputs to matching and ranking processes:

1. The new situation
2. The purpose the retrieved case will be put to
3. Recalled cases
4. Indexes of recalled cases
5. Reasonable criteria for match

The new situation is, of course, the new problem or situation that the reasoner is trying to reason about. The goal of matching and ranking procedures is to find an appropriate match for this situation.

The purpose the recalled case will be put to, the second input to the evaluation process, is represented by the reasoner's current reasoning goal. The reasoner might want to construct a part of a solution, evaluate a proposed solution or interpretation, project outcome, explain an anomaly, and so on.

The third input to ranking procedures is the set of recalled cases, those that must be ranked for usefulness. Some retrieval schemes collect a whole group of partially-matching cases and present them to the ranking processes. Others interleave retrieval and ranking.

The fourth input, the indexes associated with each of the recalled cases, can take several forms. Sometimes indexes take the form of importance values associated with dimensions of the case's description. These are used by context-sensitive numerical ranking schemes to compute a match score. Some matching and ranking procedures focus on indexes as conceptual identifiers of cases as they determine which of several cases has the potential to be the most useful match. The preference scheme presented at the end of this chapter uses indexes this way. The role of indexes in matching and ranking will become more clear as the procedures that use indexes for ranking are presented.

Reasonable criteria for match tell matching and ranking procedures when they should stop and return the best they have found so far. One can be aiming to find the "best" or "most useful" match, taking all aspects of context into account and requiring that the entire set of available cases be ranked with respect to one another. Or one can be aiming to find an adequate match, adequate according to some criteria. CASEY, for example, returns the first case in which all correspondences are resolved by the causal model. In such a scheme, the first case in which an adequate degree of match is found is returned, without the need to find the best in the available set. Other reasonableness criteria (Veloso 1991, 1992) include finding a case that has the potential to predict a certain kind of specified outcome, finding a case whose solution is below a certain complexity, finding a case whose solution is of a certain kind, and so on.

9.2 THE BUILDING BLOCKS OF MATCHING AND RANKING PROCESSES

Armed now with definitions, discussion of how matching and ranking procedures work can commence. We begin with the building blocks, the pieces of the two processes that are combined with each other to create matching and ranking schemes. There are a number of issues that must be addressed to implement a reliable partial-matching scheme. We need a way of computing the degree of match of corresponding descriptors in two cases. That, in turn, requires a way of recognizing which features correspond to each other. Because the goodness of a match depends on how well the case can address the goals of the reasoner, we need a way of using the goals of the reasoner to determine and record the importance of features to a match. We take up these three issues below.

9.2.1 Finding Correspondences

Finding correspondences is done to determine which features of a new situation should be matched to which features in a stored situation. The features that should be matched are, in general, those that play the same functional roles. Equivalence of functionality can be determined several ways:

- By noticing that the two values fill the same slot or share a common predicate relationship
- By using commonsense reconciliation heuristics
- By noticing that two values play the same structural roles in the two representations
- By using evidence provided in a causal model to determine the functional roles of descriptors

When Two Values Fill the Same Slot

In the easiest situations, and as a first step, correspondences can be found by simply noting correspondences in the representations of an old and new case. Two values may fill the same slot in frames that correspond to each other or two values embedded in a set of predicate clauses may play the same role in corresponding predicate clauses. Figure 9.2 shows an example of each of these. In the frame representation, we know the two `green salad` in the two representations correspond because both fill the `side-veg` slot, the `host` designations correspond, the `ingredients` designations correspond, and so on. In the predicate representation, we can identify the correspondences by matching the predicates in each clause. We know `beef` corresponds to `tofu` because both are arguments of the `include` predicate. Similarly with `spicy` and `mild` (both arguments of `taste`) and `stir-fry` and `stir-fry` (both arguments of `preparation`).

When representations are set up so that slots or predicate clauses are defined functionally and at the level required for matching, this means of computing correspondences works very well. In JULIA (Hinrichs 1992), for example, slots correspond to the functional and structural components of the artifacts being designed. Functional slots hold information that provides constraint on structural components. Because JULIA is designing menus for dinners, its frame representations have functional slots corresponding to such things as eaters, cost, cuisine, ingredients, and serving style and structural slots corresponding to the structural components of a meal (appetizer, salad course, main course, dessert). Each of these is, in turn, broken down into its functional and structural components. The frame representations in Figure 9.2 show some of JULIA's slots in their descriptions of the main courses from two meals. Agents and descriptors are functional components; objects are structural components. The ingredients designation under descriptors will provide constraint on the various dishes under the objects slot; when propagated, tomato will be designated as a necessary ingredient in at least some dishes.

When a new situation is defined unambiguously according to functional and structural components, JULIA has an easy time determining correspondences between new situations and stored cases. Eaters correspond to eaters, the appetizer dish corresponds to the appetizer dish, and so on.

But, often, mapping similarly named slots and predicates to each other is only a good first step in determining correspondences, and sometimes, it is a mistake. CASEY's representations illustrate both complexities. Figure 9.3 shows the problem description part of one of CASEY's case representations. CASEY names its slots according to the functions they play in describing a case. Its problem description slot, for example, holds the signs and symptoms of a patient needing diagnosis. There are many kinds of signs and symptoms, each playing different roles depending on what the diagnosis is. Thus, it is difficult to further subdivide them into more functionally motivated subslots until after the problem has been solved. Items within the slot are thus undifferentiated by function.[3]

Thus, though the slot problem description is a functional slot, it is functional at a different level than is needed for matching cases to each other. It works well in designating to the reasoner what should be taken into account in coming up with a diagnosis. On the other hand, matching cases to each other requires determining the correspondences between each of the items in that slot and items in the same slot of a recalled case. To do this, CASEY attempts, as a first step, to match clauses with the same predicate. But, as the CASEY example at the beginning of this chapter shows, correspondences computed this way can be mistaken, and a more sophisticated means of determining correspondences is necessary.

Even when a representation is set up to parallel the functional structure of normal cases, it may still be inadequate for representing oddly structured cases. When that happens, some of its slots might be overloaded, while others are unfilled. Consider, for example, two cases like that from JULIA (Figure 9.4). In the left-hand case, JULIA is representing a case in which two main dishes were served rather than the normal one. The main-dishes slot, which normally has one filler, has been broken into two parts. In addition, the side-dishes slot, which normally is broken into a vegetable dish and a starch dish, is undifferentiated. Although each of a normal meal's components was present in this case, the meal was structurally odd. Nonetheless, it can provide suggestions toward more normally configured meals if the correspondences between its pieces and those of a new well-structured case can be ascertained. The right-hand case is also odd. Its meal structure is that of a normal case, but though most of

---

3. Some have pointed out that this is a poor representation and that I should not use it here. My claim is that this is the best representation for the problem description that can be done *before solving the problem*. One cannot divide the signs and symptoms into functionally similar subcategories (or subslots) until one knows the role they are playing. One could, on the other hand, use slots for each of the attributes instead of listing them as attribute-value pairs. But that would be an equivalent representation to this one, which bundles all of the attribute descriptions together. Such slots would not be functionally motivated, and correspondence procedures would have to find correspondences between slots instead of correspondences between attribute-value pairs. It would be the same process, with all the same complexities and needs.

PARALLEL FRAME REPRESENTATIONS

```
            Case101                              New Situation
isa: main-course                      isa: main-course
agents:                               agents:
    eaters:                               eaters:
        host: jlk                             host: jlk
        guests: research-grp                  guests: all-the-inlaws
descriptors:                          descriptors:
    cuisine: vegetarian                   cuisine: vegetarian
    ingredients: tomatoes                 ingredients: tomatoes
    service: buffet                       service: family-style
objects:                              objects:
    main dish: tomato tart                main dish:
    side-dishes:                          side-dishes:
        veg-dish: green salad                 veg-dish: green salad
        starch-dish: pesto pasta              starch-dish:
```

PARALLEL PREDICATE REPRESENTATIONS

```
(include beef)           <------------>   (include tofu)
(taste spicy)            <------------>   (taste mild)
(preparation stir-fry)   <----->          (preparation stir-fry)
```

FIGURE 9.2 Parallel Representations Make Computation of Correspondences Easy

```
Problem description:
    (patient-name "natalie") (age 62) (sex female)
    (dyspnea on-exertion) (orthopnea absent) (chest-pain anginal)
    (anginal unstable) (syncope/near-syncope none) (palpitations none)
    (nausea/vomiting absent) (cough absent) (diaphoresis absent)
    (hemoptysis absent) (fatigue absent) (therapies none)
    (blood-pressure 146 81) (heart-rate 86)
    (arrhythmia-monitoring normal) (resp 14) (temp 98.3)
    (appearance anxious) (mental-status conscious)
    (jugular-pulse normal) (pulse slow-rise) (auscultation s2 murmur)
    (s2 soft-a2) (murmur systoic-ejection-murmur)
    (apex-impulse laterally-displaced) (parasternal-impulse normal)
    (chest clear-to-auscultation-and-percussion) (abdomen normal-exam)
    (extremities normal-exam) (ekg lv-strain normal-sinus)
    (cxr calcification cardiomegaly) (calcification mitral aortic-valve)
    (cardiomegaly lv)
```

FIGURE 9.3 A Problem Representation from CASEY

```
PROBLEM                                        CASE
-----------------------------------------      --------------------------------
ISA m-main-course                              ISA m-main-course
AGENTS                                         AGENTS
  EATERS                                         EATERS tom
    HOST tom
    GUESTS mike richard
DESCRIPTORS                                    DESCRIPTORS
  CUISINE mid-eastern-cuisine                    CUISINE greek-cuisine
OBJECTS                                        OBJECTS
  DISHES                                         DISHES
    MAIN-DISHES                                    MAIN-DISHES baba-ghanouj
      MAIN-DISHES-1 baba-ghanouj
      MAIN-DISHES-2 skewered-lamb & eggplant
    SIDE-DISHES tabbouleh hummus                 SIDE-DISHES
                                                   VEG-DISH hummus
                                                   STARCH-DISH lemon-potatoes
                                                 DRINK retsina
                                                 BREAD pita-bread
```

FIGURE 9.4   Cases from JULIA with Unfilled and Overloaded Structural Slots

JULIA's meals have host and guests as eaters, this one was not served to guests, so though there were eaters, there was no host or guest. Its eaters slot is undifferentiated.[4]

There are thus two circumstances when matching similarly named slots and predicates is inadequate:

- When a slot is filled by a list of fillers undifferentiated with respect to their function (as in CASEY's representations)
- When a stored case has overloaded and/or unfilled structural slots (as in JULIA's representations)

The first circumstance is a result of not using a representation that differentiates descriptive features from one another by function, as in CASEY. The second is a result of using a func-

---

4. Again, it has been pointed out that perhaps this is merely a poor representation—that a better one wouldn't have this problem. Again, I claim that it is the best representation available. When problems and solutions are ill structured, there may not be any one representational structure that works for all situations. It would be unwise, for example, for the representation of a meal to anticipate that a meal could have two main dishes and to include slots for that in every case representation. Most meals will be filled in with only one main dish. Others will have more than two. No matter how much space one leaves for main dishes, for example, some case will have more than was anticipated. Better is this flexible type of representation—its normal structure accounts for the normal structure of meals, but it can also deal with oddly structured ones. It can do this because its slots are named according to the functional roles they play. One can be flexible within such a structure to the extent that component roles are consistent, even if the number of components playing each role is variable.

tionally differentiated representation that can't cover oddly structured cases. The overloading that results from forcing oddly structured cases into highly structured representations is equivalent to the undifferentiated features in the first circumstance. The difference tends to be in degree of overloading. In JULIA, for example, one tends to see two or three values in an overloaded slot. CASEY's undifferentiated slots (e.g., `problem description`), by contrast, can have dozens of descriptors in them.

Two means of compensating are presented. JULIA uses commonsense reconciliation heuristics. CASEY uses evidence rules based on a causal model.

Using Commonsense Reconciliation Heuristics

There are several reasons why the slots in representations of similar cases might not obviously correspond to each other (Hinrichs 1992).

- The number of features may be different. Some cases have more or fewer features than others, as shown in the examples above. A meal, for example, can have any number of courses and dishes. A patient can have any number of signs and symptoms.

- The depth of representation in two cases can be different. Some cases might be represented at the level of individual actions, others more abstractly. We can describe meals, for example, according to their menus or according to the sequence of eating actions that took place.

- Cases are represented from different points of view. A meal might be a case by itself, or it might be embedded in a dinner party.

JULIA uses four commonsense reconciliation heuristics to identify correspondences (Hinrichs 1992). I have added a fifth (number 4).

1. Defined slots map directly.
2. Prefer mappings between feature values that have the same functional role.
3. Prefer mappings between feature values that satisfy the same constraints.
4. Prefer mappings between feature values that are the same or more similar.
5. Multiple problem features may map onto a single, more general, case feature, and vice versa.

The first heuristic tells us to go with the correspondences that are obvious. If two slots are named the same way, assume their values correspond. It also tells us that structure of the representation counts, that is, that if all else fails, differentiated subslots of a slot go with the parent slot. If we are trying to determine correspondences between the two cases in Figure 9.4, this would allow us to map `eaters` on the left-hand side (including `host` and `guests`) to `eaters` on the right. It allows us to map the main dishes on the left-hand side to those on the right, cuisine on the left to that on the right, and side-dishes on the left to those on the right. It allows us to make initial correspondences, but we are still left with sets corresponding to each other and without knowing which items in each set correspond to which items in the other one (e.g., does tabbouleh on the left correspond functionally to hummus or lemon-potatoes on the right?).

The second heuristic allows us to use knowledge about functional role to make further correspondences. We know, for example, that broccoli is a vegetable. Thus, if we see it undifferentiated in a side-dishes slot, we can guess that it corresponds to the item in the veg-side slot of another case.[5]

The third heuristic specifies that knowledge of constraints should be used to ascertain correspondences. If we know that elements of two cases have the same constraints on them, we can guess that they correspond. For example, if the main dish in the new situation is constrained to be vegetarian and the old situation had two main dishes, lamb curry and vegetable curry, this heuristic tells matching processes that the vegetable curry corresponds to the main dish in the new situation. This heuristic is similar to semantic similarity criteria in ACME (Holyoak and Thagard 1989). It is also implemented in MEDIATOR.

The fourth heuristic specifies that in differentiating which things should be matched to each other, sameness and obvious similarity count. Using this heuristic, the hummus on the left can be mapped to the veg-dish on the right, leaving tabbouleh to be mapped to the starch-dish. Of course, similarity is what this is all about, and one could interpret this heuristic as circular. It is not meant to be so. Rather, it designates that mappings between things that are the same or obviously similar should be preferred if they have already been found to fill the same functional role.

Finally, the last heuristic allows multiple items to be mapped onto one and vice versa. It is this heuristic that gives matching functions permission to map both baba ghanouj and skewered lamb and eggplant on the left to baba ghanouj on the right. It also gives permission for matching functions to map the combination of hosts and guests on the left to the one eater on the right.[6]

Using a Causal Model

When a causal model is available, it can provide additional guidance in distinguishing which features of a new situation and a retrieved case play the same functional roles. This is especially important in domains where functional role is undifferentiated in the representation and where each feature can play several different functional roles. This is the situation we saw in the Newman-David case at the beginning of the chapter. In that situation, "pulse" was playing

---

5. It is a heuristic like this that allows CHEF to make correspondences between its various include predicates. If, in one dish, it needed to include beef and include broccoli, and in a new situation, it needs to include tofu and include snow peas, it must decide which of the includes correspond to which in order to know how to reinstantiate its old recipe. Knowing that broccoli and snow peas are both vegetables and that beef and tofu are both protein foods allows it to do this.

6. When multiple features from a new situation map onto a single feature in a case, it is probable that the recalled case will be able to suggest a solution only to one of the features of the new situation and another case will be needed to compute the value of the other. For example, if a meal planner wanted a meal with one vegetarian dish and one lamb one, then the right-hand case, which has only a vegetarian main dish, will be able to provide a suggestion only for the vegetarian main dish. Another case will be needed to suggest a value for the lamb dish.

different roles in the cases being matched. In one, where the pulse was normal, it played the role of a normal body function. In the other, where the pulse was abnormal, it played the role of support for the hypothesis of slow ejection. In order to determine the degree of match of the two cases, it was necessary to make clear the functional roles of "pulse" in the two cases.

As we saw in discussing that case, when descriptive features of two cases are very close to each other in value, we can often assume that they correspond. When they are far from each other in value, however, there is greater chance that they are playing different functional roles in the solution, and assuming that the two values correspond and that their degree of similarity should be part of the aggregate match score can be a mistake. Although the slow-rise pulse in David's case was qualitatively different from the normal pulse in Newman's case, the lack of a match on these features was not relevant to the overall degree of match, because the slow-rise pulse was consistent with the diagnosis the old case had proposed. Normal pulse in the old case was playing a different functional role than slow-rise pulse in the new case, and although the two have the same descriptive name (pulse), they do not correspond to each other functionally.

CASEY shows us how to use a causal model to determine functional correspondence. CASEY begins by assuming that equal values filling the same slots or filling the same role in two predicate clauses correspond to each other. It then uses its causal model to reconcile differences between the old and new problem representations. It accepts a case as a match to a new situation if the differences between the new situation and the old case are consistent with the solution from the old case. If the causal model cannot resolve the differences, the old case is rejected as a match.

The implementation of the process in CASEY is through application of general-purpose *evidence rules* (Koton 1988a, 1989). Evidence rules take as input a difference between the old case and the new situation, the old solution, and the relevant causal model. One or several evidence rules are associated with each type of difference. One is chosen. It uses the causal model and the old solution to try to resolve the difference between the old and a new case and to find mapping for the difference it is given. In short, these rules know how to use the causal model to find ways of making differences between two cases consistent with the old solution (the one proposed by the recalled case). If the features of the new case are consistent with the solution to the old case, it is a good solution to the new case. Figure 9.5 shows the evidence rules defined in CASEY.

Before getting into their details, there are some terms that need defining. The middle columns in Figure 9.5 designate several different descriptions of features. Features can be present, absent, and missing. *Present* means that there exists a value for the feature in question in the representation. *Absent* is a particular species of a feature being present. When a value is absent, the representation specifies that the feature does not exhibit itself in a case. In Figure 9.3, both coughing and nausea/vomiting are shown as absent. Syncope, however, is marked as having value none. It is present in the representation, but with a value stating that there is little of it. This is different from a value of absent. *Missing* means that a feature is not in the representation for a case and nothing is known about its value. In Figure 9.3, there is no value for orthostatic-change. Its value is unknown, missing from the representation. Missing and absent have a special relationship. When a value is absent in either the new situation or the

Rule Name	Old Case Value is	New Case Value is	Action
Same Qualitative Region	V_1	V_2	Accept if V_1 and V_2 in same region
Rule Out	Present	Present & Incompatible	Rule Out Correspondence
Other Evidence	Present Supports State S	Missing	Find Another Support for S
Unrelated Old Case	Not Used	Missing	Ignore
Supports Existing State	Missing	Present	Find Support in Old Case
Unrelated New Case	Missing	Present Not-Used Abnormal	Mark as Unexplained
Normal	Missing	Present	Ignore
No Info in Old Case	Missing	Absent	Assume Absent
No Info in New Case	Absent	Missing	Assume Absent

FIGURE 9.5   Evidence Rules: Using a Causal Model to Reconcile Differences Between Two Case Representations

retrieved case and missing in the other one, it is generally safe to assume that it is absent where missing.[7]

The first two heuristics, same qualitative region and rule out, deal with situations in which two values filling the same descriptive role are different from each other. Same qualitative region says that if the values are in the same qualitative region, they should be accepted as corresponding equal values. Rule out says that if the values are incompatible (not in the same qualitative region), then they do not correspond to each other and some other evidence of consistency of the new value should be found. Age 65 and age 72, for example, are both ages fitting the qualitative region old on CASEY's scale of ages, so they can be matched to each other. Age 30 and 65, on the other hand, are in different qualitative ranges and cannot be matched to each other. Unstable anginal pain and within-hours unstable anginal pain are within the same qualitative pain region and do match each other. Slow-rise pulse and normal pulse are in different qualitative pulse regions and cannot correspond.

When values filling the same descriptive clause in the representation are within the same qualitative region, CASEY assumes they correspond and that they are a good match to each other. Otherwise, it treats values in both the old and new cases as differences and tries to explain each one using its other evidence heuristics.

CASEY's other evidence heuristics deal with missing information, either in the stored case or in the new one. In general, when some feature is in the old case but not in the new one, evidence rules question whether the missing feature is crucial evidence for some piece of the

---

7. The presumption of the diagnostician when a value from a previous case was missing is that it would have been irrelevant to the diagnosis anyway. Therefore, it is assumed that its value in the new situation is also irrelevant. The presumption when a value is missing in the new case and was absent in the old one is that if it had an odd value (in the new case), it would have been noted on the record. Because the value was normal in the old case, it can be safely assumed that it was irrelevant to the old diagnosis and can be safely ignored in the new situation.

old solution. If so, other features of the new case that could provide alternative support for that crucial piece of the old solution are sought. Other evidence is invoked when some feature supporting a piece of the solution (e.g., a diagnostic state) in the old case is missing in the new one. It looks for some other feature of the new case that could support that state (e.g., another possible manifestation of that diagnostic state). For example, limited cardiac output can manifest itself as dyspnea on exertion or syncope on exertion or both. If the old case shows dyspnea on exertion and the new one does not but does show syncope on exertion, this evidence rule identifies both as playing the same functional role (supporting limited cardiac output). The fact that dyspnea is missing in the new case is considered inconsequential.

On the other hand, if some feature of the old case did not contribute to the old solution and is missing in the new case, Unrelated old case says to ignore the missing information. No info in new case is invoked when the value of some dimension in the old case is absent and there is no value in the new case. It assumes that the value is absent in the new case also. For example, if coughing was absent in the old case and we know no value for coughing in the new case, this heuristic says that we can assume no cough is present.

When some feature is in the new case but not in the old one, other evidence rules are invoked. In general, when this happens, evidence rules look for something in the old solution that explains the new value. Supports existing state looks for some support in the old case for a new feature not in the old case. For example, aortic valve calcification is a possible manifestation of aortic valve disease. If aortic valve calcification is present in the new case and we have no information about it in the old case, aortic valve disease in the old solution provides support for the aortic valve calcification in the new case. When no supporting evidence for a value in the new situation is found, and that value is in an abnormal range, Unrelated new case marks it as an unexplained feature—some feature whose explanation will need to be added to the old diagnosis if it is otherwise consistent with the new situation. On the other hand, normal says to ignore a value in the new case with no support from the old solution if it is in the normal range. No info in old case says to ignore a value of absent in the new case if it is missing in the old case. The rationale here is that if the value is not recorded, we can assume it was absent there also.

In order to support the use of evidence rules, a model needs to show which features (signs and symptoms) and solution states (diagnostic states) can support evidence of which other features and solution states. CASEY's causal models record causal relationships among signs and symptoms and diagnostic states and among several diagnostic states. Diagnostic states are aware of how they tend to manifest themselves in signs and symptoms. Signs and symptoms are aware of the diagnostic states they imply. Diagnostic states are aware of which other diagnostic states they cause and are caused by. In addition, numerical and other scales are separated into qualitative regions. Two values within the same qualitative region are considered close matches. Figure 9.6 shows part of CASEY's model of the cardiac system.

The Newman-David example from the beginning of this section gives an illustration of how evidence rules and causal models work together to compute correspondences between features and to judge consistency of differences between an old case and a new situation. Figure 9.7 shows the differences between the two cases and the evidence rules that reconcile those differences. All differences are judged insignificant using the evidence rules.

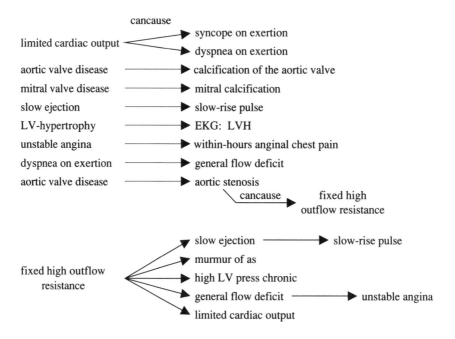

EKG: normal sinus and LV strain is qualitatively the same as EKG: normal sinus and LVH.
Age 62 and up is the same qualitative region.
Pulse-rate 55–80 is in the normal range.
Pulse-rate 81–100 is in the slightly high range.
Temperature 97.5–99 is normal range.
Angina unstable and angina within-hours and unstable are qualitatively the same.

FIGURE 9.6   Part of CASEY's Causal Model

Computing Correspondences Across Domains

When cases are within the same domain, finding correspondences between their parts takes some effort, as shown above. When they are in different domains, the process is even harder. Yet, cross-contextual reminding and suggestions can be quite powerful in reasoning. Consider, for example, the chess and football example given in chapter 6, a chess expert looking at a football game and noticing the opportunity to set up a fork situation—the opposing team can respond in two different ways, and whichever they choose, the one they did not choose gives the defending team the opportunity to move forward. Representations of the two situations have quite different surface roles in them—two teams in opposition versus two players, a field for playing versus a board with pieces, and so on. Seeing the correspondences between the two situations requires understanding them both in terms of their abstract descriptions—as competitive games, with two sides in opposition, a set of rules, a set of playing pieces, and a playing

DIFFERENCES FOUND BETWEEN CASES

No.	*Feature Name*	*Value in old case*	*Value in new case*
1	Age	72	65
2	Pulse-rate	96	90
3	Temperature	98.7	98.4
4	Orthostatic-change	absent	
5	Angina	unstable	within-hours & unstable
6	Mean-arterial-pressure	107	99.3
7	Syncope	none	on exertion
8	Auscultation	murmur of AS	
9	Pulse	normal	slow-rise
10	EKG	normal sinus & LV strain	normal sinus & LVH
11	Calcification	none	mitral & aortic

APPLYING EVIDENCE RULES

- Same Qualitative Region: 1, 2, 3, 5, 10
- No Information: 4
- Unrelated Old Case Feature: 6
- Supports Existing State: 7, 9, 11 (aortic)
- Other Evidence: 8
- Unrelated New Case Feature: 11 (mitral)

FIGURE 9.7 Evidence Rules Explain the Differences Between Two Cases

area. Understanding each in this way allows the functions of the components of each situation to be ascertained and correspondences to be worked out.

In general, the methods already presented for finding correspondences work when slots or definitional predicates have the same names or when their functional roles can be ascertained fairly easily. In cross-domain situations, and even in some within-domain situations, this is not the case. Commonsense reconciliation and use of a causal model fall short under two circumstances:

- When slots or definitional predicates have different names
- When computing the function of some role and its filler requires complex inference

Both are present in the chess and football example.

Putting Abstractions into the Representational Vocabulary

Within the case-based reasoning community, the approach to computing such correspondences has been to anticipate the kinds of cross-contextual remindings that will arise and then to define the contents of a representational vocabulary that will cover correspondences between these kinds of situations. The vocabulary from the Universal Indexing Frame (UIF) (Schank and Osgood 1990), discussed in chapter 6, gives a way of doing this for intention situations (i.e., situations involving planning and goal fulfillment), regardless of domain. Cases are represented using a vocabulary of goals and plans and interactions between people. Whether the domain is chess, football, or interpersonal relationships, the same representation vocabulary and the same structure is assigned to each case. Correspondences can thus be found using commonsense heuristics. In essence, the abstractions needed to notice that components of two cases are playing the same functional roles are built into the representation. Chess and football, as competitive games, both represent situations of goal conflict. Whenever there is a goal conflict, there are two opposing sides, there is a goal in conflict, and there will be certain plans available to achieve the goal. The players, rules, strategies, and so on, of each game fit these roles.

Structure Mapping

But such an analysis has not been done for every abstract domain, and some weak methods are necessary for explaining the way correspondences can be found when they are not known a priori. The analogical reasoning community has suggested a method called *structure mapping* (Gentner 1983, 1988; Falkenhainer 1988). Under structure matching, the features of cases are mapped *structurally* to find correspondences. Features that share a common structural tie in each situation are matched to each other regardless of semantics. The hope is that if a value plays the same role as another structurally, then it will play a similar role functionally also.

A favorite structure mapping example comes from understanding physics. Most of us go into a physics class understanding a lot about water flow. We know about water flowing through conduits, the most familiar of which are streams and pipes, and we know that some sort of conduit must connect a source and a sink for the water to flow between them. Based on that understanding, we can infer a lot about electricity, if we can ascertain the correspondences between objects and processes in the two domains.

There is a system to coming up with such correspondences. The most important, perhaps, is that correspondences between common relations should be found before attempting to find correspondences between objects (derived from Collins and Burstein 1989; Gentner 1983). In looking at plumbing and electricity, we first try to make correspondences between the relationships like `connect` before we try to figure out whether a pipe corresponds to a wire or a battery. The intuition here is that objects that are related to other objects in similar ways are likely to correspond to each other. The account derives from observations of people that show that the analogies they find useful tend to involve "rich, inter-constraining systems of mappings between two domains, rather than a set of independent correspondences" (Black 1962; Gentner 1980, 1983; Holyoak 1984).[8]

Two kinds of constraints guide the finding of correspondences, called *mapping*.

1. Selection constraints specify requirements for the mapping:

   ■ Only relational commonalities count. Thus, no correspondences are sought for isolated object descriptions in a representation unless they are involved in a larger relational structure.

   ■ Among the relational commonalities, the highest-order causal relations specify which relational commonalities to pay attention to. This is called the *systematicity principle* (Gentner 1983).[9] Intuitively, the systematicity principle states that connected systems of relations are mapped to each other in finding correspondences, rather than concentrating on isolated objects or relations.

2. Structural consistency constraints specify preferences when choices can be made in a mapping:

   ■ Consistent, one-to-one object correspondences

   ■ Consistency in the mapped dependency structure

An example will make this clearer. Figure 9.8 illustrates a simple water flow situation at the top and an analogous heat flow situation at the bottom (taken from Gentner 1988). In the water flow case, we see a pipe connecting a small vial and a large beaker. The beaker has more water, the result is water flowing through the pipe into the small vial. In the heat flow situation, we see a silver bar with an ice cube on the end sitting in a mug of hot coffee. The reasoner already understands that the rate of water flowing from the beaker to the vial is a function of the pressure difference between the two vessels and has just been told that *heat is like water*. It needs to figure out the relationship between heat flow and water flow. The reasoner uses its understanding of water flow to understand the flow of heat from the coffee to the ice cube by way of the bar. This requires setting up correspondences between the two situations.[10]

---

8. Quote and references from Clement and Gentner 1991, pp 91–92.

9. *Highest-order* causal relations are those that connect other high-order relations to each other. A first-order relation takes objects as arguments. A second-order relation takes at least one first-order relation as an argument. An nth-order relation has at least one $(n\text{-}1)$th-order relation among its arguments. In Figure 9.9, for example, the relation cause is the highest order. It has a first-order relation (flow) and a second-order relation (greater) as arguments, making it a third-order relation.

10. This example may be confusing to some people, because its task seems different from what we have been discussing up to now. This is an example of trying to compute correspondences after being told that similarity exists for the purpose of learning a set of new facts. Up to now, the task has been to determine correspondences after partially-matching cases have been retrieved for the purpose of choosing a best or good-enough case to reason with. The tasks are indeed different, but the subtask of finding correspondences is the same. In both situations, a partial match has been proposed, some subset of correspondences are already known, and the full set of correspondences must be found.

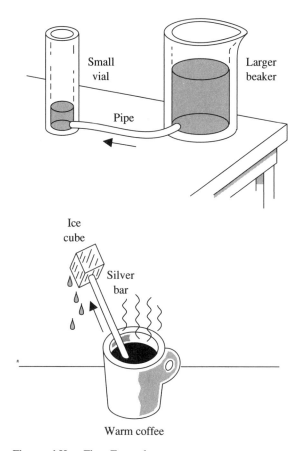

FIGURE 9.8   Water Flow and Heat Flow Examples

Figure 9.9 shows the representations a reasoner might have of both situations. We can see that the representation of heat flow, the new situation, is far less complete than the representation of water flow, the well-known case. The process of setting up correspondences includes the adding of relationships between representational units that are already known. Structure mapping tells us to start by attempting to find correspondences to the highest-order relations of the well-known item. The `cause` relation at the top of the water flow representation plays that role. There is no `cause` relation in the heat flow example yet, but there are clauses in that representation that correspond to the ones in the water flow situation that `cause` relates to each other. Thus, the `cause` relation is added to the heat flow representation, and the `greater (pressure(beaker) (pressure (vial))` clause is mapped to `greater (temp (coffee) temp (ice cube))` and `flow (beaker, vial, water, pipe)` is mapped to `flow (ice cube, coffee, heat, bar)`. Having made that correspondence, object and relationship correspondences can be made. We see that `pressure` corresponds to `temp`, `water` to `heat`, `pipe` to `metal bar`, `beaker` to `coffee`, and `vial` to `ice`. Systematicity guides choice of object and relationship

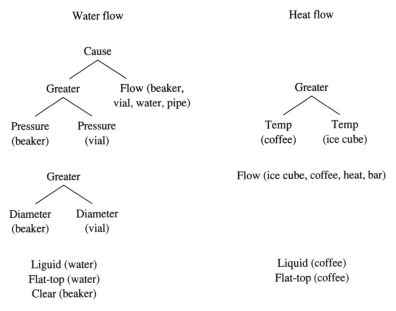

FIGURE 9.9 Representations of Water and Heat Flow

correspondences and also determines which relations get attended to. Because the diameters of the beaker and vial don't participate in the constellation of relations governed by the highest-order relation, no attempt is made to find corresponding features in the heat flow situation.

This methodology has some important features. Correspondence is based on the structural features of descriptions rather than the specifics of their content. This makes it broadly applicable across domains where correspondences have not been well studied. In addition, the systematicity principle is intuitively appealing—it prefers deeper correspondences to shallower ones. Superficial similarities are considered for correspondence only in the context of deeper relational similarities.

There are several complexities and caveats in using structure mapping, however. For example, there was an implicit assumption in the example that any case would have just one constellation of important relations associated with it and that that set would always guide the finding of correspondences. On the contrary, cases might have several different constellations of important relations, and a choice may need to be made about which to focus on. Even the water flow example has this characteristic. In addition to knowing that the difference in pressure between beaker and vial causes water to flow through the pipe, we also know that differences in their diameters affect the rate of pressure change in the two vessels. Were we to have a new situation in which *heat capacity* were important, then the system of relations surrounding that causal relation would be the more appropriate one to focus on in setting up correspondences.

Falkenhainer (1988) shows that choosing an appropriate system of relations to focus on is dependent on the goals of the reasoner. He also shows that systematicity is difficult to apply when knowledge is ambiguous or lacking, and he provides a more knowledge-based methodology for structure mapping that deals with those problems. Those building systems to do cross-domain case-based reasoning will find his methodology useful.

9.2.2 Computing Degree of Similarity of Corresponding Features

Once it is known which features correspond to each other, the degree of similarity between corresponding features can be computed. There are several methods available for computing the degree of similarity of two values:

- Comparison based on placement in an abstraction hierarchy
- Computation of distance on a qualitative scale
- Computation of distance on a quantitative scale
- Comparison of the degree to which features play the designated functional role

Using an Abstraction Hierarchy

When using an abstraction hierarchy to compute degree of similarity, it is computed in terms of the *most specific common abstraction* (MSCA) of the two values. The more specific the most specific common abstraction, the better the match.

Using an abstraction hierarchy and relative ranking, one pair of values matches better than another if the MSCA of the first is more specific than the MSCA of the second. Suppose, for example, that we have sparrow and robin filling corresponding roles. The most specific common abstraction might be bird in a simple abstraction hierarchy (see Figure 9.10). Comparing robin and cat, the most specific common abstraction might be animal. Because bird, the MSCA of sparrow and robin, is more specific than animal, the MSCA of robin and cat, it is a better match. Computing relative MSCA requires computing MSCA for each pair of values and then computing MSCA for the resulting MSCAs.

Computing an absolute ranking of specificity involves assigning *specificity values* to all nodes in the abstraction hierarchy. If a score of 0 means least specific, and 1 is most specific, then robin and sparrow, which are most specific, might be assigned the value 1, while cat,

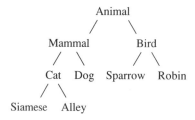

FIGURE 9.10   A Simple Abstraction Hierarchy

dog and bird, which are less specific, might be assigned 0.6. Mammal, which is still less specific, might be assigned 0.4, while animal is assigned 0.2. The score of the partial match is the specificity value of the MSCA. Comparing sparrow and robin, the score of the MSCA is 0.6. Comparing cat and robin, the score of the MSCA is 0.2.

Notice that neither of these methods counts distance in the abstraction hierarchy. Unless an abstraction hierarchy is perfectly balanced semantically, there is good reason to avoid counting distance. In places where the hierarchy is more densely populated, similar values will tend to be physically farther from each other than in more sparsely populated parts of the hierarchy. Measuring degree of match based on specificity alleviates that problem.

A problem arises in abstraction hierarchies when items are abstracted several different ways. This could result in several different MSCAs for the same two values. Some way of determining which are the right branches of the abstraction hierarchy to follow in computing MSCA is needed. Context or problem-solving goal may sometimes provide this. Failing that, a means of ranking sets of MSCAs is needed.

Qualitative and Quantitative Distance

Another way of measuring degree of match is by measuring the distance between two values on a qualitative scale. If two values are within the same qualitative region, then they are considered equal. Otherwise, the distance between their qualitative regions provides a measure of their match score. CASEY, for example, compares ages using qualitative regions. Ages 60 and up is the *old* range, 40 through 59 is *middle-aged*, and 20 through 39 is *young adult*. Using this scheme, ages 62 and 75 match each other exactly, as do ages 62 and 70, 40 and 55, 40 and 45, and so on. Ages 40 and 62 are one qualitative region apart; ages 35 and 65 are two qualitative regions apart. The more qualitative regions separate two values, the lower the match score.

Using qualitative regions to measure the degree of match of quantities makes a lot of sense when small differences in quantity are irrelevant to degree of match. A problem that arises with qualitative ranges, however, is that the degree of match is inaccurate at the edges of the ranges. For example, 39 matches 62 as well (or badly) as 40 does, but because 39 is in one qualitative region and 40 is in another, their match scores when compared to 62 will be different. A possible solution to this problem is to check whether two values relative to each other are near the edges of their qualitative regions and to adjust relative degrees of match based on that. Another is to make qualitative regions overlap each other. If *middle-aged* is defined as 35 through 62 and *old* is defined as 55 and up, for example, putting borderline values into two categories, then qualitative matching can be made more accurate.

Another way to measure two quantities qualitatively is to compute the differences between the quantities and then assign the difference to a qualitative difference. For age, for example, a difference of one to four years might be one region, while a difference of five to eight might constitute a different region, and so on.

Qualitative measurement of degree of match might not involve quantities at all. Many values we think of only in qualitative terms. Students might be highly motivated, moderately motivated, slightly motivated, or not motivated at all, for example. Each of these values is a qualitative value on a qualitative scale. The distance between two qualitative values on a scale can be computed either by counting the number of qualitative values between two values being compared, or by assigning each region a numerical value and comparing those.

One might also compare values qualitatively by comparing the attributes of two values. Lasagne, for example, is a pasta dish of Italian cuisine that includes ricotta cheese; mozzarella cheese; large flat pasta; tomato sauce flavored with garlic, pepper, basil, and oregano; and ground beef. Manicotti is a pasta dish of Italian cuisine that includes ricotta cheese, mozzarella cheese, large tubes of pasta, and tomato sauce flavored with garlic, pepper, basil, and oregano. Comparing them based on their descriptions, we see that they are similar except for the shape of the pasta and the inclusion of beef. Computation based on attributes results in creation of a comparison structure that points out similarities and differences. Implementations that compare based on attributes use either frame or microfeature (Domeshek 1991b) representations.[11]

Another way to compute qualitative distance is to measure the quality of the chain of inferences linking two values to each other. PROTOS does this as part of its knowledge-based matching scheme. This scheme will be discussed in chapter 13.

Finally, numerical values can be compared numerically. The larger the (normalized) distance between two values, the smaller their degree of match.

Maintaining Consistency

Any two dimensions of a case may be compared using different means of comparison. Age might be compared qualitatively, for example, while type of animal, another slot of the same representation, may need to be compared using a hierarchy. It is important to make sure that match scores, no matter how computed, are consistent with one another across dimensions. Huge differences should get similar low scores; small differences should get similar high scores. An absolute score of 0.5, for example, should mean the same degree of match no matter which dimension is being scored and which scoring method is being used. If 0 is the score for no degree of match and 1 the score for perfect match across one dimension, then each dimension should be scored the same way before adjusting for importance of dimensions.

When a Boulder Is Used as a Chair: Judging Degree of Similarity Based on Performance of a Function

The matching techniques described so far work when items being matched are qualitatively similar. Another set of issues arises, however, when the items to be matched are semantically far from each other. Correspondence techniques, for example, might allow a program to notice that a boulder and a chair are being used for the same function and therefore correspond. That having been decided, however, none of the techniques for matching that we have described will be very good at determining the relative similarity of a boulder to two different chairs or of a chair to two different boulders. CASEY's method finesses this problem by assuming that

---

11. Computation of this sort is a kind of dynamic hierarchical approach to comparison. The hierarchical approach shown above relies on a semantic network or other hierarchical structure's being in place and relating items to each other. Comparing qualitatively by attributes allows the same sort of comparison to be done but doesn't depend on an in-place semantic network to do the work.

if two qualitatively different things are shown to correspond by a causal model, then they match. Degree of match is never computed beyond that. The assumption here is that if two items have been found by a causal model to correspond in function, and if all other components of the match are also accounted for, then the goodness of the match can be assumed.

It is important in some applications, however, to be able to determine which of several possible matches of this sort is better. Is the case that has a huge boulder in it a better or worse match than the one with the chair-size boulder? Of course, the answer depends on more than whether the boulders and chairs are good matches, but it does require that some judgment be made about the goodness of match of each boulder to the chair. We currently have no good answers to this, noting only that matching of this sort will require determining what function of the object being matched is shared by the two objects and computing in some way the degree to which the new item is able to carry out that function. Argumentation, which is discussed in chapter 13, would be a beginning to answering this question.

9.2.3 Weighting Dimensions of a Representation: Assigning Importance Values

A function that computes degree of match can only be as good as the knowledge it has of the importance of fields or dimensions. The importance associated with each field tells us how much attention to pay to matches and mismatches in that field when computing how good a match is. Importance can be assigned statically, or it can be computed dynamically, taking into account aspects of the context in which the match is happening. It can be assigned globally, over a large set of cases, or it can be assigned more locally, over a small set of cases. At the most fine-grained local level, there may be several ratings of importance associated with each dimension of each case.

A global assignment of field importance requires an analysis of cases in the domain to determine which dimensions of a representation tend to be the important ones for a match. These importance values are then attached to fields of the representation, and the degree of match of any two cases to each other is computed using these assigned values.

One way to assign importance values is to have a human expert assign them as the case library is being built. The expert might have some feeling about which dimensions and combinations of dimensions make good predictors. For example, when the Battle Planner (Goodman 1989) is determining how closely a case matches a new situation, it ranks the ratio of the strengths of the two sides of a battle very high, while the individual strengths of the sides are ranked quite low. This assignment of importance means that, all other things being equal, a case that is very similar in the ratio of strengths of its two sides is a very good match, able to predict strategies that work and point out strategies that have failed. On the other hand, if the strength of one side in a new situation matches the strength of a side in a case, there is less reason to think it a good match. The strength of one side is not as good a predictor of strategy as the ratio of strengths of the two opponents.

One problem with this ranking scheme is that it is hard for people to assign ratings beyond estimates of relative ranking. On the other hand, research on certainty factors showed that fine-grained determinations were not necessary. The same seems to hold true of importance values assigned to dimensions. REMIND (Cognitive Systems 1992) solves this problem by having experts designate importance of a field by assigning the equivalent of qualitative values such as "most important," "very important," "important," "ignore," and so on. Each is associated with a number that the system uses for its computations. The specifications are not exact determinations of importance, but they capture relative importance and seem to work well.

MEDIATOR overcomes this problem by assigning importance rankings in a hierarchical way. Rather than trying to assign importance to each descriptor independently, it groups descriptors according to which component of the case they are describing. Components of the case are assigned importance rankings, and individual descriptive features of each component are assigned importance rankings within the context of the component. The aggregate match score is computed by first computing a match score for each component and then computing a match score for the case based on the degrees of match of the components.

Given MEDIATOR's task and domain, similarity of arguments is more important than similarity of disputed objects, and both are more important than similarity of disputants. For disputed objects, functional descriptors such as splitability are more important for ranking than descriptive descriptors such as color. Functional descriptors are thus given higher importance within the context of disputed objects. A hierarchical ranking scheme can be implemented easily when a frame system is used for representation. Frames provide the hierarchy, and ranking of any field is within the context of the frame it is a slot in. Match scores are computed by beginning at the bottom level of the frame representation, computing match scores for each dimension of those frames, aggregating those scores to compute a score for the frame, aggregating frame scores to compute a score for the next frame up, and so on until a complete score is computed.

Another way to assign importance values is to do a statistical evaluation of a known corpus of cases to determine which dimensions predict different outcomes and/or solutions best. Those that are good predictors are then assigned higher importance for matching.

A single static value for importance works well enough when there is little or no variation in the importance of case dimensions across problems. For some tasks and in some domains, however, the importance of features varies with the context of the match. Consider, for example, a mediator using a case library of baseball players and their salaries to determine fair salaries for new players. In order to determine a fair salary for a new player, he recalls other similar players, looks at their salaries, and computes the salary for the new player based on the salaries of those players and the differences between this new player and those recalled. The features of players that the mediator pays attention to in determining the similarity between a new player and an old one are different depending on what position the new player plays.

When he is trying to decide the fair salary of a pitcher, for example, he recalls other pitchers with similar earned-run averages, numbers of shutouts, and other statistics particular to pitchers, and he pays less attention to batting and fielding statistics. When he is trying to compute a fair salary for a fielder, on the other hand, similarity is based on fielding and hitting credentials (e.g., fielding percentage, agility, number of assists, strength of throw for fielding; batting average, number of RBIs, number of stolen bases for hitting). Clearly, a single globally assigned importance value for each descriptive dimension of a baseball player will not support judgment of similarity for this mediator as well as an assignment of importance values that is sensitive to the new player's role on the team.[12]

Taking this example one step further, in some situations even more sensitivity to context is needed to determine the relative importance of features in judging similarity. Let's suppose that the mediator has computed what he thinks is a fair salary for a new player, and now he wants to validate the goodness of the salary he has computed. One way to do that is to recall players with similar salaries to make sure that this new player's salary is consistent with other salaries across the team. Here, the most important feature to concentrate on in choosing the most useful cases from the case library is the salary of other players. The mediator needs cases in which salaries are similar. After cases are recalled, players will be compared to each other based on relative performance to determine if the proposed salary is an appropriate one.

Assignment of multiple importance ratings to dimensions of a case's description can be done easily by building on the idea of assigning a global importance value to each dimension of the case representations. Several different importance values are computed and assigned for each case dimension, each corresponding to a different construal of context. Continuing with the baseball example, the dimension "batting average" might be highly ranked for the goal of computing a salary when the new player is a fielder, ranked considerably lower when the same goal is active but the position of the new player is pitcher, and ranked very low or zero when the goal is to validate a derived salary. Similarly, the dimension "earned run average" is ranked high when the goal is to derive a salary for a new pitcher, ranked zero when the new player plays some other position and when the goal is to validate a derived salary. Figure 9.11 shows a set of dimensions on which baseball players are described and their importance values in judging similarity across a variety of contexts.

In other situations, the importance of dimensions cannot be computed a priori but is better computed on the fly when a set of partially-matching cases is made available, taking into account the importance of each dimension within that set of partially-matching cases and the sort of outcome each tends to predict and, from that, attempting to compute how important each dimension is in the current situation. This is a more complicated process than those suggested above, and is perhaps more appropriately done in trying to understand situations well before problem solving rather than while trying to retrieve cases that can suggest good solutions. It does seem appropriate, however, to point out that the importance of dimensions does sometimes need to be computed on the fly.

HYPO (Ashley and Rissland 1988a) implements this process using three phases. First, dimensions are clustered according to the interactions they have with other dimensions, and a hierarchy of clusters is formed. The occurrence of combinations of dimensions in each of the partially-matching cases is catalogued to do this. In the second phase, the effects of each cluster are determined by looking at the outcome of each case in each cluster. Some clusters will tend to predict positive outcomes, some negative, and some will predict positive or negative

---

12. It gets more complicated than this. For example, depending on whether the pitcher is a relief pitcher or a starting pitcher, number of saves is more or less important. And, of course, one year's statistics are not enough; the player's performance over time is also important. Baseball aficionados will have to excuse me for leaving such complexities aside.

	goal=compute salary position=pitcher	*goal=compute salary position=fielder*	*goal=evaluate salary*
name			
position	high	high	
age	moderate	moderate	moderate
experience	moderate	moderate	
height			
weight			
salary			very high
# shutouts	high		
earned run avg	very high		
innings pitched	high		
strikeouts	high		
saves	moderate		
fielding %age		high	
agility	moderate	very high	
# assists		high	
strength of throw	moderate	high	
batting average	low	very high	
slugging average	low	very high	
rbi's	low	high	
home runs		high	
stolen bases		very high	
strikeouts at bat	low	high	
doubles		moderate	
triples		moderate	

FIGURE 9.11   Assignment of Importance Values for Multiple Construals of Context (Blank spaces designate an importance value close to or equal to zero)

outcomes more strongly than others. From this clustering, the factors that are important in the new situation are extracted. In the final phase, hypothetical situations similar to the new one are created, and the importance of factors is tested.

The description here of this process is dense, and the process itself remains esoteric for now, having been implemented only in HYPO and only in the legal domain. This sort of analysis of what is important can be used to determine which features of a new situation are more important in judging usefulness of partially-matching cases. It seems most useful when a reasoner needs to figure out what to pay attention to in a problem description, so that it can come up with a solution that makes sense. That process will be described in more detail in chapter 13.

9.3 PUTTING IT ALL TOGETHER

The building blocks of matching and ranking procedures are the processes discussed above: finding correspondences between the cases, computing degree of match of corresponding values, and assigning or computing degree of importance of dimensions of a representation. Figure 9.12 lists the components and the several types of procedures for carrying each one out.

It is now time to consider the ways in which these building blocks can be combined. In the sections that follow, several different matching and ranking procedures are presented. First, the easiest numeric matching scheme and the way it can be integrated into a simple static ranking scheme is discussed. Then its shortcomings are presented, along with some easy ways to overcome them. Two dynamic matching and ranking schemes are then presented. Each adds additional capability but also additional complexity to matching and ranking processes.

The procedures to be presented are of three kinds: numeric, heuristic, and mixed. Figure 9.13 summarizes. Numeric procedures depend on a numeric *evaluation function* that uses relative importance of dimensions and the degree of match of each to compute a match score. Heuristic procedures presented are of two types. *Evidence procedures*, such as those CASEY uses, provide one type. Here, no ranking is done; rather, the first case found to match adequately according to the available causal model is returned. Because this procedure has been discussed in detail as a building block for the matching process, it is not discussed again here. The other heuristic procedure applies *preference heuristics* over the set of cases being ranked to sift out the most useful of the cases according to a set of preference criteria.

FINDING CORRESPONDENCES

- Based on structural correspondence
- Based on functional correspondence
- Across domains

COMPUTING DEGREE OF SIMILARITY BETWEEN CORRESPONDING FEATURES

- Based on placement in abstraction hierarchy
- Based on a qualitative or quantitative scale
- Based on functional role

ASSIGNING IMPORTANCE TO DIMENSIONS

- Globally, over the whole library
- Based on purpose case will be put to
- Based on importance in previous instances

FIGURE 9.12 Building Blocks of Matching and Ranking Schemes

NUMERIC PROCEDURES:

■ Nearest-neighbor matching and ranking using a numeric evaluation function

HEURISTIC PROCEDURES:

■ Evidence rules identify a good-enough match
■ Preference heuristics sift the set of available cases according to specified preferences

COMBINED HEURISTIC AND NUMERIC PROCEDURES:

■ Exclusion first, ranking by either numeric or heuristic procedures
■ Heuristic choice of importance criteria, application of numeric matching and ranking procedures

FIGURE 9.13   Schemes for Selecting Cases

Other procedures combine heuristic and numeric approaches. In one approach, heuristic *exclusion criteria* are applied to the set of available cases to delete those cases that can easily be found not to provide useful matches, and then one of the matching or ranking procedures is applied to the rest. In the other approach, importance criteria are chosen heuristically, and numeric evaluation procedures use those criteria to match and rank.

Heuristic choice of importance criteria makes a numeric procedure more or less context-sensitive. The simplest way to use a numeric evaluation function is to assign importance criteria globally. Under this scheme, importance criteria are assigned to each dimension of the representation and applied consistently over the entire case library, independent of what a case will be used for and independent of the idiosyncrasies of the case. Importance criteria can also be assigned more locally, however, providing more context sensitivity. Dimensions can be assigned different importance depending on the purpose to which a case will be put, providing sensitivity to the reasoner's goal. Alternatively, they can be assigned locally to each case, taking its idiosyncrasies into account, making matching sensitive to what features have been important in the past. Or a combination of the two methods can be used, assigning several matching criteria to each case and choosing according to the goal of the reasoner.

9.3.1 Matching and Ranking Using a Numeric Function: Nearest-Neighbor Matching

When a case-based reasoner is responsible for achieving only one kind of reasoning goal, computing the degree of match can be a fairly straightforward process that uses a numerical evaluation function. A single global set of importance values is assigned to dimensions of the case library. Every feature in the input case is matched to its corresponding feature in the stored or old case, the degree of match of each pair is computed, and based on the importance assigned to each dimension, an *aggregate match score* is computed (Figure 9.14). Ranking

For each feature in the input case,

- Find the corresponding feature in the stored case
- Compare the two values to each other and compute the degree of match
- Multiply by a coefficient representing the importance of the feature to the match.

Add the results to derive an *aggregate match score*.

This number represents the aggregate degree of match of the old case to the input.
A case can be chosen by choosing the item with the largest score.

FIGURE 9.14   Easy Numeric Matching and Ranking Algorithm (Nearest-Neighbor)

procedures order cases according to their scores, and higher scoring cases are used before lower scoring ones. This is called *nearest-neighbor matching*.

Several early case-based reasoners implement versions of this algorithm, including MEDIATOR and PERSUADER. Each of the CBR shells on the market include this simple algorithm. In general, in these systems, corresponding dimensions are found by mapping slots with the same names to each other. Values along each dimension are compared using whichever of the comparison procedures is appropriate: qualitative comparisons when qualitative ranges are available, numerical correspondences when values are numbers, and assessment using an abstraction hierarchy when one is available. Each dimension is assigned a degree of importance; the degree of match in each dimension is multiplied by the importance of the dimension, and the products are added up.

REMIND's (Cognitive Systems 1992) implementation of this simple algorithm is shown in Figure 9.15. In REMIND, both importance and dimensional degree of match are represented as numerical values between 0 and 1. Closer matches have values closer to 1; poorer matches closer to 0. Similarly, an importance ranking of 1 is higher than a lower importance ranking. The aggregate match score is computed by summing the products of the importance of each field multiplied by the degree of match of values in the field. To normalize the scores, they are divided by the sum of the importance rankings.

The set of importance values assigned to each dimension are inserted into the formula in Figure 9.15 to derive the *evaluation function* used to compute aggregate degree of match. The aggregate match score is computed by applying the evaluation function to the dimensional match scores computed for each dimension.

$$\frac{\Sigma_{i=1}^{n} \, w_i \times sim(f_i^I, f_i^R)}{\Sigma_{i=1}^{n} \, w_i}$$

where w_i is the importance of dimension (slot) i, sim is the similarity function for primitives, and f_i^I and f_i^R are the values for feature f_i in the input and retrieved cases, respectively.

FIGURE 9.15   A Numerical Evaluation Function

	Player1	*Player2*	*Player3*	*New*
name	White	Grey	Black	Green
position	shortstop	outfield	3rd base	2nd base
age	27	28	28	31
experience	91 (games)	54	236	103
at bats	231	107	733	300
height	72	72	71	72
weight	160	185	175	200
salary				
agility	good	moderate	high	moderate
batting avg	268	243	291	263
slugging avg	294	346	411	375
rbi's	14	14	79	36
home runs	0	2	13	7
stolen bases	3	6	3	1
strikeouts	35	15	100	51
doubles	2	5	41	12
triples	2	0	4	1

FIGURE 9.16   Several Sample Cases from the Baseball Library and the New Situation

We can use the baseball example to illustrate. Let us assume the case library has three players in it, as shown in Figure 9.16. And let us assume the mediator using this case library is attempting to derive a fair salary for a new player, shown in the right-hand column of that figure. Let us also assume that the qualitative value very high in Figure 9.11 corresponds to the value 1.0, that high corresponds to 0.8, that moderate corresponds to 0.4, low corresponds to 0.2, and no assigned importance value corresponds to an importance of 0.

Our goal is to judge the closeness of fit of each case in the case library to the new situation. We do that by comparing the new situation to each of the cases in the library and computing a match score for each. Because our new player is a fielder, and we want to derive a salary for him, we use the degrees of importance associated with the middle column of Figure 9.11. Figure 9.17 shows, in its first column, the numerical importance value for each dimension. In its other columns, it shows the degree of match of the value in the new case to the value in each old one. The bottom row shows the match score when the function in Figure 9.15 is applied.

Using a numeric evaluation function of this sort, ranking cases is quite simple. Cases with higher scores are ranked higher than those with lower scores. This scheme is called *nearest-neighbor ranking*. Cases whose descriptions are most similar to a new situation are ranked higher than those whose descriptions are less similar. In the baseball example, Player2 comes out as most similar to the new player and the one whose salary will be used to compute a salary for the new player.

	Importance of dimension	Degree of Match		
		Player1	Player2	Player3
name	0			
position	.8	.8	.6	.8
age	.4	.8	.8	.8
experience	.4	.8	.2	.2
height	0	1	1	1
weight	0	.6	.8	.7
salary	0			
agility	1	.7	1	.5
batting average	1	1	.9	.8
slugging average	1	.4	.8	.8
rbi's	.8	.2	.2	.2
home runs	.8	0	.2	.4
stolen bases	1	.2	.1	.2
strikeouts	.8	.4	.2	.3
doubles	.4	0	.3	0
triples	.4	.5	.5	.3
match score	8.8	4.26	4.48	4.18
normalized match score		.484	.509	.475

FIGURE 9.17 Importance of Each Dimension and Degree of Match in Each Dimension for Each Case

This example was simple enough to be able to show how numeric evaluation works, but it is also simple enough to show some of the problems with blindly applying numerical evaluation schemes. Readers should notice that the similarity scores for all three players were quite close. According to the metric used, each is about equally similar to the new situation, but Player2 is a little more similar. When the scores for cases across the case library are this close, there are three possible explanations. Either the cases are, indeed, all quite similar to one another, matching criteria have not been chosen well, or both. If cases are all similar to one another, then either more cases need to be collected to allow a more balanced set of suggestions to be put forth by the case library or some better means of distinguishing cases must be found (i.e., better similarity or matching criteria—importance criteria and dimensional match criteria—are needed). If cases really aren't that similar to each other but the matching functions say they are, then, again, better matching criteria are needed.

Matching criteria, in turn, can be poor for three reasons. Either the wrong importance values are assigned to dimensions, the matching of values within a dimension is being done poorly, or the wrong dimensions are being compared. In the baseball case, it is the last of these: Raw numbers are being compared to each other (e.g., number of home runs, number of strikeouts) when comparison should be made along a normalized view of the dimension. Normalizing in the baseball domain means dividing raw scores by number of games the player has played or the number of times he's been at bat. Normalizing home runs by number of times at bat, for example, would show us that the new player's home run percentage is higher than that of the other players (zero for Player 1; 1.8 percent for Player2, 1.7 percent for Player3, and 2.3 percent for the new player). Normalizing the number of strikeouts could show us that the new player strikes out considerably more than the players he is compared to—his strikeout average is 17 percent; those of the other players are between 13.6 percent and 15.1 percent.

Often, when the wrong dimensions are being compared, it means that the indexing vocabulary has been chosen badly. Additional analysis is needed to find the right dimensions for indexing.

Other times, dimensions for representation are chosen correctly, but importance values associated with dimensions lack sensitivity to context. It may be appropriate to make evaluation criteria more fine-grained and local (e.g., compare the new player to other players based on the particular strengths of each player rather than based on a normalized set of criteria). Or, better heuristics for choosing matching criteria may be needed. Sections 9.3.3 and 9.3.4. discuss these options.

9.3.2 Adding Exclusion to the Ranking Procedure

A numerical evaluation function can compute degree of match of several cases, but it can only rank them—it cannot recognize that some cases should not be considered at all. The way to deal with this problem in the context of numeric evaluation is to add an *exclusion* step to the ranking procedures before performing numeric evaluation. An exclusion step looks for *differences* between cases that are known to predict that a retrieved case will not be useful.

MEDIATOR (Kolodner and Simpson 1989) did this. Before comparing cases for their degree of similarity, it first excluded cases that had mismatches in important places. Recall that MEDIATOR resolved everyday resource disputes in commonsense ways. One type of difference that requires exclusion is a difference between the goal relationships in two cases. If the goals of disputants in one case are in competition and those in another case are complementary, then the match is excluded. Competing goals cannot both be fully achieved (e.g., two kids want the same candy bar; two countries want the same land mass). Complementary goals might both be achievable with a bit of ingenuity (e.g., one person wants the fruit of an orange, the other its peel; one country wants to maintain its integrity, another wants its borders secure from attack). The kinds of solutions used when goals are in competition do not work when goals are complementary. Thus, mismatch on this dimension shows that a recalled case cannot provide a solution to the new situation.

After excluding those cases with important mismatches, MEDIATOR determines the degree of match of the remaining cases to the new situation using a numeric matching scheme. It assigns numeric importance values to each of its dimensions, and it computes the degree of match along each dimension using an abstraction hierarchy. It chooses the case that scores highest to reason with first.

PROTOS (Bareiss 1989a) does the same, using *censors* to rule out a potential match before matching functions are applied. The difference between PROTOS's and MEDIATOR's approaches is that PROTOS does its exclusion during the retrieval phase. Exclusion is a process that mediates between retrieval and ranking. Retrieval processes retrieve potentially useful cases. Matching and ranking functions are asked to validate usefulness of cases and/or choose the most useful in the given set. Though both PROTOS and MEDIATOR use heuristics to exclude some potentially matching cases from being considered by matching and ranking procedures, PROTOS's censors exclude cases from being retrieved from memory and therefore from being among the cases that are passed to matching and ranking procedures. MEDIATOR, by contrast, uses exclusion after retrieval to hone down the set of cases that matching procedures are asked to match and rank.

9.3.3 The Need to Take Context into Account in Ranking

Although the numerical evaluation method is very simple, it is important to keep in mind that it is only as good as the importance ratings assigned to the dimensions. If retrieval is to be based on the usefulness of cases, or the purpose they will be put to, then importance ratings must be assigned taking purpose into account. When a case library is to be used for only one purpose and the relative importance of different dimensions to a good match is consistent across cases, assigning one set of importance values to every dimension will work. But, as described earlier, when cases are to be used for several different purposes, each of which requires focus on different aspects of cases to determine which is most appropriate, several different sets of importance values must be assigned. Indeed, whether or not a numerical evaluation of similarity is done, when cases are to be used for several purposes, several different criteria for matching might be necessary.

The baseball example shows this well. The mediator who wants to compute fair salaries for baseball players may need to use one criterion for judging similarity when dealing with pitchers, another when dealing with catchers, and another when dealing with outfielders. And he may want to use completely different criteria when attempting to check the consistency of his computations than when doing the computations themselves. When a reasoner will be used for many different reasoning purposes or in several different reasoning contexts, it may need to have several different means of evaluating the goodness of its partial matches. We continue with a more detailed discussion of what context is and how it affects matching.

Recall the meal-planning example from the introduction to this part of the book. A host was planning a meal. The host's case library held four cases, all of which were equally similar to the new situation, taking only similarity of features into account. Without knowing what reasoning the host wanted to do, it was impossible to know which of those cases was the best match. Knowing the reasoning the host wanted to do, however, made it obvious which case was the best one to retrieve. When planning the main dish, the two cases that suggested main dish solutions were best. When evaluating the proposed solution, the one that could help project outcome was best. When trying to figure out how to adapt a main dish with cheese for someone allergic to dairy products, the case that directly addressed that issue was best.

That example showed that the purpose to which a case will be put after retrieval plays a large role in judging whether it should appropriately be retrieved. A large component of context that needs to be considered in determining which of several cases are more appropriate ones to retrieve is that purpose, or the reasoner's goal.

Another determiner of context in matching and ranking cases is what was important in each old case. Cases keep track of the manner in which components of a situation have acted in combination with other components in the past. When a new situation shares some combination of features with an old case that were important to its outcome or important to the way it was solved, the old case can be more helpful than if it shares just random features.

Who the particular guests are, for example, may not generally be significant in predicting reasonable meals. An analysis of factors responsible for outcomes would probably show that the best global predictors of what to serve are the eating restrictions of the guests, the degree to which a guest is adventurous, and the tendencies of the guests to like or not like spicy food. We can use such an analysis to set up importance values, assigning these fields high importance. But after some particular experience, we may find that some combination of features of a case that are not represented well by the available importance values serve as a significant predictor of success for situations of that sort. After Anne came to dinner and was served grilled trout, for example, the host in the previous example found out that Anne does not eat fish. Though we might not want to change the generally applicable evaluation procedures to accommodate this idiosyncrasy, it is certainly worthwhile to be able to notice that in this particular kind of situation (i.e., one where Anne comes to dinner), serving fish will result in a poor outcome.

Taking only the goal of the reasoner into account in judging similarity is inadequate to this task, because the tendencies of different representational dimensions to contribute to a solution (the importance values in an evaluation function) don't tell us anything about what was important in any particular case. The following example shows the difficulty of using a global or generally applicable evaluation function to retrieve cases in which certain idiosyncratic features are important to pay attention to in judging similarity. Here, the most useful case is the one in which Anne is a guest, but it is difficult to define similarity criteria that both support the goal of evaluating a partial solution and allow this case to be noticed as the most useful one for the purpose.

A host is planning a meal. Anne is a guest. It is summer. Salmon will be served. It will be prepared by grilling. The host is trying to evaluate this portion of the menu. The case library holds several similar cases, among them are the following:

Meal1: It was summer; the meal had to be easy to prepare; grilled trout was served; Anne was a guest; Anne didn't eat because she doesn't like grilled fish.

Meal5: It was summer; the meal had to be easy to prepare; grilled salmon was served; the guests were a group of people from work. Everyone raved about the meal.

Meal6: It was summer; the meal had to be easy to prepare; grilled hot dogs were served; Anne was a guest. All went well.

Each case matches the new situation more or less to the same degree. All can provide at least some help in evaluating the proposed plan. Meal1 tells us that Anne will not like this meal. Meal5 tells us that people will tend to like grilled salmon, but it cannot predict the potential disaster that Meal1 helps the reasoner to avoid. Meal6 tells us that all will turn out well if grilled food is served but is clearly not as useful as either Meal1 or Meal5.

It would be hard, if not impossible, to get a generally applicable evaluation function to choose Meal1 as an appropriate candidate for retrieval without also having it pull out a number of other meals where grilled fish was served or where Anne was a guest. The guest list cannot be used as the determining factor—if it were, Meal6 might be judged equally suitable (something grilled was served to Anne, and she liked it). Nor can what was served be considered the important factor—if it were, every meal in which grilled fish of some sort was served would be judged equally useful. Rather, it is the combination of features in that particular experience that determine what is important in judging usefulness. The facts that Anne was a guest and that some sort of grilled fish was served, *occurring together in combination*, are what point out that this case is more useful than any others where Anne was a guest or where grilled fish was served.

One could write an evaluation function that combined guests and food served as an important factor when taken together, but that's not exactly what the case above predicts. In general, the combination of guests and food served will not be predictive unless the reasoner has had many experiences serving food to the same people over and over again and, then, only if the results of those experiences tended to cover a wide space. That is, if most of the time the combination of guests and food does not predict anything special about the outcome, then giving that combination high status in an evaluation function will not work well. On the other hand, it is worth giving high status to the fact that Anne (a particular person) was a guest and that fish (a particular food) was served. This one instance of the combination of guest and food served makes an important prediction.

One could add this combination to the set of criteria that similarity-judging procedures use. Though that would take care of this situation, it would still be inadequate overall. Other idiosyncratic combinations of features might still not be covered in the function. A gas grill, for example, might do a fine job of cooking meats but might not cook fish as nicely as charcoal does. We might want our similarity-judging procedures to pay attention to the fuel when fish is being grilled but not at any other time. The point is that there are infinite combinations of factors that can justify decisions or that can predict results. The job of keeping a generally applicable set of matching criteria up to date over time is difficult. As experiences are collected, more and more important idiosyncratic combinations of features might be found. Updating a single evaluation function so that it is always reliable is complex, if not impossible. Furthermore, even if one could be found and if it could be maintained, the complexity of applying it would make it inappropriate. Matching and ranking procedures are applied over and over again in a case-based system. They need to be computationally simple. An evaluation function that does the extra work of checking criteria for idiosyncratic cases all the time is necessarily more complex than it needs to be.

In order for matching functions to continue to be effective after new facts about the world are discovered, procedures that judge similarity must be updated over time. But updating a generally applicable set of criteria as additional combinations are discovered is clearly the wrong way to go about that. An alternative way is to evaluate each case for usefulness based on the particular combinations of features that were responsible for its decisions or its results and, in effect, to assign importance values to the dimensions of individual cases. These locally applicable values can then be used instead of the more generally applicable values when a case is idiosyncratic. In this way, the idiosyncrasies of particular situations can be taken into account in judging similarity when necessary, but they don't overburden the generally applicable means of evaluation.

Let's go back to the example to see how that works. First, we must assume that Meal1 designates which of its features are responsible for its results. Those that are responsible are that Anne was a guest and fish was served. It is these two features that are given primary importance in the match between the new situation and Meal1. Meal5 also designates which of its features are responsible for its result, in this case, the fact that salmon was prepared by grilling. In matching the new situation to Meal5, it is this feature that is assigned primary importance in the match. Meal1 and Meal5 are both judged useful, though by invoking different importance values. Both fit needed criteria, and both are made available to procedures making the decision about what to serve.

Of course, it can get more complex still, because, depending on the reasoning context, different feature combinations might be more important in judging goodness of fit than others. The case in which Anne didn't eat the fish might also hold information about what was done to recover: Hot dogs were put on the grill at the last minute. If a host served fish to a guest who did not eat fish and was trying to figure out a quick way to get the guest something to eat, remembering this case would help. But it would have to be judged similar along lines appropriate to recovering from the failure of serving fish rather than along the dimensions used above (those useful for evaluating a situation). A case might need the equivalent of several different sets of matching criteria associated with it—one for each use to which the case can be put.

Another issue that might be taken into account in judging usefulness is the extent to which the new case can be predicted to achieve the intended outcome. What's necessary here is for the reasoner to know what outcome it needs to achieve. The ranking process then is a compare-and-contrast process. The predictions of each retrieved case are projected onto the new situation. Projected outcomes are then compared to each other and the case belonging to the best projected outcome is chosen.

A doctor, for example, may be trying to decide which of several treatments to use on a patient. To make that decision, he might try to project the outcome of each. Choice of a treatment (and choice of a case to continue reasoning from) is based on which treatment is likely to deliver a more desirable outcome. In effect, he chooses the best case by using each to compute a solution and then choosing the best solution.

In the remainder of this chapter, we will explore schemes for judging similarity and ranking the usefulness of cases that take matching context into account. The simplest method, and the one alluded to in previous sections, is to assign multiple importance values to dimensions, making assignments in a contextually sensitive way and using numerical evaluation functions to compute match scores. Alternatively, one can label cases with their important features and the contexts in which each combination is important and then use preference heuristics to find the most useful cases. In a third alternative, one could do a relative comparison of several cases with one another and argue about which is likely to allow the best results. The first two methods are discussed here. The third is left for chapter 13, where interpretive case-based methods and the role of cases in persuasive argumentation is discussed.

9.3.4 Making Ranking Dynamic Through Multiple Assignments of Importance

The easiest way to implement a context-sensitive evaluation scheme, as alluded to in the baseball example, is by using several sets of importance criteria, each associated with conditions stating the circumstances under which it should be used. In practice, this can be done in several ways.

- Partition the case library, assigning a different set of importance criteria to each partition.
- Associate different importance criteria with different reasoning goals.
- Associate one or more sets of importance criteria to each case, each associated with a different task it can provide guidance for.

When only one reasoning goal will be served by a case library, but what is important varies with the type of new situation, the case library can be partitioned according to type and each partition assigned a different set of importance values for its case's dimensions. Let us return to the problem of determining salaries for baseball players. Cases in the case library might describe players and the salaries they get. Because different features of players are useful in ranking the worth of pitchers and fielders, it makes sense to partition the case library according to whether players are pitchers or fielders and to attach a different importance values to the dimensions describing each. As noted in a previous discussion, importance criteria associated with pitchers will give high importance to those dimensions characterizing successful pitching, emphasizing judging similarity based on those features that are important for success in pitching. Importance criteria associated with the fielding partition will give high importance to features important for fielding. Alternatively, if different skills are needed for each particular position, it is appropriate to partition the case library according to positions of players, assigning a different evaluation function to each. Another example comes from football or soccer. One judges defensive players differently than offensive ones. It therefore makes sense to partition the case library according to whether players play defensive or offensive positions, assigning to each partition importance values appropriate to comparing its players to each other.

The REMIND case-based reasoning shell (Cognitive Systems 1992) supports such partitioning through the use of what it calls *prototypes*. A prototype represents a partition of the case library, and each has a different ranking of case dimensions associated with it.

If multiple goals are to be supported by a case library, however, then partitioning by type is not enough. Cases in each partition might be evaluated for similarity differently depending on the reasoning goal they were being called on to support. To accommodate different reasoning goals, different evaluation functions can be associated with different reasoning goals.

When criterion for judging similarity vary both with the goal being addressed and the type of case, importance values are assigned taking both into account. Figure 9.11 shows that for baseball.

But even that is not enough when cases are highly idiosyncratic, as the example of Anne not eating grilled fish shows. For such circumstances, associating one or more sets of importance criteria *with each case* in the case library makes sense. Each set of values designates the purpose (reasoning goal) it serves and emphasizes those dimensions of the case that, if they match well, suggest that the case can serve that reasoning goal. In general, to do this, explanation-based methods of choosing indexes are applied, and those dimensions chosen as indexes are given high importance values.

9.3.5 Using Preferences to Implement a Relative Ranking Scheme

Implementing evaluation functions numerically is appealing for many reasons. Computations are quite simple and straightforward. Computations are of absolute degree of match and therefore require no references to the degree of match of other cases. When important components of context are taken into account in evaluation functions, a useful enough case is often found. Evaluation is easy to manage and is fast, both of which are important in building working systems. Indeed, using numeric evaluation functions to rank cases will probably be the method of choice for most applications of case-based problem solving.

On the other hand, the method has deficiencies. It is not guaranteed to be accurate, nor do the match scores it computes give any indication of why the match is a good one, something that is important in some applications.

Another way of implementing dynamic evaluation is by using a relative matching scheme—ranking cases with respect to one another rather than computing individual match scores. One way to do this ranking is with a preference scheme. In a preference scheme, several different means of ranking are played off against one another. Preference rules state, "All else being equal, choose the one with the following traits."

Such a scheme uses preference heuristics as filters. Partially-matching cases are sent through each filter in turn. The filter either chooses a set of cases that it prefers, or it allows the whole set through. In this way, the set of partially-matching cases is never whittled down to nothing. The case or set of cases most preferred by filters is returned. Cases that can address the reasoner's goal are preferred over others, if they exist, but if there are no cases that address that goal, cases that match on other features are retrieved.

Setting up such a scheme requires two considerations:

- Which preferences should be used?
- In what order should the preferences be applied?

Because goodness of match depends on a combination of the goals of the reasoner and the degree to which features of partially-matching cases were important in deriving their solutions or affecting their outcomes, preferences should, at a minimum, address these two aspects of matching context. This set of criteria, when applied, selects out cases that have the potential to provide guidance to a reasoner. Thus, these seem to be the criteria that should be applied before any others. Some cases that pass these tests might be better than others, however. Other preferences can choose the cases that are better, if that is important, or selection can be at random from the cases with these essential qualities.

All other things being equal, cases that suggest better answers and/or allow easier reasoning are preferred over others. When constructing solutions, cases that are easy to adapt to the new situation are preferable to those that are harder to adapt; cases that suggest cheaper solutions are preferred over those that suggest more expensive ones; and those that suggest solutions that are more likely to succeed are preferred over those that suggest less likely to succeed solutions. When evaluating, those that are more specifically similar to the new situation are preferred over less specific matches. In general, one chooses preference heuristics for those conditions that are both important to discriminate on and easy to compute.

PARADYME (Kolodner 1989) provides one implementation of a preference scheme. It uses six preferences heuristics to rank its cases, divided into three sets.

- For choosing cases that can address the reasoner's goal
  1. Goal-directed preference
  2. Salient-feature preference

- For pragmatically choosing better ones from that set
  3. Specificity preference
  4. Ease-of-adaptation preference

- For choosing among the rest
  5. Frequency preference
  6. Recency preference

Goal-directed preference is responsible for making sure that the retrieved case can address the purpose of the retrieval well; those cases that can best address the problem solver's goals are preferred over others. *Salient-feature preference* allows the relative similarity of a new case to an old one to be judged in the context of the old case. It is based on the principle that we should use experience to tell us which features of a new situation are the ones to focus on. PARADYME prefers cases that share a full combination of important features with the new problem over cases whose matching features are more randomly scattered.

These two preferences make up a minimal set. Together, they choose cases that can best address the reasoner's goal. Goal-directed preference chooses cases that can address the reasoner's goal. Salient-feature preference chooses from those the ones that match best on combinations of features important to achieving that goal.

PARADYME's next set of preference heuristics choose cases from that set that have the potential to result in better answers or that will allow easier computation of a solution. *Ease-of-adaptation preference* is based on the principle of utility and is specific to the needs of case-based reasoning. A case that is easier to adapt to a new situation is better than one that is harder to adapt. This heuristic says to prefer cases whose solutions are easier to adapt than those whose solutions are harder to adapt.[13] *Specificity preference* states that a more specific match

---

13. Alas, it is hard to say more than this about computing ease of adaptation. Though we know ease of adaptation is an important choice heuristic for determining which of several cases are better, there are currently no general-purpose criteria available for judging how hard or easy a case is to adapt.

is better than a less specific one. Cases that match more specifically are preferred over less specific matches. PARADYME has several ways to judge specificity. First, a case is a more specific match than another if the features that match in the less specific case are a proper subset of the features that match in the more specific case. Thus, a probe is more specifically matched by a case that matches all its features than one that matches only a subset. Second, a case matches more specifically than one of its ancestors in memory's generalization hierarchy. For example, a particular Italian meal is more specific than a generic Italian meal. Third, a case matches more specifically if the probe matches features in more of its parts. A meal, for example, is matched better if the new situation matches aspects of both its main course and its appetizer course than if it matches aspects of only one of those.

The final set of heuristics, those applied last, choose from the set of cases that are left after pragmatic concerns are taken care of. *Frequency preference* and *recency preference* are based on two principles psychologists have discovered—items that are referenced more frequently are more likely to be recalled than other similar items, and items that have been referenced more recently are more likely to be recalled than other similar items (all else being equal).

PARADYME has one set of preference heuristics implemented, but for any particular application, there might be others that are useful. For example, when solutions have widely varying costs of execution, preferring cases that suggest cheaper solutions is a pragmatic concern. This preference belongs in the second set, those that address pragmatics. A system that is aiming toward novel solutions might use a preference that selects weirder solutions over more normal ones. If it is not concerned with cost, then cost preferences would not be used.

Use of preferences is the first relative ranking scheme we have seen, and it presents different constraints than do the absolute schemes. The full set of candidate cases is ranked with respect to one another at once, and the ranking can be used only after some other procedure for retrieving candidate cases from the case library has already been run. There is no good way to interleave such ranking with retrieval. This has its advantages and disadvantages. A disadvantage is that full search of the case library needs to be carried out before ranking is done. Search procedures can't stop when they've gotten a good-enough case. If retrieval must be very efficient, then relative ranking procedures should only be used when retrieval of candidate cases is itself an efficient process. PARADYME was originally implemented on a SIMD-parallel machine. Initial retrieval was a parallel process that ran in time linear to the number of clauses in the description of the new situation. It retrieved all cases that partially matched the new situation. Application of preferences was a parallel process that ran when retrieval of partial matches was complete. Though parallel machines are not the only ones that can do retrieval quickly, it is worth bearing in mind that relative ranking procedures are particularly appropriate for parallel implementations.

In general, relative ranking schemes tend to require more computational power than absolute ones do, so it makes sense computationally to do the ranking of cases with respect to each other after a substantial set of candidate partially-matching cases is retrieved. The practice has been to use a coarse indexing scheme to retrieve partially-matching cases, using a finer-grained scheme during ranking. PARADYME, for example, retrieves partially-matching cases from the case library based on similarities between recorded features. All cases that match along recorded dimensions are retrieved.[14] Its cases are annotated with fine-grained indexes, chosen by the explanation-based index selection method, and they are the ones used when evaluating which of the several cases can be most useful.

The major advantage to ranking cases after initial retrieval has been carried out is that retrieval can be made flexible. In PARADYME, for example, retrieval of a case that can address the reasoner's current goal is preferred, and indeed, one of these can usually be found if the case library is large enough and indexed well. But retrieval of something that matches well but does not directly address the reasoner's current goal is also possible when no case is available that can address that goal. Cases that match on more relevant features are preferred over those that match on random features, but if none are available, then those that match best on other features are recalled. In addition, one can easily change secondary matching criteria using a preference scheme by adding, deleting, or changing preferences.

After so much discussion in this and previous chapters of the importance of goals to retrieval and the need to retrieve cases that address the reasoner's goal, it might seem strange to list flexibility of retrieval as an advantage. Indeed, for most applications, retrieval of a case that can best achieve the reasoner's current goal is the best way to achieve good answers quickly. From a cognitive point of view, however, allowing only goal-directed retrieval seems counter to intuitions. We all get reminded of cases from time to time that don't obviously address what we are trying to accomplish, yet sometimes they provide very useful information. Use of a preference-based relative ranking scheme begins to provide an explanation of how that might happen.

9.4 SUMMARY

Retrieval processes retrieve from the case library a set of potentially useful cases, all of which partially match the new situation. Matching and ranking processes choose the best, most useful, or good enough, cases from among that set. Building blocks include the finding of correspondences between cases, computing degree of similarity of corresponding features, and assigning importance values to dimensions of cases. Methods of matching and ranking are only as good as the available building blocks. If a system tries to match values that are not in correspondence, it won't compute good match scores. If importance ratings are not sensitive enough to context or if dimensional matches are not consistent, then match scores will be unreliable.

Finding correspondences can be done by several means. In general, methods begin by assuming that similarly named slots and similarly named predicates correspond. When values filling corresponding slots or filling arguments in a clause don't match, however, methods for finding correspondences begin to question the correspondence. Either commonsense reconciliation heuristics or causal heuristics are used to complete the set of correspondences. When a

---

14. PARADYME's retrieval scheme is actually somewhat more complicated than this. Retrieved cases must have similarity in their core descriptors (the ones that describe the type of case) and also must share idiosyncratic descriptors. In addition, shared descriptors must include context-setting descriptors and scene-specific descriptors. For example, if the case library holds records of medical patients, then cases retrieved initially must share diagnosis designations (core descriptor) and signs and symptoms (idiosyncratic descriptors), both of which are context-setting. They must also share scene descriptors, for example, the same test was carried out in both.

new situation and a case it is being matched to are from different domains, problems arise, because representations will tend to share only a small subset of their slots or predicates. Designing a representational structure and vocabulary that spans domains and structure mapping are two ways of finding correspondences across domains.

Dimensional matching can be done by several methods: comparison based on placement in an abstraction hierarchy, computation of distance on a qualitative scale, computation of distance on a quantitative scale, and comparison of the degree to which features play the designated functional role.

Assigning importance to case dimensions is another key to selecting the most useful cases. Importance of a dimension to a match depends on its overall impact with respect to achieving the reasoner's current goal and its specific impact in individual cases. There is a full spectrum of methods for assigning importance values. They can be assigned globally over the entire case library (independent of context); assigned to partitions of the case library; assigned locally on a case-by-case basis; assigned several to a case; or computed on the fly at retrieval time.

Putting it all together, there are several kinds of methods for choosing useful cases. The easiest way of choosing is to use a numerical nearest-neighbor procedure that combines importance of each dimension with its degree of match and sums the scores to create a match score for each case. One chooses the case with the best score. Such a scheme can be made more or less sensitive by assigning importance values in more or less context-sensitive ways and heuristically choosing an appropriate set of importance values for each match.

Heuristic means of choice include choosing a case that shows sufficient evidence that it can be useful and using preference heuristics to sift through the set of potentially matching cases according to a set of preference criteria. CASEY's model-based evidence heuristics, also used to find correspondences, provide an example of the first kind of procedure; any case that passes the tests of the evidence rules can be returned to the case-based reasoner for use. PARADYME's preference method provides an example of the second kind.

Other methods for choosing useful cases combine numerical and heuristic methods. Already mentioned is the method of choosing a set of importance values heuristically and then running numerical matching and ranking procedures. Another combination method applies censors or exclusion criteria to available cases to exclude those that can easily be shown not to be applicable. An available matching or ranking method is then applied to the remainder of the set.

10

Indexing and Retrieval

Previous chapters have discussed selection of indexes, means of organizing a case library, algorithms for searching that case library, and a means of determining how well a case in the case library matches a new situation. The processes are used both to insert new cases in the case library and to retrieve cases that can help the reasoner reason about a new situation. Figure 10.1, a copy of the figure from the introduction to this section of the book, shows how these processes interact to allow retrieval and update to happen. A case is analyzed and its indexes extracted, the case library is searched, and the case is either added in identified places or the cases in those places are retrieved. Finally, the most useful of the retrieved cases are selected out for further use.

Each of these individual processes has been discussed, and one of the things that should have become clear in those discussions is that the relationships between these processes are complex. Achieving accuracy and efficiency during retrieval is a function of the index selection procedures, the organizational structures, and the search processes in combination. In this chapter, we revisit indexing to look at its effect on retrieval.

There are several topics covered in this chapter. First is the assessment of a new situation before and during retrieval to determine where similar cases might reside in the case library. The chapters about indexing discussed the means by which one chooses indexes for cases when adding them to the case library. Given a complete case, that is, one whose problem had been solved and/or where feedback about outcome was available, one examines the effect of the situation description on the solution to choose some types of indexes and the effect of the situation description and solution on the outcome to choose other types.

In reasoning about new situations, we would like to select out of the case library the cases that have the most to contribute to the new situation. In the best of all worlds, we would

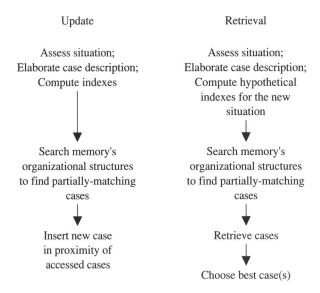

FIGURE 10.1   Update and Retrieval Processes

be able to do that if we could choose for the new situation the indexes it would have if it were already in the case library. Because new situations are only partially specified, however, that is impossible. Given only a description of a problem situation, for example, we can't easily choose out those features that are more important for choosing its solution—we don't know what the solution is yet, and figuring out what is important to computing it is part and parcel of the problem that needs to be solved. In general, because new situations are only partially described and partially understood, we may not be able to accurately specify some of their important derived features, those that might discriminate a relevant case from the others in the case library. Retrieval of useful cases sometimes requires making educated guesses about what some of those descriptors are. **Situation assessment** is the process of sizing up a new situation and determining what the indexes for a similar case would be if it were in the case library. It is an incremental and cyclical process. Part of the work happens before search, part happens during search, and if initial assessment has proven too inaccurate or incomplete to allow useful cases to be retrieved, part happens after search.

The second topic we cover is the implementation of indexes. Chapter 8 shows that one way to implement indexes is as the labels on the arcs of discrimination networks and redundant discrimination networks. Chapter 9 shows that indexes can be implemented as weights attached to dimensions of cases and used by numeric evaluation functions. Indexes can also be implemented as annotations or labels attached to cases designating which of its features contributed to its solution or outcome.

Finally, we discuss the achievement of accuracy, efficiency, and flexibility in retrieval.

10.1 SITUATION ASSESSMENT: CHOOSING INDEXES FOR RETRIEVAL

When we add a new case to the case library, the process of choosing its indexes is a process of assessing what the case could be useful for and in what situations. We begin with a full description of a situation, and in choosing indexes, we select out some descriptors as identifying ones.

During retrieval, our goal is to retrieve cases that have the potential to allow good inferences to be made about a new situation. We want to find cases that are most similar to the new situation along dimensions deemed to be the most important ones. We do this by, in essence, imagining what the indexes for the new situation would be if it were well understood and then finding cases in the case library that are indexed the same way.

But there is a disadvantage at retrieval time that isn't there at update time. When we begin to reason about a new situation, we normally don't understand it very well. An assessment process that can size up the situation is needed to guess what its indexes might be.

Consider, for example, the assessment a program like CYRUS must do. It is asked about a situation in which the secretary of state of the United States was talking to some news reporters. In order to recall the event, it must assess the situation. Was it a diplomatic meeting, a briefing, a press conference, or a friendly get-together? Each has a different description, is indexed differently, and is found in a different organizational structure. Alternatively, it is asked about a visit from a friend/colleague from a foreign country. It must retrieve that event. Is it a friendly visit? a colleagial visit? a visit from a foreigner? an instance of good friends spending quality time together? a instance of a house guest creating extra work? a chance to go to a great restaurant? a chance to show off the interior decorating? something else entirely? Again, depending on the interpretation the program gives the new situation, different potential indexes will be chosen for it, some prohibiting retrieval because nothing matches, others resulting in retrieval of cases different than expected. Either situation might be interpreted according to one, many, or all its different renderings. Each may be interpreted differently at different times. Each may be interpreted differently depending on who is doing the interpreting.

Situation assessment, or **situation analysis**, is the process of sizing up a situation. It includes figuring out what kind of situation the new one is, what is important about it, and what else may be true about it besides what is patently obvious. In situation assessment, the raw details of a situation are interpreted and analyzed, and a coherent rendering of the situation is produced. The rendering is more complete than the raw situation, but it is subject to the idiosyncrasies of the reasoner. One person's rendering of a situation may be different from another person's. One computer program's rendering might be different from another's. The rendering of the situation might also be inaccurate. With incomplete information, we often make poor inferences. Thus, several renderings of the situation might be needed before a satisfactory one is found.

Nonetheless, deriving some coherent rendering of a new situation, whether consistent with somebody else's rendering or not, is necessary for case retrieval, for two reasons:

■ The raw representation of a new situation may not sufficiently match anything in the case library. This happens when a new situation is described along dimensions different from those used as indexes or descriptive features of cases in the case library. Elaborating the description of the new situation in order to bridge the gap between its description and descriptions of cases in the case library may be a necessary prerequisite to retrieving any cases at all.

■ The raw representation of a new situation may be so generally described that it matches large numbers of items in the case library that are very different from each other, and there is no good way of determining which are better than others. Elaborating the situation allows a reasoner to distinguish which of the many partially-matching cases has the potential to be most useful.[1]

Some examples from CASEY and JUDGE will illustrate:

CASEY is trying to diagnose a new case. It has a detailed description of the new patient's signs and symptoms. But cases are indexed in the case library according to the diagnostic conditions of the patients.

JUDGE is attempting to sentence a teenager who has killed somebody during a fight. It knows the sequence of events that led to the killing. It knows who was involved and where it happened. But cases are indexed in the case library according to the motivations of the killers, the degree of escalation of violence, and other "calculated" features.

Our guidelines for indexing cases tell us that cases should be indexed by features and feature combinations that are both usefully predictive and concrete enough to be recognized. A feature that is concrete enough to be recognized is one that is either observable or can be computed with very little inference. The problem we see in both these examples is that although the features used for indexing are good predictive features and concrete enough to be recognized, they are not directly observable. Deriving such features requires at least some effort.

This tension between predictiveness and observability is a common one. It would not do to limit indexing to observable features, because opportunities to remember useful cases that are similar along unobservable dimensions would be lost. For the same reason, one cannot limit indexes to only those predictive features that are observable. The more observable an index is, the more easily it can be used. But the more predictive an index is, the more useful it is.

This is the dilemma in CASEY. Signs and symptoms are directly observable and concrete. But combinations of signs and symptoms are not the most predictive case features. The

---

1. When using a discrimination network under these circumstances, traversal stops prematurely at an internal node without reaching a leaf node holding a case. Sometimes, when this happens, all cases below that internal node make the same prediction, and any one could be retrieved and used. Other times, however, the cases below the internal node each make different predictions. Some way of traversing further through the memory is needed to distinguish which of those cases are better matches. Derivation of case features that would allow such traversal to happen allows that.

same disorder can manifest itself in many different ways. And the same combinations of symptoms can show up in several different disorders. Because the case library is not large enough to be representative of every different way a disorder can manifest itself, retrieval and matching based on similarity of signs and symptoms is not accurate enough to be useful. Signs and symptoms are predictive in CASEY only in the context of diagnostic states (disorders). Thus, its cases are indexed primarily by combinations of diagnostic states in a patient's diagnosis. Similarity of signs and symptoms only makes sense within that context.

This arrangement poses a severe problem at retrieval time. CASEY must diagnose patients given only each patient's signs and symptoms, but it needs to use diagnostic states in order to retrieve useful matching cases. CASEY resolves this problem by inferring *plausible* diagnostic states of a new patient based on the patient's signs and symptoms. It retrieves cases based on plausible diagnostic states, and in a later step, it uses its evidence rules to rank retrieved cases for closeness of fit by comparing their symptoms in the contexts of diagnostic states.[2]

JUDGE's (Bain 1986) dilemma is similar to CASEY's. Predictive features in the domain are not directly observable. In JUDGE's domain, however, the computations necessary to derive predictive features are quite extensive and expensive to compute. Computing the motivation of a defendent, for example, requires, among other things, analysis of his state of mind when going into the fight, who started it, and what goals and emotions that may have evoked. JUDGE derives necessary predictive features before it attempts case retrieval, however, because without such interpretation, it would be unable to retrieve usefully similar cases.

Whatever the reasons are that situation assessment is needed, it is accomplished through an elaboration process. Derivable features of the case are computed, and those features, along with the original description, are used for retrieval and matching.

Elaboration can be done in several different ways. Inference procedures might be associated with dimensions specifying how they can be inferred from given information. CASEY knows that plausible diagnostic states can be inferred by looking up known symptoms in the causal model and retrieving from it the diagnostic states they imply. JUDGE has a procedure for computing the motivation of defendants and another for computing the degree of violence of a crime. Another way to elaborate a situation description is to recall cases similar to it and infer that it has the features of similar cases.[3]

The concept of elaboration itself is simple. One starts with a partial description of an item and makes plausible inferences to add to the description. Its complexity comes from two places. First, a single elaboration might require significant computational power and/or time. Computing the motivation of criminals, for example, is a complex operation. Second, there may be large numbers of possible elaborations that can be carried out, each of which takes at least some power and time. Together, the needed computational power could be immense. Inferring a plausible diagnostic state is an easy computation for CASEY, for example, but the more symptoms are known about a patient, the more of these inferences must be done. For

---

2. The description of CASEY's *evidence rules* and the way it uses them for matching is in chapter 9.

3. Of course, this can be a circular kind of reasoning, and care must be taken not to fall into circularity in using this method.

these reasons, we need some way of determining which elaborations are worth computing. The complexity of elaboration comes in considering how it can be controlled.

When elaboration is expensive, as in JUDGE, or potentially extensive, as in CASEY, it must be controlled in an intelligent way, weighing the benefits of the computation against its costs. It makes sense for CASEY to derive all plausible diagnostic states before attempting retrieval because it is a cheap operation and one that is required for accurate retrieval. With only signs and symptoms available as descriptors, it would be impossible to judge which of several partially-matching cases was most usefully similar. JUDGE's elaborations are much more complex than CASEY's, but JUDGE, too, must do those that are necessary for accurate retrieval. Because its elaborations are computationally complex, however, JUDGE needs to be sure that it does only the derivations that are absolutely necessary.

How can we know which elaborations are the right ones? The trivial answer is that those elaborations that are necessary to enable retrieval are the ones that must be done. We can figure out which are the right ones by looking at processes that compute indexes for cases. Those dimensions that are used to index cases in memory are, obviously, the ones that are needed to enable retrieval. But there may be few enough items in memory that not all such elaborations need be done. Or, some one or a few elaborations may be enough to determine which is the best-matching case—not all possible elaborations may be needed.

The control problem in situation assessment is the problem of figuring out which elaborations should be carried out. In a system where few elaborations are needed and all are inexpensive, this is not an issue, as all elaborations can be done. But when some elaborations are expensive, when there are many elaborations that could be done, and when elaboration could be inaccurate, some control of the process is needed.

Situation assessment can be controlled by a three-tiered process. Before search is attempted, the set of dimensions known to be necessary for good retrieval is elaborated. We will refer to this process as *context setting*. The dimensions to be elaborated during context setting are generally designated on a checklist. CHEF, CASEY, and JUDGE all perform context setting. During search, elaboration is done on an as-needed basis, using the case library to designate which dimensions it needs elaborated so that it can discriminate among several items in memory. We will refer to this process as *context refinement*. ANON (Owens 1989b, 1993), CASCADE (Simoudis 1991b, 1992), and several programs that use discrimination networks perform context refinement. After search, the set of items retrieved is examined to see if they are indeed as useful as they could be. If not, the situation is reassessed, and search is attempted again. We will refer to this process as *redefining the context*. PROTOS and AUTHOR (Dehn 1989) (a short-story writing program) redefine their contexts as a result of analyzing what they find during search. Depending on the needs of a reasoner, one or all of these processes might be used for elaboration. CYRUS uses a combination of all three methods, and the methodology called *validated retrieval* (Simoudis 1991b, 1992), implemented in CASCADE, uses the same process to achieve both of the latter two effects.

10.1.1 Before Search: Context Setting Using a Checklist

Before search is attempted, it is often advantageous to assess the new situation sufficiently to identify its predictive dimensions. When the case features needing elaboration vary little from problem to problem or situation to situation, the easiest way to control derivation of needed features is to specify to the program which dimensions should be elaborated. The program can then compute those dimensions before it attempts retrieval.

CASEY, for example, always computes plausible diagnostic states before attempting retrieval. JUDGE always computes motivations of fighters, the degree of escalation of violence, and so on, before attempting retrieval. CYRUS, whose cases span many different types of situations, always infers the type of a new situation (e.g., diplomatic meeting, briefing, diplomatic trip, state dinner) before attempting retrieval.

Under this scheme, the hard work is done by the knowledge engineer or applications builder. It is up to that person to determine which dimensions are the ones that require elaboration and to judge the cost and benefit of elaborating each one. In general, elaborations that must be done prior to searching memory correspond to case dimensions that serve as *primary* indexes or identifiers for cases. CYRUS, for example, uses type of situation to group cases in redundant discrimination networks, and without type, it would not be able choose a redundant discrimination network to search. Type of situation is a primary index. CASEY's primary indexes are its diagnostic states—other features, such as signs and symptoms, serve as identifiers only within the context of that primary designation. Those dimensions that partition the case library into large groups, each of which has distinctive kinds of solutions or results, are the primary indexes. These indexes, which tend to be most predictive of solutions or outcomes, are also the ones whose values need to be known before retrieval begins.

Implementation of this scheme involves giving the program a checklist of dimensions to elaborate, along with procedures for carrying out those elaborations, or providing it with a list of strategies that can be run to carry out elaboration. The program can then run down the checklist or the strategy list and do each of the required computations.

JUDGE, CASEY, CYRUS and CHEF all use checklists of dimensions. JUDGE's checklist includes the motivations of the defendant and the degree of violence of the incident. JUDGE uses procedures associated with each of these dimensions to compute, for each new situation, its values along these dimensions. It then moves on to retrieval. CASEY's checklist includes in it just one thing: diagnostic states. It uses its procedure for computing diagnostic states to compute plausible diagnostic states for each new situation before attempting to do retrieval. CHEF's checklist designates that it should anticipate potential problematic interactions between its goals. It does this, using a case-based method, before attempting to retrieve cases that can help it solve its problem. CYRUS uses something that looks more like a checklist of strategies. Before retrieval, CYRUS elaborates only one thing: type of situation. It has a set of heuristics called *component-to-context instantiation strategies* that it uses to infer the type of a situation before attempting retrieval. It runs down that list to infer the situation type.

Though all these programs use a global checklist to control elaboration, checklist-based elaboration can be made sensitive to context. For example, elaboration checklists or strategies can be associated with particular kinds of tasks the system does, so that it can specialize its elaboration to its task. Different dimensions may be appropriately elaborated when a reasoner is retrieving cases to help with explanation, for example, than when it is retrieving cases to help with critiquing. Or elaboration checklists can be associated with different types of cases, similarly to the way index-selection checklists are associated with different types of cases in CYRUS (see chapter 7).

10.1.2 During Search: Incremental Context Refinement

The second means of controlling derivation is to derive features as needed during retrieval. When needed derivations vary from problem to problem, this makes sense. One way to do this is to use memory's content and organization to guide elaboration. The process can be a static or a dynamic one. The static version of the process uses memory's discrimination networks to guide elaboration (Kolodner 1983a, 1984). Discrimination networks and redundant discrimination networks are traversed by asking the questions on the nodes of a new situation and then traversing the branch whose label best matches the answer derived from the new situation. Often the answers to questions asked by a discrimination network are already known, and answering the question means looking up an answer. When the answers to questions are not yet known, they are derived. Memory's questions tell the reasoner which elaborations are necessary and when to do them.

Consider, for example, the discrimination network in Figure 10.2, repeated from chapter 8. Let us assume that we are attempting to solve a dispute between two children who both want the same avocado. The first question in the network asks what kind of dispute we are looking for. If we have not yet specified the dispute type, memory tells us that this is an important dimension to elaborate. We compute the type for this dispute and determine that it is a physical dispute. The next question asks what the disputant goal is. We already know that it is ownership, and we follow that branch. Next we are asked which piece of the object we are concerned with. Again, we don't know, but we make the necessary inferences and infer that they both want the fruit of the avocado. Moving on, the next question asks the type of object. We match to type fruit and retrieve the Orange Dispute.

The dynamic version of the process retrieves all partially-matching cases and suggests useful elaborations based on the similarities and differences of those cases (Owens 1989b,

FIGURE 10.2   A Prioritized Discrimination Network

1993; Simoudis 1992). Those elaborations are carried out, retrieval is attempted again, and if additional discrimination is needed to find one or a small set of well-matching cases, the process is repeated. In both Owens's and Simoudis's schemes, the memory tends to be flat (unorganized), and retrieval of partial matches is a parallel operation. All cases that partially-match the new item are retrieved. Discrimination is then done on the fly. Cases are analyzed for their similarities and differences, and those dimensions that can discriminate some set of partially-matching cases as better matches than the others are chosen for elaboration. An elaboration might be chosen because it divides the set of available cases in equal portions, or it might be chosen because it can identify a specific useful case. Alternatively, it might be chosen because it can divide the set of available cases along dimensions relevant to the reasoner's current reasoning goal.

Consider, for example, the following illustration from Owens's (1988) ANON. ANON is asked for advice about the probable results of a situation in which a task is to be carried out with a limited and insufficient amount of a necessary resource—a sparse and quite abstract description of a situation. ANON finds four proverbs[4] that all match this specification.

1. A pig with two owners is sure to die of hunger.
2. Grasp all, lose all.
3. If you run after two hares, you will catch neither.
4. If you buy meat cheap, when it boils you will smell what you have saved.

Because they are about several different kinds of situations, and each predicts different results, ANON needs to discriminate among them, determining which is more appropriate to the current situation. ANON therefore preceeds to identify the dimensions of the new situation that, if known, would allow it to determine which is more applicable. A dimension that can discriminate is the type of resource. Two of the proverbs are about a capability as a resource, one is about money as a resource, and one is about owners as a resource. It therefore asks for the type of resource (by asking specifically whether capabilities are spread too thin) and is told that, indeed, not enough capability is the problem. It finds two proverbs, numbers 2 and 3 above, both of which give the same advice—if you don't have enough of some needed capability, you will fail if you try to do everything that needs to be done.[5]

---

4. ANON stores proverbs rather than cases in its library. Proverbs are the advice gleaned from individual cases. They are generally stated in terms of real-world items and processes, and though they don't give all the details of a case, they tend to be concrete enough that they play a similar role. ANON uses proverbs to give advice about planning situations.

5. ORCA (Bareiss and Slator 1991, 1992; Slator and Bareiss 1992) implements a different version of the dynamic process to help users specify cases well. The user describes his or her case as best he or she can to the system. ORCA retrieves from its library the case that best matches this partial description. It then compares the retrieved case to the new situation, extracting from the retrieved case those types of situation descriptors that are not specified in the new situation and that have been predictive previously. It asks its user to specify the new situation better along those dimensions. It continues in this way until a full description of a situation is derived. This process is similar in spirit to Norman's (Norman and Bobrow 1979) incremental elaboration process and to the problem specification process implemented in RABBIT (Williams et al. 1982), which provided a sort of case-based interface to a database.

The situation above is a simple one. A small set of items is found, and one useful discrimination is found that can divide the set. The process becomes more complex when there are several possible elaborations that could be done at any time. A validated retrieval example (Simoudis 1991a) will show that.[6] Validated retrieval, described briefly in chapter 8, is used for diagnosis. The elaborations that are generally needed after partially-matching cases are retrieved are those that can validate or rule out the diagnosis suggested by retrieved cases. Here, the system is trying to diagnose what is wrong with an automobile. It knows that the car is a Mazda, model 626, model year 1985, with a 2.0 liter EFI engine, and mileage of 51,293, and that the problem is that the car won't start. It retrieves four partially-matching cases, each of which suggests a different problem and repair. Figure 10.3 shows the new problem and the four cases that are retrieved.

When we examine the cases that are retrieved, we see that four different validations are suggested, requiring four separate elaborations: determining the fuel level, determining the condition of the gas gauge, determining the condition of the fuel injector, and determining the condition of the gas pump. When several elaborations are suggested, some are generally more useful than others, and some are generally more expensive than others. Checking the fuel level, for example, is easier (cheaper) than checking the condition of the gas gauge or the gas pump, both of which require at least some dismantling of the car. With no additional information about which problem is more common, it makes sense to try the cheaper elaborations (e.g. by carrying out tests) before more expensive ones. If one of these serves to ascertain which case is the best match, the more expensive ones can be avoided. When information about probability is available, it, of course, must be considered in addition to expense of computation in determining which elaboration to do first. An expensive elaboration might be worth doing if it is highly probable that the case it goes with is the best match.

Both redundant discrimination schemes and dynamic schemes generally suggest a set of elaborations at any time, not just one. Some have the potential to be more fruitful than others. Some might be so expensive that, even if potentially fruitful, they wouldn't be worth computing except as a last resort. Some means of guiding choice of what to elaborate is needed, whether the scheme is static or dynamic. The rule of thumb, of course, is that the benefit of any elaboration should outweigh its cost. The question is one of how to make sure that happens.

Two different schemes have been invoked to provide that control. Under one scheme, procedures that build memory's organizational structures make sure discriminations are entered into networks in order of priority. Under the other scheme, control is imposed at retrieval time, using functions that compute the relative worth and the relative cost of elaborations that are requested. The first is appropriate in static discrimination schemes with limited redundancy. The second is appropriate in dynamic schemes and when discrimination networks are highly redundant.

When control is handled by procedures that build memory's organizational structures, discrimination is restricted at the time the network is being built so that at retrieval time only important paths are ever followed. So, for example, one way to provide control is to make sure that questions asked in the discrimination network are in order of importance, with most

---

6. Validated retrieval is implemented in several computer-related troubleshooting domains. The example given here, however, is a simple one that shows well what validated retrieval is about.

CASE 1

make:	MAZDA	**model:**	626	**model year:**	1988
engine type:	2.0L EFI	**mileage:**	12,498		

problem: Engine is stalling.
val. proc.:   The fuel injector was clogged→Condition of fuel injector.
repair: Cleaned the fuel injector.

CASE 2

make:	MAZDA	**model:**	626	**model year:**	1984
engine type:	2.0L EFI	**mileage:**	67,183		

problem: Engine does not start.
val. proc.:   The car had a broken gas pump→Condition of gas pump.
repair: Replaced the gas pump.

CASE 3

make:	MAZDA	**model:**	626	**model year:**	1987
engine type:	1.8L EFI	**mileage:**	23,077		

problem: Engine does not start.
val. proc.:   No fuel existed in the tank→Check fuel level.
repair: Filled the gas tank.

CASE 4

make:	Toyota	**model:**	Camry	**model year:**	1987
engine type:	2.8L	**mileage:**	45,774		

problem: Not good gas mileage.
val. proc.:   Leaky fuel line→Condition of fuel line.
repair: Replaced the part of the fuel line with the leak.

(a) Cases in CC's case base

NEW PROBLEM

make:	MAZDA	**model:**	626	**model year:**	1985
engine type:	2.0L EFI	**mileage:**	51,293		

problem: Engine does not start.

(b) The surface features of a car problem

FIGURE 10.3   A New Problem and Several Cases for Validated Retrieval

important questions at the top. With a network set up this way, one can be sure that the questions discrimination networks ask are all relevant ones. Another way to provide control is to discriminate in the network only along truly important dimensions. No discriminations on more mundane dimensions are done. Again, if discrimination is restricted in this way, we can be sure that only important elaborations will ever be requested by memory.

There are advantages and disadvantages to schemes like this. The advantage, of course, is that only important derivations are ever requested by memory. The disadvantages are more plentiful. First, as discussed in chapter 8, it is hard, if not impossible, to set up a discrimination network perfectly, especially when new items are added to it dynamically over time. Though the network will tend to discriminate well initially, there is no guarantee that it will continue to discriminate efficiently as it grows. Second, it is hard to deal with missing information in such a network. When some value cannot be derived, the network provides no guidance on how to proceed without that information. Finally, such a scheme imposes a fair amount of rigidity on retrieval. Cases can be retrieved based only on a priori computations of the importance of their features. There is no way to retrieve a case based on features not known to be important descriptors at the time the case was inserted into the memory.

Despite its drawbacks, there are many applications in which such a scheme is entirely appropriate.[7] If it is expected that any feature that is needed can be derived, then missing features is no problem. If the costs of computations are not high, then a network that adheres to real-world importances of dimensions is not necessary. If new items are rarely added to the network, and if it can be set it up to discriminate according to the priorities of dimensions, then again, these disadvantages don't count for much. Finally, if all predictions about the usefulness of a case can be made before it is added to the memory, then the rigidity of the scheme is not an issue.

The other means of control is to provide it at retrieval time. Under this scheme, when several elaborations are suggested, a set of processes judge the cost and potential benefits of each. Elaborations whose potential benefits outweigh the costs are carried out. ANON does this by keeping track of the *discriminating power* and *cost* of inferring each dimension of its representations (Owens 1993). Discriminating power is the extent to which a feature divides a set. ANON chooses to elaborate the dimension with the least cost and most utility in terms of discriminating power and function. For example, if the system is operating in a resource-constrained situation and needs to infer a recovery strategy, it prefers to elaborate those dimensions that are discriminating with respect to the resources used for recovery, preferring dimensions that are cheaper to derive over those that require more computation. There are, of course, many technical issues still to be ironed out. How do we represent utility? How do we judge it? How do we measure cost? And so on. The research world has not answered these questions. For many applications, however, satisfactory implementations based on the general framework just presented are not difficult to design.

10.1.3 After Retrieval: Redefining the Context

Situation assessment is the understanding piece of case-based reasoning. It is the process that evaluates a situation to determine where in memory knowledge useful to dealing with a new situation may reside. Indeed, we can't solve a problem well unless we understand the problem and the situation it is embedded in. But our understanding of a problem may evolve over time, and the initial assessment we make of a situation may not be a good one. An initial interpreta-

---

7. However, these disadvantages do discount the scheme as cognitively plausible.

tion of a situation may prove not to be fruitful when solving a problem, and some other interpretation may be necessary. Situation assessment procedures might then have to reassess or redefine the situation.

Consider, for example, the following situation: A mediator is trying to help Israel and Egypt come to an agreement over ownership of the Sinai Desert. The mediator assesses the problem as a physical dispute, that is, a dispute over an object, the Sinai. Based on this assessment, he sees ownership as the key, and based on his experiences mediating ownership disputes, he suggests the land be split down the middle, giving half to Israel and half to Egypt. Egypt and Israel both protest. Sticking with the same interpretation of the situation, the mediator tries to find another way of dividing the land that will work—making sure the divisions are worth the same amount, making sure each country is ceded historical and religious places in the Sinai that are important to it, and so on. Neither Egypt nor Israel is satisfied with any of the suggestions. Eventually, the mediator figures out that he is on the wrong track, and he tries to reassess the situation. If it isn't an argument over ownership of an object, then it must be a different kind of argument. He sets himself the task of figuring out what kind of argument it is.

This reassessment task is what we are referring to as redefining the context. When we redefine context, we change the values of one or several *primary descriptors* of the case—those that are the most predictive. For the mediator in this example, and for the MEDIATOR program, the type of argument is a primary descriptor; each suggests several solution frameworks. For PROTOS, diagnostic categories are its primary descriptors. CYRUS's primary descriptors are its types of events. During retrieval, we try to stick with primary descriptors that were chosen before retrieval, and we elaborate or refine other descriptors of a new situation. When we find that method is not allowing us to retrieve cases that solve our problem, the next step is this one—redefining the primary descriptors.

Few case-based programs do this, and there is not a lot of methodology to present about how to do it. Those programs that do redefine their context, however, provide illustrations of how it can be done.

MEDIATOR and PROTOS both use a case-based methodology to reassess their situation and to redefine their context for search. Both reassess in response to failures. When MEDIATOR fails to come up with a solution that its clients agree to, it asks itself why it failed. Its first attempt to answer that question is case-based. It looks to see if it has ever failed in a similar way previously. If so, it looks to see if its new failure is of the same sort. When MEDIATOR fails to solve the Sinai Dispute appropriately the first time, for example, it remembers the Orange Dispute. There, the failure to derive a good solution came from misunderstanding the goals of the disputants. MEDIATOR asks itself whether there are other goals Israel and Egypt might have in addition to ownership. Each time MEDIATOR elaborates a problem description due to failure, it also checks to see whether the problem should be redefined. In this case it should. Rather than being a dispute over a physical object, it is a political dispute—a dispute over goals themselves.

PROTOS reassesses its context definitions as a result of failed validation. PROTOS's first step is to guess at a diagnosis for its new situation using knowledge associating situation descriptors with diagnostic categories. The chosen diagnostic category becomes its primary descriptor or context for search. PROTOS then attempts to validate its diagnosis by matching its new situation to cases with the chosen diagnosis. When an attempted match fails, PROTOS is left with a designation of the differences between the new situation and the one it attempted to match to. Some differences are minor and suggest that match to a different case within the same diagnostic category be attempted. Others are indicative of the need to choose a different diagnostic category. If any of its differences indicate that need, it chooses the new diagnostic category as its hypothesis and repeats the process from there.[8] The process itself will be clearer after more detailed discussion of PROTOS in chapter 13.

CYRUS redefines its context using context-definition heuristics. Some of these heuristics know how to infer the type of a situation from given components. For example, it knows that situations in which diplomats from several different countries talk to each other are likely to be `diplomatic meetings`. It knows that a situation in which a diplomat travels to a foreign country is likely to be a `diplomatic trip`. Other strategies know how to infer the type and details of an event related to the one it is focusing on. For example, `diplomatic trips` are normally for the purpose of `negotiation` and normally contain within them one or more `diplomatic meetings` and several state ceremonies, such as `welcomes` at the airport and `state dinners`. When asked a question, CYRUS's first task was to assess the situation. Based on its assessment, it searched its memory for similar cases. If it was not successful, or if it wanted additional cases, it reassessed the situation and searched again. Reassessment meant either using its first set of strategies to come up with an alternative type of event or using its second set of strategies to search for a related event that, if found, would point to the type of event it was actually looking for.

Suppose, for example, that CYRUS is trying to remember the dates of one of Cyrus Vance's trips to Israel. It begins by searching for diplomatic trips to Israel. But there may be too many for it to find the one it is looking for without additional detail. There may not be additional detail about the trip itself that allows this trip to be discriminated from other ones (because the information that is available is not of the type used for indexing trips). But the additional information that is available might allow some other type of event to be recalled that would provide a pointer to the trip. Suppose, for example, that the system is told that during this trip, Vance visited a particular museum. Changing the context to `museum visit` and searching for the specified one might result in retrieval of an event that happened during that trip. Either the museum visit will supply the dates, or it may include information in it (e.g., the time of year or who was with Vance) that, when added to the original specification of the trip, will allow the appropriate trip to be retrieved.

Because CYRUS's strategies address the retrieval of events for the purpose of fact retrieval rather than for the purpose of problem solving, I will not give more detail about its strategies. More detail can be found in Kolodner (1983a, 1983b, 1984). What is important to take away from this discussion are two things: first, that reassessing a situation is sometimes necessary because all the information needed for assessment is not available initially at retrieval time, and second, that reassessment can be done in a case-based way or through the use of elaboration strategies.

---

8. PROTOS's difference links allow this to happen. Difference links associate cases with each other and are labeled by relevant differences between the cases they connect.

10.2 IMPLEMENTING INDEXES

Discussions about search, matching, and situation assessment show that indexes play several different roles in case-based systems. Their first role is in **identifying** or **labeling** cases. When thought of this way, we talk about indexes as *describing the situations in which the case can provide guidelines in the future*, and we think of indexes as playing the function of *conceptually discriminating* cases from other similar ones. Thinking about indexes this way usually results in taking an explanation-based approach to choosing indexes, and indexes are then the features or combinations of features in the case that were responsible for solving some piece of the case in a certain way or for determining some aspect of its outcome.

The second role indexes can play is as **search restrictors**. As search restrictors, indexes *label arcs in memory's organizing structures* and physically discriminate cases from each other. In this role, they act as traffic police, directing and restricting search through the case library.

Their third role is as **importance indicators**. In numerical ranking schemes, remember, each dimension of representation is given an importance rating. One measures how closely a new situation matches a case in the case library by taking into account a combination of the importance value of each dimension and its degree of match. Those cases in which a small number of important dimensions match well are considered better matches than those in which large numbers of less important features match well. The *importance ratings attached to a case's dimensions* are its indexes.

Several of the algorithms that have been presented make clear the role indexes play. The questions in discrimination networks and redundant discrimination networks correspond to attributes of a case; their answers correspond to values. The indexes of a case are a set of attribute-value pairs. It is not hard to see how they can be used to construct or search a discrimination network. A good discrimination network uses the indexes of cases as its questions and answers. Indexes in discrimination networks play both the identifier and search restrictor roles. In looking at some parallel algorithms, it is also easy to see the role of indexes. Using a flat memory and a parallel scheme, the action is in the matching functions. The indexes of a case are its more important (predictive) features, and they are the ones designated as more important in determining degree of match. Depending on the algorithm, indexes play the identification role or the role of importance indicator. Numeric ranking algorithms, too, make clear the way they use indexes. Indexes, recorded as importance values associated with dimensions of the case representation, allow ranking functions to determine which of several partial matches are better than others. Indexes play the importance indicator role here.

In the first implementations of case memories (e.g., CYRUS, IPP, MEDIATOR, CHEF), cases were organized using discrimination networks or redundant discrimination networks, and indexes played both identifier and search restrictor roles simultaneously. They were chosen as identifiers and then attached to the arcs of discrimination networks used to organize cases in the case library. In retrieving cases from the case library, only those paths where descriptors of the new situation match indexes in the memory are followed, restricting search to those portions of the case library most likely to contain a match. This keeps search to a minimum but inhibits flexibility (more on this subject in the next section).

In more recent implementations (e.g., PARADYME, ANON, CASCADE, Abby), these two roles have been separated. Indexes are used only in their identifier role. Retrieval algorithms retrieve partially-matching cases independent of any physical indexing scheme. Indexes are used to identify which of the partially-matching cases are likely to be the most useful ones. As claimed in chapter 8, this change in outlook has arisen largely as a result of the availability and existence of massively parallel machines. In a parallel implementation, search through the case library can be done in reasonable time without putting restrictions on the paths that can be followed. When restrictions on search are removed, more flexible retrieval can be supported without losing the precision of the serial methods.

Indexes have been implemented in several different ways, each corresponding to a role that indexes play. Implemented as physical indexes in a discrimination net or other discrimination scheme, they guide and direct search through case memory. When they act as conceptual discriminators or identifiers, they live as annotations on cases designating their *combinations of salient features* and can act as preferences when choosing a best case. Indexes can also be built into evaluation functions, where the most important features are given the highest weights.

Our implementations often combine several of these methods. MEDIATOR, for example, uses indexes to create a discrimination scheme. During retrieval, it uses these indexes to direct its search through the case memory, allowing it to focus on retrieving only cases with known potential to be useful. However, it usually recalls several cases using this scheme and must sort them out to find the best ones. It uses a numerical evaluation function for this, assigning to some dimensions of its case representation more importance than others.

10.3 ACHIEVING EFFICIENCY, ACCURACY, AND FLEXIBILITY

One of the most important issues when choosing indexing and retrieval methods is the effect of different schemes on retrieval accuracy, efficiency, and flexibility. Efficient serial search requires that search be restricted to those portions of the case library that are likely to provide useful cases. In serial search schemes, indexes are used to discriminate cases from each other and to partition the case library appropriately. The need for efficiency seems to imply that indexes should be fairly restrictive so that little of the case library needs to be searched. The need for accuracy, however, implies that indexes used for discrimination and partitioning should be sufficiently rich so that cases that are retrieved are useful. When accuracy is a requirement, indexes should be chosen with usefulness in mind. Indexing should be on features that alone or in combination predict that the case can make a useful suggestion in a new situation.

Flexibility implies another set of constraints. An indexing scheme that is flexible can be used easily in a variety of situations. Though it may have been constructed with some use in mind, the more flexible a scheme is, the more useful it will be when used for something other than what was anticipated. A special case of this happens when we read a book, a story, or a newspaper article, or when we hear a story or about some event. Because we are not experiencing the event or reading the story in the context of needing to get an answer to something, we can anticipate some, but not all, of the situations in which it could usefully be retrieved. If we indexed only by the needs we could anticipate, we wouldn't be able to retrieve the situation later under unanticipated circumstances. To compensate, we might index the situation based on descriptive features associated with our best understanding of it. They may not discriminate the situation well from others, but they describe it sufficiently richly that there's a chance for partial matching of the case under a variety of future circumstances. A need for flexibility, then, implies indexing cases richly according to their descriptive features.

In chapter 7, two schemes for choosing indexes were discussed. Tendency-based schemes use as indexes all those features of a case that have tended to be important ones for identifying cases in the past. Identifying the indexes for a case is a process of running down a form or checklist and filling in values for each dimension on the list. The composite index that results describes the situation quite richly, though it can include both highly discriminating features of the case and those that are merely descriptive, and it may exclude some features of a case that are not usually important to keep track of but in some case were. Explanation-based schemes attempt to identify the kinds of situations in which the case is likely to provide useful guidance and to assign as indexes distinguished combinations of features that, if seen together, describe a kind of situation in which the case will be useful. A case may have several of these indexes. Explanation-based indexes discriminate better than checklist-based indexes do, describing precisely the situations in which a case can productively be used.

Whether checklist-based or explanation-based methods should be used in a system depends largely on the nature of the cases, the nature of the domain, and the nature of the tasks that cases need to support. Of particular importance is the difficulty of computing indexes and the predictiveness of features. In some domains, computing indexes in an explanation-based way is prohibitively complex or impossible. This may be because the domain is not well understood. Or it could be that it is well understood but too complex to take everything into account. For those domains, checklist-based methods are the only way. When the system supports certain specific reasoning tasks, checklists should be optimized to the tasks, including those dimensions that are predictive for each task.

In other domains, it is easy to compute indexes in an explanation-based way, but it may or may not be better to do that than to index cases more completely using a checklist. In some domains, the presence of individual features in a situation predicts nothing, but some combinations of features, if seen together, are highly predictive. If a domain is like that and explanation-based selection of indexes is easy, then indexes should be computed by explanation-based methods. In other domains, it is hard to predict which combinations of features will recur, and indexing must be on all features that tend to be predictive ones. In other domains, a single case might be useful in a variety of situations, only a few of which can be predicted at the time the case is entered into the case library and any of which could come up in the future. Or it may be impossible to predict all the situations in which a case should be retrieved. Even if explanation-based indexing were easy in such domains, it would be too restrictive to use by itself. In these situations, we opt for completeness in the indexing scheme, using a less discriminating but more complete set of features as indexes. If, in addition, we want to optimize a system for particular tasks, we might use both explanation-based and checklist-based indexes.

CHEF uses a combination of checklist-based and explanation-based methods for this reason. It begins by using a checklist that tells it which individual features of cases are likely to be important ones. It builds a discrimination network based on those, prioritizing it for the task of choosing solutions to problems. As it gets experience, however, it finds that its cases don't all lead to successful results. In order to become a better problem solver, it needs to keep track of the kinds of situations in which failures are likely to occur. This requires explanation of its failures. Once explanations have been derived, applying explanation-based methods to choose indexes is simple (coming up with the explanation is the harder part). CHEF thus uses explanation-based methods of index selection to choose additional indexes for its cases. Because these indexes are used to retrieve cases that can help it anticipate failures, CHEF uses these indexes to build another discrimination net, prioritized for that task. Its explanation-based indexes optimize it for anticipating failures.

Explanation-based methods tend to promote choice of more restrictive but more accurate and discriminating indexes, while checklist-based indexing, which indexes cases by the broad range of features that tend to be predictive ones in a domain, results in less restrictive, more flexible, but also less accurate indexing. Networks with explanation-based indexes in them will tend to be smaller and therefore more efficient networks. The cases they retrieve tend to be highly accurate ones (i.e., very good matches) for the purposes of some reasoning task that the network supports. Networks with checklist-based indexes will tend to be larger, because the indexes of any case contain many more features. They are both bushier and deeper and therefore less efficient to search. However, their cases will be retrievable in a wider variety of situations, not merely in the anticipated ones.

There is also variability in the accuracy and flexibility afforded by checklists, however. Checklists can contain a wide variety of descriptive features, some that discriminate well, others that describe well. Or, they can contain only features that are relatively more discriminating. The more restrictive a checklist is, the more accurate and efficient retrieval will be (assuming those features on the checklist are the most discriminating features). The more coverage the checklist provides, the more flexible retrieval will be, but many cases will generally be retrieved, and a ranking scheme will need to be used after retrieval to sort the better matches out.

There is thus an interesting interaction between discriminating power of indexes and flexibility of retrieval. The more specific its indexes are about situations in which a case should be retrieved (i.e., the more discriminating power they have), the less ability a system will have to retrieve cases in support of unanticipated tasks. When indexes describe cases in more detail, retrieval in support of anticipated tasks may be less efficient, though not necessarily less accurate; however, unanticipated tasks will be better supported.

This interaction results in a tension between designing a retrieval system for usefulness and designing one for flexibility. And indeed, the indexing schemes in most case libraries have been designed either for usefulness or for flexibility but not for both. CYRUS's case library was designed for flexibility. There was a need to retrieve cases in response to unanticipated questions. It uses a checklist-based indexing scheme, and its checklists include a wide variety of descriptive features. CHEF, on the other hand, had the task of planning, and it chooses indexes for its cases using explanation-based indexes in a way that makes planning work well. The Universal Index Frame was derived with flexibility in mind. The checklist it provides is chock-full of descriptive features, and there is no effort to winnow out combinations of features that identify a case as having a particular lesson to teach. Cases are about social situations, and though each has a lesson to teach, there are a variety of situations in which each could usefully teach its lesson. Anticipating all of them would be impossible. The UIF provides a way of indexing each case richly by a combination of domain-independent and domain-specific descriptive features. Flexibility is obtained from rich descriptive indexing based on careful analysis of the domain-specific and domain-independent dimensions appropriate for describing cases.

One could, of course, combine a flexible scheme with a more discriminating one in a hybrid approach. Consider, for example, a system that knows about several different kinds of advice it has to give but that might be asked for advice about a variety of other topics also. It might use a checklist approach to index cases flexibly but use a more discriminating approach to index cases for the tasks that it recognizes each is useful for.

One can also think of coarse- and fine-grained indexes and their implications for the efficiency, accuracy, and flexibility of retrieval. Coarse-grained indexes tend to be more abstract in their descriptions; fine-grained, more specific. If chosen based on predictive strength, coarse-grained indexes tend to be useful in retrieving cases that are approximately in the right ballpark, while fine-grained indexes tend to retrieve well-matching cases.[9] Explanation-based indexes tend to be fine-grained; checklist-based indexes can be coarse-grained or fine-grained. Using a coarse-grained indexing scheme, retrieval is efficient, but it isn't necessarily accurate. Many cases that match on abstract features but not on important details might be retrieved. Additional reasoning must be done to choose the best of the retrieved cases. And it is quite possible that some useful cases might be missed using a coarse-grained approach. Fine-grained indexing is more accurate but less efficient. But the two modes of indexing can often be combined profitably, using coarse-grained indexes to retrieve a set of potentially useful cases and fine-grained discriminations for ranking those cases. CASEY provides the best illustration of such a scheme.

There is also a relationship between the ease of computing indexes and the efficiency of retrieval. When an indexing scheme uses features as indexes that are difficult to recognize, computationally complex, or time-consuming to derive, the process by which these features are derived will slow retrieval considerably. Some of those features may be most useful in retrieving good matches, however. Some retrieval schemes make the use of such features as indexes easier than others. As the discussion at the beginning of this chapter showed, prioritized discrimination nets, for example, can be used to control when such features are derived. When such features are used as indexes in a discrimination network, they are only derived for a new case when they are encountered in the network. That way, an expensive feature won't be derived for all cases but only those for which there is a chance that it is a useful descriptor.

But, as was discussed earlier, other retrieval schemes can also be used to control such derivation. Validated retrieval (Simoudis 1991b, 1992), recall, searches initially using a coarse-grained indexing scheme, finding cases that are in the right ballpark. It examines those to see which expensive features are worth deriving. To make such a scheme workable, of

---

9. Note, however, that though surface features are specific, they are not guaranteed to retrieve useful cases. Sometimes, surface features make irrelevant fine-grained distinctions that inhibit good retrieval.

course, features used in the initial coarse discrimination should be easily recognizable or easy to derive.[10]

10.4 SUMMARY

This chapter has covered the relationship between indexing and retrieval. The first topic it covers is situation assessment. Earlier chapters about indexing discussed methods for choosing indexes for cases to be inserted in the case library. This chapter focuses on the problems inherent in choosing indexes during retrieval. During retrieval, the indexes a new situation would have if it were in the case library are computed. This allows retrieval and matching functions to make educated guesses about which parts of the case library to search, ultimately allowing search and matching to be carried out effectively. The process is called situation assessment.

Situation assessment is the process of interpreting and elaborating the description of a new situation, figuring out what kind of situation it is, what is important about it, and what else may be true about it besides what is patently obvious. Because indexing schemes can't anticipate every way a new situation might be described, situation assessment procedures are needed to bridge the gap between representation and indexing schemes used in the case library and the representation of a new situation. Elaboration schemes may be procedure-based or case-based. Some elaborations require much computational power and/or time; others are simpler. Because some elaborations are expensive to carry out, and because elaboration can be extensive, some means of control must be placed on situation assessment so that only those elaborations that have the potential to be most fruitful are computed.

Because the knowledge that is available when solving a new problem may be incomplete, situation assessment is generally carried out in several stages. Before retrieval, checklist-based control can be used to infer values along those dimensions that are known to be important to accurate retrieval. During retrieval, elaboration is done on an as-needed basis. When more discrimination is needed, search processes can be defined to ask for the information they need in order to discriminate. After search, if retrieved cases don't solve the problem, the situation might need to be reassessed, and retrieval may need to be carried out again.

Also covered is the implementation of indexes. In previous chapters, we could discuss what an index is and methods for choosing them, but without knowing the kinds of algorithms used for retrieval, discussion of implementation would have been impossible. Indexes can be implemented in three different ways. They can be implemented as the questions and labels in discrimination networks and redundant discrimination networks. In that role, they guide and direct search only to those places in the case library likely to hold similar cases. Indexes can also be implemented as identifying labels on cases. In parallel schemes, where restriction of search is not needed, implementing indexes this way allows retrieval processes to first retrieve partially-matching cases based on all specified features and then to narrow down the set to those that match on labeled dimensions. Finally, indexes can be implemented as the import-

---

10. Note the slightly different meaning of coarse-grained here. Rather than referring to abstract derived descriptors, it refers to easily available or easy-to-compute descriptors. If one thinks of coarse-grained as those features that retrieve cases within the right ballpark, one can think of these two conceptions as different implementations of the same concept.

ance values that numerical ranking schemes use. Systems can use one or more methods for implementing indexes; it is not uncommon to use a redundant discrimination network to direct search and then to use a numerical ranking scheme to select out the best of the retrieved cases.

Finally, efficiency, accuracy, and flexibility were discussed. Efficiency is the speed with which a system can retrieve cases. Accuracy is the degree to which retrieved cases can be used to achieve the designated reasoning goal of the reasoner. Flexibility is the degree to which cases can be retrieved to address unanticipated reasoning goals. The means of choosing indexes that is used affects efficiency, accuracy, and flexibility. In general, the more specific an indexing scheme is, the more accurate and efficient retrieval will be, but the less flexible. Flexibility is achieved by indexing on large numbers of descriptive features, but flexible schemes tend to produce less efficient and less accurate retrieval and to require ranking functions to select out from the set of retrieved cases those that can achieve the reasoner's goal.

PART IV

Using Cases

In previous chapters, representation and access of cases has been presented in considerable detail. In this section, we look at the ways in which cases are used in reasoning. There are several different ways cases are used. Sometimes, solutions from cases are adapted to solve new problems. Other times, retrieved cases are used to interpret a situation in context. Still other times, cases are used to point out potential problems with solutions or to project their results. Chapter 11 discusses the many different ways adaptation can be done; ten methods for adaptation are presented. Chapter 12 discusses how adaptation processes can be controlled, that is, deciding what, in an old solution, needs to be modified and deciding which adaptation strategy is most likely to produce an acceptable result. Chapter 13 discusses case-based interpretation processes, both those used to classify or interpret a situation and those used to project the results of carrying out problem-solving solutions. Chapter 14 addresses control issues inherent in systems that use several cases to reason or that solve complex problems.

11

Adaptation Methods and Strategies

Because no old situation is ever exactly the same as a new one, old solutions must usually be adapted to be made applicable to new situations. In adaptation, one manipulates a solution that isn't quite right to make it better fit the problem description. Figure 11.1 gives a definition.

Adaptation might be as simple as substituting one component of a solution for another or as complex as modifying the overall structure of a solution. Consider, for example, one of JULIA's problems:

> JULIA must create an Italian meal that is cheap, easy to prepare, and vegetarian. Based on a composite case that we'll call "generic Italian meal," it decides that the meal should include antipasto, pasta, a main course, and dessert. It breaks the problem into component parts and begins to work on the main course, which provides the most constraints on other parts of the meal. Based on some previous case, JULIA suggests that lasagne be served as the main dish of the main course. It is easy to prepare, cheap, and Italian. But it does raise two problems in the new situation:
>
> 1. There is a conflict between having lasagne as the main dish and having a pasta course, because main ingredients are not supposed to be repeated across courses.
> 2. The lasagne suggested has meat in it, conflicting with the requirement for a vegetarian meal.
>
> JULIA solves the first problem by deleting the pasta course from the structure of its solution. It solves the second by adapting lasagne to make it vegetarian. It does this by deleting the secondary ingredient that violates the vegetarian constraint (meat), creating vegetarian lasagne. It could also have adapted this part of the meal by finding a replace-

INPUT:

- A problem description
- A not-quite-right solution
- The problem description that goes with the solution (optional)

OUTPUT:

- A solution that fits the problem description

METHOD:

- Adjust the not-quite-right solution to make it appropriate as a solution to the described problem

FIGURE 11.1   Adaptation

ment for lasagne that has lasagne's desirable properties and is also vegetarian, perhaps finding spinach lasagne during this process.

The first adaptation is a structure modification. One component of the solution (the pasta course) is deleted from the suggested solution. The second adaptation is a simple transformation. The suggested recipe for lasagne is transformed to make it vegetarian.

The example from JULIA shows how an old solution is adapted before it is actually tried out in the world. Adaptation might also be applied to a solution that proves to be faulty. We call this kind of adaptation *repair*. Repair is often hypothetical; that is, it is reasoning about what should have been done to avoid the fault. Consider, for example, one of CHEF's problems:

> CHEF has just created a recipe for beef and broccoli. When it tries it out, it discovers that the broccoli is soggy. It explains to itself that the broccoli was soggy because it was cooked too long and looks at its recipe to see why it was cooked so long. It was cooked along with the beef, which requires a longer cooking time than does broccoli. CHEF proposes that the broccoli be cooked separately from the beef after the beef is cooked and that before the broccoli is done the beef be put back into the wok to make it hot.

Here, CHEF tries out its recipe and asks itself how it could have avoided the problem. The result of its reasoning is a new recipe for beef and broccoli in which (it is hoped) the broccoli will remain crisp. The repair CHEF did to its old recipe is structural: it changed the order of the steps and added a new one. When repairs are inserted into the memory as cases, they allow a reasoner to avoid repeating its mistakes. Once CHEF indexes this hypothetical recipe in memory, for example, it has it available to guide it the next time it makes a stir-fried dish with meat and a crispy vegetable. Of course, repairs that have been tried out in the world and found to work are more reliable than hypothetical repairs. A case library might contain both kinds, giving more credence to those that are tried and true than to hypothetical ones, or it might store only those that it knows to be reliable.

As we have seen, the whole structure of a solution can be adapted or some piece of the solution can be adapted without changing overall solution structure. And adaptation can happen during solution formulation or after feedback derived from projecting the results of a solution or carrying it out in the world has pointed out a problem in need of repair. Adaptation can take several forms: something new might be inserted into the old solution, something might be deleted from it, some item might be substituted for another, or some part of the old solution might be transformed.

In this chapter, we present ten methods by which adaptation can be done:

SUBSTITUTION METHODS:

1. Reinstantiation
2. Parameter adjustment
3. Local search
4. Query memory
5. Specialized search
6. Case-based substitution

TRANSFORMATION METHODS:

7. Commonsense transformation
8. Model-guided repair

OTHER METHODS:

9. Special-purpose adaptation and repair
10. Derivational Replay

The six substitution methods substitute values appropriate for the new situation for values in the old solution. *Reinstantiation* is used to instantiate an old solution with new objects. For example, CHEF uses reinstantiation to create a chicken and snow peas recipe from a recipe for beef and broccoli. Chicken is substituted for beef everywhere in the recipe, and snow peas are substituted for broccoli. *Parameter adjustment* is a heuristic for adjusting numerical parameters of an old solution. It relies on specialized heuristics that relate differences in input specifications to differences in output. JUDGE (Bain 1986), for example, uses parameter adjustment to sentence a criminal to a shorter sentence than another criminal because the crime was less violent. *Local search* provides a way of searching an auxiliary knowledge structure for a substitute for some old value or structure that is inappropriate for the new situation. If in an old menu, one served oranges for dessert but they are not available, local search allows the reasoner to search the semantic network of foods to find a close relative of oranges (say apples, another winter fruit) that can serve as a substitute. *Query memory* means asking either auxiliary knowledge structures or the case memory to return something with a given description. In *specialized search*, both auxiliary knowledge structures and case memory are also queried, but specialized search heuristics are used to guide memory search. *Case-based substitution* uses other cases to suggest substitutions. CLAVIER is the program that first implemented case-based substitution, but the best intuitive example, perhaps, comes from the meal-planning domain. A meal planner that has determined that the lasagne it is planning for the main dish is inappropriate may choose a substitute by recalling other Italian meals with pasta as a main dish.

Transformation methods are used to transform an old solution into one that will work in a new situation. In *commonsense transformation*, commonsense heuristics are used to replace, delete, or add components to a solution. A commonsense heuristic called "delete secondary component," for example, can be used to transform lasagne into vegetarian lasagne. *Model-guided repair* is transformation guided by a causal model. Reasoning about devices, whether for diagnosis or design, can often be guided by a model.

Special-purpose adaptation and repair heuristics are used to carry out domain-specific and structure-modifying adaptations not covered by the other methods. These heuristics are indexed by the situations in which they are applicable. CHEF, for example, uses a specialized adaptation heuristic to insert a "defatting" step to any recipe that includes duck. JULIA uses specialized adaptation heuristics to modify the structure of its solutions. One such heuristic knows how to remove redundancies from a structure; another recognizes when two functionally similar components must both be included in a solution. Such heuristics can also implement strategies for repairing solutions after they have been carried out and failed. CHEF uses specialized repair heuristics for this purpose. Each is a rather abstract strategy for repairing a faulty solution, indexed by the type of failure it repairs.

Special-purpose adaptation heuristics are often implemented as *critics* and controlled through use of a rule-based production system. Critic application also provides a way of implementing parameter adjustment, commonsense transformation, and model-guided repair. CASEY's model-guided repair heuristics are implemented as critics, as are PERSUADER's parameter adjustment heuristics.

Derivational replay is the process of using the method of deriving an old solution or solution piece to derive a solution in the new situation. Using derivational replay, a reasoner solving a probability problem would use the same set of steps that were used previously to solve a similar problem. Derivational replay can also be used to derive pieces of solutions. Like case-based substitution, derivational replay provides a case-based means of doing adaptation.

Some adaptation methods rely on commonsense knowledge, others are based on causal models, others use knowledge specific to a task or domain, and others combine one or more of these sources. Some are used for substitution; others, for transformations of various kinds. Some change values in a solution; others operate on its structure. Figure 11.2 shows where each method fits along each of these dimensions. In our discussions of adaptation methods, we will present the knowledge each method uses and the adaptation tasks they are able to perform.

Method	Guidance	Task	Operates on
Reinstantiation	structural	substitution	values
Parameter adjustment	commonsense	substitution	values
Local search	specialized, commonsense	substitution	values, structure
Query memory	specialized	substitution	values, structure
Specialized search	*ad hoc,* commonsense	substitution	values, structure
Case-based substitution	cases	substitution	values
Commonsense transformation	commonsense	transformation	values, structure
Model-guided repair	causal	transformation, substitution	values, structure
Specialized adaptation and repair heuristics	specialized, commonsense, causal	substitution, transformation	values, structure
Derivational replay	cases	substitution, transformation	values, structure

FIGURE 11.2   Adaptation Methods

11.1 SUBSTITUTION

Substitution is the process of choosing and installing a replacement for some part of an old solution. There are many different kinds of substitutions. A component of an old solution can be substituted, the amount of some component can be substituted, or a whole group of components or amounts can be substituted at the same time. Consider, for example, the meal planning situation presented in chapter 1:

> A meal planner is planning a meal for a group of people including Elana, a vegetarian who is allergic to milk products but will eat fish, Nat and Mike, two meat-and-potatoes men, and several other people, including Anne. There will be about twenty people total. The meal should be inexpensive, easy to make, and use the tomatoes from my garden. It is summer.

Suppose that the meal planner is reminded of this meal:

> The AI research group came to dinner at REC's house, about thirty people. He wanted the meal to be inexpensive and easy to make. He served an antipasto, lasagne, broccoli, and ice cream for dessert. It was summer. The guests sat on the patio to eat. There was lots of beer and lemonade to go around.

There are several substitutions that must be made to adapt this solution above to the new situation. First, several roles are filled differently. The host is different, and the guests are different. Second, the lasagne is inappropriate for vegetarians. Substitution of a vegetarian lasagne recipe for the one used would solve that problem. Third, the amount of each item and ingredient necessary for a group of twenty is different from what is necessary for a group of thirty. Fourth, there are not enough tomatoes used in the proposed dishes. Some substitution for broccoli could solve that problem.[1]

Several different substitution methods are used to do these four adaptations. The first, substitution of several roles, is done by reinstantiation. The framework for the old solution is reinstantiated, substituting the new roles for the old ones all at once. The second, substitution of a vegetarian recipe for the usual one, can be done by local search, a methodology of searching memory's abstraction hierarchies in the neighborhood of the item needing substitution for one that is appropriate to the new situation. Alternatively, it might be done by case-based substitution, finding another Italian meal with vegetarian pasta as the main dish and substituting that dish for the lasagne. The third, substitution of amounts, is done by parameter adjustment. Based on differences between the two problem specifications (one has twenty people, the other thirty), specialized parameter adjustment heuristics are applied to fix the amounts in the output. In this case, the amounts needed for the new case are roughly two-thirds what was needed in the first. The fourth, substitution of some vegetable dish with tomatoes in it for the broccoli, can be done by querying memory directly for such a dish, by doing a specialized search using a search heuristic that knows where in memory to look to find dishes of a particular kind, or by case-based substitution.

In the next subsections, we discuss each of these substitution methods.

11.1.1 Reinstantiation

Reinstantiation is used when the frameworks of an old and new problem are obviously the same but roles in the new case are filled differently than roles in the old one. In reinstantiation, one takes an old solution and substitutes new role bindings for old ones. In the example above, reinstantiation is used to substitute the new host and guests for those designated in the old case. Several case-based reasoners employ reinstantiation. When CHEF creates a chicken and snow peas recipe based on its beef and broccoli recipe, it substitutes chicken for beef and snow peas for broccoli using reinstantiation. The *meat* role of beef and broccoli is filled by chicken, and the *vegetable* role is filled by snow peas to create the new recipe. When MEDIATOR solves the Orange Dispute by recourse to the Candy Bar Dispute, it uses reinstantiation to substitute the orange for the candy bar and the sisters (who want the orange) for the kids (who wanted the candy bar).

There are two things the reasoner must know or compute in order to do reinstantiation:

1. Correspondences between roles in the old case and the new one
2. An abstracted (variablized) framework for the old solution

---

1. There are other adaptations that should or could be done. For now, we ignore them to concentrate on the role of substitution.

Problem: Roles in the new case are filled differently than in the old.
Solution: Substitute role bindings in the new case for those in the old one. This is a three-step process:

- *Abstract* the framework of the old problem and solution.
- *Compute correspondences* between the roles in the two problem statements.
- *Instantiate* the framework of the old problem and solution based on computed correspondences.

FIGURE 11.3   Reinstantiation

Figure 11.3 shows the set of steps necessary for reinstantiation.

Reinstantiation is easiest to use when the framework for an old problem and solution are already known and when roles are specified in the representation of a problem. MEDIATOR's problem representations have both these qualities, making both computation of role correspondences and abstraction easy. Its problem representations designate the functional roles of its descriptors, thus computation of role correspondences requires only pairing up items that fill the same already designated functional roles. Thus, for example, if the old case specifies that a candy bar was the disputed object and the description of the problem in the new case specifies that an orange is the disputed object, candy bar and orange are recognized as corresponding roles. Figure 11.4 shows parts of two of MEDIATOR's cases. It is easy to see how the corresponding roles can be assigned.

MEDIATOR's case representations are specified as collections of abstract frames and their role bindings, as can be seen in Figure 11.4. Thus, abstraction means extracting those frames from the old case and noting correspondences between bindings in problem and solution frames. The Candy Bar Dispute, for example, specifies its problem as a `physical dispute` between disputants `child1` and `child2` and disputed object `candy-bar1` and specifies its solution as an application of `Divide Equally` to parties `child1` and `child2` and object `candy-bar1`. The abstraction created from this representation substitutes variables for each of the role fillers, as shown in Figure 11.5, and assigns values to each of those variables based on the way they were filled in the case.

Given these representations, let us explore how reinstantiation works in solving the Orange Dispute based on the Candy Bar Dispute.

1. The abstraction of the old problem and solution are extracted from the Candy Bar Dispute, resulting in the abstraction in Figure 11.5.
2. Correspondences between the roles in the old and new case problem descriptions are computed. Here, the set of disputants `child1` and `child2` correspond to the set of disputants in the Sinai Dispute: `sister1` and `sister2`, and the disputed object `candy-bar1` corresponds to disputed object `orange1`.
3. The solution portion of the abstraction is reinstantiated with the new role bindings, resulting in the solution:

```
Divide Equally
    parties: sister1, sister2
    object: orange1
```

A more refined solution is also available and can be computed by instantiating Divide
Equally using those variable bindings. Figure 11.6 shows the steps in Divide Equally. Figure
11.7 shows what its steps look like when instantiated using those variable bindings.

OLD CASE: THE CANDY BAR DISPUTE
```
Goal: resolve dispute
Situation description:
    isa: dispute-situation
    disputants: child1, child2
    disputed object: candy-bar1
    dispute:
      stated goals:
        (goal child1 (possess child1 candy-bar1))
        (goal child2 (possess child2 candy-bar1))
      inferred goals:
        (goal child1 (ingest child1 (piece candy-bar1)))
        (goal child2 (ingest child2 (piece candy-bar1)))
Solution:
    plan: M-DIVIDE-EQUALLY
parties: child1, child2
object: candy-bar1
    predictions:
        if-results-ok:
            ((ingest (actor child1) (object piece1))
             (ingest (actor child2) (object piece2)))
```

NEW PROBLEM: THE ORANGE DISPUTE
```
Goal: resolve dispute
Situation description:
    isa: dispute-situation
    disputants: sister1, sister2
    disputed object: orange1
    dispute:
      stated goals:
        (goal sister1 (possess sister1 orange1))
        (goal sister2 (possess sister2 orange1))
      inferred goals:
        (goal sister1 (ingest sister1 (fruit orange1)))
        (goal sister2 (ingest sister2 (fruit orange1)))
```

FIGURE 11.4 Representation of (Pieces of) Two cases from MEDIATOR

```
Goal: resolve dispute
Situation description:
   isa: dispute-situation
   disputants: &party1, &party2
   disputed object: &object (isa &object food)
   dispute:
     stated goals:
        (goal &party1 (possess &party1 orange1))
        (goal &party2 (possess &party2 orange1))
     inferred goals:
        (goal &party1 (ingest &party1 (piece &object)))
        (goal &party2 (ingest &party2 (piece &object)))
```

FIGURE 11.5 Abstraction of the Candy Bar Dispute

In the easiest cases, reinstantiation is a process of substituting new values for old ones by instantiating an old framework with new values. However, there are three circumstances that complicate reinstantiation:

■ When representations are not explicit about a framework for an old solution

■ When representations are not explicit about the functional roles of descriptors

■ When several roles play the same function

Reinstantiation is easy in the MEDIATOR because frameworks for old solutions are explicit in its representations. Thus, the first step of reinstantiation, abstraction, is simple.

The second reason reinstantiation is easy in the MEDIATOR is that its representations specify explicitly the functional roles of descriptors. We know that the candy bar plays the *dis-*

```
Isa: Plan
Parties: &char1, &char2
Props: &object, &cutting-obj
Steps:
   step1: Use &cutting-obj to divide &object in two;
          resulting in &piece1 and &piece2
   step2: Give &piece1 to &char1
   step3: Give &piece2 to &char2
Results:
   (dirty &cutting-obj)
   &object is in two pieces
   (possess &char1 &piece1)
   (possess &char2 &piece2)
Expectations:
   &char1 and &char2 will do the expected thing with &object
```

FIGURE 11.6 Divide Equally

```
Isa: Plan
Characters: sister1, sister2
Props: orange1, &cutting-obj
Steps:
    step1: Use &cutting-obj to divide orange1 in two;
           resulting in orange-piece1 and orange-piece2
    step2: Give orange-piece1 to sister1
    step3: Give orange-piece2 to sister2
Results:
    (dirty &cutting-obj)
    orange1 is in two pieces: orange-piece1 and orange-piece2
    (possess sister1 orange-piece1)
    (possess sister2 orange-piece2)
Expectations:
    sister1 and sister2 will do the expected thing with orange1
```

FIGURE 11.7 Divide Equally When Instantiated Using Role Bindings of the Orange Dispute

puted-object role and that the children, as a group, play the *disputants* role. Because functional roles are explicit in the representation, it is easy to compute the correspondences between roles in old and new cases (step 2 of reinstantiation). Though it is easiest to compute correspondences if functional roles are explicitly specified, there are other ways to compute correspondences if the numbers of items needing correspondence is small:

- Match *most-similar* items to each other using memory's abstraction hierarchies (semantic networks) as a guide.
- Match items to each other based on constraints provided by the old case.

CHEF uses the first method to find correspondences. Figure 11.8 shows CHEF's representation for beef and broccoli. As can be seen, although CHEF's representations make variables and the framework they fit into explicit (making the abstraction step easy), they do not specify the functional roles of variables. Nowhere, for example, does the representation state that beef is playing the meat role or that broccoli is playing the vegetable role. CHEF's problem representations don't make functional roles of descriptors obvious, but because the set of possible correspondences between variables in the old and new situations is small, memory's abstraction hierarchies can be used to compute which role fillers are most similar to each other. We shall consider the following problem description and the semantic network shown in Figure 11.9 to show how this works:

(style stir-fry) (taste savory) (include chicken) (include snow-peas)

We shall also assume that CHEF has been reminded of its recipe for Beef and Broccoli (because it is stir-fried and has savory taste). The task is to determine what chicken and snow peas correspond to in the beef and broccoli case. The method is to look in the semantic network to see which descriptors in the two cases can play similar functional roles. Looking in the semantic network in Figure 11.9, we see that the representations of chicken and beef are

Problem: (style stir-fry) (taste savory) (include beef) (include
   broccoli)

Solution: beef and broccoli

```
(ingredients
   ingr1 (beef lb .5)
   ingr2 (soy-sauce tablespoon 2)
   ingr3 (rice-wine spoon 1)
   ingr4 (cornstarch tablespoon .5)
   ingr5 (sugar spoon 1)
   ingr6 (broccoli lb 1)
   ingr7 (salt spoon 1)
   ingr8 (garlic chunk 1))
(actions
   act1 (chop object (ingr8) size (matchhead))
   act2 (shred object (ingr1))
   act3 (marinate object (result act2)
                in (& (ingr2) (ingr3) (ingr4) (ingr5) (ingr8))
                time (20))
   act4 (chop object (ingr6) size (chunk))
   act5 (stir-fry object (result act4) time (3))
   act6 (stir-fry object (result act3)
                time (3))
   act7 (add object (result act4) to (result act6))
   act8 (stir-fry object (result act7) time (.5))
   act9 (add object (ingr7) to (result act8)))
(style stir-fry)
```

FIGURE 11.8 A Case in CHEF: Beef and Broccoli

closely related, in that both are protein foods of a meat type. They are thus found to correspond. Similar reasoning results in the correspondence between snow peas and broccoli.
Notice that in order for this process to work well, the semantic network has to be set up so that
items that can play the same functional role are situated closely together in the net.

The third complication occurs when several roles play the same function. The MEDIA-
TOR example we have been using shows this complication. Though the two children play the
same functional role in the problem statement (disputant), they play two different roles in the

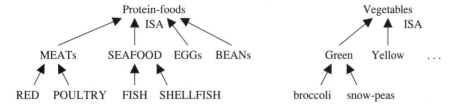

FIGURE 11.9 Representation and Organization of Chicken, Beef, Snow Peas, and Broccoli

solution (one is the `cutter`, the other the `chooser`). It is easy to substitute roles in the problem descriptions (step 2 of reinstantiation) but harder to reinstantiate the old solution appropriately (step 3). Which of the two sisters should cut the orange, and which should choose her half? In this case, constraints provided by the old case solve the problem. The cutter needs to understand the situation (constraint provided by `one cuts, the other chooses`), and in the Candy Bar Dispute, this was implemented by choosing the older child as the cutter. Following the same guidelines, the older sister can be chosen as the cutter in solving the Orange Dispute.

Though there are methods available for computing abstractions and correspondences when representations do not make them obvious, it is important to keep in mind that as abstraction and computation of correspondences get hard, adaptation by reinstantiation becomes less than ideal. In fact, when representations don't make frameworks and roles obvious, it becomes hard to recognize that role substitution will work.

When frameworks and functional roles are specified, reinstantiation is quite simple. However, there are still several tasks it cannot do. It cannot adjust parameters, nor can it adapt structural features of a solution. Thus, if snow peas need to be cooked a shorter time than broccoli, an additional adaptation step is necessary after reinstantiation to make that adjustment. Nor can reinstantiation add a step to a recipe stating that the chicken should be deboned or substitute cutting with a knife for breaking when the Candy Bar Dispute suggests splitting the orange in two and giving one half to each disputant. Additional adaptation steps after reinstantiation are necessary to effect structural changes in an old solution.

11.1.2 Parameter Adjustment

Parameter adjustment is a technique for interpolating values in a new solution based on those from an old one. That is, given an old solution and a new case that differs by some degree from it, the old solution is modified to the extent that the two cases differ from each other. For example, a crime that is more heinous than a previous one requires a harsher sentence. A wage contract that gave a certain wage based on the standard of living in one community is appropriate in another community to the extent that the wage is adjusted to meet the standard of living in the new community.

In **parameter adjustment**, changes in parameters in an old solution are made in response to differences between problem specifications in an old and a new case. It is a two-step process. First, the old and new problem descriptions are compared and their differences extracted. Then **specialized adjustment heuristics** are applied to the old solution to create a new one. Adjustment heuristics capture the relationships between problem features and solution parameters. Figure 11.10 summarizes the process.

Several case-based reasoning programs use parameter adjustment as a method of adaptation. PERSUADER (E.P. Sycara 1987a; K. Sycara 1988a) uses parameter adjustment to adjust the numerical values of an old contract to bring them into line with a new situation. When PERSUADER constructs a new labor-management contract based on some old one, for example, it adjusts percentage raises in salaries and benefits based on differences between cost of living in the location of the old contract and the location of the new dispute. If an old contract was signed in a location where cost of living is high and has risen faster than the norm, but the new dispute is in a place where cost of living is not rising as fast, a smaller percentage wage

Problem: Parameters in the new case are different from those in the old one.
Solution: Adjust the old solution as follows:

- *Compare* the old and new problems and extract differences.
- For each difference, *apply a specialized adjustment heuristic* to the old solution to create a new one.

FIGURE 11.10 Parameter Adjustment

increase is in order in the new contract. JUDGE (Bain 1986) uses parameter adjustment to adapt an old sentence for a crime to a new situation.

Figures 11.11 and 11.12 show examples of parameter adjustment heuristics used by each program. Examining PERSUADER's heuristics, we see that it has some heuristics that adjust a set of parameters all at once based on differences between the old and new situations, while others are specialized to particular parameters. We can also see that often extensive interpretation is necessary to calculate the differences between the old and new cases. Though comparisons of cost of living or inflation rate require only table lookup, the differences referenced in JUDGE's heuristics require inference about outcomes, intent, justification of intent, amount of force, and escalation of force, none of which are immediately available in the raw description of a crime.

An example will illustrate how parameter adjustment is done. In it, JUDGE is attempting to sentence Ed, who has just killed Moe in a fight.

> **New problem**: Moe struck Ed several times. Ed was slightly hurt. Ed struck Moe several times. Moe fell down. Moe struck Ed several times, breaking Ed's nose. Ed stabbed Moe with a knife one time, killing Moe.

JUDGE remembers another case, crime3:

> **Old case**: Hal struck Gary several times. Gary was slightly hurt. Gary struck Hal several times. Hal fell down. Hal hit Gary very hard several times, breaking Gary's ribs. Gary shot at Hal with a gun several times, killing Hal. Gary's sentence, for murder, was a term of imprisonment of not less than twenty-five years.

JUDGE compares the two problem descriptions: In both crimes, the victim was killed. Although results were the same in both situations, the outcome in the newer crime was accidental and involved a less severe intent. Ed's action did not demonstrate as extreme a force as Gary's action. Gary's intent, shown by repeated shooting, was more severe than Ed's, and so on. The old crime, crime3, was substantially worse.

Using an **extreme-force heuristic,** JUDGE adjusts the old sentence of twenty-five years to fifteen years (more or less 50 percent of the old sentence).

It is clear from these rules and examples that application of at least some parameter adjustment heuristics requires deep comparisons between the old and new cases. Whenever

REINSTANTIATING A COMPETITOR'S CURRENT CONTRACT

IF the closest case is a competitor's
THEN

- IF the contract is current AND the competitor's position-in-industry has remained unchanged
  THEN

  □ For economic demands, transfer the percent change from the retrieved contract to the proposed contract AND
  □ for noneconomic demands, transfer the contract language from the retrieved contract to the proposed contract directly

  ELSE adjust the percent change or contract language in the direction opposite to the change in the competitor's competitive position.

- Apply area differentials to the resulting values.

ADJUSTING FOR INFLATION RATE (AN AREA DIFFERENTIAL)

If inflation-rate is different in the two locales, compute the percentage difference in inflation rate, and adjust the percentage wage increase from the old case by that amount.

FIGURE 11.11   Two of PERSUADER's Parameter Adjustment Heuristics (Sycara 1987a)

Conflicting comparison, same crime: IF one crime had a worse outcome but a justified intent, and the crimes are not immediately different, THEN use the old sentence.

Conflicting comparison, different crime: IF one crime had a worse outcome but a justified intent, and the crimes are immediately different, THEN increase or decrease the old sentence by 25 percent as appropriate.

Intent and outcome different or similar result, same crime: IF both outcome and intent were worse in one crime or one crime had a worse intent but otherwise the crimes were similar, and the crimes are not immediately different, THEN increase or decrease the old sentence by 25 percent as appropriate.

Intent and outcome different or similar result, different crime: IF both outcome and intent were worse in one crime or one crime had a worse intent but otherwise the crimes were similar, and the crimes are immediately different, THEN increate or decrease the old sentence by 50 percent as appropriate.

Extreme force, same crime: IF extreme force appeared in one crime without offsetting justification, and the crimes are not immediately different, THEN increase or decrease the old sentence by 50 percent as appropriate.

Extreme force, different crime: IF extreme force appeared in one crime without offsetting justification , and the crimes are immediately different, THEN increase or decrease the old sentence by 75 percent as appropriate.

FIGURE 11.12   Several of JUDGE's Parameter Adjustment Heuristics (Bain 1989)

extensive inferencing must be done, some control must be placed on the inference process. There are two different ways case-based reasoning problems deal with this:

- They keep a checklist of comparisons that are always made before parameter adjustment (JUDGE's method).

- They maintain a list of parameter adjustment heuristics, each of which knows, in general, under what circumstances it is applicable. Check each one in turn, and for each that is potentially applicable, do the comparisons it requires (PERSUADER's method).

The first method is appropriate in domains where cases are always compared across the same dimensions; the second serves to partition the set of possibilities when making all comparisons would be prohibitive. The sample rule from PERSUADER, for example (see Figure 11.11), is applicable when the retrieved case is a contract of a competitor company. Under those circumstances, it is appropriate to compare cases on the currency of the old contract, the competitor's position in the industry, and area differentials. We discuss this issue in more detail in the section on choosing what to adapt.

It is important to note that parameter adjustment is an interpolation method and only that. Parameter adjustment heuristics cannot be used to create a solution from scratch. Rather, their power is in guiding the generation of a new solution from an old one. PERSUADER cannot use parameter adjustment to create a new contract, but it can use parameter adjustment to adjust an old one to fit new demands. Similarly, JUDGE cannot use parameter adjustment to sentence an offender "from scratch;" parameter adjustment allows it to calculate a sentence based on an old one.

As can be seen from the discussion of parameter adjustment, these specialized heuristics look a lot like production rules. In fact, they are often implemented that way.

11.1.3 Local Search

Reinstantiation substitutes a whole set of roles in a case at once, but sometimes it is necessary just to substitute some small part of an old solution to make it work in the new case. Substituting vegetarian lasagne for lasagne is an instance of this. Consider another example, a case from JULIANA (Shinn 1989). JULIANA is attempting to create a meal for vegetarians, wants to make it French cuisine, and wants to prepare it by stewing. It recalls a meal whose main dish is bouillabaisse. Though most of the meal is appropriate for the new case, bouillabaisse has meat and fish in it, items that vegetarians won't eat. JULIANA solves the problem by looking in its abstraction hierarchy of dishes to find a substitution for bouillabaisse (see Figure 11.13). Walking up the network from bouillabaisse, it finds French stews. Walking down from there, it finds ratatouille, a vegetarian stew. Substitution of vegetarian lasagne for lasagne can be done similarly if there is a recipe for vegetarian lasagne close to lasagne in memory's abstraction hierarchies.

Local search is the process of searching in an abstraction hierarchy in the environs of a concept for some close relative that could be substituted for it (Figure 11.14). It is generally used when an old solution is almost right for the new case and could be made to fit with some

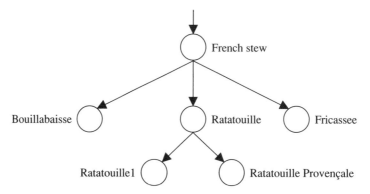

FIGURE 11.13   Semantic Network in the Environs of Bouillabaisse

minor substitution. In its simplest form, local search looks first at siblings of the old element to see if any of them work, then at cousins, and so on. Unrestricted local search is inefficient, however, and guidelines for moving up and down the hierarchies are necessary.

To see that these guidelines are necessary, consider the abstraction hierarchy from PLEXUS in Figure 11.15 (Alterman 1986, 1988). This hierarchy represents the relationships between several goals and plans and specializations of plans. For the purposes of this presentation, the important thing to notice about this memory is that many of the nodes have multiple parents in the hierarchy.

Now, consider the following problem. PLEXUS is about to take the subway in New York City for the first time. It remembers taking the subway in San Francisco (BART). Steps involved in doing that are to (1) buy a ticket, (2) enter the station using the ticket for entry, (3) ride the train, and (4) exit using the ticket to exit. PLEXUS attempts to apply its BART plan to riding the New York subway and looks around for a ticket machine (the normal way of buying a ticket in BART). It doesn't find one.

PLEXUS must find a substitution for ticket buying that is applicable to the new situation and that will let PLEXUS continue with the rest of the plan. A pure local search would look for siblings and then cousins of buy BART ticket in the net. Buy BART ticket has several siblings: buy theater ticket is a sibling through buy ticket, and use change machine is a sibling through use money machine. Though the multiplicity of parents and siblings in this network is not overwhelming, it is not hard to imagine a network in which each node has sev-

---

Problem: Some element of the solution doesn't fill the needs of the new problem.
Solution: Substitute another value by searching for a close relative in memory's abstraction hierarchies. In general, the steps involved in local search are the following:

- *Abstraction:* walking up hierarchies
- *Refinement:* walking down hierarchies

FIGURE 11.14   Local Search

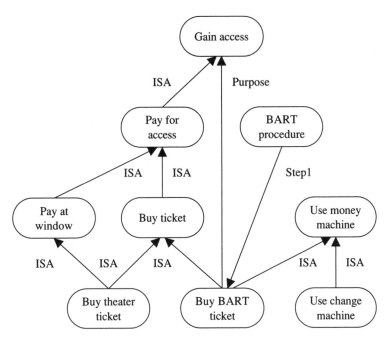

FIGURE 11.15 An Abstraction Hierarchy from PLEXUS

eral parents and many siblings and cousins. Checking all of them for applicability could be quite expensive.

The problem, then, is how to control navigation up and down the network to find a substitution. PLEXUS provides several specialized answers for planning domains. For example, when substitution is necessary because of failing preconditions, PLEXUS gives us the following guidelines:

Abstract: Move up the abstraction hierarchy toward the *purpose of the failing step* until the point where the failing condition has been abstracted.
Refine: Find a concrete descendant of that concept that can be substituted.

Other reasons for substitutions provide other guidelines for abstraction and refinement.

Using these guidelines, PLEXUS substitutes for the failing buy BART ticket step by traversing toward gain access, the *purpose* of buy BART ticket, until lack of a ticket machine (the failing precondition) is abstracted out. This puts it at buy ticket. Refining downward, it finds buy theater ticket (usually done at a window). Trying that out in the environment of the New York subway station it is in, it finds a window and goes up to it to buy a subway ticket (a reinstantiation of buy theater ticket).[2]

---

2. Not quite right yet—it will have to buy a token rather than a ticket—but the substitution does put it in the right ballpark.

On examining the PLEXUS example in more detail, we find that whereas PLEXUS provides guidelines for traversing up the abstraction hierarchies, its guidelines for moving back down are not as concrete. It merely specifies trying all the descendant nodes until a good one is found. This deficiency can be corrected by indexing nodes by features that predict their usefulness. The refinement step can then be an index-following step in many cases, where indexes direct the reasoner toward the most promising concrete descendants. `Buy theater ticket`, for example, might be indexed off of `buy ticket` by `locale = theater` and/or `there is a ticket window in sight`, while `buy BART ticket` might be indexed by `locale = BART station` and/or `there's a ticket machine in sight`. Using this indexing scheme, `buy theater ticket` is the preferred refinement when a ticket window is in site, while `buy BART ticket` is preferred when a ticket machine is seen.

Several case-based reasoning programs use local search as a method for making substitutions. PLEXUS, as we have seen, provides concrete guidelines to the abstraction and refinement processes, telling them where they are allowed to look for a substitution. SWALE (Kass and Leake 1988), like PLEXUS, provides several different guidelines for movement through the abstraction hierarchies, each associated with a fix it is trying to make. One called **twk-generalize-anomaly** is used when it is trying to find a more general concept to substitute for a specific inappropriate one:

> **Twk-generalize-anomaly:** Abstract the anomalous concept in the old case until a concept that also describes a corresponding object in the new problem is encountered.

We can see how this is used if we consider SWALE's trying to explain the *Challenger* disaster by reference to Jim Fixx's death. The space shuttle *Challenger* has just blown up. SWALE remembers Jim Fixx, a jogger who, in the prime of his life, died after running because of a previously unknown heart ailment. In attempting to apply this explanation to the *Challenger* disaster, SWALE finds that the *Challenger* has no heart. Applying twk-generalize-anomaly, it searches upward in its hierarchies for a concept that describes an internal part of the *Challenger* that might be analogous to a heart. It finds `pump`, a generalization of `heart` that describes a space shuttle component. SWALE's explanation based on this and other adaptations is that the *Challenger* exploded due to a previously unknown defect in a pump.

Other programs that use local search provide no specific guidelines for traversing abstraction hierarchies but do provide guidelines about how far to look (e.g., JULIANA, JULIA). Though it is well known that this is not a particularly meaningful way to control local search (Brachman and Schmolze 1985), it has been useful in some programs in ensuring that they don't spend all of their resources attempting local search. When local search is cut off by this control scheme, other search methods are attempted instead.

11.1.4 Query Memory

Local search is an appropriate means of finding a substitution if one exists in memory's hierarchies in a locale where it can easily be found (i.e., close to the item to be substituted for). Though it is often possible to set up networks that make this easy, if memory's hierarchies are to be used for several purposes, it is not possible to predict the relationships every concept might have to every other one, and local search won't be sufficient. **Query memory** can be useful in these circumstances.

For illustration, consider again the picture of JULIANA's memory (Figure 11.13) and the following problem: JULIANA must plan a meal in which the main dish is stew. It remembers a meal with bouillabaisse. After remembering this meal, it told that there will be several meat-and-potatoes men coming. Bouillabaisse is too strange for such picky eaters. Local search turns up ratatouille (a vegetable stew), not appropriate for meat-and-potatoes men, and fricassee, another light French stew, also not appropriate. Stews for meat-and-potatoes men are not located in memory close to bouillabaisse. Local search might find one if it were allowed to search broadly enough, but such a broad search can be quite expensive. Moreover, though a broader search can be counted on to find answers more often than a narrow search, no arbitrary cutoff for a local search can be guaranteed to find answers all the time.

When local search won't work, it is sometimes possible to construct a partial description of an item that would make a good substitution and to search directly for that. Continuing with the example, JULIANA asks memory to find a dish with meat and potatoes as ingredients that is prepared by stewing. When memory is asked directly for that, it returns the suggestion `Irish stew`.

How does this work? Rather than searching in the local environs of an already known concept, query memory asks retrieval processes to search memory's abstraction hierarchies from the top to find the partially specified item. The particular search method to be used depends on the organization of the memory, as explained in chapter 8. If abstraction hierarchies are indexed (as in CYRUS), then the indexing structure can be used to guide search. On a parallel machine, indexing may not be necessary. If memory is of any substantial size, then query memory can only be as efficient as downward traversal.

11.1.5 Specialized Search

Query memory gives memory a partial description of something it should try to find and asks memory to find it. **Specialized search** (Figure 11.16) goes one step further: it gives memory instructions about *how* to find a needed item. Figure 11.17 shows some of the specialized search heuristics SWALE (Kass and Leake 1988) uses.

An example (Kass 1989a) will illustrate. SWALE is trying to find an explanation for Len Bias's death. Len Bias was a healthy all-star college basketball player who died unexpectedly of a heart attack. SWALE is reminded of the Jim Fixx case. Jim Fixx was a jogger who seemed to be in good health but died of a heart attack after running. After his death, doctors found that

---

Problem: Some element of the solution does not fill the needs of the new problem
　　　　AND local search is inapplicable or yields no answer.
Solution: Give memory instructions about how to look for an alternate.

FIGURE 11.16 Specialized Search

- To find an action done by a particular actor, look for the common things that actor does by first finding the common thematic roles that person plays and then finding the actions common to people in those roles.

- To find what could have caused something, look for the caused event in the consequent of a causal rule and hypothesize the antecedent.

- To find an implement a person might have used, look for instruments the actor normally uses by first finding the common thematic roles that person plays and then finding the implements handled in that role.

FIGURE 11.17   Some Specialized Search Heuristics from SWALE

he had a heart defect that had gone undetected. The assumption was that the jogging put undue stress on his heart, causing the heart attack.

Based on the Jim Fixx case, SWALE can hypothesize that Len Bias had a previously undetected heart defect, and that jogging put undue stress on his heart, causing the heart attack.

Len Bias, however, was not a jogger. SWALE notices this contradiction and seeks to replace jogging in the Jim Fixx explanation with something more appropriate to Len Bias that can fill the same role. In other words, it asks itself, What did Len Bias do that prompted the heart attack?

To answer this question, SWALE attempts to find an action that Len Bias did often that could put stress on the heart. There are many different ways one could enumerate the activities of Len Bias. To put some control on this process, SWALE uses a specialized search heuristic called Substitute Action: Actor Theme to guide search. Specialized search heuristics guide search procedures to look in memory in places where answers are likely to be found. In this case, search heuristics are told to look at the *thematic roles* Len Bias plays in his life and, for each of those, consider actions specific to that role.

The first role SWALE looks at is Bias's role as a basketball player. Basketball players normally do practice shots and wind sprints. Because doing wind sprints is a kind of running (as is jogging), SWALE can identify it as an action with the potential of putting stress on the heart. SWALE therefore proposes that Len Bias's heart attack was provoked by his doing wind sprints, which put too much stress on his heart (which had an unknown defect), causing the heart attack.

This problem might have been solved by local search, searching in the environs of jogging in the semantic network for activities that Len Bias does that could prompt a heart attack. Why is specialized search better? Using local search to attempt a substitution for jogging in the Jim Fixx explanation would yield a large number of activities related to jogging. For each of them, the reasoner would have to ask two questions: Is this something Len Bias does? and Could this prompt a heart attack? Using specialized search instead, only those activities that Len Bias is known to do are considered. For each of these, of course, the reasoner must ask whether it could prompt a heart attack. But specialized search is better for two reasons. First, fewer substitutions are considered (there are fewer activities specific to Len Bias than related to jogging). Second, for each substitution that is considered, fewer questions must be asked of it. The search itself directs memory to find only items that fulfill one of the requirements.

Is specialized search always more efficient than local search? There are several things to consider in determining that. First is the cost of the search. Which costs more, a simple local search or a specialized search? The answer may be different in each memory. In general, however, the broader one allows the local search to be, the more costly it is. Specialized search, by its nature, is meant to be cheap. Second is the cost of the questions we must ask of what is found. Does it cost more to ask the questions we must ask of items found by local search or those found by specialized search? In the Bias example, it is obviously cheaper to ask questions after specialized search because the questions that need to be asked are a subset of those needed for local search. In general, this will be the case, because specialized search will look for items that are as close to what is needed as possible. Third is the chance of finding something useful. If semantic networks are set up just right, a small local search might yield an answer quickly. If not, then in some cases local search may not be able to yield an answer at all in a reasonable period of time. Specialized search is more likely to find a potentially reasonable answer quickly because it directs search to appropriate places in memory.

To give a case-based reasoner specialized search capabilities, two things must be done:

- Specialized search heuristics must be defined.
- Applicability criteria must be associated with each heuristic.

Search heuristics should be defined that can help in finding all types of items that will be requested on a regular basis and that have a well-known method of being found. In addition, the reasoner must be given guidelines on when to try each heuristic. Specialized search is as efficient as the specialization makes it. Thus, the description of when each heuristic should be used should be concrete and recognizable. Heuristics might be indexed by those criteria, or some other method of access can be used.

11.1.6 **Case-Based Substitution**

Local search is appropriate for finding a substitute if one exists close by in memory's hierarchies, and specialized search is good for finding substitutes in well-known places. Sometimes the best place to find a substitute, however, is in another similar case. **Case-based substitution** (Figure 11.18) looks for a substitute by finding a case that can suggest an alternative. In the example in the introduction to this section, case-based substitution was suggested to find a vegetarian substitute for lasagne. Rather than searching the set of pasta dishes for a vegetarian one similar to lasagne (as query memory would do), the set of cases that include pasta dishes is searched to find an appropriate alternative. Another case might, for example, suggest substituting manicotti for lasagne.

Problem: Some element in the solution does not fill the needs of the new problem
AND local search is inapplicable or yields no answer.
Solution: Find a case that can suggest an alternative. Extract that alternative and use it.

FIGURE 11.18   Case-Based Substitution.

The big question that arises here, of course, is why not use the case that provides the alternative suggestion in the first place? The answer is that though that case can suggest a useful alternative, it might not provide the best overall match to the new situation. An example from CLAVIER will both illustrate the substitution method and illustrate this point.

Given a set of composite parts to cure in an autoclave (a large convection oven), CLAVIER (Hennessy and Hinkle 1992) must derive a set of layouts that cure everything, such that the parts in each layout will cure in the same amount of time. CLAVIER has just retrieved a case that suggests how several of the high-priority parts might be laid out in the autoclave for curing. All the parts in that layout except one match parts CLAVIER must cure. CLAVIER must find a substitute among its parts-to-be-cured for the one unmatched part.

CLAVIER does this by looking in its case library for *pieces of similar cases* that can suggest substitutes. It does this by searching for cases with pieces similar to the piece of the initially retrieved case that needs revision. In CLAVIER, the tables in the autoclave represent a case's pieces. CLAVIER therefore looks for cases with tables in them similar to the one that needs fixing.

Figure 11.19 shows the inputs and outputs of the process. The first column shows the initially retrieved case and its unmatched part. The fourth column shows cases retrieved from the case library that can suggest substitutes. The darkened parts of those cases are the pieces of those cases that partially match the table in the initially retrieved case that held the unmatched part. Note that CLAVIER finds three such cases, all of which have a piece that matches the three matching parts from the initially retrieved case and that has a different part in the place where the unmatched part was located. Note also the second column, which shows CLAVIER's context for searching the case library for a substitute. *Context determination* is the process of specifying what to look for in the case library. It will be discussed in more detail later.

Next CLAVIER examines the suggestions made by retrieved cases and chooses the most appropriate one. First, it narrows the suggestions. We can see that two of the suggestions were for pieces of a case that were in the same relative location in the autoclave as the piece from the intially retrieved case needing revision. The other case's piece was located in a different place in the autoclave. CLAVIER prefers the suggestions made by cases where the case piece had a more similar spatial context. Thus, there are two suggestions made: the H-shaped part and the parallelogram-shaped part. Because there is an H-shaped part of high priority in CLAVIER's list of items to be cured, it chooses to substitute that part.

There are two steps to the case-based substitution process:

1. Find cases with pieces similar to the piece that needs revision.
2. Choose a substitute from among the suggestions.

In the first step, appropriate cases are retrieved from the case library. In the second step, their suggestions are extracted and evaluated, and one is chosen.

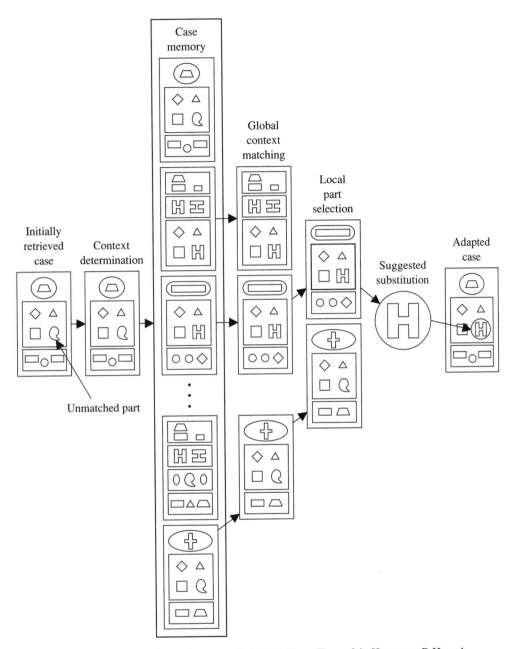

FIGURE 11.19 Case-Based Substitution in CLAVIER. From Figure 2 in Hennessy, D.H. and Hinckle, D. (1992), "Applying Case-Based Reasoning to Autoclave Loading," *IEEE Expert* 7(5), pp. 21–26.

As shown in this example, finding cases requires deriving a description of cases that should be searched for. Initial case retrieval looks for cases whose problem specifications are similar to that of the new situation; case-based substitution looks for cases that have parts that are similar to a part of the solution-in-progress that needs revision. Similarity is judged across solution components, and only some aspects of the old solution should appropriately be compared. A meal planner looking for a substitute for lasagne in an Italian meal will be looking for a meal with Italian cuisine that has pasta as a main dish and that has side dishes similar to those that have already been chosen but will be little concerned with the dessert or appetizer that was served previously. CLAVIER is concerned with finding a case that has a table similar to the one that is incomplete in its solution-in-progress. It doesn't care a lot about the rest of the layout.

In order to find appropriate cases, two things are necessary:

- A system must be able to construct a description of what it is looking for.
- Cases must be indexed to allow retrieval based on the contents of their parts.

Constructing a description of cases to look for is called *context determination* in CLAVIER. Context determination means figuring out specifications for the kinds of cases that, if retrieved, could potentially suggest good substitutions. The designers of CLAVIER found that there are two components to this specification: a partial description of the kinds of case pieces that, if found, would help, called *local context*, and a description of the more *global context* that case piece should be embedded in to be useful. Local context in CLAVIER is the spatial context associated with the table that has the unmatched piece—what else is on the table and where in the oven the table is located. Global context includes relevant information about the remainder of the layout. In CLAVIER that includes the type of composite material used in other parts in the load, the type of mold being used (e.g., steel or aluminum), and a general description of the types of parts in the load (e.g., beams, ribs, stiffeners). These describe the general heat-up characteristics of items in the load. The working hypothesis here is that the best substitutions will share globally similar characteristics in addition to being descriptively similar (Hennessy and Hinkle 1992).

In addition to CLAVIER, JULIA and CELIA each do case-based substitution. JULIA's specifications of case pieces include as local context the other dishes in the courses of the meal that it is focusing on and as global context such things as the cuisine of the meal, the formality of the meal, the required ease of preparation, and the way in which it will be served (e.g., buffet). CELIA, which diagnoses automobile malfunctions, uses as local context the reasoning goal it is attempting to carry out (e.g., verify a hypothesis) and the actions that have been done so far in that attempt. As global context, it includes the type of car and year it was made, previous reasoning goals that are still unachieved, and previous hypotheses that have been shown to be faulty.

Important to being able to access pieces of cases is an indexing mechanism that allows that to happen. What is necessary is an indexing scheme that indexes cases according to descriptions of their case pieces. Chapter 5 discusses two ways this might be done. One possibility is to break cases into pieces and index their pieces separately. Using this method, each case piece is indexed according to the situations in which it is expected to be useful. Important to this indexing scheme is that case pieces be indexed not only by their own descriptors but also by relevant parts of the context in which they are embedded. The second method is to index cases according to both the situations in which the entire case ought to be retrieved and those in which its component parts should be retrieved. There is no hard-and-fast rule for which of these is more appropriate. CLAVIER and JULIA index by the second method; CELIA indexes by the first. The important thing is that case pieces be accessible and that they be accessible through a combination of their local and global context.

11.1.7 Memory Organization Requirements for Substitution Methods

Several of the methods discussed depend on abstraction hierarchies holding the kinds of concepts that need substitution. In previous chapters, we have addressed the organization of cases in memory, but we have left mysterious the organization of what many call *semantic memory*. In a traditional approach to semantic memory, concepts are organized hierarchically in semantic networks. Each concept knows all its children concepts (instances links) and each knows its parents (isa and inst links). Figures 11.13 and 11.15 are standard traditional semantic networks.

Semantic networks are good for storage economy and provide good support for feature inheritance. But they have a problem: Traversal down the hierarchy is unconstrained. One can get out all descendants of a parent node, but in its traditional formulation, one cannot concentrate on one or a subset of descendants. As a result, search for a concept within a traditional semantic network can be quite expensive. If search methods used for case-based reasoning are to be efficient, some additions to the traditional formalism are needed. What we propose is to add indexed links, like those used to organize case memories, to the semantic network that can guide traversal downward. Such links allow control of query memory and the refinement step of local search.

The illustration of PLEXUS's memory in Figure 11.15 can be used to illustrate. There are currently no downward labels in that network. If we look at the buy ticket node, for example, we see that it has two children—buy theater ticket and buy BART ticket. If we index buy theater ticket by features from the environment that predict its applicability and we also index buy BART ticket by features that predict its applicability, then either can be accessed directly from buy ticket without having to check the applicability of each of buy ticket's children. Both might be indexed by a description of the visual environment (existence of a booth with a person in it for buy theater ticket; existence of a ticket machine for buy BART ticket), and they might also be indexed by the situations in which they tend to be applicable (going to the theater and going to the movies for buy theater ticket; taking the subway for buy BART ticket). Indexing of this sort would allow efficient traversal of memory's semantic networks based on a description of what is being searched for or a description of the situation described by a case.

11.2 TRANSFORMATION

Substitution is appropriate if there already exists an item or concept that can be substituted for some inappropriate value. But it cannot be used if the item required does not yet exist. Nor can it be used for insertions or deletions of extra items in an old solution.

Consider, for example, a case-based reasoner that needs to plan a kosher meal.[3] Due to a variety of other requirements on the meal, it is reminded of a meal where lasagne was served. Lasagne, however, is not kosher. In particular, it mixes milk and meat in the same dish. If memory knows of a lasagne recipe with no milk or no meat, it might be substituted for the lasagne in the old meal. But let's suppose that memory knows of no such dish. It could substitute something completely different for the lasagne, or it could figure out a way to make the lasagne fit the constraints of being kosher, that is, a way to *transform* it to fit the constraints of the new situation.

How can this transformation work? Some simple commonsense guides us in this process. If the dish cannot contain both milk and meat products, then either one or the other must be deleted or substituted. Because meat is a secondary ingredient of the recipe, one possibility is to delete it using a transformation heuristic called delete secondary feature. Another possibility is to substitute for meat something else that could fulfill the same function (using a transformation heuristic called substitute feature). This requires, first, determining meat's function, and then finding a substitute using one of the substitution methods. If we look at meat as a protein provider, we can substitute tofu or fish for it. If we look at it as a texture provider, then we can substitute something like spinach or eggplant.

Alternatively, the problem could be solved by leaving the meat in the lasagne and taking out the milk products (cheese and butter). Cheese is a primary ingredient and thus cannot be deleted. Butter is a secondary ingredient, but it provides a necessary function beyond just being a dairy food (keeps the lasagne from sticking to the pan), so it cannot be deleted. Substitutions for both those ingredients can be made, however (using substitute-feature). A substitute for cheese that has the same taste and texture is tofu-cheese (a tofu product), and a substitute for butter that keeps things from sticking and has the same texture is nondairy margarine.

Transformation can also be guided by a causal model. Consider, for example, the following case that CASEY (Koton 1988a) had to solve. CASEY's new patient is named Newman. He is 65, a male, exhibits dyspnea on exertion, has anginal chest pain, and so on. Figure 11.20 shows more of his signs and symptoms. CASEY's is reminded of an old patient named David, who had limited cardiac output due to aortic valve disease. A full explanation of his condition can be found in Figure 11.21. CASEY's task is to diagnose or explain Newman's heart problem. What would be ideal would be to simply be able to transfer the explanation of David's problem to Newman. For a variety of reasons, however, the explanation of David's heart problem cannot be transferred intact to explain Newman's problem. In particular, their ages, pulse rates, body temperatures, angina, mean arterial pressure, syncope, pulse, and other signs are different. Some features evident in David are not seen in Newman, and vice versa.

---

3. Kosher meals contain no food items known to be not kosher and may not contain both milk and meat products. Not kosher items include pork, shellfish, the byproducts of each of these, and any meat product that has not been slaughtered and rendered in the ritual way.

New problem: Patient: Newman

History: age = 65, sex = male, dyspnea on exertion, orthopnea absent, chest-pain angi-nal, anginal within-hours unstable, syncopy/near-syncope on exertion, palpita-tions none, nausea/vomiting absent, cough absent, diaphoresis absent, hemptysis absent, fatigue absent, therapies none

Lab findings: ekg lvh normal-sinus, cxr calcification, calcification mitral aortic-valve

Vital signs: blood-pressure 138 80, heart-rate 90, arrhythmia-monitoring normal, resp 20, temp 98.4

Physical exam: appearance nad, mental-status conscious, jugular-pulse normal, pulse slow-rise, apex-impulse normal, para-sternal-impulse normal, chest clear-to-aus-cultation-and-percussion, abdomen normal-exam, extremities normal-exam

FIGURE 11.20 A New Case for CASEY—Newman

CASEY uses *model-based repair strategies* to adapt the explanation of David's case to Newman. Because Newman's syncope on exertion (dizziness) can be explained by limited cardiac output, a state already in the explanation of David's problem, for example, CASEY inserts syncope on exertion into the explanation it is working with and connects it causally to limited cardiac output. Because slow-rise pulse can be explained by slow ejection, already in the explanation it has started with, CASEY inserts that into the old explanation and

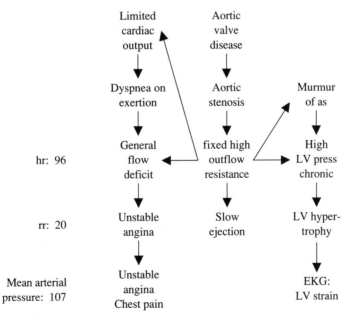

FIGURE 11.21 The Solution to One of CASEY's Cases—David

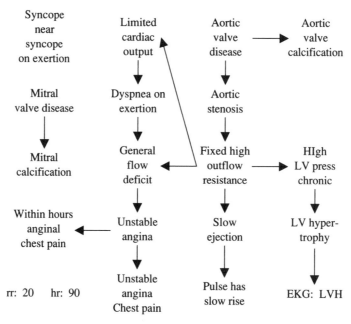

FIGURE 11.22   Causal Explanation of Newman's Problem—Derived by Repairing the Explanation of David's Problem

connects it causally to slow ejection. To do these insertions, CASEY uses a model-based repair heuristic called add evidence. Add evidence is used whenever some feature in the new case that was not in the old one is supported by some state in the explanation of the old case. A causal model describing which states cause which other ones is consulted to make this determination. In solving the case of Newman, CASEY refers to its causal models of cardiac behavior to make ten adaptations to the explanation of David's condition. In addition to adding evidence, CASEY knows how and when to remove and substitute evidence, to add and remove states, and to add links. Figure 11.22 shows the solution CASEY builds using model-guided repair.

Transformation is the process of transforming an old solution to fit the new situation by making deletions or insertions, or transforming some element of the old solution by deleting some part of it, inserting some new element, adjusting the amount of something, or making a substitution. Model-guided repair, which reasons based on a causal model to suggest an adaptation, can be used for transforming either the structure of a solution or some value. Commonsense transformation uses general-purpose commonsense heuristics for adapting values needing transformation.

11.2.1 Commonsense Transformation

The example shows that commonsense transformation (Figure 11.23) uses a small set of heuristics that use knowledge about the relative importance of different components of an item to

Problem: Some element of the old solution violates the constraints of the new situation AND no substitutable item exists.

Solution: Transform the element using commonsense transformation rules. Such rules use knowledge about the relative importance and functions of different components of an artifact.

FIGURE 11.23   Commonsense Transformation

determine whether deletions or substitutions should be done. There are several requirements for making commonsense transformation work:

- Systems must be able to identify the component of the item being transformed that is in need of repair.
- Representations must separate out primary from secondary components of artifacts.
- Representations must maintain internal relationships between elements of problems being solved.

To see the importance of each of these, consider again the lasagne example. Lasagne violates the kosher constraint by including both milk and meat products. In order to transform the lasagne recipe to make it kosher, it is necessary to identify what needs to be transformed. This requires, first, identifying the violation and, second, identifying what needs to be done to remove it. The violation here is of a constraint that specifies a combination of ingredients that should not be used together. Removing a violation of a combination restrictor requires deleting one or the other of the items in the restricted combination.

JULIA (Hinrichs 1992), which this example is taken from, uses a reason maintenance component to identify inconsistencies in its solutions. The process works like this:

- JULIA *transfers* its old solution to the new case.
- JULIA's constraint propagator *propagates constraints* stemming from its new problem specification into the transferred solution.
- JULIA's reason maintenance system *notices violations.*
- JULIA's adaptation engine applies commonsense transformation heuristics to get rid of the violations.

How does it work for this example? The old solution is lasagne, defined as an Italian food with ingredients pasta, ricotta cheese, mozzarella cheese, beef, tomato sauce, oregano, garlic, basil, and pepper. The new problem specification states that the meal must be kosher, according to the constraint specified in Figure 11.24. Propagating the piece of the constraint that states that milk and meat products cannot both be used in the same meal, JULIA finds that the ingredients list of lasagne violates it. It thus identifies the *ingredients* of lasagne as needing transformation. The constraint itself, which specifies a proscribed combination, is used to identify that either deleting the milk products or deleting the meat products will suffice.[4]

---

4. JULIA uses resolution in this step to identify what needs changing.

```
(and (doesnt-contain (?ingredients) obviously-non-kosher-food required)
     (not (and (contains (?ingredients) meat required)
               (contains (?ingredients) dairy-product required)
               required)
          required)
     required)
```

FIGURE 11.24   JULIA's Representation of the Kosher Constraint

JULIA is now ready to make its repair. It has at its disposal several transformation heuristics, shown in Figure 11.25. It is because of the knowledge these heuristics need that representations need to specify which components of an item are primary and which are secondary. Primary components are those that in some way define the artifact—you can't have lasagne without the lasagne noodles and the ricotta. Secondary components play support roles but don't define the dish. The beef is in this role. Because JULIA knows which ingredients of dishes are primary and which are secondary, it can effect substitutions and deletions in a sensible way.

These heuristics also require that internal relationships between components of an object be maintained. This is necessary to effect appropriate substitutions. The ricotta cheese in lasagne, for example, provides protein and also provides a liquid texture. It wouldn't make sense to substitute beef for the ricotta cheese, because, although the beef provides protein, it cannot provide the necessary liquid texture. It makes no sense to substitute beef for the mozzarella because that provides another kind of texture that the beef can't provide. Figure 11.26 shows the representation for lasagne that JULIA uses that makes clear both the importance and the role of components of an object.

Using this representation and these heuristics, JULIA has several choices for transforming the lasagne into a kosher dish. It can focus on the role of the beef as a protein provider and find a substitution for the beef using a local search, perhaps turning up vegetarian-burger. It can focus on the role of the beef as a texture provider, deciding that its role as a protein provider is unimportant, and find a substitute for beef that provides similar texture (perhaps by finding another dish similar to lasagne that has spinach or eggplant in it). Alternatively, it can decide that neither the protein role nor the texture role of the beef is important and use delete

Delete secondary component: A secondary component that does not serve a necessary functional role can be deleted.

Substitute component: Replace any component with another that can fulfill the same functions.

Add component: Add needed components, making sure their effects don't counter the necessary functions of other components.

Adjust the amount of a component: Do this in response to needed results.

FIGURE 11.25   Some Commonsense Transformation Heuristics

LASAGNE
```
isa: pasta-dish
cuisine: italian-cuisine
main-ingredients:
    ingr1: tomato-sauce
            function: liquid, sauce, taste
    ingr2: lasagne-noodle
            function: texture, structure
    ingr3: ricotta-cheese
            function: taste, sauce, protein
    ingr4: mozzarella-cheese
            function: taste, texture, protein
secondary-ingredients:
    ingr1: egg
            function: binding
    ingr2: ground-beef
            function: texture, protein
seasonings: (salt pepper oregano basil garlic)
cost: cheap
ease-of-prep: easy
taste: mild
```

FIGURE 11.26   Representing Importance and Role of Components

`secondary` component to delete the beef from the dish. Alternatively, it can focus on the milk products—the two kinds of cheeses—and use `substitute component` to find substitutions for those. Its substitution for the ricotta must be able to help form a liquid sauce, and its substitution for mozzarella must be of similar texture (i.e., runny).

11.2.2 Model-Guided Repair

Whereas commonsense transformation relies on commonsense knowledge of regularities in the world, **model-guided repair** is a method for transformation that relies on knowledge of the causal connections of some type of system or situation. Because high blood pressure and irregular heartbeat, for example, are both known to result from clogged arteries, high blood pressure can be replaced by irregular heart rate in an old solution in which irregular heart rate was thought to result from clogged arteries. Model-guided repair is a collection of heuristics that access causal models to transform an old solution to make it fit the new situation. The heuristic used to replace irregular heart rate with clogged arteries, for example, is called `substitute-evidence`. This heuristic says that if two states can provide evidence for the same other state, they can be substituted for each other. When used in the example above, this heuristic examines the causal model explaining cardiac behavior to find if they could both provide evidence for some state. It finds that they do and therefore effects the substitution.

As in parameter adjustment, repairs made using model-guided repair derive from evaluation of the differences between the description of the old problem and that of the new one.

Problem: Features of the old case are different from those in the new one, and a causal model describing the relationships between solution components is available to reason from.

Solution: Adjust the old solution as follows:

1. *Compare* the old and new problems and extract differences.

2. *Evaluate* differences between the old and new problems using the available causal model and *characterize* the differences.

3. For each difference, *apply the appropriate model-guided repair heuristic* to the old solution to create a new one.

FIGURE 11.27 Model-Guided Repair

First differences are evaluated with respect to the model and classified by type. Then repairs associated with each difference are made. There are two major differences between parameter adjustment and model-guided repair, however. First, parameter adjustment can only adjust values and quantities of values. Model-guided repair can be used to transform the structure of an old solution or to repair some component. Second, the specialized adjustment heuristics in parameter adjustment are specialized to particular kinds of parameters in particular domains. They encode what seems to work but are based on no hard model. Model-guided repair heuristics are general-purpose and are based on our knowledge of causality. There is one associated with each type of change one can make in a causal explanation. Particular causal models accessed by the general-purpose heuristics serve to specialize the heuristics to particular domains. Figure 11.27 shows the steps required to make a model-guided repair.

Two programs that make extensive use of model-guided repair are CASEY (Koton 1988a, 1989) and KRITIK (Goel 1989, 1991b). CASEY uses model-guided repair for a diagnosis task: to adapt the causal explanation of a previous patient's heart ailment to the specifics of a new situation. KRITIK uses model-guided repair for two tasks: to design new devices based on the design of old ones, and to create causal explanations of how a new device works based on the causal explanation of the device it was based on.

CASEY's repair heuristics are closely associated with its *evidence heuristics*, explained in chapter 9. As was discussed there, CASEY's evidence heuristics evaluate the differences between an old and new problem to determine if two cases could be made to match. They thus implement step 2 of model-guided repair. CASEY has repair heuristics associated with each evidence heuristic that know how to carry out the repair that is necessary to make an old solution fit a new situation. Figure 11.28 shows the relationships between CASEY's evidence heuristics and its repair strategies.

Both evidence rules and repair rules in CASEY deal with the causal connectedness of explanations. Evidence rules attempt to find evidence for new symptoms in the explanations of old cases. Repair strategies fix the old explanations to reflect those relationships.

Let us go back to the example in section 11.2 and examine how it is solved. First, the case-based reasoner must notice the differences between the old and new cases (shown in Figure 11.29). There are three classes of differences:

- Different values filling the same field (e.g., age, pulse rate)
- Descriptors in the old case that are not in the new one (e.g., syncope)
- Descriptors in the new case that are not in the old one (e.g., orthostatic change)

Second, evidence heuristics classify those differences with respect to the causal model that is available. As discussed in chapter 9, CASEY classifies differences 1, 2, 3, 5, and 10 as being in the same qualitative region. It identifies 6 as an unrelated old case feature, finds that 7 and 9 both support some state in the old solution, that 8 provides other evidence for some state already in the old solution, and that 11 is an unrelated feature in the new case. It has no information on 4. Finally, to adapt the old explanation to the new cases, CASEY applies the repair heuristics associated with each of these classes of differences. Figure 11.30 shows the repair heuristics it applies. After applying those heuristics, CASEY ends up with the explanation found in Figure 11.21.

CASEY deals with causal models at the level of movement from state to state. But causal models can include more than that. In particular, some causal models record the mechanism that makes the state change happen. For example, a cooling system might change a liquid from a warm to a cool state by means of passing it through a series of cooled pipes. Faults in the system show themselves in the states of the objects but need to be tracked down to mechanisms that failed. CASEY assigns blame for symptoms to components of a system (e.g., the aortic valve is calcified); faults can also be explained by mechanisms causing the faulty component (e.g., the chemical mechanism that takes calcium away in the blood is inhibited). For some applications, explanations of faulty mechanisms are not necessary; for others they can provide useful guidance for adaptation. KRITIK shows how knowledge of causal mechanisms can guide adaptation.

KRITIK implements model-guided repair for the task of design and has defined repair heuristics that address the mechanisms behind a change of state. An example from KRITIK (Goel 1989) will show the need for knowledge about causal mechanisms in guiding repair and

Evidence Rule	Repair Strategy
Rule-out	Remove-state
Other-evidence	Remove-evidence
Unrelated-oldcase-feature	Remove-evidence
Other-evidence	Add-evidence
Supports-existing-state	Add-evidence
Same-qualitative-region	Substitute-evidence
Supports-existing-state	Add-state
Add-state	Add-link
Unrelated-newcase-feature	Add-measure

FIGURE 11.28   CASEY's Repair Strategies

No.	Feature Name	Value for Old Case	Value in New Case
1	Age	72	65
2	Pulse-rate	96	90
3	Temperature	98.7	98.4
4	Orthostatic-change	absent	unknown
5	Angina	unstable	within-hours & unstable
6	Mean-arterial-pressure	107	99.3
7	Syncope	none	on exertion
8	Auscultation	murmur of AS	unknown
9	Pulse	normal	slow-rise
10	EKG	normal sinus & lv strain	normal sinus & lvh
11	Calcification	none	mitral & aortic

All differences are judged insignificant by evidence rules.

- 1, 2, 3, 5, 10 same qualitative region
- 4 no information
- 6 unrelated oldcase feature
- 7, 9 supports existing state
- 8 other evidence
- 11 unrelated newcase feature

FIGURE 11.29 Differences Between Two of CASEY's Cases

Substitute-evidence hr:90 hr:96
Remove-evidence mean-arterial-pressure:107
Add-evidence within-hours unstable-angina
Remove-evidence murmur-of-as
Add-evidence slow-rise slow-ejection
Remove-evidence lv-strain
Add-evidence lvh lv-hypertrophy
Add-evidence aortic-calcification aortic-valve-disease
Add-state mitral-valve-disease
Add-evidence mitral-calcification mitral-valve-disease

FIGURE 11.30 Repairs Effected by CASEY on the Solution to David

BEGIN FUNCTION CoolSulphuricAcidHighAcidity
GIVEN:

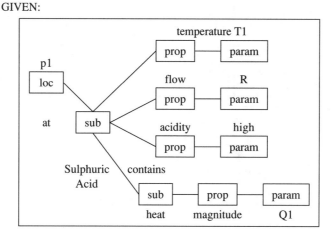

MAKES:

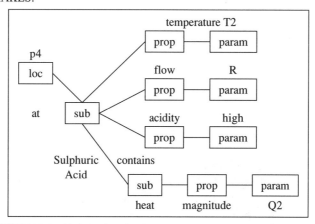

END FUNCTION CoolSulphuricAcidHighAcidity

FIGURE 11.31   A Problem Description from KRITIK—Design a Sulfuric Acid Cooler with the Properties Shown

the way KRITIK uses that knowledge. KRITIK is designing a device to cool high-acidity sulfuric acid in liquid form. Its problem description is shown in Figure 11.31. KRITIK is reminded of an old design for a nitric acid cooler shown in Figure 11.32; it cooled low-acidity nitric acid in liquid form. A portion of KRITIK's causal explanation of how the nitric acid cooler works is given in Figures 11.33 and 11.34. Examining the specifications in Figure 11.31

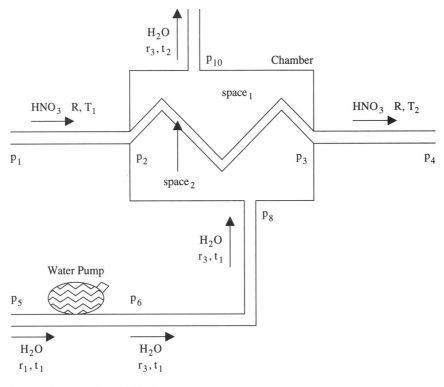

FIGURE 11.32   A Nitric Acid Cooler

and comparing them to the initial specification at the top of Figure 11.32 and the final specification at the bottom of Figure 11.34, we can see that though there are similarities between the requirements of the new case and the old one, there are also two differences. The new case uses a different kind of acid ("nitric acid" becomes "sulfuric acid") and has a property (high acidity) not specified in the old case.

KRITIK treats adaptation of the old design as a credit assignment problem. It views the design for the nitric acid cooler (the old case) as having failed to deliver the desired function of cooling sulfuric acid and attempts to find the structural faults responsible for the failure. To solve this problem, KRITIK uses the functional specification of the nitric acid cooler (the retrieved case) as an index to access the causal mechanisms responsible for achieving its function (among them, the mechanisms shown in Figures 11.33 and 11.34). Then it uses the functional differences between the nitric acid and sulfuric acid coolers to access applicable modification plans.

Modification plans are associated with the kinds of differences there are between artifacts; each plan gets its knowledge from the specifics of the materials, properties, and mechanisms comprising those differences. The modification plan used for this adaptation, for example, is one of the family of **substance-property-difference plans**. The one used here knows

BEGIN BehaviorCoolNitricAcid-1

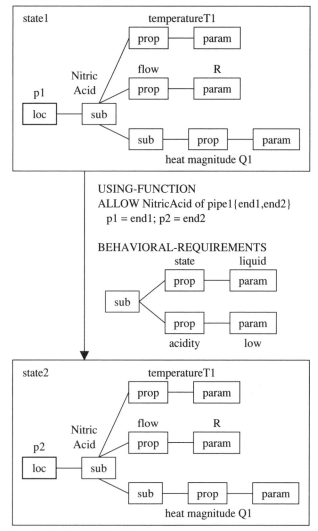

END BehaviorCoolNitricAcid-1

FIGURE 11.33 A Portion of the Explanation of How the Nitric Acid Cooler Works

how to transform old designs to deal with the particular property *acidity* of liquid substances. This plan is akin to a specialized-search heuristic. It looks for potential faults responsible for a mechanism's failure to accommodate the designated property, in this case cooling of a high-acidity substance. Knowledge of high-acidity substances and their requirements for cooling guide the search. Applying this heuristic and using knowledge about high-acidity substances,

BEGIN BehaviorCoolNitricAcid-3

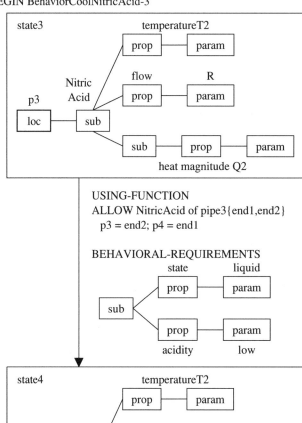

USING-FUNCTION
ALLOW NitricAcid of pipe3{end1,end2}
  p3 = end2; p4 = end1

BEHAVIORAL-REQUIREMENTS

END BehaviorCoolNitricAcid-3

FIGURE 11.34   Explanation of the Nitric Acid Cooler

KRITIK discovers that the pipes in its nitric acid cooler (pipe3(p3,p4) in Figure 11.34) allows the flow of low-acidity substances but not high-acidity ones. Having identified this fault, the plan's next step is to generate a new functional description of the faulty component (it should allow the flow of high-acidity substances) and to query memory for such a component. It then effects a substitution.

Whereas CASEY uses a general model of a device and general-purpose evidence rules to create new explanations of malfunctions from old ones, KRITIK uses a combination of causal models of particular devices and functional descriptions of components to discover what makes an old device inappropriate for carrying out newly specified functions. KRITIK's causal models of physical devices annotate state transitions with the causes responsible for the transition. Its models explain the cause for a state transition in terms of a function of a device component, a structural relation between components, a physics principle, or a qualitative parametric equation. Though such knowledge is not necessary to identify faulty states, it is necessary to identify faulty mechanisms and to find ways of repairing them.

11.3 SPECIAL-PURPOSE ADAPTATION AND REPAIR HEURISTICS

The methodologies presented so far are general-purpose methods for carrying out adaptations. They are domain-independent, though they often rely on domain-specific knowledge. They are the *weak methods* for effecting adaptation. Experience in artificial intelligence has shown, however, that though weak methods are broadly applicable, application of knowledge specific to a domain often produces better results with less effort. The same is true in adaptation: special-purpose adaptation heuristics, when they exist, provide powerful guides for adaptation. Special-purpose adaptation heuristics typically guide three different kinds of adaptation:

- Domain-specific adaptation
- Structure modification
- General-purpose repair

Domain-specific adaptation refers to substitution and transformation rules specific to some problem domain. For example, chefs know that oregano can be replaced by a marjoram and thyme combination if oregano is not available. This is an adaptation specific to cooking. Domain-specific adaptation can best be illustrated with an example from CHEF (Hammond 1986a, 1989a). One of its domain-specific heuristics tells it that duck must be defatted before cooking. Attached to the concept *duck* in memory is a rule that says, "When stir-frying duck, defat it before cooking." Whenever the concept duck is encountered during problem solving, this heuristic is checked for applicability. If it is applicable, it is fired, and a defatting step is inserted in the recipe under construction.

This particular domain-specific adaptation heuristic modifies the structure of an old solution by inserting a new item into the structure. Structure modification is another function that special-purpose adaptation heuristics often carry out. Though we have many general-purpose methods for substituting values in old solutions, we have identified little in the way of general-purpose structure-modifying methods. Model-based repair is the only general-purpose method we've identified so far. Case-based adaptation, discussed in the next chapter, can also effect changes in structure. But most structure-modifying adaptations are implemented using special-purpose adaptation heuristics.

TWO BIRDS WITH ONE STONE

IF the function of a component part is redundant
  AND = there's no other reason for that component,
THEN delete it.

DIVIDE AND CONQUER

IF a slot cannot be filled because of overconstraint
  AND = overconstraint is due to constraints generated from
              individual members of a group,
THEN attempt to increase choice by splitting the overconstrained slot
              and partitioning the constraints.

FIGURE 11.35 Some Special-Purpose Adaptation Heuristics from JULIA

The domain-specific adaptation heuristic from CHEF shown here effects modifications to old solutions. But not all structure-modifying adaptation heuristics are domain-specific. JULIA uses special-purpose adaptation heuristics to make commonsense transformations on the structure of old designs. Examination of several of JULIA's heuristics will illustrate (Figure 11.35). *Two birds with one stone* is used to delete a structural part of a solution that is redundant. *Divide and conquer* expands the structure of an old solution by adding extra component parts that duplicate some part that is already there but in a way that allows all constraints to be satisfied. Some examples will illustrate.

JULIA is trying to plan a cheap, easy-to-prepare Italian meal. Based on its composite of Italian meals, it decides to serve an antipasto salad as the first course, then a pasta course, then the main course, and then dessert. It next sets itself the task of specifying the main course and, in the process, lasagne is suggested as a main dish. Though lasagne is easy to prepare, cheap, and Italian, it is a pasta dish. Serving it as a main dish would duplicate the function of the pasta course. JULIA applies *two birds with one stone* to delete the pasta course from the meal's structure.

JULIA is now trying to plan a meal for several guests who include a vegetarian allergic to milk products and someone who only eats "normal" food. Propagating these requirements into the meal, JULIA constrains the main dish to not include milk or meat or fish as ingredients and to have ingredients and combinations of ingredients that are common to American dinners. JULIA is unable to find a way of fulfilling these constraints—dishes common to American dinners all have meat, fish, or milk products in them. Dishes without milk, meat, or fish are not acceptable as "normal" food. *Divide and conquer* is applied, and it suggests serving two main dishes rather than one, one to fulfill the constraints of the vegetarian, another to fulfill the constraints of the traditional eaters.

Special-purpose adaptation heuristics are also used to guide general-purpose repair of a solution. Repair, remember, is adaptation that is carried out in response to feedback showing that a solution is faulty. Feedback might be obtained by evaluating the solution in some way (e.g., by projecting its results using a causal model) or by carrying out the solution and observing the results. When feedback about a solution is gathered, there is often more information available about how a solution must be changed to work than before feedback is obtained. When we taste a dish and it is too sour, for example, we know that it must be adapted to change its sweetness. Though repair can be carried out by many of the strategies and methods described up to now, some heuristics are applicable only during repair and not during earlier adaptation. In particular, the strategies CHEF uses to repair failed plans fall into this category.

CHEF is aware of approximately a dozen types of planning failures, all characterized primarily by the kinds of interactions plan steps can have with each other (e.g., side effect disables condition) and secondarily by the specifics of the interaction (e.g., the particular condition is balance). Planning failures index repair strategies appropriate to their repair. The intent in CHEF is to characterize repair strategies so that they are generally applicable across planning domains. Each strategy is indexed by the kinds of planning situations in which it is applicable, and each exists as a special-purpose heuristic.

One particular planning failure it knows about, for example, is when a side effect of an early plan step disables some condition necessary for a later plan step to work. For example, leavening in a baked dish will make the batter rise only if the amount of leavening and liquid in the batter are appropriately balanced. This is a condition necessary for the baking step to succeed. But, if in adding strawberries to a recipe, one inadvertently adds extra liquid to the batter, the balance will be off. A side effect of adding strawberries is that it disables the balance condition necessary to make the baking succeed. CHEF calls this planning failure `side-effect:disabled-condition:balance`, and it has several repair strategies associated with this condition:

`alter-plan:side-effect`: Use an action to achieve the initial goal that doesn't cause the offending side effect (e.g., add the taste of strawberries without the liquid).

`alter-plan:precondition`: Find an alternative to the blocked step that doesn't require the violated conditions (e.g., find a way to make batter rise that does not require balance between liquid and leavening).

`recover`: Put a step after the action that caused the side effect that will remove the offending state (e.g., find a step to remove the liquid that results from chopping the strawberries, and insert it before the batter is baked).

`adjunct-plan`: Add a new step to run concurrently with the plan that will allow it to satisfy the goal despite the violation (find a step that will allow baking the batter to have the desired effect).

`adjust-balance:up`: Adjust the imbalance by adding more of what there is less of (e.g., add more leavening to balance the liquid).

`adjust-balance:down`: Adjust the imbalance by deleting some of what there is too much of (e.g., get rid of some of the liquid).

Each also has cases associated with it illustrating the different ways each of the abstract strategies have been carried out. When CHEF encounters a planning failure in which a balance condition is disabled by a side effect of a previous step, it runs through these strategies, evaluating which are possible, and chooses one to apply. It uses the illustrative cases to determine how to apply the strategies and to help it judge whether they are applicable or likely to be productive.

INCREASING CHOICE:
```
IF slot is splittable,
   AND there are more than two unsatisfied constraints that derive from
      characters,
   AND those constraints can be divided into two disjoint sets along
      character-derived boundaries based on constraint incompatibility,
THEN generate two new subslots of the original slot, migrate the
      partitioned constraints to the new slots and schedule the new slots to
      be refined.
```

RECOGNIZING SLOT SPLITTABILITY:
```
IF slot represents a group,
   AND the slot is not itself a generated slot (ie, avoid infinite loops)
   AND the number of values stored in the slot does not exceed the
      prescribed cardinality in the slot description,
THEN the slot is splittable.
```

RECOGNIZING CONSTRAINT INCOMPATIBILITY:
```
IF two slots have identical arguments but inverse constraint types,
   OR they have identical constraint types but disjoint argument ranges,
THEN they are incompatible.
```

FIGURE 11.36   Divide-and-Conquer Inferences

In looking at the presented heuristics and their application, it is important to note that some are easier to apply than others—that is, some are easily identifiable as applicable; others require extensive inference before their applicability can be determined. For example, it is easier to notice that the average age of workers is old (if it is recorded) or if duck is being used in a recipe than to notice that the function of a component part is fulfilled by another component or that a failure is due to a side effect of an early step.

The ease with which the applicability of a special-purpose heuristic can be recognized is a factor in several different ways to control their application. One method, when the applicability of a heuristic is easy to recognize, is to implement the heuristics as *critics*. A critic, as first implemented in NOAH (Sacerdoti 1977) and HACKER (Sussman 1975), is a repair rule that is specialized to a particular kind of repair. A critic's antecedent allows it to recognize the need for a repair. Its consequent designates how to fix the problem. CHEF's heuristic for adding a step to defat duck fits this description. Critics can be implemented two different ways. When applicability is cheap to recognize, critics can be kept in a list, and applicability of each critic in the list can be checked each time a change is made to a solution. Alternatively, critics can be indexed by their applicability conditions and fired when those conditions are present. CHEF implements its domain-specific adaptation heuristics as critics. PERSUADER implements its parameter adjustment heuristics, which are also implemented as critics, using a list (to be discussed in more detail in the next chapter).

When the applicability of a special-purpose heuristic is hard to ascertain, they need to have associated with them some criteria for knowing when they might be applicable. That is, they need to be indexed by features most likely to predict their applicability. After being accessed through their indexes, their applicability conditions are checked to see if they can be applied. Consider, for example, the critic *divide and conquer* in JULIA (see Figure 11.35). In order to ascertain its applicability, a long string of inferences is necessary. Figure 11.36 shows some of them. The string of inferences is only triggered, however, when JULIA's reason maintenance system notices an overconstrained slot. In effect, the critic is indexed by the description `overconstrained-slot`. Similarly, *two birds with one stone* is triggered when a constraint ruling out duplication of components is violated. CHEF's general-purpose repair heuristics are indexed for the same reason. Though they are powerful when applicable, recognizing their applicability is complex; therefore, they are indexed by the kinds of failure situations in which they are applicable, and only when such a situation is encountered is their application attempted.

Another way to control application of critics is to group them by function. PERSUADER, for example, has special-purpose adaptation heuristics that serve several different purposes. Some are used for parameter adjustment early in the reasoning. Others are used later for anticipation of potential problems. Still others are used to compensate for changes. Because PERSUADER has its critics grouped by function, it can schedule those critics that require inference to determine their applicability to run only under appropriate circumstances. Another thing PERSUADER does to ensure that applicability of special-purpose heuristics is as cheap as possible is to leave flags around during processing that hold the information it needs for later adaptation. If it makes a change that changes equitability, for example, it sets a flag stating that. It maintains its state rather than having to compute it. The next chapter will discuss in detail the many different ways that application of adaptation methods and heuristics can be controlled.

11.4 DERIVATIONAL REPLAY

Each of the adaptation methods described up to now fixes an old solution to fit a new situation. Sometimes, however, it is more appropriate to recompute a new solution or partial solution using the same means by which the old solution was computed. Recall for a moment doing calculus or physics homework. The teacher had worked out some examples on the blackboard during class, or alternatively, some examples had been worked out in detail in the book. The exercises at the end of the chapter usually asked us to apply what was in the previous examples. Many of us did that by finding a previously worked out example and following its step-by-step procedure, substituting in the values from the new problem.

We call this process *derivational replay* (Carbonell 1986). Figure 11.37 shows the method. In derivational replay, solution creation is guided in a case-based way. Whole solutions can be computed by derivational replay, as happens in calculus class, or parts of solutions can be calculated this way.

Consider a problem from JULIA. JULIA is planning a vegetarian meal for someone allergic to milk products. Because it is early spring and asparagus is in season, it proposes serving an asparagus soufflé. But the soufflé has cheese in it. JULIA wonders how it can adapt

Problem: Some element of the old case does not fit the needs of the new case.
Solution: To compute a substitute element for the new case, recall how the old value
was computed and replay that computation.

FIGURE 11.37   Derivational Replay

the soufflé to make it acceptable and remembers a meal in which it adapted a tomato dish with cheese as a secondary ingredient by deleting the cheese (see chapter 5, Figure 5). JULIA repeats this inference process.

Derivational replay was first implemented in a program called ARIES (Carbonell 1986), a forerunner of PRODIGY/ANALOGY (Carbonell and Veloso 1988; Veloso and Carbonell 1989, 1993a). ARIES replayed the entire previous set of reasoning steps from a previous case to compute an answer to a new problem. This more complete method was called *derivational analogy*. Derivational analogy is useful when intermediate computations must be done to derive an answer from the problem statement, and when the results of those intermediate computations are dependent on the *constants* in the problem, and constants in the old and new cases are not the same. This happens when solving a new probability or calculus problem based on an old one. In general, it is true in many planning situations. PRODIGY/ANALOGY takes advantage of derivational analogy to create plans in a variety of domains, some of considerable complexity.

Derivational analogy also happens in doing some kinds of design. If, for example, a small change in specifications propagates through the entire design, it makes sense to use derivational analogy to solve the problem. BOGART (Mostow 1989a; Mostow and Barley 1987; Mostow, Barley and Weinrich 1989, 1992) and DIOGENES (Mostow 1989b, 1992; Mostow and Fisher 1989) do that for design.

Based on our experience, however, and based on our observations of people solving problems, we believe that in most cases, full derivational analogy is unnecessary. Though it cuts down the work in finding operators to apply in solving a problem, it still requires that all computations be done from scratch. It is often useful, however, to compute intermediate values in ways they have been computed in the past.

In order to apply derivational replay, a case must record more than just old solutions. In particular, it must record the inferences or computations that resulted in the solution and the reasons why those inferences were appropriate. If these two items are recorded for each part of a solution, the reasoner can check to see if the old inference chain or computation is appropriate in the new situation and, if so, apply it. Illustrations of JULIA's case representation in chapter 5 show how such knowledge can be recorded.

11.5 SUMMARY

Several methods for doing adaptation have been presented, along with the knowledge each needs to get its job done. The six substitution methods include reinstantiation, parameter adjustment, local search, query memory, specialized search, and case-based substitution. Commonsense transformation and model-guided repair are used to effect transformations. Special-purpose adaptation heuristics are useful for effecting domain-specific adaptations, structure-modifying adaptations, and general-purpose repair. Derivational replay provides guidelines for computing answers the way they have been computed in the past.

Adaptation results in several kinds of changes to an old solution. Its structure might be changed, or some value in it might be substituted. Adaptation processes are used to fit a previous solution to a new problem and to repair solutions that are found to be faulty after criticism or after trying them out in the world.

Still needing discussion are several control issues: choosing what to adapt, choosing an adaptation method, and the order in which to apply adaptation procedures if there are several that are applicable. These will be discussed in the next chapter.

12

Controlling Adaptation

Specifying adaptation methods and strategies is in many ways easier than controlling their application. Though it is easy to apply a well-specified adaptation method, it is harder to know when each of the methods should be applied. The programs written by researchers addressing adaptation issues show this problem well. SWALE, for example, has a huge library of adaptation methods (mostly of the local and specialized search varieties), and it is able to apply them well, but only if a person tells it which method to apply. Similarly, any adaptation method it applies can suggest large numbers of solutions. It is up to the user of the program to choose the one he or she thinks is most appropriate.

There are a variety of heuristic methods developed by researchers to help guide adaptation. In one approach, differences between the problem specification in the new problem and that in the remembered case are used to point out what needs to be adapted, while adaptation strategies associated with each of the classes of differences are chosen to carry out the adaptation. In another approach, a checklist is used: the system runs down its checklist to see what needs adapting and has adaptation methods attached to each kind of feature needing adaptation. In still another approach, the program waits to see what goes wrong when carrying out a plan, then analyzes the failure and applies adaptation strategies particular to the type of failure encountered. Still another approach uses recalled cases to figure out what needs to be adapted and applies adaptation methods suggested by the cases.

There are three big issues that must be addressed in looking at control of adaptation processes:

1. How can a reasoner know what to adapt?
2. How can a reasoner choose an adaptation method to use for that adaptation?

3. What kind of guidance is available to adaptation methods to move them toward the right kind of adaptation?

Every case-based reasoning program that does adaptation combines a means of choosing what to adapt with some means of doing the adaptation. Each is chosen according to the needs of the task and domain and according to the knowledge available for guidance. We will first address the issue of choosing something to adapt, then look at how to choose an adaptation method to carry it out. In both discussions, we will consider the knowledge necessary to guide the processes.

It should be noted up front that sometimes choosing what to adapt and choosing an adaptation method cannot be separated. In fact, sometimes the separation can be harmful—aiming the reasoner only toward component modifications when structure modifications would be more appropriate. We separate the two issues for explicatory purposes only, and at the end of the chapter, we consider two methods of control that combine the two choices: case-based adaptation and critic application.

12.1 IDENTIFYING WHAT NEEDS TO BE FIXED

PERSUADER is trying to put together a contract agreeable to both the union and the company management. It remembers a similar situation and the contract that goes with it. How can PERSUADER know which parts of the old contract need adaptation for the new situation? PERSUADER uses a checklist to guide it in doing a standard set of comparisons between the old case and the new one. The result of those comparisons is a list of items needing adaptation. It performs those adaptations and then uses another checklist of potential problems to help it foresee standard problems before they occur. It adapts for each of those. It then asks memory to return cases that could propose other potential problems and adapts for those.

JULIA is trying to create a meal for twenty people, some of whom are vegetarians. It should be easy to make and cheap. It remembers the lasagne dinner it served to a large group of people once. The normal lasagne recipe, which includes beef as an ingredient, won't feed vegetarians. How can JULIA identify the lasagne as an offending part of the old solution? For that matter, how can it identify the meat component of the lasagne as the problem with lasagne? And once it does, what should be adapted—the meat component or the lasagne itself? JULIA uses the support of a reason maintenance system and a constraint propagator to determine what in an old solution needs to be adapted to fit a new situation. When JULIA installs lasagne in the "main-dish" slot of the "main course," the reason maintenance system notices that one of its ingredients, meat, violates a posted constraint. JULIA then knows to do adaptations that will remove that violation.

JULIANA must plan a meal for a set of overweight kids. It must be cheap, easy to prepare, satisfy a variety of tastes, and so on. It remembers a nursing home meal for convalescing patients. That meal had to be high in calories. JULIANA chooses what to adapt by comparing the descriptions of the old problem and new one, looking for differences. It applies adaptation strategies appropriate to the differences. Because the first meal was high calorie and the second needs to be low calorie, it adapts the old solution to get the extra calories out. Fried chicken becomes broiled chicken; whole milk becomes skim milk.

There are six methods that we have discovered for identifying what in an old solution needs fixing to fit a new situation:

1. Differences in problem specifications point to a need to fix parts of an old solution (CASEY, JULIANA).

2. A checklist identifies standard problems that, if present, must be fixed (JUDGE, PERSUADER).

3. Inconsistencies between the proposed solution and stated goals and constraints of the new problem are identified and point to a need for fixes (JULIA, JULIANA, CLAVIER).

4. Projection of the results of a solution points to problems that must be repaired (KRITIK, PERSUADER, JULIA).

5. Causal analysis of the results of carrying out a solution points to failures that must be repaired (CHEF).

6. Adaptations done previously point to a need for compensatory adaptations (PERSUADER).

12.1.1 Using Differences Between Problem Specifications

Adaptations to old solutions compensate for the partial match between a new problem and an old case. When connections can be made between aspects of a problem specification and those in the solution, differences between problem specifications can be used to identify changes that must be made in an old solution and to guide the adaptation that makes those changes.

Consider CASEY. In previous chapters, we've seen how CASEY matches a new situation to an old case and how it does adaptation. There are three kinds of differences between two problem statements that CASEY, and any other matcher, must deal with:

1. Slots in the two problem specifications might be filled differently
2. Features in the new problem might be missing in the old one
3. Features in the old problem might be missing in the new one

During matching, CASEY uses its evidence rules to explain discrepancies between an old case and a new situation. It does this, in effect, by seeing if the old diagnosis could hold given the new information. It considers whether a new feature missing in the old case can be explained by a state in the old solution, whether a feature of the old case missing in the new one is necessary to the old solution, and so on. The result of this reasoning is a set of differences between the old and new problem that point to changes that must be made in the old solution to make it fit the new situation. Once that is done, CASEY applies its repair strategies to effect the changes. Because repair strategies are linked to the differences pointed out by evidence rules, choice of repair strategies is easy.

Using a causal model (as CASEY does) is one way to make clear the connections between features of problems and features of solutions. Another way is by means of parameter adjustment heuristics created specifically to bridge that gap. Parameter adjustment heuristics specify how changes in a problem specification translate into changes in the solution. A more violent crime requires a longer sentence (JUDGE). A higher cost of living requires a higher salary (PERSUADER). Though neither of these two systems chooses what to adapt by means of looking at differences between problem specifications, one could imagine that either could be controlled in that way. Differences between problem specifications would first be extracted, and for those where slots in the two problems are filled differently, parameter adjustment heuristics could be applied. The twist here, however, is that parameter adjustment heuristics can only handle differences in slot fillers. They cannot handle features missing in an old or new situation, so some other method is needed to deal with those.

In general, the systems that use differences between problem specifications to choose what to adapt also use those differences to choose adaptation strategies themselves. This linkage, however, is not absolutely necessary. JULIANA, for example, uses differences between problem specifications to decide what to adapt, but then it chooses its adaptation methods in several later steps.

An example from JULIANA will illustrate. JULIANA must plan a winter school lunch for overweight kids with chicken as a main dish. Because it is an institution, the food must be cheap and easy to prepare, and it must satisfy a variety of tastes. JULIANA remembers a summer nursing home meal for convalescing patients who need high-calorie fare. That food also had to be cheap and easy to make and had to satisfy a variety of tastes. The meal included milk, fried chicken, green beans almondine, whole wheat bread, and melon.

The differences between the two problems include the season in which the meal is being served (summer previously, winter currently) and the special diet being catered to (high-calorie previously, low-calorie currently). The old solution must be changed to accommodate the new season and the special diet. But we still don't know which particular pieces of the old solution must be changed. JULIANA identifies those by examining the justifications for decisions is made in constructing the old meal. In particular, it looks for those pieces of the old solution that were chosen taking season and diet into account. Those are the ones that need adaptation. If we look at the old case, we see that fried chicken was served because it was high in calories; the almonds were added to the green beans for the same reason; and whole milk, high in calories (as well as nutrition), was chosen as the drink. Melon was chosen because it is a summer fruit. JULIANA identifies those parts of the meal as pieces that need adaptation to fulfill the new constraints. The calories must be taken out of the chicken, green beans, and milk, and the fruit must be appropriate to the current season.[1]

In JULIANA and CASEY, both the differences between the old and new cases *and* connections between problem features and solution features work together in guiding choice of what to adapt. The examples show that though differences between the old case and the new situation are important in making that decision, differences are not enough, by themselves, to

---

1. We don't go into the adaptations themselves here. Briefly, however, JULIANA effects the adaptations by first attempting standard substitutions for the offending articles—whole milk becomes low-fat milk; green beans are steamed. It then does the harder refinements by a combination of local search and derivational replay. Local search for a low-calorie chicken dish yields broiled chicken. Derivational replay yields grapefruit as the fruit.

allow a reasoner to choose what to adapt. There are two processes that are necessary to using differences to choose what to adapt:

- Finding differences between an old case and a new situation
- Recording connections between problem descriptions and solutions

Identifying differences between an old case and a new situation was discussed in chapter 9, about partial matching. There we discussed the process of identifying which parts of old cases correspond to which parts of new situations. The process can be done using a causal model (as in CASEY), by structure mapping (Gentner 1983), or by using commonsense reconciliation heuristics (as in JULIA).

Recording connections between problem descriptions and solutions has not been addressed yet. There are two types of connections between problem descriptions and solutions that might be recorded:

- The ways in which situation descriptions and solutions tend to be related
- The actual connections between old situation descriptions and derived solutions

Using differences to guide choice of what to adapt requires that actual connections between old situations and solutions are recorded. Parameter adjustment heuristics record the ways situation descriptions and solutions *tend* to be related (e.g., worse crimes tend to result in harsher sentences), providing just enough information to allow adaptations to be carried out. But, as the examples show, parameter adjustment heuristics do not hold enough information in them to guide choice of what needs to be adapted. *Actual* connections between old situation descriptions and solutions are necessary for that.

CASEY records both types of connections: its old solutions record the specifics of the way internal states of a patient led to manifested signs and symptoms (i.e., old solutions record connections between their problem descriptions and solutions), and the causal model of the heart records causal connections one would expect in general. CASEY's evidence rules use a combination of these two kinds of knowledge to determine what needs adaptation. JULIANA records the relationships between old problem descriptions and solutions by storing justifications for its previous decisions: for example, the frying method was chosen for preparing the chicken because a high-calorie meal was required, melon was chosen because it was summer.[2] As shown above, these connections plus the differences between the two cases allow JULIANA to choose what needs adaptation. JUDGE and PERSUADER, by contrast, keep track of only the way problem and solution components *tend* to be related (in their parameter adjustment heuristics). CASEY and JULIANA can use differences between old and new cases to choose what to adapt; JUDGE and PERSUADER can use those differences only to effect adaptation.

---

2. This is done by attaching appropriate traces of the reason maintenance system to each piece of a solution.

12.1.2 Using a Checklist

Using differences between old and new situation descriptions is a useful way to identify what needs adaptation, but there are several circumstances that make computation of all differences between an old case and a new situation infeasible. First, when case descriptions are large, it can be inefficient to compute all the differences between problems and solutions. Second, when the important features that guide adaptation require complex inference to be derived, differences in surface features might not point to appropriate adaptations. We see the first problem in PERSUADER, the second in JUDGE.

In problem domains with either of these features, choice of what to adapt has been controlled through use of *adaptation checklists*. This method chooses what needs fixing by checking to see if standard problematic situations have arisen. In doing this, the need to fully compare problem descriptions is alleviated. An adaptation checklist records a set of tests that check the appropriateness of a solution. Each test can identify a different aspect of an old solution that requires fixing to fit the new situation. Items on the adaptation checklist often have one or a small set of standard fixes associated with them that can be applied if the test shows a potential problem with the old solution. Examples from PERSUADER and JUDGE will illustrate.

PERSUADER's problem specifications are large, and comparing old and new specifications to each other on all dimensions would be time-consuming. However, in PERSUADER's domain (labor-management disputes), there are two standard sets of problems that generally need fixing when attempting to apply an old contract to a new situation.

- Differences between important old and new case situation descriptors point to parameter adjustments that must be done.
- Several easily identifiable common problems arise in carrying out contract clauses, each of which points to a need for adaptation.

PERSUADER's first adaptation checklist therefore guides comparison of the situation descriptions of the old case and new situation along dimensions relevant to creating a good solution that usually need modification when attempting to fit an old solution to a new situation. Those standard dimensions include, among other things, cost of living, position of the company in the industry, industry differentials, job classifications, and inflation rates. When choosing what to adapt, PERSUADER walks down this checklist, comparing, for each, the values from the old case and the new situation and checking for discrepancies. For each, where there is a difference, it applies parameter adjustment heuristics appropriate to the dimension to modify the old solution appropriately. This adaptation checklist allows PERSUADER to identify and carry out the "easy" fixes that must be made.

PERSUADER's second adaptation checklist holds well-known and easily identifiable problems that commonly arise in carrying out solutions: for example, the company cannot afford the suggested contract; the salary in the suggested contract is incompatible with similar jobs in the same area. PERSUADER uses this second adaptation checklist to identify harder problems that must be fixed. If a test shows a potential problem with a suggested solution, PERSUADER tries to fix that problem, either by running one of the methods associated with that problem or by searching for a case in which the same problem arose and examining the way the problem was handled there. When a contract costs too much, for example, there are several options: lower the cost of the contract by lowering salaries and benefits, lower the cost of the contract by lowering costs, or pass the cost on to the buyer. Lowering the cost of the contract by lowering salaries and benefits is a standard means of fixing this problem, and this method is associated with the problem. The other two options are associated with cases in PERSUADER's case library.

JUDGE, which sentences juvenile criminals, uses a checklist for control because the standard set of important differences it needs to account for in its adaptation require complex inference. Blindly comparing old and new cases along surface features (e.g., who hit who) in JUDGE's domain is not sufficient for determining what needs adaptation and by how much. In JUDGE's domain there are a standard set of solution parameters that tend to need adaptation to make an old solution fit a new crime, however, the most important one being the criminal's sentence. Its checklist has this item on it. The test associated with this solution parameter knows that the harshness of a sentence depends on the criminal's motivation in carrying out the crime, the degree of violence shown, whether or not the degree of violence paralleled that of the victim, and so on. It computes these inferred dimensions for both the old and new case, compares the cases on these dimensions, and, based on those computations and comparisons, calls a parameter adjustment heuristic to adjust the old sentence to fit the new crime.

An adaptation checklist holds a set of tests that can be used to identify potential problems with a suggested solution. PERSUADER's first checklist identifies problems by identifying relevant differences between problem descriptions in an old case and a new situation. Its second checklist holds tests for identifying standard problematic qualities of a solution. Among other things, JUDGE's checklist holds a test that can identify if a sentence from a previous case is too hard or soft for a new situation. If a test on a system's adaptation checklist identifies a weakness in a proposed solution, its associated methods are run in an attempt to fix the problem. This might mean simply running an appropriate parameter adjustment heuristic, as in JUDGE and PERSUADER. It might mean attempting to choose between several associated methods, as PERSUADER does when using its second checklist. Or it might mean choosing an adaptation method from among the whole set available to the program.

12.1.3 Using Inconsistencies Between the Old Solution and Stated Goals

Another means of identifying what needs to be adapted is to compare the proposed solution to the goals and constraints of the new situation, finding inconsistencies. The solution is then adapted to remove those inconsistencies or violations. CLAVIER does this by identifying items in the suggested solution that are not in its problem specification. It then attempts to substitute something that is in the problem specification for the item that is not. CLAVIER can do this because the mapping from problem specification to solution components is straightforward—the same items (parts to be cured in the autoclave) appear in both specifications.

For domains in which descriptions in problem specifications are different from those in solution specifications the task is harder, however. In JULIA, for example, problems are described in terms of constraints describing attributes of items that will be in the solution; solutions hold concrete items. For example, a meal might be described as needing to be vegetarian, a rather abstract description that means that no item in the meal should have meat as an ingredient. A means of translating between the abstract constraint and its implications for individual items in the solution must be provided to notice descrepancies between problem specifications and proposed solutions.

The combination of a constraint propagator and a reason maintenance system is useful for doing this. The constraint propagator is responsible for propagating high-level (abstract) constraints into low-level (concrete) requirements. When given the constraint to accommodate vegetarians, for example, the constraint propogator is responsible for propogating a constraint to each item in the solution stating that meat must be ruled out of its ingredients. The reason maintenance system is responsible for noticing if constraints based on problem specifications violate suggested solutions.

This is JULIA's method. The steps are as follows:

1. *Transfer* the old solution to the new case.
2. *Propagate constraints* of the current problem statement into the solution structure.
3. *Notice violations*.
4. *Adapt* to get rid of violations.

Let us consider the lasagne problem again to see how this works. JULIA is planning an Italian vegetarian meal for a large group. It must be cheap and easy to prepare. JULIA recalls a cheap, easy Italian meal for a large group of people: an antipasto salad appetizer, lasagne and green salad for the main course, and ice cream for dessert.

JULIA transfers the old solution to its new case. It then propagates the constraints of the current problem statement into the solution. A *rule-out meat* constraint is propagated from the *vegetarian* constraint in the problem statement to the ingredients slot of each dish in the solution. Two violations are identified by the reason maintance system: the meat in the antipasto salad and lasagne both violate the *rule-out meat* constraint. The ingredients slots of the two dishes are singled out for adaptation to remove these violations.

Using this method, the solution proposed by an old case is checked for consistency with the goals and constraints of the new situation. Comparison of differences between problem descriptions is avoided. Using a checklist also alleviates the inefficiency of comparing problem descriptions to each other, but it aims adaptation only toward aspects of a solution that are known beforehand to be potentially problematic. Using a constraint propagator and reason maintenance system to identify components of an old solution needing modification allows choice of what needs to be adapted to be done on an individual basis for each case, allowing adaptation for both common and less common problems.

There is, however, a hidden complexity of this and several other of the methods presented here. When a violation is identified, we know approximately what to adapt, but there are, in general, several choices. In the example, the ingredients of lasagne are identified as being inconsistent with stated goals. We can fix this inconsistency by deleting or substituting ingredients of lasagne, in effect, transforming the lasagne to fit the new situation, or we can decide that the lasagne itself is faulty and should be replaced by something whose ingredients won't violate new constraints. How can this decision be made? In short, substitutions are attempted before transformations (because substitution is, in general, easier), and easier substitutions are tried before harder ones. A deeper discussion of these issues is in section 12.2.1.

12.1.4 Using Solution Projections

Another means of identifying what needs fixing is to project potential problems with a suggested solution. The intent is to identify anything that might go wrong in carrying out a suggested solution and then to repair it so those problems will be avoided. PERSUADER's second adaptation checklist is a first step at doing this. The tests in its checklist test for the potential for problems that are known to occur frequently when deriving new labor contracts. For example, because it knows enough about companies involved in negotiations to compute what they can afford, and it can compute how much a contract costs, it is able to project whether a contract is feasible economically for a company. If not, it attempts to fix the contract to make it more economically feasible.

Though checklists can be quite useful, the problem with them is that they can deal only with commonly known issues. They can't grow easily as the experience of the reasoner grows. Using the checklist method to guide adaptation, each new problem that is identified would have to be added to the checklist in order to make sure it could be anticipated in the future. But even with easy ways to do this, the efficiency of a checklist quickly erodes if it has to hold both common problems and obscure ones. Recall that in using a checklist, a program checks a suggested solution for the presence of each potential problem on the checklist. It makes sense to check suggested solutions for common problems, but it makes little sense to check old solutions for every obscure problem that might arise, especially if many are of little consequence.

Some other method of identifying more obscure problems with solutions is needed. Identifying inconsistencies between stated goals and solution components, described in the previous section, is one way of doing this. It can be used to identify inconsistences between specifications, but it cannot be used to identify problems that arise in carrying out solutions. These problems are more hidden and cannot be identified by merely comparing specifications to each other.

To see that this is so, consider again the problem in chapter 1. A host is planning a meal for a large group of people. She recognizes at the start that some people eat no meat or poultry, one is allergic to milk, and others are meat-and-potatoes men. She knows she must come up with a meal that all will eat. But she doesn't remember initially that her friend Anne, who is also coming, doesn't eat fish. When she considers serving tomato tart, the inconsistencies between the cheese in the tart (solution component) and the need to accommodate a guest allergic to milk products (constraint in the problem specification) can be easily noticed. But the problem with serving grilled salmon is harder to identify. It is consistent with all the specified constraints of the problem specification.

It is only when the host begins projecting the effects of serving the salmon, considering what the solution might look like when it is carried out, that she realizes that grilled salmon might not be a good solution either. As she is projecting the effects of, or evaluating, the solution, she remembers a meal where Anne was served fish and didn't eat it. She is alerted by that recalled case to a constraint that was not part of the original formulation of the problem but that nevertheless is liable to have an impact on the solution's potential success.[3]

For at least some situations, then, identifying the potential problems with a suggested solution requires projecting the outcome of the solution and evaluating its effects. Such reasoning should allow rare but important problems to be detected efficiently. Three methods for doing this have been identified. KRITIK (Goel 1989, 1991b) uses a causal model to project effects of its suggested solutions. PERSUADER and JULIA use case-based means of projecting.[4] The third method involves simulation of the suggested solution to derive its expected outcome.

Model-Based Projection

In model-based projection, the results of a solution are predicted by simulating the effects of a solution based on a causal model of how it ought to behave. Suppose, for example, that we have a causal model of how a car's fuel system works. We might have noticed that there was little fuel getting to the carburetor and conjectured that there was either a leak or a clog in the fuel line. As a result, we decided to fix the problem by changing the hose. Before we turn the car back on to see how it works, we want to check the fix in our heads. Our model tells us that the hose acts as a conduit between the gas tank and the carburetor and that the gas pump applies a force to the gas at the gas tank side of the hose, providing it with the pressure it needs to travel as far as the carburetor. Because we have no reason to believe that the fuel pump is not working, we therefore predict that with the new hose, which is clear of defects, the pump will force fuel into the hose, which will take the fuel to the carburetor. This "in the head" reasoning about how the device will work is model-based projection.

To do model-based projection, it is necessary to have a model available. When it is available, the process of projecting is equivalent to the process of running the model (DeKleer and Brown 1984; Kuipers 1984; Rieger and Grinberg 1977). In some situations, however, model-based projection requires constructing a model. Model construction is necessary when the reasoning process has generated a new type of artifact. If one modifies an existing fuel system, for example, the causal model associated with the old fuel system will no longer hold. If the hose length is shorter, for example, but the pressure exerted by the fuel pump is the same, then the fuel will arrive earlier to the carburetor. If fuel injectors replace the carburetor, then large por-

---

3. In many real-world situations, at least some of the constraints on a situation are not specified. In other situations, there are so many possible constraints that many are purposely not considered in initially solving a problem. In those situations, the most important constraints are used to solve the problem, and others are considered only when evaluation procedures show them to be important. That is what we see here. Anne's dislike of grilled fish, for whatever reason, is not part of the original formulation of the problem. It is such specialized knowledge that perhaps it sits only in the one case where she didn't eat grilled fish and does not reside with general knowledge about Anne. It is taken into account only when the peculiarities of a situation require it.

4. What JULIA and PERSUADER do in projecting outcomes is similar to what CHEF does to anticipate problems. CHEF doesn't use its case-based projection to guide adaptation, however—it uses the results of case-based projection (in its *anticipation* step) to augment its problem description, thereby allowing it to retrieve cases that can help it avoid the potential problem without needing extra repair.

tions of the old model will no longer hold. Before projecting the results of the new fuel system, a new causal model representing the way the new fuel system works must be constructed.

When a new artifact has been designed by modifying an old one, a new causal model can be constructed by modifying the old one. That is, we can figure out how a new artifact is supposed to work by projecting changes to the old artifact onto the causal model associated with that artifact. If we shorten a hose, for example, then we must change the causal model to show the fuel arriving earlier. If we replace the carburetor in a fuel system by fuel injection, then we must also replace the description of the carburetor in the causal model of the fuel system with a description of a fuel injection system.

KRITIK's model-based projection process takes three inputs (Goel 1989):

- The function desired in its new design
- The function delivered by and the structure of a known design (the one from which it is constructing its new design)
- The candidate modifications to the old design that will allow the new artifact to deliver the new function

Its output is an evaluation of whether the candidate modifications to the old design will deliver the desired function when executed. It does this by first modifying the old causal model to make it consistent with the ways in which the old artifact is to be adapted and then running the model, checking to make sure it achieves the desired function with no ill effects.

KRITIK makes changes to old causal models by means of *model-revision plans* (also called *modification-evaluation plans*). Each model-revision plan is indexed by the type of structural modification it is applicable to. That is, adaptations to an artifact are achieved by modifying the structure of the old artifact. Each type of modification to an artifact requires a different kind of modification to the associated causal model. When one replaces one substance with another one, for example, the associated causal model must reflect that replacement. To be an accurate model of the new artifiact, the model must also record descriptive differences between the old substance and the new one that have the potential to result in different behaviors. If we replace nitric acid by sulfuric acid in the artifact itself, for example, the causal model reflects that well if it both records the replacement and records that the sulfuric acid is a high-acidity substance. The degree of acidity in a substance is informative of the behavior of a device; high-acid substances will corrode some materials faster than will low-acid substances, for example.

Given the modifications that are scheduled to be made to an old artifact, KRITIK accesses appropriate model-revision plans and carries them out on the old model to create a causal model the parallels the intended behavior of the newly designed artifact. KRITIK's model-revision plans are of several types:

- *Substance modification plans* change a causal model to reflect the substitution of one substance for another one (e.g., ethanol for gasoline). They do two things. First, they substitute the new substance for the old one in the causal model. Then, they record descriptive differences between the old and new substance.

■ *Component modification plans* change components in a causal model.

   □ *Component modality change plans* change the modality of components by first sub-stituting the new modality for the old one and then replacing behavioral states asso-ciated with the old modality with those associated with the new one.

   □ *Component parameter adjustment plans* adjust the value of a component to corre-spond to a new specification.

   □ *Component replacement plans* replace a component with some function with another component that has the same or a different function. They also replace the descrip-tive properties of the old component with those of the new component.

■ *Relation modification plans* change the structure of a causal model. They might *invert a relation* or perform a *series-to-parallel conversion* or a *parallel-to-series conversion*. These plans do fairly complicated manipulation of primitive relations in a causal model.

■ *Substructure deletion plans* know how to delete specific substructures from a causal model. In *component deletion*, a component whose function is no longer needed is deleted from a causal model. An auxiliary task in doing these deletions is to compose the remainder of the components appropriately.

An example will illustrate. KRITIK is attempting to design a sulfuric acid cooler. It has, in the past, created a working nitric acid cooler, and it has the specs for that cooler on hand. In modifying the nitric acid cooler to cool sulfuric acid, it needs to replace nitric acid by sulfuric acid, and because sulfuric acid is more acidic, it has decided to replace the pipes in the nitric acid cooler by pipes that are appropriate to high-acid liquid. It does this using model-guided repair heuristics (described in chapter 11). As a follow-up step, in order to project the effects of its new design, KRITIK must create a causal model for it. KRITIK does this by modifying its causal model of the nitric acid cooler. It uses a *substance modification plan* to replace nitric acid by sulfuric acid in the model and a *component replacement plan* to replace the old pipes with the new ones. The substance modification plan also adds to the model the specification that sulfuric acid has high acidity, while the component replacement plan records the acidity that the new pipes can withstand.

Having effected these changes to the causal model, KRITIK runs the model to simulate the behavior of the newly designed artifact. It concludes that all is well. Note that had only the substance substitution been done in creating the new artifact (i.e., no change in the pipes), the causal model would have been changed only by doing a substance modification—changing the substance and noting its new properties and their needs. Running a simulation using this model would have found the design inadequate, pointing out that the pipes in the cooler were inadequate to the task of carrying a high-acid substance.

Case-Based Projection

When causal models are available, they provide an accurate means of projecting the effects of a solution. But in many domains, causal models are not available or are not accurate enough for projection. In these domains, case-based projection in often useful. Simply put, cases are recalled that have solutions similar to the suggested one, and their outcomes are examined to see if they are consistent with the intent of the new situation. If not, and if it seems as though the poor outcome could also result in the new situation, the suggested solution is repaired so that the poor outcome is avoided.

This procedure is illustrated in the meal-planning example. The host recalls cases with solutions similar to the proposed one. In one case she recalls, a set of guests, including Anne, was served grilled fish. Its outcome is examined to see if it is consistent with the intent of the new problem. What happened in that instance was that Anne did not eat the fish. This is inconsistent with the intent of the new problem—to accommodate the tastes of all the guests. A potential poor outcome (Anne not eating) is identified, as is the reason why that might happen—Anne doesn't like fish. This new piece of information is added to the problem specification, and the solution is repaired taking it into account.

Another example from JULIA will further illustrate. JULIA has just decided to serve lasagne to a group of graduate students who will be coming to dinner. It attempts to evaluate its solution, and it recalls a case in which graduate students were invited to dinner and corned beef and pastrami sandwiches were served. Several students who were vegetarians had only bread and salads to eat. Because the lasagne has meat in it, if there are also vegetarians among the students who are coming this time, they will not be able to eat. JULIA considers whether any might be vegetarians. There are some coming. Remembering the old case points out the sorts of potential problems that might occur and the circumstances in which they might happen. The reasoner considers whether there is also the potential for such a problem in the new situation and, if so, is given the chance to fix it before the solution is actually carried out.[5]

PERSUADER augments its checklist-based control of adaptation with a similar case-based component. It uses its adaptation checklist to identify common problems that its suggested solution might be harboring, but it identifies more obscure problems by case-based projection. Though a company's not being able to afford a contract is a common problem with contracts, younger workers' unhappiness about attention given to the demands of old workers is less common and not on its checklist. This problem does, however, exist in several cases, each indexed by the description of situations in which the same problem is likely to occur. Let's suppose that one case in the case library describes a situation in which there were many young workers in the work force and fewer older workers, that layoffs were imminent, and that the contract suggested used strict seniority to determine who should be laid off. The younger workers were unhappy with this solution and threatened to strike if they were not taken care of

---

5. The actual means by which JULIA makes this happen is through use of its reason maintenance and constraint propogation subsystems and querying of its client. It notices that the fact that some people were vegetarians was responsible for the previous failure and asks its client if there will be vegetarians this time. When it finds there will be, it adds the vegetarian constraint to its problem description. The constraint propogator propogates the constraint down to the dishes, as described in previous sections, finding that the lasagne is inconsistent with that constraint, and JULIA is alerted that fixing the lasagne is necessary to make this meal acceptable. Note, however, that JULIA is alerted to the need to add this new constraint by its reminding of the first grad-student dinner. The constraint-propagation and reason-maintenance subsystems can figure out what to repair and carry out the repair only after being alerted to the need by case-based projection procedures.

better. If, in a new situation, there are many young workers, the proposed contract favors older workers by having seniority take precedence at layoff time, and layoffs are imminent, this old case will be recalled, pointing out that problem. The old case might also suggest a solution (e.g., laying off senior people when junior ones are more useful to the company but giving a very generous severance that includes full pension before retirement age).

Simulation-Based Projection

The third method for projecting the effects of a solution is simulation. In many domains, simulation programs exist that can successfully be used to project effects. If a case-based system were designing a bridge, for example, it would be appropriate for it to call a simulation program to make sure the supports it designed for the bridge would withstand weather and traffic conditions. As when a model or a case is used to project effects of a solution, when a simulation shows a potential defect with a proposed solution, the solution must be fixed to take that defect out.

Projection Revisited

The major problems in repairing solutions based on projections are to determine responsibility for potential poor effects (blame assignment) and to figure out how things can be changed to produce improved results. A full analysis of either process is beyond the scope of this book, and in many situations, they are simply too hard to implement in a computer program. In many situations, however, there are relatively simple ways to do both things. There are three relatively easy ways to do blame assignment. Case-based blame assignment is one of those; if an old case records what was responsible for its failure, a system can consider whether such a situation is possible in the new case. Using a causal model is another way to find why something might go wrong; a major issue here is deriving an appropriate model, but once one is derived, the explanation for potential failures (e.g., pipes can't carry high-acid substances) is derived as a result of running the model. A simulation can often be examined to determine which parameters led to the ill effects. Cases, models, and simulations can also often help with figuring out what needs fixing and can sometimes suggest means of effecting the fix, as shown in the examples. A way to help systems get better at these processes is to extract advice about poor solutions from experts and to incorporate the explanations of the experts into both the content and indexes of poorly solved cases, allowing case-based projection to take the lead in projecting results. Case-based projection will be discussed again in chapter 13.

12.1.5 Carrying Out a Solution and Analyzing Feedback

In using solution projections to identify what needs fixing, one tries to anticipate as well as possible what *could* go wrong and then to compensate before actually carrying out a solution. Another way to identify what needs fixing in a solution is to actually carry out a solution, analyze the outcome, and reason about how it could have worked better. MEDIATOR and PERSUADER, two mediation programs, both use this means of identifying needed repairs. After coming up with a solution plan, each proposes its plan to its clients. Its clients either approve or disapprove, citing some problem with the solution. If they disapprove, MEDIATOR and PERSUADER both analyze what was responsible for the failure and repair their solutions accordingly.

CHEF's means of choosing repairs is also meant to implement this approach. After creating a plan (recipe), CHEF carries out the steps of the plan (by means of a sophisticated simulator; it has no means of actually cooking) and examines the results. If results are not what it is expecting, it does a causal analysis to find what could have caused the unexpected results. It then reasons about how the results could have been avoided and repairs its plan accordingly.

The steps involved in analyzing feedback after execution are, in principle, very much like those used when projecting results and then fixing a solution to avoid poor projections. The major difference, of course, is that once a plan has been carried out, it is often impossible to retract its ill effects.

12.1.6 Using Adaptation History: Compensatory Adaptation

When balance of some sort is necessary in a solution, adaptations to an old solution might create imbalances that must be fixed. Our best examples of this come from PERSUADER's domain: labor mediation. A solution must be equitable to both sides of a dispute. Old solutions, because they have been accepted by both parties in a previous dispute, are considered equitable. Changes that must be made to fit an old contract to a new situation, however, might change that equity. If a company can't afford the old equitable solution, for example, one way to fix the problem is to cut the salaries of employees. This solves the problem of inability to pay, but the solution favors the company, creating an inequity.

Some adaptations must be done to right imbalances created by previous adaptations. We call these *compensatory adaptations*. They may be implemented by several different adaptation methods. The need to do them can be flagged by application of an adaptation strategy that creates an imbalance, or, if it is easy to check for imbalances, by checks made after a solution is created. PERSUADER knows that some of its adaptations result in inequities. When it uses an adaptation heuristic that results in an inequity, it leaves a note around specifying the sort of compensation that must be done. It also has a means of computing the relative happiness of employer and union with a contract, giving it an effective means of computing the degree of inequity. If the "inequity flag" is on or if its computations show it that an inequity has been created, it applies compensatory adaptations to restore balance.

Inequity is not the only way previous adaptation can influence the need for later adaptation. Any adaptation that removes one inconsistency or addresses one difference might insert another inconsistency, requiring additional adaptation. For example, an adaptation that JULIA does in response to needing to remove meat from a dish might insert an ingredient that another guest is allergic to. It is important that a case-based reasoner evaluate the effects of its adaptations and take care of new inconsistencies that appear. Some of those inconsistencies can then be taken care of by applying the same adaptation cycle over again (e.g., JULIA, in noticing another inconsistency, adapts to get rid of it). Other inconsistencies, such as dealing with inequity, require a separate adaptation step.

12.2 CHOOSING AN ADAPTATION STRATEGY

Once the need for adaptation has been identified, a method of effecting the adaptation must be chosen. Several of the methods that identify what needs to be adapted also identify how adaptation ought to be done. Some checklists, for example, point to parameter adjustment strategies and other adaptation methods appropriate to making a necessary fix. For the most part, however, after identifying what needs changing, a reasoner must then figure out how to change it. There are several issues that come up here:

- Identifying exactly what to change
- Finding an appropriate adaptation or repair strategy
- Choosing between several appropriate adaptation strategies

The methods discussed earlier are good for identifying faulty pieces of cases, but they are not always as good at identifying exactly what changes should be made. For example, though they can identify that the meat in a lasagne to be served to vegetarians is causing a problem, they cannot determine whether the meat should be replaced by something else, whether it should be deleted, whether the lasagne should be replaced by something else, or whether the reasoner should rethink its choice of Italian cuisine.

Nor can those methods identify which of the several adaptation strategies should be used. Lasagne can be made vegetarian several different ways, for example, by deleting the beef, by substituting a soy product that tastes like beef, by substituting a variety of vegetables for the beef, or by simply finding another lasagne recipe without meat.

These next sections address the issues listed earlier. I shall try to give separate answers to each of the three questions, but it will be evident early on that the answers are quite integrated with each other. The answer to what, exactly, ought to be adapted often depends on how easy it is to do an adaptation. Choosing between several adaptation methods depends partly on a judgment of how good their solutions might be, and partly on how easy they are to carry out, a sort of cost-benefit analysis.

12.2.1 Choosing What Gets Adapted

Earlier I referred to a problem with adapting lasagne. Identifying the beef in the lasagne as being inconsistent with the vegetarian constraint is only the first step in identifying what needs to be adapted. One might adapt the lasagne recipe by substituting something for the beef, one might adapt the main course of the meal by substituting something different for the lasagne, or one might adapt the whole structure or essence of the solution in progress by deciding that Italian cuisine isn't appropriate. How can a reasoner determine which is the best adaptation?

The best answer I can give to this question is to try easier adaptations first. It is generally easier to find substitutions than to effect transformations. It is easier to find substitutions for items that are less connected to others than for those that are more connected. The more similar two items are to each other along relevant dimensions, the simpler a substitution will be. On the other hand, the more central a component is to what it is part of, the less appropriate it might be to replace it. Structural adaptations might be more appropriate under those circumstances.

Though all these qualities must be taken into account in deciding what to adapt, they interact with one another in complex ways, making specification of a general algorithm for deciding what to adapt impossible. The lasagne example will be used show those interactions.

We begin by recalling that substitution is easier than transformation. Taking that rule of thumb into account, it is appropriate to attempt to find a substitute for lasagne before trying to transform the lasagne by substituting or deleting components. This seems reasonable until we consider that transforming the lasagne can happen by substituting one of its ingredients—replacing the beef with something vegetarian. Why should it be easier or more appropriate to replace lasagne in the main course of the meal than to replace the beef in the lasagne? By the same token, we should also ask why it is more appropriate to attempt to fix the suggested solution by replacing the lasagne in the main course before attempting to replace the main course the lasagne is part of by another main course.

The answer to these questions hinges on the relative connectedness of the item to be adapted. In general, it is easier to make substitutions for items that have fewer constraints connecting them to other components of a solution than for those with many connections. The ingredients of a dish are heavily connected to other ingredients in the dish, the cooking method being used, ingredients of other dishes being served, and so on, often by unarticulated aesthetic constraints. A dish itself has connections to other dishes it is related to, as its ingredients do, but has few other connections. In general, then, it will be easier to substitute one dish for another than to transform the way a dish is made.

On the other hand, a course of a meal has connections to other courses and to meal descriptors that a dish, by itself, might not have. That is, an entire course of a meal might satisfy some large, important set of specifications, while a particular dish that is part of that course only satisfies some of those. That would make it easier to find a substitution for a dish than for a whole course. But some dishes play such a central role in the course of a meal that they are actually more connected to other meal components than is the course itself. A dish that is central to a course of a meal might satisfy all the constraints that the course satisfies and, in addition, have connections to other dishes in the course. Under these circumstances, it might be better to replace the entire course rather than substituting a dish.

Also important in determining what to adapt is the availability of substitutes and how closely a given substitute mimics the qualities of the item it is being substituted for. If, for example, there existed a beef substitute that tasted like beef, had the textural qualities of beef, and had the nutritional qualities of beef, but was vegetarian, the easiest adaptation would be to substitute this beef substitute for the beef in the lasagne, despite the fact that the beef is highly connected to other ingredients in lasagne.

We can summarize as follows:

Connectedness of an item to other component parts of a solution affects the potential ease of carrying out an adaptation. The more connected an item is, the harder it will be to adapt it.

Centrality of an item to the solution component it is part of affects both the ease and the appropriateness of an adaptation. Because central items tend to be highly connected to other parts of a solution, they might be hard to find substitutes for. It is therefore less appropriate to replace a central component than to transform it in a minor way. If a central component cannot be transformed minimally to fix an inconsistency, it might be more appropriate to replace the whole piece of the solution it is part of than to find a replacement for it.

Closeness of a substitute mitigates the effects of both the other dimensions. A substitution that might be hard to carry out because of the density of connections to other items in a solution is made easy by the availability of a close substitute. An adaptation that might seem inappropriate because of centrality might be deemed appropriate by the availability of a close substitute.

12.2.2 Finding an Appropriate Adaptation or Repair Strategy

How can a case-based reasoner identify a set of adaptation strategies that are potentially appropriate for carrying out an adaptation or repair? There are several ways.

- Some methods for identifying what needs to be adapted have associated with them means of carrying out the adaptation.
- Some items are associated with close substitutes.
- Some adaptation heuristics are indexed according to the situations in which they are applicable.

As shown earlier, several of the methods that identify what needs to be adapted also identify how to carry out the adaptation. Some checklists, for example, point to parameter adjustment heuristics and other adaptation methods appropriate to making a necessary fix. Evidence heuristics in CASEY, used for partial matching, are each associated with repair heuristics that know how to accommodate particular kinds of differences between two problem specifications. Cases used to point out potential problems with solutions also often point out means of making repairs.

Some items themselves point to a means of carrying out an adaptation. For example, some food items in JULIA have close substitutes associated with them, indexed by the constraint that the item often violates. Milk, for example, indexes "low-fat milk" by the constraint "low calorie." Beef indexes "veggie-burger" by the vegetarian constraint. When an item has been singled out as violating a constraint, JULIA checks whether there is an appropriate well-known substitute for it and, if so, attempts to adapt by substitution.

Another way adaptation strategies can be identified as potentially applicable is by indexing them according to the situations in which they are applicable. Special-purpose adaptation strategies, recall, are indexed this way. One heuristic we discussed, for example, came from CHEF and stated that when duck is being stir-fried, a step of defatting the duck should be inserted in a recipe before the duck appears in any other step. This heuristic, we stated, should be indexed by the fact that the method of cooking is stir-frying and the ingredient being used is duck. Indexing it this way allows this heuristic to be recalled whenever duck is being stir-fried.

When we discuss indexing special-purpose adaptation heuristics, the same major issues arise that arise when discussing the indexing of cases. What vocabulary for indexing should we be using? Should we be indexing only by the specifics of situations in which adaptation strategies are useful, or are there some more generally applicable ways of indexing adaptation strategies? Certainly, as in indexing cases, it would be nice if we could index adaptation strategies so that their indexes were easily recognizable and also generally applicable.

Many special-purpose heuristics are truly special-purpose, applying only to situations in which specific features are present. CHEF's critic for defatting duck is one of these; it is applicable only when duck is being prepared using the stir-fry method. Others, though still special-purpose, are more broadly applicable. CHEF's heuristics for altering plans, for example, are applicable to different kinds of planning situations, independent of the particular planning domain. KRITIK's heuristics for altering designs of artifacts are applicable to design problems, independent of domains, as are some of JULIA's heuristics for structure modification.

Two schemes have been suggested for indexing adaptation strategies in a generally applicable way. Indexing strategies by the failures they fix is implemented in CHEF. Indexing strategies by the differences they address is implemented in KRITIK.

Recall that CHEF is a case-based planner with two adaptation steps. It adapts old plans to create new ones using reinstantiation and parameter adjustment, indexing critics that implement those two processes by the specifics of the situations they address (e.g., what cooking method is being used, what ingredients are being used). It repairs its plans after they have been shown to fail by applying a set of general-purpose repair strategies associated with well-known planning failures.

CHEF indexes its repair strategies by the kinds of failures they fix. Many of the strategies shown in the previous chapter, for example, are applicable to situations in which a necessary condition has been disabled by a side effect of a previous planning step. Others were specific to the disabled condition's being *balance*. CHEF indexes its repair strategies using a vocabulary for failures that represents the interactions plan steps can have with each other (e.g., side effect disables condition) and the specifics of the interaction (e.g., the particular condition is balance). The intent in CHEF is to characterize repair strategies so that they are generally applicable across planning domains.

In order to use an indexing vocabulary such as CHEF's, a system must be able to characterize its failures along these dimensions. CHEF includes in its reasoning a process of evaluating feedback from its plans that results in a characterization of the ways the plan steps interacted with each other. A discussion of the ways in which planning failures can be identified can be found in Hammond (1986b, 1989a).

KRITIK (Goel, 1989, 1991b) indexes adaptation strategies according to the differences in functional specifications of artifacts that must be accommodated by adaptation strategies. Its adaptation strategies represent *families* of plans for generating structural modifications to an artifact, each applicable to a specific type of functional difference.

Substance-property difference plans, for example, are used to modify an old design to compensate for a difference in the property of a substance, for example, degree of acidity. In general, these plans accomplish their goal by making either component parameter adjustments, component modality changes, or component replacements. Plans associated with specific substances and their properties are more specific about the particular changes that are appropriate to compensating for their differences. When degree of acidity of a substance goes up, for example, components that come in contact with the substance must be replaced by components that are not harmed by contact with high-acid substances.

Design of the sulfuric acid cooler will illustrate. Recall that this artifact must accommodate sulfuric acid, a highly concentrated acid. The case KRITIK remembers is of a cooler for nitric acid, a less acidic substance. KRITIK compares the specifications for the two coolers, noting that in the new situation there are two differences.

- The substance to be cooled is different.
- The degree of acidity of the substance to be cooled is different.

It must change the design of the old cooler to accommodate these two differences. Because the second of these is a substance-property difference, it calls on its substance-property-difference plan to carry out the modification. That plan, in turn, calls on a plan specific to acidity. This plan looks for components of the old artifact that are to come in contact with the substance, examines each to see if it is harmed by a high-acid substance, and calls for replacing those components that can be harmed with components that can function well with high-acid substances. To carry out this plan, the specification of the old artifact (its causal model) is consulted, and the pipes are singled out as allowing the flow of only low-acid substances. They are therefore replaced.

KRITIK has several families of adaptation plans. The substance family of adaptation plans includes substance difference, substance-property difference and substance-parameter difference plans. The component family includes component difference, component-modality difference, and component-parameter difference plans. Each works similarly to the illustration. Each family of plans is indexed by the kind of difference it must adapt for. Each plan in the family is indexed by the particular type of difference it deals with. Each adaptation plan makes use of specific component and substance information found in the causal model of the old plan to carry out its adaptations.

12.2.3 Choosing Between Several Adaptation Methods

Using checklists, indexing, and specification of substitutes, a reasoner can identify a variety of potentially applicable adaptation heuristics and strategies that can be used to carry out the necessary adaptation. We must now consider the means by which the reasoner can decide which of the many strategies is most applicable. As in determining exactly what to adapt, there are general guidelines that we can state and illustrate but no general-purpose algorithm that we can present. The guidelines are as follows:

- Try more specifically applicable adaptations before more general ones. This allows those more likely to provide better solutions to be attempted first.

The most specifically applicable adaptations are those indexed by the concrete descriptors of the new situation and those pointed to by the methods that choose what to adapt. These will tend to be special-purpose adaptation heuristics and parameter adjustment heuristics. They might also include well-known substitutions. More specifically applicable adaptations will tend to result in the most appropriate solutions, provide the most concrete instructions for adaptation, and be the easiest to apply.

- Attempt easy strategies before harder ones. This guideline aims the reasoner toward putting as little effort as possible into adaptation.

Common sense tells us that if we can get a good solution by an easy strategy, we shouldn't bother putting in the effort to use a harder strategy. Thus, we prefer easier strategies over harder ones. Local search, parameter adjustment, and specialized search are easy for two reasons. Little or no analysis is necessary to choose one of these methods. They are easy to apply.

- All other things being equal, choose strategies that have more likelihood of succeeding over those that are more prone to failure.

Again, common sense tells us that it is more productive to use strategies that are likely to succeed than those that are prone to failure. On the other hand, some strategies with high failure rates may, when they succeed, produce solutions that are far superior to those produced by other strategies.

- Move to more generally applicable and more complex strategies only when specifically applicable and simple strategies fail.
- Use strategies prone to failure only when the potential for a good solution from such a strategy is far higher than the potential from other strategies, when the consequences of failure are low, or when there is a good chance that the potential for failure can be caught with little effort or cost before the solution is deployed.

These two guidelines are corollaries to the other guidelines and perhaps seem unnecessary to state. One tries those strategies more likely to give better solutions first, attempting easier ones before more complex ones, moving to more complex and less specific strategies only after the easy and applicable ones have been shown not to yield sufficient results. One tries risky strategies only when one can afford to.

Discussion is needed here of two things: what makes an adaptation strategy complex and how one can judge the risks inherent in carrying out an adaptation strategy.

An adaptation method can be complex because much analysis is necessary to figure out *that* it should be applied or because much analysis is necessary to figure out *how* to apply it. When much analysis is necessary to determine that a strategy is applicable, analysis and choice of the strategy are done only when there is reason to believe that the strategy is necessary. CHEF chooses its repair strategies only after it experiences failure. When initially adapting an old solution to fit a new situation, it does only easy adaptations (reinstantiation, parameter adjustment, and special-purpose critic application), waiting to do the analysis necessary to apply harder ones only after it knows they are needed. JUDGE and PERSUADER do only the complex analysis they know is necessary to effecting a good solution, and they control which analysis they will do by means of a checklist. In controlling which analysis they will do, they also control which adaptation strategies can be chosen.

When a strategy requires much complex analysis in order to be applied, simpler strategies are preferred unless the complex one is known to be one that can provide a good answer. Adjusting a sentence in a criminal case, for example, requires complex analysis, but the analysis is done because it is crucial to deriving a good solution. If we look at the repair strategies associated with recovering from side effects, we see that some are more abstractly stated than others. Recover, for example, is quite abstract, as is alter-plan:precondition. They give guidelines, but much reasoning is needed to figure out the specifics of making the strategy work. Adjust-balance:up, on the other hand, requires less work for application. If a solution can be found by applying it, the work of attempting application of the other strategies can be skipped.

How can a reasoner know how much effort will be needed to apply a strategy? There is no principled answer to this that anybody in the case-based reasoning community has put forth yet. We might examine strategies and make our best judgments and perhaps annotate each with a difficulty factor. Alternatively, we might keep records of how hard strategies have been to apply and judge complexity based on those. Or we can count operations required to carry out the adaptation and judge complexity based on those.

There is less to say about how a reasoner can know whether or not a strategy is risky. One might keep track of its rates of success and failure, recording particularly the circumstances in which the strategy has failed. In general, however, such predictions are quite hard to make. There are so many specialized factors associated with adaptation methods that there are no general methods we know of for predicting their risk of failure well.

12.3 CHOOSING WHAT GETS ADAPTED AND THE METHOD OF ADAPTATION IN TANDEM

The discussion so far has separated choice of what needs to be adapted from adaptation itself, as if the two are separate processes. This is a useful distinction for purposes of discussion. It is often useful in implemented systems. But there are some times, as we've seen in the discussion, when the separation is hard or impossible to make, or when having two separate steps could be detrimental to good adaptation. There are several reasons we might not want to separate the two processes.

- A problem can be identified, but choice of what to adapt is not straightforward. This might be for one of several reasons:

  □ Choice of what to adapt depends on the adaptation methods available.
  □ Choice of what to adapt depends on availability of known substitutes.
  □ Several adaptations are available, some structural modifications, some component-part modifications. Identifying a component part to modify (usually easier) can prohibit better structural modifications from being considered.

☐ It is impossible to designate a component part for modification. Rather, a structural modification is necessary.

■ The appropriate adaptation is so stereotyped and obvious that there is no need to separate choice of what to adapt from how to do it.

In previous discussion, I have alluded to the ways in which choice of what should be adapted and choice of an adaptation method can be combined. Some checklists point to adaptation strategies as they choose *what* to adapt, for example. In this section, I make the combination of the two steps more explicit and present three methods that explicitly integrate them. Case-based adaptation and adaptation based on execution-time feedback are useful when choice of what to adapt is not straightforward. Critic application is useful when the connection between a problem and its repair is stereotyped.

12.3.1 Case-Based Adaptation

In case-based adaptation, guidance for adaptation, both what to adapt and how, is given by a previous case. My favorite example of case-based adaptation is presented in the first chapter. There, a host who is considering serving tomato tart as a main dish must adapt it for a guest who is allergic to milk products. Remembering a previous instance of adapting a dish with cheese by substituting tofu-cheese tells the host how to adapt the tomato tart.

In this example, a previous case is used to guide adaptation after the item needing adaptation has been identified by some other means. That is, the system already knows that the cheese in the tomato tart violates its *rule-out cheese* constraint and that it must adapt the tomato tart. The case it remembers tells it how to do the adaptation. It also tells it which specific piece of the old solution to adapt to fix the inconsistency.

PERSUADER presents another good example. PERSUADER is trying to create a contract for Jung Products, a company producing health products. Using several precedent cases, it derives a ballpark solution. Guided by its adaptation checklist of possible problems that might come up, PERSUADER checks to see if Jung Products can afford the proposed solution and finds that it can't.

PERSUADER must fix the contract. It knows the problem it must fix: the contract is too expensive. But it does not know exactly what part of the contract must be fixed or how to do it. It attempts to apply the one heuristic associated with contracts being too expensive: lowering the benefits package given to the employees. But it finds that this will be unacceptable. It therefore attempts to find cases that can suggest solutions.

PERSUADER remembers three cases with `inability to pay economic package` (the problem with this contract). One case involves a company that produces a similar product, is in the same geographical area, and must consider the same issues in its economic package. The problem was solved there by using a plan called `pass the extra cost to the consumer`. PERSUADER finds that plan applicable and adds it to its solution.

When cases are recalled while evaluating a proposed solution, they also can direct adaptation. Consider another piece of the example in chapter 1. The reasoner proposes to serve grilled salmon and is considering the goodness of that solution. She remembers a meal where

Anne was served grilled fish and didn't eat it; hot dogs were put on the grill at the last minute to feed Anne. Remembering that case in the course of evaluation causes the reasoner to consider potential failures that might arise. It also proposes a solution, which the reasoner might or might not choose to take advantage of; the case remembered here proposes that Anne be fed hot dogs. Should the reasoner decide to take this suggestion, the proposed solution can be adapted easily.

These examples are interesting for a variety of reasons. First, a previous case points out both what should be adapted and how to do the adaptation. When potential problems with solutions are identified, by whatever means, it is not always clear exactly what should be fixed to alleviate the problem. When a case is available to guide adaptation, it shows both what to adapt and how to do the adaptation. Another thing that should be noticed in the two examples is that no particular slot in the buggy solution was ever singled out to be fixed. Rather, the suggestions made by the cases change the structure of the proposed solution rather than adapting any of its component parts. Had either system been constrained to do its adaptation by adapting component parts of its buggy solution (e.g., the economic parts of the Jung contract, the main dish of the meal), the solutions suggested by cases would have been missed. Sometimes, as in the PERSUADER case, adaptation of structure rather than of the components of a solution produces more creative or novel solutions than can be derived by adapting components. Using previous cases to guide adaptation can promote novel adaptations.

The ability to do novel adaptation is one of the things that distinguishes novices from experts. Presumably one way to acquire such expertise is to collect cases in which novel adaptation is done. Seeding a case library with such cases is useful for tasks in which adaptation is idiosyncratic.

12.3.2 Using Execution-Time Feedback

In most of our discussions, we have focused on reasoning separately from action. When plans are carried out, however, feedback from the world often points to a need for adaptation. PLEXUS (Alterman 1988) was the earliest case-based reasoner to use feedback from the world to guide adaptation. PLEXUS, recall, is a commonsense planner that reasons about riding subways. Using its plan for riding BART in San Francisco, it attempts to ride a New York subway. Its BART plan tells it to buy a ticket from a ticket machine, but it looks around and cannot find one. This violates its expectations, telling it that a change in its plan is needed. It must adapt its plan so that a ticket machine is not necessary.

Knowing what the problem is, however, doesn't tell PLEXUS what to adapt. An analysis of the type of problem this is does point the way, however, to a method for performing adaptation. As illustrated in the previous chapter, PLEXUS uses a local search method specific to the problem of failing preconditions to find a step to substitute for the one it can't do.

Adaptation as a result of execution-time feedback is becoming an important issue as intelligent systems move from being planners to actually being part of the world. PLEXUS provides us with one means of using execution-time feedback for control: classify the problem encountered and use an adaptation strategy appropriate to the problem type. Though many of the methods above can be applied to control execution-time adaptation, additional research is needed to uncover other methods specific to execution-time control.

12.3.3 Using Critics to Control Adaptation

When the need for an adaptation is obvious and the method for doing the adaptation is standard, application of critics can choose both what to adapt and the adaptation method in one step. HACKER (Sussman 1975), a forerunner to case-based programs, used critics to deal with these situations. A single critic had a means of identifying a particular type of problem and held a procedure for fixing it.

For many problems, critics are the optimal way of implementing adaptation methods. CHEF's adaptation critics, for example, identify easily identifiable problems and fix them. The critic `defat-duck`, for example, is turned on whenever duck is used in a stir-fry recipe. Were CHEF to also know about roasting, it might have another critic associated with duck that inserts a step for pouring off fat after roasting is done.

A principle about critics that must be remembered, however, is that they are useful only if (1) identifying the situations in which they can be applied is inexpensive and (2) little deliberation is necessary to choose a method for carrying out the suggested adaptation. CHEF illustrates this principle. CHEF uses critics during its planning stage to insert and change the order of steps in standard ways, but critics are not useful in CHEF for repair of plans that don't work. The reason for that is twofold. First, much reasoning is necessary to identify problems. Doing that reasoning once is preferable to checking the applicability conditions of many complex critics. Second, each failure that is identified might be fixed in a variety of ways, and choice of the means of repair depends on a variety of other features of the situation.

Perhaps the lesson to be derived from this principle has to do with specificity of the methods available. Domain-independent guidelines for effecting adaptations, such as adding more of something or taking out something to restore imbalance, are too general to act as critics. Experience applying these general rules, however, can suggest particular fixes that work in particular situations (e.g., add more egg white if a soufflé won't rise). These standardized repair rules are entirely appropriate as critics. When adaptations can be standardized for a domain, critic application makes control of adaptation easy.

12.4 FLOW OF CONTROL

The discussion of adaptation in these two chapters has made several claims with implications for control of the adaptation process.

- The full cycle of adaptation includes modifying an old solution in relatively simple ways, evaluating the proposed solution by projecting results and fixing it appropriately, and analyzing the outcome after execution and repairing the solution if it failed.
- Sometimes, a sequence of adaptation methods, applied in the right order, works well.
- The process of adaptation often requires trying several adaptation strategies until a good solution in found. Easy-to-apply and specifically applicable methods take preference over more complex and more generally applicable ones.

What are the implications of combining all these? Does every case-based reasoner have to do all the steps in an adaptation cycle? As with many of the questions that come up in considering how to build a case-based system, there are no hard-and-fast answers to these questions. Their answers largely depend on the circumstances. In some domains, easy modifications are all that are necessary; in others, one would not be happy with a suggested solution unless there had been some analysis of its potential effects. In some, evaluation of the results of carrying out a solution is crucial; in others, those results are not available. In general, however, the flow of control of adaptation happens like this:

- Reinstantiate (variable substitution)
- Modify reinstantiated solution, making easy fixes

  □ Identify needed fixes
  □ Adapt appropriately, preferring easier and more specific methods over others

- Evaluate proposed solution and repair as necessary

  □ Project effects
  □ Identify necessary repairs
  □ Repair appropriately

- Compensate for adaptations (if necessary)

  □ Identify necessary compensations
  □ Adapt appropriately, preferring easier and more specific methods over others

- Collect and evaluate feedback, and repair as necessary

  □ Collect feedback
  □ Identify problems
  □ Repair appropriately

The list begins with the easiest of adaptation methods—reinstantiate the old solution for the new situation. The process continues with easy modifications, then projects the results and makes necessary repairs, then compensates for any inequitable changes that have been made. It is then time to carry out the solution and, if feedback is available, analyze feedback and repair the solution such that it would have worked.

Systems that solve problems by doing multiple adaptations of the solution to a single old case (e.g., CHEF, KRITIK) and those that use multiple cases to construct solutions (e.g., PERSUADER, JULIA) go through a process similar to this. An example from PERSUADER shows how the sequence works for a system that uses multiple cases in the course of its problem solving. PERSUADER is handed the following problem (from Sycara 1987a):

> The present contract negotiation is Marta company contract negotiations The
> negotiations are at an impasse, which I will try to resolve Looking to pro-
> pose a contract that is acceptable to Marta union and Marta company
>
> The inpasse resulted from the following:
> Marta union has made the demands:
>   (12% wage increase) (6% increase in pensions)
> Marta company has responded with the proposals:
>   (1% wage increase) (0% pension increase)

PERSUADER first searches memory for similar contract situations.

> Trying to establish prevailing practices...
> Searching memory for similar collective bargaining experiences...
>
> Searching memory for current competitors' contracts...
> Failed to find current competitors' contracts...
> Failed to find past competitors' contracts...
> Having found industry contracts...
> Consider contracts with same job classification: Bus-driver
> Consider those with successful negotiations
>
> The contract I am considering is the Redhound Company contract

PERSUADER reinstantiates the old solution for the new situation and applies parameter adjustment heuristics using a checklist.

> For the wage demand, my reasoning is:
> The company's present wage value $6.50 is below
>   wage average ($8) for the industry by 18.7%
> This could be modified by area statistics
> Since the cost of living in Atlanta differs from
>   the national average by -2%,
>   the 18.7% is modified by 2% to become 16.7%
> Redhound's old wage value, $8, was below the
>   wage average ($8.50) for the industry by 6.27% ...
>
> I am considering a wage change of 12% since this is less
>   than the change of 15% granted by Redhound
>
> For the pension demand ...

In its next step, it evaluates the proposed solution, attempting to anticipate what might be wrong with it and to fix those things. It uses a checklist here, also, to identify potential problems. Here, it checks to make sure the company can afford the economic package.

> Considering the company's finances ...
> If economic conditions do not change for the Marta company
>   it cannot afford the present economic package.

```
Trying to recall similar impasses, namely impasses
   with the same impasse issue M-ECON-PKGE
   and the same impasse cause INABILITY-TO-PAY

Looking at the plan called "try to reduce the cost of wages"
   which was used successfully to break impasse 16274656...

Looking at the plan called "increase price of product"
Seems applicable
```

There is no need to compensate for adaptations done previously because none of them changed the balance of equity for either party to the dispute. PERSUADER thus goes on to try out its solution, presenting it to the two parties, collecting feedback, and, based on feedback, repairing its solution.

PERSUADER talks privately to the two parties.

```
Do you MARTA UNION accept the contract?
yes

Do you MARTA COMPANY accept the contract?
no
```

PERSUADER considers why the company might not accept the contract, has a further discussion with the company, and determines that the company finds the cost of the contract too high. It is now ready to repair its solution by trying to find a way to decrease costs. It cycles through its list of heuristics for decreasing costs, finding that reducing the costs of pensions will work.

```
Looking at the plan "try to reduce the cost of pensions"

With respect to pensions, since the bargain unit
   consists mainly of young workers, a reduction in
   pension seems acceptable.

The proposed pension increase is 2%.
```

PERSUADER presents this solution to the disputing parties and collects more feedback to evaluate its new solution, again asking the union and company if they accept the contract. This time the union will not accept the contract. PERSUADER forms a hypothesis about the reason for the union's unhappiness and continues by attempting additional repairs. PERSUADER continues collecting feedback and attempting repair until it either comes up with an acceptable solution or the best one it is capable of. If a solution it considers good is not acceptable to some party, PERSUADER attempts to persuade that party of the appropriateness of the solution.

12.5 SUMMARY

In general, there are four major decisions that must be made in carrying out adaptation:

- Identifying what needs fixing
- Identifying what part of the faulty solution should be changed to carry out the fix
- Identifying applicable adaptation methods and/or heuristics
- Selecting an adaptation strategy and carrying it out

Identifying what needs to be fixed can be done by a variety of methods. Sometimes differences between problem specifications point to a need to fix parts of an old solution. Checklists can be used to keep track of standard problems, that, if present, must be fixed. A reasoner that can notice inconsistencies between its current goals and a proposed solution knows to fix the inconsistencies. Projecting potential results of a solution is a way of pointing to needed fixes. One fixes a solution so that the predicted problems are mitigated or disappear. Some adaptations point to a need for compensatory adaptations. Finally, after a solution is carried out and fails, an analysis of the failure can help a reasoner figure out what should have been different for the solution to succeed.

Knowing what needs fixing is not the same thing as identifying the exact changes that must be made in a proposed solution. When CHEF knows that the balance between its leavening and liquids must be fixed, it must still do additional reasoning to figure out what change to make in a recipe. It might change its solution by upping the amount of leavening, by decreasing the amount of liquid, or by adding some new ingredients. Deciding which parts of a case to change to make a fix depends on the ease of changing a particular part of the solution, the degree to which that change will carry out the needed fix, and the centrality and connectedness of the pieces to be changed. Changing a central item might detract from the identity of the solution (e.g., if you take the cheese out of pizza, is it still pizza?). A highly connected piece of a solution might be difficult to change.

Appropriate adaptation heuristics and methods are found several different ways. Some methods for identifying what needs to be adapted have their means of carrying out the adaptation associated with them. For example, some checklists have adaptation heuristics associated with them. Some items are associated with close substitutes, making substitution an appropriate method. And some adaptation heuristics are indexed according to the situations in which they are applicable.

When several adaptation methods are available, a reasoner must choose among them. Two simple preference heuristics serve as guidelines for this process. First, more specifically applicable adaptations are preferred over more general ones. Second, easier-to-apply strategies are preferred over more complex ones.

Though these decisions have been presented as if they are separate steps in the process of controlling adaptation, it is important to keep in mind that they can be interleaved with each other. Case-based adaptation, the use of execution-time feedback, and critic application are three methods that combine choice of what to adapt with choice of an adaptation method.

We must also keep in mind that adaptation is an incremental process. Several adaptations might be carried out in sequence to effect all the changes that are necessary to make a proposed solution appropriate. Some of those adaptations are carried out before evaluation takes place; others are carried out after evaluation of an entire solution is done. Evaluation might be based on projection of the results of a soluton, or it might be based on feedback from actually carrying out a solution, or both. The adaptation that is done as a result of evaluation is often called repair. For many complex problems, both adaptation and repair are needed to effect good solutions.

13

Using Cases for Interpretation and Evaluation

George, who is about to turn thirteen, is arguing with his overprotective parents about going to the movies to see *Little Shop of Horrors*. They don't want him to go.[1]

> **George**: That's not fair. You let Sarah see that movie. (Sarah is his older sister.)
> **Parents**: Sarah is three years older than you.
> **George**: Why does that make a difference?
> **Parents**: You're not mature enough for that movie.
> **George**: Noah's parents let *him* go see it. (Noah is George's best friend.)

This argument is not unlike the persuasive arguments we all engage in from day to day. George is taking one side of the argument (I want to go to the movies). His parents are taking the other (You can't). Each is trying to convince the other that his side is the right side. As George counters his parents' objections, he justifies his arguments by citing cases he's encountered that make his point. His parents should let him see the movie because they let his sister see it. If Noah is mature enough to see the movie, then so is he. His parents, in turn, point out the differences between the cases George cites and his own case, because the differences help make their points. By comparing and contrasting this new situation to several old ones, George and his parents will eventually come to some agreement about whether George can see the movie.

Comparing and contrasting new situations to old ones is the hallmark of interpretive case-based reasoning. Intepretive case-based reasoning is a process of evaluating situations or solutions in the context of previous experience. George is attempting to force his parents to

---

1. Example adapted from (Ashley 1990, 196–201), based on his Ph.D. dissertation.

reevaluate their stand on his going to the movies by presenting them with several cases that he thinks are important as context.

Evaluation in context is something we do every day. Members of university admissions committees evaluate the potential of applicants to make it in their school by comparing them with other similar students who have and have not done well. Doctors distinguish between patients having one illness and another similar one. Is this patient a schizophrenic with depression or a depressive with psychosis? Is the patient suicidal? Is this the kind of arthritis that responds to drug A or the kind that responds to drug B? Parents must evaluate in context every day: Is it okay to bring my child's toy wagon into the park when the sign says that no vehicles are allowed? My son says he has a sore throat. Should I keep him home from school or send him and see what develops? My daughter wants to see a scary movie. Is this one appropriate for her, or will she cry and run out the way she did the last time?

The first step in the evaluation process is to remember old situations that are like the new one. We then ask ourselves whether this new situation is enough like an old one that it can be interpreted the way the old one was. Is my son's complaint that he's sick like other ones he's made when he's just tired, or is it more like those he makes when he is really sick? In what ways is this new applicant similar to those who have done well in graduate school? In what ways is he similar to those who have done less well?

We also ask what differentiates the new situation from old similar ones so that we can ascertain whether or not the old interpretation is likely to hold. Perhaps an applicant is like some who have not done well (e.g., his grades and GRE scores are low like theirs). On the other hand, he has extensive experience, maturity, and drive that most of those students didn't have; maybe that means we shouldn't pay attention to those similarities. Perhaps the movie my daughter wants to see is like others she's walked out of scared and crying. But perhaps she has changed since then (e.g, has become more mature), rendering the interpretation based on the old situations unsuitable. To determine if she will get scared and cry at this one, I have to consider in what ways this situation is like others she's been in, in what ways it is different, and whether those differences are enough to convince me that she won't be too scared this time. This requires considering similarities and differences between this movie and others she's seen and also considering similarities and differences between my daughter when she saw those movies and my daughter now, because those are the two major factors determining whether she will get scared or not.

Cases are used for interpretation and evaluation by professionals and laypeople, by children and grown-ups, by experts and novices, for commonsense reasoning and for reasoning in expert domains, for interpreting situations and while solving problems. Cases provide a useful basis for interpreting new situations because there are often so many unknowns that no straightforward means of evaluation is available. Is George mature enough for *Little Shop of Horrors* or not? There's no hard-and-fast measure of his maturity or of that required for the movie that can be used to make that decision. What grade point average is necessary to make it in graduate school? It depends on the circumstances.

Cases make up for our lack of knowledge and are useful for evaluation and interpretation because, in general, the world is consistent. Two kids who are best friends are probably as mature as each other, and if the movie was okay for one, it's probably okay for the other one. If two movies are equally scary, my daughter is likely to have the same reaction to both. Two students with the same background and same grade point average are likely to perform similarly in college.

At the same time, interpreting new situations based on old ones provides a way of maintaining consistency and equity over time. The legal system is based on that premise. If the law treats similar cases alike, it is equitable. Precedent-based mediation is also based on that premise. In labor mediation, the standard procedure for suggesting new agreements is to begin with an old precedent-setting agreement and to modify it to fit the new circumstances. Agreements are in the form of contracts, and a signed contract is considered equitable because both sides agreed to it. When an old contract is modified in favor of one side, compensatory modifications in favor of the other side are also done to maintain that equity.

In chapter 1, we listed and discussed three different tasks interpretive case-based reasoning was useful for: justification, interpretation, and projecting effects. Justification means showing cause or proof of rightness of an argument, position, or solution. Interpretation means trying to place a new situation in context. Projection means predicting the effects of a solution. These tasks, in turn, support a variety of reasoning goals. Classification, situation assessment, and solution evaluation and repair are the most pervasive.

What all these tasks have in common is argumentation. To justify, interpret, or project, the reasoner compares and contrasts the new situation to old cases. Some will support one interpretation or effect. Others will support a different one. Argumentation is the process of creating coherence from the many divergent views cases might support. In argumentation, the reasoner sorts through the similar cases and divides them into those that support and those that oppose the possible interpretations or effects and, on the basis of that sorting, comes up with a conclusion. The cases used to come up with that conclusion can be used to justify it.

Persuasive argumentation using cases is something we all do day by day. We do it when we try to convince someone of our position on an issue. And we do it when we try to convince ourselves of the rightness of a solution or when we try to weigh the costs and benefits of several possibilities against one another. The process of creating persuasive arguments is called *adversarial reasoning:* making persuasive arguments to convince others that we or our positions are right.

The majority of research in adversarial reasoning has concerned itself with legal reasoning. American law is based on cases. Though laws exist, the concepts they refer to tend to be *open textured;* that is, what the concept means depends on the context in which it is used. Concepts that are parts of laws are interpreted in a situation-dependent way. A sign on an office building that says No Dogs Allowed, for example, probably does not refer to seeing-eye dogs; rather, it refers to dogs who are people's pets. The concept "dog," though seemingly well defined, is quite ambiguous in this context. Suppose, for example, that a blind person's doctor was in this building, and that she was unable to see him because the guard would not let her in with her seeing-eye dog. The owner of the building might argue that *dog* means *dog* and he doesn't want dogs in his building. He might refer to several cases of his throwing out people who came in with their pets. The blind person, in turn, would argue that her dog was not a dog but her eyes, and that she could not gain access to her doctor without the dog. She would then cite several cases in favor of regarding seeing-eye dogs as eyes, not dogs, for example, by showing that seeing-eye dogs are allowed in courtrooms and in hospitals, where pet dogs are not allowed.

As in law, many of the concepts we encounter every day are open textured. That is, they cannot easily be defined in terms of necessary and sufficient conditions. Whether something fits into a category or not depends a lot on context. The seeing-eye dog in the example is just one illustration of the difficulty of defining categories by necessary and sufficient conditions and expecting them to work at all times. Seeing-eye dogs are certainly dogs—they fit all the necessary and sufficient conditions—but they should not be treated like dogs in many situations because of important extenuating circumstances. One could certainly redefine the category dog to mean "usually pet dog, except for a blind person," but there are several problems with this. First, for many purposes, the seeing-eye dog is a dog. It needs to be taken out for walks like other dogs. It needs to be fed like other dogs, and it eats the same things. It looks like a dog and sounds like a dog. Second, there are many exceptional kinds of dogs—those that are part of a fire crew, those that perform in a circus, and so on. Under some circumstances, each should be considered the same as other dogs; under other circumstances, each should be treated as special. Almost any single definition of dog we might write would fail under at least some circumstances. What seems more appropriate is a means of defining the nuances of the category "dog" according to the different contexts it is used in.

Open-textured concepts are pervasive. Most natural categories and many complex human-created categories cannot be defined by necessary and sufficient conditions (Hampton 1979; Rosch and Mervis 1975; Smith and Medin 1981). One famous example of such a category is the concept *chair*. The prototypical chair is used to support a person in a seated position and has a back and seat attached to each other and supported by four legs, but there are chairs missing one or more of these properties that we still recognize as chairs. Even worse, some chairs don't have any of the physical properties at all (e.g., beanbag chairs), and others cannot be used functionally. Yet we recognize all of them as chairs. How do we do that? Psychologists (Rosch 1978; Medin 1983; Medin, Dewey, and Murphy 1983) hypothesize that we remember many examples of each concept, some more prototypical, some less prototypical. As we engage in the recognition process, we match the new item to examples we are familiar with, assigning to the new item the category of the object it is most similar to. Evidence seems to back this up—experimental subjects classify more prototypical objects faster than they classify less prototypical ones. (Rosch 1978).

Compare-and-contrast procedures, then, are used naturally by people as they recognize the world around them and classify its constituents. New items are compared to well-known ones, and when a sufficient match is found, the new one is classified as the old one was. PROTOS implements this process in the domain of diagnosis of hearing disorders. PROTOS receives a description of a hearing disorder as input. Its first step is to guess what category the new problem fits into by looking at how the important features of the new case overlap with important features of categories of hearing disorders it knows about. This guess is PROTOS's first hypothesis about what category the new case fits into. PROTOS verifies its hypothesis by comparing the new case to exemplars in the hypothesized category to see if it can find a good match. If it finds a match, it chooses that category for the new case. However, PROTOS is also aware of the kinds of classification mistakes that are commonly made in its domain. In particular, it knows instances of examples that have been misclassified because of strong similarity to cases in the wrong category. If it finds that the new case matches one of these *failure cases*, it makes a new hypothesis—that the new case is an instance of the category this failure case was an instance of. It repeats the matching process in that category, continuing until it finds a good match.

The case-based classification procedure PROTOS implements models the largely unconscious automatic processing we do as we recognize objects in the world around us. Notice, however, that it was implemented in and applied to an expert domain—recognizing hearing disorders—a seemingly more strategic process than recognizing objects we see around us. Classifying using prototypes is not only a natural process that helps people get around in the commonsense world, but it is also a powerful decision-making procedure that allows people to make technical decisions. For example, although the manual psychiatrists use (*DSM-III,* American Psychiatric Association 1980) for diagnosis attempts to define its categories using necessary and sufficient conditions, it is hard to cover the borderline cases that way and nearly impossible to distinguish borderline cases of several similar disorders from each other. Those psychiatrists who use the manual well treat its descriptions of diagnostic categories as prototypes, add to that their own experiences and those culled from casebooks, and use the combination of the prototypical descriptions and exemplars to distinguish similar diagnostic categories from each other as they diagnose (Kochen 1983). PROTOS shows how machines can use similar procedures to make classification decisions in circumstances where necessary and sufficient conditions cannot be used to define the categories.

There are several problems we run into in doing this. First, if the meaning of concepts changes in context, then how do we keep track of what some concept means? Second, how do we figure out which classification a new instance falls into? The legal system has taken care of these problems by using cases. In law, one keeps track of what a concept means by saving the situations in which it was interpreted one way or another and using those as illustrations of its meaning. Concepts are not defined by necessary and sufficient conditions but by scenarios. One decides if a new examplar fits the definition by matching it against those that do and those that don't and determining which it is most similar to. When the new concept is shown to be enough like some already interpreted examplar, it is interpreted the same way. Much of the "action," then, is in the process of determining what a new exemplar is most similar to.

PROTOS's prototype-based classification procedure has the basics of this process embedded in it. PROTOS compares new cases to old ones it knows about. It keeps track of its own confusions, thus allowing the system to notice when its first hypothesis might not be the right one—a simple form of contrasting. What PROTOS is missing with respect to argumentation is strategies for weighing evidence for and against a series of conclusions. It can rule *out* some category based on a poor match, it can rule *in* some category based on a good match, and it can decide that it ought to be considering another category, but it cannot consider the pros and cons of several decisions to analyze which is best. It is these kinds of strategies that we normally think of when we think about argumentation.

This is where legal argumentation comes in. Lawyers argue every day using cases. Some argument strategies they use are prescribed and taught in law schools; other strategies have been honed by individual lawyers over time. HYPO, which models the argumentation lawyers do, not only determines which cases are most similar to its new situation, but it also does the full range of actions that we call argumentation. That is, it uses its cases to create cogent and coherent arguments in support of some position or another, and it creates hypothetical cases, or alternative scenarios, that it can use in its arguments when real cases it needs to make its points don't exist.

Many of the reasoning processes used by lawyers give us insight into a process of argumentation that can be used to evaluate the goodness, soundness, or validity of solutions and their alternates. In particular, argumentation procedures can provide the basis for critiquing solutions to problems before presenting them for use in the world. Strategic planners do such critiquing as they create plans. Teachers do this sort of critiquing as they create lesson plans. Generals do critiquing of this sort as they create battle plans. All problem solvers that plan for contingencies must do at least some critiquing to ascertain which contingencies to plan for.

Critiquing, however, has not received a lot of attention in AI or cognitive science approaches to problem solving. The reason is that for many years the tradition within AI circles has been to work on less-than-realistic problems and to treat the world as closed. The *closed-world assumption* assumes that the reasoner, whether person or program, knows everything it needs to know to solve a problem. If it doesn't know something, the assumption is made that either the something isn't true or isn't important. When real-world complexity is brought into problem solving, however, the closed-world assumption ceases to be useful. When problems are complex, we do not always have all the information we need while solving a problem to ensure its successful solution. There may be too many things to take into account, so the problem is solved by taking a simplified view of the world. In addition, some things may just not be known or not known accurately. And some things the problem solver may not realize it is important to take into account. And worst of all, something out of the control of the reasoner might change the world in unforeseen ways.

One way human problem solvers deal with such complexity is to critique solutions as part of the problem-solving process. Not only do they formulate solutions, but they also **run scenarios** (Goel and Pirolli 1989) to critique those solutions before they try them out in the world. One way to do this is to recall similar situations in which similar solutions were carried out. The outcome of those situations can be projected on the new one, allowing the outcome of its solution to be predicted. Another way is to create hypothetical scenarios in which the outcome can be easily predicted and to project those outcomes on the new situation. The critiquing process requires more than mere projection, however. What's hard, in particular, is that different scenarios can be used to predict different outcomes. Which should the reasoner believe? This is where argumentation comes in. In addition to projection, the reasoner must determine which of the old or hypothetical cases are indeed similar enough to the new one for the projection to make sense. Comparing and contrasting new situations and their solutions to old ones for the purpose of determining if an old outcome can apply to a new situation is one area in which argumentation can aid problem solving.

In fact, this process has the potential to help problem solvers in several different ways. First, it can point out what the potential problems with a proposed solution are, pointing the way toward repairing solutions appropriately. Second, it can point out what might be changed to make a good solution better. Third, scenarios used during critiquing can serve as justifications for whatever solution is decided on. Fourth, it can help the problem solver realize what is important to pay attention to in future problem solving.

In this chapter, we explore the processes inherent in argumentation and interpretive case-based reasoning. We focus on three processes:

1. Exemplar-based classification
2. Case-based argumentation strategies in support of situation assessment
3. Case-based projection of outcome in support of critiquing problem-solving solutions

For each, we discuss the process and any special requirements it puts on retrieval and indexing.

13.1 EXEMPLAR-BASED CLASSIFICATION

Classification is the process of determining what category some object fits into. In case-based or exemplar-based classification, categorization is done by finding the exemplar most similar to the new item and assigning the new item its classification. There are two major parts to the process: identifying or finding exemplars to match to and carrying out the match itself. In principle, either of these processes could be done by choosing search and match procedures from among those presented in previous chapters. Thus, the actual processes by which exemplar-based classification is done are not particularly interesting in and of themselves. What is interesting and important to address, however, are two things: the fact that case-based processes can be used for classification and efficient ways for these processes to work in combination with each other to classify. I will not attempt to present every combination of processes that might be efficient for carrying out exemplar-based classification; rather, I will present one program, PROTOS, that carries out the process accurately and efficiently and discuss why it works well.

Recall that PROTOS works in the domain of audiology; it diagnoses hearing disorders. It takes as input a description of the symptoms and test results of a patient and identifies the disorder the patient has. Its classification process is a sort of generate-test-debug (Simmons and Davis 1987; Simmons 1988) process. It begins by using surface features of its new case to make an initial hypothesis about the disorder the patient has. It attempts to verify the hypothesis by finding an exemplar from that category that matches its new case well. To do that, it chooses one exemplar from the category to use to begin its process and attempts to match its new case to that. If its new case and the exemplar it chooses match each other well, it is finished. If not, its debug cycle begins. Using the results of its match, it chooses an alternative exemplar that might be a better match to its new case. The new exemplar might be from the same category, or it might be from another one. PROTOS's process is summarized in Figure 13.1.

What makes classification hard, in general, is that the descriptions of items we want to classify usually are in terms of visible descriptive features, but we often need to evaluate similarity in terms of less visible features, often defined by function. A horizontal platform on a piece of furniture, for example, can be interpreted as a seat or as a tabletop, depending on the other properties of the object. This problem is equivalent to the situation assessment problem discussed in chapter 10.

- Based on surface features of the new case, identify categories it is likely to be in and select the most likely. The chosen category is the current hypothesis.
- Select a similar case from the category.
- Evaluate the similarity of the new case and the exemplar. If similar enough, the hypothesis holds.
- If not similar enough, use the results of the match to identify relevant differences between the new case and the chosen exemplar. Use those differences to choose a new exemplar. Continue from previous step.

FIGURE 13.1   PROTOS's Exemplar-Based Classification Algorithm

PROTOS deals with the problem by making its first hypotheses based on surface features but using a knowledge-based matching process that knows how to evaluate functional similarity to both verify its hypotheses and guide subsequent hypothesis formation. Though its first hypotheses are based on surface descriptions of items, knowledge gained in the matching process can be used to guide later hypothesis formation if memory indexes its cases in ways that allow that. Thus, though it might begin by thinking of the horizontal platform as a horizontal platform, after matching it may be able to think of it as a seat. Further discussion of how PROTOS carries out its steps will make this clearer.

Step 1: Make an initial hypothesis.   PROTOS uses surface features of its new case to identify a set of candidate categories. As in CASEY, each of the symptoms PROTOS is familiar with has associated with it a set of categories it is usually present in. Horizontal platform, in the domain of furniture, for example, has associated with it the categories chair, table, bench, and stool. In the audiology domain, `ac-reflex-u(normal)` is associated with `normal-ear` and `possible-menieres`, while `tymp(a)` is associated with `normal-ear`, `possible-menieres`, `cochlear-age`, and `bells-palsy`. PROTOS uses its associations, called *reminding links*, to generate a list of all the plausible categories for the new case. It then narrows the plausible list to a set of most likely categories by choosing those categories from the list that are predicted most strongly by surface features. It chooses the most highly favored as its first hypothesis. If it runs into a dead end using the first category it chooses, it returns to this step and chooses the next strongest category on its list.

Figure 13.2 shows an example from the audiology domain. The left side of the figure shows the set of features describing a new case (p8590R). The right side shows the set of categories hypothesized in this first step. The middle section shows associations between symptoms (on the left) and categories that this category list was derived from. When we combine the evidence, `normal-ear` and `possible-menieres` are most strongly favored (strengths of associations are not shown here but play a role in ordering the categories). PROTOS chooses `possible-menieres`.[2]

---

2. Both `normal-ear` and `possible-menieres` are predicted about equally strongly. PROTOS chooses `possible-menieres` because there are enough abnormal symptoms (e.g., `air(mild)`) to disqualify `normal-ear`. PROTOS effects this *censoring* of `normal-ear` by means of the *censor links* in its memory.

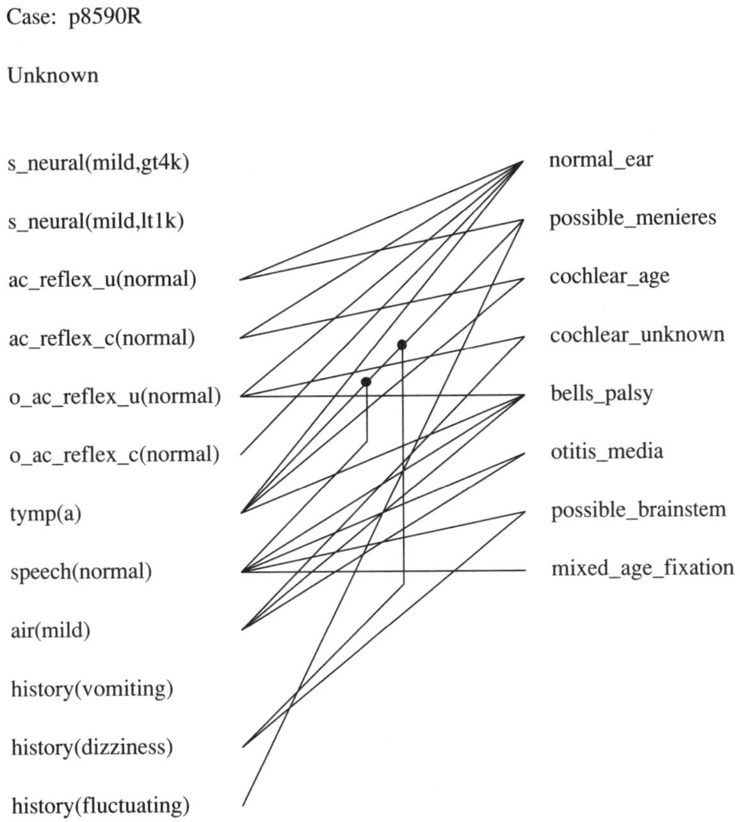

Case: p8590R

Unknown

FIGURE 13.2   A New Case and the Plausible Categories It Evokes

Because only surface features are available at this point, categories choosen in this first step may not be the best hypotheses. These categories, however, provide a starting point for the classification process. In later steps, better knowledge is derived about the new case, allowing better hypothesis formation. The first step provides a starting point for deriving the knowledge needed to continue the process. Other case-based reasoners (e.g., CHEF) apply situation assessment heuristics in their first step to reformulate the case description in such a way that appropriate cases can be found immediately in memory. In making its initial hypothesis based on a case and then reformulating later based on differences between its new case and its chosen one, PROTOS performs situation assessment in a case-based way.

Step 2: Select the most on-point case from the chosen category.   PROTOS does this using *prototypicality links*, which link categories with cases that are typical of the category. Strong prototypicality links link categories to cases that are highly prototypical. Weak protypicality links link categories to less typical cases. Bird, for example, is linked by strong prototypocality links to robin and canary and bluebird, by weak prototypicality links to owl and penguin. PROTOS chooses a case to begin its search by choosing the most highly prototypical case in the category. When an exemplar chosen in this step is neither a good match nor a predictor of other exemplars (step 4), PROTOS returns to this step and chooses another exemplar (the next most prototypical).

Step 3: Evaluate the degree of similarity between the new case and the chosen exemplar.   PROTOS makes its initial choice of a case based only on available surface features, but in this step it begins to bring deeper knowledge into the classification process. Associated with each of PROTOS categories is a model with two kinds of knowledge:

- A functional and causal description of items in the category
- Associations between functional components of those items and their implementation in specific real-world cases of those items

The category chair, for example, has associated with it a model that states that chairs have as their function holding a person, and that this is enabled by the combination of a seat, a backrest, and a seat support. It knows that chair 2 is made of wood and has legs that act as seat support, while chair 1 is made of metal, has a pedestal that acts as seat support, and also has armrests that are associated with holding a person and wheels, which are spurious to the chair's functioning. Figure 13.3 shows PROTOS's rendition of this model.

PROTOS uses its model to guide the matching process. It begins by matching those descriptors from the new case that match descriptors from its exemplar case exactly. This allows it to assign functional descriptions to parts of the new case. It then attempts to assign unmatched descriptors to functional parts of the exemplar that are not already assigned.

Suppose, for example, that PROTOS has only one chair in its chair category, chair 2. This is the one made of wood with four legs. It has chosen chair as the most plausible category for a new item, this time one with a seat, a back, and a pedestal. PROTOS will first match the seat in the new case to the seat in chair 2 and the back in the new case to the back in chair 2. It has nothing, however, to match the pedestal to. It looks at the functions of the leftover parts in chair 2, however, and finds that the legs, which are unmatched, play the role of seat support. It considers whether a pedestal could play such a role. If its knowledge tells it that, indeed, a pedestal can act as seat support, it considers its match successful. If its knowledge tells it that the pedestal cannot act as seat support, it considers the match a failure. If it is missing knowledge about whether a pedestal can act as seat support, it asks its expert collaborator.

Step 4: Reformulate hypothesis.   If the match process is not successful, PROTOS attempts to derive a better hypothesis based on feedback from the match. It uses features of the new case that are not matched in the exemplar and features of the exemplar that are not matched in the new case to point it to a better exemplar. It does this by way of *difference links*. Difference links connect cases to cases according to the differences between the item the link is emanating from and the item it is pointing to. They can connect cases within the same category or across categories. Figure 13.4 shows the difference links that connect chair 1 and chair 2, two cases in the same category (`chair`). PROTOS finds a new exemplar by following rele-

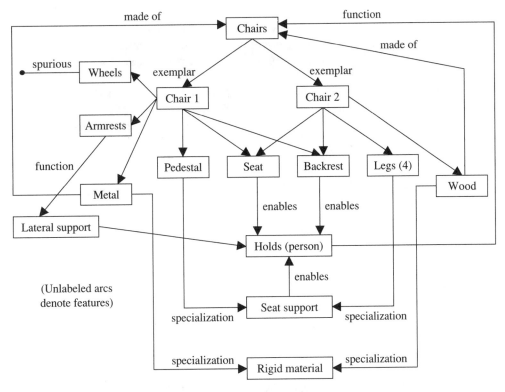

FIGURE 13.3   A Simple Model from PROTOS

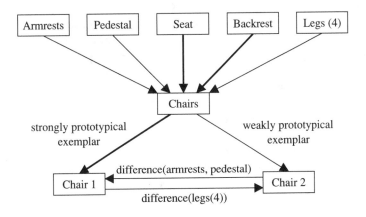

(Unlabeled arrows denote remindings. Line weight indicates strength.)

FIGURE 13.4   Difference Links

vant difference links from its current exemplar. These links point to cases that are different from that exemplar in the same way the new case is different from it.

The process continues by choosing one of the cases pointed to by a difference link as the new current exemplar and returning to step 3. If matching is unsuccessful and no difference links are available, PROTOS returns to try out cases pointed to by prototypicality links in previous cycles, and if none are available, it returns to the list of categories chosen in step 1, chooses the next category on its list, and continues the cycle.

Using PROTOS's method, successful classification depends on three factors:

■ Knowledge-based matching functions that judge similarity based on functional, causal, and correlational correspondences

■ Rich semantic linking between exemplars in its case library, based both on surface features and features derived in the course of matching

■ A failure-driven knowledge-acquisition process that is integrated with its classification process and that updates both functional knowledge used by matching functions and links between cases

Matching functions have already been discussed here and in chapter 9. The other two factors require more attention, however.

We begin with PROTOS's semantic linking. Steps 1, 2, and 4 of the classification process depend on linkages between descriptors, categories, and cases. PROTOS's memory has four kinds of links that allow it to choose exemplars for comparison.

Associative links (actually called *reminding links* in PROTOS) associate features with categories and exemplars. They are used in step 1 for hypothesis formation. Associative links are weighted by the likelihood of the feature's being associated with the category.

Censor links (which were not discussed earlier) provide negative associations. They allow PROTOS to rule out hypotheses predicted by associative links.

Prototypicality links associate categories with their prototypical exemplars. There are two kinds of prototypicality links: strong ones and weak ones. These links are used to choose an exemplar from a category for matching. Strongly prototypical exemplars are preferred. Weakly prototypical exemplars are chosen for matching only if attempted matches to strongly prototypical exemplars both fail and produce no alternative hypotheses.

Difference links record important differences between exemplars and allow movement from exemplar to examplar during the classification process. They are labeled by the difference between the two items they connect. Difference links can connect two exemplars from the same category or exemplars from different categories. Thus, when they are used in step 4 to suggest a new exemplar, they can either suggest an exemplar from the same category, keeping the current hypothesis intact, or they can suggest an alternative category, in effect, reformulating the hypothesis.

- If a case is misclassified, then
  - ☐ Request new domain knowledge from the teacher
  - ☐ Reassess the remindings that suggested the exemplar
  - ☐ Learn censors
  - ☐ Try again
- If a case is classified well, but PROTOS finds the match weak, then request explanations of featural equivalence.
- If a case is classified well and a very strong match to the chosen exemplar, then discard the new case and increase the prototypicality of the case it matched.
- Add any other well-classified cases to the category as exemplars and learn from them new associative links.
- If the case was initially misclassified but is now correctly classified, then install difference links between the original and new exemplar.

FIGURE 13.5 PROTOS's Learning Heuristics

Associative links provide linkages based on estimated probabilities of descriptive features being associated with categories; difference links allow movement from hypothesis to hypothesis based on features that have been found to be important to focus on in particular contexts. The difference links we have shown have all been surface features, but there is no reason why difference links can't be labeled by features derived in the course of matching. The success of hypothesis reformulation is dependent on the presence and accuracy of difference links.

It is the use of difference links that gives PROTOS the capability of finding good matches for new cases. But that capability requires that difference links be installed in memory in the first place. PROTOS installs those links as a result of its failure-driven knowledge acquisition process. When it fails to categorize a case well on its first try, it engages in a dialogue with an expert that allows it to both refine its functional and general knowledge and add links to its memory. Inability to find a match, misclassification of a new case, and recognized weaknesses in matches that the expert has approved alert PROTOS that it needs to learn something new. PROTOS asks the expert for input in those areas. In addition, misclassification alerts PROTOS to confusions that might arise in the future, and it installs difference links to account for those. Its learning process is summarized in Figure 13.5.[3]

Whenever a new case is added to memory, difference links are made to any cases it incorrectly or suboptimally matched during problem solving. In general, PROTOS recognizes the need to install difference links when it misclassifies an item on an early try and then classifies it well later. When that happens, it installs difference links between the exemplar it had originally incorrectly matched the new case to and either the new case or the exemplar it is merged with. The links are labeled by features the teacher points out as important. Alterna-

---

3. Note: Well-classified cases are those that are correctly identified as being in a category, either because the system classified them as such or because the teacher supplied the classification.

tively, they could be labeled automatically by all features of both the new case and the exemplar that are not accounted for in the match, later removing those that turned out not to be useful (a process that requires a longer training time).

13.2 CASE-BASED INTERPRETATION

Exemplar-based classification works when a model exists that can be used for matching and when it is easy to identify items in the real world with concepts in the concept world. For example, as long as it is easy to look at an object and recognize that its horizontal platform is a seat, PROTOS can identify the object as a chair. But exemplar-based classification can only be as good as its matching procedure, and good matching procedures rely on well-articulated (though not necessarily complete) models of the items they are attempting to match. Otherwise, they can match only based on the similarities of surface features.

Exemplar-based classification methods are insufficient, however, when no model is available, when at issue is which model should be used for matching, or when at issue is whether something fits a description of a hard-to-define component of a given model. An exemplar-based classification procedure cannot determine, for example, whether an item that it has identified as a chair should be considered a work of art or a piece of furniture. And if it cannot easily recognize that a portion of an object it is looking at is a seat, then it cannot recognize a chair.

When a model is not available to use in matching (i.e., there is no domain theory), when the terms that define the model do not have agreed-upon definitions, and when there are many competing models, making which model to use a major issue, processes that can weigh evidence for and against a hypothesis are needed. We can go back to the example at the beginning of this chapter to make clear the need for such processes and to examine what they need to accomplish and how.

Recall that George, who is almost thirteen, is trying to convince his parents that he should be allowed to see *Little Shop of Horrors* (Ashley 1990), which is rated PG, meaning that parental guidance is suggested in determining whether children can see it. There are many arguments he could make. He could argue that he is a teenager, not a child, and use a PROTOS-like approach to point out that "almost thirteen" is in the category teenager. To do that, he would either find a case in "going to a PG movie" category in which someone almost thirteen was allowed to go or a case in the "teenager" category in which the child was almost thirteen. He could argue that he has the appropriate maturity to see the movie, again using a PROTOS-like approach, finding a case of another child of equal maturity being allowed to see a similar movie. This is what he does, in fact, when he points out that Noah's parents let him see the movie. Alternatively, he could argue about the fairness of being allowed to see the movie and justify that with a case showing that someone he is equivalent to was granted a similar wish. This is his strategy in pointing out that his sister Sarah was allowed to see the movie.

George is up against several hurdles. First, there are many different arguments that could be made. Which issues should he focus on? Second, there are many competing models defining common terms. George's definition of mature is different from his parents' definition. It isn't enough to show that he's mature by his model. He either has to show he is mature according to their model or show that his model is the more appropriate one. Third, there are no models for some terms. How, for example, can one show *fairness*?

Case-based, or exemplar-based, classification provides a piece of the argumentation process, but it is surrounded and controlled by strategies for argumentation that determine which case-based classification should be attempted. These strategies need to both decide how to direct an argument initially and then respond to challenges put forth against the argument. George argues fairness by citing his sister's being allowed to see the movie, and his parents respond with the difference between George and his sister (age and level of maturity). George continues the argument where his parents led it—this time arguing that indeed he is mature enough. George's task is twofold: to keep the argument under control (i.e., keep it associated with issues that he can respond to) and to choose cases that can hold up his side of the argument best.

As stated earlier in the chapter, we all do this sort of adversarial argumentation every day, both in commonsense kinds of situations and when we are playing the role of technical experts. Should I take the new job? Should I let this student into graduate school? Should I let my daughter go to overnight camp for four weeks, or is two weeks good enough? Should I drive in by the normal route, which was full of traffic yesterday, or should I take an alternative route? Which strategic direction is better for the company? We need to hire two people but have money only for one—should we hire a person who is expert in one of the areas where we need expertise or one who knows a little about each but is expert at neither? If the first, which area should she be expert at?

Making justifiable arguments to support one or another decision is a process of recalling old cases and comparing and contrasting them to the new situation to determine which of several outcomes is most likely. The cases used for analysis are the same ones that can be used to justify whatever decision is made. Ashley lists a variety of case-based processes that comprise the argumentation process (Ashley 1990, 25–26):

- Comparing a problem situation to a past case to justify by analogy the conclusion that the same decision should be reached

- Distinguishing the problem situation from a past case to justify the conclusion that it should *not* be decided analogously

- Arguing that a particular case does not provide a compelling justification for deciding the problem situation by comparing it to counterexamples, cases just as similar to the problem situation but in which different outcomes were reached

- Posing hypothetical cases as examples and counterexamples in which the purported comparisons or distinctions would or would not justify the desired result

- Combining comparisons to and constrasts with many cases into an argument about how the problem situation should be decided and evaluating the strength of the competing arguments

These processes, in turn, require consideration of a variety of comparative features of cases (Ashley and Rissland 1988a):

Factual similarities and differences relative to the current situation: Which cases share more features with the current problem situation (are most on point)? Which share less?

Outcomes: Of the cases that are most on point, how do their outcomes compare? If comparably on-point cases have conflicting outcomes, what are their differences relative to the current situation?

Uses: Which cases make stronger points? Which will make an argument difficult? Which distinguish other cases that must be considered? Which point to extremes?

Potential relevance to the current fact situation: Which cases are nearly on point? Might any of those cases jog the memory of the reasoner to look for and discover new facts and arguments about the current situation?

Significance to other parts of the argument: What are the cases and connections when the current situation is viewed from a different slant?

Possible variations: What new cases and connections come into view when the facts of the current situation are changed hypothetically? How do the connections change when features are added, subtracted, exaggerated, or combined with those of neighboring cases?

The case-based reasoning community has looked to law as the domain to examine to figure out how these processes can be carried out, and the model of adversarial reasoning implemented in HYPO (Ashley 1990), a legal reasoning program, is arguably the most comprehensive of those studies.[4] In the rest of this section, HYPO's approach to these processes will be presented.

HYPO's adversarial reasoning process takes as input a description of a new case, called the *current fact situation* or *cfs*. Its output is an evaluation of who the winner of the case should be and a set of arguments for and against that outcome. An input, for example, might be that George, who is almost thirteen and in seventh grade, wants to see *Little Shop of Horrors*. If HYPO argued this case, it would determine that George should win and present an argument citing fairness and maturity that argues for George's being allowed to go, anticipates and counters the objections of his parents, and is justified by a set of cited cases. HYPO's process for argument creation has six steps:

1. *Analyze* the new situation for relevant factors.
2. Based on these factors, *retrieve* cases.
3. *Position* the retrieved cases with respect to the new one.
4. *Select* the most on-point cases, both pro and con.
5. *Generate three-ply arguments* for each of the issues.
6. *Test* the analysis using hypotheticals.

---

4. A more recent case-based approach to legal reasoning can be found in Branting's GREBE (Branting 1991a, 1991b, 1991c, 1991d).

The first step assesses the current fact situation to extract its important features. With important features available, HYPO retrieves similar cases. In the third step, it clusters those cases according to the points they make. Some cases will point to the outcome being evaluated; others will point to some other outcome. Some cases in each cluster will be more on point than others. That is, they will share more with the new situation than other cases do. These cases, which will frame the arguments to be constructed, are selected out in step 4.

The work of creating arguments is done in step 5. Those cases that are most on point are used to try to support the chosen outcome. But there are almost always differences between those cases and the new situation. In general, differences point out holes in the argument that can be created, and it is up to the arguer to anticipate counterarguments that can be set up based on these differences and to be able to counter those arguments. A three-ply argument consists of an argument for some claim followed by a counterargument arising from a problem with that claim, followed by a counter to the counterargument supporting the original claim. In step 6, the strength of the argument created in step 5 is tested by applying it to hypothetical variants of the problem situation that weaken or strengthen the argument.

13.2.1 Analyzing and Retrieving Cases: Dimensions, Indexing, and the Case Analysis Record

Discussion of exactly how these processes can be carried out requires discussion of the knowledge structures used for representation and organization of cases. HYPO uses *dimensions* to represent the predictive features of cases. Cases are indexed in the case library by their dimensions. It uses a *case analysis record* to record its analysis of a case. It uses a *claim lattice* to cluster and organize cases retrieved in step 2. The claim lattice allows HYPO to easily see the relationships between cases it has recalled. This, in turn, enables the creation of good arguments.

A dimension, in HYPO, is a factor that has been found to influence outcome of cases. Dimensions are specific to particular domains and are associated with claims that can be made within that domain. The "going to the movies" domain, for example, has dimensions age, lateness of showtime, movie-rating, emotional maturity, homework burden, location, and night of the week. The "maturity" claim ("Of course, I'm old enough") has associated with it emotional maturity, age, and movie rating. The "fairness" claim ("You let my sister do it, I should be allowed also") has associated with it lateness of showtime, location, and night of the week. When making an argument about maturity, one focuses on the maturity set of dimensions. When making an argument about fairness, one uses the fairness set. The legal trade secrets domain has as dimensions competitive advantage gained, voluntary disclosure, non-disclosure agreements, and so on. Figure 13.6 shows some of the dimensions in the trade secrets domain.

Depending on the value a case has along each dimension, there is more or less chance (all other things being equal) of an outcome arising. For example, the older a child is, the more chance he will be allowed to go to the movies, while the more homework he has, the less chance he will be allowed to go. The existence of a nondisclosure agreement favors an outcome of illegal nondisclosure, while the less voluntary a disclosure, the more an outcome of legality of actions is favored. Good cases to use in an argument are those that point to the

The plaintiff's position is strengthened to the extent that

Brought-Tools: The plaintiff's former employees brought the plaintiff's notes, diagrams, tools to the defendant.

Competitive-Advantage: The defendant's access to the plaintiff's secret information gave the defendant a competitive advantage.

Disclose-Secrets: The plaintiff did not voluntarily disclose his secrets to outsiders.

Noncompete-Agreement: The plaintiff's employees had entered into nondisclosure agreements.

Bribe-Employee: The defendant bribed the plaintiff's employees to switch employment.

Vertical-Knowledge: The plaintiff's secrets were not simply about customer business methods.

FIGURE 13.6 Sample Dimensions from HYPO's Trade Secrets Domain. From Figure 1 in Ashley, K.D. and Rissland, E.L. (1988), "A Case-Based Approach to Modeling Legal Expertise," *IEEE Expert*, 3(3), pp. 70–77.

---

favored outcome and whose values on each dimension are either equal to the new situation or differ in the direction that makes the new case look more inclined toward that outcome.[5]

Cases tend to be described in terms of visible descriptive features; dimensions tend to be more interpretive and are derived from more visible features. A legal case might be described in terms of the size of the company, the number of people disclosed to, the amount of money lost by the party bringing the suit, the time that went into developing a product, the size of the customer base, and so on. Dimensions combine and interpret these descriptors, capturing their relevance. *Competitive advantage*, for example, is computed based on time it took the defendant to make a product compared to the time it took the plaintiff. If the defendant developed the product more quickly, there is the suggestion that the defendant used the shortcut provided by the plaintiff's confidential information. One assumes that the larger the difference in development time, the more advantage was gained through confidential information.

Dimensions hold four kinds of knowledge:

- *Prerequisites* are tests that can be performed to determine if a new situation can be described by the dimension. For example, the prerequisites of the *bribe employee* dimension are that the two corporations involved in the lawsuit compete with respect to a product and that the defendant gained access to confidential product information belonging to the plaintiff by luring the plaintiff's former employees away to work for the defendant and disclose that information.

---

5. Technically, HYPO's use of dimensions is slightly different than given here. HYPO does not actually reason about the chance of an outcome arising. Rather, it reasons about the relative strengths of arguments. An argument is strong to the extent that a case is more convincing along some dimension than some other case in which a desired outcome happened.

- *Focal slots* point to descriptors that are most important in determining the magnitude of the dimension. To compare two cases on a dimension, their focal slots are compared. The *bribe employee* focal slot is the bribe itself—what the defendant offered the plaintiff's employees to entice them away. The magnitude of the dimension depends on the magnitude of what is in the focal slot; the more enticements, the higher the magnitude of this dimension.

- *Comparison methods* specify how to use focal slot information for comparison. In general, comparison methods specify how to find or compute focal slots, how to compare two values (e.g., set inclusion, less than, greater than, something versus nothing), and how to interpret the results of the comparison with respect to an outcome. For example, supposing that the focal slot on the dimension *maturity* is *age*, the comparison method would specify that age be looked up, that comparison be done by means of numerical comparison operators, and that increase in maturity is correlated with increased permission to go to the movies.

- Dimensions *index* cases and point to the cases they index. *Bribe employee* indexes two cases: *Telex* v. *IBM* and the *Midland Ross* case.

Cases in the case library are described in terms of their dimensions and indexed by their dimensions. New situations are analyzed to derive their dimensions in step 1 of the argumentation process. Each dimension's prerequisites are tested in the new situation to see if they apply. Once it is determined which dimensions a new situation has, cases indexed by that dimension are retrieved in step 2.

The full representation of a new case in HYPO has three parts to it:

- The current fact situation
- Its dimensions
- The case analysis record

The *current fact situation* is the surface description of the situation being analyzed. It includes information such as descriptions of the people involved, descriptions of the organizations involved, the location of the situation, and other factual information relevant to the issues at hand. Figure 13.7 shows the English version of the current fact situation for HYPO's case *Telex* v. *IBM*. It is represented internally in a frame representation (similar to Figure 4 in chapter 5).

The *case analysis record* records information derived in the course of analyzing a case. HYPO begins constructing the case analysis record during steps 1 and 2 of the argumentation process. The case analysis record keeps track of which dimensions a case has, which descriptors of the case are most relevant to those dimensions, which dimensions it almost has (near-miss dimensions), which claims can potentially be made, and which cases are likely to be relevant to argumentation. Near-miss dimensions are those where most, but not all, of the prerequisites for the dimension are fulfilled. HYPO records new information in its case analysis record as it is derived. Figure 13.8 shows a case analysis record for a new situation. Information in the case analysis record is used for retrieving old cases, for organizing them in the claim lattice (to be discussed later), and for constructing arguments.

An attorney's corporate client (IBM) complains that Telex has been misappropriating trade secrets with respect to IBM's Merlin disk-drive system. Specifically, IBM complains that

- Telex offered IBM's Merlin project engineers large salaries, stock options, and bonuses (one for $500,000) as inducements to join Telex (Bribe-Employee).

- All former IBM employees had entered into nondisclosure agreements with IBM to keep IBM's trade secret information confidential (Noncompete-Agreement).

- Because of its access to IBM trade secrets, Telex developed its competing products in substantially less time and at lower expense (Competitive-Advantage).

FIGURE 13.7 The Current Fact Situation for *Telex* v. *IBM*. From Figure 2 in Ashley, K.D. and Rissland, E.L. (1988), "A Case-Based Approach to Modeling Legal Expertise," *IEEE Expert*, 3(3), pp. 70–77.

13.2.2 Positioning and Selecting Cases: The Claim Lattice

Argumentation procedures need to keep track of the similarities and differences between cases. HYPO uses a *claim lattice* for this job. The claim lattice is a graph that organizes cases retrieved in step 2 so that their similarities and differences are made explicit and so that their usefulness can be easily recognized. Cases in the claim lattice are more or less on point to the problem situation; some have desirable outcomes, some have undesirable ones; some can be used to create arguments, others are troublesome for argumentation; some are very useful, some not as useful. All, however, are related in some significant way to the new situation.

The claim lattice is a hierarchical structure created by comparing relevant dimensions of retrieved cases with relevant dimensions of the new situation. At the root of the claim lattice is the new situation itself. At the next level are those cases that share independent subsets of the dimensions of the new situation. Below that are cases that share a subset of those dimensions. As the claim lattice is traversed downward, cases share smaller and smaller subsets of dimensions with the new situation. Those near the top of the lattice are more *on point* than those farther down. Figure 13.9 shows a claim lattice HYPO generated for the case represented by the case analysis record in Figure 13.8.

Applicable factual predicates: exists-corporate-claimant, exists-confidential-info, employee-switched-employers, and so forth
Applicable dimensions: Agreed-Not-To-Disclose, Bribe-Employee, Competitive-Advantage.
Near-miss dimensions: Brought-Tools, Disclose-Secrets, Vertical-Knowledge
Potential claims: Trade secrets misappropriation, breach of nondisclosure agreement
Relevant CKB citations: Midland Ross, Data General, Structural Dynamics, Raycorp vs. Tronic, Modern Controls

FIGURE 13.8 A Case Analysis Record. From Figure 3 in Ashley, K.D. and Rissland, E.L. (1988), "A Case-Based Approach to Modeling Legal Expertise," *IEEE Expert*, 3(3), pp. 70–77.

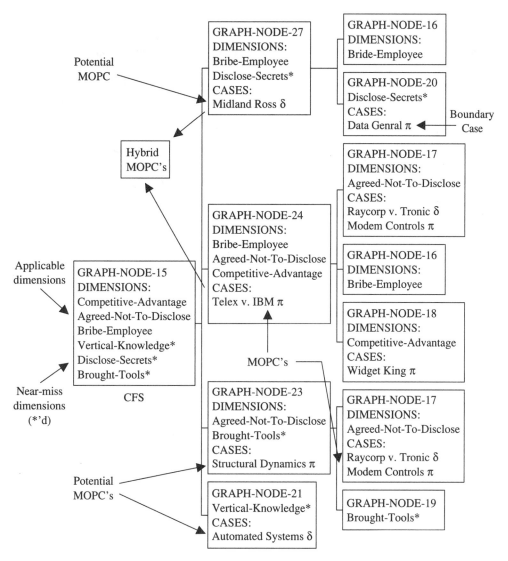

The root node represents the cfs and its D-list (asterisks indicate dimensions that are near misses as to the CFS). Successor nodes contain pro-plaintiff or pro-defendant cases, involving trade-secrets-misappropriation claims, that are on point to the cfs. Nodes closest to the root that do not have near-miss dimensions contain mopcs; otherwise, they may contain potential mopcs. Leaf nodes are least on point. Each major lattice branch that contains MOPCs represents one way of arguing about the CFS. MOPCs may be counter examples to cases with opposite outcomes in successor nodes. Boundary cases exemplify extremes along particular dimensions. Hypothetical hybrid MOPCs combine features of different MOPCs that hold for plaintiff and defendant. Potential MOPCs suggest fruitful hypothetical variants of the CFS.

FIGURE 13.9 A Claim Lattice from HYPO. From Figure 4 in Ashley, K.D. and Rissland, E.L. (1988), "A Case-Based Approach to Modeling Legal Expertise," *IEEE Expert*, 3(3), pp. 70–77.

Both existing dimensions of a new situation and its near-miss dimensions are used to retrieve cases and build the claim lattice. Thus it holds in it both cases that can be used to create arguments and those that have the potential to be used to create arguments. Near-miss dimensions, indexing potentially useful cases, can be used to point out information that may be missing from the current fact situation. When the relevant information is gathered, cases with the near-miss dimension that is satisfied become available for argument construction. In Figure 13.9, near-miss dimensions in the new situation are marked by an asterisk (*).[6]

A claim lattice is appropriate for arguing one claim. If there are several to be argued, separate claim lattices need to be set up for those. Arguing for George, for instance, requires separate claim lattices for arguing maturity and fairness. In the *Telex* v. *IBM* case, there are two claims that must be argued: trade secrets misappropriation and breach of a nondisclosure agreement. Each claim to be argued may have different dimensions important to it. The claim lattice shown is for trade-secrets misappropriation.

Nodes in the claim lattice are organized according to the degree of overlap of dimensions of the new situation and dimensions of old cases. Nodes are labeled by the subset of dimensions they represent, and each node may hold several cases. Cases at any node may argue either side of a claim. That is, they can point to several different outcomes. Legal cases in a node of a claim lattice might have been won by the plaintiff or the defendant. Some nodes are present in the lattice more than once, because their dimensions represent subsets of the dimensions of several nodes at a higher level.

Arguments are created by finding cases that are most on point, using them as the framework for an argument, using differences between them to anticipate counterarguments, using cases with an opposite outcome to support the counterargument, and then using cases with the outcome of the most on-point case to counter the counterargument. This will become clearer later. Some cases are more useful in support of an argument than others. For example, some cases can be considered *trumping cases*. They get at the holes in an argument and more. Trumping cases are particularly useful when they point to a desired outcome, troublesome when they point to an undesirable one. The claim lattice not only organizes cases according to their similarity to the new situation, but it also helps the reasoner to determine which are the more useful or potentially useful cases for argumentation.

There are several different kinds of cases in a claim lattice, each used for different purposes in argumentation:

■ *Most on-point cases*, or *MOPCs* are those that share a maximal set of *real* dimensions with the current situation. In the claim lattice shown, that includes *Telex* v. *IBM, Raycorp* v. *Tronic,* and *Modern Controls*. Most-on-point cases that have the desired outcome are used to formulate arguments. Each branch of the lattice that contains one of these represents one way of arguing the claim for the current situation.

---

6. A later implementation of HYPO used two claim lattices, one with only existing dimensions of the new case and the other with both existing and near-miss dimensions. The first is used to pick MOPCs (most on-point cases). The second is used to choose potential MOPCs. The change was done for two reasons: the claim lattices with the near-misses were getting too big to show the user, and the algorithm for picking MOPCs could be made simpler (Ashley, personal communication).

■ *Potential most on-point cases* are those that share the most real and near-miss dimensions and are not most on-point cases. In the figure, that includes *Midland Ross, Structural Dynamics,* and *Automated Systems.* Though these cases can't be used as the framework for an argument, they can be cited to make appropriate counterpoints or to support arguments made by the most on-point cases. In addition, potential MOPCs suggest hypothetical variants of the current situation that might be useful in making a point and dimensions to find out more about.

■ *Examples* are cases that have a desirable outcome for the arguer. Those that are most on point are used to frame arguments. Those less on point are used to support arguments.

■ *Counterexamples* are cases that have an undesirable outcome for the arguer. Those that are more on point (i.e., share more with the new situation) are particularly troublesome to arguing the desirable outcome. Counterexamples and potential counterexamples (those that would be counterexamples if there were a few more facts present) help the reasoner to anticipate arguments that will arise from the other side.

13.2.3 Generating and Testing Arguments

An argument in HYPO has three components (Ashley 1990, 62–63):

1. A *point* is made on behalf of one party in the dispute in favor of some outcome. A point has three parts:

    ■ A *conclusion* in favor of some outcome

    ■ *Justification* for the conclusion in the form of a citation to a prior case

    ■ *Rationale* for the justification in the form of an analogy between the new situation and the cited case

2. A *response* on behalf of the opponent or opposing outcome that *counters* the original point. It has at least one of the following components:

    ■ A statement *distinguishing* the new situation from the cited case

    ■ Citation of *counterexamples* to the cited case

3. A *rebuttal* on behalf of the first party favoring the original outcome and responding to the response.

These three components together comprise a *three-ply argument.*

Making a point: The point of a three-ply argument is made by consulting the claim lattice and choosing from it a most on-point case that favors the outcome being argued for. That case becomes the justification for the conclusion. Drawing an analogy between a cited case and a new situation means pointing out their similarities—in particular, the ones that are important to the point being made. These are, in general, the cited dimensions. Thus, the similarities between the cited case and the new situation become the rationale for the justification.

Using the claim lattice in Figure 13.9, if we are arguing for the defendant (the one being sued), there is only one choice of a case to use: *Raycorp* v. *Tronic*. In that case, the defendant won even though the employee who disclosed information signed a nondisclosure agreement. The rationale is that in both cases, there was agreement not to disclose. This point is not very strong, but it is well formed, and there is no stronger point that can be made based on the currently known facts (Ashley and Rissland 1988).

Response: Responses can be of two sorts: *distinguishing* the cited case and the new situation and *citing counterexamples* to the cited case. Distinguishing means pointing out differences between the cited case and the new situation that show that the cited case may not be very good justification for the conclusion, and sometimes even showing that it justifies the opposing position. There are two kinds of differences that can be cited to distinguish a cited case from a new situation:

- Different positions along shared dimensions
- Unshared dimensions

When George cites his sister's seeing *Little Shop of Horrors* and his parents reply that she is older, they are distinguishing on the basis of different positions along a shared dimension. The dimension (age of viewer) is shared by the cited case and the new situation, but it has a different value for each. George, in citing that case, was trying to gloss over that difference. His parents, in distinguishing, point it out. When the difference along a dimension favors the opposing outcome, the difference is a *distinction*. To compare values on dimensions to each other, HYPO compares the values in the dimension's *focal slots* according to the interpretation information in the dimension's *comparison method*.

Unshared dimensions are dimensions that one case has but the other doesn't. In the legal example we've been considering, the new situation can be distinguished from *Raycorp* v. *Tronic* by two unshared dimensions: competitive advantage and bribed employee. That is, in the new situation, but not in the old one, the defendant's access to the plaintiff's product information saved it time and expense, and the defendant paid a former employee of the plaintiff to switch employment. Unshared dimensions that are appropriate for distinguishing are those that favor the opposing side.

Counterexamples are cases that share many of the same dimensions with the new situation that are shared by the cited case, but in which there was an opposite outcome. Looking at the claim lattice in Figure 13.9, we see that *Modern Controls* shares the same dimensions with the new situation that *Raycorp* v. *Tronic* shares with it but that the opposing side won. It is a counterexample to *Raycorp* v. *Tronic*. We also see that *Telex* v. *IBM* shares the same dimension with the new situation that *Raycorp* v. *Tronic* shares with it, and it also shares two other dimensions with the new situation. This makes *Telex* v. *IBM* a *more on-point counterexample* to *Raycorp* v. *Tronic*.

There are four kinds of responses that can be made using distinguishing information and counterexamples. *Trumping* a point means citing a more on-point counterexample to show that the opposite conclusion should be reached. A *partial counter* response cites a counterexample even though it might not trump. It points out that there are reasons to counter the argument.

A *disparaging* response attacks the significance of the argument made by the cited example by citing boundary counterexamples. Boundary counterexamples are those that support an outcome but very weakly. If George reminds his parents that they once before let him see a PG movie, when, in fact, they don't usually let him see such movies, he is citing a boundary counterexample. It makes his case by showing the inconsistency of his parents' argument but makes it very weakly. In general, a boundary counterexample pushes on a boundary. It is the weakest case for a side along a particular dimension but a case in which that side still won. In one of HYPO's nondisclosure cases, for example, the plaintiff won even though there were disclosures to six thousand outsiders. This case provides a very weak argument for the plaintiff along this dimension.

An *alternative explanation* response asserts that a comparison is not fair because there are other features, not shared by either the current case or the cited case, that justify the result. It is the weakest of the responses.

Rebuttal: One rebuts by responding to the response by either distinguishing or citing counter-counterexamples.[7] If the response showed that a set of dimensions not included in the original cited case is important to the solution, for example, one could present a case in the rebuttal with those dimensions that supports the conclusion of the original point. If the response points out a difference on a dimension, one can rebut by finding a case with the same difference that supports the conclusion of the original point. In general, one will find such cases in the claim lattice in the branch that the response case came from. When such cases are found, they can be used to distinguish the response case from the original case (as HYPO does) or presented to counter the rebuttal.

A problem arises, of course, when the response is a trumping one, that is, when a more on-point counterexample is used. That requires a different kind of response. One might be able to counter by distinguishing or trumping again, but in general, strong arguments justified by existing cases will be difficult to make. One way to deal with such situations is by proposing *hypothetical* variants of the new situation to show that the trumping case doesn't really hold. George, for example, might argue by pointing out that if he were two months older (i.e., already thirteen), this argument wouldn't even arise. His hypothetical would be used to point out the absurdity of using absolute age as a sign of maturity.

Alternatively, hypotheticals can be used to suggest that a counterexample can be trumped by the original situation. HYPO proposes a hypothetical variant of the current fact situation that is more on point than the counterexample. When presented to a user, this spurs the user to see if those features really are present in his or her current fact situation.

Using hypotheticals: When a case does not exist to make a needed point, an arguer may create one and use the hypothetical case the same way a real case would be used. Hypotheticals are used for a variety of purposes in argumentation (Rissland 1986; Ashley 1990):

- They allow an arguer to explore issues in greater detail than reality allows, often teasing out hidden assumptions. A hypothetical case, for example, might allow the

---

7. HYPO doesn't actually use counter-counterexamples. It would be easy, however, to add them.

arguer to zero in on which of several features is the important one to focus on by pitting competing features against each other. Or it might allow exploration of the meaning of some rule or statute. By exaggerating strengths or weaknesses in a case, or by eliminating features, using hypotheticals allows focus on particular parts of a situation.

■ They allow an arguer to control the course of an argument by focusing attention on the issues present in the hypothetical.

■ They allow an arguer to present, support, and attack positions that reality would not allow, in order, for example, to test the consequences of tentative conclusions, to take an assertion to its limits, or to explore the meaning of a concept.

The explorations enabled by using hypotheticals are particularly useful in testing the arguments that can be made using real-world cases. HYPO tests its arguments by creating relevant hypotheticals and seeing if the arguments generated so far still apply.

One way to create hypotheticals is by modifying real cases. Useful kinds of modifications include making a near-miss dimension apply, strengthening or weakening a case along a dimension, and making extreme cases. HYPO has five heuristics for generating hypotheticals from real cases (called *the seed case,* Ashley 1990):

1. Pick a near-miss dimension and modify the facts to make it applicable. To do this, HYPO modifies the seed case by filling in a missing prerequisite for the near-miss dimension. A useful near-miss dimension for George to focus on, for example, is maturity. The prerequisite for this, in his parents' eyes, is that he already be a teenager. Using this heuristic, George's age is modified to be thirteen. In using this case to argue his point, George will point out that the modification he needed to make to the situation to create a situation they would agree to was slight, hence they should give in to his desires.

2. Pick an applicable dimension and make the case weaker or stronger along that dimension. This is done by changing the value in the dimensions focal slot. Often, this is done relative to some target case. This heuristic can be used by George to create the same hypothetical. If George knows that his parents will let him see *Little Shop of Horrors* when he is a teenager and he is only two months from turning thirteen, then it is advantageous for him to create a hypothetical in which he is two months older than now and to argue that he would be allowed to see it under those circumstances and it really isn't much of a difference. The difference here between application of the first heuristic and this one is that one focused on the maturity dimension, the other on age. That they both ended up making the same hypothetical happens because of the close relationship between those two dimensions.

3. Pick a dimension related to a relevant dimension and apply one of the other heuristics to it. Dimensions are related when they favor different outcomes and both appear in the same case. George's sister, for example, may have a lot of homework (favoring not going to the movies) but be older (favoring going) and still be allowed to go the movies on a school night. George may use this case to point out to himself that amount of

homework, an unfavorable feature, may nevertheless lead to a favorable result. Picking up on that, he might modify his description of the current situation to include in it that he has little homework.

4. Pick an applicable dimension and make the case extreme on that dimension. An arguer might do this to focus attention on the extent to which a dimension has to hold to be relevant to an outcome. For example, in Supreme Court arguments about whether a religious display is appropriate on government property, justices relied on several extremes. They asked if leaving only the religious part in made a difference. They asked if taking out all the blatantly religious parts made a difference. This was in order to determine the extent to which percentage of religious content made a difference (Ashley 1988).

5. Pick a target case that is a win and, using the first two heuristics, move the seed case toward it to create a near-win. In this way, an arguer can examine what sorts of changes need to be made in a losing situation to turn it into a winning one.

HYPO decides which hypotheticals to create by comparing a seed case (either its current situation or one of the cases it has cited in an argument) with a description of a target it would like to achieve. For example, after the *Telex v. IBM* case is used to trump the argument made by the *Xerox v. SCM* case, HYPO might want to generate a counter to the trump case, one that includes its dimensions but in some way that favors the defendant winning. It sends the trump case to the hypothetical case generator along with a specification of a target specifying the dimensions that need to be filled in and the targeted outcome. Using knowledge about those dimensions and the values along them that favor different outcomes, HYPO would call the second heuristic several times to modify the values in the specified dimensions.

13.3 CRITIQUING SOLUTIONS: CASE-BASED PROJECTION

Case-based interpretation methods are for more than just classification and law. The interpretive reasoning processes we have been discussing give us insight into the process of argumentation that can be used to evaluate the goodness, soundness, or validity of problem-solving solutions. We can use what we have learned from our investigations of law to implement case-based analysis procedures that can project the results of their solutions before carrying them out in the world, allowing them to be repaired before they are executed. In addition, an understanding of these processes is allowing us to create systems that can work along with people to help them assess the pros and cons of several different solutions and decide which is best. This assessment of solutions based on the outcomes of other cases is the process we call *case-based projection*.

The simplest illustration of case-based projection comes from the meal planning domain and was presented in chapter 1. The host has just decided to serve grilled salmon to a group of eaters, some of whom don't eat milk products and others of whom eat only "normal food." The host runs a scenario. "Suppose I serve grilled salmon," she asks herself. "What will happen?" But how can she guess what will happen? There is no standard numerical simulation that can be run. There is no causal model that can be run. Recalling similar cases may be the only way.

She therefore attempts to recall other cases in which grilled salmon or something similar was served to these or similar guests. This is when she is reminded of the case in which Anne, who is one of the guests, was served grilled fish and refused to eat it. The case-based interpretation process must now begin. The host must consider whether this meal is another one that Anne won't eat. What was it about the fish that made Anne not eat it? Is that same thing true of the fish I will serve now? Answering these questions may be simple (Anne simply doesn't like fish), or they may require the full power of adversarial reasoning.

Critiquing a solution to a problem requires two steps: generating likely outcomes and evaluating which of those outcomes is likely to occur. The case-based generation of potential outcomes itself is fairly simple. If we index cases according to dimensions that were responsible for their outcomes, then the set of cases that can generate potential outcomes can be collected by analyzing the current case for its relevant dimensions and, using the case (including its problem description and solution) and its dimensions as a probe into memory, retrieving applicable cases. The outcomes of those cases can then be projected onto the new situation by using adaptation heuristics to adapt their specifics to the specifics of the new situation. The hard part comes in determining which of those several outcomes is most likely. This is where argumentation strategies play a role.

Consider, for example, a strategic planning situation. Executives of a small manufacturing company are trying to map the company's future. There is a small amount of capital to invest and several possible ways to use it. The additional resources could be put into development in an already strong part of the company, development in another part of the company that is not strong but would nicely complement the company's strengths if it were, attempts to increase sales of already existing products, acquisition of a small related business, and so on. In doing strategic planning, the executives first generate possibilities for investment. They've already come up with several possible directions, and they add to the possibilities they've already come up with by consulting other cases where companies in similar industries with similar financial situations were faced with similar decisions. In one recalled case, for example, a company invested in several market surveys before making major commitments of the sort these executives are doing—looking into the future market, how their designs and potential designs stacked up against those of competitors, how their manufacturing facilities stacked up against those of competitors, and so on. Several companies brought in a business consultant before making major decisions about where to put resources.

Next, they project the potential results of each possible direction. They do this by recalling cases in which each of the possibilities was carried out, looking at the results in each of those cases, and adapting those results to the new situation. In one case, for example, a company put its extra resources into sales of existing products, only to find out six months later that they were no longer competitive because they had not accelerated development enough to keep up with competitors. In two situations, a company acquired a struggling company in the same business that was more advanced in its design but lacked manufacturing and marketing resources. In one of those situations, the acquisition was a failure and the acquiring company nearly went under—as part of the contract, the acquiring company had agreed to keep the design team of the acquired company separated from the design team of the acquiring company, and the overhead of supporting two design teams had been too much. In the other case, the merger had gone quite well—the design teams of the two companies had been merged, as had their marketing teams and the manufacturing facilities. In the case in which the marketing survey was done, the company put off making investment decisions but made a sound one in the end. The companies that brought in business consultants had mixed results: in some, where the consultant had done a good job of understanding the company's vision, culture, and financial state, decisions had been sound; in others, where the consultant had not done as thorough a job, the suggestions made had not been good ones; in some, where the future of the industry was easy to ascertain, suggestions from consultants had been good ones; in others, where the future was harder to project, consultants had not been particularly helpful.

The decision about which direction(s) to go in requires several considerations. Should they bring in a consultant or not? Comparing and contrasting their own situation to those in which consultants were brought in can help in answering this question. Is it more like those in which bringing in a consultant was a good choice or more like those in which it was a poor choice? Other cases suggest the need for a marketing survey. Will doing a survey be useful to them or not? Comparing and contrasting their own situation with those in which a survey was useful and those in which it was not will help here. Somewhere along the way, whether they do a survey or not, whether they bring in a consultant or not, they must consider the effects of each of the possibilities. Will a merger negatively or positively affect their company, and is there a way to ensure that it will have a positive effect? Comparing and contrasting the new situation to those in which mergers were done helps answer this question. If only sales are increased, will the whole company suffer six months down the road? Comparing and contrasting this case to the one in which that happened will help make that projection.

Comparing and contrasting requires knowing which differences and similarities affect results. Is the size of the company important to outcome? What about the culture of the company? If so, which aspects of culture? What about the size of the available resources? Each evaluation might require focus on different dimensions. Deciding if a merger will work, for example, might require consideration of the culture of the two companies and whether their design teams are mergeable. Deciding if development needs a boost requires consideration of where it is compared to that of competitors. And so on.

Making such decisions requires a tremendous amount of world knowledge. It might seem overwhelming to think about getting such knowledge into the computer. It might also seem inappropriate to have the computer make decisions of the sort that are needed in these examples. There are many judgments required, and we might not want automated systems making such judgments. On the other hand, those making such decisions would be greatly aided by having databases of cases at their disposal as they are making their decisions.

Projecting the effects of solutions in situations where there are many unknowns is a task that has the potential to be carried out well by the combination of a human decision maker and a computer library of cases. We can imagine the computer providing cases for a human user to take advantage of in creating arguments for or against outcomes and in refining proposed plans. If cases suggest solutions and report results of carrying out those solutions in other situations, the person using the program can use those cases to project possible outcomes, to decide which is likely to occur, and to decide what changes in a proposed plan might make positive outcome more probable.

There are several things we can learn from HYPO and PROTOS about building systems that can help somebody make arguments to project outcomes. The first set of lessons is about the presentation of cases to users. Because argumentation is a process of comparing and contrasting items to each other, the set of items to be compared and contrasted should be made available to users. Because some cases count more than others, cases should be presented in a way that makes their relative usefulness apparent. Because knowing which cases can support each outcome is crucial to creating a good argument, cases should be presented such that they are positioned according to the outcome they project. When a user is trying to decide whether to use a consultant, for example, cases can be clustered according to whether a consultant was used or not; what the end result of using the consultant was; and what dimensions of the situations led to those results. HYPO uses its claim lattice to organize cases for presentation. There may be other ways.

Another set of lessons comes from the knowledge that augments cases in making an argument. HYPO shows us the role played by dimensions that influence outcome in judging the outcome of a solution. HYPO uses dimensions to index cases, to compare cases, and to create hypotheticals. If dimensions important for comparison are made available to a user, they can also help him or her decide which of several projected outcomes is more likely. A program seeded with dimensions by an expert can be used by a novice to evaluate a new situation. A program that helps a user do strategic planning for business, for example, would tell users that when trying to decide if a consultant should be used, they should compare and contrast situations based on dimensions such as the size of the company, the amount of the investment, and the business experience of the strategic planners. For deciding on whether a merger will work, it tells users that dimensions such as different aspects of the culture of the company, the amount of debt of the company to be acquired, the relative sizes of the two companies, and whether the new company complements the old one in areas of strength are the important ones to consider in comparing and contrasting situations to each other. And so on.

The REMIND tool for building interactive case-based reasoning systems (Cognitive Systems 1992) provides facilities for building systems that can help users critique solutions to problems. It embodies both the lessons learned from interpretive CBR programs. It provides facilities for presenting cases to users in a useful way and facilities for making the dimensions of a domain and their influences available to users. It has been used to implement applications in a variety of domains requiring decision support, including advisement on whether to make loans, advisement on battle planning, and several strategic planning domains. Systems retrieve and present partially-matching cases from their case libraries so that users can easily see the basis of each partial match, which are the better matches, and which factors, if changed, would make a difference. The tool presents influential dimensions of the domain to users in the form of influence diagrams.

Consider, for example, a simple application built with REMIND[8] that can help someone assess the value of his or her house. In our example, a user is trying to decide if it is more worthwhile to build an addition onto her house or to move. The house in question was bought ten years ago for $200,000; is in Newton, Massachusetts; has three bedrooms, two and a half baths, a total of seven rooms; and is on a half-acre lot. The owner is thinking about spending approximately $90,000 on the addition of two bedrooms, a bath, and another family room, bringing the total to five bedrooms, three and a half baths, and ten rooms total. To make her

---

8. Thanks to Claudia Colan of Cognitive Systems, Inc., for generating the accompanying figures.

```
╔══════════ Case Editor : MLSDemo : Default View ══════════╗
║ [Previous][ Next ][ Jump To ][ New ][ Copy ][ Delete ]      ║
║ 203 cases ( Case 203 is Hypothetical, id = 203 )            ║
╟────────────────────────────────────────────────────────────╢
```

Asking Price	n/a	City	Newton

House Style	Split-Level	Amenities	
Bedrooms	5	Air Conditioning?	True
Bathrooms	3	Attic?	False
Half Baths	1	Corner Lot?	n/a
Total Rooms	10	Eat-in Kitchen?	True
Lot Size	Half Acre	Landscaped?	True
Exterior	Wood	Master Bath?	True
Garage	Two-Car	Swimming Pool?	False
Basement	Slab	Porch or Deck?	True
Roof	Asphalt Shingle	Security System?	True
Tax	n/a	Wooded Lot?	False

FIGURE 13.10   A New Problem Situation

---

decision, the owner projects the market value of the house after the addition. She describes her house (after the addition) to the system as shown in Figure 13.10 and asks the system to recall similar houses.

The system recalls eleven cases and describes their relationship to the new situation, as shown in Figure 13.11. Six are valued at well over what the owner needs her house to be worth, three are valued at the lowest end of what she requires, and two are valued well below what she needs her house to be worth. If the house is valued close to the lowest valued ones, then the addition is not worth making—it would be more cost-effective to move. If it is valued closer to any of the others, the addition is worthwhile. Determining the value for the house with an addition requires figuring out whether it will be more like the lower valued houses or more like one of the higher valued ones. Comparing and contrasting is in order. The owner chooses to examine the highest priced house first. Figure 13.12 shows descriptions of her current house (with its addition) and the highest priced house side by side, presented in such a way that comparisons can easily be made.

In comparing the houses to each other, however, the owner doesn't know which are the important fields to focus on. She asks the system which fields should be compared to each other and how much each counts by calling up an influence diagram (called a *q-model* in REMIND) that shows which descriptive fields influence the asking price of a house and how much influence each has. We see in Figure 13.13 that city is the biggest factor determining asking price and that number of bedrooms is also important. Aesthetic factors count but are not

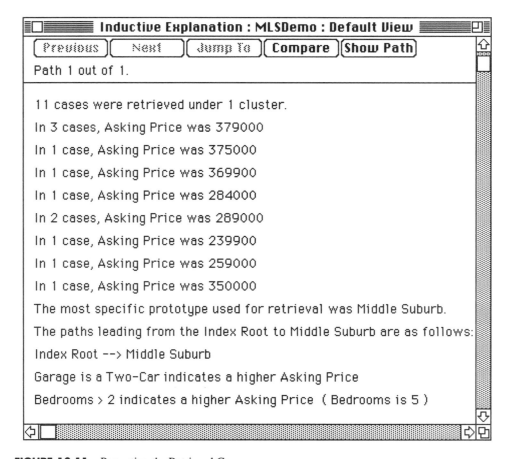

FIGURE 13.11   Presenting the Retrieved Cases

as important, nor are safety and transportation as important. Comparing her house to the highest-priced house, she sees that the differences are in the attic, the basement, the number of baths, and the number of bedrooms. Her house will be worth less than the highest priced house because it has one fewer bedroom, no attic, and no basement but more because it has an additional bathroom. Taking all that into account, she assumes that though her house will not be worth $379,000 after the addition, it will not be worth a lot less than that. She continues by comparing her house to the other houses that have been retrieved, and based on each, she computes a rough estimate of the value her house will have after the addition.[9] She finds that the two low priced houses are both in Dedham, a lower priced suburb and that her house is more comparable to the other houses in Newton. She finds that her house has an advantage over the houses that are worth approximately what she needs hers to be worth—her house has one more

---

9. REMIND will do that also if an adaptation formula is provided to it. One clicks the *adapt* button at the top of the comparison screen to tell the system to run its formulas.

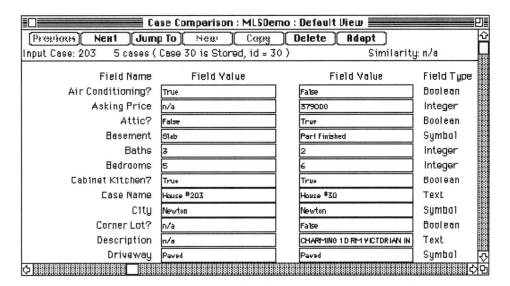

Field Name	Field Value	Field Value	Field Type
Air Conditioning?	True	False	Boolean
Asking Price	n/a	379000	Integer
Attic?	False	True	Boolean
Basement	Slab	Part Finished	Symbol
Baths	3	2	Integer
Bedrooms	5	6	Integer
Cabinet Kitchen?	True	True	Boolean
Case Name	House #203	House #30	Text
City	Newton	Newton	Symbol
Corner Lot?	n/a	False	Boolean
Description	n/a	CHARMING 1 D RM VICTORIAN IN	Text
Driveway	Paved	Paved	Symbol

FIGURE 13.12   Comparing Two Cases to Each Other

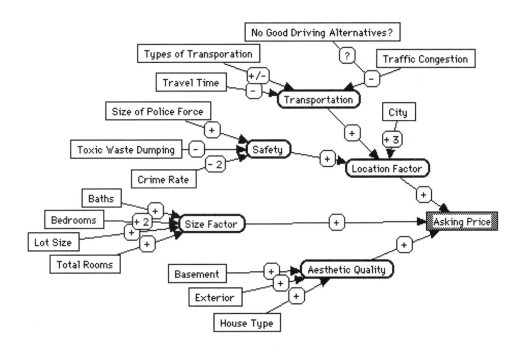

FIGURE 13.13   Influence Diagram Showing Which Dimensions Are Relevant to Outcome

bedroom than one, a bigger lot than another, and is in a higher priced suburb than the third. Based on the comparisons, it looks as though her house will be worth at least $300,000 after the addition, which makes the addition worthwhile.

Required for this analysis were two inputs: a library of cases and an analysis of the factors that are important in judging outcome. The system's job is to present cases and factors to users on demand. But someone must enter them into the system first. REMIND provides two kinds of tools: *acquisition tools* for entering cases, factors, indexes, and other knowledge into a system and *presentation tools* for interacting with clients making use of a system's contents. To the extent that cases are available and that factors and their relative influences can be derived and are entered by experts, REMIND and other systems like it can be useful in building interactive systems for projecting likely outcomes and evaluating their effects.

Where do available methods fall short? The major shortfall of existing methods is that though they can be used to evaluate situations based on an already generated set of influential dimensions, they cannot be used to determine, for a new kind of situation, which of its dimensions are the important ones. Consider, for example, the host who is trying to determine if Anne will eat grilled salmon. She must determine what caused Anne not to eat the grilled trout and compare the new situation to the old one based on that explanation. But our case-based methods can't help the host figure out, on the fly, what was wrong with the grilled trout. Any one or several of its attributes could have been at fault. Perhaps the problem was that it was fish. Perhaps the problem was that it was grilled. Perhaps the problem was that it was a whole fish. Perhaps the problem was that its head was attached. Perhaps it was the texture of the fish. Even worse, attributes of the world might have been to blame. Perhaps the problem was that Anne was pregnant then and fish made her feel nauseated. As long as we know which dimensions are the important ones, we can build a case-based system to help with argumentation. If part of the problem is figuring out which are the important dimensions in any situation, then, though case retrieval will help a user make a decision, the basis for supporting case-based argumentation will be absent.

13.4 SUMMARY

Interpretive case-based reasoning is the process of comparing and contrasting a new situation to old ones in order to better understand it, evaluate it, or project its effects. The first step in the process is to recall cases that are like the new one. We then ask whether the new situation is enough like an old one that it can be interpreted the same way the old one was. We also examine what differentiates an old case from a new situation to ascertain whether or not an old interpretation is likely to hold. Cases make up for our lack of knowledge about the world and are useful for evaluation and interpretation because, in general, the world is consistent. Interpretive case-based reasoning is used for three tasks: classification, situation assessment, and projection of outcomes.

Case-based classification is best exemplified by PROTOS, which diagnoses hearing disorders by finding the case in the case library that is most similar to the new one and assigning the new case the same classification. It begins by making an initial hypothesis about a classification based on surface similarities. A knowledge-based matching procedure is then used to confirm the initial hypothesis. It attempts to match the new situation to a case from the chosen category. Mismatches turned up by matching procedures allow PROTOS to find a better case to match to, either within the same category or in another one. This method is successful due to a combination of its knowledge-based matching, rich semantic linking between exemplars, and a failure-driven knowledge acquisition process.

Exemplar-based classification works when a model exists that can be used for matching. But when a model is missing, argumentation must be added to the interpretive model. Argumentation is the process of making justifiable arguments to support one or another decision. It is implemented with compare-and-contrast procedures. HYPO implements interpretive reasoning and augumentation in the domain of case law. A new situation is analyzed for its relevant factors, and cases are recalled. Recalled cases are positioned according to whether they support the desired outcome in the new situation. The most on-point cases (pro and con) are chosen to anchor argumentation, and three-ply arguments are created by using a most on-point case to make a point, one with an opposing outcome to counter the point, and one with the desired outcome to counter that. Arguments, in turn, are compared to each other to make a final interpretation. This interpretation may be tested with hypothetical cases.

Case-based interpretive methods are also useful for projecting the outcome of a situation—for example, for strategic planning. Although no automated systems have been built to do this, both PROTOS and HYPO give guidelines for building interactive systems that can help people with this task. Such systems should make the cases to be compared and contrasted to each other available to people in a way that makes their relative usefulness apparent. They should also make available to people the partial model of the domain that can be used to judge the closeness of fit.

14

Using Cases: Some Additional Issues

Israel and Egypt both want the Sinai. MEDIATOR wants to settle the dispute. It assumes that they both want ownership of the land itself, and it attempts to *derive a solution*. It is reminded of the Korean Conflict, resolved by dividing the land mass in two, giving half to each side in the conflict. Based on that case, it proposes dividing the Sinai equally between Israel and Egypt.

Next MEDIATOR presents its solution and gets feedback. It is told that neither country likes this solution. Its goal now is to *explain the expectation failure*. It remembers the Orange Dispute. In this case, two sisters wanted the same orange. Their mother divided it in half, giving one half to each girl. One threw away the peel and ate the fruit. The other threw away the fruit and used her peel to bake a cake. The mother realized that she had misinterpreted the goals of the second girl (a wrong-goal-failure).

MEDIATOR explores whether in this case, too, there might have been a wrong goal failure, that is, a failure to interpret the goals of the disputants correctly. It finds that this could in fact be the case and sets itself up to find out the goals of Egypt and Israel. Based on further feedback, MEDIATOR decides that Israel wants the Sinai for security reasons, Egypt for integrity reasons.

Its goal now is to *derive a solution*, this time based on the newly understood case. It remembers the Panama Canal Dispute. In this case, both the United States and Panama want the Panama Canal Zone, the U.S. for security reasons, Panama for integrity reasons. It is solved by giving security rights to the U.S. and land rights to Panama. Based on this case, MEDIATOR proposes giving Israel security rights to the Sinai and giving Egypt land rights.

An architectural firm was given the task of designing a Manufacturing Research Center for Georgia Tech. The task was to design a building in which people would engage in high-tech manufacturing research. It had to include areas where manufacturing could be done, and it had to include office space. The manufacturing areas had to be easily changeable, allowing easy insertion of new machines and reconfiguring of machines already there. It had to allow for chemical, as well as mechanical, procedures. Terry Sargent, the chief designer, reports that his inspiration in designing that building came from several places.[1] He traveled all over the world, surveying flexible manufacturing centers, factories, and research centers. From the traditional shape of factories came the shape of the building—long and narrow with silos at the corners. Inspiration for the decoration on the facade came from a chocolate-manufacturing building—the decoration on the building was reminiscent of the activities inside. Inspiration for placement of offices, labs, and other work areas came from another building. The Pompidou Center provided the inspiration for the management of the building's utility systems—visible and colorful. And so on.

As we can see in the examples, multiple cases often need to be considered in conjunction in solving problems. There are several reasons why. In general, however, it boils down to this: Each of several cases might address different issues that need to be addressed in the solution of a single problem.

Sometimes, as in the MEDIATOR example, different cases are needed for each of several reasoning tasks. One case or set of cases might help the reasoner anticipate potential problems, another might help in creating a solution, and still another might help with tracking down and perhaps repairing a reasoning error. Multiple cases are also necessary when a single case can solve only part of the new problem, as in the architectural example. This latter situation is common when a problem to be solved is very large, as, for example, in architectural design. One case might suggest a piece of the solution, another case another piece, and so on. It is also common when problem solving and execution are interleaved with each other. In these situations, the conditions that make a case applicable can change as execution proceeds. For example, a case that a doctor recalls might suggest a diagnosis. Following up on that hypothesis, the doctor might use the same case to suggest a test to be done to confirm the diagnosis. If the test results are different from those in the remembered case, however, that case becomes insufficient or useless in guiding interpretation of the results of the test, the doctor's next step. Recalling some other case or set of cases at that point will be more useful to the doctor than sticking to the one that made the initial suggestions. Multiple cases are also used for checking consistency. Figure 14.1 summarizes this list.

Whatever the reason for using multiple cases, there are several control issues that arise that are not present when problem solving centers around one case. One issue is targeting retrieval of cases for the different reasoning goals and tasks the reasoner is using cases for. We discussed in retrieval chapters how the goals of the reasoner influence choice of appropriate cases. Here we review that discussion and look at where those goals come from, how they can be scheduled, and how they can be used to, in effect, control the case-based reasoner.

Another is the issue of focusing on appropriate parts of old cases during reasoning. A single case can be large, and only a piece of it might be useful in addressing a reasoner goal. For example, MEDIATOR's primary focus when it is attempting to derive a solution to the Sinai Dispute is on the solution part of the Korean Conflict. When it is attempting to explain why its solution to the Sinai Dispute failed, its focus is on the failure explanation part of the

---

1. Personal communication, from a talk delivered at Georgia Tech in March 1992.

- One for each of several problem-solving tasks
  - □ To aid in interpretation
  - □ To suggest a solution
  - □ To warn of the potential for failure
  - □ For evaluation
  - □ To explain a failure
  - □ For repair

- To derive different parts of a single solution
- When integrating planning and execution
- For checking consistency

FIGURE 14.1   Reasons for Needing Multiple Cases

Orange Dispute. Though other parts of each case might be examined in the process of making a case-based inference, the reasoning goal determines where focus begins.

Another issue is the derivation and maintenance of reasoning goals. Where do they come from? How can they be scheduled? How does their scheduling interact with case-based reasoner functions? A particular special kind of task that cases are used for is case-based anticipation of problems that might arise in a situation. This is one of the hallmarks of case-based reasoning, that as a natural part of reasoning, cases in which problems arose previously are remembered and supply warnings. Our discussions so far have been centered on how to use cases to suggest solutions and to interpret situations. Here we discuss the processes by which cases can be used to warn of potential problems.

We then try to fit all the processes together—case-based reasoning processes that interpret a new situation and extract its indexes, retrieve cases, and use them, and goal scheduling processes that guide sequences of calls to the case-based reasoner.

Finally, the merging of pieces of solutions is another major issue for consideration. Adaptation addresses the modification of a single solution to fit a new situation. Other issues arise when parts of multiple cases are pieced together.

Overall, this chapter addresses the complexities involved in using multiple cases for problem solving.

14.1 USING REASONING GOALS TO GUIDE CASE-BASED PROCESSES

In general, when multiple cases are used, each has a different function. Usually the reasoner is working on some reasoning task or goal, and some case can help it address that goal. When the reasoner moves on to a new task or goal, another case might provide more appropriate guidance. Building from that notion, several case-based reasoners use **reasoning goals** to guide and control use of multiple cases during reasoning. Reasoning goals determine what kinds of cases to retrieve from the case library and how to apply them.

- Which cases to retrieve
- How many cases to retrieve
- How to focus on an appropriate part of a large case
- Whether to use adaptation or interpretive methods

FIGURE 14.2   The Kinds of Guidance Reasoning Goals Can Provide

We already have discussed the role reasoning goals and the reasoner's task play in retrieval. It is important that cases retrieved from the case library are those that can best address the reasoner's goal. Retrieval processes are thus informed of the reasoner's goal; and search, matching, and ranking functions use that information to find and choose appropriate cases. Chapters 8 and 9 explain how that can be done. Reasoning goals can also be used to guide several other case-based reasoning processes. Because some reasoning goals require several cases and some only one, reasoning goals can give guidance about how many cases to retrieve. When a case is large, and only some small part of it is needed to achieve the current reasoning goal, the goal provides guidance for focusing on an appropriate part of the case. And, we have seen several different types of case-based inferences. Sometimes adaptation is in order; at other times interpretive methods are. Reasoning goals also determine which kinds of case-based inferences should be made. The full list can be found in Figure 14.2.

In previous chapters, we've discussed some of those goals. In the discussion of indexing, three kinds of reasoning goals were presented, each with different indexing guidelines.[2] *Solution-creation* goals are those whose achievement results in creation of a piece of a solution to a problem. Achievement of *explanation* goals results in the creation of an explanation for some phenomenon. *Evaluation* goals call for interpreting a situation or projecting the effects of a solution. In this discussion, we will refer to common goals from each of these categories. For example, some common solution-creation goals are deriving a solution or a piece of a solution, choosing what to adapt, choosing an adaptation method, and repairing a solution. Common evaluation goals include interpreting a situation, choosing a classification, and anticipating a failure. Explaining a failure and generating a hypothesis are two kinds of explanation goals.

Consider, for example, the tasks of deriving a solution, explaining a problem-solving failure, evaluating a solution, and repairing a solution. Figures 14.3, 14.4, 14.5, and 14.6 show the guidance each of these reasoning goals provides to case-based reasoning processes.

Deriving a solution or part of a solution.   When the reasoner is trying to derive a solution or a part of a solution, the part it is attempting to derive provides focus for the case-based reasoner. The reasoner looks for cases that are similar along dimensions necessary to make inferences about the designated part of the problem. When PERSUADER is focusing on deriving seniority clauses for a contract, for example, it attempts to find cases in which seniority clauses were an issue. It thus looks for cases in similar industries and locations in which the goals of the union and the company on seniority issues match those in the new case. It would also be appropriate to look for cases that match along other dimensions that have been found

---

2. These have also been called *reasoning tasks*.

DERIVING A SOLUTION OR PART OF A SOLUTION

The reasoner must solve a problem or part of a problem.

- Reasoning goal = derive solution (focus)
- Search:
  - □ Search for cases similar along the dimensions necessary to solve the designated part of the problem.
  - □ Prefer cases that also have solutions similar to the partial solution in the current case (if there is one).
  - □ One case is sufficient.

- Focus on
  - □ The previous solution or the part of the previous solution designated by focus

- Reasoning:
  - □ Adopt and adapt the old solution or the designated part of the previous solution based on differences between the old and new problem situations.

FIGURE 14.3   Deriving a Solution: Guidance to Case-Based Reasoning Processes

EVALUATING A SOLUTION

The reasoner has come up with a solution; it must evaluate it.

- Reasoning goal = evaluate solution
- Search:
  - □ Search for similar solutions; prefer those with similar problem statements.
  - □ Search for similar problem descriptions.
  - □ Several cases are necessary.

- Focus on:
  - □ Outcomes

- Reasoning:
  - □ Check whether old problem outcomes are likely to show up in the new case; check to be sure that old good outcomes are also possible.
  - □ Spawn processes to adapt/repair the solution to avoid problem outcomes, and evaluate again.
  - □ In case several outcomes are judged possible, compare and contrast possibilities to decide which outcomes are likely.
  - □ In case no possible outcome is perfect, compare and contrast outcomes to decide which is most favorable.

FIGURE 14.4   Evaluating a Solution: Guidance to Case-Based Reasoning Processes

EXPLAINING A FAILURE

The reasoner has just received feedback telling it about a failure. It must explain it.

- Reasoning goal = explain failure
- Search:
  - Search for a similar situation with a failure.
  - Search for a similar failure.
  - Only one is needed.

- Focus on
  - the previous failure and its explanation

- Reasoning:
  - Adopt and adapt the previous explanation based on differences between the current and previous failures.

FIGURE 14.5   Explaining a Problem-Solving Failure: Guidance to Case-Based Reasoning Processes

REPAIRING A FAILURE

The reasoner must repair a failure.

- Reasoning goal = repair failure
- Search:
  - Search for similar failures in similar types of situations.
  - Search for similar failures.
  - Search for similarly explained failures.
  - Only one case is necessary.

- Focus on:
  - the previous failure and its repair

- Reasoning:
  - Adopt and adapt the previous repair based on differences between the old and new failure situations

FIGURE 14.6   Repairing a Failed Solution: Guidance to Case-Based Reasoning Processes

to be good predictors of the specifics of seniority clauses. When JULIA is trying to decide what to serve for dessert, it looks for cases with dessert requirements that are similar to its current ones. It may need a dessert specific to the season of the year, with specific caloric restrictions, or to complement a certain kind of food. It looks for cases that match its requirements.

After cases are recalled, focus is on the part of the previous solution designated by the goal's focus. When seniority is the focus, for example, the seniority part of the old solution is consulted to complete the solution in the new situation. Similarly, when JULIA is trying to decide what to serve for dessert, it concentrates on the dessert portion of the meal it recalls.

The case-based reasoner then attempts to adapt the designated part of the previous solution based on differences between the old and new problem situations. PERSUADER, when trying to complete seniority clauses in a new case, attempts to adapt the seniority clauses of the old case to the new situation. JULIA, when trying to complete the dessert portion of a meal, attempts to fit the old dessert to the new situation.

Evaluating a proposed solution.
After a solution is complete or after some portion of it has been completed, evaluation is done. Interpretive reasoning is necessary to achieve this reasoning goal.

As illustrated in chapter 13, when attempting to evaluate a solution in a case-based way, it is often appropriate to compare and contrast the new situation to a whole series of cases. The interpretations suggested by those cases are analyzed with respect to each other to come up with a final evaluation. To evaluate a meal plan in a case-based way, for example, JULIA would remember a series of cases, each with different outcomes. For each outcome, JULIA would consider whether it was a possible outcome for its current case. If some poor outcome was possible, JULIA would attempt to fix it. If evidence was conflicting or if each fix created some new problem, JULIA would need to use a method similar to HYPO's to weigh the evidence and decide which outcome was best.

In evaluation, cases with solutions similar to the proposed one are recalled, with preference given to those cases that have similar problem statements. The process then continues as suggested in the previous paragraph and as described in chapter 13. Another way to do evaluation is to recall cases with similar problem descriptions and compare their solutions.

Explaining a problem-solving failure.
When a reasoner needs to explain a failure, it has, in general, solved a problem, attempted application of the solution in the world, and gotten feedback telling it about a failure.[3] Similar situations with similar failed outcomes will be able to help it explain its new failure. If none of those can be found, similar failed outcomes might also be useful. Only one case is necessary, though if the explanation from that case does not seem applicable, or if several competing explanations are being sought, then other cases might also be used. After recalling a case, the reasoner focuses on the previous failure and its explanation. Adaptation procedures are used in an attempt to adapt the previous explanation to the new situation.

An example will illustrate. The MEDIATOR has just attempted to solve the Sinai Dispute. As you may recall, its first solution was to divide the land mass equally between Egypt and Israel. This solution was based on an assumption that both parties wanted the land in order to own it. The MEDIATOR receives feedback telling it that neither Israel nor Egypt likes this

---

3. Alternatively, it might have simulated the world to get feedback or it may have used case-based means of criticism to predict failure. The same explanation procedure is in order whether the failure already occurred or was about to and no matter what means was used to determine that.

solution. It now has the goal of explaining the failure. It looks for similar kinds of situations with similar failures and is content with finding one. In this case, it finds the Orange Dispute. The two situations were similar in that a compromise solution was being sought, disputants wanted ownership of a property, and the plan Divide Equally was attempted. And in both the plan failed.

MEDIATOR focuses on the failure in the previous case and the explanation of the failure. It attempts to transfer the old explanation to the new case. The old failure was found to be a wrong goal inference. That is, the goals inferred were wrong. MEDIATOR considers whether this might also be so in the new situation. It does this by first checking the consistency of the old explanation to the new case and then refining (adapting) the explanation as needed to fit the new situation. Indeed, a wrong goal inference could be the problem, because MEDIATOR had not been told the goals of Israel and Egypt; it had inferred them. The old solution is reinstantiated using the new parties, providing the explanation that MEDIATOR inferred wrong goals for Israel and Egypt with respect to the Sinai.

Repairing a solution.   Once failures are explained, they must be repaired. This subgoal too can provide guidance to the case-based reasoner. PERSUADER, for example, can fix a negotiations impasse based on the way it has repaired similar ones in the past.

When attempting to repair a failure, it is appropriate for the reasoner to search for similar failures in similar types of situations; failing that, similar failures or similarly explained failures. The reasoner then focuses on the previous repair, determines if it seems applicable to the current situation, and, if so, attempts to adapt it to fit the new situation.

My favorite meal-planning example will illustrate. A host has just planned a meal whose main dish is tomato tart. She has just found out that one of the guests is allergic to milk products. She considers whether the tomato tart can be adapted to fit the constraints set by that person. She remembers another meal whose main dish had cheese as a main ingredient and one of the guests was allergic to milk products (a similar failure in a similar type of situation). She concentrates on the repair; in that case, when she served yuppie pizza, she substituted tofu-cheese for cheese in some of the pizzas. She applies this repair in the new situation also.

Once we propose that case-based reasoning be guided by reasoning subgoals, there are several issues we must address.

■ What, exactly, are all the subgoals, and what guidelines are associated with each?
■ Where do subgoals derive from?
■ How can subgoals be chosen and managed?
■ How do we integrate goal scheduling and case-based reasoning?

The first question we have begun to answer by providing examples of several subgoals and the guidance they provide. Additional detail about this and the remaining issues will be presented after discussion of anticipating the potential for failure, a special kind of reasoning goal.

14.2 ANTICIPATING POTENTIAL PROBLEMS AND OPPORTUNITIES FOR ENHANCEMENT

One of the most important uses cases can be put to is the anticipation of failures before they occur. Failure cases that are remembered in the course of reasoning can be used to alert the reasoner to the possibility of failure. A teacher, for example, who remembers what went wrong previously in presenting some lesson, can plan to make sure the same thing doesn't happen again. An architect who remembers a problem with a previous building can design the new building so that the problem is avoided.

Remembering cases that predict failure can happen almost any time during problem solving. Some problems can be foreseen based only on a description of a new situation. Other problems become evident as a solution is being worked out. Others become evident only after a solution is worked out and its potential results are considered.

Anticipating potential failures can happen as a result of intentional or unintentional search. Some very careful problem solvers attempt to foresee potential problems before beginning problem solving, several times during the process, and as a part of evaluating a complete solution. Others attempt to predict potential problems only after a complete solution is worked out. Others choose some subset of these points to check for the potential for failure of a solution they are putting together. At times when they want to check for a potential problem, they call on memory to recall similar situations in which problems occurred. For each, they consider whether the failure could happen in the new situation and, if so, take whatever measures are appropriate to avoid it.

Other problem solvers don't intentionally check for problems at all. Rather, they wait until failure cases are recalled. Failure cases recalled at any point during problem solving are examined to see what they predict, and action is taken if appropriate. Whatever the custom, any time cases are recalled from memory, there is a chance that failure cases will be recalled. When a failure case is recalled, the reasoner needs to examine that case and the failure it predicts and check to see if the same failure could happen in the new situation.

When anticipating failures is intentional, the case-based reasoner begins by searching for cases that are similar in description and partial solution (if it exists) to the new case and in which a failure occurred (Figure 14.7). When CHEF is attempting to create a recipe using chicken and snow peas, for example, it remembers the beef and broccoli case during its failure anticipation step. The two cases are similar in their problem descriptions: in both the goal is to create a dish using a meat and a crisp vegetable by the method of stir-frying. In addition, the beef and broccoli case was initially a failure. The broccoli was soggy, a violation of the goal of having a crisp vegetable.

Reasoning continues with focus on the previous failure and its cause, if the cause of the failure is known. The reasoner uses that information to decide whether the problem could repeat in the current situation, and if so, elaborates the problem description in such a way that the failure can be avoided or uses the recalled failure to point to a piece of the new solution that must be fixed. Continuing with the chicken and snow peas example, CHEF considers whether sogginess of snow peas is a potential problem in the new case, decides that it is, and

ANTICIPATING FAILURES

The reasoner wants to anticipate potential problems so it can avoid them.

- Reasoning goal = anticipate problems
- Search:
  - □ Search for similar cases that failed.
  - □ Return all cases that are sufficiently similar.

- Focus on (for each):
  - □ the previous failure and its cause (if known)

- Reasoning (for each):
  - □ Could this problem happen here?
  - □ If so, elaborate problem description appropriately, and if necessary, fix solution appropriately.

FIGURE 14.7   Anticipating Failures: Guidelines for the Case-Based Reasoner

elaborates the description of the chicken and snow peas problem by specifying that it should avoid creating soggy vegetables (equivalent to making sure that the vegetables are crisp). During solution derivation, this annotation causes CHEF to prefer cases in which soggy vegetables were known to be a potential problem and were avoided and in which crisp vegetables were a specified goal.

When anticipation happens later in problem solving and a partial solution already exists, this step might also include a call to adaptation strategies to fix the partial solution appropriately before going on. When JULIA discovers that one of its guests will not eat the grilled fish it has planned for a main dish, for example, it elaborates the problem description to specify that people who don't eat fish should be accommodated. It also spawns a subgoal to fix the problem that is already in the solution.

When anticipation is unintentional, that is, when a failure case has been recalled as a side effect of some other call to retrieval processes, the process is the same, but the retrieval step is left out.

Cases can also be used to anticipate *opportunities* to be taken advantage of. Consider, for example, a teacher who had always taught her foliage class in the spring when new green leaves were abundant on the trees. One year, however, she had to teach it in the fall. As she was used to doing, she took the class into the woods, where large varieties of leaves could be found. This time, however, the students were not only finding leaves, but they were also finding nuts and berries and observing chipmunks and squirrels that were collecting the nuts and carrying them away. Taking advantage of an opportunity to enhance her lesson, she hurriedly got the class together for a broader discussion of natural changes during the autumn season, including in her discussion changes in leaves, changes in the trees they grow on, and the ways in which animals depend on the nuts and berries dropped by the trees in the fall to live through the cold winter.

Now it is fall and the teacher is getting ready again to teach her foliage classes. She is reminded of last year's experience. Last year, she included lessons about changing leaves, berries, and animals in a rather haphazard way when they came up. Remembering that experience this time, she anticipates that these issues will arise again and plans for them. Anticipating the issues that will come up before going into the woods alerts her to the set of things she ought to prepare for, and she prepares better than she had previously. She plans discussions about autumnal changes before going on the field trip, she plans nut-gathering and animal-watching activities along with the leaf-gathering activities, and she plans for further discussion upon return.

In general, cases can help with anticipating opportunities when they achieve multiple goals present in a situation that are not normally achieved simultaneously or when they point out new goals that are achievable in the context of known ones. The teacher in the example was planning to achieve the goal of learning about leaves with her class. The recalled case showed her that the opportunity for also learning about nuts and berries and the animals that eat them was present in the planned situation and could also be achieved.

The intentional method of anticipating opportunities is a process of looking at a situation and asking what else it allows. One way to do this is by asking memory for cases in which this situation was encountered and in which more than what is planned was accomplished or in which things other than what is planned were accomplished. A teacher, for example, might ask memory for experiences taking kids on hikes in the woods. Some will illustrate leaf gathering, the currently planned activity. Some of those, such as the case recalled above, might show other activities that can be done at the same time. Other cases will illustrate other woods activities. Some might show rock examination, for example, and some might show following the paths animals make in the woods. For each, the teacher can consider what will work in combination with her planned activity. Having particular instances available for examination will allow her to answer many of the questions that will come up in those deliberations: how much time the extra activity will take, what age group it is appropriate for, and so on. Some cases recalled this way will also show potential problems encountered by teachers who take kids for walks through the woods—a sprained ankle in one situation, poison ivy in another, kids walking away from the group in another. Problem situations are dealt with using the guidelines presented.

Another way to anticipate the added opportunities a situation allows is by focusing on particular things that are normally allowable. For example, a teacher may, as common procedure, examine experiences she is about to give her students to figure out the whole set of principles that are illustrated. As a next step, she might consider which of those principles seem worth emphasizing by asking memory for cases in which those principles are presented. Cases, presumably, will point out the difficulty of making each presentation or getting each point across, providing the teacher with the data she needs to decide which principles are worth pursuing. Though cases aren't used for anticipation itself, they are used to determine which anticipated opportunities should be grabbed.

Like anticipating failures, anticipating opportunities can be an intentional or an unintentional process. That is, the reasoner may consciously set anticipation of potential opportunities as a goal, carrying out the procedures just outlined. Alternatively, the reasoner may consider potential opportunities only when some call to the case retriever results in retrieval of a case that achieves more than what the reasoner is currently considering.

14.3 DERIVING SUBGOALS

We now know many of the reasoning goals and tasks that case-based reasoning can support. An issue we have not yet tackled, however, is how a reasoner can keep track of which subgoals to pursue. Reasoning subgoals can be derived from several possible sources:

- A set script of reasoning goals given to the program
- Problem reduction
- Case-based derivation
- Combinations of the above

Scripts of subgoals.   Most of the early case-based reasoning programs derived their reasoning subgoals from a set script. MEDIATOR, for example, began by attempting to elaborate the problem description, went on to classify the problem, then moved into the planning phase, first establishing planning policies, then choosing an abstract plan, then refining it and making predictions about its outcome. It continued by trying the solution out in the world and collecting feedback, analyzing the feedback for failure or success of the solution, and in case of failure, classifying the failure, repairing it, and attempting solution again.

CHEF also used a preset script of reasoning subgoals to guide the reasoner. First it attempted to anticipate the potential for failures (its situation assessment goal), then choose a plan, then adapt it, then try it out in the world and get feedback, then explain the failure if one occurred, and then repair it.

There are several different ways a script of subgoals can be derived. MEDIATOR's set was derived by examining the subgoals set up by traditional problem solvers (most notably plan instantiation problem solvers) and using those to guide the case-based system, CHEF's were set up with case-based planning in mind, and PERSUADER's were set up keeping in mind the way people do PERSUADER's task.

Hammond derived CHEF's reasoning subgoals by considering what cases are particularly good for and what is necessary for using cases for planning. The reasoning ran as follows: Cases are useful for anticipating problems and for suggesting solutions. Using a case to derive a solution requires adaptation. Thus, reasoning subgoals include anticipating potential failures, solution suggestion, and adaptation. Because a problem might not be solved the right way first time around, explanation and repair are also in CHEF's subgoal script.

PERSUADER's goals were also preset but were chosen in a different way, by examining the way people do the task PERSUADER had to do. Because labor negotiation, PERSUADER's task domain, is commonly done by a precedent adjustment method, Sycara was able to examine the way people used precedents and adjusted them in the course of their everyday deliberations. She found that they first recalled precedent-setting cases, adapted them based on easy and obvious differences, examined them and corrected for commonly recognized potential problems, and compensated for any inequities introduced in previous steps. After a solution was derived, it was presented to the disputing parties for acceptance. If it was not accepted, impasses were examined and repaired, and if repair was impossible, the negotiator attempted persuasion. The script of reasoning subgoals PERSUADER uses follow this pattern.

Problem reduction.   Other case-based reasoners derive their subgoals with problem reduction methods. Each of JULIA's reasoning goals, for example, knows how it can be broken down into subgoals to be achieved. A meal is created by a process of solution derivation followed by evaluation. Each of those reasoning goals knows the subgoals that need to be achieved in order to achieve it. `Refine-meal`, for example, a high-level solution derivation goal, can be achieved by achieving the subgoals `refine-descriptors`, `refine-main-course`, `refine-other courses`. Each of those in turn knows the subgoals it can be broken into. What keeps JULIA from being a problem reduction problem solver is that it attempts to use case-based reasoning to achieve each of its goals, and only when cases cannot help it to achieve an entire subgoal does it break the subgoal into its component parts.

In Carbonell's (1983) original transformational analogy approach to reusing experience, reasoning goals were derived through problem reduction, using means-ends analysis. His more recent ARIES (Carbonell 1986) and PRODIGY (Minton 1988; Minton et al. 1989; Veloso and Carbonell 1989, 1993) do the same.

Case-based derivation.   The third method for deriving subgoals is case-based derivation. Using this method, one breaks a reasoning goal into its component subgoals by following the breakdown used in previous cases. ARIES (Carbonell 1986) was the first program to derive subgoals this way. ARIES solved problems by achieving subgoals in the same order they had been done in some previous similar case. The subgoal structure of old cases was derived either from other cases or by means-ends analysis. JULIANA (Shinn 1988b, 1989) also derives its subgoals from other cases.

Combining methods.   A combination of methods can also be used to derive subgoals. In some domains, it might be appropriate to provide a script of subgoals for "normal" cases, switching to case-based derivation for more novel ones. If a system's cases are those it has solved itself (as in, e.g., ARIES and CASEY), then a combination of problem reduction and case-based derivation might be appropriate. ARIES and PRODIGY, for example, prefer to use cases to derive their subgoals, but if no case is available, they apply means-ends analysis to the task.

14.4   TYPES OF REASONING GOALS AND TASKS

Previous discussions have pointed out some of the reasoning tasks and subgoals that come up in reasoning, but up to now we have not attempted to present the whole set. The discussion about the sources of subgoals, however, now allows better presentation of reasoning tasks and goals. Three sources of reasoning subgoals were suggested:

■ Tasks required, in general, for problem solving or understanding

■ The reasoning tasks of case-based reasoning

■ Reasoning tasks required by a task domain

Each view of problem solving that has been put forth by the artificial intelligence and cognitive science communities has included a number of steps. Plan instantiation (Friedland 1979), for example, designates classifying a problem, choosing an abstract plan, and incremental refinement as its steps. Means-ends analysis (Newell and Simon 1963; Ernst and Newell 1969) designates noticing differences, deciding which difference is the most important, choosing an operator to reduce the difference, and so on, as its steps. Other approaches designate elaborating the problem description, establishing planning policies, choosing an abstract framework, making predictions about outcome, and so on, as problem-solving steps. Approaches to language understanding also designate subgoals that must be fulfilled to complete understanding. The methodologies put forth for solving problems and understanding situations are one source of reasoning tasks and subgoals.

Case-based reasoning provides another set of reasoning tasks and subgoals. Anticipating the potential for failure and the potential for advantageous opportunities are two tasks cases support well. Though not commonly part of the vocabulary in traditional approaches to problem solving and understanding, these are reasoning tasks we all use cases for as we get around in the world from day to day. The two major case-based reasoning tasks, adaptation and interpretation, each have their own subtasks, which can also be thought of as reasoning subgoals: choosing what to adapt, choosing an adaptation method, selecting a case to base an argument on, creating a hypothetical, and so forth. In addition, case-based reasoning integrates learning into the problem-solving cycle. It would not do to reuse cases if we didn't keep track of the effects of solutions and evaluate which were the good and which were the poor ones. Thus, case-based reasoning also suggests as reasoning subgoals explanation of failure and repair.

Finally, the reasoning that must be done to solve problems in particular domains provides domain-specific kinds of reasoning goals. An architect has to analyze the structure of a building, make sure the heating and air conditioning system is adequate, and so on. A teacher has to evaluate whether a lesson is at the right level of detail. A mediator has to use old contracts as precedents but modify them based on differences in circumstances, has to maintain equity, has to confer with the parties to a dispute, and so forth. A judge needs to evaluate the consistency of a sentence about to be handed down. Domain-specific reasoning is also a source of reasoning goals.

Obviously, presentation of the full set of guidelines for each of these reasoning subgoals is impossible. The important thing is for knowledge engineers to be aware of the subgoals they need their systems to carry out and to design indexing schemes, specifications for retrieval, heuristics for focus, and adaptation and/or argumentation strategies that are appropriate to achieving those goals.

14.5 **GOAL SCHEDULING**

The next question we address is the scheduling of reasoning goals. Many of the goals that arise in reasoning are scheduled goals. Some can be scheduled far ahead of their use. Others get scheduled on an as-needed basis. A careful planner, for example, schedules the evaluation phase of reasoning before getting there because he or she can anticipate that it is a necessary task. Explanation of a failure, on the other hand, doesn't get scheduled until a failure needing explanation occurs. Though goals such as this one might not be scheduled until the need for them arises, we can anticipate when the need for them will occur and where they fit into the entire goal cycle. The need to explain a failure happens after a solution is attempted in the world, feedback is received, and feedback signals failure. The feedback-interpretation subgoal can schedule explanation of failure as a result of its own deliberations.

The timing and need for other reasoning goals, however, cannot be as easily anticipated. Anticipation of the potential for failure is one of these. We can schedule anticipation steps in a script of subgoals, but there is no guarantee that there will not be too many or too few of them or that they will occur at optimal times. CHEF, for example, schedules failure anticipation early in its reasoning, before it begins its planning. As a result, it is able to anticipate problems that have occurred previously that can be recognized on the basis of input only. But some problems cannot be anticipated until much problem elaboration has been done and a partial solution has been generated. Others cannot be anticipated until a plan is being carried out and the telltale signs of impending failure are seen. The need for extra liquid in a stir-fry recipe, for example, might not become obvious until the stir-frying is actually being carried out. Anticipation previous to that may be possible if heat and humidity conditions, size of the pan being used, and the temperature of the burner being used are known, but these features, like others in the world, are not easily measured or cannot be recognized until late in deriving a solution. It is thus impossible to know, in setting up the goal scheduler, exactly when failure anticipation is most appropriate.

A good example of anticipation that cannot happen until late in reasoning comes from JULIA. JULIA is planning a meal for a group of people including some vegetarians, some meat-and-potatoes men, and others. JULIA decides to serve grilled salmon for dinner. At this point, JULIA remembers serving grilled fish to Anne (one of the guests) the previous summer. Anne would not eat the fish, and hot dogs were put on the grill for her at the last minute. JULIA is able to remember this case because its salient features are all matched in the new situation: Anne is a guest, and grilled fish will be served. The combination of these features predicts the potential for a plan failure.

The only way JULIA could have anticipated this problem to begin with would have been to (1) store the information that Anne doesn't eat fish in the representation for Anne and use it in solving the problem or (2) look for instances of invited guests' not eating things before beginning to solve the problem. Neither is optimal. Had JULIA had the information about Anne's likes and dislikes stored, it would have used that information in solving the problem. But it didn't have it stored. Perhaps it should have, but making sure information is in all the places it needs to be in memory with all the appropriate connections and associations intact is a big chore. Some information is bound not to be where it is needed sometimes. JULIA could have searched for cases in which there was something that not all the guests ate, but that is a lot of work. JULIA's method instead is to assume everything is as expected unless a particular problem can be anticipated based on specifics of the situation. As specifics are added to the situation (i.e., as the problem is solved), more potential problems can be anticipated.

A goal scheduler that can deal with all these scheduling considerations must at least be able to start with a reasoning goal or sequence of reasoning goals and derive new ones from the old ones as they are carried out. This allows it to deal with goals whose sequence can be anticipated and goals that can be derived in the process of achieving other goals. It must, in addition, be augmented with some means of accommodating goals that arise on the fly, for example, those that are suggested by chance remindings. There are several ways to deal with this problem:

- Include steps in the control structure at various times to look for cases that can predict potential problems and opportunities.
- Augment the scheduler with opportunistic control.
- Make the control structure a suggest and evaluate cycle.

Let us discuss each option.

Anticipating problems at scheduled times.   This is CHEF's method. It is certainly the easiest way to deal with anticipation. Once or several times in the script of reasoning subgoals, an anticipation subgoal is inserted. As stated earlier, however, it is impossible to know exactly when failure anticipation will be possible and most productive.

Augmenting the scheduler with opportunistic control.   Another solution is to add an opportunistic component to the goal scheduler, that is, a reasoning component that keeps its eyes open, so to speak, for opportunities that require new goals to be spawned. This component runs concurrently with the goal scheduler. It recognizes the opportunity to anticipate a potential problem and avoid it in the upcoming solution whenever a case with an undesirable outcome is retrieved. Adding this component to the goal scheduler results in a scheduler that normally works on goals that are derived from scripts, other goals, or cases, but that interrupts its flow of control whenever a case with a potential problem is recalled.

Of course, there are problems with such a regime, the biggest one being that in some situations, interruptions can overwhelm other reasoning. One way to deal with this is to give the opportunistic component some rudimentary means of determining whether an interruption is worth making. Another way to deal with the problem is to allow interruptions only at certain times, for example, only at the end of sequences of well-connected subgoals, never between them. Another way is to provide the reasoner with the means of determining how important each of its goals is. The opportunistic component would add a goal to the goal queue, but the goal scheduler would carry it out only if it was more important than other pending goals. One means of doing this is suggested in MEDIC (Turner 1989b, 1989c), a case-based diagnostic program that integrates execution and planning.

Making the control structure a suggest-and-evaluate cycle. Another way of dealing with issues that come up in making a program opportunistic is to make it quasi-opportunistic; that is, put the opportunism into the control structure but in a way that ensures that failures will be anticipated at appropriate times. This solution is, in effect, a compromise between the first two. JULIA does this with a *suggest-and-evaluate* cycle. Each time some solution derivation subgoal is completed, an evaluation subgoal is run. When this subgoal is run, the memory looks for cases that can help it anticipate problems and opportunities. If any are found, the guidelines for anticipation are followed. In either case, reasoning then continues where it left off.

14.6 INTEGRATING THE GOAL SCHEDULER WITH THE CASE-BASED REASONER

The final topic in discussing the integration of a goal scheduler with a case-based reasoner is the calling sequence. This is simple. Each time a reasoning goal needs to be achieved, the goal scheduler calls the case-based reasoner, specifying three pieces of information:

- The description of the new problem or situation
- If available, the already derived partial solution to the problem
- The current reasoning goal

The case-based reasoner takes it from there.

14.7 WHEN TO USE A GOAL SCHEDULER

Every case-based reasoner has some sort of scheduler, though some are simpler than others, and some exert more control than others. Scripts of reasoning subgoals are implemented in some systems in a program that calls the case retriever at appropriate times. CHEF, JUDGE, CASEY, PERSUADER, and MEDIATOR all work this way. CHEF, for example, begins by anticipating failures, continues by retrieving a case that can suggest a solution, then adapts it, then predicts results, then tries its solution out in the world, then analyzes its results, and then effects repairs. It calls the case-based reasoner with appropriate designation of its problem description for each case-based reasoning step. MEDIATOR begins by elaborating the problem description and continues by choosing planning policies, choosing an abstract plan, refining it, predicting results, trying it out, and so on. It, too, calls case-based reasoning processes with appropriate designations of its problem description. For each of these programs, because the script of reasoning subgoals is constant from problem to problem, there is no need for a dynamic goal scheduler. Rather, a program with the order of the subgoals built into it calls the case retriever as needed.

A dynamic goal scheduler is needed when reasoning subgoals can change from problem to problem. JULIA, for example, tries to solve its problems by remembering a single case that can provide a framework for an answer and adapting from there. But it is usually not able to find one such case. If it can't find one, it spawns subgoals, each focusing on solving a different part of the problem. It attempts to achieve each of those subgoals by retrieving and adapting a case, and it often does, but when it is not successful, it breaks the problem down further and spawns appropriate subgoals.[4]

Once a goal scheduler is being used to keep track of problem decomposition, it is trivial to augment it to take care of other scheduling issues. JULIA's goal scheduler was easily augmented to create the suggest-and-evaluate cycle. Each time a goal is added to the scheduler, a check is made to see if an evaluate goal should also be added. A goal scheduler can also be easily augmented to support situation assessment. When memory needs more information to continue a search, the request can go to the goal scheduler, which can interrupt achievement of the goal it was attempting, schedule the elaboration goal at the head of the goal queue, and choose a method for carrying it out. Augmentations to allow opportunistic anticipation of potential problems is also relatively easy. When a failure case is encountered, a message can be sent to the goal scheduler to schedule a critical evaluation of it.

Different goal-related issues come up in implementing interactive systems. Experience has been that explicitly scheduling reasoning goals for a user is annoying, and that instead, it is important to make sure that the user's reasoning goals are anticipated in building a system in such a way that they are easy to address. A person using a system to aid in evaluating a solution is going to want to designate what is important to focus on in retrieving cases, to see the differences between a retrieved case and the new situation, to see the relative degree of match of the retrieved cases to the new situation, to try out adaptations, and so on. These are the things that should be provided for that task. People using systems to design large artifacts, such as buildings will want different things from a system. At a mimimum, they will want to designate a piece of the building they are focusing on and see how their design goal has been accomplished in other instances and what problems have arisen as a result. People using systems for contingency planning will want potential problems pointed out to them in an easy-to-recognize way. On the other hand, in a system that is teaching how to do a task, it might be advantageous to explicitly show users what the appropriate reasoning goals are and give them the option of choosing one they want to carry out or explore.

14.8   A NEGLECTED COMPLEXITY: MERGING PIECES OF SEVERAL SOLUTIONS

Discussion in this chapter has focused on control issues involved in using several cases to solve a problem. But some difficult conceptual issues have been avoided. In particular, it is not always easy to merge the partial solutions from several different cases. In planning the different parts of a meal, for example, a meal planner may have Chinese food suggested by one case and French food suggested by another. Using procedures suggested up to now, the second sug-

---

4. I will not comment on which kind of goal scheduler to use. Depending on scheduling needs, anything from a simple queue to a prioritized agenda might be appropriate.

gestion would be noticed as a violation of the first. Either one cuisine would be ruled out because of the violation, or one or both would be modified to accommodate the other. In the end, one cuisine or the other would prevail for the meal, different cuisines would be used for different courses, or a compromise cuisine (say, French Vietnamese) would be chosen for the meal.

The reasoning necessary to accommodate these widely differing proposals can be extensive. Remembering cases and making minor adaptations are both fairly simple processes. Dealing with inconsistencies like the one in this situation seems far more complex for several reasons. First, the amount of adaptation necessary is extensive, far more so than in most of the other examples we have looked at. Second, there are large numbers of possibilities that need to be considered along the way, and these possibilities must somehow all be suggested. Up to now, we've counted on cases to do suggesting and counted on adaptation strategies to refine suggestions. It seems here that we want adaptation strategies to suggest compromises. Third, at least some of the possible solutions seem to have a creative component. Switching to French Vietnamese cuisine and substituting Vietnamese versions of Chinese and French dishes already chosen seems somehow more creative, perhaps more elegant, than other solutions we have looked at up to now.

If we examine the adaptations that are necessary to get to any of the possible solutions, we will see that the adaptation strategies provided can handle them. Query memory, for example, might be used to find a cuisine that has both French and Chinese characteristics. Once that is found, local search might be used to find dishes to substitute for the chosen ones. The issue is not so much applying adaptation strategies as it is figuring out which ones to apply.

Merging the partial solutions to many cases is, in general, a more complex and creative process than adapting a single old solution to fit a new situation because the suggestions made by multiple sources might conflict with one another. It is, however, a common case-based process, one reported quite often by expert problem solvers who work on complex problems. Sometimes argumentation procedures are appropriate to determine which of several suggestions is a better one, but often the goal is to integrate the best parts of several solutions.

The best illustration of a computer program that merges parts of several cases is JULIA (Hinrichs 1992). Its constraint propagator maintains records about the relationships that must hold between the parts of its cases. Its reason maintenance system notices violations and points out when adaptation must be done. Its adaptation engine carries out adaptations. Those three processes, in combination, provide the bare minimum of support for merging pieces of several cases.

But there is something unsatisfying about putting so much of the responsibility for merging into processes that are outside the case-based reasoner. The idea behind case-based reasoning, after all, was that cases would provide guidance so that the work of computationally more complex processes would be held to a minimum.

The jury is still out on ways to simplify this process. Indeed, there is little research in this area. Observations of experts, however, point to a process of creating a *frame* for a solution, a case-like entity that records relationships between parts of a proposed solution but is more abstract than a case itself. Framing a problem generally means choosing some set of its specifications to concentrate on and deriving a framework that becomes more refined over time. The same architect discussed earlier, for example, recalls designing a long-term hospice facility for cancer patients. It needed to have many of the facilities hospitals have and, in addition, house patients for long periods of time. He chose to focus on the long-term care and the fact that patients would be bedridden most of the time. Concentrating on that, he inferred that they would be bored and feeling bad, and he wanted to give them all a view to the outside that would provide them with something beautiful to look at. Based on that, he decided to design a long, narrow building with all the patient rooms around the perimeter and looking out into the woods. This frame gave him a basis for specifying constraints on other parts of the building: siting of the building (should have views on long sides), placement of the parking lots (where they wouldn't spoil patient view), placement of the hospital facilities (in the internal part of the building), and so on.

JULIA uses the equivalent of a frame to integrate the suggestions made by several cases. It uses "meal prototypes," each of which describes the common characteristics of a type of meal, to get started. Once it decides on standard American cuisine, for example, it knows that there will be an appetizer course followed by a salad course followed by a main course that includes meat and two vegetables, followed by dessert. For French cuisine, it knows that salad comes after the main course. For vegetarian cuisine, it expects the salad along with the main course and fewer side dishes. Its meal prototypes frame the solution for it, allowing it to query the case library with a general description of each piece of the meal it is trying to fill in. Its framing minimizes the tasks of its support processes. Without the framing step, they would have to work much harder. In fact, without the framing step, JULIA's processing would look a lot like decomposition-recomposition approaches to problem solving.

A frame plays the same role in computing complex solutions that cases play in simple situations. Each provides a place to get started in solving the problem. Rather than starting from scratch, one starts with a general idea of what the answer looks like and proceeds by refining or modifying the parts. Framing minimizes decomposition processes and allows recomposition (merging) to be efficient. Of course, JULIA greatly simplifies this problem; its frames reside in its memory. The architect in the example above created his frame. We still don't know how frames can be created on the fly.

14.9 SUMMARY

In this chapter, we addressed the issues involved in controlling a complex case-based reasoning process, especially when using multiple cases during problem solving. In general, when multiple cases are needed, it is to achieve a series of reasoning goals. Reasoning goals can be used to provide guidance to the case-based reasoner in a number of areas: they provide suggestions of how many and what kind of cases to retrieve, they help the reasoner focus on appropriate parts of a large case, and they tell the reasoner which case-based reasoning method to employ.

Reasoning goals may derive from a variety of places: from the specific steps employed in carrying out a task, from the steps employed in carrying out a general reasoning process, or from the steps employed in carrying out case-based reasoning. A program's reasoning goals can be specified in a script that is followed for each problem that is solved, they can be derived through goal decomposition methods, or they can be derived in a case-based way.

A special kind of reasoning goal that cases support is anticipation of potential problems and opportunities. When failure cases are recalled, they advise the reasoner to check to see if a similar failure could arise in the new situation. If so, the reasoner can carry out measures to avoid the failure. When a reasoner recalls cases that achieve more than the reasoner wants, they advise the reasoner that more can be achieved and prompt the reasoner to consider how much more is appropriate.

If many cases are used in the course of solving a single problem, and if goals control the retrieval and use of cases, then goals must be scheduled in a way that makes sense. Most important in a case-based environment is that the goal scheduler not be so dogmatic in its ways that it does not allow anticipation of potential failures.

A neglected issue in case-based reasoning is the merging of pieces of several solutions to create a solution to a new problem. Merging partial solutions to many cases is more complex than adapting simple solutions because the suggestions from multiple sources might conflict with each other. Systems that have been successful at doing such merging have been able to frame their solutions at the abstract level before moving on to specifics. Up to now, such frames have been built into systems as abstract cases. A challenge for the case-based reasoning community is to discover how to create frames on the fly, much as human problem solvers are able to do. Such a capability will allow our case-based reasoners to produce more innovative and creative solutions.

PART V

Pulling It All Together

The past ten chapters have discussed the component parts of a case-based reasoner, focusing on issues associated with each. In the closing section of the book, we focus again on the case-based reasoner as a whole. Chapter 15 looks at issues that come up in designing and building a case-based system. Chapter 16 summarizes, concludes, and presents challenges and opportunities. The Appendix can also be thought of as belonging in this section. It lists over seventy case-based reasoning systems that have been built over the past ten years. The major features of each are enumerated, and may of the entries list lessons learned in the course of research or development.

15

Building a Case-Based Reasoner

In the curricula of many design disciplines, the properties of artifacts to be designed are emphasized at the expense of the design process itself. Students going through the courses graduate knowing all about the artifacts but little about the process of designing a new one. Up to now, this book, too, could be faulted for such behavior. Each chapter has discussed a different piece of a case-based reasoner or issue in case-based reasoning, presenting the circumstances under which each is useful, but the interactions between the parts and the criteria for choosing among the many ways of doing different tasks that take those interactions into account have been given short shrift.

In this chapter, I try to address the many issues that come up as a knowledge engineer is designing a case-based system. Many of the design decisions the knowledge engineer will encounter are explored, and an attempt is made to give guidelines for making those decisions. Some attention is also given to the ways in which one decision affects others, but it is impossible to foresee all the possible interactions between the parts. In an attempt to remedy that situation, the Appendix presents lists of attributes of several running case-based systems and, for each, lists its accomplishments and what led to those effects.

Most of the systems that have been presented (e.g., CHEF, CASEY, JULIA, KRITIK) have been automated problem solvers. Presented with a problem description, they go through the steps of deriving a solution, sometimes asking a person to make decisions about preferences. Automated systems have all the knowledge they need to solve a problem built into them—the means of judging similarity, adaptation heuristics, knowledge (commonsense or causal) needed to make matching and adaptation procedures work, and so on. They also have built into them the set of steps they must follow to derive a solution. CHEF knows, for example, to first anticipate potential problems, then retrieve a case that suggests a solution, then adapt it, then try it out in the world, and so on. JULIA knows to attempt to find a case to achieve its current reasoning goal and, if it can't, to break the goal into several subgoals. It also knows *how* to break its goals into subgoals. They also have built into them all the support processes that are needed to make the automated case-based reasoner work. JULIA has, for example, a constraint propagator and a reason maintenance system supporting its case-based reasoner. Systems also might have hooks to other reasoners that can help them out if case-based reasoning is failing. CASEY, for example, can call the Heart Failure Program if it has no case available to guide its problem solving.

But some problems are too hard to automate or inappropriate for automation—because the knowledge needed for adaptation is too undefined or because there is too much of it, because preferences are important, because value judgments or aesthetic judgments are needed, or because problems are very large. In these circumstances, an interactive aiding system is more feasible. Several of these have been introduced, for example, the Battle Planner, ARCHIE-2, CLAVIER, and CANASTA.

In an aiding system, the case-based reasoner augments the memory of a person solving a problem. The system provides cases, and perhaps other support. The human user makes the hard decisions based on those cases—which cases to use, which adaptations to apply, which potential problems to address, and so on. Aiding systems can be built to help experts or to help novices. They are particularly useful in helping novices, putting at their fingertips the expertise that they have not yet had the opportunity to acquire.

A third kind of case-based system is used for training. The ASK systems (Ferguson et al. 1992), mentioned in chapter 2, are used this way. In a case-based training system, cases can be used for two purposes: as example problems for the student to work on and as illustrations of general guidelines that need to be taught. In the ASK systems, for example, both cases and guidelines are resident in the systems. The system presents both to trainees, using cases to illustrate the ins and outs of guidelines. These are the newest kind of case-based system and the least discussed in this book. In addition to a well-indexed case library, such systems need guidelines for structuring training sessions.

No matter which kind of case-based reasoner one has in mind, there are a number of questions that must be considered in designing the system.

- Should case-based reasoning be used?
- Which tasks should case-based reasoning be used for, and which tasks should use some other kind of reasoner?
- What sort of support is needed to make the chosen tasks work?
- Should the system be automated, or provide support for a human reasoner?
- If providing support for a human reasoner, what level of support should it provide?

The next several sections will discuss these issues.

Once all that is done, the details of building a system must be addressed. Perhaps the most important issue to deal with here is building the case library—collecting, representing, and indexing cases. Chapters 5 and 6 discuss case representation, and chapters 6 and 7 discuss available indexing methods, but the issues that have not yet been addressed with respect to building the case library are methodologies for collecting cases, which cases are appropriate to collect, the appropriate grain size for cases, and the pragmatics of assigning indexes. These issues are addressed in this chapter.

Another issue that has not been addressed yet is that of case library maintenance, especially in the context of interactive systems. What kind of support is needed to continue to collect cases after a case-based reasoner is out in the field? How can one make sure that outcomes are recorded for new cases? What kind of support is needed to maintain a good set of indexes on cases—both on newly collected ones and on those already in the case library as they get used and their utility is ascertained? One might call these learning issues, and indeed they are in an automated case-based system. In this chapter, these issues will be addressed from the point of view of keeping a case library up-to-date. In the final chapter of the book, learning itself will be addressed.

Finally are the set of issues that determine whether a system will be used or not—issues of human-computer interaction. People will use an interactive system only if they are comfortable using it and if it provides them what they need. The last major section of this chapter addresses human-computer interaction issues. Suggestions are made about building systems for browsing a case library and training systems, with particular emphasis on making the interaction between human and computer natural and beneficial to problem solving.

Another issue not yet addressed is the interaction of case-based processes with other reasoning processes. Most of the systems presented so far have been purely case-based (e.g., CHEF, CASEY, KRITIK). Others have had processes in support of case-based reasoning integrated into them (e.g., JULIA, KRITIK). Some have called on other kinds of reasoners as necessary; CASEY, for example, calls on the model-based Heart Failure Program to solve problems it can't solve. Other systems have case-based reasoners among the different kinds of reasoners they include. For example, CYCLOPS (Navinchandra 1988, 1991), which designs landscapes, uses both case-based and rule-based components. It moves from one to another of its reasoners until it finds one that can solve its problems. ROUTER (Goel and Callantine 1992; Goel, Callantine et al. 1991) combines case-based and model-based components similarly for route planning. CABARET (Rissland and Skalak 1989, 1991) combines rule-based and case-based reasoning and includes strategies for deciding which is better to use at any time. It often is appropriate to integrate a case-based reasoner with other kinds of reasoners. Some tasks a system does might be done easily by one kind of system, others by another. Normative problems may be solved easily using rules; more complicated problems may be solved more easily using cases. There is little to say, in general, however, about such integrations beyond what has been said in other sections of the book; thus, this topic is not covered in this chapter.

A caveat is perhaps in order here. Case-based reasoning is still relatively young. Though it has much promise, there have been few industrial-strength systems built to date. Thus, the engineering of case-based systems has not yet received as much attention as has the engineering of, say, rule-based expert systems. It is therefore impossible to lay down concrete rules for building them; only general guidelines are available. This chapter might, therefore, frustrate those who thought they would finally find out how to build these systems. The best advice I can give to such people is this: Read this chapter for its guidelines, and then use what you've learned in the rest of this book, your experience in building other sorts of intelligent systems, your experience in engineering large systems, and your best creative capabilities and imagination to make it work. As more case-based applications are built, more concrete guidelines for building case-based systems will be developed. It will be possible then to write a book about engineering case-based systems.

15.1 FIRST THINGS FIRST: WHEN SHOULD A CASE-BASED REASONER BE USED?

The first thing that must be considered in building a case-based system is whether or not case-based reasoning is appropriate to the task at hand. If cases are hard to collect, for example, building a case-based reasoner will be difficult. If provably correct solutions are required, heuristic methods may not be the best way to get to them. On the other hand, when little concrete knowledge is available about a domain but expert practitioners exist, a case-based reasoner may be the simplest kind of expert system to build.

The first line of attack in deciding whether case-based reasoning is an appropriate method for solving a problem may be to look at its advantages and disadvantages. If its advantages are preferred and its disadvantages are inconsequential for a task, then case-based reasoning is the way to go. Case-based reasoning has several advantages.

- *A case-based system can easily be made to learn.* In case-based reasoning, problem-solving efforts are cached to save future work . Learning is, in effect, a natural consequence of problem-solving efforts. Case-based systems can be engineered to add to their capabilities or adapt to small changes in their environments by continuing to collect cases and insert them into the case library after the system is fielded.

- *When using case-based reasoning to solve problems, solutions can be justified by the cases they are derived from.* The cases used to solve a problem provide grist for both justifying derived solutions and analyzing their probable outcomes. In a domain where it is difficult to evaluate solutions objectively, case-based reasoning has the advantage of providing illustrations of the effects of particular solutions and kinds of solutions.

- *Case-based reasoners can easily be designed to anticipate potential problems as a natural part of their reasoning.* Unsuccessful experiences with past solutions can be used in case-based systems to anticipate possible problems that might result from solving a problem a certain way. In general, this capability adds efficiency, allowing solutions to be partially debugged before they are carried out. In some domains, anticipating problems that might arise when carrying out a solution plan is critical.

- *Case-based reasoning provides a way for humans and computers to interact to solve problems.* Case-based reasoning is inspired by human behavior. However, when we look at the processes involved in CBR, we see that some are easier for people, while others are easier or more appropriate for computer. People, for example, are good at creative adaptation but poor at remembering the full range of applicable cases, either because they tend to be biased in their remembering or because, as novices, they have not yet had the experiences they need to solve some problem. Computers can augment the memory limitations of people, providing for them the cases they would otherwise not remember. Case-based reasoning provides a way of using the best qualities of both human and computer for solving problems.

■ *Knowledge acquisition for a case-based system is natural.* Communication between system and domain experts can use concrete examples rather than piecemeal rules. Experts find it difficult to report the knowledge they use to solve problems. They are, however, quite at home reporting their experiences and discussing the ways in which cases are different from one another. Their experiences can be coded as cases. The differences they talk about help with both indexing cases and recording knowledge that adaptation heuristics can use.

In addition, the applicability of case-based reasoning to the task in question should be considered. Chapter 3 details the ways in which case-based reasoning provides advantages for design, diagnosis, planning, and interpretation tasks. If case-based reasoning's contributions are needed in an application, it should be considered.

A comparison of case-based reasoning and other reasoning methods might also be considered. Case-based reasoning has advantages over knowledge-intensive heuristic methods in several circumstances.

■ Case-based reasoning should be considered when it is difficult to formulate domain rules but cases are available.

Formulating rules is particularly difficult in weak-theory domains (Porter, Bareiss, and Holte 1990), those in which domain knowledge is incomplete, uncertain, or inconsistent. It is tedious, and perhaps difficult, to formulate rules when there is a great deal of variability in the appearance of situations that have the same outcome. For all these kinds of situations, case-based systems are advantageous.

CLAVIER is perhaps the best example of a successful system built under these circumstances. Laying out parts for curing in an autoclave is a black art. Some experts exist who can do it well, but equations for deriving airflow in an autoclave don't exist. Nor is it easy to articulate rules. Cases of successful loading of the autoclave form the best model of the domain that exists. Many layout problems have this characteristic. Recently relayed to me was the example of laying out air ducts for a mobile air conditioning system. Several experts do it well, but the company wanted to use those experts for other things and build a program that would help less experienced people do the layouts. Analysis of the problem showed that it would take two to three years to capture the knowledge of these experts and put it into a rule-based or numerical-based system. The reason: the domain model is not yet known—it must be derived before either of these methods can be used. It seems a task well suited to case-based reasoning, however. Experts are available who already do the task quite well, they seem to use a case-based approach, and their cases are available.

■ Case-based reasoning should be considered when rules that can be formulated require more input information than is normally available. This may be because problems are incompletely specified, because they are ill defined, or because the knowledge needed by rules is simply not available at problem-solving time.

PROTOS is an example of such a system. Though one could, in theory, formulate rules for diagnosing hearing disorders, such rules don't work very well for several reasons. Most important, there is not enough knowledge about the domain itself to formulate general-purpose rules that make reference to knowledge available in situations. Because the knowledge needed in rules (i.e., the specifications in their antecedents) is not available in descriptions of situations or is expensive to derive, even rules that can be formulated can't be easily used. The rules that could be derived tended to be specific to patterns of symptoms—rules, in effect, corresponded to prototypical cases. It was more advantageous to build a system that emphasized partial pattern matching than to try to capture every pattern of symptoms in rules.

- Case-based reasoning should be considered when it is expensive to use rules because the average rule chain is long.

CASEY provides the best illustration of this phenomenon. CASEY is built on top of the Heart Failure Program (Long et al. 1987), a model-based program implemented using rules, that diagnoses heart defects. When we compare the number of accesses to model knowledge that each program had to do for a set of two dozen cases, we see that CASEY was always two to three orders of magnitude more efficient when it had a case in its case library that was sufficiently similar to the new situation.

- Case-based reasoning should be considered when generally applicable knowledge is not sufficient to solve a problem, either because the knowledge that is necessary changes with context or because some of the knowledge needed to solve a problem is used only under special circumstances.

Sometimes what is needed to solve a problem is known, but when it should be used is unknown. Trying it out all the time when it is useful only sometimes is wasteful. Case-based reasoning provides a natural way of specifying the applicability of such knowledge, contextualizing it for appropriate use. Attaching special-purpose knowledge to a case as part of the knowledge that allowed the case to be solved makes it accessible whenever that case is retrieved (presumably under other conditions where that knowledge should be used). In real life, we see this among professionals of all kinds. Asking directly for retrieval of an obscure piece of knowledge might yield no results, but asking the expert to solve a problem in which that knowledge is necessary and in which he or she has used the knowledge previously to solve another problem will result in its recall.

My favorite example of this is one in which a psychiatrist diagnoses a patient without taking into account a key physical symptom. (Psychiatrists, after all, are used to looking at psychological symptoms—looking at physical ones is, in general, at a lower level of priority.) He diagnoses the patient incorrectly, with a subsequent lack of success during treatment. After further analysis (when treatment doesn't work), he realizes that he should have taken that symptom into account initially. Taking it into account allows the correct diagnosis to be made and correct treatment to be prescribed. Though he knew the effects of the symptom, he had neglected to use his knowledge during diagnosis. The second time he saw a similar patient with that symptom, however, he was reminded of the first case. It keyed him in to using the appropriate knowledge from the beginning, and he used his knowledge about the effects of the symptom to make a correct diagnosis right away.

■ Case-based reasoning should be considered when a case library already exists.

CLAVIER, again, is probably the best illustration of the advantages of having an available case library. A first version of CLAVIER was implemented and running very quickly using the available case library. Especially when using a commercially available case-based reasoning shell, most of the work in building a system goes into collecting cases and indexing them. If a case library is already available, a good part of that effort is made unnecessary. A problem that arises in using available case libraries, however, is that cases might be described in an inappropriate language. Case-based reasoning requires indexing by predictive features of a case, some of which are surface features, others deeper derived features. If an existing library describes its cases only along surface features, building a useful case library from it will require analyzing the cases to extract descriptors that are most advantageous for indexing.

Case-based reasoning is also often applicable when other computational methods are either unavailable or overcomplex.

■ When no fast computation method exists for *deriving a solution* from scratch, case-based reasoning allows new solutions to be derived from old ones.

This advantage is really a variation of the first advantage of case-based reasoning over other heuristic methods. If a fast computational method exists, and if it can give optimal rather than satisficing solutions, then certainly it should be used rather than taking a case-based approach. If, however, computational methods are unavailable or prohibitively complex (to implement or to carry out), then case-based reasoning might provide a solution. CLAVIER and CASEY are our best examples of this. In CLAVIER's domain, little enough is known about airflow in an autoclave that derivation of rules and derivation of other numerical computational methods is too hard, but the task does get done satisfactorily by people taking a case-based approach. CASEY's situation is slightly different. The knowledge is available to formulate a model of the domain, but there are no efficient computational methods available to use that knowledge to derive solutions.

■ When there is no fast computational method for *evaluating a solution*, or when there are so many unknowns that available methods for evaluation are unusable or difficult to use, case-based evaluation allows evaluation to be done anyway.

When solving problems in complex real-world domains, at least some information is generally unknown. Yet, we may need to evaluate solutions to the best of our ability. Many computational methods for analyzing solutions require that most knowledge is known. For example, a structural analysis program that evaluates the structural integrity of a bridge might require that the user supply information about wind velocity, number of cars expected to be on the bridge at any time, maximum water depth, minimum water depth, and so on. Some of these values may be unavailable. Under those circumstances, it is up to the engineer using the program to guess, to the best of his or her ability, what those values are. The availability of similar cases might allow that estimation to be made easily. In other situations, no computational methods are available at all. For those circumstances, cases provide a means of projecting outcomes anyway, and those projected outcomes are evaluated against the specifications of the problem.

Several caveats go with each of these analyses, however.

■ Case-based reasoning requires cases.

Much of the effort in building a case-based system goes into case collection. If it is impossible or especially difficult to collect cases, then case-based reasoning will be difficult, or impossible, to use. If cases don't yet exist, a case-based system can't be built. If cases are impossible to collect because those who know them are unavailable, or because they don't yet exist, then, again, building a case-based system is inappropriate.

On the other hand, a case-based approach can be applied to keep track of the experiences in a domain, building a library over time that can eventually be put to use in an automated, aiding, or training system. For example, engineers at Georgia Tech are grappling with design problems associated with waste disposal. Because of their toxicity, batteries should not be disposed of in general-purpose landfill or other disposal sites. They need to be extracted and disposed of separately. Because of their limited availability or cost, other components of an artifact may need to be extracted for recycling (e.g., gold). This set of requirements suggests designing with *disassembly* in mind. This has not been done in the past, however, so a case-based system to aid with design for disassembly is infeasible. On the other hand, if experiences designing for disassembly are collected in a case library, then eventually the collected wisdom can be made available to those without specific experience.

■ For case-based reasoning to be useful and reliable, cases with similar problem statements should have similar solutions.

Case-based reasoning is based on the premise that situations recur in a predictable way. Adaptation modifies old solutions to fit new situations by keeping the gist or framework of an old solution intact and revising it in fairly trivial ways based on the differences between the new and old situation. Interpretive reasoning is also based on the premise that old situations and new ones will behave similarly. If a domain is discontinuous, that is, if similar situations require wildly different kinds of solutions, then case-based reasoning cannot apply. Adaptation will not be applicable, and interpretive reasoning will not be reliable.

■ Case-based solutions are not guaranteed to be optimal.

The full solution space is usually not explored in a case-based system, hence optimal solutions may be missed. This is, of course, a problem for any heuristic method and not peculiar to case-based reasoning. When optimal solutions are necessary, heuristic reasoning might not be the way to go. On the other hand, case-based reasoning may be usable despite the need for optimal answers if heuristics can be adapted to more fully search the case library. Moreover, it should be remembered that in an open world (i.e., when at least some important knowledge about the world is unknown when a solution is created), case-based reasoning provides a means of anticipating what is unknown and, as such, constitutes a means of dealing with uncertainty that may be necessary in creating optimal solutions. If much is unknown, cases can help a reasoner deal with uncertainties and ambiguities of the real world.

■ Case libraries require considerable storage space. Case-based reasoning requires a large database memory to store cases.

15.2 WHICH TASKS AND SUBTASKS SHOULD THE CASE-BASED REASONER SUPPORT?

Every problem-solving task has several parts to it. In design, for example, problems need to be broken into parts, interactions between the parts have to be maintained, each part has to be solved, the design as a whole must be assessed for completeness, and so on. A case-based reasoner might be appropriate for some parts of a task but not appropriate for others. In design case-based reasoning may be used to suggest solutions, to assess the solution, and to suggest the interactions between parts of a solution, but not for maintaining interactions between parts as the solution evolves or breaking the problem into component subproblems.

In building a reasoner, it is important to assess what the component parts are to the reasoning process, to determine which of those parts will be the responsibility of the case-based reasoner, what support the case-based reasoner needs to get its job done, and which kinds of reasoners will have responsibilities for the remainder of subtasks. Which support processes the reasoner needs depends on the particular retrieval, index assignment, similarity assessment, and adaptation methods chosen for each. Readers should refer back to appropriate sections of the book as they are considering support processes. We concentrate here on determining which subtasks of the reasoning process the case-based reasoner should be used for.

There are several ways problems need to be looked at to determine which subtasks case-based reasoning should be responsible for. We need to consider the *overall task* the reasoner is responsible for and the *domain* in which it is carrying out the task, together called the *task domain*—for example, design buildings, plan lessons, diagnose heart diseases—and look at how that is naturally broken into component parts. We might also consider the *type of task* the reasoner is engaged in—for example, design, diagnosis, interpretation, planning—and the way that is naturally broken into component parts. Task analysis takes all this into account in determining how common problems in the domain can be broken into component parts. Another way to break the overall task into component parts is to consider the *generic tasks case-based reasoning is used for*: anticipating problems, constructing solutions, evaluating solutions. We also need to consider the *functions cases can most profitably be put to*. For example, cases can be used to help elaborate problem descriptions, as a basis for adapting and merging solutions, as the basis for deciding what to compare in several solutions, and so on.

15.2.1 Analysis of the Task Domain

When we think in terms of the reasoner's task, there are two questions we ask:

- How does the task break into subtasks?
- For each subtask, is a case-based approach natural, or is there some other method that is computationally more simple or that provides better accuracy?

We try to break the task into subtasks to see where the complexity lies, to see what a reasoner has to cover, and to see which pieces case-based reasoning is applicable to. An aiding system, for example, might be aimed toward helping someone with more complex tasks. Complexity, of course, can mean many different things, and we'll leave further discussion of how to judge and deal with complexity to the discussion on automation.

Breaking the task into subtasks gives the system designer a feel for the lay of the land. Sometimes that means finding out the full range of tasks that have to be covered in a program to make it complete. Other times, it allows the designer to focus on some aspects of the task that are particularly important. When we look at architectural design, for example, we see that the ability to do the conceptual part of the design well, the part where priorities are set and the solution is framed, is what separates novices from experts. If we are building a system to help novices, we might concentrate first on supporting that piece of the design process.

Knowing what type of task it is helps with task analysis. For example, we know that design has a conceptual phase, a preliminary phase, and a detailed phase, and we know approximately what design tasks are done in each phase. For diagnosis, we know that the real-world process interleaves data collection, hypothesis derivation, and hypothesis evaluation.

How to do a task analysis is beyond this book, but let me provide some examples. When we watch teachers planning lessons, we see them establishing a set of objectives, framing the kind of lesson they want to teach, filling in details to create a lesson plan, and then projecting its results, modifying the plan as necessary as a result of projections. When we watch battle planners, we find that they use standard military doctrine to create a solution and then assess it by projecting its solution and fixing the plan appropriately. When we watch designers of buildings, we see them first attempt to better understand what the client has in mind, then to prioritize specifications and focus on the high-priority ones, derive a framework for a solution from that, and then hop around from piece to piece in the framework fleshing it out. This is the level of task analysis necessary at this point.

After breaking the task into subtasks, we assess, for each, whether a case-based approach is natural or if there is some other method that is computationally more simple or appropriate. Case-based reasoning, for example, may not be able to provide the level of accuracy needed for some subtasks. Programs that can do some tasks may already exist. A program that mixes case-based reasoning with other methods will use case-based reasoning for those subtasks it is appropriate to and other methods for other tasks.

15.2.2 Generic Case-Based Reasoning Tasks

Another way to assess what tasks the reasoner should support is to examine the generic tasks case-based reasoning is good at and to determine which of those is necessary for the new situation. Recall that there are several generic tasks case-based reasoning supports: constructing solutions, anticipating failures, and evaluating solutions. To decide which of these is appropriate in a reasoner, several questions should be asked.

- Where is the complexity in the task to be accomplished? Is it in deriving a solution initially? Evaluating solutions? Anticipating effects? Repairing solutions?
- How much is known in advance about the problem situation? Are there things that will be known at execution time that are not known at the time a solution is being derived?
- Are there many obscure ways in which a solution could fail, or is a reasonable-looking solution almost always a good one?

In general, the more complex piece of the problem is the one that needs to be concentrated on in system design. In building the Battle Planner, for example, designers found that the major complexity was in evaluating solutions and repairing them. Coming up with initial solutions was fairly trivial. They therefore put their efforts into helping users evaluate and repair solutions.

In general, when knowledge about the state of the world is missing at solution-creation time, anticipating effects and evaluating solutions is particularly important. For example, good lesson plans take into account the kinds of interactions with students that are likely to come up during a lesson. The extent to which these are anticipated determines the extent to which the lesson can be taught flexibly. A teacher who anticipates the antics of students during a lesson might be able to plan to incorporate those antics into the lesson. A teacher who has not anticipated antics might be stymied by them, making the lesson less effective than it ought to be. A teacher who anticipates student questions can work out solutions or methods of coming up with solutions before class. A teacher who anticipates the things that will be hard in a lab can plan to have extra help available during the necessary time; one who has not anticipated will plan a less effective lab session. In design, too, anticipating effects and criticizing solutions is important. The more anticipation is done up front, the better a design can incorporate features that will make manufacture, maintenance, and use easy. When anticipation is important, case-based support should be provided.

In some domains, by contrast, nearly everything is known at solution-creation time and detecting potential failures is easy. When a reasonable solution can be expected to succeed, case-based support for evaluation is probably unnecessary.

15.2.3 Functions Cases Can Profitably Fulfill

Functions cases should be put to depend on the extent to which cases can provide a basis for making decisions and the extent to which a reasoner needs to get better at those tasks over time. In PERSUADER, for example, cases that provide guidance for adaptation allow idiosyncratic problems with solutions to be identified and adapted for. In using cases to guide adaptation, PERSUADER is able to increase its repertoire of adaptation methods with experience. Using cases to guide adaptation makes a lot of sense in this domain. In MEDIATOR's domain, cases can be profitably used to disambiguate and elaborate problem descriptions, a necessary subtask of mediation. Using cases to do these tasks allowed MEDIATOR to get better at disambiguation and elaboration over time.

15.3 WHAT DEGREE OF AUTOMATION SHOULD BE USED?

Case-based reasoners can be fully automated, or they can provide varying degrees of aid to a human user. At the simplest, an aiding system acts as a case retriever, providing cases to a user who uses the cases to reason. But an aiding system can provide other forms of support also, for example, help with adaptation or help with evaluation. Help with adaptation generally involves carrying out adaptations when asked. Help with evaluation generally means showing the user the factors that should be considered during evaluation and clustering cases to make comparison easy.

The degree of automation a case-based system ought to have requires further assessment of the task it will be applied to. There are several questions the knowledge engineer must ask in doing that assessment:

- How much creativity is required to derive solutions?
- How much complexity is involved in evaluating solutions and effecting repairs?
- Are aesthetic judgments or value judgments necessary?
- Where does a person working on this task have trouble? Which parts are easy?

15.3.1 Consideration 1: Required Creativity

Consider the task of planning meals for a nursing home. There are two subtasks: coming up with a meal aimed toward the general population of the institution and catering to the many patients on special diets. In some nursing homes, any meal that gives the required nutrition and is easy to make, regardless of taste, aesthetics, or variety, is satisfactory. In other nursing homes, there is a commitment to good taste, aesthetics, and variety, in addition to a commitment to good nutrition and a preference for easy-to-make meals.

Planning meals for the first type of nursing home is easy. Almost any combination of foods that is nutritionally sound will work. Each case in the case library can be assumed to provide that. Patients on special diets can be taken care of easily by doing simple substitutions and adaptations of the normal meal. A breakfast consisting of some instantiation of protein food, toast, fruit, milk, and hot drink would be quite satisfactory on a day-to-day basis in such a nursing home. Patients on low-fat diets would get the low-fat substitution for milk (skim milk). Those on a low-cholesterol diet would get low-fat cottage cheese or yogurt as their protein food. And those without teeth would have their toast ground in the blender and their protein food in an almost-liquid form (e.g., runny scrambled eggs). Such meals are easy to plan. JULIANA was quite successful at planning such meals.

What makes this task easy is two things. First, a library of cases is available, and little smart discrimination of cases is needed to retrieve a satisfactory one. Second, once cases are retrieved, the adaptation needed to come up with a satisfactory set of meals is straightforward and fairly trivial. Adaptation to create the general-purpose meal requires only simple computations: adjusting quantities of ingredients for the number of people being fed, substituting new recipes for old to provide a touch of variety, and substituting in-season ingredients for out-of-season ones. Catering to patients on special diets is also easy: simple substitutions and adaptations of the main meal will, for the most part, suffice.

Planning meals for the second type of nursing home is different. A variety of breakfast foods and combinations of foods are required from day to day. Some combinations are easy for the kitchen to adapt for patients on special diets; others are harder. Runny eggs and ground-in-the-blender toast will not be allowed on the menu. Some other way of taking care of special-diet patients is required.

This problem is harder because more complex adaptation is required. Adaptation strategies can be complex because their applicability conditions are not well defined or because they are not easily expressible or well known. The dietician in the second situation is asked to create adaptation strategies on the fly, to figure out how to use abstractly defined adaptation strategies, and to apply adaptation strategies in situations they were not specified for. When adaptation is not well defined, the process of deriving a solution requires creative thought. People are often (but not always) good at creative adaptation. Computers have not been able to autonomously reason creatively enough yet.

One kind of problem where creative adaptation tends to be needed is in design of items with many parts. Often, the solution to such problems requires blending or merging of solutions to pieces of many other problems, and complex adaptation is needed to make the pieces fit together well. It has not been easy to discover the adaptation heuristics that creative designers use to put such solutions together.

If satisfactory solution of a set of problems requires only a good case library and an easily programmable set of adaptation strategies and heuristics that have well-defined applicability conditions, then an automated case-based reasoner can be counted on to derive satisfactory answers if the case library is available.

If applicability of adaptation strategies cannot be easily defined, if the adaptation strategies themselves are not easily expressible and well known, if adaptation strategies can be expressed only in very abstract terms (requiring much reasoning for operationalization), or if good answers require applying adaptation strategies in ways other than the prescribed way, then an automated system will not do a good job of deriving solutions.

A system that retrieves cases and leaves the adaptation to a person will, in general, be more appropriate in these circumstances. When adaptation strategies can be defined and are easily applied, but their applicability conditions are not well known, the system might in addition carry out the adaptations specified by the human user. When applicability conditions are known but application is difficult, the system might suggest adaptations to the user.

15.3.2 Consideration 2: Complexity of Evaluating Solutions and Effecting Repairs

As in deriving solutions, the degree to which the process of evaluating solutions is well defined determines whether an automated or interactive system is more appropriate. Recall that case-based evaluation requires several kinds of knowledge:

- Knowledge of the factors to be focused on in evaluation
- Knowledge of the priorities of factors with respect to each other
- Knowledge about the extent of influence each factor has on a solution and on different parts of the solution
- Knowledge of what influences the values of factors and their influences on each other

When each of these kinds of knowledge is well known and well defined for some task, an automated case-based evaluative component can be built.

More often than not, however, it is too hard to define each of these kinds of knowledge precisely. Though a reasoner might be able to determine to what extent each of the factors plays a role in a solution, it is often more appropriate or easier to have a person weigh the relative merits of factors against one another. When aesthetics, value judgments, or idiosyncratic preferences determine how good a solution is, it is especially important to have human users making the decisions.

Evaluation of solutions often leads to repair, and here, too, the complexity of choosing and effecting repairs determines whether it can be done automatically by a system or needs to be guided or done by a person. When detected problems have a one-to-one correspondence with repair (adaptation) methods and repair methods are easily applied, a system can be given full responsibility for repair. If making decisions about which repair method to apply is easy, again, a system can do it. Often, however, choosing repair methods and applying them is not so straightforward. When choosing a repair method is difficult but carrying it out is easy, the user can be asked to choose the method, and the system can carry it out. Similarly, when choosing the method is easy but carrying it out is not straightforward, roles can be reversed. And when both are difficult, the user should do it, though possibly with suggestions made by the system.

15.3.3 Consideration 3: Need to Consider Aesthetics, Values, and/or User Preferences

When value judgments, aesthetic judgments, or idiosyncratic user preferences are important to creating or evaluating a solution, aiding systems are preferred. Computers have not yet proved themselves capable of aesthetic judgments, it is too dangerous to have computers make value judgments, and when idiosyncratic preferences are important, users generally prefer to be in control.

15.3.4 Consideration 4: Locus of Complexity

Different reasoning tasks have their complexity in different places. For some tasks, coming up with a ballpark solution is easy, but specializing that ballpark solution to the new situation is difficult. Army generals, for example, can use prescribed doctrine to easily come up with a battle plan for any situation. Making that battle plan work for a particular situation, however, requires considerable deliberation.

One way to determine where the complexity lies in a task is to compare the behavior of novices and experts doing a task. The places where novice and expert behavior are similar are probably the easy parts of the task. Those where novice behavior is significantly different or results in poorer solutions are generally the parts of the task where the complexity lies. Soldiers, as well as generals, for example, can come up with battle plans based on prescribed doctrine. But novices have trouble predicting whether a plan will work and what might need to be done to it to make it work. The obvious place to provide help is with the evaluation and repair task.

In other situations, deriving an initial solution is quite difficult, sometimes because of the sheer size of the solution space, sometimes because of the complexity of the interconnectedness of the solution. This happens often in design, where many different things that interact with one another must be taken into account. Here, it makes sense to help the user deal with interactions between the parts.

In general, when a person is included in the decision-making loop, the system should be responsible for helping the person make difficult decisions, providing whatever aid is needed.

In addition, tasks need to be divided between a system and a person in a workable way.[1] Here, it makes sense to think of machine and person acting together as a unit. What must necessarily be done by the person is assigned to the user. What is easy for the computer can be given to the computer. If something is easy for both computer and person, then which has responsibility depends on several things. First, human users should have to do any part of the problem that is required to deal with some other task that is assigned to the human. Second, if the task is boring for a person and not a necessary human task, then the computer should do it. Third, if the decision requires value judgment, aesthetics, or other preferences, the person should do it. Fourth, if the person and computer are going to interact well with each other, each must be given enough responsibility to keep on top of the problem.

15.4 BUILDING AND MAINTAINING THE CASE LIBRARY

Though there has been much discussion of case representation and choice of indexes, little has been said about collecting cases themselves. There are two major issues here: collecting a good set of cases and methods for collection. In addition, we return to the pragmatics of case representation: their grain size and content.

---

1. The field of human-machine systems (previously called man-machine systems) is devoted to dealing with this issue. Readers should consult that literature if dividing tasks between user and computer is a critical part of what they are doing (e.g., Rasmussen, Pejtersen, and Goodstein 1992; Sheridan 1992; Sheridan and Ferrell 1974; Sheridan and Johannsen 1976). This paragraph, of necessity, glosses over many of the important findings of that field.

Case collection has two phases: initial collection of cases, or *seeding* of the case library, and testing of the case library to make sure it provides the required coverage and reliability. The result of testing and subsequently refining the case library is that the library is *trained* for the tasks it will support. Training, itself, is a lifelong process—one that, in general, needs to continue throughout the life cycle of a system.

15.4.1 Collecting Cases: Which Ones?

Three general principles guide case collection.

1. Cases should cover the range of reasoning tasks the system will be responsible for doing or supporting.

2. Over this range of reasoning tasks, cases should cover the range of well-known solutions and well-known mistakes.

3. Collecting cases is an incremental process—we do the best we can to provide coverage initially, and then we find out what's missing by trying to use the cases that have already been collected.

In general, cases need to be collected according to the needs of the reasoner, that is, based on the reasoning tasks and goals it will do or support. Cases in the case library should provide as much coverage as possible about both achieving reasoning goals and the obstacles that are likely to be encountered in achieving them—the range of well-known solutions and mistakes. But a case-based system, like an expert, needs to be given time to grow. No matter how careful we are at initially seeding the case library, there will be some problems that are beyond its capabilities. As those are encountered and the limits of the case library are found, new cases need to be added to fill the gaps. Interestingly enough, the very cases that the system can't solve, when added to the case library (with the help of an expert), can generally play that role.

Though the first pass at building a case library is unlikely to provide full coverage, an organized approach to determining the kinds of cases that need to be collected can result in good coverage. Providing coverage on the range of problems that will come up requires, first, a task analysis, looking at the subtasks and subgoals that must be accomplished or achieved. Cases are then collected to illustrate means of accomplishing those subgoals and anticipating and avoiding their pitfalls. The following guidelines suggest how this can be done.

1. For each subgoal your system will have or support, collect cases that illustrate how to achieve both solutions themselves (e.g., paint the trim red) and well-known methods for arriving at solutions (e.g., the color of the trim is complementary to the color of the walls). If there is a range of well-known ways to achieve some subgoal or to accomplish some task, cover all of them in the cases. Index cases that illustrate *solution methods* by the combination of the subgoal(s) they achieve and the circumstances under which they provide a solution method appropriate to achieving the subgoal(s). Index cases that illustrate *solutions* by the combination of the subgoal(s) they achieve and the circumstances under which they provide appropriate solutions to the subgoal(s).

2. For each subgoal, delineate the well-known problems that crop up in achieving it. These include obstacles to achieving the subgoal and well-known mistaken solution methods and mistaken solutions. To support anticipating problems and avoiding failure, collect cases that point out potential problems, indexing them by the combination of features that predict failure. To support avoiding those problems, make sure some of these cases record what was done to avoid the problem. To support repairing problems once they happen, make sure some cases include the means by which problems were repaired, indexing these cases additionally by a description of their outcome and also a description of the problem they repair. If multiple repairs are possible, collect cases that cover the set. Though the well-known problems that crop up should be collected before training a system, lesser-known problems can be delineated, and cases illustrating them can be collected during training—as a result of noting the failures of the system.

3. For each subgoal, delineate what common good and poor solutions look like. (Good solutions will already have been delineated by the first guideline. Poor solutions might have been delineated by the second.) To support evaluation of solutions, collect cases that illustrate both good and poor solutions to each subgoal. Index each by outcome descriptions and features that predict outcome.

Following these guidelines, a case library will have cases in it that (1) suggest methods for achieving each subgoal or task the reasoner must achieve, (2) suggest solutions to problems, (3) list obstacles that might be encountered in achieving each goal, (4) warn against certain solutions, (5) illustrate what good and bad solutions look like, and (6) project outcomes for solutions. A system with this range of cases can do the full range of case-based activities: anticipating problems before they happen, planning to make sure they are avoided, repairing problems that do occur, deriving successful solutions easily, and evaluating solutions. Of course, not all case-based reasoners need to do all these tasks, and knowledge engineers should choose the subset of these guidelines appropriate for the tasks their systems are assigned.

In addition, an advantageous way of managing case collection is to go for depth of coverage in one area initially rather than going for overall breadth. This allows for early evaluation of system performance.

15.4.2 Achieving Coverage and Reliability

After an initial case library is built, it must be tested, as must be done in building any large system. In initially building the case library, or *seeding* it, one tries to provide coverage of common methods and problems. In the *testing and training* phase, gaps in the case library and inadequacies of the original cases and indexing scheme are exposed, and each is fixed.

There are three kinds of problems that are exposed during testing.

1. Gaps in the library's coverage are found.
2. Inadequacies of the indexing scheme are found.
3. Inadequacies in the contents of cases in the case library are found.

When cases in the case library are inadequate for solving a new problem, a gap in the library's coverage is exposed. As gaps are found, the library must be augmented with cases that fill those gaps. Usually, the problem the library was inadequate for provides a good case for filling a gap. Sometimes, to provide coverage several simpler cases are needed in addition to the new one.

Another problem that is exposed in this training phase is inadequacy of the indexing system. This is discovered when cases that should have been retrieved in response to a new situation are not recalled, often resulting in an inability to solve a new problem or in derivation of a poor solution. When this happens, indexes on the cases that should have been recalled need to be refined.

A final problem that can be exposed during testing is the inadequacy of the contents of cases that are recalled from the case library. Some cases might be recalled at appropriate times but the reasoner may not be able to derive from them the full extent of advice that they ought to be able to provide. In these situations, the contents of the individual faulty cases must be refined.

Testing and refining of the case library generally requires knowledge of the tasks and domain the case library supports. Refining of indexes and cases can be done manually, or programs can help. PROTOS, for example, interacts with a human expert to refine its indexes and to install new cases in its case library.

As in building any large system, testing must be done in several phases. One tests the case library on typical cases first to make sure that what's in there is retrievable at the right times and provides good advice. One then tests it on more novel problems, filling in exposed gaps. The system is then ready for alpha and beta testing, testing in the kinds of situations in which it will be exposed when put to work. First trials of the case library should probably be done in-house using "friendly" users. After in-house evaluation and collection of additional cases, a system becomes ready for the equivalent of beta testing—testing it in the field.

Does it ever end? Does a case library ever become complete? The answer depends on the complexity of the problem and parallels the expectations we have of human experts. Fairly simple tasks can be covered relatively completely, and we would expect that a fully tested, mature case-based system applied to a simple problem would be successful most of the time. As the complexity of a task increases, however, our expectations should be those we would have of human experts. If the domain is huge (e.g., medicine), we expect a person to be expert at a subset of it (say, endocrinology) but to be able to use commonsense to solve some problems outside of that specialty. Even within specialty areas, there are some problems that are common and straightforward and can be solved by the specialist, others that are more novel and require the specialist's specialist (e.g., an endocrinologist who specializes in growth disorders). Even the specialist's specialist will find some problems harder to solve than others. Some will require looking in resource books for obscure knowledge; others will require piecing together disparate knowledge and experience; others will require trial and error; others, the creation of a new experimental paradigm under which to conduct more research. Specialists can solve problems to the extent of their expertise, and as their expertise grows, so does the range of problems they can address. Training, in complex domains and for complex tasks, is a lifelong endeavor.

It is the same with a mature case-based system. A system will be able to perform to the extent of coverage of its expertise (cases in its case library and available adaptation strategies), and as its expertise is strengthened, so is the range of situations it can reason about. It is up to those collecting cases to make sure that the cases collected eventually cover the expected range of expertise of the system. It is up to the user to expect no more from a system than he or she would from a human expert. We all (machines and people) have limits.

Building a mature case library is thus a many-phased process. We begin by systematically collecting cases and continue by testing the coverage and reliability of those cases, giving the system harder and harder tests as it evolves. The full extent of coverage and reliability in a case library, then, depends at least as much on the representativeness and rigor of the trials the system is put through before being put in the field as it does on the coverage of the cases the system is seeded with. To some extent, the degree of work that has to be done in the testing stages depends on how carefully the system has been seeded. But no matter how careful the seeding has been, there are liable to be many gaps that cannot be discovered until the system is tested on representative problems.

This suggests that, though system builders should be systematic in collecting cases to seed a new case library, there is no need to aim toward creating a perfect case library first time around. Guidelines for collecting cases are aimed toward creating a case library of *well-known* solutions, pitfalls, and repairs. Idiosyncratic solutions and problems can be added in a later pass. Of course, what seems idiosyncratic to one person might be well known to another person. That's not a problem. Cases representing some set of common methods, solutions, and pitfalls in some area are enough to seed a case library. As those are used, it becomes clear what those cases don't cover and where the gaps are in the case library. The cases that fill exposed gaps can then be collected. The important thing is that case libraries be rigorously tested using the kinds of problems that will come up when the system is put into the field.

15.5 MAINTAINING THE CASE LIBRARY

As case libraries are used, they must be maintained. Even after much initial testing, when a case library is used in the field, it may be discovered that some indexes are inaccurate, that some cases are incomplete, or that some coverage is missing. This may happen for several reasons.

- Novel situations that did not come up in the course of initial testing might be encountered.
- The purpose to which the system was to be put might evolve.
- The nature of experiences in the domain the library is associated with might change over time.
- The case library's purpose might be to track the experiences for a new and maturing domain or task.

Whatever the reasons, maintaining the integrity of the case library is a natural life-cycle event for a case-based reasoner.

As in testing and training the case library, changes may need to be made in the case library for several reasons. There may be gaps in the case library, exposed when a new situation arises for which no recalled cases can provide a solution. The problem here might be that cases that could have helped were not recalled or that the case library holds no such cases. When cases that should have been recalled are not recalled, indexes must be updated on those cases so that they are recalled in the future. When no appropriate cases reside in the case library, the new situation, after being solved by a human expert or some other computer system, is added into the case library. As new cases and indexes are added to the case library, the repertoire of situations the case-based reasoner can handle will grow.

Alternatively, the suggestions provided by some cases may become obsolete or inadequate. As a case library is used, some of its cases may be found to make poor or inadequate suggestions. A solution derived from a case or set of cases may fail or give poorer results than expected. When this happens, several things might have to be done. First, the indexes of cases that were used in deriving the poor solution might need to be updated, taking into account the situation in which its suggestion was inapplicable. Second, cases that were used in deriving the poor solution might need to be deleted or their contents made more easily usable. Third, the new situation, in which a previously used solution failed, must be installed in the case library, along with any other cases that are needed to provide necessary coverage.

Much of what needs to be done to maintain a system is the same as what is done while it is being tested. As during testing, when situations that the case library cannot handle are encountered, a human expert can be brought in to analyze those situations and make appropriate changes to the case library and its indexing. Alternatively, a computer program that can assign blame and explain failures might be able to do the job (e.g., as CHEF does). Or a person and computer can work together, as PROTOS does.

There are, however, several additional complexities in maintaining a case library that are not present as it is being built and tested.

- Making cases out of situations that the case library has proposed solutions to
- Authorizing updates to the case library
- Propagating changes in a case library around to the many locations where the same library is being used
- Taking outdated cases out of the case library

The cases put in a case library as it is being seeded are generally complete experiences—their solutions and outcomes are already known. When a system is in the field making suggestions or solving problems, however, cases start out incomplete—after solving a problem, only its description and solution are known but it is unknown how that solution behaved when applied. Only after a suggested solution is carried out can its outcome be recorded; thus, until the results of carrying out a solution are known, a case is incomplete. Until results are in, we don't know if the new situation is so much like old ones that it can be forgotten or if it is novel enough that it should be installed in the case library. Case libraries can mature only if novel cases are added as appropriate.

The passage of time between when a solution to a problem is suggested and when its outcome can be reported requires some additional bookkeeping that is not necessary when complete cases are added all at once. To do a reliable job of adding new cases to the case library as it is being used, systems need to keep track of their partial cases (those for which they have computed or suggested solutions) and collect feedback about the outcomes of those cases to make them complete. Then, either the system or a human expert needs to examine those cases to make sure they are being solved appropriately. Those that add coverage to the case library can be added. Those that suggest problems with the indexing or content of cases already in the case library can act as prompts for debugging the cases and indexes that the case library already holds.

Gathering feedback is sometimes the most important and complex of the things that have to be done to maintain and refine a case library. Gathering feedback can be simple or complex. For some problems, feedback can be gathered automatically by sensors that can read the environment. For others, asking a human operator what happened is sufficient. In other situations, however, the best feedback comes from a variety of sources, and collecting it might be a project in and of itself. The best designs, for example, take into account all users in every phase of the life cycle of the artifact being designed. Feedback about a building, for example, might be gathered from those involved in its construction, those who use the building after it is built, those who maintain it, and those who remodel it later. For many tasks and domains, the power of the case-based reasoner comes from the feedback it can provide about how things have worked in the past. If such power is needed, some way of collecting such feedback should be devised and implemented.

There are thus a number of different kinds of changes that can be made in a case library. Cases already in the library can be refined to make them easier to use, their indexes can be changed, cases can be added to the case library, additional feedback information can be added to cases that are already in the case library, and cases can be found to provide poor information and deleted. A case library that is allowed to grow over time with the experiences of those who use it can act as a corporate memory for an organization. Experiences of employees in one unit of a company can be passed on easily to other employees of the company by putting them into a case library.

But developers should be aware of the organizational problems they need to deal with in maintaining a case library. In particular, the issue is, When should changes to a case library be made, and who should make them? Making changes in the case library is perhaps more of a bookkeeping and social headache than a conceptual issue. However, doing it right can make a big difference in the reliability and usefulness of a case library. If just anybody can make changes in a case library functioning in a production environment, the case library can become unreliable quickly. But if users are prohibited from customizing a case library to their needs, the case library may be less useful than it ought to be. If users can customize only their own copies of the case library but have no way to pass that information on to other users, then discoveries that might be useful to an organization as a whole won't be able to have the impact they could. Means of authorizing global changes to a case library and propagating those changes in reasonable time are needed if a system is to perform at its best.

In some applications, only experts will be using systems, and it will make sense for any user to be able to change or augment the library. In other situations, only novices will be using the system. Here it makes more sense to save up the problems that have been solved using the case library for an expert to sort through. The expert will decide which cases belong in the case library, which show that more coverage is needed, which are exactly like cases already in the library, and so forth. In situations where the same case library is used in multiple locations, some protocol for collecting library changes from multiple locations and propagating changes to all them will need to be set up.

15.5.1 Collecting Cases: How?

We know how to discover which cases need to be collected. We focus now on methodologies for collecting cases and for making sure that the proper information is collected about each. Cases can come from several different places: an existing database, case books, file cabinets, magazines, textbooks, automated problem-solving systems, interactive problem-solving systems, and human experts. Collecting from each makes different demands on the case collector.

The first source of cases we consider is existing databases. CLAVIER is the best example of one of those. Its initial case library was built based on a small database (written on note cards) that had already been collected. As it was used, new situations that were encountered were added to it as cases. Several help-desk applications are currently being built based on existing databases. The biggest issue in collecting cases from databases is making sure that cases have the kinds of data in them that allow similarity to be judged reliably. Sometimes the important features of a case for indexing and judging similarity require values along dimensions that are not recorded in the database. When this is true, those dimensions must be added to the representation.

For example, the Battle Planner needs to judge similarity based on the relative strengths of the two sides in a battle rather than their absolute strengths. If a case library were being constructed from a set of database records that recorded absolute, but not relative, strength, then converting those database records to a good case representation would require deriving the missing, but necessary, dimensions. Here, that means adding a field designating relative strength to the representation, computing the relative strengths of the two sides, and inserting the computed value into the new field in the representation.

A similar issue comes up in collecting cases from books and file cabinets. It is often necessary to interpret those cases, to fill in missing dimensions, to create summaries, and to partition cases into appropriate chunks. Representations of houses in architectural digests, for example, usually record square footage and cost. A case representation may require a qualitative measure of cost or a cost per square foot. These may need to be derived from the absolute information given in the digest. Representations of buildings in file cabinets, by contrast, tend to overwhelm with the specifics of their information. Summarization is necessary so that each case can be presented effectively to users. And, a single case in a set of file cabinets may be more appropriately represented as a set of smaller cases, each associated with a different aspect of the design.

In doing such interpretations, guidelines concerning case representation and indexing are followed.

- Cases should have a lesson to teach.
- Cases should be indexed according to the situations in which they can provide guidance.
- Cases need to record in their machine-readable representations at least what is needed for indexing.
- Cases need to include in them enough information to get their point across.[2]

Other guidelines are commonsensical. One shouldn't have so much in one case that the reasoner can't easily determine the case's point. Thus, if a case has many separate lessons to teach, it might be better represented as several different cases, each with one or a small number of lessons in it. Such smaller cases may be connected to one another using pointers if they depend on one another or if some sequence of them is useful for reasoning.

Cases can also be collected from a problem-solving system, whether automated or interactive. In general, one must describe a problem to a system in order for it to be able to solve the problem. Thus, the problem description in such cases is normally well described. In an automated system, the system knows why it made the decisions it made and which knowledge about the problem it used in making its decisions. Thus, in an automated system that keeps track of why it made its decisions, adequate information ought to exist in the case description for indexing the case. Chapter 7 explains how this can be done in an automated way by explanation-based index-selection methods. When problems are being solved interactively by a combination of human and machine, it may not be possible to collect all the information needed for indexing; thus, some of the same interpretation that must be done on cases collected from books, magazines, and file cabinets must be done to establish good indexes for such cases.

Finally, the most fruitful source of cases is often human experts themselves. One collects cases from human experts by asking them to recall their experiences. To get experts to relate the particular kinds of cases that need to be collected, some prompting is generally in order (e.g., tell me about particular building facades you've liked; tell me about the ones you think have worked most poorly; tell me about others that are like this one but worked better). Often, experiences related by experts are incomplete. This requires additional prompting (e.g., Why do you think it worked so poorly? What would you have done instead?).

Books about knowledge engineering and building expert systems (e.g., Hayes-Roth, Waterman and Lenat 1983) have hints in them for getting experts to talk, and those hints are often applicable to collecting cases from experts also. For example, it is often worthwhile to take a story the expert has just told you, perturb it just a bit, and ask what he or she would have done in that case. The expert may have an actual case to talk about or may solve a problem on the fly, either way allowing collection of additional cases.

---

2. Some cases are used by systems to reason; others are presented to people to reason with. Cases might thus hold a combination of machine-readable and other documentation. The full content of a case needs to be enough to reason with. The way that content is represented depends on who will be using it. Many recent interactive system present cases to people using video or as a combination of graphics and canned text. The case content (video, pictures, text) has to be adequate for a person to learn something useful from it. The machine-usable part of the case, however, needs to include only enough to index cases well.

Sometimes it is useful to interview several experts at the same time. They jog one another's memories, and a profusion of stories emerges. Such case collection is a two-step process. The group meeting helps the experts think of cases, but individual sessions with the experts are often necessary to fill in additional details about the cases they relay in the group. During summer 1992, for example, three science teachers joined the SCI-ED project (Kolodner 1991b) to relate their experiences teaching science. Group meetings were held in the mornings, each day discussing a different topic, for example, assessing student performance, breaking students into groups, dealing with failures of experimental procedures to work. As they talked to one another, each teacher related his or her experiences, and the other teachers chimed in with stories about similar situations. A wide range of stories emerged, but they were incomplete. In the afternoons, the teachers filled in details about the stories they had told in the morning, details necessary for indexing, for removing ambiguity, and for concrete illustration—for example, how, exactly, to carry out the methods being discussed, the circumstances in which a method might be used, other times it has been used and what resulted, background needed for another teacher to follow the same procedure.

Though experts are generally happy to relate their experiences, some warnings that might counter frustrations are in order. First, stories related by experts are almost never complete or detailed enough the first time they are told. Often, it is impossible to get experts to tell complete stories. We've found that this is not, in general, a problem. Sometimes stories are too incomplete to be usable, but often, although stories are incomplete, they are sufficient. In general, experts tell stories in very much the same way they would relate them to colleagues. If a story has enough in it for a colleague to walk away with a lesson learned, then the case is sufficiently expressed. The knowledge engineer must, however, query the expert about the situations in which each story's lesson should be recounted. This will allow the story to be indexed properly.

This seems a counterintuitive claim—that cases don't need complete information to be useful. As AI people, we are trained to want our systems to have complete knowledge about every item they hold, but completeness often isn't necessary. For a case to be useful, it needs to include enough information to index it well and to make sense of and make use of its point.

Second, some stories experts tell don't look like cases because the experts emphasize general guidelines over the specifics of an experience. This was a frustration for our own group as we began collecting cases for the SCI-ED project. Teachers told us many stories, but they also told us some things that sounded like general rules. Teachers at SciTrek, the science museum in Atlanta, for example, told us that in sequencing activities for children, it's better to start with low-tech and move to high-tech activities—that once the children are involved in the high-tech activities, it's a letdown for them to return to the low-tech ones. They also told us that you should never give for homework anything that must be done to make another lesson successful. We found that each guideline, however, was attached to one or more experiences the teachers had had, some successful and some not. To go with the high-tech low-tech sequencing guideline, for example, they told us about the way their course had been sequenced the previous summer and the better way it was currently sequenced. The guideline was on their minds because they had just recently derived it based on their observations about what had worked and what hadn't. We used both their stories and their guidelines in our system—using the guidelines as the lessons illustrated by the stories, and using the stories to illustrate and allow access to the rather abstract guidelines. The result of this experience is that SCI-ED includes both stories and general guidelines in it, but no guideline is ever put into the system without at least one, and usually several, stories to illustrate it.

Experts report guidelines for a variety of reasons. There may be general guidelines that cover the common or easy situations, or the expert may have recently derived a generalization of some sort from a set of experiences. Alternatively, the expert may use guidelines during presentations and therefore feel comfortable relating them. Such guidelines should neither be ignored nor allowed to predominate. Often, even when general guidelines can be given, they are too abstract to be operationalized easily. For example, we may not know what high-tech and low-tech mean without examples, and without examples, we may not be able to figure out which sorts of things are appropriate for homework assignments and which are not.[3]

Guidelines provided by experts during case collection can be thought of as general methods for achieving subgoals. Thought of this way, they can be used to guide collection of cases that operationalize the guideline—cases that show the several ways that a particular solution method can be carried out. For example, when teachers told us that grouping adolescent girls and boys together didn't work well, we asked them to tell us about the groupings they had encountered, what resulted, why they thought that happened, what they thought might work better, what they did to change things, how that worked, and so on, collecting a variety of experiences of groupings that work and those that don't.

A warning should also be given about the veracity of such guidelines. Sometimes the guidelines that experts think they use are applicable in only a subset of situations, and sometimes presented guidelines are inconsistent with one another. For example, in addition to telling us that adolescent boys and girls shouldn't be grouped with each other, teachers also told us that groups of adolescents shouldn't include only girls. Taking these two guidelines at face value, there is no way to put girls into groups—one guideline states that they can't be put with boys, and the other states that they can't be put with girls. Using these two guidelines to guide collection of cases, however, we found that the first applies to shy, quiet girls who are unsure of themselves in scientific environments and the second applies to groups of girls who are already good friends. But we also noted that in some circumstances, both guidelines seem to apply (e.g., when there is a group of shy, quiet girls who are unsure of themselves and also good friends). Some cases we collected distinguished what to do in situations where both guidelines seem to fit. Thus, even with guidelines available, it is useful for problem solvers to see cases that illustrate what works and doesn't work in the situation they are in. Seemingly conflicting guidelines, by themselves, are too confusing for any reasoner, human or machine, to use in solving problems.

---

3. As another example, readers can go back to the places in this chapter where they feel they need more concrete examples to know exactly how to carry out my guidelines. In general, they will find terms or instructions in those places that are hard to operationalize. In those places, readers would have felt more comfortable if I had presented a variety of examples to illustrate the ins and outs of making the instructions work. Perhaps this is the right place to apologize for those lacks.

15.5.2 Collecting Cases: What Constitutes a Case?

The final issue we attend to with respect to case collection is exactly what constitutes a case. Several guidelines with respect to this issue have been presented earlier in this section.

- A case presents an experience or situation that makes at least one point or teaches at least one lesson.
- A case needs in it enough information to make its point clear and usable. A reasoner should be able to derive benefit from the contents of a case.
- A case needs in it enough information to be indexed well.
- If a case makes too many points, it may be difficult to use. It may be worthwhile to divide such cases into several smaller cases that may then be connected to one another through pointers of appropriate kinds.

Still, there are some additional points to make about the constitution of cases.

First are implications about a case's contents. If a case is to be useful for anticipating problems or evaluating solutions, it must include outcome information. This was a point made in chapter 5 that bears repeating. When a case holds a description of a problem situation and the way that situation was solved or handled, it can be used to propose solutions to problems. Unless cases also hold information about what happened as a result of carrying out their solutions, however, there is no way for a reasoner to distinguish whether a suggested solution is good or not, to anticipate problems that might arise, or to use cases to project what might happen when a solution is carried out. It is often tempting to include in cases only problem descriptions and solutions, and indeed, for some case-based reasoners in some domains, this is sufficient. It behooves the developer, however, to consider whether outcome information is important to the task the case-based reasoner must do and to include such information in cases if it is needed. A help-desk application that only knows what solutions were suggested, for example, will repeat the same poor suggestions over and over to unsuspecting users. If the system also had some indication of whether its suggestions were working and under what circumstances they were failing, it could tailor its responses better.[4]

A second issue is the form of cases. This was discussed in chapter 5 also but bears repeating here. Cases need to be represented in a form that makes them usable to their users. If a case library's users are computer programs, then cases should have their entire contents represented symbolically in a form the program can manipulate well. If, however, a case library is to be used by people, the information in its cases should be represented so that human users can peruse them easily. Sometimes this means representing a case's contents as stories told in the language users speak. Some parts of a case's contents are best presented through drawings or photographs. Sometimes video clips provide a good way of representing their contents;

---

4. Related to this is a case collection issue. It is tempting to collect only cases with positive outcomes. But in order for a system to adequately anticipate problems and evaluation its solutions, cases with both positive and negative outcomes need to be present in the case library.

sometimes graphs and charts are necessary; other times, a combination of presentation means is needed.

The content of a case that needs to be presented to a user and the content that has to be represented symbolically are two different things. One needs to represent symbolically only those parts of a case that the computer needs to use. Other parts of the case can be represented in nonsymbolic ways. All cases need to have those parts of their descriptions that are used for indexing represented symbolically, because the computer is responsible for case storage and retrieval in all case-based systems. Beyond that, however, which parts are represented symbolically is dependent on the responsibilities of the case-based reasoner. If it needs to carry out adaptations, for example, then any parts of a case's description that are needed to successfully carry out an adaptation should be represented symbolically.

In our own group, we learned this lesson the hard way (Goel, Kolodner et al. 1991; Pearce et al. 1992; Domeshek and Kolodner 1991). In the original ARCHIE, we tried to use symbolic representations for everything. ARCHIE was supposed to help architects design office spaces. But its case representations were both too unwieldy and too unfamiliar for human experts to make use of, and the complexity and completeness that we insisted on in its symbolic representations made it hard for us to collect more than a handful of cases in the year of its development. In ARCHIE-2 (Domeshek and Kolodner 1992, 1993), only the indexes are machine-readable; the content of cases is in a format architects find easy to interact with. Though architects and other designers made polite noises about the original ARCHIE, they are quite excited by the potentials implied by ARCHIE-2. Though ARCHIE had a half dozen cases after over a year of work, we were able to collect and index several hundred cases in ARCHIE-2 once the qualities of cases and indexes were defined.

Finally, it is worth focusing on the narrative nature of cases. The cases we hear in conversations are stories that people tell to make relevant points. Such stories describe situations that teach lessons. They are used in conversation to suggest solutions, warn against solutions, suggest approaches to a problem, warn against certain approaches, and suggest what might happen in the future. We can view cases in a case library just as we view such stories. Stories hold our attention to the extent that they stick to their point and eventually make it. If they ramble and don't make their point easily, our attention drifts. Stories are useful to the extent that they hold just the right amount of information and are told at the right times. A story told at the wrong time bores us, as does a story with too much information. One with too little information makes us wonder why it was told.

This view of cases as narratives that teach lessons is instructive. It tells us about the tone cases in a system should have. Just as a story emphasizes some facts over others to make its points, so must cases emphasize some facts over others. Cases shouldn't just be conglomerations of facts about a situation—they are useful to the extent that they tell a story at the right level of detail to provide good advice at the right times.[5] Thinking of cases as stories that make a point provides some intuition about what to include or emphasize in case descriptions and indexes.

---

[5]. This, too, was a problem in ARCHIE—its cases were complex configurations of facts about a building, and the stories they told were hard to find.

15.6 CASE PRESENTATION AND HUMAN-COMPUTER INTERACTION

One of the major issues that must be addressed in building interactive systems is structuring the interaction between person and machine. When the machine is at the beck and call of the user, responsible only for responding to human queries, structuring interaction is easy. The user is provided with some way of asking questions of the computer, and the computer responds. When the needs of interaction become more complex, however, so too do the complexities of structuring that interaction.

Consider, for example, a system whose responsibility it is to help a person browse a library of cases or records, a relatively simple task. In browsing, a user looks around a library, trying to discover what is there or looking for some items that might be of particular interest. When a library is large, randomly looking at items in the library doesn't work—the browsing requires some structure. We can see the need for structure if we think about browsing the local branch of the public library. Because books that are about the same subject are near one another, we can look at one or a few books in a section of the library to get a feel for what is in that section, continuing to look at books in that section if they interest us or moving on to another section of the library if not. If the library wasn't structured this way, we wouldn't be able to browse it so easily.

To build a system to help someone with browsing, then, we have to impose some kind of structure on the items being browsed, making it easy for the user to see which items in the library are similar to the one he or she is perusing. We might also think about providing access to items that are related to the one being perused. A person browsing a library of historical events, for example, might next want to see another similar event, more about the one he or she is currently looking at, other events that happened at the same time, events that came before and led to this one, or events that came after, possibly resulting from this one. A person browsing a library of lesson plans and looking at a particular one might want to see other lesson plans on the same topic, other uses of the plan he or she is looking at, lesson plans that teach follow-up material, those that teach prerequisite material, and so on. Or, the user might want to concentrate on one aspect of the lesson plan, looking at other ways of carrying it out, expected results of carrying it out, materials addressing its topic, and so on.

A useful browsing system is likely to anticipate the needs of a user, perhaps taking the initiative in laying out for the user what he or she is likely to want to see next. Structuring the interaction between user and machine in a browsing system requires knowing what the needs of the user are likely to be. Similar issues come up in structuring interactions between users and computers in other kinds of systems. In the interactive case-based systems built to date, three models guide the structure of human-computer interactions to make them natural for the user.

- The domain under which the task is being carried out (Domeshek and Kolodner 1992)
- The task the user is engaged in (Ferguson et al. 1992)
- A model of conversation and conversational transitions that is appropriate to the purpose of the system (Schank 1977)

In general, the models work in combination with each other in any particular interface. A system will interact naturally with a user to the extent that the domain, task, and conversational models match that of the user. When the match is good, the options made available to the user at any point will correspond to what the user expects. The shared context of task, domain, and conversational models is meant to provide a basis for meaningful and useful communication.

Within the case-based reasoning community, several interactive systems that use conversational, task, and domain models to structure human-computer interaction have been built. For example, the ASK systems (Ferguson et al. 1992) simulate a conversation between a novice (the user) and an expert (the system). The interface anticipates the kinds of questions the novice might ask the expert in a specific context (i.e., having just heard a particular story or having entered the system at a particular point) and presents to the user those for which it has answers. The user chooses from that set to converse with the system. The system then answers as an expert speaking to a novice. The conversational model suggests the types of interactions the user might have with the system, and the task the user is engaged in and the domain in which it is being carried out suggest the content of the interactions. The conversational model might suggest, for example, that a user will want to know about the kinds of problems that come up when carrying out some plan that is the topic of conversation. The task and domain models know the particular problems that come up when carrying out a particular plan and list those problems on the screen. The user asks a question of the system by moving to a menu that features problems that arise and clicking on the particular problem he or she is interested in knowing more about. Figure 10 in chapter 2 shows a typical screen from an ASK system.

ARCHIE-2's (Domeshek and Kolodner 1992, 1993) conversational model is a forum of colleagues discussing common sets of issues. ARCHIE's task is design of artifacts. Its conversations, then, are issues oriented and centered on the artifact being designed. Its domain is design of buildings. ARCHIE presents the set of items that can be conversed about to the user by showing a schematic (graphical design plan) of a building with annotations attached to it. Each is marked according to the design issue, artifact component, and artifact subsystem it is about. The user designates a design issue and piece of the design that he or she wants to concentrate on by pointing and clicking on an annotation. The system then makes available the particular story about the building that the user designated, the design specs for that piece of the building, the guidelines guiding design of that piece of the building, and other instances of using the same guideline in similar circumstances. In essence, it anticipates that the user will want more detail about this topic, and it makes that detail available as a virtual conversation between colleagues working under similar circumstances and trading stories with each other. The user may choose to look at any of those or to use the description of the design story he or she is currently focusing on to construct a better description of the issues he or she is interested in (equivalent of changing the topic). Figure 11 in chapter 2 shows a typical screen from ARCHIE-2 and some of the options the user has for browsing.

SCI-ED's (Kolodner 1991b) task is planning science lessons. Its conversational model, like ARCHIE's, is a forum of colleagues. But its task, planning, requires it to converse about thematic issues that come up in planning (similar to the ASK systems) and in particular, to focus on potential problems that might arise while carrying out a plan. Its interface has two modes: one that suggests plans and the specific problems that have been encountered with each, another that focuses on issues of concern to teachers, concentrating on ways of dealing with those issues and the implications of each. The interface, like ARCHIE-2's, allows for trading of stories among colleagues, but rather than centering on an artifact, it helps the user to center on and identify the types of potential problems that might arise as plans are being carried out. Figure 15.1 shows one of SCI-ED's screens.

The big issues in building such interfaces are to select appropriate task, domain, and conversational models and to integrate these models with one another in the interface. Unfortunately, though several systems have been built, there is little in the way of general principles for integrating such models in an interface that structures interactions between people and machines in natural ways. We can, however, relate the issues that we have addressed in deriving individual systems and make suggestions about dealing with each.

Is there a metaphor (familiar to the user) for describing the task the system will support, and can that metaphor be reified in the user interface?[6]   One metaphor for browsing a case library, hypertext system, or database is the metaphor of *browsing in a bookstore or a library*. We look around to see what is there, eventually zeroing in on a part of the library where we think we will have the most interest. We then move around to other areas of the library that have related materials. When we find an area with books that are of interest, we examine those books more closely.

Making such a browsing metaphor work requires anticipating the items a user will consider related to one another, that is, anticipating the transitions a user will want to make from item to item during browsing. The model of the task the user is working on while browsing provides one set of clues for determining what items are related to what other ones. The structure of an item the user is reasoning about as he or she browses the interface provides another set of clues. The ASK systems and SCI-ED use a model of the task to determine which items in the case library are related. ARCHIE-2 uses a combination of the task and the artifact being reasoned about.

A metaphor for getting quickly to the information one wants is the *table of contents* metaphor. One looks in the table of contents of a book to find the chapter most likely to hold the information one wants. One then goes to that chapter and browses it. Another metaphor for quick access is the *book index* metaphor, equivalent to the card catalog metaphor. We look in the index to a book or in a card catalog in the library to find the place where the information we are looking for is most likely to reside, and we begin our search there. Each of the systems discussed also provides one or both of these kinds of access. The ASK systems and SCI-ED give users a menu of interests to examine when they enter the system and use their designations of interest to direct them to an appropriate part of the case library. ARCHIE-2 guides users in using its indexing vocabulary to designate what they are interested in.

What interface-level tasks will the user use the system for?   In browsing, the interface-level task is simple: looking at items. An interface for browsing, then, needs to allow users to easily examine its items. They should be presented nicely, with important information first, and so on. This requires discovering the sorts of presentations the user finds most useful. Other interface-level tasks have other requirements.

------

6. The term metaphor comes from discussion with Albert Badre.

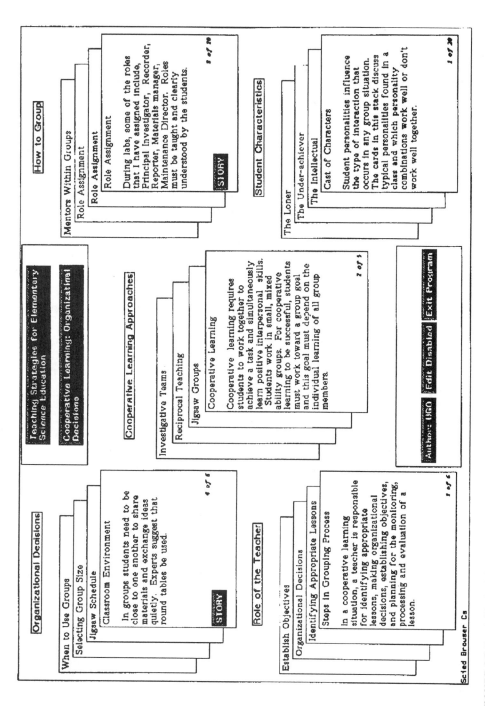

FIGURE 15.1 A Typical Screen from SCI-ED

What kinds of transitions are there between the interface-level tasks? An interface should support both the tasks that the user will use it for and the transitions between them. The complexity in browsing is in the transitions between looking at different items. Thus, for the browsing task, we study the movements a user makes or might want to make between items in the library, and we build an interface that makes those movements easy—that anticipates the movements the user will want to make. In each of the systems discussed earlier, this means displaying for the user what other similar and/or related items reside in the library and allowing the user to choose one. Dealing with this issue requires identifying different types of transitions between interface-level tasks a person uses the case library for and the ways each can be supported in an interface. These are the same transitions that we said it was necessary to designate to make the *browsing the library* metaphor work. They can be determined by looking at the reasoning task the user is engaged in while using the system and the structure of the items the reasoner is reasoning about.

What broader reasoning task is the user engaged in when using the computer system? Knowing what reasoning task the user is engaged in when using the system allows the conversation between the user and the system to be tailored to the user's needs. In particular, as stated earlier, the task the reasoner is engaged in while using a browsing system provides specifics about which transitions between examination tasks should be anticipated in the interface. In browsing, knowing what the user means to do with the things that are examined allows the system to anticipate what the user will want to see next. A person engaged in conceptual design or contingency planning, for example, will want to use examples of poor outcomes to anticipate problems that might come up in a design or plan. Once problems are anticipated, the user is likely to want to find ways to bypass those problems. If the system knows the task, the system can make sure that the user is given the option of moving from examining items that can help with anticipating problems to examining those that can help fix problems once they are identified. Different tasks will be naturally supported in different ways. We need to identify tasks, and for each, the several ways of supporting it.

What role is the system playing? In the ASK systems, designed to train novices at doing some task by allowing them to browse the set of issues they need to learn about, the system plays the role of expert teacher. In ARCHIE and SCI-ED, designed to aid users at a task they already know how to do, the system plays the role of moderator. The role of the system with respect to the user can suggest viable conversational models. For example, an expert teacher can answer questions, pose problems to a student, look over a student's shoulder as he or she solves a problem and make suggestions, and so on. There are one or several models of interaction associated with each type of interaction.

What level of initiative should the user take? What level of initiative should the system take? A system can dictate what the human user should do next, a user can take sole initiative, letting the system know what he or she wants it to do, or initiative can be shared. In browsing, there are a number of things a person might want to see next, and people will differ in what they want to see. Thus, it would be unnatural for a system to dictate what the user should see next. But a system that can anticipate what the user is likely to want to see and provide appropriate choices makes sense. Initiative is taken by the user, with the system anticipating the user's needs. In some training systems, by contrast, it may make more sense for the system to take more initiative in conversation.

What sorts of individual interactions and presentations are most natural and beneficial for the user?   In some situations, textual presentation of information makes sense; in others some sort of visual presentation is more natural; in others a combination is needed. Cases need to be presented to users in ways that allow users to easily take them in, understand them, and glean their points. If users are used to looking at certain kinds of visual representations as they do their tasks, then the most natural ways of presenting cases might involve using those sorts of visual representations. Designers, for example, are used to reading and creating drawings. When they tell each other stories, they use a combination of drawings and words to make their points. System designers should take note of the ways in which their users interact naturally with each other in designing presentations.

It should be noted that the issues that arise in building interactive case-based systems are not a whole lot different from those that arise in building other interactive systems. Browsing systems, whether case-based or of some other sort, need to anticipate the needs of their users. Training systems, whether case-based or some other sort, need to structure interactions naturally with their users. The same holds true of any aiding system that someone might build. Users can get used to almost any interface that we build for them, but some will allow them to get their jobs done easily, and others will make it more difficult. If we want our interactive systems to interact with users in a beneficial way, then we will have to figure out how the task the user is working on and the domain he or she is working in effect interaction, and we will have to define the kinds of conversations a user can have with a system.

15.7 SUMMARY

Case-based problem-solving systems can be fully automated or interactive, requiring the talents of both the human user and the computer. They can be used to solve problems or for training. Whatever the choice, the single biggest factor in making the case-based system work is its case library. The nitty-gritty requirements for building a case library include collecting cases and indexing them; testing the coverage of the case library, its indexing scheme, and the usefulness of suggestions made by individual cases; maintaining the integrity of the case library over time by collecting new cases and gathering feedback; and, if the system is interactive, designing an interface that makes interaction between the human user and the system natural, beneficial, and easy.

16

Conclusions, Opportunities, Challenges

Case-based reasoning is both a cognitively plausible model of reasoning and a method for building intelligent systems. It is grounded in commonsense premises and observations of human cognition and has applicability to a variety of reasoning tasks, providing for each a means of attaining increased efficiency and better performance.

Case-based reasoning integrates problem solving, understanding, learning, and memory into one framework. Because more specific knowledge provides more easily usable advice than abstract knowledge, the model advocates attempting use of the most specific knowledge available to reason before attempting to apply more abstract knowledge. Because using bigger chunks of knowledge to reason is more efficient than piecing together many smaller chunks, it advocates attempting use of the biggest chunks of knowledge available before attempting application of smaller chunks of knowledge. The most specific biggest chunks of knowledge we have available to us as people are our experiences, and case-based reasoning identifies the reasoning we do based on recalled experiences as the primary reasoning process.

Recalled cases are used both to interpret situations and to solve the problems they pose. The common ways we reason with cases are to adapt old solutions to fit new situations, to use the outcomes of old situations to warn of the potential for failure in a new situation, to compare and contrast cases to each other and to a new situation in order to interpret a new situation or critique a solution, and to merge pieces of several cases to form new solutions.

This model of reasoning guides us in building case-based systems. The case library acts as memory in our systems. It may hold just cases or cases and the general knowledge derived from them. Cases can record specific situations or can represent composite, prototype, or even abstractly defined situations. Whatever they are, items in the case library are indexed such that they can be recognized as applicable when appropriate. The indexes of a case are based on an interpretation of the case and analysis of the kinds of situations in which that interpretation would prove beneficial in guiding reasoning.

Situation assessment procedures provide understanding capabilities in our systems. They analyze and interpret new situations to extract a rendering consistent with case representations and indexes in the case library. Search, matching, and selection algorithms retrieve cases from the case library, using the description of a new situation as a retrieval key to retrieve similar cases and the task the reasoner is engaged in as a means of selecting useful cases from among those. Adaptation heuristics make old solutions fit new situations. Interpretive procedures allow cases to help with situation assessment and analysis of the pros and cons of proposed solutions. When reasoning is complete, a new case, representing the new experience, is added back into the case library, allowing enhanced reasoning in future similar situations.

The quality of a case-based reasoner's reasoning depends on several things:

- The experiences it has had or those that have been put into its library
- Its ability to understand new situations in terms of those old experiences
- Its adeptness at adaptation
- Its adeptness at evaluation and repair
- Its ability to integrate new experiences into its memory appropriately

Any case-based system, whether automated or interactive, needs to deal with these five issues. In interactive systems, it is the combination of capabilities possessed by the system and the user that determine how good the solutions of the combined human-machine system will be. The design of an appropriate interactive system depends on the capabilities of the human users who will use it. The system needs to provide what the human user is uninterested in or does poorly.

Much of this book has concentrated on the component parts of a case-based system that achieve the capabilities listed here. A case-based reasoner is more than the sum of its parts, however. Certainly, we must understand each of the parts and how they work, but now that those parts are understood, we must also examine the case-based reasoner as a whole, looking for what emerges when those component parts are put together. In the remainder of this concluding chapter, we do that in three parts.

We begin by examining learning in the case-based reasoning paradigm. Learning is both the major emergent behavior of a case-based reasoner and a behavior that we aim all the reasoner's component parts toward supporting. A case-based reasoner gets more efficient over time as a result of collecting more experiences and indexing them properly. It can get more effective over time if, in addition, it analyzes the effects of its solutions and keeps track of what worked and didn't work and why. There are few special processes needed to make learning happen in a case-based system. Effective learning can happen as a by-product of the reasoning and memory update. We examine how learning emerges in that way and then consider enhancements to case-based reasoning that can make learning even more effective.

We continue by drawing conclusions about the behavior one can expect from a case-based reasoner and the situations in which it is advantageous to build case-based systems—the state of the art in building case-based reasoning systems.

Finally, we consider the opportunities and challenges posed by case-based reasoning and the open research questions. There are some areas that we already know need more attention, for example, the merging of pieces of disparate cases and the creation of highly novel solutions in the research arena and the development of protocols for case library creation and maintenance in the engineering arena. In addition, when we look to the future, we can see the potential of case-based reasoning in many areas that have not been considered. Each area of opportunity poses challenges for the paradigm. We end with this set of open questions.

There are two other ways readers can pull together the things they've learned separately in the last ten or eleven chapters. One way is by rereading or skimming chapters 1 through 4, this time keeping in mind the technical details, issues, and approaches presented about each of the component parts. The other way is by examining the Appendix. It holds a case library of case-based reasoning systems. Most interesting, perhaps, are the lessons learned from working on many of these systems. Some are lessons about how to make users want to use a system; others are lessons about what can be accomplished by combining various retrieval, indexing, and adaptation alternatives; others are lessons about case collection and case representation.

16.1 CASE-BASED REASONING AND LEARNING

A case-based reasoner learns primarily by accumulating new experiences in its memory and indexing them appropriately. Learning is, thus, to at least some extent, an emergent behavior that arises from the case-based reasoner's normal functioning. On the other hand, the extent of learning a case-based reasoner can do is dependent on the range of experiences it has had, its ability to explain and repair failures, its ability to explain its successes, and its ability to generate good indexes. The better competence a reasoner has in doing those tasks, the more effective a learner it can be.

Consider, first, for example, range of experience. A reasoner does not learn merely by performing the same task over and over again. The broader the range of experiences it has had, the broader the range of situations it will be able to reason about. On the other hand, a reasoner that is broad but not deep may not be able to recognize the subtleties of a situation. The more subtle the differences between the cases a reasoner has experienced, the more competent it will be at recognizing those subtle differences and making more relevant and specific inferences.[1]

A system that is asked to solve a problem outside its range of experience might be able to apply adaptation heuristics to solve it based on some case or cases it already knows, or it might fail. If it is able to solve the problem, entering the new situation and its solution into memory as a case will allow the reasoner to solve such problems more efficiently in the future—there will be less adaptation needed. If it fails to solve the problem, the reasoner might or might not be able to learn by itself. Whether it can learn and how much it can learn will depend on the feedback it has available to it, the explanatory procedures it has available for interpreting that feedback, and its ability to do repair.

---

1. These maxims hold true whether the cases that are being accumulated and added to a case library are those the case-based reasoning system has solved by itself or cases are added by a knowledge engineer. As stated in chapter 15, a case library should be seeded with cases that represent the range of responsibilities the reasoner will have and the range of situations in which those responsibilities will have to be carried out.

A system that can explain its failures and figure out how it could have avoided the problem can insert the new situation into its case library, indexing it to enable itself to recognize in the future that a failure situation is imminent and to avoid it. If, in addition, the reasoner can figure out what would fix the problem, that information can be inserted into the case, and the case can be indexed so that its repair can be recalled as a potential solution in similar situations.

In addition, when failure cases are appropriately indexed in a case library, they help a reasoner realize what it should pay attention to in a situation. If a reasoner has been introduced to a variety of situations that differ in subtle ways, has been allowed to fail, and has been able to explain its failures, it has the opportunity to become quite accurate in its reasoning—failure cases it is reminded of will point out to it what it should be paying attention to as it reasons and aim it toward an appropriate solution. PROTOS's difference links enable this kind of reasoning. MEDIATOR's and CHEF's storage of both failed cases and their repairs enables them to focus their attention wisely.

One shouldn't be surprised to notice such behavior in a system that is exposed to subtly different situations. One might want to take advantage of this learning behavior while initially training a system (or a person). PROTOS is trained this way. When it is unable to recognize or explain its mistakes by itself, its human trainer fills in the missing knowledge.

The ability to explain why solutions succeed is also advantageous for a reasoner. Explaining why solutions succeed results in indexes being chosen for a case that reflect the full range of situations in which it can be useful. Indexes chosen based on such explanations allow a reasoner to recognize opportunities for reusing its old solutions. They can also give reasoners the ability to recognize opportunities for achieving background goals. Several case-based planners that integrate reasoning and action (e.g., TRUCKER, RUNNER, EXPEDITOR) concentrate on the indexing necessary to recognize such opportunities.

Each of these capabilities allows the reasoner to choose indexes wisely for new cases when they are added to the case library, the most important capability for enhancing case-based reasoner performance. Cases that are accumulated are only as good as the indexes associated with them. It is the indexes, after all, that allow retrieval under designated circumstances. But indexing new cases in the case library is not the only indexing issue we must address in case-based learning. Another important learning issue is the re-indexing of cases that are already in memory. When a case is recalled and proves inappropriate (either because it cannot be used or because it is used and results in a failure), one might want to re-index the case so that it is no longer recalled in situations such as the current one. When it is pointed out to a reasoner that it should have used a case it did not recall, that case should be re-indexed so that it will be recalled in the future in similar situations. When use of a case points out something new about it that was not known previously, it should be re-indexed to reflect that new knowledge. PROTOS and CELIA both re-index their cases in these circumstances. So do several other systems we have not focused on in the book (e.g., AQUA).

In addition to the learning that happens as a natural consequence of reasoning, one can think about enhancing a case-based system with learning capabilities designed to make its components work more efficiently. For example, one could put controls on which cases are added to a case library so that retrieval can be kept as efficient as possible. One could have a reasoner learn which solutions are costly to carry out and which are inexpensive (to enhance its selection of cases), which elaborations are costly to carry out and which are inexpensive (to make situation assessment more efficient), and so on. One can also use cases to enhance general knowledge.

Consider, first, the controls one might put on accumulation of cases. Some cases added to a case library might add to the library without adding to the capabilities of a system. Such cases might or might not affect the efficiency of retrieval, depending on the retrieval algorithm. They certainly require additional storage capacity. Sometimes it is worthwhile to make decisions about whether a new case belongs in the case library or not. It belongs if it allows the reasoner to do something it could not do before or to become more efficient at something it did before. Or, a reasoner could be proactive about accumulating cases. If a reasoner knows there are some things it is incapable of or has trouble with, it can seek to put itself in situations in which it will acquire appropriate cases, or it can look out for cases that can help it with its troublesome tasks.

IVY (Hunter 1989a, 1989b, 1990; Ram and Hunter 1992) and AQUA (Ram 1990a, 1990b, 1991, 1993; Ram and Leake 1991) accumulate those cases they need to enhance their reasoning. IVY diagnoses liver diseases from X rays. It adds to its case library those cases that it encounters that help it with tasks that it knows it has had problems with in the past. Sometimes it is unable to differentiate between several diagnoses, for example. When that happens, it generates a goal for itself to learn that differentiation. It recognizes any case that can help it achieve that goal as a significant addition to the case library. AQUA, which reads news stories, generates questions as it is reading—questions about the motivations of those it is reading about. If it cannot find answers in the article it is reading, the knowledge acquisition goal generated in the course of understanding remains active as it reads later stories. It recognizes as significant any story it reads that addresses that goal.

Notice that learning in these systems is proactive and controlled and is guided by the needs of the reasoner. Each system generates knowledge goals and accumulates those cases that can help it achieve those goals. IVY needs its new cases to help it diagnose; AQUA needs the new cases it accumulates to help it understand a situation it is confused about. In addition, much of the reasoning that must be done to learn happens in the normal course of the problem solving or understanding the program does. There is little specialized mechanism that is built-in just for learning. Both programs generate their knowledge acquisition goals in the process of reasoning. They use them as they continue reasoning about the current case or article. If the knowledge acquisition goal is not satisfied by the current situation, it remains active to guide later learning.

Another set of enhancements that several researchers in the case-based reasoning community have addressed are those that enhance situation assessment. In situation assessment, the reasoner elaborates a situation description to make its description fit other case descriptions in its case library, to allow further traversal of memory structures, or to differentiate between several cases competing for retrieval. Some elaborations are costly, requiring either complex inference or complex action; others are less expensive. A system that keeps track of the cost of each of its elaborations and the degree to which each is advantageous can guide its situation assessment procedures in elaborating the most useful features and preferring those that are less costly. ANON's and CASCADE's procedures for doing this were presented in chapter 9.

Cases can also be used to increase general knowledge. Programs that use redundant discrimination networks and shared feature hierarchies (e.g., CYRUS, MEDIATOR, PERSUADER, JULIA), for example, accumulate generalizations as they add to their case libraries. Such generalized knowledge is useful in controlling indexing and in making elaborations during situation assessment. IVY, ANON, and CELIA keep track of the knowledge they need as they reason. They accumulate not only cases but also general knowledge they know they need that is embedded in those cases. Though these systems rely primarily on cases to reason, they each also use some other knowledge, and each has a complex control structure. When they are aware of some piece of knowledge they need to enhance their control structures or to enhance other means of reasoning, they derive that from cases also.

Overall, accumulating the right cases, extracting the appropriate knowledge from them, and making sure cases are indexed advantageously results in several different enhanced performance behaviors:

- The ability to perform in more situations
- Increased efficiency in familiar situations
- Increased ability to cope in problematic situations
- Increased ability to take advantage of opportunities as they arise

16.2 CONCLUSIONS

The combination of reasoning and learning behavior in a case-based system, the emphasis on cases as the preferred form of knowledge, and the ability of cases to hold experience-acquired associative knowledge leads to several conclusions about applicability and capability of case-based reasoning.

CBR allows autonomous systems to deal with tasks that are not easily formalizable. In many domains, the rules, or hard knowledge, of the domain have not yet been formalized (e.g., CLAVIER's domain). In other domains, the formalization is so abstract that it is hard to use, because there is so much variation in the way abstract concepts show themselves (e.g., in PROTOS's domain). CBR allows problem solving in such domains by basing reasoning on experience in the domain rather than on formal models. Cases capture associations between situations, solutions, and outcomes, capturing an informal understanding of the domain at a concrete level.

For some tasks, CBR complements model-based or rule-based reasoning. We saw this in several domains and across several tasks. In reasoning about devices, for example, causal models provide much knowledge about how devices work, but they don't organize their knowledge in a way that makes design of new devices or debugging of existing ones efficient. Case memories, on the other hand, organize device knowledge in a way that facilitates generation of solutions. Cases associate symptoms with diagnoses for debugging, associate design goals and constraints with design plans for design. Their indexes capture the situations in which one would use the associations captured in any particular case. Cases can easily suggest solutions; the causal knowledge found in models lends itself most easily to choosing indexes for cases, guiding adaptation, and verifying solutions. CASEY and KRITIK provide two examples of the complementarity of case knowledge and model knowledge. Legal reasoning provides an example of the complementarity of case knowledge and knowledge captured in general-purpose rules. In law, rules exist, but they are expressed in terms of ill-defined concepts, concepts that can be defined only within specific contexts. Unless those concepts can be defined, the rules cannot be used. Examples, in the form of cases, illustrate the meanings of ill-defined concepts.

CBR systems are efficient and accurate in situations they are familiar with.
When similar problem statements call for similar solutions, case-based reasoning has shown itself efficient and accurate when asked to solve problems similar to those it has seen before. CASEY and HYPO showed this vividly over fairly small case libraries. More recently, CLA-VIER and PRODIGY/ANALOGY have illustrated efficiency and accuracy in more complex problem-solving situations and over larger case libraries. Of course, there are requirements in keeping a case-based reasoner accurate and efficient. The effects of carrying out a case's solutions must be analyzed, and cases must know how well their previous solutions worked and in what ways they failed. If failure cases are allowed to remain in a case library without such annotations on them, the case-based reasoner would repeat poor solutions as easily as it repeated good ones, decreasing overall accuracy and believability. In addition, good indexing is important. The efficiency of a case-based reasoner is dependent on the accessibility of its cases—indexes on new cases should not hurt accessibility.

Because case-based reasoning provides a commonsense, intuitive model of problem solving, knowledge acquisition is facilitated in a case-based system. People can easily report the cases they use to reason and the cases they have encountered on the job. Those who have built case-based and rule-based systems for the same tasks have reported that building the case-based system was substantially easier (e.g., CASCADE, PRISM). Of course, cases are not the only knowledge a case-based reasoner has. It might also have semantic networks representing the relationships among its representational concepts, a causal model to guide adaptation, special-purpose adaptation heuristics, and so on. Overall, however, experience has been that knowledge acquisition is an easier task in a case-based system than in other systems.

Because case-based reasoning is a natural, intuitive process for people, interactive aiding systems that help a user solve a problem work well. As stated previously, such systems can do retrieval only, acting to augment the human user's memory, or they can provide tools for situation assessment, for choosing the most appropriate cases from those retrieved, for adapting retrieved solutions or for trying out adaptations, for comparing and contrasting, for deciding what is important to focus on, and so on. It is important, in developing such systems, to think of the human user and the machine together as a combined case-based reasoning system. Keeping this in mind, one provides for the person what the person requires to get the job done. In more situations than we expected, this means giving the human problem solver a great deal of autonomy—providing the human with choices to examine rather than

just one case or solution, allowing the human user to designate what he or she wants to do next, and so on. Many of the lessons learned listed in the Appendix are about what it takes to make people comfortable using a case-based aiding or advisory system.

Case-based systems can provide corporate memory for an organization.   When case-based systems are augmented by the experiences of those who use them, they can become a corporate memory for the organization that is using them, allowing personnel to share their experiences. CLAVIER is our best illustration of this phenomenon to date.

Case-based systems can easily be engineered to avoid mistakes made previously and, when that's not possible, to repair their mistakes.   A case-based system can avoid mistakes when its case library holds cases illustrating failure situations. One avoids mistakes by indexing failure cases so that they can be recalled when the mistake is about to arise, before it happens. The extent to which the reasoner can avoid previously made mistakes depends on the way those cases are indexed. The better a case's indexes correspond to the range of situations the case is applicable to, the better at avoidance the system will be. But indexes must also be concrete enough to be recognizable in the full range of situations the case is applicable to in order for the case to be fully useful.[2] When indexes are represented too abstractly, or when the full range of situations in which a case is applicable can't be anticipated, a case might not be recalled at times when it could predict failure. If cases also record the way in which failures are repaired and are indexed according to the kinds of situations in which such repairs are appropriate, then, though a system might not be able to avoid every mistake, it will have the opportunity to use cases to help it repair its mistakes.

Case-based reasoners can easily be engineered to notice and grab opportunities once they have shown themselves.   Grabbing opportunities is the flip side of avoiding mistakes. Mistakes are things that go wrong—unpleasant surprises. Opportunities are pleasant surprises. The ability to recognize opportunities arises from noticing, analyzing, and indexing cases in which pleasant surprises occur. Sometimes positive things happen that were unexpected and not planned for. A father who notices that reading a particular book to his child relaxes the child and makes it easy for her to sleep might want to repeat reading this book when he must get his child to sleep quickly. Indexing the situation by both the goal he planned to achieve and the one that was achieved but not planned for will allow that. Noticing these situations, and noticing what it was about the situation that allowed the unexpected positive things to happen provides grist for indexing the case so that the reasoner can anticipate and take advantage of the added opportunity. Other times, a reasoner creates opportunities for itself. For example, a planner that interleaves one task with another creates for itself a new plan that combines the achievement of several goals. Having created that new plan, it can take advantage of it at a later time when it has both goals at the same time again.

---

2. That is, the symbols used for indexing must represent concepts that naturally arise in descriptions of situations or in the normal course of reasoning, and they must cover the full range of applicability of the case.

Case-based systems can learn from their experiences and are useful in situations in which learning is important. This summarizes the last section and also the last two conclusions. In a case-based system, performance is enhanced by reusing old solutions in new situations and by anticipating, and thereby avoiding, problems that have arisen in the past. It is further enhanced by noticing pleasant surprises and indexing them to enhance opportunities in the future. Learning happens, for the most part, as a by-product of other reasoning. Storing new experiences in the case library allows reuse of old solutions. Noticing and analyzing failures and storing that analysis along with the cases they go with allows avoidance of previous failures. Of course, indexing must be done keeping learning in mind. Cases must be indexed in ways that facilitate those behaviors that are expected of a system.

16.3 CHALLENGES AND OPPORTUNITIES

Over the past few years, the academic case-based reasoning community has been creating case-based systems with more and more sophisticated capabilities. Systems have been built that can do sophisticated scheduling, design, planning, and legal reasoning. In the commercial world, the first case-based systems have been fielded and are finding acceptance. There is thus great reason for optimism. As in the creation of any new technology, however, there is a gap between the sophistication of academic case-based reasoners and those that are actually fielded. The fielded systems use simple case representations and the simpler of the implementation procedures, and the majority of the effort in building these systems goes into their interface. Often, this is because the techniques developed in the academic world are overspecialized or have not been made to work in real-world environments. In addition, there are many issues that research in case-based reasoning has not yet solved.

There are thus several kinds of challenges that await us in the coming years in bringing case-based systems to their full potential. Some are knowledge engineering issues, those that must be confronted to make the building and fielding and use of case-based reasoning systems easier. Others are technological issues, those that must be confronted to make case-based reasoning scale up, in size of case library, in speed of retrieval, in ability to deal with multiple domains, and so on. Others have to do with expanding the capabilities case-based reasoning can provide through the further exploration of fundamental issues.

16.3.1 Knowledge Engineering Issues

We need tools! We need tools for making case collection easier, tools for making indexing easier, and tools for designing case-based systems of various kinds; tools for building automated systems and tools for building interactive ones; tools for building planning systems, tools for building design systems, tools for building scheduling systems, and so on; tools to help with creations of solutions and tools to help with evaluation; tools to help with adaptation and tools to help with merging. Systems that have been built in academia, though sophisticated, don't have the robustness needed for commercial systems. Tools provided by current commercial systems support case acquisition and case retrieval well, and some support simple adaptation and evaluation. They have proven quite useful in building help-desk applications and other applications that primarily require retrieval. But none are up to supporting the complexities of sophisticated planning, design, or scheduling. Fielded systems in those areas have all been built from scratch. The know-how being collected by people building those systems needs to be migrated into the next generation of general-purpose tools.

We need better methodologies for case collection.   In chapter 15, I presented guidelines for seeding a case library, hints about how to collect cases, and reassurances about the times it gets hard. Just as methodologies were created for knowledge acquisition in rule-based expert systems, we need methodologies for interviewing experts and collecting cases.

We need tools and protocols for case library maintenance.   Who can update a case library? When does it get done? How can it be managed in a distributed system? These and other issues confront those whose systems have multiple users in multiple locations. In order for a case library to function well as a corporate memory, in order for it to become better over time or provide more advice over time, it must be augmented with its experiences. But in an interactive system, it is hard to know whether results are due to suggestions made by a system or to the capabilities or lack of capability of those adapting or carrying out system-provided suggestions. There must be a protocol for deciding which cases should be added to a case library, and tools are needed to make the process easy. In addition, in a widely dispersed system, the same issues arise that arise in large distributed database systems. The case library must be updated without getting in the way of users using it at the time.

16.3.2 Scaleup: The Major Technological Issue

The biggest technological issue is scaleup. How can we make the retrieval algorithms that work for hundreds of cases work efficiently enough for tens of thousands of cases?

One approach is to speed up retrieval through the use of parallel retrieval schemes. It is necessary, in such solutions, to make sure that partial-match capabilities are not lost and that search is not sped up at the expense of selection. Parallel retrieval schemes that disallow partial match along case dimensions require representations that capture dimensions of partial match in their specifications[3] Parallel search processes that retrieve large numbers of cases move the burden of choosing appropriate cases from search algorithms to selection heuristics. Unless selection can also be made efficient, parallel search will not be sufficient for scaleup. Some approaches currently being attempted use graph-matching algorithms to speed up retrieval (e.g., CADET, CAPER).

Another approach is to simplify the structure of representations so that matching procedures can be made efficient. Representations must be able to fully express whatever concepts an index needs to convey, but perhaps without the embeddings that make matching difficult. Abby's approach to simplifying representations is to represent concepts as sets of binary microfeatures and to represent indexes as vectors of microfeatures. An approach to simplifying representations, coupled with parallel search schemes, may work quite well.

---

3. See discussion in chapter 8, section 3.

Another approach is to organize case libraries in database systems, depending on the database to provide efficient retrieval. Some in the community believe that current database systems are sufficient for allowing this to happen, and indeed, for some implementations they are. In case-based browsing systems, such as the ASK systems, ARCHIE, SCI-ED, and ORCA, the connections between cases are hard-wired after an initial phase of capturing the relationships between cases. Partial matching is done only when the system is being built, not at browsing time. Existing database implementations are probably sufficient for achieving efficiency in systems such as these.[4] When much partial matching must be done in the normal course of reasoning, however, existing approaches may not have enough power. Even with simplified representations (e.g., vectors of microfeatures), current technology may not be up to it—vectors of microfeatures are much larger than database records commonly in use. Database and case-based reasoning researchers need to work together to determine the kinds of features a database that supports case-based reasoning must have and to create new database paradigms.

Another approach to the scaleup problem has been to have reasoners store only those cases that it knows expand its capabilities in significant ways. Rather than storing all cases that are encountered, only those that achieve a potential goal of the reasoner in a new way or significantly speed up processing are stored. This is AQUA's and IVY's approach. Effort is needed to determine which cases to keep in such a scheme, a one-time cost, but less effort is required at retrieval time (a repeating cost). Implementation of such a scheme requires determining the processing trade-offs one wants to make. Should cases that only speed up processing without changing the answers that are obtained be kept? How much should a case speed up processing before it is worth keeping? The answers to these questions depend on whether retrieval time or adaptation time are more important to make more efficient and whether conservation of time or conservation of space is more important. Should cases that suggest hard-to-derive solutions that repeat very infrequently be kept? It depends again on the space-time trade-offs one needs to make. Within the machine learning community, this issue is called the *utility problem*. We want to accrue only as much knowledge (here, cases) as will help the system reason better in the future without degrading performance. To solve the utility problem, one must define the dimensions upon which utility is measured.

16.3.3 Fundamental Issues and Enhanced Capabilities

Finally, we examine the challenges that arise from attempting to enhance the capabilities of case-based reasoners and from carrying their implications into new arenas. Throughout the book, questions have arisen to which only commonsense answers or guidelines have been provided, for example, the automatic derivation of indexes, the extraction of cases from a dynamic environment, the level of abstraction of indexes. Deriving better solutions to this set of problems will be required before we can bring our case-based systems to their full potential. This section addresses those fundamental issues and introduces some additional challenges.

---

4. Of course, it would be nice to move beyond hard-wired relationships, allowing creation of dynamically changing systems.

Indexing Issues

Automating index selection.   As stated in chapter 7, our automated index selection procedures are not as good as people yet, except for narrow situations in which all the knowledge needed for explanation of failure and explanation-based selection of indexes is built-in. In particular, what is missing are general-purpose methods for analyzing situations and extracting from them explanations of why they failed and why they succeeded. Systems with special-purpose explanation facilities in them (e.g., CHEF) are able to do a good job of choosing their own indexes, but general-purpose mechanisms have not yet been achieved. This provides a major challenge as we attempt to enhance our case-based systems.

Determining the optimal level of abstraction for indexes.   The presentation of guidelines for index selection states that they should be concrete enough to be recognizable and abstract enough to provide coverage; that is, concepts used as indexes should be those that are naturally encountered or derived in the normal course of reasoning. We use our intuitions to determine this as we index cases by hand. We could, in theory, use the models of reasoning processes built into our case-based systems to have automated systems determine this level automatically, but it has only been done in several specialized situations. We need general-purpose methods for accomplishing this task. We may also need additional research to refine the commonsense set of guidelines.

The presentation of guidelines also stated that indexes should be predictive and make useful predictions. We used that guideline to formulate a procedure for choosing indexes based on the points a case can make and the situations in which it can make those points. The specifications that arise from following that procedure combine readily available surface descriptors of a situation with derived more abstract descriptions of situations. It is clear that both surface and abstract features play a role in indexing, that indexes can describe objects and concepts in a situation and their relationships to one another. From the pragmatic point of view, we see the need for indexes to convey all these things. But we still don't know the relative importance of each or whether there are general-purpose preference relationships that ought to be derived to help with ranking of partial matches.

Determining general-purpose indexing vocabularies.   For the most part, we must derive vocabularies for indexing for each new domain and task we tackle. The UIF provides a general-purpose vocabulary for social situations. We need more attempts of this sort, both within specific domains and across domains. We need to derive both vocabulary for domains and better methodologies for analyzing domains and tasks and extracting their relevant descriptors.

Cross-domain reminding and use of cross-domain cases.   Allowing systems to analogically use cases from other domains to solve their problems is another enhancement we are attempting but haven't achieved yet. The UIF was an attempt to represent cases from different domains using a universal vocabulary. It shows promise in intentional domains, but few systems actually use cases from domains other than their own. And the UIF doesn't address the representation of cases from outside the realm of social situations. A particular area where cross-domain retrieval would be useful is design. Many of the innovations in design come from applying the lessons from one domain to another. We must develop a means of automatically retrieving cross-domain design cases before our case-based systems can do this. This requires that we identify the abstract descriptors (vocabulary) that tie descriptions of artifacts together. Work is beginning on this endeavor (e.g., in ARCHIE-2 and KRITIK-2), but there is much more to be done.

Manipulating Cases

Deriving innovative or creative solutions, merging pieces of many old solutions with one another. We are beginning to be able to derive innovative solutions in our case-based systems by merging the pieces of several old cases. JULIA does that, as does CADET. But we still don't know the full range of needs for making that happen. Our systems are innovative when we can provide them with an overall solution framework for holding pieces of several cases together and when the pieces don't interact strongly with one another. But we still don't know how to derive frameworks—the ones our systems use now are built-in. Deriving truly creative solutions requires that we study further the processes of brainstorming, merging, solution evaluation, and cross-domain analogy.

Adaptation rules for new domains and tasks. Chapter 11 presented ten different means of adaptation. Some, such as reinstantiation, local search, and derivational replay, are general-purpose methods. Others, such as the application of special-purpose heuristics, are domain- and task-specific. Others, such as parameter adjustment and model-guided repair, are general-purpose but require specialized, domain-specific knowledge. The list of approaches to adaptation gives us a start as we attempt to derive adaptation heuristics for new domains. But it is not yet enough. In particular, we still are not able to fully list the kinds of adaptations special-purpose heuristics need to cover—the domain-specific ones, the task-specific ones, and those associated with adapting the structure of solutions. Better characterization of the kinds of adaptation rules that fill this miscellaneous category is needed before we can give knowledge engineers full guidelines for creating case-based systems.

Deriving important dimensions for comparing and contrasting on the fly. Our case-based interpretation systems, those that evaluate situations and solutions, do a fine job when seeded with important dimensions of their domain. But sometimes the important part of evaluation is figuring out which idiosyncratic features are the ones to focus on. In real life, we often are not told what the important dimensions for comparison are—we have to figure them out. We don't know how to make our systems do that yet. We can use the example from chapter 1 to illustrate. Recall that Anne did not eat grilled whole trout when it was served to her, and we are now considering serving fish at a meal Anne will be coming to. We need to determine if she will eat it or not and whether there is some kind of fish that she will eat. This might require us to figure out on the fly which features of the situation influence whether Anne will eat fish. Comparing that situation to others, we might find that we've seen Anne eat fish that was shaped differently, prepared differently, a different color, was filleted, tasted like chicken, had a different consistency, and so on. Here, it is the comparison we make to other situations that points out which features potentially determine outcome. Based on that, we reason some more about which ones do, in fact, determine outcome. Our interpretive systems can't yet do that. Related to this problem is the strategic posing of hypothetical situations. Our systems can do it for limited domains, but not in general.

Case Representation

Extracting cases from continuous situations.   Most of our case-based reasoners use cases that have discrete start and end points. In chapter 5, we discussed the extraction of cases from continuous situations, for example, the long-term operation of a system or the long-term interleaving of numerous actions. I gave guidelines for identifying cases in such environments, for artificially putting start and end points on some pieces of the situation. More attention is needed here, however. This is particularly important if we want our case-based reasoners to guide the behavior of robots.

Optimum size and connectivity of cases.   Also in chapter 5, we discussed the ways cases can be broken down into component parts, giving guidelines but no hard rules. This is another area where more work is needed. In many different applications, it is useful to have access to the pieces of cases independently of the whole case (e.g., in design, in situations where planning and action are interleaved). There are currently many different approaches to representing cases this way (see chapter 3). All allow pieces of cases to be independently accessed, and all maintain connections between the parts. Some break cases into parts according to the goals being addressed (e.g., CELIA, SCAVENGER, RUNNER); others, in terms of an artifact being reasoned about (e.g., CADET); others, along both dimensions (e.g., ARCHIE-2). As we build more and more capable design and planning systems, we will need to define more concretely the ways in which cases should be broken down, the ways in which the pieces can be accessed and used, and the kinds of connectivity between pieces of cases that it is necessary to maintain.

Determining the optimal level of abstraction for cases.   Most of our case-based reasoners use descriptions of real situations to reason from. Some (e.g., SWALE) use a combination of descriptions of real situations and more abstract patterns describing common situations. Others (e.g., ANON) use abstract patterns only. Still others (e.g., SCAVENGER) use composite or prototype cases, those that describe common situations but in concrete terms. It is clear that descriptions of cases need to include both specific information about the situation and information derived in the course of reasoning about the situation. If one kept only the originally available information about a case and did not also save the new things that were derived about it, one would be defeating the purpose of case-based reasoning—reuse of old experience. One would, instead, need to rederive all derived information each time' it was needed. Thus, case descriptions themselves generally include both concrete descriptive information (some of it surface features) and abstract descriptors.

The issue here is the operational level of a description that one needs in order to easily reason with it in a case-based way. Though case-based reasoning was derived as a methodology for reasoning using cases, the same adaptation and comparison procedures that are used to reason with cases can be used to reason with and about abstract descriptions of situations—to a point. And it is this point that is in question here. There is little difference between a specific situation description that says that a particular runner, Jim Fixx, jogged and then died of a heart attack because an unknown heart condition was triggered by the exercise, and a more general description that says that a person who was known to be in good shape was jogging, which he normally does, and died of a heart attack because an unknown heart condition was triggered by the exercise. The general description holds everything in it that we feel we need to know in order to understand the situation. We might be able to do case-based reasoning with a still more abstract description that tells us that an athlete who was in good health died during exercise of a heart attack because an unknown heart condition was triggered by the exercise. Again, we can do that because the abstract description is held together well by a rather well defined explanation. On the other hand, an abstraction such as "joggers can die of heart attacks," though less abstract, seems harder to use for reasoning.

Though we can identify by intuition the descriptions of situations that seem to have caselike qualities, work for the particular tasks we need to use them for, can be retrieved easily with the kinds of indexes we've discussed up to now, and can be manipulated using adaptation strategies we've already discussed, we don't have any hard rules or guidelines about which are useful and which are not.

Other Challenges

Combining case-based and model-based knowledge and reasoning. Model-based and case-based reasoning have the potential to complement each other quite well. But more work must be done to make that vision a reality. We know how to use the knowledge in causal models to choose indexes, to guide matching, and to guide adaptation, but we have not yet built a seamless reasoning system that can use models and cases interchangeably to reason— one in which models and cases hold the same kinds of knowledge and are accessed interchangeably by memory access procedures, in which model knowledge is applied in "normal" situations and in which cases supplement the domain theory, allowing it to remain robust around its edges. Doing this may or may not be necessary for building robust systems—we can use cases by themselves to do that, using prototype cases to represent normal situations. But it is of interest in understanding case-based reasoning's cognitive model more fully.

Building effective case-based interactive systems. Making people and machines interact well in a case-based environment is another opportunity and challenge. We have begun to develop guidelines for building composite human-machine case-based systems, but, so far, we have built systems that work without knowing fully the reasons why or how to advise others to do the same. This, in fact, is a problem that is right for a case-based reasoning approach. Case-based reasoning is good in weak-theory domains, and design of interactive systems is certainly an area in which theory is not available. If we collect enough examples of interactive systems that work and those that don't, we will be able to advise designers about their designs and perhaps eventually work out general guidelines.

Corporate memory. In the places where it has been attempted, case-based systems have been a valuable resource as a kind of corporate memory. But our approaches to corporate memory have been hit-and-miss so far. We know that a case library provides a corporate memory for the particular domain and task the system addresses. As we think about a larger vision of corporate memory, we may move beyond what case-based reasoning itself provides, needing to provide additional enhancements.

Case-based reasoning as a general architecture for cognition. Many people in the case-based reasoning community see case-based reasoning as much more than a methodology for building systems. We see it as providing a paradigm for analyzing cognition and for approaching new problems in cognition. For example, researchers are taking case-based approaches to design (e.g., JULIA, CADET), planning (e.g., CHEF, PLEXUS), explanation (e.g., SWALE), creativity (e.g., in CADET, Creative JULIA, ARCHIE-2, and KRITIK-2), introspection (e.g., in META-AQUA and Meta-ROUTER), and situated activity (e.g., SCAVENGER, RUNNER), using a case-based approach to investigate the cognition of each task. In approaching each task, there are assumptions made that cases and large-scale patterns play a large role in the knowledge representation and guidance of reasoning, that access to knowledge (whether case knowledge or general knowledge) is a crucial issue to contend with and that hierarchical organizations of general knowledge and cases and specification of indexes provide the first pass at confronting that issue, that the evolution of behavior over time (learning) is important to address, that the manipulation of cases and large-scale patterns is the crucial reasoning process to describe and define, and that special attention should be paid to failure.

But we haven't yet articulated case-based reasoning's paradigm well enough for the broader community to have that same appreciation of its possibilities as a paradigm for addressing issues in cognition, nor have we yet done a good enough job of showing experimentally its basis in human cognition. More experimentation must be done to show that case-based reasoning is not merely a plausible model but one whose predictions hold up when we test them in people. This will require a great deal of analysis. Analysis so far has concentrated on cases as a useful form of representation, on MOPs as an organizational structure, and on the use of abstract concepts as indexes (see chapter 4). But we must be more precise about the predictions the model makes and the processes it entails and allows. How can we interpret things that fall outside the scope of the model? How do we know when they merely tell us something is missing or not well enough specified? When do they tell us there is something fundamentally wrong?

It is not entirely clear what the optimal level of description for the theory will be. It can be defined now in terms of high-level processes. Indeed, Schank's (1982) *Dynamic Memory* was the first attempt to do that. Chapter 4 in this book gives the current understanding of the model. Situation analysis precedes and is interleaved with retrieval, which is interleaved with case manipulation, and so on. Case manipulation is of several kinds: adaptation, merging, compare and contrast. But can the model be defined at an implementational level, the way SOAR is, for example? Should it be defined at such a level? Defining the full cognitive model well as a general model of cognition remains a challenge, one that I hope will be met in the near future.

Implications for training and education. Finally, if we take case-based reasoning seriously as a cognitive model, it has implications for training and education. Training and education systems don't solve problems; they teach the human user. If people normally solve problems in a case-based way, then it makes sense to train them by putting them in the range of situations they will encounter on the job, helping them to solve those problems, and helping them to index those experiences in ways that will allow them to easily recall the right ones later on. People tend to remember things that are presented concretely and couched in many examples; people tend to remember those things that are presented in compelling ways; and storytellers—those who present cases well to people—seem to be most effective in getting people to pay attention and remember. We also know that learning happens at the edges of what we know and is facilitated by having the need to learn. Educational systems based on the case-based paradigm will put students in situations in which they have the opportunity to create their own learning goals and then make presentations in the form of compelling stories. The theory of indexing we have developed under the case-based reasoning paradigm can be used to index these stories according to the learning goals they support, the pedagogy they support, and the specifics of situations in which they will make their points most compellingly. Though much is known about the implementation and implications of building automated and interactive systems, there is still much to discover about the best ways to take advantage of the case-based reasoning paradigm in developing systems and methods for training and education.

Case-based reasoning as a cognitive model has other implications for training and education beyond the computer systems one might build. Using case-based reasoning as a model to analyze how people learn might allow us to propose (noncomputer-based) training methods, strategies for effective education, and guidelines for textbook writing.

16.4 THE FUTURE

The future of case-based reasoning, then, leads in many possible directions: the creation of tools for building case-based systems more easily, more powerful case-based systems for tasks such as design, diagnosis, scheduling, and planning and systems that use cases for education and training. Case-based reasoning is moving into the real world, from research to a methodology for building real-world systems. It is also moving in the direction of being a viable contender as a general cognitive architecture. This book provides the current state of the art in the field. More research and more development are needed to bring case-based reasoning to its full potential. I hope this book and the lessons it teaches will be useful in bringing that future to fruition.

Appendix: A Case Library of Case-Based Reasoning Systems

ABBY

References:
Major: Domeshek 1991a, 1991b, 1991c, 1993
Other: Domeshek 1988, 1989, 1990

Reasoning task: advice-giving (warning, suggesting)

Domain: lovelorn problems (and related social situations)

Automated or interactive: interactive
User hand-codes probe index (using graphical editor)
Program responds with case, presented as canned text
User interprets (and applies or ignores) text
User asks for next-best reminding or reformulates probe

Short description: ABBY is a case-based lovelorn advisor, designed as a study in indexing. It is a simple "retrieve and respond" system that picks a story out of memory and presents the text to the user

Research emphasis: developing an indexing vocabulary for describing social situations, parallel retrieval mechanisms, tools for managing a large case library

Reasoning processes
Situation assessment method: human codes probe indexes
Indexing based on: intentional analysis of situation (variation of UIF)
Retrieval algorithm: simulated parallel network retrieval
Organization of case: feature→story network (or matrix)

      Matching process: nearest-neighbor match
      Method for selecting among retrieved cases: highest partial match score
      Adaptation methods: none

Sources of cases: collected from newspapers, books, and interviews

Architectural highlights: simulated parallel matching over fixed-size feature-vector indexes

Lessons learned: The construction of content theories of representation involves commitment to a component theory—a listing of the system's representational dimensions and vocabulary items with some underlying simple featural definitions of those items. Development of the component theory itself gives feedback on the quality of representations even before taking the further steips required to define the detailed inferential connections between the terms that will transform the initial component theory into a full-fledged content theory.

ACBARR

References: Ram et al. 1993; Moorman and Ram 1992

Reasoning task: robot navigation

Domain: simulated obstacle-ridden world

Automated or interactive: automated

Short description: ACBARR uses a case-based method for dynamic selection and modification of behavior assemblages for a navigational system. The case-based reasoning module is an addition to a reactive control system and provides flexible performance in novel environments without extensive high-level reasoning that would slow the system down. It has been evaluated through simulation on several different environments known to be problematic for reactive control systems.

Research emphasis: CBR for tasks requiring continuous, on-line, real-time performance, indexing with simple perceptual inputs, learning of important environmental features for indexing

Reasoning processes
      Highlights: uses cases to adapt solutions dynamically during performance, uses a short-term memory to detect when a new or different case might be needed
      Cases used for: behavior suggestion, behavior adaptation, environmental assessment
      Indexing based on: environmental and movement information, based on perceptual input and internal monitoring of system's movement and progress
      Retrieval algorithm: flat memory, serial search
      Matching process: nearest-neighbor
      Method of selecting among retrieved cases: high score

Adaptation methods: case-based substitution, derivational reply

Architectural highlights: AuRA architecture augmented with CBR; learning and performance integrated and continuous

Lessons learned: Case-based reasoning allows a reactive system to derive the benefits of high-level reasoning without sacrificing real-time response and fast performance, leading to better real-time performance. It allows the system to learn about and adapt to its environment dynamically, drawing on the power of analytical learning without sacrificing the speed of similarity-based comparisions.

ANON

References: Owens 1990, 1991, 1993

Reasoning task: situation assessment

Domain: plan failure situations

Automated or interactive: interactive

Short description: ANON is a demonstration of a memory organization scheme for matching abstract characterizations of situations against concrete situation descriptions. The purpose of the program was to demonstrate the role of memory in controlling inference. Given a brief list of features characterizing a situation, the program found the most appropriate abstract characterizations of the situation (in the form of advice-giving proverbs) and, based on those, interacted with the user to determine which additional abstract features also characterized the situation. See chapter 10 for more detail.

Research emphasis: selection of an appropriate indexing vocabulary for characterizing plan failures; use of a parallel architecture for search

Reasoning processes
    Indexing based on: combination thematic and situation-specific vocabulary derived from a functional analysis of failure detection and repair
    Situation assessment: interleaved with search, guided by dynamic evaluation of the descriptors necessary to differentiate between competing cases
    Retrieval algorithm: flat memory, parallel search
    Organization of cases: large, flat space of labeled cases
    Matching process: nearest-neighbor
    Method for selecting among retrieved cases: situation assessment, interleaved with search, points out descriptors necessary to differentiate between competing cases; Next descriptor chosen for elaboration by an information-theoretic balancing of inference cost against information utility of each needed feature

Case representation: cases are abstract rather than specific; and take the form of common advice-giving proverbs

AQUA

References: Ram 1990a, 1990b, 1991, 1993; Ram and Leake 1991

Reasoning task: story understanding, motivational analysis, explanation

Domain: terrorism

Automated or interactive: automated

Short description: AQUA reads newspaper stories. It asks intelligent questions in an effort to understand novel aspects of incoming stories, uses those questions to focus the understanding process, and learns by answering its questions and asking new ones. Cases in its memory guide the process.

Research emphasis: case-based explanation, focus of attention during understanding, learning through incremental revision of existing knowledge, recognizing interestingness

Reasoning processes
    Highlights: understanding = read + explain + learn
    Cases used for: explanation, learning, question asking
    Situation assessment method: checklist (find anomalies)
    Indexing based on: anomaly characterization + situation characterization + character stereotype characterization
    Retrieval algorithm: discrimination net traversal
    Organization of cases: multiply indexed discrimination net
    Matching process: match input situation to consequents of explanations; if matched, abductively infer antecedents
    Method for selecting among retrieved cases: believability, applicability, relevance, verification, specificity
    Adaptation methods: none

Knowledge sources: XPs, decision models, MOPs, character stereotypes, goals, plans, beliefs, mental states, physical states, etc.

Architectural highlights: uniform question-based architecture for integration of tasks
    Reasoning subtasks: understanding = read + explain + learn
    Means of choosing the next task to work on: subgoaling + opportunistic triggering of tasks when associated questions are answered

ARCHIE

References: Goel, Kolodner et al. 1991; Pearce et al. 1992

Reasoning task: aiding design

Domain: architectural design (office buildings)

Automated or interactive: interactive (see description below)

Short description: ARCHIE is an interactive design-aiding system for architectural design, built using REMIND. It supports contruction and evaluation of solutions. Users specify their problem description and/or solution description; the system retrieves and displays past designs and provides suggestions and warnings. In support of evaluation, the system computes potential outcomes and retrieves and displays past designs with similar outcomes. See description of ARCHIE-2 for new work on this project.

Research emphasis: building a case library in a complex domain; developing an indexing vocabulary in support of design

Reasoning processes
> **Cases used for:** design generation and design criticism
> **Situation assessment method:** user describes situation
> **Indexing based on:** design goals, outcomes, and situation descriptors
> **Retrieval algorithm:** nearest-neighbor and qualitative retrieval
> **Organization of cases:** cases clustered around similar design goals and outcomes
> **Matching process:** nearest-neighbor
> **Method of selecting among retrieved cases:** highest match score, but user can browse through all retrieved cases
> **Adaptation methods:** none; adaptation is left to the user
> **Means of choosing the next task to work on:** user specification

Sources of cases: domain experts, architectural journals and magazines, post-occupancy evaluations of existing buildings

Lessons learned: Design cases can be very large and need to be decomposed into smaller units. Libraries of design cases can be useful but may need to be supplemented with other types of design knowledge. Practical design support systems need usable interfaces to allow easy access to relevant information. Keep it simple.

ARCHIE-2

References: Domeshek and Kolodner 1991, 1992, 1993

Reasoning task: supports browsing through a library of design documentation, stories, and guidelines

Domain: architectural design (courthouses)

Automated or interactive: interactive

Short description: ARCHIE-2 is a story-based hypermedia browsing system in support of design. The user specifies his or her interests to the system, and the system offers relevant documentation, stories, and guidelines for perusal. Stories and guidelines are organized graphically around design plans to allow easy transition between stories that are about the same building. They can also access multiple stories that illustrate the same guideline. Users can also easily request stories that are related in topic to one they are looking at. See chapters 2 and 15 for more details.

Research emphasis: indexing vocabulary for cases about artifacts, design of design-aiding systems, tools and methodologies to support construction and management of large case libraries

Reasoning processes
    Cases used for: solution construction, evaluation
    Indexing based on: artifact component, functional subsystem, and design issue that case/story makes point about, augmented with stakeholder and life-cycle information
    Retrieval algorithm: nearest-neighbor match
    Organization of cases: flat library, partitioned by presentation type: story, guideline, or design description
    Matching process: nearest-neighbor
    Method for selecting among retrieved cases: high score
    Adaptation methods: none

Sources of cases: cases collected from professional building evaluations; vocabulary developed in concert with trained architects

Lessons learned: Case presentation and segmentation matter. When cases are large, they must be segmented for easy understanding by a user. ARCHIE-2 segments cases according to the points they make. Users engaged in a creative process want browsers they can use to look things up; they don't want to feel that the system is making authoritative suggestions to them.

ASK systems

References: Ferguson et al. 1992; Bareiss 1992; Schank et al. 1991

Reasoning task: user-directed exploration of stories and guidelines describing a task and/or domain

Domains: ASK-Tom: trust bank consulting; ASK-Michael: industrial development; Advise-the-President: presidential decision making (specifically the Iran hostage crisis); Trans-ASK: military transportation planning; The Book of Water: a growing encyclopedic knowledge base about water and the water industry; ASK Little Village: social services in a working-class Latino neighborhood of Chicago

Automated or interactive: interactive

Short description: ASK systems are hypermedia systems designed to replicate aspects of conversation with an expert. A user identifies an area of interest and is presented with initial information. This may generate follow-up questions that are pursued via a graphical browsing interface. ASK systems are rationally organized memories of cases and other information for user-directed exploration. See chapters 2 and 15 for more detail. See also the entry on TaxOps.

Research and development emphasis: the organization of knowledge bases around task and conversational models

Reasoning processes

    Highlights: the model-based memory organization

    Cases used for: user exploration

    Situation assessment method: user-driven

    Indexing based on: task, domain, and conversational models

    Organizational structure: links between related cases

    Retrieval algorithm: follow the links between cases

    Matching process: none (connections between cases are hard-coded)

    Method for selecting among retrieved cases: user-driven

    Adaptation methods: none (ongoing work on bridging techniques to "adapt" the user's perception of a case)

Sources of cases: experts and practitioners in the domain

Lessons learned: A simple organization of cases coupled with an engaging user interface successfully replicates important aspects of conversation with an expert.

Battle Planner

References: Goodman 1989

Reasoning task: projecting the results of actions for plan evaluation

Domain: land warfare battle planning

Automated or interactive: interactive

Short description: The system is built from an existing database of over 600 historical battles. Each case includes about 60 separate pieces of information describing the battle, as well as textual commentary from an expert's evaluation. The user describes a battle situation and chosen battle plan. The system retrieves cases to project the outcome. The user uses this information to revise her battle plan. Chapter 2 holds additional detail.

Research emphasis: accurate projection using previous experience; interactive systems that allow novices to benefit from the experience of experts

Reasoning processes

    Highlights: inductively-derived decision tree indexes cases

    Cases used for: projection, evaluation, and suggestion of alternative courses of action

    Situation assessment method: case-based projection

    Indexing based on: inductively derived indexes based on a simple qualitative model of the domain

    Retrieval algorithm: binary decision-tree traversal

    Organization of cases: a two-tiered memory organization with primary tier based on expert-defined categories of cases organized around a case-prototype hierarchy and secondary indexes that form binary discrimination trees whose leaves are clusters of cases that share a common outcome.

    Method for selecting among retrieved cases: user decides

Knowledge sources: existing databases of information, qualitative models of the domain, expert organized hierarchies of symbolic information, formulas for deriving secondary features from primary features

Lessons learned: Induction provides an effective technique for index generation in interpretive CBR systems. Simple qualitative information is very helpful in improving indexing accuracy without requiring extensive domain modeling.

BOGART

References: Mostow 1989a; Mostow and Barley 1987; Mostow, Barley, and Weinrich 1989, 1992

Reasoning task: replay stored design plans to solve new problems

Domain: circuit design

Automated or interactive: interactive

Short description: BOGART helps a user to design circuits. The user describes his or her new situation to the system, retrieves a design plan from the library, and selects a portion to replay. BOGART decides which decisions are applicable to the new situation and replays them. The user makes further decisions that are needed to complete the design.

Research emphasis: use of derivational reply in detailed design

Reasoning processes
    Cases used for: creating new designs
    Situation assessment method: user
    Indexing based on: no indexing; user selects case from list
    Retrieval algorithm: none
    Organization of cases: list
    Adaptation methods: derivational replay; BOGART replays only the steps of an old
        case whose preconditions are still satisfied, and can therefore produce an
        incompletely refined design, which the user then completes using VEXED

Architectural highlights: top-down refinement model of design

Lessons learned: The applicability of derivational replay to design seems to be dependent on the applicability of the top-down refinement model of design to the design problem. BOGART was applied to a mechanical design task, but it didn't help much, because the task was ill suited to the top-down refinement model—it was really a parameter design problem.

BROADWAY

References: Skalak 1992

Reasoning task: case retrieval and explanation

Domain: selection of automobile for purchase

Automated or interactive: automated

Short description: BROADWAY uses a procedural representation of cases. Cases are represented as knowledge sources in a blackboard architecture. Case knowledge sources define local neighborhoods of similarity and are triggered if a problem case falls within a neighborhood.

Research emphasis: procedural case representation and retrieval

Reasoning processes
> **Highlights:**   retrieval responsibility is imposed on the cases themselves by including similarity metrics in the case representation; cases are active entities, rather than responsive to external procedures; retrieval is distributed among cases rather than being a centralized process
>
> **Cases used for:**   solution generation and explanation
>
> **Indexing based on:**   local similarity metrics representing different senses of similarity appropriate to regions of the case space
>
> **Retrieval algorithm:**   individual case knowledge sources activate themselves when a problem case falls within a local neighborhood
>
> **Organization of cases:**   dimensioned blackboard spaces
>
> **Matching process:**   nearest-neighbor according to locally defined similarity metric
>
> **Method for selecting among retrieved cases:**   cases sorted according to the number of different perspectives from which they are similar
>
> **Adaptation methods:**   none

Lessons learned: Local similarity metrics may be relied upon for retrieval in weak domains where a global similarity metric is not available. Cases may be usefully represented as dynamic knowledge sources in a blackboard architecture.

CABARET

References: Skalak and Rissland 1990, 1992; Rissland and Skalak 1991

Reasoning task: interpretive reasoning in support of argumentation

Domain: domain-independent shell, instantiated in an area of tax law

Automated or interactive: automated, with an interactive system development tool that includes a case browser and an interactive interface for control settings

Short description: CABARET is a domain-independent shell that integrates rule-based and case-based reasoning to facilitate applying rules containing ill-defined terms. The integration of these two reasoning paradigms is performed via a collection of control heuristics that suggest how to interleave case-based methods and rule-based methods to construct an argument to support a particular interpretation.

Research emphasis: mixing reasoning paradigms in support of interpretive reasoning

Reasoning processes
> **Cases used for:**   interpretation of open-textured terms in rules
> **Situation assessment method:**   cases elaborated based on checklist of dimensions
> **Indexing based on:**   rule-firings, factors, and case dispositions
> **Organization of cases:**   flat
> **Method for selecting among retrieved cases:**   retrieved cases partially ordered by relevant factors in a claim lattice
> **Adaptation methods:**   none

Architectural highlights: Forward-chaining rule-based control module, forward- and backward-chaining production system, and an augmented HYPO-style case-based reasoner work together. Each reports its progress to a central control module, and each monitors general progress of the others. Specifications to retrieval algorithms are based on what is needed to make the next argument move.

Lessons learned: Case-based reasoning and other reasoning paradigms may be integrated via control heuristics that capture reasoning strategies and argument strategies. Cases can be compared on the basis of how they perform under a rule set, as well as on the basis of purely case-based dimensional analysis.

CABER

References: Barletta and Mark 1988; Simoudis, Mendall, and Miller 1993

Reasoning task: failure recovery

Domain: failures in automated machinery

Automated or interactive: interactive

Short description: CABER assists the operator of a milling machine in recovering from machine failures that arise in the process of manufacturing. The user describes a problem, and the system retrieves cases, asking questions of the user to determine which of the retrieved cases is most appropriate. The repair plan in the selected case is presented to the user. CABER automatically adds cases to its case library, employing explanation-based indexing (EBI) to choose its indexes. Caber uses real cases of milling machine failures collected from Cincinnati Milacron, Inc.

Research emphasis: explanation-based indexing, recovery from failure

Reasoning processes
> **Cases used for:**   failure recovery
> **Indexing based on:**   explanation-based indexing procedures using knowledge about the structure and behavior of machines
> **Situation assessment method:**   memory-guided
> **Retrieval algorithm:**   redundant discrimination network search, incremental based on memory-guided situation assessment
> **Organization of cases:**   hierarchy with class/subclass relationships

    Matching process: exact matches between obtained features and the corresponding features of the new problem required to traverse the network

    Method for selecting among retrieved cases: selecting the case whose repair plan has the highest probability of resolving the new problem based on past effectiveness of the plan in addressing similar problems

    Knowledge sources: structure and behavior of milling machines, effectiveness of repair actions

Lessons learned: Creating case from existing problem reports that were provided by the milling machine manufacturer was difficult and time-consuming because of the lack of relevant information in the problem reports. A domain expert was needed to interpret the contents of each problem report, complementing the information included in each report, and providing the structure and behavior knowledge used by the system.

CABINS

References: Miyashita and Sycara 1993

Reasoning task: scheduling, repair-based optimization

Domain: manufacturing

Automated or interactive: automated

Short description: CABINS acquires user's scheduling preferences in the form of cases and reuses them to generate high-quality schedules and to reactively manage schedules in response to unexpected environmental events. In the knowledge acquisition phase, the user interacts with CABINS to (1) select repair heuristics to improve suboptimal schedules, (2) evaluate the acceptability of repairs, and (3) provide explanation for unacceptable repair results. In performance phase, CABINS uses the results of its acquired experience to perform repair-based scheduling in predictive and reactive situations. CABINS contains over 4000 cases, which took only 10 hours to collect.

Research emphasis: acquiring user preferences and constraints and incorporating them into the scheduling process

Reasoning processes

    Highlights: integrates CBR with constraint propagation techniques to do time-dependent and resource-constrained reasoning

    Cases used for: solution generation, solution evaluation, failure avoidance and recovery, failure explanation

    Situation assessment method: evaluation based on checklist of criteria

    Indexing based on: abstractions of domain relations and constraints

    Retrieval algorithm: serial search of flat memory

    Organization of cases: flat

    Matching process: nearest-neighbor, using conjunctive features

    Method for selecting among retrieved cases: best score

> **Adaptation methods:**   constraint violations point to need for adaptation
>
> **Means of choosing the next task to work on:**   activities in the schedule repaired in order of expected schedule improvement

Lessons learned: Comparative controlled experimentation with a number of scheduling methods and with respect to various optimization criteria has shown that a case-based approach can (a) reliably acquire user preferences in a domain without a causal model and (b) outperform other methods in both predictive schedule generation and reactive response to unpredictable execution events.

CADET

References: Navinchandra, Sycara, and Narasimhan 1991a, 1991b; Sycara et al. 1992; Sycara and Navinchandra 1989a, 1989b, 1991a, 1991b, 1992

Reasoning task: design of small mechanical devices

Automated or interactive: automated

Short description: CADET is a case-based design tool that uses index elaboration (situation assessment) as a means for finding and synthesizing entire cases or parts of cases. Its indexing is in terms of abstract behaviors. New devices are created by synthesizing the behaviors of pieces of known devices. CADET's abstract indexing and situation assessment procedures allow it to generate innovative design alternatives and to retrieve and synthesize device parts across domains.

Research emphasis: generation of design alternatives for mechanical devices through merging pieces of several old designs

Reasoning processes
> **Cases used for:**   solution generation
>
> **Situation assessment method:**   behavior-preserving elaboration operators interleaved with search processes
>
> **Indexing based on:**   behaviors of devices
>
> **Retrieval algorithm:**   database finds all records that match each arc in the index graph; maximal matching graph algorithms find the minimum number of cases that can be used to satisfy the given design goal
>
> **Organization of cases:**   directed acyclic graphs representing behaviors of devices are normalized into a relational database
>
> **Method for selecting among retrieved cases:**   retrieved cases judged for lowest cost and weight and ease of synthesis
>
> **Adaptation methods:**   avoids adaptation by synthesizing only those parts of prior designs that are directly relevant to the given goal; in addition, some parametric adjustment and local search.

Sources of cases: interviews with designers, design handbooks, *Encyclopedia of Mechanisms*, *How Things Work*, *The Way Things Work*

Architectural highlights: a blackboard architecture with modules for elaboration, user interaction, constraint checking, case storage and retrieval, materials adaptation; control directed to parts of the given behavior specification that are unsatisfied.

Lessons learned: The larger the database, the better. Situation assessment, done in a principled way, is very powerful.

CADSYN

References: Maher and Zhang 1991

Reasoning task: design

Domain: structural design of buildings

Automated or interactive: primarily automated reasoning, user interaction to confirm or revise decisions made by system

Short description: CADSYN, a hybrid CBR design model, integrates case-based reasoning with problem decomposition and constraint processes. Solutions are derived by finding the most relevant previous design situation and transforming the potential solution to fit the new design situation using a domain specific constraint satisfaction approach. Design cases were acquired from drawings of building projects designed by a local engineering consulting company. Behavior of CADSYN is currently being reviewed by design experts. A related project is looking at case organization and flexible indexing.

Research emphasis: design case representation as a hierarchy of subsystems and case transformation by a domain-specific constraint-satisfaction approach

Reasoning processes
    Cases used for: solution generation
    Situation assessment method: expert-provided
    Indexing based on: design specifications
    Retrieval algorithm: hierarchical search
    Organization of cases: hierarchy produced by conceptual clustering based on design problem specifications
    Matching process: exact matching as hierarchy is traversed
    Method for selecting among retrieved cases: numerical evaluation
    Adaptation methods: structural adaptation, constraint satisfaction, special-purpose adaptation heuristics

Knowledge sources: specific design situations (cases), generalized decomposition domain knowledge, design constraints

Architectural highlights: combines CBR and decomposition

Lessons learned: Design data cannot be collected from drawings alone. Drawings need to be interpreted by engineers involved in a project. Drawings by themselves do not make design criteria explicit.

CASCADE

References: Simoudis and Miller 1990; Simoudis 1991a, 1991b, 1992

Reasoning Task: failure recovery

Domain: device drivers of the VMS operating system

Automated or interactive: interactive

Short description: CASCADE assists front-line engineers in recovering from crashes of the VMS operating system that are due to device driver failure. The user describes a new problem to the system, and the system retrieves cases that suggest repairs. The user selects a case and carries out its repair. CASCADE's initial case memory was created from a set of 200 problem reports obtained from one of Digital Equipment Corporation's customer support centers. CAS-CADE uses a bi-directional retrieval method called validated retrieval.

Research emphasis: to define an efficient retrieval method that can operate in domains where initial descriptions of problems are sparse and non-discriminating

Reasoning processes
> **Cases used for:**   choice of a failure recovery method
> **Situation assessment method:**   interleaved with search; more below
> **Indexing based on:**   available descriptive features and derived validating features
> **Retrieval algorithm:**   validated retrieval—retrieve those cases that appear to be most relevant based on available descriptive features; for each, derive features that can validate the usefulness of the case, using newly derived features to retrieve additional cases; continue, returning cases that match well
> **Organization of cases:**   two discrimination networks, one based on available features, the other based on validating ones
> **Method for selecting among retrieved cases:**   user, based on system ranking of cost of carrying out repair
> **Adaptation process:**   none

Lessons learned: Significant domain-specific knowledge is necessary for similarity assessment and validation. Knowledge acquisition is facilitated through the use of cases, but the knowledge engineer's role is not eliminated. Each domain expert has his or her own action model and uses cases differently; thus presentation of all alternatives to the user is necessary.

CASEY

References: Koton 1988a, 1988b, 1989

Reasoning task: explanation, diagnosis

Domain: heart failures

Automated or interactive: automated

Short description: CASEY combines CBR and causal reasoning to provide a causal explanation of a patient's heart disease symptoms. It uses case-based reasoning to recall and remember problems it has seen before, and it uses a causal model of its domain to justify reusing previous solutions, to guide their adaptation for the new situation, and to solve unfamiliar
problems. It is built on top of the Heart Failure Program (Long et al. 1987) and uses its causal
model. Additional detail can be found in chapters 2, 9, and 11.

Research emphasis: speed-up of model-based reasoning

Reasoning processes
> **Highlights:**   combines CBR with model-based reasoning
> **Cases used for:**   matching, adaptation
> **Situation assessment method:**   checklist-based control
> **Indexing based on:**   importance of features to the causal explanation of each patient
> **Retrieval algorithm:**   redundant discrimination network
> **Organization of cases:**   prioritized redundant discrimination network
> **Matching process:**   evidence heuristics and a causal model; see chapter 9
> **Method for selecting among retrieved cases:**   causal model
> **Adaptation methods:**   model-guided repair; see chapter 11

Knowledge sources: model of the heart, derived for Heart Failure Program

Lessons learned: CBR can frequently produce the same results as a model-based expert
system in significantly less time.

CELIA

References: Redmond 1989a, 1989b, 1989c, 1990a, 1990b, 1991, 1992

Reasoning task: diagnosis, learning

Domain: automobile diagnosis

Automated or interactive: automated diagnosis, interactive learning

Short description: CELIA learns from an instructor by predicting the expert's actions and
explains how the steps relate to each other. As a result of this process, CELIA retains the example as a case. The parts of the case (snippets) can be used individually for future prediction and
explanation. When CELIA cannot explain the instructor's actions, then, with the instructor's
help, CELIA tries to learn knowledge about the relevant device and about the goals involved in
the task. See chapter 4.

Research emphasis: acquiring cases, learning indexes, combining case-based and other reasoning methods

Reasoning processes
> **Cases used for:**   generating solutions, explaining, choosing indexes
> **Situation assessment method:**   case-guided inquiry

> **Indexing based on:** reasoning goals along with all associated features initially, those found to make relevant predictions later
> **Retrieval algorithm:** serial search
> **Organization of cases:** flat
> **Matching process:** reasoning goal takes priority, qualitative distance along some dimensions, degree of overlap in others, importance of dimensions associated with each case and snippet
> **Method for selecting among retrieved cases:** preference method

Reasoning subtasks or subgoals: specific to diagnosis and repair—clarify complaint, verify complaint, generate hypothesis, test hypothesis, interpret test result, repair, test repair

Lessons learned: During early learning of a task and domain, case acquisition, by itself, significantly enhances performance. When failure occurs, both learning a new case and reindexing the old one that failed are necessary. Experts' examples can provide a good start in seeding a case memory if the student actively processes and explains the examples. Dividing cases into linked goal-centered snippets allows both efficient solution of problems that have been previously encountered and case-based solution of novel problems.

CHEF

References: Hammond 1986a, 1986b, 1987, 1989a

Reasoning task: planning

Domain: recipe creation

Automated or interactive: automated

Short description: CHEF is a case-based planner in the domain of recipe creation. Given a set of planning goals, it assesses the situation by remembering cases that can help it anticipate what might go wrong. It adds to its problem specification based on that. It then retrieves and adapts a case from its library of recipes to create a recipe for the new situation. It runs the new plan (recipe) through its simulation program and records its results. In the next step, it explains any failures that resulted and repairs its plan, creating one that avoids those problems. It records the repaired plan in its case library, making it available during later reasoning. For more detail, see chapters 2, 8, 10, and 11.

Research emphasis: a case-based approach to planning

Reasoning processes
> **Highlights:** situation assessment before planning
> **Cases used for:** situation assessment, solution generation, repair
> **Situation assessment method:** case-based projection
> **Indexing based on:** prioritized constraints and factors known to cause failures
> **Retrieval algorithm:** discrimination net search

Organization of cases: several prioritized discrimination nets, one for each reasoning task, TOPs for organizing repairs

Matching process: exact match while traversing discrimination net

Method for selecting among retrieved cases: none

Adaptation methods: reinstantiation, special-purpose critics, special-purpose repair heuristics

Reasoning goals: anticipate, retrieve, adapt, repair

Means of choosing the next task to work on: set script

Knowledge sources: cases, TOPs, and associated repair strategies

CLAVIER

References: Barletta and Hennessy 1989; Hennessy and Hinkle 1992; Hinkle and Hennessy 1990; Mark 1989

Reasoning task: design and evaluation

Domain: autoclave loading, spatial arrangements

Automated or interactive: interactive

Short description: CLAVIER generates autoclave load schedules by working interactively with a user. It presents a graphic depiction of recommended layouts, along with a prioritized list of parts waiting to be cured. The user enters or adjusts part priorities and selects from recommended layouts. The user can modify recommended layouts, in which case CLAVIER critiques the new (adapted) layout by comparing it with the other layouts in the case library. CLAVIER uses cases three ways: as constraints in its heuristic planning and scheduling module, to determine allowable layouts within the autoclave, and to help validate manually-adapted cases. CLAVIER has been in continuous use at Lockheed since 1990. It began with 20 cases and now has over 300. Chapters 2 and 11 have additional detail.

Development emphasis: applying CBR to a real-world problem and exploring the interactions between planning and scheduling

Reasoning processes
Cases used for: generating layouts, generating schedules, critiquing adaptations
Situation assessment method: user specifies situation
Indexing based on: parts, part locations, and part orientations
Retrieval algorithm: flat memory, serial search
Organization of cases: flat
Method for selecting among retrieved cases: based on number of parts matched and priorities of matched parts, user chooses from among above-criterion solutions
Adaptation methods: in early version, case-based substitution; in later version, user manually adapts and CLAVIER critiques

Source of original cases: files of subject-matter expert

Lessons learned: It is important to provide automatic support for maintaining the correctness of the database and avoiding case duplication. It is important to provide a complete environment for supporting users, in addition to the knowledge-based parts of a system.

The Compaq SMART System

References: Acorn and Walden 1992

Reasoning task: customer support help desk; diagnosis and repair

Domain: Compaq hardware and software running on Compaq machines

Automated or interactive: interactive

Short description: Using CasePoint, from Inference Corporation, the system helps Compaq customers diagnose and repair hardware and software problems. The user describes his or her problem, and the system retrieves cases. To determine which of the retrieved cases are most appropriate, the system questions the user to find the values of differentiating features. The problem description is iteratively refined and the most relevant case is recalled. The case library is used simultaneously by up to 60 users at a time. The case library is stored in a SQL database. A team of case engineers maintains the system.

Development emphasis: need to make shared knowledge available to customers so that problems can be solved faster and more easily

Reasoning processes
    Cases used for: solution creation
    Situation assessment method: incremental query to user to find values to discriminate between competing cases
    Indexing based on: checklist of features
    Retrieval algorithm: serial search of library partition
    Organization of cases: SQL relational database management system
    Matching process: nearest-neighbor
    Method for selecting among retrieved cases: high score
    Adaptation methods: none

Architectural highlights: multiple readers and writers to case library

Lessons learned: Case-based systems cannot build themselves on the fly by merely adding cases as they happen. "Library engineering" is needed to ensure organized, graceful growth of the case library.

CYCLOPS

References: Navinchandra 1988, 1991

Reasoning task: design debugging

Domain: layout design, landscape architecture

Automated or interactive: interactive

Short description: CYCLOPS combines constraint-based solution generation with case-based debugging and repair for design of landscapes. Cases are instances of repair. They have several parts to them: the problem needing repair, the repair that was carried out, the reason the problem arose, the reason the repair worked. Match procedures use a systematicity-based matching principle, which often yields innovative solutions through analogy. The system is controlled by an A* search algorithm. CYCLOPS was the first application of CBR to design.

Research emphasis: integration of A* and CBR for design

Reasoning processes
    Cases used for: design debugging and repair
    Indexing based on: description of problem situation, features responsible for the problem situation
    Retrieval algorithm: serial search retrieves cases that partially match on indexed features
    Organization of cases: flat
    Matching process: systematicity-based structure mapping
    Method for selecting among retrieved cases: alternatives placed on the A* search tree and selected by A*'s optimality criteria
    Adaptation methods: case-based identification of problems and case-based solution suggestion

Architectural highlights: CBR and search process communicate via a blackboard, with the A* algorithm providing control

Lessons learned: There are some solutions a case-based reasoner can come up with that a pure search method is not configured to find; in particular, solutions created by cross-domain analogy.

GREBE

References: Branting and Porter 1991; Branting 1991a, 1991b, 1991c, 1991d

Reasoning task: interpretation, projection of effects

Domain: legal reasoning

Short description: GREBE uses legal cases and legal and commonsense rules to identify and explain the possible legal consequences of factual situations

Research emphasis: techniques for integrating rules and cases; techniques for retrieving and integrating cases represented as semantic networks

Reasoning processes

 Highlights: reasons using "snippets" of cases: collections of facts relevant to individual inference steps in a precedent's explanation

 Cases used for: classification, explanation

 Situation assessment: elaboration for the purpose of improving match

 Indexing based on: goals, structural characteristics of snippets

 Retrieval algorithms: incremental best-first matching over entire case library followed by match refinement

 Organization of cases: organized by "is an exception to" links and structural difference links

 Matching process: structure matching

 Method for selecting among retrieved cases: degree of structural similarity after case elaboration

 Knowledge sources: explanations of legal precedents, commonsense rules, taxonomic hierarchies among predicates

Architectural highlights: fully integrates rule-based reasoning (RBR) with CBR

Choosing next reasoning goal to work on: Structure matching generates subgoals of inferring facts that would improve match; RBR generates subgoals of finding precedents of concepts in rule antecedents that match the current facts.

Lessons learned: Explanation is improved by a control strategy that permits RBR and CBR to be freely interleaved, by matching of case "snippets" rather than entire cases, and by use of highly expressive representations of cases. However, highly structured case representations make matching difficult. Though representations need to be fully expressive, flat structure enhances matching efficiency.

HYPO

References: Ashley 1989, 1990, 1991; Ashley and Rissland 1987, 1988a, 1988b; Rissland and Ashley 1986; Rissland 1986

Reasoning task: case-based interpretation and argumentation

Domain: legal reasoning, trade secrets law

Automated or interactive: mostly automated

Short description: HYPO evaluates problem situations by comparing and contrasting them with cases from its case library. It generates legal arguments citing the past cases as justifications for legal conclusions about who should win in problem disputes involving trade secret law. HYPO's arguments present competing adversarial views of the problem and it poses hypotheticals to alter the balance of the evaluation. HYPO uses dimensions as a generalization scheme for accessing and evaluating cases. Its computational definitions of relevant similarities and differences and techniques for selecting the best cases to cite in support of a point and as counterexamples enable it to make contextually sensitive assessments of relevance and salience without relying on either a strong domain theory or a priori weighting schemes. See chapters 2 and 13 for more details.

Research emphasis: modeling legal argument

Reasoning processes

>**Reasoning highlights:** see chapter 13
>
>**Cases used for:** situation assessment; argument generation
>
>**Situation assessment method:** cases compared to past cases in terms of dimensions
>
>**Indexing based on:** dimensions (predictive factors for a domain)
>
>**Retrieval algorithm:** retrieve any case indexed by a dimension that applies to or is a near miss to the problem
>
>**Organization of cases:** flat, indexed by dimensions
>
>**Method for selecting among retrieved cases:** sort cases into a claim lattice, and select cases that share maximal subsets of dimensions with problem

Lessons learned: A computational model of argument can be implemented and employed to select and organize relevant information for a user.

Internal Analogy

References: Hickman and Larkin 1990; Hickman and Lovett 1991

Reasoning task: heuristic search in problem solving

Domain: DC-circuits, fluid statics, and geometry theorem proving

Automated or interactive: automated

Short description: Internal analogy transfers both success and failure experiences from a previously solved subgoal that is contained in the same problem as the current subgoal. The appropriate level of partial match is learned through feedback from previous analogical reasoning. Because internal analogy allows for transfer at varying levels of granularity, transfer happens in an efficient compiled manner except where the adaptation process flexibly applies internal analogy or other general problem-solving methods recursively.

Research or development emphasis: effective within-trial transfer and learning a better partial-match metric through experience

Reasoning processes

>**Cases used for:** solution generation and adaptation
>
>**Indexing based on:** characteristics of the problem-solving goal and initial state
>
>**Retrieval algorithm:** least-deviant-first search through memory subject to resource limitations
>
>**Organization of cases:** goal tree, similar to derivational analogy
>
>**Matching process:** match on goals and preconditions of goals
>
>**Method for selecting among retrieved cases:** case that deviates the least along goals and preconditions

    Adaptation methods: recursive use of internal analogy
    Knowledge sources: class hierachy, deviation weights
    Means of choosing the next task to work on: goal decomposition

Lessons learned: Learning the similarity metric through experience and transferring experience at variable levels of granularity increase efficiency of a problem solver. It is advantageous to examine the way a subgoal has already been achieved within the current problem-solving episode in addition to looking at the ways it has been achieved in other instances.

IVY

References: Hunter 1989a,b,c, 1990; Ram and Hunter 1992

Reasoning task: diagnosis

Domain: lung tumor histology

Automated or interactive: automated

Short description: IVY explores the idea of the "paradigm case," one that can represent a whole class of cases, aiming to identify such cases and store only those in its memory. IVY diagnoses lung tumors, improving its diagnostic performance by using failure explanations to generate learning goals. Incoming cases that satisfy one or more of those goals are stored. IVY uses a model of its diagnostic process to explain its failures. The ability to reason about its own reasoning is crucial in generating explanations for failures, which in turn identify which future cases will be stored, where they will be stored, and what they will be used for.

Research emphasis: handling large numbers of cases by identifying small numbers that can significantly improve performance

Reasoning processes
    Cases used for: identifying potentially relevant diagnoses; specifying general disease classes to more specific diagnoses; differentiating between competing diagnoses
    Indexing based on: observable input features; inferred input features; representation of internal processing
    Retrieval algorithm/organization of cases: pointers to cases stored at various places in "semantic" (noncase) memory; pointers built when cases are stored and derive from knowledge that caused the case to be recognized as worth remembering
    Matching process: tests conditions attached to case pointers
    Method for selecting among retrieved cases: multiple cases used
    Adaptation methods: none

Lessons learned: Some cases are more useful than others. Cases of high expected utility can be identified as they occur, and this provides a mechanism for focusing attention on aspects of experience that are truly worth remembering. In order to focus learning productively, a program needs to represent and act upon specific desires for knowledge. It is possible (and perhaps necessary) to use an internal characterization of the learner's own reasoning processes to identify knowledge that is needed to improve its reasoning ability.

JULIA

References: Hinrichs 1988, 1989, 1992; Hinrichs and Kolodner 1991

Reasoning task: design

Domain: meal planning

Automated or interactive: automated, with user selecting preferences

Short description: JULIA does design in the domain of meal planning. It uses cases to propose plausible solutions, decomposing the problem as necessary and posting constraints to guide synthesis. JULIA exploits a repertoire of adaptation methods to transform previous meals and dishes in order to meet constraints on the current problem. These adaptation methods are used both to modify previous cases and to repair previous decisions that have been invalidated by constraints that arrive late. Chapters 2 and 11 have more detail.

Research or development emphasis: plausible reasoning and design

Reasoning processes
>   **Cases used for:** proposing solutions and parts of solutions
>   **Situation assessment method:** checklist of important features guides problem elaboration
>   **Indexing based on:** specifications in problem descriptions
>   **Retrieval algorithm/organization of cases:** redundant discrimination nets
>   **Matching process:** heuristic matching rules permit partial matching of types, components, and ranges while network is being traversed
>   **Method for selecting among retrieved cases:** preference procedure
>   **Adaptation methods:** common-sense transformation, special-purpose structure-modifying heuristics
>   **Knowledge sources:** cases, constraints, design plans, and qualitative preferences

Architectural highlights: hierarchical architecture that includes modules for goal scheduling, case retrieval, adaptation, and constraint posting, built upon a substrate of reason maintenance

Lessons learned: Because design specifications are usually incomplete, inferences may be unsound, and design processes must be responsive to new facts and specifications that arrive late. JULIA's integration of case-based reasoning and constraint posting enables this ability.

KRITIK

References: Goel 1989, 1991a,b, 1992; Goel and Chandrasekaran 1992

Reasoning task: design

Domain: physical devices (e.g., simple electrical circuits, heat exchangers)

Automated or interactive: automated

Short description: KRITIK uses model-guided repair to synthesize new designs from old ones. Model knowledge is good for identifying needed fixes in a design and verifying that a design works, but it is inefficient for design synthesis. Cases are used in KRITIK for design synthesis, and adaptation procedures use model knowledge to identify needed fixes in a preliminary design, to suggest fixes, and to choose indexes for cases. Each design in KRITIK has a model of its behavior associated with it. KRITIK creates models for newly-created designs by adapting old models. Chapters 11 and 12 hold more detail.

Research emphasis: integration of model-based and case-based reasoning for design

Reasoning processes
    Cases used for: design plan generation
    Indexing based on: functions delivered by the stored designs
    Retrieval algorithm: select out based on indexes
    Organization of cases: flat, with one layer of indexes
    Matching process: nearest-neighbor
    Method for selecting among retrieved cases: domain-specific heuristics
    Adaptation methods: model-guided repair, see chapter 11

Knowledge sources: cases, models, knowledge about specific functions

Reasoning subtasks or subgoals: case retrieval, design adaptation, model revision, design verification, redesign, case storage

Lessons learned: Case-based reasoning is an efficient and effective method for solving simple design problems when case-specific models are available to guide the adaptation process. Domain models can provide the vocabulary for indexing cases.

MEDIATOR

References: Simpson 1985; Kolodner and Simpson 1988, 1989

Reasoning task: planning

Domain: mediation

Automated or interactive: automated

Short description: MEDIATOR's task was to resolve disputes over resources. It used case-based reasoning for a wide variety of tasks: for situation assessment, several planning steps, diagnosis of reasoning errors, and repair of failed plans. Like traditional problem solvers, MEDIATOR was always aware of the reasoning subgoal it was working on and had available to it "from-scratch" inference rules or methods that it could use to achieve each one when appropriate cases were not available. MEDIATOR was one of the earliest case-based reasoners and the first to integrate the use of multiple cases. See chapters 3 and 14 for more detail.

Research emphasis: variety of tasks cases can be used for in reasoning

Reasoning processes

    Cases used for: situation assessment, solution generation, diagnosis of reasoning errors, repair

    Situation assessment method: case-based projection or special-purpose elaboration rules, guided by a checklist

    Indexing based on: checklist of problem features

    Retrieval algorithm/organization of cases: redundant discrimination net

    Matching process: exact match while traversing discrimination net

    Method for selecting among retrieved cases: exclusion, then weighted similarity metric

    Adaptation methods: reinstantiation, case-based refinement

    Reasoning goals: elaborate, choose plan, refine plan, present to client, evaluate feedback, diagnose errors, repair, repeat

    Means of choosing the next task to work on: set script

Knowledge sources: cases, hierarchy of plan frameworks

Architectural highlights: a goal-directed, problem-solver-directed application of the case-based reasoner; the current subgoal was important in focusing in on the relevant part of the recalled case and applying the right type of case-based inference

MEDIC

References: Turner 1988a, 1989a, 1989b, 1989c

Reasoning task: planning

Domain: diagnosis of pulmonology disease

Automated or interactive: automated

Short description: MEDIC uses generalized cases, called schemas, to plan and execute a sequence of mental and physical actions for diagnosing lung disease. Its schemas are of several kinds, corresponding roughly to MOPs, scenes, and TOPs. MOP-like schemas describe disease entities and hold procedures for diagnosing them. Scene-like schemas describe signs and symptoms and hold procedures for recognizing them. TOP-like schemas hold strategic knowledge about diagnosis. Schemas hold both descriptive knowledge about the entity they represent and processing knowledge that is used to activate other schemas. They are arranged in packaging and generalization hierarchies like MOPs, allowing the same kind of access. This allows MEDIC to choose reasoning procedures in a context-sensitive way. MEDIC's agenda control mechanism allows it to interleave planning and execution, responding appropriately to things that come up in its environment and allowing it to continue reasoning while it is waiting for additional information to become available. The approach was intended for highly reactive environments and was thus far more complex than needed for diagnosis. However, descendants of MEDIC are being used for robotic control.

Research or development emphasis: CBR for a task in which planning and execution are interleaved, handling unanticipated events

Reasoning processes
    Highlights: context-sensitive choice of procedures for reasoning; all aspects of reasoning are schema-based (takes MOPs to their utmost)
    Cases used for: generation of reasoning tasks and subgoals
    Indexing based on: situational features, surface as well as deep
    Retrieval algorithm/organization of cases: redundant discrimination networks, modified to allow better control of search
    Matching process: custom matching, criteria built into schemas
    Method for selecting among retrieved cases: preference heuristics

NETTRAC

References: Brandau, Lemmon, and Lafond 1991; Kopeikina, Brandau and Lemmon 1988

Reasoning task: planning and execution monitoring

Domain: traffic management in public telephone networks

Automated or interactive: interactive

Short description: NETTRAC acquires and uses cases to manage traffic in public telephone networks. NETTRAC is invoked by real-time events in the network or by user intervention. Problems in this domain may extend over hours or days, and the system must monitor conformance with (case-generated) expectations for the duration of the problem. Because of continuous changes in the network (e.g., new technologies), the system must learn just to maintain stable performance. In addition to automatic case learning, NETTRAC learns components of a domain model by observing user modifications to its recommended plans. Multiple induced decision trees are used for indexing and retrieval so as to simplify learning of new indexing as cases accumulate.

Research emphasis: CBR for continuous situations and drifting domain; user-guided learning; NETTRAC is a development prototype

Reasoning processes
    Highlights: uses multiple decision-trees (built by ID3-like algorithm) for initial category indexing and final selection; cases consist of multiple, snapshotlike feature vectors representing monitoring milestones
    Cases used for: classification, index-induction, run-time planning and monitoring
    Situation assessment method: domain-specific procedures
    Indexing based on: domain-specific features, in ID3-like decision trees
    Retrieval algorithm: multiple ID3-like decision trees
    Method for selecting among retrieved cases: domain-specific similarity metrics
    Adaptation methods: domain-specific procedures

Sources of cases: expert network managers

Lessons learned: Highly structured cases make everything complicated. General-purpose adaptation methods are not worth the effort in this domain (confirming similar observations, e.g., CLAVIER). CBR appears to be ideal for building advisory "learning apprentice" systems.

ORCA: the Organizational Change Advisor

References: Bareiss and Slator 1991, 1992; Slator and Bareiss 1992

Reasoning task: retrieval for the purpose of advice giving

Domain: organizational change consulting (redesigning business units in the event of merger/acquisition, corporate restructuring, etc.)

Automated or interactive: interactive

Short description: ORCA is a consulting aid and advice-giving program that interacts with a consultant to gather information about a client, and then tells stories that are analogous to the client's situation. ORCA's stories help the consultant consider realistic problem-solving alternatives. ORCA builds a picture of the problem situation incrementally by comparing and contrasting it with multiple stored cases. As more stored cases are retrieved, questions are raised and posed to the consultant user, more is learned about the problem, and ORCA's interpretations become more "on-point." The ORCA consultation continues, from story to story, as long as the user believes it to be worthwhile to answer questions and view cases.

Reasoning processes
    Situation assessment method: need for additional information suggested by retrieved cases; user provides information needed
    Indexing based on: descriptive features of business situations and inferable abstract problem descriptions
    Retrieval and organization: ORCA's memory is a network of domain features, abstract problem descriptors, and stories, all connected by "reminding" links; when a question is answered, activation is sent across the links, and the activation levels of each element are used to order them onto their own agendas
    Method for selecting among retrieved cases: presented cases must share both observable surface features and abstract problem types

Sources of cases: business publications, interviews with experts

Lessons learned: Representing stories by their proverbial content is both useful and problematic. On the one hand, proverbs are a natural way for humans to characterize experience, and this is a key feature of any indexing scheme that has any hope of "scaling up." On the other hand, stories of sufficient complexity will strike different people in different ways on different days, and this means that stories will be indexed in terms that not everyone can agree on. Perhaps this is the best we can hope for when the domain is so complex that no answer is ever really "right."

Parse-O-Matic

References: Goodman 1991

Reasoning task: natural language parsing

Domain: stock screening questions

Automated or interactive: automated

Short description: Parse-O-Matic, built at Cognitive Systems using a predecessor of REMIND, uses a case library of over 50,000 micro-cases to create a semantic representation of an English language stock-screening question. It is implemented using a blackboard-based working memory in conjunction with a reactive architecture. It uses an early-commitment strategy and does on-the-fly correction when early assumptions (such as resolution of ambiguous words and attachments) are incorrect. Word-sense and morphological disambiguation, pronominal reference, and elision are all handled in an integrated manner. A micro-case is an individual action performed in the course of reasoning.

Emphasis: use of cases encoded as temporal sequences of micro-cases, comparison of accuracy, speed, and knowledge-engineering time for creation and maintenance of case-based and rule-based systems

Reasoning processes
    Cases used for: suggesting action to perform
    Situation assessment method: task-specific
    Indexing based on: descriptors needed to choose an action or distinguish between
        several actions
    Retrieval algorithm: binary decision-tree traversal
    Organization of cases: binary decision tree
    Method for selecting among retrieved cases: none needed; retrieval algorithm ensures that all retrieved cases predict the same action
    Adaptation methods: local search

Knowledge sources: morphological analysis rules, spelling correction heuristics, frame-based blackboard, case library of previously parsed requests, action application mechanism.

Lessons learned: Decomposing a derivation of a semantic representation into individual actions (micro-cases) and iteratively retrieving and applying the next most appropriate action is more accurate than trying to reuse an entire previous derivation. This system was built in about half the time required to build a rule-based system with comparable accuracy.

PERSUADER

References: K. Sycara 1987a,b, 1988a,b

Reasoning task: generating compromise solutions

Domain: labor negotiations

Automated or interactive: automated, with feedback from users

Short description: PERSUADER combines case-based reasoning and decision-theoretic techniques to come up with acceptable partial goal satisfaction resolutions in labor negotiations. A user describes a labor dispute to the system. It creates a new solution using the best precedent-setting case it can find, augmenting that solution with pieces of solutions from other cases when necessary. It does "easy adaptations" as it is initially creating a solution, and after it has put together a ballpark solution, it does harder ones, attempting to anticipate what might go wrong. It presents its solution to the disputants, who provide feedback that gets incorporated back into the problem description. PERSUADER then uses failure cases in an attempt to repair the proposed solution. Decision-theoretic techniques are used to ensure that repairs move the solution in a positive direction. See chapters 11 and 14 for more detail.

Research emphasis: CBR for situations in which only partial goal satisfaction can be achieved

Reasoning processes
   Cases used for: solution generation, adaptation, failure avoidance and recovery, creating models of other agents
   Indexing based on: predictive features in labor negotiation
   Retrieval algorithm/organization of cases: redundant discrimination net
   Method for selecting among retrieved cases: distance in multidimensional similarity hierarchies
   Adaptation methods: parameter adjustment, case-based adaptation

Lessons learned: Combining CBR with decision-theoretic techniques ensured that adaptations moved solutions in positive directions (made them more acceptable to disputants).

PLEXUS

References: Alterman 1986, 1988

Reasoning task: commonsense planning and acting

Domain: everyday world

Automated or interactive: automated, with feedback

Short description: PLEXUS modeled a situated agent making and carrying out a commonsense plan. The assumption is that much of an agent's day-to-day activities are routine, and that agents get around in the world by adapting previous routines (cases) during interaction with the world as a result of a comprehension process that builds a description of the external world and noticed violations of the expected routine. Thus, maintenance of a library of customized routines for an agent's normal activities should simplify future action under normal, or slightly varying, circumstances. Examples of such routines are riding the bus to work, renting a video from the local shop, eating at a favorite restaurant, and calling from the office telephone. PLEXUS modeled the execution-time adaptation such an agent needs to carry out in making its way through the world. Adaptation was done by finding an action to substitute for the one that could not be carried out, and choice of that action was made based on input provided from the external world.

Research emphasis: execution-time adaptation, situated action

Reasoning processes
  Indexing based on: salient features of the world that distinguish one routine from another
  Retrieval method: follow semantic links
  Organization of cases: semantic network
  Internal structure of cases: partonomies, roles, and causal knowledge, with each part and role also organized into categories
  Adaptation: local search; see chapter 11

Knowledge sources: the external world, semantic memory, and case (routine) memory

PRIAR

References: Kambhampati 1993; Kambhampati and Hendler 1992; Kambhampati et al. 1993

Reasoning task: plan modification, adaptation and reuse

Domain: hierarchical nonlinear planning; tested in blocks world and process planning for automated manufacturing

Automated or interactive: automated

Short description: The ability to modify existing plans to accommodate externally-imposed constraints can improve efficiency of planning. PRIAR embodies a theory of incremental plan modification and reuse suitable for hierarchical nonlinear planning. The causal and teleological structure of plans generated by a planner are represented in the form of an explanation of correctness called a "validation structure." Individual planning decisions are justified in terms of their relation to the validation structure. Plan modification is formalized as a process of removing inconsistencies in the validation structure of a plan when it is being reused in a new or changed planning situation. Repair of inconsistencies involves removing unnecessary parts of the plan and adding new non-primitive tasks to the plan to establish missing or failing validations. The result is a partially reduced plan with a consistent validation structure, which is then sent to the planner for complete reduction. During this phase, called refitting, a minimum-conflict heuristic, again based on the validation structure of the plan, is used to ensure conservative modification.

Research emphasis: case-based planning for complex situations

Reasoning processes
  Highlights: disciplined use of causal structures to guide all phases of plan modification and reuse
  Cases used for: initial plan generation

Indexing based on: causal analysis

Retrieval algorithm: validation structure–based similarity metric

Method for selecting among retrieved cases: degree of match between the causal structure of the previous plan and the specification of the new problem

Adaptation methods: retractions using validation structures, followed by extensions using a from-scratch planner

Knowledge sources: causal structure of the plan, domain theory in the form of action operators

PRISM

References: Goodman 1990

Reasoning task: text classification and routing

Domain: interbank financial telexes

Automated or interactive: automated

Short description: PRISM, built using REMIND, uses a case library of over 9600 preclassified telexes to classify interbank financial telexes. The text of a new telex is run through a lexical pattern matcher to tokenize it, and the set of tokens is used for matching. The content-based classification of the retrieved telex is adapted using bank-specific information about departments and employees so that the telex can be routed. PRISM has been in continuous daily operation at Chase Manhattan Bank since October, 1989, and was the first commercially deployed CBR system.

Development emphasis: fast, accurate classification of text; comparison of efficiency, accuracy, and time required to create and maintain rule-based and case-based systems

Reasoning processes

Cases used for: classification

Situation assessment method: lexical pattern matching

Indexing based on: an inductively derived discrimination tree whose features account for variance in the classification of previous texts

Retrieval algorithm: binary decision-tree traversal algorithm

Organization of cases: cases organized into a binary decision tree; leaf nodes are clusters of texts sharing the same classification; internal nodes are binary discriminations based on the presence or absence of tokens and classes of tokens in the text

Method for selecting among retrieved cases: none needed; all retrieved cases have the same classification

Adaptation methods: special-purpose heuristics determine what needs adaptation; other special-purpose rules carry out adaptation

Source of cases: 9600 preclassified interbank financial telexes

Lessons learned: This case-based system took one-quarter the time that it took to build an equivalent rule-based system, with better accuracy (77%) overall. Case-based systems, because they are data-driven, are also more maintainable and reliable.

PRODIGY/ANALOGY

References: Veloso 1991, 1992; Veloso and Carbonell 1989, 1993a, 1993b, 1993c; Carbonell and Veloso 1988

Reasoning task: planning and learning

Domain: demonstrated in a variety of domains

Automated or interactive: automated

Short description: PRODIGY/ANALOGY integrates derivational analogy and means-ends analysis to handle large complex planning problems. The case library is seeded by cases solved by the general-purpose problem solver. Cases are represented as derivational traces of problem-solving episodes, each capturing the subgoaling structure, the explored failed alternatives, and pointers to applied control knowledge. PRODIGY/ANALOGY replays the reasoning done in previous cases, adapting for partial match between new and past situations, and coordinating the integration of multiple retrieved cases through use of the recorded subgoal structure. Learning occurs by accumulation and flexible reuse of cases.

Research emphasis: scaling up of derivational analogy; both complexity of cases and number of cases

Reasoning processes
    Cases used for: guide search in general problem solving
    Indexing based on: footprinted initial state and goal interactions
    Retrieval algorithm: returns a reasonable match rather than enforcing finding of the best match
    Organization of cases: hash tables and redundant discrimination networks
    Method for selecting among retrieved cases: chooses good enough cases based on footprinted similarity metric
    Adaptation methods: multicase replay of problem-solving traces (derivational replay)

Architectural highlights: integration of drivational analogy/case-based reasoning with general purpose planning

Lessons learned: Integrating general-purpose problem solving with CBR has been effective in solving complex problems. Cases reduce general-purpose search; domain knowledge and general problem solving identify appropriate indexes for cases and act as a fall-back engine when adaptation fails. PRODIGY/ANALOGY was tested with a case library of over 1000 cases each with up to 250 decision steps. It scaled up well.

PROTOS

References: Bareiss 1989a; Bareiss, Porter, and Murray 1989; Bareiss, Porter, and Weir 1988; Porter, Bareiss, and Holte 1990

Reasoning task: heuristic classification (e.g., routine diagnosis)

Domain: audiology

Automated or interactive: automated reasoning with interactive knowledge acquisition in the event of failures

Short description: PROTOS learns to perform heuristic classification under the guidance of an expert teacher who provides the system with information needed to rectify problem solving failures. It implements an alternative approach to case retrieval, using weak domain knowledge to connect cases to each other in a case library. PROTOS tightly integrates problem solving and knowledge acquisition through its memory links. PROTOS' classification method is a type of hypothetico-deductive reasoning, frequently used by human diagnosticians. See chapters 2 and 13 for more.

Research emphasis: classification in weak-theory domains; automated knowledge acquisition driven by problem-solving failures

Reasoning processes
    Cases used for: confirming classifications, suggesting alternative classifications
    Situation assessment method: none, requires complete description
    Indexing based on: learned associations between situational features and classifications, learned prototypicality ratings of cases, learned differences between similar cases
    Retrieval algorithm: same as classification algorithm, see chapter 13
    Organization of cases: organized in categories and ranked in order of prototypicality; difference links connect similar cases with significant differences
    Matching process: knowledge-based pattern matching

Knowledge sources: cases and partial domain theory

Lessons learned: A relatively straightforward case-based approach sufficed to acquire the knowledge required to perform diagnostic classification at an expert level. A case-based approach may be required to handle the tremendous variability present in instances of real-world categories.

REMIND CBR Shell
Cognitive Systems, Inc.

References: Cognitive Systems 1992

Reasoning task: prediction, classification, fault diagnosis, help-desk, data mining

Domain: generic tool

Automated or interactive: interactive

Short description: REMIND provides facilities for rapid prototyping and deployment of CBR applications. A key feature of REMIND is the ability to augment case representation with domain knowledge. REMIND includes facilities for importing data from existing databases, designing custom forms for the display and manipulation of data, building semantic hierarchies that define abstractions over symbolic data, deriving abstract features from more primitive data, building a qualitative model of a domain to guide index generation, inductive indexing of cases, browsing through retrieved cases, and validating the accuracy of a CBR application. REMIND runs on a variety of hardware platforms. A C-function library allows integration of CBR applications into other systems.

Development emphasis: generic classification and prediction facilities within the case-based framework and associated tools and user interfaces

Reasoning processes
> **Indexing based on:**   conceptual categories of cases defined by an expert; inductively derived discriminations guided by a qualitative model of a domain, abstract derived features defined by expert-supplied heuristics, and abstractions over symbolic values; expert-supplied assessment of importance
> **Retrieval algorithm:**   decision-tree traversal and/or nearest-neighbor
> **Organization of cases:**   clusters sharing common characteristics and/or flat memory
> **Matching process:**   nearest-neighbor
> **Method for selecting among retrieved cases:**   user browses all, is made aware of nearest-neighbor match score
> **Adaptation methods:**   special-purpose expert-supplied heuristics.

Knowledge sources: cases, expert-supplied qualitative models, symbol hierarchies, heuristics for deriving abstract features from more primitive ones, induction, expert-supplied heuristics for adaptation

ROUTER

References: Goel and Callantine 1992; Goel, Callantine et al. 1991

Reasoning task: robot navigation—path planning

Domain: college campus

Automated or interactive: automated

Short description: ROUTER integrates traditional model-based methods for robot navigation with a case-based method. It also suggests how spatial models of the navigation space can provide answers to some issues in case-based navigation. It uses a hierarchically organized spatial model to index cases and to organize the case memory. It uses model-based repair to adapt past plans and to verify new ones. ROUTER uses a flexible control architecture that allows for opportunistic selection and integration of the case-based and model-based planning methods. A distributed version further explores cooperation between model-based reasoning and case-based reasoning in a parallel and distributed environment.

Research emphasis: the role of topographic models of space in path planning and in organizing and indexing path-planning cases

Reasoning processes
> **Cases used for:** plan generation and adaptation
> **Indexing based on:** locations and neighborhoods in the navigation space
> **Retrieval algorithm:** nearest (spatial) neighbor
> **Organization of cases:** around neighborhoods in the navigation space
> **Adaptation methods:** rather merging: combining solutions from multiple cases, combining partial solutions generated by model-based and case-based components

Lessons learned: Domain models can provide a scheme for organizing the case memory; probing the case memory can provide clues to whether case-based or other methods should be used.

SCAVENGER

References: Alterman, Zito-Wolf, and Carpenter 1991; Zito-Wolf and Alterman 1990, 1992

Reasoning task: plan acquisition; case acquisition

Domain: operation of everyday mechanical and electronic devices

Automated or interactive: automated, interacts with the world

Short description: SCAVENGER is an adaptive planner. It learns plans for using everyday mechanical and electronic devices, such as photocopiers and telephones, by operationalizing instructions received from a person or manual. It attempts to carry out instructions on a device and adapts and refines them as necessary based on interaction with its environment. Its multicase plan representation facilitates accumulating and organizing procedural knowledge derived from experiences. The multicase partitions episodes into their component decisions, allowing individual access to novel components of an example while avoiding redundant storage of common components. It is a kind of "generalized" procedure, but not a generalization, as the details of examples are retained. It is efficient to access, and it facilitates the merger of knowledge from multiple examples.

Research emphasis: representing procedures to allow access to their constituent parts, procedure acquisition, adaptation and plan refinement

Reasoning processes
> **Cases used for:** plan generation, expectation generation
> **Indexing based on:** goals, plan being carried out, step in plan

Retrieval algorithm/organization of cases: case library is partitioned by the multi-case structure; within each partition, retrieval is by best-match on primarily first-order features

Matching process: recursive numeric similarity function

Method for selecting among retrieved cases: high score

Adaptation methods: local search, extension of PLEXUS's method

Knowledge sources: cases, semantic memory, library of instruction patterns

Lessons learned: When a CBR system interacts with the world, it can identify the kinds of problems that arise and the kind of knowledge that it needs to perform realistically. Choice of procedural representation significantly affects the performance and generality of such a system. Indexing vocabulary should be concrete enough to be recognized in the course of normal activity.

SQUAD: Software Quality Control Advisor

References: Kitano et al. 1992

Reasoning task: advising

Domain: software quality control

Automated or interactive: interactive

Short description: SQUAD is a large-scale, corporatewide case-based system for software quality control. A user describes a problem to the system, and SQUAD retrieves cases with a similar problem. If the user is not satisfied, he or she redescribes the problem and continues the search. Cases are collected from throughout NEC corporation. The case library currently holds 20,000 cases and increases at the rate of 3,000 cases per year. Cases are stored in a relational database, and a nearest-neighbor similarity metric is used to choose appropriate cases. Each case corresponds to a software quality control activity done by NEC engineers, and the SWQC group is in charge of maintaining the case library.

Emphasis: knowledge-engineering process for acquisition of large numbers of cases, flexible and robust case representation and retrieval, use of a relational database for case storage and retrieval, integration of a case library with a mainstream information system, use of software engineering techniques (the CASE method) to build CBR applications

Reasoning processes

Cases used for: solution generation, warning

Situation assessment method: users incrementally refine queries

Retrieval process: SQL queries are posed to the database, each associated with a similarity measure for nearest-neighbor match

Organization of cases: relational database

Method for selecting among retrieved cases: all made available

Sources of cases: software quality control engineers submit after each activity forms whose format corresponds to a case in the case library; 160,000 employees involved; 15,000 have made case reports

Lessons learned: Substantial organization support is needed for a project of this magnitude; flow of information and processing between organizational units must be well defined. In this case, the activity was well supported and commanded by the president/CEO and board members. A system this large needs speed. This architecture can acquire speed easily with a massively parallel machine.

SWALE/ACCEPTER

References: Kass and Leake 1988; Kass, Leake and Owens 1986; Leake 1991a, 1991b, 1992a, 1992b; Schank and Leake 1989

Reasoning task: explanation of anomalous events

Domain: death and destruction

Automated or interactive: SWALE automated; ACCEPTER interactive

Short description: SWALE generates explanations of anomalous events in news stories. Upon detecting an anomaly, it retrieves prior explanations, evaluates their appropriateness, and adapts them for the new situation. Cases are represented in terms of their causal dependencies, allowing retrieval based on similarities in causal structure. The resulting cross-domain retrieval allows generation of creative explanations. ACCEPTER evaluates explanations based on their relevance to the targeted anomaly and their usefulness in achieving the overarching goals of the reasoner. ACCEPTER outputs descriptions of flaws in explanations to choose a best explanation chosen from among several and to guide further adaptation.

Research emphasis: explanation, cross-domain indexing, evaluation

Reasoning processes
    Cases used for: suggesting explanations
    Situation assessment method: comparison of new events to standard stereotyped
        anomaly patterns
    Indexing based on: anomaly characterizations, unusual features
    Retrieval algorithm/organization of cases: flat memory, indexed one- level deep,
        retrieval based on indexes
    Method for selecting among retrieved cases: relevance to anomaly, plausibility of
        suggested explanation, usefulness
    Adaptation methods: local search, specialized search, search heuristics indexed by
        anomaly vocabulary
    Knowledge sources: cases, anomaly patterns, explanation patterns, adaptation strate-
        gies, requirements for useful explanations

Lessons learned: Cases can be used to better understand poorly-specified input situations. Retrieval of the best cases requires access to the internal structure of cases, not just their raw facts. Cases in the form of stereotypes play a useful role, especially in explanation. CBR has much potential for explanation, making explanation-construction inexpensive and guiding a reasoner to focus only on those kinds of explanations that have proven useful in similar contexts in the past.

Other Systems

The systems in this section of the appendix are preliminary, never got fully implemented, are similar to other more fully explained systems in the Appendix, or are explained well in the text, or I was unable to gather enough details about their inner workings and lessons learned to make a useful longer entry.

AskJef (Barber et al. 1992) is designed to help software engineers in designing human-machine interfaces. The user specifies a design problem, and the system retrieves a set of cases and orders them in terms of their relevance. The user can browse through the cases and associated design principles, guidelines, domain object descriptions, and prototypical errors. Cases from other domains are available by asking for further illustrations of design principles and guidelines. Design examples are represented graphically and decomposed temporally. The different types of knowledge are cross-indexed to enable the designer to navigate through the system's memory to gain an understanding of the range of interface design problems or to get help with a particular problem. AskJef uses text, graphics, animation, and voice to make its presentations. AskJef gets its greatest advantage from organizing cases around abstract principles and guidelines. Designers like to refer to such guidelines, but they are often too abstract to make operational without much experience. Cases are useful in AskJef in making design guidelines and principles concrete. AskJef was a joint project between Georgia Institute of Technology and the NCR Corporation. It was built using Toolbook and Art-IM on an IBM-compatible PC.

ASP-II (Alexander and Tsatsoulis 1991) analyzes the electromagnetic compatibility of complex, co-located communication systems. Given a description of a collection of communication systems, ASP-II retrieves complete or partial cases or skeletal plans. It adapts the cases or instantiates the skeletal plans to generate a detailed plan about how to perform analysis to determine the electomagnetic compatibility of the full communication systems. Its contribution is in the integration of case-based and skeletal planning. It uses domain-specific special-purpose critics for adaptation and merging.

Bidder's Associate, built by Klein Associates, Inc., is a case-based aiding system used by process engineers as an aid in bid preparation. It is currently in use at Enginetics, a manufacturer of jet engine parts located in Dayton, OH. The process engineer enters specifications for the part in question, and the system responds with a list of similar parts previously manufactured by Enginetics. Each has information associated with it about the resources needed, time required, and cost incurred in manufacturing these similar parts. Process engineers at the company report that Bidder's Associate improves bid quality and reduces the time needed to formulate a bid. Bidder's Associate runs on a personal computer.

CAB-Assembly (Pu and Reschberger 1991a, 1991b) uses cases to guide heuristic search in the domain of assembly-sequence generation for manufacturing. Given a product (consisting of several parts) and descriptions of its final configuration, CAB-Assembly proposes to assemble two parts at a time based on previous cases. The case library stores failures as well as successes, and the system is able to propose correct search paths most of the time. When search proceeds in a wrong direction, it can be caught by previously failed cases. Cases greatly increase the capability of heuristic search, suggesting good search paths and helping the reasoner to avoid blind alleys. CAB-Assembly's indexes are based on geometrical and spatial relationships.

CAPER (Kettler et al. 1992, 1993) is a case-based planner in the domains of transport logistics and automobile construction. Its emphasis is on parallel retrieval from a large case library and on the merging of several subplans to create a plan. CAPER attempts to recall a single old plan that will achieve its target goals. For any goals the retrieved plan does not address, additional plans or plan fragments are retrieved. This is repeated until all goals are achieved. The retrieved plans are then merged, possibly with adaptation. Cases are represented as collections of component plans stored as graphs. Retrieval processes emphasize subgraph matching. Initial results show considerable speedup over serial retrieval algorithms.

CAS (Consumer Advisory System [Turner 1986, 1987]) was an early case-based planner. It presented plans to consumers about how to acquire or build consumer products, in particular, bookshelves. It explained plans to the level of detail required by its users, expanding them in detail only at a user's request. CAS kept track of the preconditions for each of its plan's steps and noticed the need to adapt old plans when step preconditions were violated. Each precondition knew how its normal violations manifested themselves, and each indexed the adaptation heuristics to be carried out in the event of precondition violation.

CATO, the Case Argument Tutor (Aleven and Ashley 1992; Ashley and Aleven 1991, 1992), teaches law students basic skills in making and responding to arguments that cite cases and gives students practice in reasoning with cases. The system presents exercises to teach law students issues such as justifying a legal assertion by citing a relevant case, selecting the most relevant cases to cite, avoiding cases that can be trumped with counterexamples, and distinguishing an opponent's case. CATO poses problems to the student and provides tools to help with analyzing the problem and fashioning an answer. Students are provided with feedback in the form of explanations, examples, and follow-up problems that drive the lesson home. Cases are grouped according to Argument Context, a collection of a problem situation and cases related to the problem situation in pedagogically interesting ways. CATO includes an automatic example generator, a deductive retriever, and facilities for filtering, ranking, and storing complex examples. It chooses cases for presentation to students based on a combination of pedagogical and domain-specific relevance criteria. It is also being used as a research tool to discover a cognitive model of explaining and arguing with cases that can explain the differences between novice and expert performance in problem solving and adversarial reasoning.

CBR+EBL (Cain, Pazzani, and Silverstein 1991) uses a combination of case-based reasoning and explanation-based reasoning to make predictions about foreign trade negotiations. It retrieves cases by doing a search of the whole case library looking for the best-matching case, calculated by a numeric similarity function. Similarity criteria are associated with each case in the case library, making calculation of a match score highly context sensitive. Those features that play a part in explaining the outcome of a case are assigned higher importance than those that do not.

CBS (Bradtke and Lehnert 1988) uses cases to guide heuristic search. Given a search space and operators for moving about the space, it uses a case library of known problem solutions to guide it through the search. The case library operates as a type of evaluation function that prunes the space and facilitates search. CBS solved the 8-puzzle from arbitrary start states using a small case library of previously-established solution paths to guide its search. No additional knowledge about subgoals, chunking, or any other form of derivational abstraction was needed. The key to making it work was choosing a good indexing strategy. Rather than indexing cases by raw placement of the pieces, they were indexed by derived descriptions including several descriptions of adjacency and several descriptions of patterns.

CHASER (Cuthill 1992; Cuthill and McCartney 1992a, 1992b) is a legal case-based reasoner that performs issue spotting and precedent retrieval for a restricted class of situations in the tort law domain. CHASER uses a combination of common sense, tort law and cases to derive definitions of legal principles, to decide which principles and issues are relevant in the new situation, and to identify points of disagreement between the new situation and previous precedent. CHASER constructs arguments for plaintiffs based on this analysis and retrieved cases. CHASER has been tested on three different types of situations, varying each ten different ways. Its case library holds thirty-five cases.

CHIRON (Sanders 1991a, 1991b) incorporates hierarchical and case-based planners, which cooperate to produce plans in the domain of personal income tax planning. Plans are based on "safe harbor" plans, standard conservative prototypes that are likely to succeed, with adaptations suggested and constrained by previous cases. Output includes both plans and HYPO-style arguments supporting the plans.

COOKIE (McCartney 1990, 1993) plans the preparation of meals, and along with DEFARGE, its execution monitor, monitors their preparation. Planning is done by adapting cases; a plan can be produced from multiple or partial cases. Learning is through adding its experiences to its case base. Problem specification is done interactively with a user; plans are generated automatically and then adapted interactively. Execution is done via interaction between the system and a cook. COOKIE's cases are uninterpreted, i.e., they contain, and are indexed by, the raw details of a situation rather than higher-level interpretations of the situation. This has been found to be especially useful in recording execution, as it is not always possible to interpret effects at the time they happen.

CREANIMATE (D. Edelson 1991a, 1991b, 1992; Edelson et al. 1993) uses cases for instruction. Students learn about the design principles associated with various animal behaviors. Using those principles, students design new animals by modifying existing animals. During a discussion of how well adapted the animal is, CREANIMATE presents videos of animals in the wild that illustrate the principles under discussion. CREANIMATE includes a task environment and a storyteller. The task environment engages the student in a motivating task that motivates him or her to want to find out about certain things. The storyteller capitalizes on these opportunities for learning by presenting cases that help students to learn from the situations they encounter in the task environment. CREANIMATE's research emphasis is on indexing and retrieval strategies for serving pedagogical goals.

Creative JULIA (Kolodner and Penberthy 1990) investigates the role of case-based reasoning in creative design. Its creative process is an iterative brainstorming process involving recall of cases that might solve the new situation, evaluation of each for the pros and cons of its solution in the new situation, and use of the results of that evaluation to add constraint to the problem specification and the solution specification. Of particular interest in that process is specification of a retrieval process that allows brainstorming and the role of evaluative procedures in incrementally refining a problem specification. A retrieval process for brainstorming seems to need relaxed preference criteria for choosing which of the many accessed cases are worth considering. The issue in evaluation is where the criteria for evaluation come from. Several sources were identified: constraints of the new problem situation, well-known esthetic criteria, and criteria arising from the evaluation of previous similar designs. The initial implementation figured out what to do with leftover rice. More recent studies are in the areas of architectural design, algorithm design, design of lesson plans, and design of small mechanical devices.

CYRUS (Kolodner 1983a, 1983b, 1984, 1985) predates case-based reasoning but was co-developed with MOPs as a cognitive model of the storage and retrieval of large numbers of events in a memory. CYRUS stored and retrieved events in the life of Cyrus Vance, who was then Secretary of State of the United States. Retrieval was in response to questions posed by a user. CYRUS's elaboration strategies allowed it to bridge the gap between characterizations of events in questions and characterizations of the same events in memory, providing the first set of situation-assessment mechanisms. Its memory was organized as a redundant discrimination network and it chose its indexes by means of a checklist created by examining which dimensions of the domain tended to make inferential predictions. More detail on CYRUS can be found in chapters 4, 8, and 10.

DEJAVU (Bardasz and Zeid 1991, 1992) is a domain-independent design assistant. It acquires design process models from a designer as new problems are solved. Over time, as the system becomes knowlegeable in the domain of deployment, it acts as a design assistant, retrieving past design cases suitable for reuse in response to a user-specified problem specification. It follows a top-down decomposition design model, and solutions are usually composed of a combination of user-suggested and retrieved design cases. The adaptation module works interactively with the user toward integrating these design suggestions into a cohesive whole. Its initial implementation is in a mechanical design domain. DEJAVU uses redundant discrimination nets and does fine-grained indexing based on large numbers of features taken from the design specification. The major lesson learned is that using large numbers of unprioritized fine details as indexes can be overwhelming to redundant discrimination schemes. This could be fixed by interpreting situations to extract their most important descriptors and, based on that, prioritizing the indexes.

DIOGENES (Mostow 1992; Mostow and Fisher 1989) resynthesizes heuristic search algorithms using derivational replay. When given a new specification for an old algorithm, DIOG-

ENES uses derivational replay to extract those portions of it that still apply and to connect them together appropriately. The user completes the algorithm by adding in additional transformations that are needed. DIOGENES extends BOGART's procedures, handling transformations that rearrange existing structure in a plan.

EXPEDITOR (Robinson and Kolodner 1991) takes a case-based approach to the learning of new plans for getting around in the world. Beginning with a set of simple plans, EXPEDITOR responds to its needs to get around in the world, in the process interleaving its known plans to achieve conjunctive sets of goals and learning the situations in which its plans fail. Its memory is organized in a MOP-like structure, and the storage of annotations about failure in these structures allows it to get better at explaining its failures, repairing them, and avoiding them. EXPEDITOR combines planning and action and uses feedback from the world to recognize which plans are applicable.

IPP (Lebowitz 1983a, 1983b) was a precursor to CBR but was co-developed with MOPs and CYRUS and explored many of the memory issues that arise in making large numbers of cases available for reasoning. IPP and RESEARCHER (Lebowitz 1986a), its descendant, read news stories and built up a memory of those stories, organizing the stories in redundant discrimination networks, creating generalizations as they built their memories, and using those generalizations for some of their language understanding tasks. Understanding processes became progressively more memory-based in each system; items being represented became progressively more complex. IPP's domain was terrorism stories; its cases (terrorism episodes) were relatively unstructured and undetailed. RESEARCHER read patent abstracts about disk drives; its cases (descriptions of disk drives) were represented in the form of hierarchical structures and had much detail. UNIMEM (Lebowitz 1986a, 1987), their descendant, concentrated on generalization, using memory's contents to control the explanations created by generalization processes. Its representations were again simple, and it worked in a variety of domains. These programs are not strictly case-based programs, but they do integrate memory processes with other reasoning processes. The major lesson learned is that for such processing, a large memory is necessary—500 cases were not nearly enough. The second lesson learned is that representations should be kept as simple as possible. Although they must be fully expressive, simplicity of form allows easy examination and matching.

JUDGE (Bain 1984, 1986, 1989) assesses situations and assigns sentences for juvenile criminals. It takes as input a description of a fighting situation that resulted in death, and it must sentence the offender. Crimes are described in terms of the actions of the participants. But to sentence the offender, JUDGE needs to infer the circumstances behind the killing (e.g., who started the fight, how violent it was, fear factors) and the chances of the offender repeating his violent action. JUDGE assesses the situation and then adapts a solution from a previous similar situation to derive a sentence in the new case. After deriving a sentence, JUDGE tests its consistency by deriving a sentence from a second case (either the second best match or the case the retrieved case was derived from) to make sure the sentence is consistent with other previous decisions. See chapter 10 for more details.

KRITIK2 (Stroulia and Goel 1992; Stroulia et al. 1992) is a descendant of KRITIK. Like KRITIK, it designs simple physical devices. KRITIK2 augments KRITIK in several ways.

Foremost, it emphasizes the use of generic teleological mechanisms, such as cascading, for non-parametric adaptation, adding to the set of general causal mechanisms available to aid the adaptation process. As a result of the addition of these mechanisms, KRITIK2 must organize several types of abstract cases in its case library. It uses MOP-like structures to organize its model knowledge and case knowledge, integrating the two types of knowledge with each other to allow uniform access and differentiating out MOP-like and TOP-like models. The addition of this new type of causal knowledge allows blame assignment and repair in a broader range of situations than KRITIK allows. Its many kinds of adaptation procedures and its TOP-like structures for organizing domain-independent causal knowledge aim it toward the ability to do creative design based on cross-domain analogies.

MEMORABILIA (Oxman 1993a, 1993b, 1993c) stores architectural design cases that have the status of precedents and makes them available to students who are learning design. A design precedent is a recognized outstanding example of a particular type or style of design. The user presents his or her design issue to the system by filling in a form, and the system searches for relevant design cases. The user may also browse the library of cases. Designs are represented as stories (natural-language descriptions) linked to appropriate illustrations. The system's cases concentrate on spatial organization, usually taught early in the design curriculum. Its cases represent museums and similar types of buildings. Work on MEMORABILIA is aimed toward creating a universal indexing vocabulary for design similar to the UIF.

META-AQUA (Cox and Ram 1992; Ram and Cox 1993) uses schema-like cases called meta-explanation patterns (meta-XPs), to reason introspectively about its own reasoning processes and the knowledge used by these reasoning processes as it carries out a performance task (in this case, story understanding). In introspective multistrategy learning, a reasoner introspects about its performance on a reasoning task, identifies what it needs to learn to improve its performance, formulates learning goals to acquire the required knowledge, and pursues its learning goals using multiple learning strategies. Meta-XPs provide a uniform representation for reasoning and learning tasks and subtasks, making it easy to add new learning strategies and reasoning tasks to the system. Meta-XPs capture domain knowledge, indexing knowledge, knowledge about carrying out reasoning processes, knowledge for selection of reasoning processes, and knowledge for selection of learning processes. A simple planner collects and combines reasoning goals suggested by meta-XPs.

The MLS Library, built by Cognitive Systems, Inc., using REMIND, helps buyers appraise their homes and locate homes that meet their specifications. For appraisal, users define the characteristics of the house they want to appraise and then perform a retrieval to look for comparable houses. They pick the best-matching house from those retrieved and ask the system to adapt its price to calculate an asking price for the house in question. For house-hunting, users select the features of their dream house and then define a set of weights for those features that are most important to them. A nearest-neighbor retrieval is performed to find close-matching houses to visit. The MLS Library uses several kinds of organizational and retrieval techniques. For appraisal (an evaluative task), it uses a prototype hierarchy followed by an inductively created decision tree. For house-hunting (a generative task), it uses a search of the whole case library, using a numeric evaluation function to choose the best cases. Figures associated with the house appraisal example at the end of chapter 13 come from the MLS Library.

NNable (Laffey, Machiraju, and Chandhok 1991a, 1991b), developed at Apple Computer, is an environment for supporting the performance of "knowledge workers" and provides a corporate memory to benefit the community of "knowledge workers." The CBR component, built using REMIND, is one element of this environment. The human troubleshooter uses a customized form to enter a description of the troubleshooting event, and the system retrieves archived problem-solving experiences to help the user diagnose and then repair the problem. Each case represents an entire problem-solving episode, from problem statement to final diagnosis and repair. The system is set up so that iterative use of CBR on a single troubleshooting event is supported. Cases are stored, in NNable, in a "case server" that allows multiple end user stations to retrieve cases at the same time. Retrieval in NNable uses REMIND's nearest-neighbor retrieval scheme. In this application, there was a decrease in retrieval quality when the qualitative modeling features of REMIND were used. Cases were originally collected from troubleshooters via interviews and observations, but the case library was allowed to grow naturally as it was used. The major work in building this system went into developing a vocabulary for representing cases. The vocabulary had to bridge the "language discrepancies" of different users of the system.

OCCAM (Pazzani 1989, 1990, 1991) is a learning system that combines several kinds of learning, including similarity-based generalization and explanation-based learning. It learns from its individual experiences and maintains a case library of those experiences that it accesses as it is trying to learn. Its case library is in the form of a redundant discrimination net, storing both cases and generalized cases. While most redundant discrimination networks use a similarity-based method to form their generalizations, OCCAM uses an explanation-based method if explanatory information is available. OCCAM indexes cases in memory by those surface features that are indicative of causal relationships. It uses explanation-based indexing methods if there is available explanatory knowledge. When it is unable to explain new events, it indexes them by all known features and uses similarity-based indexing methods to form new generalizations. The generalizations formed by similarity-based learning may be used to explain and index new events. OCCAM answers questions by making predictions from generalized events and retrieves precedents (cases) to support its arguments.

OGRE (Wall et al. 1988; Donahue 1989) is a domain-independent case retrieval tool. A domain expert describes a domain in terms of factors (characteristics), each representing one aspect of the domain, legal values for that aspect, a method for comparing two values of that factor, and a method for determining the importance of that factor in any given comparison. A user describes a situation to OGRE in terms of values for the factors in the domain, and the system presents the user with a list of similar cases, based on the comparison methods supplied by the expert. The user is responsible for making decisions based on retrieved cases. PC-OGRE is PC-based, built in PC Scheme. Scaleup will require a real database and better indexing than PC-OGRE has right now. The most time-consuming part of getting a system up and running with PC-OGRE, as with any case-based system, is getting users to input a sizeable case library. OGRE is used at Texas Instruments and has been evaluated by its users. Users find case retrieval to their liking. They want systems to help them, but do not trust systems to do their jobs for them. Users find retrieval and recognition of failure cases to be as important as retrieval of good solutions.

ORCA (Blidberg, Turner, and Chappel 1991; Turner 1992; Turner and Stevenson 1992), which is currently under construction, will be an intelligent controller for ocean science autonomous underwater vehicles (AUVs). It builds on MEDIC, but also draws on other work in reactive planning and autonomous control. Like MEDIC, its cases are in the form of descriptive and procedural schemas organized in MOP-like hierarchies. Its hierarchical organization of schemas allows context-sensitive reasoning and attention-focusing. Its agenda control allows a combination of planful behavior and prompt reaction to changes in the environment. ORCA uses schemas to control the whole range of robot behaviors, both high-level and low-level.

PANDA (Roderman and Tsatsoulis 1993) is a case-based design assistant in the domain of fire engines. It targets novice designers who have little knowledge of the domain and need both advice and explanations. Given a description of design goals, it selects pieces of old designs and design prototypes that satisfy most of them. It presents those to the user, and the user guides adaptation and explores design choices. Presented cases advise about design choices and predict failures. PANDA integrates the use of cases and prototypes, preferring to present cases to its users if any are available and presenting design prototypes when none are.

PRO (Lehnert 1987a, 1987b) takes as input the letters in a word and determines how to pronounce it. It creates a case library of grapheme-phoneme relations based on a training set of word-pronunciation pairs. After training on 750 words, PRO obtained a 76 percent phoneme hit rate on a test set of 100 previously unseen words. The PRO architecture exploits symbolic methods to establish a search space of possible pronunciations and localist connectionism to select a single preferred pronunciation from the resulting search space. This hybrid architecture demonstrates how a large case library of simple cases can be efficiently accessed and exploited for CBR-style problem solving.

The ReMind Help Desk, developed by Cognitive Systems, Inc. using REMIND, helps users diagnose common PC problems by examining past cases. The system has a library of 500 cases donated by GE's PC help desk. Users enter a description of their problem in natural language and also fill in a simple form. In effect, retrieval is a three-tier process. In the first step, natural language input is mapped into a concept lexicon that can be used for retrieval. Next, traversal of an inductively generated descrimination network determines abstract diagnostic categories. Finally, nearest neighbor matching determines specific diagnoses and orders the cases for presentation to the user. The user can interactively refine the match by adding further symptom information and asking for additional retrievals.

RUNNER (Hammond 1988) is an opportunistic case-based planning program that combines planning with execution. Its domain is errand-running. As it sets up new goals for itself, it finds that it cannot achieve some of them immediately but must wait for an opportunity to present itself. RUNNER indexes blocked goals in its memory according to the characteristics of situations in which the goal is likely to become unblocked (derived from the goal's preconditions). As RUNNER moves through its daily routine, its blocked goals are triggered by the changing state of the world and, as the opportunity arises, it carries them out. RUNNER is a descendant of TRUCKER and is also implemented using the notion of "opportunistic memory," but its domain is richer and it carries out a wider range of activities.

SCI-ED (Chandler and Kolodner 1993; Kolodner 1991b) is a story-based hypermedia browsing system in support of lesson planning for elementary science education. It supports a contingency planning model of lesson planning. Teachers can thus use the system to help put a lesson together (create a plan) and to critique and repair the lesson plan. The system helps teachers anticipate problems that might arise in using a plan in their classrooms, opportunities for adding additional or optional activities, and means of avoiding those problems and integrating the additional activities. Because teachers use the system outside the classroom, in order for the system's advice to be useful, it is particularly important to give teachers guidelines for recognizing when these special situations are happening or about to happen. Because many of the issues that arise in the classroom are not specific to particular lessons, teachers can also come to the system with a classroom problem in mind and receive advice on that. SCI-ED is being built after significant interaction with school system science coordinators and inexperienced teachers (who point out what teachers need help with and relate their war stories) and experienced teachers (who have a wealth of lesson ideas and advice about dealing with classroom issues). As in the ASK systems, SCI-ED holds links between the many stories, guidelines, lessons, and approaches in its library, and its interface shows users the kind of related information that is available. It uses a combination of general guidelines and compelling personal stories to make its points. See chapters 14 and 15 for more details and examples of SCI-ED's cases.

SHAMUS (Broverman 1992) is a case-based interface to a rich hypermedia document base of examples of semiconductor wafer fabrication. Wafer fabrication is a process that even most experienced engineers cannot explain well. SHAMUS provides engineers with a library of "lessons learned." Access to documents describing past similar successes and failures provides useful information in the form of "hints" and "reminders." Because users often do not have a well-specified idea as to what they are looking for when they are browsing the document library, SHAMUS provides a way for users to incrementally refine their problem descriptions, and each iteration can be fueled by knowledge gained and refined during a process of browsing related electronic documentation. Some documents provide suggestions without enough information for constructing a new solution, and this specification process also helps users find related documents that can provide additional detail. Acceptance of SHAMUS as a prototype has been high, but a lot of work was required to scale up the documentation library, to put it into hypermedia form, and to index the documents. The system was built using ART-IM's CBR kernal and uses KMS as the underlying hypermedia tool, all running on a Unix platform.

SPIEL (Burke and Kass 1992; Kass et al. 1992; Kass et al. in preparation) presents stories to students for tutorial purposes as they are learning about complex social tasks (for example, selling) in the context of a simulation system. SPIEL continuously monitors the stream of student events and simulator states, looking for opportunities to tell some story. SPIEL uses storytelling purposes, in addition to UIF-type specifications, to index its stories. Indexes are turned into production rules that can efficiently recognize storytelling opportunities in the midst of students' interaction with the social simulation. Indexes are hand-generated using an associated story indexing tool. A generic student model and a task model are used to determine appropriate storytelling strategies and the purposes that should be addressed during tutoring. The relation between a story and an opportunity to tell that story is more complex than can be captured by a simple numeric similarity metric. Thus, the right story to tell is chosen by a set of procedures that compare stories and the new situation to each other based on pedagogical guidelines. SPIEL's stories are captured on video. The system knows only the information about them that is captured in an index.

SHRINK (Kolodner 1982, 1983c; Kolodner and Kolodner 1987) was one of the earliest case-based projects and was influential in defining the case-based reasoning paradigm, but it never became a fully-implemented system. It was designed to be a psychiatric diagnostician; the intent was to use a combination of category descriptors and cases to guide diagnosis and treatment. SHRINK was to get better over time as its memory was augmented with new success and failure situations. SHRINK's contribution was a series of real-life cases that illustrated the ways in which cases were used for expert reasoning and were suggestive of the means by which expertise can be built up from experience.

TaxOps (Slator and Fidel 1993; Slator and Riesbeck 1991), one of the ASK systems, delivers expert advice to corporate tax professionals about corporate tax planning and services. Advice is in the form of "war" stories, anecdotes, and professional opinions, gathered from videotaped interviews with corporate tax specialists. TaxOps places the user within a network of these video clips and, by motivating a tour of the network, engages the user in an interactive video dialogue with these experts. The intent is to give users easy access to the corporate memory by making a "roomful of experts" available to them. The educational component of this strategy relies on the intuition that it can be instructive to hear a good story, told at the right time and with authority, particularly if the story is relevant to a task or problem confronting the student. In TaxOps, this is accomplished by a combination of case-based matching and goal-directed browsing. To initiate a TaxOps session, a user fills out a short form describing a business situation of interest. The users are given a choice of several entry points to the video clip network and are then free to navigate through the video network, viewing clips that are relevant to their purposes, and traversing to other clips along pre-set links that pose questions that are answered by connected clips. The session is guided by the structure of the network but is controlled by users, whose interest in the subject matter leads them from clip to clip. TaxOps succeeds on several levels. First, it captures a portion of a corporate memory: good stories about successes and failures that bear repeating because they are entertaining, informative, and memorable. Second, it connects the stories of different areas of expertise, and thus forms links between different areas of thought (in this case, different tax practices). Third, it reasons about real data and real cases; it makes rational associations between opportunities and services; and it does this in a way that is visible to users. Fourth, it places users into a network of experts, where they can follow their own curiosity, get answers to their questions, and interact with the experts in a nonthreatening way, without the pressure that often accompanies learning situations. Lastly, TaxOps is engaging to use: the "roomful of experts in a box" is fun to talk to.

TRUCKER (Hammond 1988; Marks, Hammond, and Converse 1988) is an opportunistic case-based reasoner that integrates planning and execution in a realistic planning situation—it lacks perfect information about its world and it is not always allowed to take its plans to completion before new goals arise. Its domain is UPS-type pick-up and delivery scheduling. It begins with a set of items it must deliver and/or pick up, and it plans a route for doing that. As it carries out its plan, it is informed of additional pickups and deliveries that it must do (new goals). Based on its knowledge of where it is, where it intends to be later in its plan, and which locations are close to each other, it integrates the new instructions into its plan, grabbing the opportunity to address each as it becomes viable. From its successes, TRUCKER learns new routes through town that allow it to efficiently schedule multiple orders in disparate locations (i.e., plans for achieving conjunctive goals). The mechanism that allows TRUCKER to opportunistically schedule new orders relies on a combination of its map, its current plan, and its memory of the way it has carried out plans in the past. As in other case-based planners, memory is used to remember past plans that are reused in new circumstances. In addition, its current plan is broken up and put into memory in pieces (each corresponding to a subgoal or conjunctive set of subgoals), each one indexed by the conditions under which it can successfully be carried out. This way, if the opportunity to carry out a later part of the plan arrives earlier than anticipated, TRUCKER can notice the opportunity and take advantage of it. This conception of memory is called "opportunistic memory."

VOTE (Slade 1991, 1992, 1993) uses case-based reasoning to simulate and predict voting decisions of members of the United States House of Representatives on given bills, using goal-based knowledge representations of a member's past voting record, political ideology, and relationships with constituency groups. VOTE generates natural language explanations for its decisions in both English and French. Indexing is shallow (inverted index) and based on the goals of the voter, his or her voting record, public norms, constituency issue agendas, and bill consequences. Cases are judged according to their potential consequences in order to choose the best out of the many retrieved. Goals and their relative importance seem to provide a computationally feasible indexing strategy when reasoning about decision making and social relationships. VOTE has also been applied to other decision domains, including going to college, buying a car, investment choices, and capital budgeting.

Bibliography

Acorn, T., and Walden, S. 1992. SMART: Support management cultivated reasoning technology for Compaq customer service. In *Proceedings of AAAI-92. Cambridge, MA: AAAI Press/MIT Press.*

Alba, J. W., and Hasher, L. 1983. Is memory schematic? *Psychological Bulletin 93: 203–231.*

Aleven, V., and Ashley, K. D. 1992. Automated generation of examples for a tutorial in case-based argumentation. In *Proceedings, Second International Conference on Intelligent Tutoring Systems (ITS-92), Montreal,* ed. C. Frasson, G. Gauthier, and G. I. McCalla. Berlin: Springer Verlag.

Alexander, P.; Minden, G.; Tsatsoulis, C.; and Holtzman, J. 1989. Storing design knowledge in cases. In *Proceedings. See* Hammond 1989c.

Alexander, P., and Tsatsoulis, C. 1991. Using sub-cases for skeletal planning and partial case reuse. *International Journal of Expert Systems 4(2): 221–247.*

Alterman, R. 1986. An adaptive planner. In *Proceedings of AAAI-86.* Cambridge, MA: AAAI Press/MIT Press.

Alterman, R. 1988. Adaptive planning. *Cognitive Science 12: 393–422.*

Alterman, R.; Zito-Wolf, R. J.; and Carpenter, T. 1991. Interaction, comprehension, and instruction usage. *Journal of the Learning Sciences 1: 361–398.*

American Psychiatric Association. 1980. *Diagnostic and Statistical Manual of Mental Disorders (DSM-III).* Washington, D.C.: American Psychiatric Association.

Anderson, J. 1983. *The architecture of cognition,* Cambridge, MA: Harvard Univ. Press.

Ashley, K. D. 1987. Distinguishing--A reasoner's wedge. In *Proceedings of the Ninth Annual Conference of the Cognitive Science Society.* Northvale, NJ: Erlbaum.

Ashley, K. D. 1988. Arguing by analogy in law: A case-based model. In *Analogical reasoning: Perspectives of artificial intelligence, cognitive science, and philosophy,* ed. D. Helman. Boston: Kluwer.

Ashley, K. D. 1989. Defining salience in case-based arguments. In *Proceedings of IJCAI-89.* San Mateo, CA: Morgan Kaufmann.

Ashley, K. D. 1990. *Modelling legal argument: Reasoning with cases and hypotheticals.* Cambridge, MA: MIT Press, Bradford Books.

Ashley, K. D. 1991. Reasoning with cases and hypotheticals in Hypo. *International Journal of Man-Machine Studies* 34: 753–796.

Ashley, K., and Aleven, V. 1991. A computational approach to explaining case-based concepts of relevance in a tutorial context. In *Proceedings. See* Bareiss 1991.

Ashley, K. D., and Aleven, V. 1992. Generating dialectical examples automatically. In *Proceedings of AAAI-92.* Cambridge, MA: AAAI Press/MIT Press.

Ashley, K. D., and Rissland, E. L. 1987. Compare and contrast: A test of expertise. In *Proceedings of AAAI-87.* Cambridge, MA: AAAI Press/MIT Press.

Ashley, K. D., and Rissland, E. L. 1988a. A case-based approach to modeling legal expertise. *IEEE Expert* 3(3): 70–77.

Ashley, K. D., and Rissland, E. L. 1988b. Waiting on weighting: A symbolic least commitment approach. In *Proceedings of AAAI-88.* Cambridge, MA: AAAI Press/MIT Press.

Bain, W. 1984. Toward a model of subjective interpretation. Yale University, Department of Computer Science Technical Report no. 324.

Bain, W. 1986. *Case-based reasoning: A computer model of subjective assessment.* Ph.D. diss., Department of Computer Science, Yale University.

Bain, W. 1989. Judge. In *Inside case-based reasoning,* ed. C. K. Riesbeck and R. C. Schank. Northvale, NJ: Erlbaum.

Barber, J.; Bhatta, S.; Goel, A.; Jacobsen, M.; Pearce, M.; Penberthy, L.; Shankar, M.; Stroulia, E. 1992. AskJef: Integrating case-based reasoning and multimedia technologies for interface design support. In *Artificial intelligence in design 1992,* ed. J. Gero. Boston: Kluwer Academic Publishers.

Bardasz, T., and Zeid, I. 1991. Applying analogical problem solving to mechanical design. *CAD Journal* 23(3): 202–212.

Bardasz, T., and Zeid, I. 1992. DEJAVU: A case-based reasoning designer's assistant shell. In *Artificial Intelligence in Design 1992,* ed. J. Gero. Boston: Kluwer Academic Publishers.

Bareiss, E. R. 1989a. *Exemplar-based knowledge acquisition: A unified approach to concept representation, classification, and learning.* Boston: Academic Press.

Bareiss, E. R. 1989b. The experimental evaluation of a case-based learning apprentice. In *Proceedings. See* Hammond 1989c.

Bareiss, E. R., ed. 1991. *Proceedings: Workshop on case-based reasoning (DARPA), Washington, D.C.* San Mateo, CA: Morgan Kaufmann.

Bareiss, E. R.; Ferguson, W.; and Fano, A. 1991. The story archive: A memory for case-based tutoring. In *Proceedings. See* Bareiss 1991.

Bareiss, E. R.; Porter, B. W.; and Murray, K. S. 1989. Supporting start-to-finish development of knowledge bases. *Machine Learning* 4: 261–285.

Bareiss, E. R.; Porter, B. W.; and Weir, C. C. 1988. Protos: An exemplar-based learning apprentice. *International Journal of Man-Machine Studies* 29: 549–561.

Bareiss, E. R., and Slator, B. M. 1991. *From Protos to ORCA: Reflections on a unified approach to knowledge representation, categorization, and learning.* Northwestern University, Institute for the Learning Sciences, Technical Report no. 20.

Bareiss, E. R., and Slator, B. M. 1992. The evolution of a case-based approach to knowledge representation, categorization, and learning. In *Categorization and category learning by humans and machines,* ed. Medin, Nakamura, and Taraban. New York: Academic Press.

Barletta, R., and Hennessy, D. 1989. Case adaptation in autoclave layout design. In *Proceedings. See* Hammond 1989c.

Barletta, R., and Kerber, R. 1989. Improving explanation-based indexing with empirical learning. In *Proceedings of the Sixth International Machine Learning Workshop.* San Mateo, CA: Morgan Kaufmann.

Barletta, R., and Mark, W. 1988. Explanation-based indexing of cases. In *Proceedings of AAAI-88.* Cambridge, MA: AAAI Press/MIT Press.

Barsalou, L. W. 1988. The content and organization of autobiographical memories. In *Remembering reconsidered: Ecological and traditional approaches to the study of memory,* ed. U. Neisser and E. Winograd. New York: Cambridge Univ. Press.

Barsalou, L. W., and Bower, G. H. 1984. Discrimination nets as psychological models. *Cognitive Science* 8: 1–26.

Bartlett, R. 1932. *Remembering: A study in experimental and social psychology.* London: Cambridge Univ. Press.

Berger, J. 1989. ROENTGEN: A case-based approach to radiation therapy planning. In *Proceedings. See* Hammond 1989c.

Bhatta, S. R., and Goel, A. K. 1992. Discovery of physical principles from design experiences. In *Proceedings of the Ninth International Machine Learning Workshop.* San Mateo, CA: Morgan Kaufmann.

Birnbaum, L. ed. 1991. *Proceedings of the International Conference on the Learning Sciences.* Charlottesville, VA: Association for the Advancement of Computing in Education.

Birnbaum, L., and Collins, G. 1988. The transfer of experience across planning domains through the acquisition of abstract strategies. In *Proceedings. See* Kolodner 1988.

Birnbaum, L., and Collins, G. 1989. Remindings and engineering design themes: A case study in indexing vocabulary. In *Proceedings. See* Hammond 1989c.

Black, M. 1962. *Models and metaphors* Ithaca, NY: Cornell Univ. Press.

Blidberg, D. R.; Turner, R. M.; and Chappel; S. G. 1991. Autonomous underwater vehicles: Current activities and research opportunities. *Robotics and Autonomous Systems* 7: 139–150.

Bobrow, D. G., and Norman, D. A. 1975. Some principles of memory schemata. In *Representation and understanding,* ed. D. G. Bobrow and A. Collins. New York: Academic Press.

Bower, G. H.; Black, J. B.; and Turner T. J. 1979. Scripts in text comprehension and memory. *Cognitive Psychology* 11: 177–220.

Brachman, R. J., and Schmolze, J. G. 1985. An overview of the KL-ONE knowledge representation system. *Cognitive Science* 9: 171–216.

Bradtke, S., and Lehnert, W. G. 1988. Some Experiments with Case-Based Search. In *Proceedings of AAAI-88.* Cambridge, MA: AAAI Press/MIT Press.

Brandau, R.; Lemmon, A.; and Lafond, C. 1991. Experience with extended episodes: Cases with complex temporal structure. In *Proceedings. See* Bareiss 1991.

Branting, L. K. 1988. The role of explanation in reasoning from legal precedent. In *Proceedings. See* Kolodner 1988.

Branting, L. K. 1989. Integrating generalizations with exemplar-based reasoning. In *Proceedings of the Eleventh Annual Conference of the Cognitive Science Society.* Northvale, NJ: Erlbaum.

Branting, L. K. 1991a. Building explanations from rules and structured cases. *International Journal of Man-Machine Studies* 34: 797–837.

Branting, L. K. 1991b. Reasoning with portions of precedents. In *Proceedings of the Third International Conference on Artificial Intelligence and Law, Oxford, England.* New York: Association for Computing Machinery.

Branting, L. K. 1991c. Integrating rules and precedents for classification and explanation: Automating legal analysis. Ph.D. diss., Department of Computer Science, University of Texas, Austin.

Branting, L. K. 1991d. Exploiting the complementarity of rules and precedents with reciprocity and fairness. In *Proceedings. See* Bareiss 1991.

Branting, L. K., and Porter, B. W. 1991. Rules and precedents as complementary warrants. In *Proceedings of AAAI-91.* Cambridge, MA: AAAI Press/MIT Press.

Brewer, W. F., and Nakamura, G. V. 1984. The nature and functions of schemas. In *Handbook of social cognition,* ed. R. S. Wyer and T. K. Srull. Northvale, NJ: Erlbaum.

Brooks, L. R.; Allen, S. W.; and Norman, G. 1989. The multiple and variable availability of familiar cases. In *Proceedings. See* Hammond 1989c.

Broverman, C. 1992. Case-based hypermedia access of "lessons-learned" to accomplish technology transfer. In *Proceedings of the IEEE Advanced Semiconductor Manufacturing Conference, Cambridge, Massachusetts.* New York: IEEE Press.

Burke, R. 1989. Understanding and responding in conversation: Case retrieval with natural language. *In Proceedings. See* Hammond 1989c.

Burke, R. D., and Kass, A. 1992. Integrating case presentation with simulation-based learning-by-doing. In *Proceedings of the Fourteenth Annual Conference of the Cognitive Science Society.* Northvale, NJ: Erlbaum.

Burstein, M. 1988. Combining analogies in mental models. In *Analogical reasoning,* ed. D. Helman. Boston: Kluwer.

Cain, T.; Pazzani, M.; and Silverstein, G. 1991. Using domain knowledge to influence similarity judgements. In *Proceedings. See* Bareiss 1991.

Carbonell, J. G. 1983. Learning by analogy: Formulating and generalizing plans from past experience. In *Machine learning,* vol. 1.

Carbonell, J. G. 1986. Derivational analogy: A theory of reconstructive problem solving and expertise acquisition. In *Machine learning,* vol. 2.

Carbonell, J. G.; Knoblock, C. A.; and Minton, S. 1991. PRODIGY: An integrated architecture for planning and learning. In *Architectures for intelligence,* ed. K. VanLehn. Northvale, NJ: Erlbaum.

Carbonell, J. G., and Veloso, M. M., 1988. Integrating derivational analogy into a general problem solving architecture. In *Proceedings. See* Kolodner 1988.

Chandler, T. N., and Kolodner, J. L. 1993. The science education advisor: A case-based advising system for lesson planning. In *Artificial intelligence in education: Proceedings of the World Conference on AI in Education (Edinburgh, Scotland).* Charlottesville, VA: Association for the Advancement of Computing in Education.

Chapman, D. 1987. Planning for conjunctive goals. *Artificial Intelligence* 32(3): 333–377.

Charniak, E., and McDermott, D. 1985. *Introduction to artificial intelligence.* Reading, MA: Addison-Wesley.

Charniak, E.; Riesbeck, C. K.; McDermott, D. V.; and Meehan, J. R. 1987. *Artificial intelligence programming.* Northvale, NJ: Erlbaum.

Cheeseman, P.; Kelly, J.; Self, Matthew; Stutz, J.; Taylor, W.; and Freeman, D. 1988. AutoClass: A Bayesian classification system. In *Proceedings of the Fifth International Machine Learning Workshop.* San Mateo, CA: Morgan Kaufmann.

Chi, M. T. H.; Bassok, M.; Lewis, M.; Reimann, P.; and Glasser, R. 1989. Self-explanations: How students study and use examples in learning to solve problems. *Cognitive Science* 13: 145–182.

Chi, M. T. H., and VanLehn, K. A. 1991. The content of physics self-explanations *Journal of the Learning Sciences* 1(1): 69–105.

Clancey, W. J. 1988. Acquiring, representing, and evaluating a competence model of diagnostic strategy. In *The Nature of Expertise,* ed. M. Chi, R. Glaser, and M. Farr. Northvale, NJ: Erlbaum.

Clement, C., and Gentner, D. 1991. Systematicity as a selection constraint in analogical mapping. *Cognitive Science* 15: 89–132.

Cognitive Systems. 1992. *ReMind Developer's Reference Manual.* Boston.

Collins, A., and Burstein, M. 1989. A framework for a theory of mapping. In *Similarity, analogy, and thought,* ed. S. Vosniadou and A. Ortony. New York: Cambridge Univ. Press.

Collins, A., and Gentner, D. 1982. Constructing runnable mental models. In *Proceedings of the Fourth Annual Conference of the Cognitive Science Society.* Northvale, NJ: Erlbaum.

Collins, G. 1987. Plan creation: Using strategies as blueprints. Ph.D. diss., Department of Computer Science, Yale University.

Collins, G. 1989. Plan adaptation: A transformational approach. In *Proceedings. See* Hammond 1989c.

Converse, T.; Hammond, K.; and Marks, M. 1989. Learning modification rules from expectation failure. In *Proceedings. See* Hammond 1989c.

Cox, M. T., and Ram, A. 1992. Multistrategy learning with introspective meta-explanations. In *Proceedings of the Ninth International Machine Learning Workshop.* San Mateo, CA: Morgan Kaufmann.

Cullingford, R. 1978. *Script application: Computer understanding of newspaper stories.* Yale University, Department of Computer Science Technical Report no. 116.

Cullingford, R. 1986. *Natural language processing: A knowledge engineering approach.* Totowa, NJ: Rowman and Littlefield.

Cuthill, B. B. 1992. *Situation analysis, precedent retrieval and cross-context reminding in case-based reasoning.* University of Connecticut, Department of Computer Science and Engineering Technical Report no. CSE-TR-92-3. Storrs.

Cuthill, B. B., and McCartney, R. 1992a. *Issue spotting in legal cases.* University of Connecticut, Department of Computer Science and Engineering Technical Report no. CSE-TR-92-1. Storrs.

Cuthill, B. B., and McCartney, R. 1992b. *Issue spotting in CHASER.* University of Connecticut, Department of Computer Science and Engineering Technical Report no. CSE-TR-92-22. Storrs.

Davis, R. 1982. Teiresias: Applications of meta-level knowledge. In *Knowledge-based systems in artificial intelligence,* ed. R. Davis and D. Lenat. New York: McGraw-Hill.

Dehn, Natalie J. 1989. Computer story-writing: The role of reconstructive and dynamic memory. Ph.D. diss., Department of Computer Science, Yale University.

DeJong, G., and Mooney, R. 1986. Explanation-based learning: An alternative view. In *Machine Learning* 1: 145–176.

de Kleer, J., and Brown, J. S. 1984. A quantitative physics based on confluences. *Artificial Intelligence* 24: 7–83.

Domeshek, E. 1988. Understanding stories in their social context. In *Proceedings of the Tenth Annual Conference of the Cognitive Science Society.* Northvale, NJ: Erlbaum.

Domeshek, E. 1989. Parallelism for index generation and reminding. In *Proceedings. See* Hammond 1989c.

Domeshek, E. 1990. Volition and advice: Suggesting strategies for fixing problems in social situations. In *Proceedings of the Twelfth Annual Conference of the Cognitive Science Society.* Northvale, NJ: Erlbaum.

Domeshek, E. 1991a. *Do the right thing: A component theory for indexing stories as social advice.* Northwestern University, Institute for the Learning Sciences Technical Report no. 26.

Domeshek, E. 1991b. Indexing stories as social advice. In *Proceedings of AAAI-91.* Cambridge, MA: AAAI Press/MIT Press.

Domeshek, E. 1991c. What Abby cares about. In *Proceedings. See* Bareiss 1991.

Domeshek, E. 1993. A case study of case indexing: Designing index feature sets to suit task demands and support parallelism. In *Advances in connectionist and neural computation theory,* vol. 2: *Analogical connections,* ed. J. Barnden and K. Holyoak. Norwood, NJ: Ablex.

Domeshek, E., and Kolodner, J. 1991. Toward a case-based aid for conceptual design. *International Journal of Expert Systems* 4(2): 201–220.

Domeshek, E., and Kolodner, J. 1992. A case-based design aid for architecture. In *Artificial Intelligence in Design 1992,* ed. J. Gero. Boston: Kluwer.

Domeshek, E., and Kolodner, J. L. 1993. Finding the points of large cases. In *Artificial Intelligence for Engineering Design, Analysis and Manufacturing (AIEDAM)* 7(2): 87–96.

Donahue, D. 1989. OGRE: Generic reasoning from experience. In *Proceedings. See* Hammond 1989c.

Doyle, J. 1979. A truth maintenance system. *Artificial Intelligence* 12: 231–272.

Duran, R. T. 1988. *Concept learning with incomplete data sets.* University of Texas, Department of Computer Science Technical Report no. AI88-82. Austin.

Dyer, M. 1983. *In-depth understanding.* Cambridge MA: MIT Press.

Edelson, D. 1991a. Why do cheetahs run fast: Responsive questioning in a case-based teaching system. In *Proceedings. See* Birnbaum 1991.

Edelson, D. 1991b. Oh, the stories I could tell: Managing an aesopic teaching dialogue. In *Proceedings. See* Bareiss 1991.

Edelson, D. 1992. When should a cheetah remind you of a bat? Reminding in case-based teaching. In *Proceedings of AAAI-92.* Cambridge, MA: AAAI Press/MIT Press.

Edelson, D.; Collins, A.; Bareiss, R.; and Kass, A. 1993. Incorporating AI into effective learning environments. In *Proceedings of the Tenth International Conference on Technology in Education, Cambridge, Massachusetts.*

Ernst, G., and Newell, A. 1969. *GPS: A case study in generality and problem solving.* New York: Academic Press.

Falkenhainer, B. 1988. Learning from physical analogies: A study in analogy and the explanation process. Ph.D. diss., University of Illinois, Urbana-Champaign.

Faries, J. M., and Reiser, B. J. 1988. Access and use of previous solutions in a problem solving situation. In *Proceedings of the Tenth Annual Conference of the Cognitive Science Society.* Northvale, NJ: Erlbaum.

Faries, J. M., and Reiser, B. J. 1990. Terrorists and spoiled children: Retrieval of analogies for political arguments. In unpublished *Proceedings of the 1990 AAAI Symposium on Case-Based Reasoning.*

Feigenbaum, E. A. 1963. The simulation of natural learning behavior. In *Computers and Thought,* ed. E. A. Feigenbaum and J. Feldman. New York: McGraw-Hill.

Ferguson, W.; Bareiss, R.; Birnbaum, L.; and Osgood, R. 1992. ASK systems: An approach to the realization of story-based teachers. *Journal of the Learning Sciences* 2: 95–134.

Fisher, D. 1987. Knowledge acquisition via incremental conceptual clustering. In *Machine learning,* vol. 2.

Forbus, K. 1988. Quantitative physics: Past, present and future. In *Exploring artificial intelligence,* ed. H. Shrobe. San Mateo, CA: Morgan Kaufmann.

Forbus, K. D., and Gentner, D. 1986. Learning physical domains: Toward a theoretical framework. In *Machine learning,* vol. 2.

Forbus, K. D., and Gentner, D. 1989. Structural evaluation of analogies: What counts? In *Proceedings of the Eleventh Annual Conference of the Cognitive Science Society.* Northvale, NJ: Erlbaum.

Friedland, P. 1979. *Knowledge-based experiment design in molecular genetics.* Stanford University, Computer Science Department Technical Report no. 79–771.

Gentner, D. 1980. *The structure of analogical models in science.* Technical report no. 4451. Cambridge, MA: Bolt Baranek and Newman.

Gentner. D. 1983. Structure-mapping: A theoretical framework for analogy. *Cognitive Science* 7(2).

Gentner, D. 1987. The mechanisms of analogical learning. In *Similarity, analogy, and thought,* ed. S. Vosniadou and A. Ortony. New York: Cambridge Univ. Press.

Gentner, D. 1988. Analogical inference and analogical access. In *Analogica,* ed. A. Prieditis. Los Altos, CA: Morgan Kaufmann.

Gentner, D. 1989. Finding the needle: Accessing and reasoning from prior cases. In *Proceedings. See* Hammond 1989c.

Gentner, D., and Forbus, K. D. 1991. MAC/FAC: A model of similarity-based access and mapping. In *Proceedings of the Thirteenth Annual Conference of the Cognitive Science Society.* Northvale, NJ: Erlbaum.

Gentner, D.; Rattermann, M. J.; and Forbus, K. D. 1993. The roles of similarity in transfer: Separating retrievability from inferential soundness. *Cognitive Psychology.*

Gick, M., and Holyoak, K. 1980. Analogical problem solving. *Cognitive Psychology* 12: 306–355.

Gilovich, T. 1981. Seeing the past in the present: The effect of associations to familiar events on judgements and decisions. *Journal of Personality and Social Psychology* 40(5): 797–808.

Goel, A. 1989. Integration of case-based reasoning and model-based reasoning for adaptive design problem solving. Ph.D. diss., Department of Computer and Information Science, The Ohio State University.

Goel, A. 1991a. Model revision: A theory of incremental model learning. In *Proceedings of the Eighth International Machine Learning Workshop.* San Mateo, CA: Morgan Kaufmann.

Goel, A. 1991b. A model-based approach to case adaptation. In *Proceedings of the Thirteenth Annual Conference of the Cognitive Science Society.* Northvale, NJ: Erlbaum.

Goel, A. 1992. Representation of design functions in experience-based design. In *Intelligent Computer Aided Design,* ed. D. Brown, M. Waldron, and H. Yoshikawa. Amsterdam: North-Holland.

Goel, A., and Callantine, T. 1992. An experience-based approach to navigational path planning. In *Proceedings of the IEEE/RSJ International Conference on Robotics and Systems, Raleigh, North Carolina.* New York: IEEE Press.

Goel, A.; Callantine, T.; Shankar, M.; and Chandrasekaran, B. 1991. Representation and organization of topographic models of physical spaces for route planning. In *Proceedings of IEEE Conference on Artificial Intelligence Applications, Miami.* New York: IEEE Press.

Goel, A., and Chandrasekaran, B. 1989. Use of device models in adaptation of design cases. In *Proceedings. See* Hammond 1989c.

Goel, A., and Chandrasekaran, B. 1992. Case-based design: A task analysis. In *Artificial intelligence approaches to engineering design,* vol. 2: *Innovative design,* ed. C. Tong and D. Sriram. San Diego: Academic Press.

Goel, A. K.; Kolodner, J. L.; Pearce, M.; Billington, R.; and Zimring, C. 1991. Towards a case-based tool for aiding conceptual design problem solving. In *Proceedings. See* Bareiss 1991.

Goel, V., and Pirolli, P. 1989. Design within information- processing theory: The design problem space. *AI Magazine* 10(1): 19–36.

Goodman, M. 1989. CBR in battle planning. In *Proceedings. See* Hammond 1989c.

Goodman, M. 1990. Prism: A case-based telex classifier. In *Innovative applications of artifical intelligence,* vol. 2, ed. A. Rappaport and R. Smith. Cambridge, MA: MIT Press.

Goodman, M. 1991. A case-based, inductive architecture for natural language processing. Unpublished paper presented at AAAI Spring Symposium on Machine Learning of Natural Language and Ontology.

Govindaraj, T. 1987. Qualitative approximation methodology for modeling and simulation of large dynamic systems: Applications to a marine steam power plant. *IEEE Transactions on Systems, Man, and Cybernetics* 17(6).

Graesser, A. C., and Nakamura, G. V. 1982. The impact of a schema on comprehension and memory. In *The psychology of learning and motivation,* vol. 16, ed. G. Bower. New York: Academic Press.

Hammond, K. 1984. *Indexing and causality: The organization of plans and strategies in memory.* Yale University, Department of Computer Science Technical Report no. 351.

Hammond, K. 1986a. CHEF: A model of case-based planning. In *Proceedings of AAAI-86.* Cambridge, MA: AAAI Press/MIT Press.

Hammond, K. 1986b. Learning to anticipate and avoid planning problems through the explanation of failures. In *Proceedings of AAAI-86.* Cambridge, MA: AAAI Press/MIT Press.

Hammond, K. 1987. Explaining and repairing plans that fail. In *Proceedings of IJCAI-87.* San Mateo, CA: Morgan Kaufmann.

Hammond, K. J., 1988. Opportunistic memory: Storing and recalling suspended goals. In *Proceedings. See* Kolodner 1988.

Hammond, K. J. 1989a. *Case-based planning: Viewing planning as a memory task.* Boston: Academic Press.

Hammond, K. 1989b. Opportunistic memory.In *Proceedings of IJCAI-89, Detroit.* San Mateo, CA: Morgan Kaufmann.

Hammond, K., ed. 1989c. *Proceedings: Workshop on case-based reasoning (DARPA), Pensacola Beach, Florida.* San Mateo, CA: Morgan Kaufmann.

Hammond, K. J., and Hurwitz, N. 1988. Extracting diagnostic features from explanations. In *Proceedings. See* Kolodner 1988.

Hampton, J. A. 1979. Polymorphous concepts in semantic memory. *Journal of Verbal Learning and Verbal Behavior* 18: 441–461.

Hayes, P. 1985. Naive physics 1: Ontology for liquids. *Theories of the commonsense world,* ed. J. Hobbes and B. Moore. Norwood, NJ: Ablex.

Hayes-Roth, F.; Waterman, D.; and Lenat, D., eds. 1983. *Building expert systems.* Reading, MA: Addison Wesley.

Hendler, James A., 1988. Refitting plans for case-based reasoning. In *Proceedings. See* Kolodner 1988.

Hennessy, D. H., and Hinkle, D. 1992. Applying case-based reasoning to autoclave loading. *IEEE Expert* 7(5): 21–26.

Hickman, A. K., and Larkin, J. H. 1990. Internal analogy: A model of transfer within problems. In *Proceedings of the Twelfth Annual Conference of the Cognitive Science Society.* Northvale, NJ: Erlbaum.

Hickman, A. K., and Lovett, M. C. 1991. Partial match and search control via internal analogy. In *Proceedings of the Thirteenth Annual Conference of the Cognitive Science Society.* Northvale, NJ: Erlbaum.

Hinkle, D., and Hennessy, D. 1990. Clavier: A case-based autoclave loading advisor. In *Proceedings: Fabricating Composites 90.* Society of Manufacturing Engineers (SME).

Hinrichs, T. R. 1988. Towards an architecture for open world problem solving. In *Proceedings. See* Kolodner 1988.

Hinrichs. T. R. 1989. Strategies for adaptation and recovery in a design problem solver. In *Proceedings. See* Hammond 1989c.

Hinrichs, T. R. 1992. *Problem solving in open worlds: A case study in design.* Northvale, NJ: Erlbaum.

Hinrichs, T., and Kolodner, J. 1991. The roles of adaptation in case-based design. In *Proceedings of AAAI-91.* Cambridge, MA: AAAI Press/MIT Press.

Holyoak, K. J. 1984. Analogical thinking and human intelligence. In *Advances in the psychology of human intelligence,* vol. 2, ed. R. J. Sternberg. Northvale, NJ: Erlbaum.

Holyoak, K. J. 1985. The pragmatics of analogical transfer. *The psychology of learning and motivation,* ed. G. Bower. New York: Academic Press.

Holyoak, K., and Thagard, P. R. 1989. A computational model of analogical problem solving. In *Similarity, analogy, and thought,* ed. A. Vosniadou and A. Ortony. New York: Cambridge Univ. Press.
Hunter, L. 1989a. Finding paradigm cases, or when is a case worth remembering? In *Proceedings. See* Hammond 1989c.

Hunter, L. 1989b. Knowledge acquisition planning: Results and prospects. In *Proceedings of the Sixth International Machine Learning Workshop.* San Mateo, CA: Morgan Kaufmann.

Hunter, L. 1989c. *Planning to learn: Gaining expertise through experience.* Yale University, Department of Computer Science Report no. YALEU/DCS/TR678.

Hunter, L. 1990. Planning to learn. In *Proceedings of the Twelfth Annual Conference of the Cognitive Science Society.* Northvale, NJ: Erlbaum.

Jones, E. K. 1989. Case-based analogical reasoning using proverbs. In *Proceedings. See* Hammond 1989c.

Jones, E. K. 1992. *The flexible use of abstract knowledge in planning.* Northwestern University, Institute for the Learning Sciences Technical Report no. 28.

Kambhampati, S. 1989a. Representational requirements for plan reuse. In *Proceedings. See* Hammond 1989c.

Kambhampati, S. 1989b. Integrating planning and reuse: A framework for flexible plan reuse. In *Proceedings. See* Hammond 1989c.

Kambhampati, S. 1993. Exploiting causal structure to control retrieval and refitting during plan reuse. *Computational Intelligence* (in press).

Kambhampati, S.; Cutkosky, M. R.; Tenenbaum, J. M.; and Lee, S. H. 1993. Integrating general purpose planners and specialized reasoners: Case study of a hybrid planning architecture. *IEEE Transactions on Systems, Man and Cybernetics* 23 (in press).

Kambhampati, S., and Hendler, J. A. 1989. Control of refitting during plan reuse. In *Proceedings of IJCAI-89*. San Mateo, CA: Morgan Kaufman.

Kambhampati, S., and Hendler, J. A. 1992. A validation structure based theory of plan modification and reuse. *Artificial Intelligence Journal* 55: 193–258.

Kass, A. 1986. Modifying explanations to understand stories. In *Proceedings of the Eighth Annual Conference of the Cognitive Science Society*. Northvale, NJ: Erlbaum.

Kass, A. 1989a. Strategies for Adapting Explanations. In *Proceedings. See* Hammond 1989c.

Kass, A. 1989b. Adaptation-based explanation: Explanations as cases. In *Proceedings of the Sixth International Machine Learning Workshop*. San Mateo, CA: Morgan Kaufmann.

Kass, A. 1989c. Adaptation-based explanation: Extending script/frame theory to handle novel input. In *Proceedings of IJCAI-89*. San Mateo, CA: Morgan Kaufmann.

Kass, A. 1990. *Developing creative hypotheses by adapting explanations*. Northwestern University, Institute for the Learning Sciences Technical Report no. 6.

Kass, A.; Burke, R. D.; Blevis, E.; and Williamson, M. 1992. *The GuSS project: Integrating instruction and practice through guided social simulation*. Northwestern University, Institute for the Learning Sciences Technical Report no. 34.

Kass, A.; Burke, R.; Blevis, E.; and Williamson, M. (forthcoming.) Constructing learning environments for complex social skills. *Journal of the Learning Sciences*.

Kass, A. M., and Leake, D. B. 1988. Case-based reasoning applied to constructing explanations. In *Proceedings. See* Kolodner 1988.

Kass, A. M.; Leake, D. B.; and Owens, C. 1986. SWALE: A program that explains. In *Explanation Patterns: Understanding Mechanically and Creatively*, ed. R. Schank. Northvale, NJ: Erlbaum.

Kettler, B. P.; Andersen, W. A.; Hendler, J. A.; and Evett, M. P. 1992. *Fast, frequent, and flexible retrieval in case-based planning*. University of Maryland, Department of Computer Science Research Report. College Park.

Kettler, B. P.; Hendler, J. A.; Andersen, W. A.; and Evett, M. P. 1993. Massively parallel support for case-based planning. In *Proceedings of the Ninth IEEE Conference on Artificial Intelligence Applications, Orlando*. Washington, DC: IEEE CS Press.

Kitano, H.; Shibata, A.; Shimazu, H.; Kajihara, J.; and Sato, A. 1992. Building large-scale and corporate-wide case-based systems. In *Proceedings of AAAI-92*. Cambridge, MA: AAAI Press/MIT Press.

Klein, Gary A., and Calderwood, Roberta, 1988. How do people use analogues to make decisions? In *Proceedings. See* Kolodner 1988.

Klein, Gary A.; Whitaker, Leslie A.; and King, James A. 1988. Using analogues to predict and plan. In *Proceedings. See* Kolodner 1988.

Kochen, M. 1983. How clinicians recall experiences, *Meth. Inform. Med.* 22: 83–86.

Kolodner, J. L. 1982. The role of experience in development of expertise. In *Proceedings of AAAI-82*. Cambridge, MA: AAAI Press/MIT Press.

Kolodner, J. L. 1983a. Maintaining organization in a dynamic long-term memory. *Cognitive Science* 7(4).

Kolodner, J. L. 1983b. Reconstructive memory: A computer model. *Cognitive Science* 7(4).

Kolodner, J. L. 1983c. Towards an understanding of the role of experience in the evolution from novice to expert. *International Journal of Man-Machine Studies* 19(5): 497–518.

Kolodner, J. L. 1984. *Retrieval and organization strategies in conceptual memory: A computer model.* Northvale, NJ: Erlbaum.

Kolodner, J. L. 1985. Memory for experience. In *The psychology of learning and motivation,* ed. G. Bower, vol. 19. Orlando, FL: Academic Press.

Kolodner, J. L. 1987. Capitalizing on failure through case-based inference. In *Proceedings of the Ninth Annual Conference of the Cognitive Science Society.* Northvale, NJ: Erlbaum.

Kolodner, J. L. 1988a. Retrieving events from a case memory: A parallel implementation. In *Proceedings. See* Kolodner 1988.

Kolodner, J. L., ed. 1988b. *Proceedings: Workshop on case-based reasoning (DARPA), Clearwater, Florida.* San Mateo, CA: Morgan Kaufmann.

Kolodner, J. L. 1989. Selecting the best case for a case-based reasoner. In *Proceedings of the Eleventh Annual Conference of the Cognitive Science Society.* Northvale, NJ: Erlbaum.

Kolodner, J. L. 1991a. Improving human decision making through case-based decision aiding. *AI Magazine* 12(2): 52–68.

Kolodner, J. L. 1991b. Helping teachers teach science better: Case-based decision aiding for science education. In *Proceedings. See* Birnbaum 1991.

Kolodner, J. L., and Barsalou, L. 1982. Psychological issues raised by an AI model of reconstructive memory. In *Proceedings of the Fourth Annual Conference on Cognitive Science.* Northvale, NJ: Erlbaum.

Kolodner, J. L., and Kolodner, R. M. 1987. Using experience in clinical problem solving: Introduction and framework. *IEEE Transactions on Systems, Man, and Cybernetics* 17: 420–431.

Kolodner, J. L., and Penberthy, L. 1990. A case-based approach to creativity in problem solving. In *Proceedings of the Twelfth Annual Conference of the Cognitive Science Society.* Northvale, NJ: Erlbaum.

Kolodner, J. L., and Riesbeck, C. K. 1986. *Experience, memory, and reasoning.* Northvale, NJ: Erlbaum.

Kolodner, J. L., and Simpson, R. L. 1984. Experience and problem solving: A framework. In *Proceedings of the Sixth Annual Conference of the Cognitive Science Society.* Northvale, NJ: Erlbaum.

Kolodner, J. L., and Simpson, R. L. 1988. *The MEDIATOR: A case study of a case-based reasoner.* Georgia Institute of Technology, School of Information and Computer Science Technical Report no. GIT-ICS-88/11. Atlanta.

Kolodner, J. L., and Simpson. R. L. 1989. The MEDIATOR: Analysis of an early case-based problem solver. *Cognitive Science* 13(4): 507–549.

Kolodner, J. L., and Thau, R. 1988. *Design and implementation of a case memory.* Georgia Institute of Technology, School of Information and Computer Science Technical Report no. GIT-ICS-88/34. Atlanta.

Kopeikina, L.; Brandau, R.; and Lemmon, Alan. 1988. Case-based reasoning for continuous control. In *Proceedings. See* Kolodner 1988.

Koton, P. 1988a. Reasoning about evidence in causal explanation. In *Proceedings of AAAI-88.* Cambridge, MA: AAAI Press/MIT Press.

Koton, P. 1988b. Integrating case-based and causal reasoning. In *Proceedings of the Tenth Annual Conference of the Cognitive Science Society.* Northvale, NJ: Erlbaum.

Koton, P. 1989. Using experience in learning and problem solving. Ph.D. diss., Department of Computer Science, MIT.

Kuipers, B. 1984. Commonsense reasoning about causality: Deriving behavior from structure. *Artificial Intelligence* 24: 169–203.

Laffey, J.; Machiraju, R.; and Chandhok, R. 1991a. Organizational memory as a support for learning and performance: Prototypes and issues. In *Proceedings. See* Birnbaum 1991.

Laffey, J.; Machiraju, R.; and Chandhok, R. 1991b. Integrated support and learning systems for augmenting knowledge workers: A focus on case-based retrieval. In *Proceedings of The World Congress on Expert Systems, Orlando, Florida.* Elmsford, NY: Pergamon Press.

Laird, J. E.; Newell, A.; and Rosenbloom, P. S. 1987. Soar: An architecture for general intelligence. *Artificial Intelligence* 33: 1–64.

Lancaster, J. S., and Kolodner, J. L. 1987. Problem solving in a natural task as a function of experience. In *Proceedings of the Ninth Annual Conference of the Cognitive Science Society.* Northvale, NJ: Erlbaum.

Lancaster, J. S., and Kolodner, J. L. 1988. Varieties of learning from problem solving experience. In *Proceedings of the Tenth Annual Conference of the Cognitive Science Society.* Northvale, NJ: Erlbaum.

Lange, T. E., and Wharton, C. M. 1993. Dynamic memories: Analysis of an integrated comprehension and episodic memory retrieval model. In *Proceedings of IJCAI-93.* San Mateo, CA: Morgan Kaufmann.

Leake, D. B. 1989. The effect of explainer goals on case-based explanation. In *Proceedings. See* Hammond 1989c.

Leake, D. B. 1991a. Goal-based explanation evaluation. *Cognitive Science* 15: 509–545.

Leake, D. B. 1991b. An indexing vocabulary for case-based explanation. In *Proceedings of AAAI-91.* Cambridge, MA: AAAI Press/MIT Press.

Leake, D. B. 1992a. Constructive similarity assessment: Using stored cases to define new situations. In *Proceedings of the Fourteenth Annual Conference of the Cognitive Science Society.* Northvale, NJ: Erlbaum.

Leake, D. B. 1992b. *Evaluating explanations: A content theory.* Northvale, NJ: Erlbaum.

Leake, D. B., and Owens, C. C. 1986. Organizing memory for explanation. In *Proceedings of the Eighth Annual Conference of the Cognitive Science Society.* Northvale, NJ: Erlbaum.

Lebowitz, M. 1983a. Generalization from natural language text. *Cognitive Science* 7(1).

Lebowitz, M. 1983b. Memory-based parsing. *Artificial Intelligence* 21: 363–404.

Lebowitz, M. 1986a. An experiment in intelligent information systems: RESEARCHER. In *Intelligent library and information systems,* ed. R. Davies. Ellis-Horwood.

Lebowitz, M. 1986b. Integrated learning: Controlling explanation. *Cognitive Science* 10: 219–240.

Lebowitz, M. 1987. Experiments with incremental concept formation: UNIMEM. In *Machine Learning* 2: 103–138.

Lehnert, W. G. 1987a. Case-based problem solving with a large knowledge base of learned cases. In *Proceedings of AAAI-87.* Cambridge, MA: AAAI Press/MIT Press.

Lehnert, W. G. 1987b. Word pronunciation as a problem in case-based reasoning. In *Proceedings of the Ninth Annual Conference of the Cognitive Science Society.* Northvale, NJ: Erlbaum.

Lichtenstein, E. H., and Brewer, W. F. 1980. Memory for goal-directed events. *Cognitive Psychology* 3: 412–445.

Long, W. J.; Naimi, S.; Criscitiello, M. G.; Jayes, R. 1987. The development and use of a causal model for reasoning about heart failure. In *Symposium on Computer Applications in Medical Care, IEEE*. New York: IEEE Press.

Machine learning: An artificial intelligence approach, vol. 1. 1983. Ed. R. Michalski, J. Carbonell, and T. Mitchell. Palo Alto, CA: Tioga.

Machine learning: An artificial intelligence approach, vol. 2. 1986. Ed. R. Michalski, J. Carbonell, and T. Mitchell. Los Altos, CA: Morgan Kaufmann.

Maher, M. L., and Zhang, D. M. 1991. CADSYN: Using case and decomposition knowledge for design synthesis. In *Artificial Intelligence in Design 1991,* ed. J. S. Gero. Oxford: Butterworth-Heineman.

Mark, W. 1989. Case-based reasoning for autoclave management. In *Proceedings. See* Hammond 1989c.

Mark, W. 1991. Software design memory. In *Proceedings of the AAAI Workshop on Automated Software Design*. San Mateo, CA: Morgan Kaufmann.

Mark, W. 1992. Adapting plan architectures. In *Machine learning methods for planning,* ed. Steven Minton. San Mateo, CA: Morgan Kaufman.

Mark, W., and Schlossberg, J. 1990. Interactive acquisition of design decisions. In *Proceedings of the Fifth Knowledge Acquisition for Knowledge-Based Systems Workshop, Banff, Alberta, Canada*.

Marks, M.; Hammond, K. A.; and Converse, T. 1988. Planning in an open world: A pluralistic approach. In *Proceedings. See* Kolodner 1988.

Marks, M.; Hammond, K. A.; and Converse, T. 1989. Planning in an open world: A pluralistic approach. In *Proceedings of the Eleventh Annual Conference of the Cognitive Science Society*. Northvale, NJ: Erlbaum.

McCartney, R. 1990. Reasoning directly from cases in a case-based planner. In *Proceedings of the Twelfth Annual Conference of the Cognitive Science Society*. Northvale, NJ: Erlbaum.

McCartney, R. 1993. Episodic cases and real-time performance in a case-based planning system. *Expert Systems with Applications* 6: 9–22.

Medin, D. L. 1983. Structural principles of categorization, *Interaction: Perception, development, and cognition*. Northvale, NJ: Erlbaum.

Medin, D. L.; Dewey, G. I.; and Murphy, T. D. 1983. Relationships between item and category learning: Evidence that abstraction is not automatic. *Journal of Experimental Psychology: Learning, Memory and Cognition* 9(4): 607–625.

Michalski, R. S., and Stepp, R. E. 1983. Learning from observation: Conceptual clustering. In *Machine learning,* vol. 1.

Minton, S. 1988. Learning effective search control knowledge: An explanation-based approach. Ph.D. thesis, Computer Science Department, Carnegie Mellon University.

Minton, S.; Knoblock, C. A.; Kuokka, D. R.; Gil, Y.; Joseph, R. L.; and Carbonell, J. G. 1989. *PRODIGY 2.0: The manual and tutorial*. Technical Report CMU-CS-89-146, School of Computer Science, Carnegie Mellon University.

Mitchell, T. M., Kellar, R. M., and Kedar-Cabelli, S. T. 1986. Explanation-based learning: A unifying view. *Machine Learning* 1(1): 47–80.

Miyashita, K., and Sycara, K. 1993. Case-based incremental schedule revision. In *Knowledge-based scheduling,* ed. M. Fox and M. Zweben. San Mateo, CA: Morgan Kaufmann.

Moorman, K., and Ram, A. 1992. A Case-based approach to reactive control for autonomous robots. In *Proceedings of the AAAI Fall Symposium on AI for Real-World Autonomous Robots, Cambridge, Massachusetts*. Cambridge, MA: AAAI Press/MIT Press.

Mostow, J. 1981. *Mechanical transformation of task heuristics into operational procedures.* Ph.D. diss., Carnegie-Mellon University (available as CMU-CS-81-113).

Mostow, J. 1983. Machine transformation of advice into a heuristic search procedure. In *Machine learning,* vol. 1.

Mostow, J. 1989a. Design by derivational analogy: issues in the automated replay of design plans. *Artificial Intelligence* 40: 119–184.

Mostow, J. 1989b. Towards automated development of specialized algorithms for design synthesis: Knowledge compilation as an approach to computer-aided design. *Research in Engineering Design* 1: 167–186.

Mostow, J. 1992. A transformational approach to knowledge compilation: Replayable derivations of task-specific heuristic search algorithms. In *Automating Software Design,* ed. M. Lowry and R. McCartney. Cambridge, MA: AAAI Press.

Mostow, J., and Barley. 1987. Automated reuse of design plans. In *Proceedings of the 1987 International Conference on Engineering Design (ICED87),* vol. 2. Boston: ASME.

Mostow, J.; Barley, M.; and Weinrich, T. 1989. Automated reuse of design plans. *International Journal for Artificial Intelligence in Engineering* 4(4): 181–196.

Mostow, J.; Barley, M.; and Weinrich, T. 1992. Automated reuse of design plans in BOGART. In *Artificial intelligence in engineering design,* ed. C. Tong and D. Sriram. Boston: Academic Press.

Mostow, J., and Fisher, G. 1989. Replaying transformational derivations of heuristic search algorithms in DIOGENES. In *Proceedings. See* Hammond 1989c.

Navinchandra, D. 1988. Case-based reasoning in CYCLOPS, a design problem solver. In *Proceedings. See* Kolodner 1988.

Navinchandra, D. 1991. *Exploration and innovation in design: towards a computational model.* New York: Springer Verlag.

Navinchandra, D.; Sycara, K.; and Narasimhan, S. 1991a. Behavioral synthesis in CADET, a case-based design tool. In *Proceedings of the Seventh IEEE Conference on AI Applications, Miami.* New York: IEEE Press.

Navinchandra, D.; Sycara, K.; and Narasimhan, S. 1991b. A transformational approach to case-based synthesis. *Journal of Artificial Intelligence for Engineering, Design, Analysis and Manufacturing, AI-EDAM* 5 (1).

Newell, A. 1992. *Unified theories of cognition.* Cambridge, MA: Harvard Univ. Press.

Newell, A., and Simon, H. A. 1963. GPS, a program that simulates human thought. In *Computers and thought,* ed. E. A. Feigenbaum and J. Feldman. New York: McGraw-Hill.

Norman, D. A., and Bobrow, D. G. 1979. Descriptions: An intermediate stage in memory retrieval. *Cognitive Psychology* 11: 107–123.

Norman, D. A.; Rumelhart, D. E.; and LNR Research Group. 1975. *Explorations in cognition.* San Francisco: Freeman.

Ortony, A.; Glore, G.; and Collins, A. 1988. *The cognitive structure of emotions.* Cambridge: Cambridge Univ. Press.

Owens, C. 1988. Domain-independent prototype cases for planning. In *Proceedings. See* Kolodner 1988.

Owens, C. 1989a. Plan transformations as abstract indices. In *Proceedings. See* Hammond 1989c.

Owens, C. 1989b. Integrating feature extraction and memory search. In *Proceedings of the Eleventh Annual Conference of the Cognitive Science Society.* Northvale, NJ: Erlbaum.

Owens, C. 1990. Indexing and retrieving abstract planning knowledge. Ph.D. diss., Department of Computer Science. Yale University.

Owens, C. 1991. A functional taxonomy of abstract plan failures. In *Proceedings of the Thirteenth Annual Conference of the Cognitive Science Society.* Northvale, NJ: Erlbaum.

Owens, C. 1993. Integrating feature extraction and memory search. *Machine Learning* 10(3): 311–340.

Oxman R. E. 1993a. Indexing of design precedents: a cognitive approach. *Design Studies.*

Oxman R. E. 1993b. PRECEDENTS: Memory structure in design case libraries. In *CAAD Futures 93.* Elsevier Science Publishers.

Oxman R. E. 1993c. Case-based design support: Supporting architectural composition through precedent libraries. *Journal of Architectural Planning Research.*

Pazzani, M. 1989. Indexing strategies for goal-specific retrieval of cases. In *Proceedings. See* Hammond 1989c.

Pazzani, M. 1990. *Creating a memory of causal relationships: An integration of empirical and explanation-based learning methods.* Northvale, NJ: Erlbaum.

Pazzani, M. 1991. Learning to predict and explain: An integration of similarity-based, theory-driven and explanation-based learning. *Journal of the Learning Sciences* 1: 153–199.

Pearce, M.; Goel, A.; Kolodner, J. L; Zimring, C.; Sentosa, L.; and Billington, R. 1992. Case-based design support: A case study in architectural design. *IEEE Expert* 7(5): 14–20.

Porter, B. 1989. Similarity assessment: Computation *vs.* representation. In *Proceedings. See* Hammond 1989c.

Porter, B. W.; Bareiss, R.; and Holte, R. C. 1990. Concept learning and heuristic classification in weak-theory domains. *Artificial Intelligence* 45: 229–263.

Pu, P., and Reschberger, M. 1991a. Case-based assembly planning. In *Proceedings. See* Bareiss 1991.

Pu, P., and Reschberger, M. 1991b. Assembly sequence planning using case-based reasoning techniques. *Knowledge Based Systems* 4 (3).

Quinlan, J. R. 1986. Induction of decision trees. *Machine Learning* 1(1): 81–106.

Ram, A. 1989a. Incremental learning of paradigmatic cases. In *Proceedings. See* Hammond 1989c.

Ram, A. 1989b. *Question-driven understanding: An integrated theory of story understanding, memory and learning.* Yale University, Department of Computer Science Technical Report no. 710.

Ram, A. 1990a. Decision models: A theory of volitional explanation. In *Proceedings of the Twelfth Annual Conference of the Cognitive Science Society.* Northvale, NJ: Erlbaum.

Ram, A. 1990b. Knowledge goals: A theory of interestingness. In *Proceedings of the Twelfth Annual Conference of the Cognitive Science Society.* Northvale, NJ: Erlbaum.

Ram, A. 1991. A theory of questions and question asking. *Journal of the Learning Sciences* 3 and 4: 273–318.

Ram, A. 1993. Indexing, elaboration and refinement: Incremental learning of explanatory cases. *Machine Learning* 10(3): 201–248.

Ram, A.; Arkin, R. C.; Moorman, K.; and Clark, R. J. 1993. Case-based reactive navigation: A case-based method for on-line selection and adaptation of reactive control parameters in autonomous robotic systems. Georgia Institute of Technology, College of Computing Technical Report no. GIT-CC-92/57, Atlanta.

Ram, A., and Cox., M. T. 1993. Using introspective reasoning to select learning strategies. In *Machine learning: A multistrategy approach,* vol. 4, ed. R. S. Michalski and G. Tecuci. San Mateo, CA: Morgan Kaufmann.

Ram, A., and Hunter, L. 1992. Goals for learning and understanding. *Journal of Applied Intelligence* 2: 47–73.

Ram, A., and Leake, D. 1991. Evaluation of explanatory hypotheses. In *Proceedings of the Thirteenth Annual Conference of the Cognitive Science Society.* Northvale, NJ: Erlbaum.

Rasmussen, J.; Pejtersen, A. M.; and Goodstein, L. P. 1992. *Cognitive engineering: Concepts and applications.* New York: John Wiley.

Read, S., and Cesa, I. 1990. This reminds me of the time when ...: Expectation failures in reminding and explanation. *Journal of Experimental Social Psychology* 26.

Reder, L. M., and Anderson, J. R. 1980. A partial resolution of the paradox of interference: The role of integrating knowledge. *Cognitive Psychology* 12: 447–472.

Redmond, M. 1989a. Combining case-based reasoning, explanation-based learning, and learning from instruction. In *Proceedings of the Sixth International Machine Learning Workshop.* San Mateo, CA: Morgan Kaufmann.

Redmond, M. 1989b. Learning from others' experience: Creating cases from examples. In *Proceedings. See* Hammond 1989c.

Redmond, M. 1989c. Combining explanation types for learning by understanding instructional examples. In *Proceedings of the Eleventh Annual Conference of the Cognitive Science Society.* Northvale, NJ: Erlbaum.

Redmond, M. A. 1990a. Distributed cases for case-based reasoning: Facilitating use of multiple cases. In *Proceedings of AAAI-90.* Cambridge, MA: AAAI Press/MIT Press.

Redmond, M. A. 1990b. What should I do now? Using goal sequitor knowledge to choose the next problem solving step. In *Proceedings of the Twelfth Annual Conference of the Cognitive Science Society.* Northvale, NJ: Erlbaum.

Redmond, M. A. 1991. Improving case retrieval through observing expert problem solving. *Proceedings of the Thirteenth Annual Conference of the Cognitive Science Society.* Northvale, NJ: Erlbaum.

Redmond, M. A. 1992. *Learning by observing and understanding expert problem solving.* Georgia Institute of Technology, College of Computing Technical Report no. GIT-CC-92/43. Atlanta.

Reiser, B. J. 1986a. Knowledge-directed retrieval of autobiographical memories. In *Experience, memory, and reasoning,* ed. J. L. Kolodner and C. K. Riesbeck. Northvale, NJ: Erlbaum.

Reiser, B. J. 1986b. The encoding and retrieval of memories of real-world experiences. In *Knowledge structures,* ed. J. A. Galambos, R. P. Abelson, and J. B. Black. Northvale, NJ: Erlbaum.

Reiser, B. J. 1988. Predictive inferencing in autobiographical memory retrieval. In *Practical aspects of memory: Current research and issues,* vol. 1: *Memory in everyday life,* ed. M. M. Gruneberg, P. E. Morris, and R. N. Sykes. New York: John Wiley.

Reiser, B. J.; Black, J. B.; and Abelson, R. P. 1985. Knowledge structures in the organization and retrieval of autobiographical memories. *Cognitive Psychology* 17: 89–137.

Reiser, B. J.; Black, J. B.; and Kalamarides, P. 1986. Strategic memory search processes. In *Autobiographical memory,* ed. D. C. Rubin. New York: Cambridge Univ. Press.

Rieger, C., and Grinberg, M. 1977. The declarative representation and procedural simulation of causality in physical mechanisms. In *Proceedings of IJCAI-77.* San Mateo, CA: Morgan Kaufmann.

Riesbeck, C. K. 1986. Direct memory access parsing. In *Experience, memory and reasoning,* ed. J. L. Kolodner and C. K. Riesbeck. Northvale, NJ: Erlbaum.

Riesbeck, C. K., and Schank, R. S. 1989. *Inside case-based reasoning.* Northvale, NJ: Erlbaum.

Rissland, E. L. 1983. Examples in legal reasoning: Legal hypotheticals. *Proceedings of IJCAI-83*. San Mateo, CA: Morgan Kaufmann.

Rissland, E. L. 1986. Learning how to argue: Using hypotheticals. In *Experience, memory and reasoning,* ed. J. L. Kolodner and C. K. Riesbeck. Northvale, NJ: Erlbaum.

Rissland, E. L., and Ashley, K. 1986. Hypotheticals as heuristic device. *Proceedings of AAAI-86*. Cambridge, MA: AAAI Press/MIT Press.

Rissland, E. L., and Ashley, K. 1987a. HYPO: A case-based reasoning system. *Proceedings of IJCAI-87*. San Mateo, CA: Morgan Kaufmann.

Rissland, E. L., and Ashley, K. 1987b. A case-based system for trade secrets law. *Proceedings, First International Conference on Artificial Intelligence and Law.*

Rissland, E. L., and Skalak, D. B. 1989. Combining case-based and rule-based reasoning: A heuristic approach. *Proceedings of IJCAI-89*. San Mateo, CA: Morgan Kaufmann.

Rissland, E. L., and Skalak, D. B. 1991. CABARET: Rule interpretation in a hybrid architecture. *International Journal of Man-Machine Studies* 34: 839–887.

Robinson, S., and Kolodner, J. 1991. Indexing cases for planning and acting in dynamic environments: Exploiting hierarchical goal structures. In *Proceedings of the Thirteenth Annual Conference of the Cognitive Science Society.* Northvale, NJ: Erlbaum.

Roderman, R., and Tsatsoulis, C. 1993. PANDA: A case-based system to aid novice designers. *Artificial Intelligence for Engineering Design, Analysis and Manufacturing (AIEDAM)* 7(2): 125–134.

Rosch, E. 1978. Principles of categorization. In *Cognition and categorization,* ed. E. Rosch and B. B. Lloyd. Northvale, NJ: Erlbaum.

Rosch, E., and Mervis, C. B. 1975. Family resemblances: Studies in the internal structure of categories. *Cognitive Psychology* 7: 573–605.

Rosenbloom, P. S.; Newell, A.; Laird, J. E. 1989. Towards the knowledge level in Soar: The role of architecture in the use of knowledge. In *Architectures for Intelligence,* ed. VanLehn. Northvale, NJ: Erlbaum.

Ross, B. H. 1986. Remindings in learning: Objects and tools. In *Similarity, analogy, and thought,* ed. S. Vosniadou and A. Ortony. New York: Cambridge Univ. Press.

Ross, B. H. 1989. Some psychological results on case-based reasoning. In *Proceedings. See* Hammond 1989c.

Ruby, D., and Kibler, D. 1988. Exploration of case-based problem solving. In *Proceedings. See* Kolodner 1988.

Rumelhart, D. E., and Ortony, A. 1977. The representation of knowledge in memory. In *Schooling and the acquisition of knowledge,* ed. Anderson, Spiro, and Montague. Northvale, NJ: Erlbaum.

Sacerdoti, E. D. 1977. *A structure for plans and behavior.* Amsterdam: North-Holland.

Sanders, K. E. 1991a. Representing and reasoning about open-textured predicates. In *Proceedings of the Third International Conference on Artificial Intelligence and Law, Oxford, England.* New York: Association for Computing Machinery.

Sanders, K. E. 1991b. Within the letter of the law: Planning among multiple cases. In *Proceedings. See* Bareiss 1991.

Schank, R. C. 1975. *Conceptual information processing.* Amsterdam: North-Holland.

Schank, R. C. 1977. Rules and topics in conversation. *Cognitive Science* 1: 421–441.

Schank, R. 1982. *Dynamic memory: A theory of learning in computers and people.* New York: Cambridge Univ. Press.

Schank, R. 1986. *Explanation patterns: Understanding mechanically and creatively.* Northvale, NJ: Erlbaum.

Schank, R., and Abelson, R. 1977. *Scripts, plans, goals and understanding.* Northvale, NJ: Erlbaum.

Schank, R.; Ferguson, W.; Birnbaum, L.; Barger, J.; and Greising, M. 1991. ASK-Tom: An experimental interface for video case libraries. In *Proceedings of the Thirteenth Conference of the Cognitive Science Society.* Northvale, NJ: Erlbaum.

Schank, R. C., and Leake, D. B. 1989. Creativity and learning in a case-based explainer. *Artificial Intelligence* 40: 353–385.

Schank, R., and Osgood, R. 1990. *A content theory of memory indexing.* Northwestern University, Institute for the Learning Sciences Technical Report no. 2.

Seifert, C. M., 1988. Goals in reminding. In *Proceedings. See* Kolodner 1988.

Seifert, C. M. 1989. Analogy and case-based reasoning. In *Proceedings. See* Hammond 1989c.

Seifert, C. M., and Gray, K. C. 1990. Representational issues in analogical transfer. In *Proceedings of the Twelfth Annual Conference of the Cognitive Science Society.* Northvale, NJ: Erlbaum.

Seifert, C. M., and Hammond, K. 1989. Why there's no analogical transfer. In *Proceedings. See* Hammond 1989c.

Seifert, C. M.; McKoon, G.; Abelson, R.; and Ratcliffe, R. 1985. Memory connections between thematically similar episodes. *Journal of Experimental Psychology: Human Learning and Memory* 12(2).

Selfridge, M., and Cuthill, B. 1989. Retrieving relevant out-of-context cases: A dynamic memory approach to case-based reasoning. In *Proceedings. See* Hammond 1989c.

Sheridan, T. B. 1992. *Telerobotics, automation, and human supervisory control.* Cambridge, MA: MIT Press.

Sheridan, T. B., and Ferrell, W. R. 1974. *Man-machine systems: Information, control, and decision models of human performance.* Cambridge, MA: MIT Press.

Sheridan, T. B., and Johannsen, G., eds. 1976. *Proceedings: Monitoring behavior and supervisory control.* New York: Plenum Press.

Shinn, H. S. 1988a. The role of mapping in analogical transfer. In *Proceedings of the Tenth Annual Conference of the Cognitive Science Society.* Northvale, NJ: Erlbaum.

Shinn, H. S. 1988b. Abstractional analogy: A model of analogical reasoning. In *Proceedings. See* Kolodner 1988.

Shinn, H. S. 1989. *A unified approach to analogical reasoning.* Georgia Institute of Technology, School of Information and Computer Science Report no. GIT-ICS-90/11. Atlanta.

Simmons, R. G. 1988. A theory of debugging. In *Proceedings. See* Kolodner 1988.

Simmons, R., and Davis, R. 1987. Generate, test and debug: Combining associational rules and causal models. In *Proceedings of IJCAI-87.* San Mateo, CA: Morgan Kaufmann.

Simoudis, E. 1991a. Knowledge acquisition in validated retrieval. *International Journal of Expert Systems: Research and Applications* 4(3): 299–315.

Simoudis, E. 1991b. Retrieving justifiably relevant cases from a case base using validation models. Ph.D. diss., Department of Computer Science, Brandeis University.

Simoudis, E. 1991c. The application of CBR to help desk domains. In *Proceedings. See* Bareiss 1991.

Simoudis, E. 1992. Using case-based retrieval for customer technical support. *IEEE Expert* 7(5): 7–13.

Simoudis, E.; Mendall, A.; and Miller, P. 1993. Automated support for developing retrieve-and-propose systems. In *Proceedings of Artificial Intelligence XI Conference, Orlando, Florida.*

Simoudis, E., and Miller, J. S. 1990. Validated retrieval in case-based reasoning. In *Proceedings of AAAI-90*. Cambridge, MA: AAAI Press/MIT Press.

Simpson, R. L. 1985. *A computer model of case-based reasoning in problem solving: An investigation in the domain of dispute mediation.* Georgia Institute of Technology, School of Information and Computer Science Technical Report no. GIT-ICS-85/18. Atlanta.

Skalak, D. B. 1989. Options for controlling mixed paradigm systems. In *Proceedings. See* Hammond 1989c.

Skalak, D. B. 1992. Representing cases as knowledge sources that apply local similarity metrics. In *Proceedings of the Fourteenth Annual Conference of the Cognitive Science Society.* Northvale, NJ: Erlbaum.

Skalak, D. B., and Rissland, E. L. 1990. Inductive learning in a mixed paradigm setting. In *Proceedings of AAAI-90*. Cambridge, MA: AAAI Press/MIT Press.

Skalak, D. B., and Rissland, E. L. 1992. Arguments and cases: An inevitable intertwining. *Artificial Intelligence and Law: An International Journal* 1: 3–48.

Slade, S. 1991. Qualitative decision theory. In *Proceedings. See* Bareiss 1991.

Slade, S. 1992. Generating explanations for goal-based decision making. *Decision Sciences* 23: 1440–1461.

Slade, S. 1993. *An interpersonal model of goal-based decision making.* Northvale, NJ: Erlbaum.

Slator, B. M., and Bareiss. E. R. 1992. Incremental reminding: The case-based elaboration and interpretation of complex problem situations. In *Proceedings of the Fourteenth Annual Conference of the Cognitive Science Society.*Northvale, NJ: Erlbaum.

Slator, B. M., and Fidel, K. C. 1993. Topical indexing and questions to represent text for retrieval and browsing. *Heuristics: The Journal of Knowledge Engineering* 6(4).

Slator, B. M., and Riesbeck, C. 1991. TaxOps: A case-based advisor. *International Journal of Expert Systems* 4: 117–140.

Smith, E. E.; Adams, N.; and Schorr, D. 1978. Fact retrieval and the paradox of interference. *Cognitive Psychology* 10: 438–464.

Smith, E. E., and Medin, D. L. 1981. *Categories and concepts.* Cambridge, MA: Harvard Univ. Press.

Spiro, R. J. 1979. *Prior knowledge and story processing: Integration, selection and variation.* University of Illinois, Center for the Study of Reading, Technical Report no. 138. Urbana-Champaign.

Spiro, R. J.; Feltovich, P. J.; Coulson, R. L.; and Anderson, D. K. 1987. *Multiple analogies for complex concepts: Antidotes for analogy-induced misconception in advanced knowledge acquisition.* Southern Illinois University School of Medicine, Conceptual Knowledge Research Project Technical Report no. 2. Springfield.

Stanfill, C., and Waltz, D. 1986. Toward memory-based reasoning. *Communications of the ACM* 29(12).

Stanfill, C., and Waltz, D. L. 1988. The memory-based reasoning paradigm. In *Proceedings. See* Kolodner 1988.

Stefik, M. 1981. Planning with constraints. *Artificial Intelligence* 16: 111–140.

Stroulia, E., and Goel, A. K. 1992. Generic teleological mechanisms and their use in case adaptation. In *Proceedings of the Fourteenth Annual Conference of the Cognitive Science.* Northvale, NJ: Erlbaum.

Stroulia, E.; Shankar, M.; Goel, A.; and Penberthy, L. 1992. A model-based approach to blame assignment in design. In *Artificial Intelligence in Design 1992,* ed. J. Gero. Boston: Kluwer.

Sussman, G. J. 1975. *A computer model of skill acquisition.* New York: American Elsevier.

Sycara, E. P. 1987a. *Resolving adversarial conflicts: An approach to integrating case-based and analytic methods*. Georgia Institute of Technology, School of Information and Computer Science Technical Report no. GIT-ICS-87/26. Atlanta.

Sycara, E. P. 1987b. Finding creative solutions in adversarial impasses. In *Proceedings of the Ninth Annual Conference of the Cognitive Science Society*. Northvale, NJ: Erlbaum.

Sycara, K., 1988a. Using case-based reasoning for plan adaptation and repair. In *Proceedings. See* Kolodner 1988.

Sycara, K. 1988b. Patching up old plans. In *Proceedings of the Tenth Annual Conference of the Cognitive Science Society*. Northvale, NJ: Erlbaum.

Sycara, K.; Guttal, R.; Koning, J.; Narasimhan, S.; and Navinchandra, D. 1992. CADET: A case-based synthesis tool for engineering design. *International Journal of Expert Systems* 4(2).

Sycara, K., and Navinchandra D. 1989a. Integrating case-based reasoning and qualitative reasoning in engineering design. In *Artificial intelligence in engineering design,* ed. J. Gero. U.K.: Computational Mechanics Publications.

Sycara, K., and Navinchandra, D. 1989b. A process model of experience-based design. In *Proceedings of the Eleventh Annual Conference of the Cognitive Science Society*. Northvale, NJ: Erlbaum.

Sycara, K., and Navinchandra, D. 1991a. Index transformation techniques for facilitating creative use of multiple cases. In *Proceedings of IJCAI-91*. San Mateo, CA: Morgan Kaufmann.

Sycara, K., and Navinchandra, D. 1991b. Influences: A thematic abstraction for creative use of multiple cases. In *Proceedings. See* Bareiss 1991.

Sycara, K., and Navinchandra, D. 1992. Retrieval strategies in a case-based design system. In *Artificial intelligence in engineering design*, vol. 2, ed. C. Tong and D. Sriram. Boston: Academic Press.

Thagard, P., and Holyoak, K. 1989. Why indexing is the wrong way to think about analog retrieval. In *Proceedings. See* Hammond 1989c.

Thornedyke, P. W., and Hayes-Roth, B. 1979. The use of schemata in the acquisition and transfer of knowledge. *Cognitive Psychology* 11: 82–106.

Turner, R. 1986. A derivational approach to plan refinement for advice giving. In *Proceedings of the 1986 IEEE International Conference on Systems, Man, and Cybernetics, Atlanta*.

Turner, R. M. 1987. Modifying previously-used plans to fit new situations. In *Proceedings of the Ninth Annual Conference of the Cognitive Science Society*. Northvale, NJ: Erlbaum.

Turner, R. M. 1988a. Opportunistic use of schemata for medical diagnosis. In *Proceedings of the Tenth Annual Conference of the Cognitive Science Society*. Northvale, NJ: Erlbaum.

Turner, R. M. 1988b. Organizing and using schematic knowledge for medical diagnosis. In *Proceedings. See* Kolodner 1988.

Turner, R. M. 1989a. Case-based and schema-based reasoning for problem solving. In *Proceedings. See* Hammond 1989c.

Turner, R. M. 1989b. When reactive planning is not enough: Using contextual schemas to react appropriately to environmental change. In *Proceedings of the Eleventh Annual Conference of the Cognitive Science Society*. Northvale, NJ: Erlbaum.

Turner, R. M. 1989c. *A schema-based model of adaptive problem solving*. Georgia Institute of Technology, School of Information and Computer Science Technical Report no. GIT-ICS-89/42. Atlanta.

Turner, R. M. 1989d. Using schemas for diagnosis. *Computer Methods and Programs in Biomedicine* 30: 199–208.

Turner, R. M. 1992. A view of diagnostic reasoning as a memory-directed task. In *Proceedings of the Fourteenth Annual Conference of the Cognitive Science Society*. Northvale, NJ: Erlbaum.

Turner, R. M., and Stevenson, R. A. G. 1991. ORCA: An adaptive, context-sensitive reasoner for controlling AUVs. In *Proceedings of the Seventh International Symposium on Unmanned Untethered Underwater Submersible Technology (Durham, NH)*. University of New Hampshire Marine Systems Engineering Laboratory, Durham, NH.

Vasandani, V., and Govindaraj, T. 1990. Knowledge representation and human-computer interaction in an intelligent tutor for diagnostic problem solving. In *Proceedings of the 1990 International Conference on Systems, Man, and Cybernetics, Los Angeles*. New York: IEEE Press.

Veloso, M. M. 1991. Efficient nonlinear planning using casual commitment and analogical reasoning. In *Proceedings of the Thirteenth Annual Conference of the Cognitive Science Society*. Northvale, NJ: Erlbaum.

Veloso, M. 1992. *Learning by analogical reasoning in general problem solving*. Carnegie Mellon University, School of Computer Science Technical Report no. CMU-CS-92-174.

Veloso, M. M., and Carbonell, J. G. 1989. Learning analogies by analogy--The closed loop of memory organization and problem solving. In *Proceedings. See* Hammond 1989c.

Veloso, M. M., and Carbonell, J. G. 1993a. Derivational analogy in PRODIGY: Automating case acquisition, storage, and utilization. *Machine Learning* 10(3): 249–278.

Veloso, M. M., and Carbonell, J. G. 1993b. Towards scaling up machine learning: Case study with derivational analogy in PRODIGY. In *Machine learning methods for planning and scheduling,* ed. S. Minton. San Mateo, CA: Morgan Kaufmann.

Veloso, M. M., and Carbonell, J. G. 1993c. Automatic case generation, storage, and retrieval in PRODIGY. In *Machine learning: A multistrategy approach,* vol. 4, ed. R. S. Michalski. San Mateo, CA: Morgan Kaufmann.

Wall, R. S.; Donahue, D.; and Hill, S., 1988. The use of domain semantics for retrieval and explanation in case-based reasoning. In *Proceedings. See* Kolodner 1988.

Waltz, D. 1989. Is indexing used for retrieval? In *Proceedings. See* Hammond 1989c.

Wilensky, R. 1978. *Understanding goal-based stories*. Yale University, Department of Computer Science Technical Report no. 140.

Wilensky, R. 1983. *Planning and understanding: A computational approach to human reasoning*. Reading, MA: Addison Wesley.

Williams, M., and Hollan, J. 1981. The process of retrieval from very long term memory. *Cognitive Science* 5: 87–119.

Williams, M. D.; Tou, F. N.; Fikes, R. E.; Henderson, A.; and Malone, T. 1982. RABBIT: Cognitive science in interface design. In *Proceedings of the Fourth Annual Conference of the Cognitive Science Society*. Northvale, NJ: Erlbaum.

Zito-Wolf, R. J., and Alterman, R. 1990. Ad-hoc fail-safe plan learning. In *Proceedings of the Twelfth Annual Conference of the Cognitive Science Society*. Northvale, NJ: Erlbaum.

Zito-Wolf, R. J., and Alterman, R. 1992. Multicases: A case-based representation for procedural knowledge. In *Proceedings of the Fourteenth Annual Conference of the Cognitive Science Society*. Northvale, NJ: Erlbaum.

Index

ABBY, 242, 311, 316, 581–82
Abelson, R.P., xv, 10, 100, 114, 133,
    138, 221, 224, 230
Abstract features, retrieval based on,
    195–96
Abstraction(s)
  of cases, 11
  level of
    for cases, 576–77
    for indexes, 199, 574
    in indexing vocabulary, 204–7,
      214–15, 218
    of UIF, 240
  in local search, 408–9
  in representational vocabulary, 342
Abstraction hierarchy, 346–47, 407,
    408, 409
ACBARR, 582–83
Accessing complex devices, 120
Access procedures, 141
Accuracy
  of CASEY, 43
  of PROTOS, 55
  of retrieval, 384–88
Achievement goals, 232
ACME, 336
Acorn, T., 598
Acquisition tools, 502
ACT*, 15

Active intentional learner, 127
Activity-based reminding, 107
Adams, N., 10
Adaptation, 17, 18, 21–22, 82, 135,
    136, 137, 393–68, 536, 564.
    See also Repair
  based on execution-time feedback,
    462
  carrying out, 452–53
  case-based, 461–62
  cases to guide, 540
  choosing strategy for, 454–60
  compensatory, 453
  complex strategies, 541
  creative, 540–41
  critics of control, 463
  defined, 7
  derivational replay, 396, 397, 435–36
  domain-specific, 431, 432, 434
  feedback analysis, 452–53
  flow of control of, 463–66
  general purpose, 431
  identifying targets of, 440–52
    in tandem with method of adapta-
      tion, 460–63
    using checklists, 444–45, 447
    using differences between problem
      specifications, 441–43

    using inconsistencies between old
      solution and stated goals,
      445–47
    using solution projections, 447–52
  methods of, 7
  special-purpose, 396, 397, 431–35,
    456–57
  structure modification, 431
  substitution, 395, 397–417, 455
    case-based, 396, 397, 398, 413–17
    local search, 395, 397, 398,
      407–10, 411, 459
    memory organization requirements
      for, 417
    parameter adjustment, 395, 397,
      398, 404–7, 434, 441–42, 459
    query memory, 395–96, 397,
      410–11
    reinstantiation, 395, 397, 398–404,
      406, 464
    specialized search, 396, 397, 398,
      411–13, 459
  transformation, 418–31, 455
    commonsense, 396, 397, 420–23
    model-guided repair, 396, 397,
      419, 423–31
  weak methods of, 431
Adaptation checklists, 444–45, 447
Adaptation critic, 46